# Using Q&A™
## 2nd Edition

# Using Q&A™

## 2nd Edition

**David P. Ewing**

**Bill Langenes**

**Revised by**
**Tom Badgett**
**Donna Dowdle**

**QUE® Corporation**

**Carmel, Indiana**

# **Using Q&A™**, 2nd Edition



Library of Congress Catalog No.: 88-61160
ISBN 0-88022-382-0



92 91 90 89 8 7 6 5 4

Interpretation of the printing code: the rightmost double-digit number is the year of the book's printing; the rightmost single-digit number, the number of the book's printing. For example, a printing code of 88-1 shows that the first printing of the book occurred in 1988.

*Using Q&A*, 2nd Edition, is based on Version 3.0 and the earlier Q&A Versions 1.0, 1.1, and 2.0.

# Dedication

To the Ewing clan—Bob, Mark, Kathy,
Bill, Mary Beth, Rita, Janet, and Tom
D.E.

To Marie, my best friend
B.L.

# Acknowledgments

The authors thank Kathy Murray, Que Corporation, for her significant work on reorganizing, rewriting, and adding material to many of the book's chapters.

*Publishing Manager*

Scott N. Flanders

*Product Director*

Karen Bluestein

*Senior Editor*

Lloyd J. Short

*Editors*

Sandra Blackthorn
Kelly Curie
Kelly Dobbs
Jeannine Freudenberger
Steven Wiggins

*Technical Editor*

George Beinhorn

*Editorial Assistant*

Debra S. Reahard

*Book Design and Production*

Dan Armstrong
Cheryl English
Carrie Torres Marshall
Jennifer Matthews
Diana Moore
Cindy L. Phipps
Joe Ramon
Dennis Sheehan
Mae Louise Shinault

Screen reproductions in this book were created by means of the InSet program from INSET Systems Inc., Danbury, CT.

# About the Authors

## David P. Ewing

David P. Ewing is Publishing Manager for Que Corporation. He is coauthor of Que's *Using Symphony*, *Using Javelin*, and *1-2-3 Macro Workbook*; author of Que's *1-2-3 Macro Library*, *The Using 1-2-3 Workbook*, and *Using 1-2-3 Workbook Instructor's Guide*; and contributing author to *Using 1-2-3*, Special Edition.

Mr. Ewing received his B.A. from Duquesne University and his M.A. from North Carolina State University. He is currently completing his Ph.D. at Purdue University. Prior to his position at Que, he was the Assistant Director of the Business Writing Program at Purdue University, where he developed course materials and trained instructors. For eight years, Mr. Ewing taught college-level writing and business communications courses. He has published articles in leading business communications books and journals and given numerous presentations at national conferences on writing and business communications.

## Bill Langenes

Bill Langenes is an independent consultant, providing marketing communications services to companies in the personal computer marketplace. He has more than 14 years' experience in marketing and communications, the last eight years of which have been spent in the personal computer industry. In addition to his marketing experience, Mr. Langenes has been the West Coast editor of *Computer Retailing* and has worked with a major software publishing company to produce promotional and training materials. Mr. Langenes received his B.S. degree from the University of North Dakota. He now lives in Saratoga, California, with his wife and two sons.

# Contents at a Glance

# Table of Contents

## II Using Q&A File

## IV Using Q&A Report

# Trademark Acknowledgments

Que Corporation has made every effort to supply trademark information about company names, products, and services mentioned in this book. Trademarks indicated below were derived from various sources. Que Corporation cannot attest to the accuracy of this information.

1-2-3, Lotus, Symphony, and VisiCalc are registered trademarks of Lotus Development Corporation.

3Com is a registered trademark of 3Com Corporation.

Apple and LaserWriter are registered trademarks, and Macintosh and AppleShare are trademarks of Apple Computer, Inc.

COMPAQ is a registered trademark and COMPAQ DeskPro 386 is a trademark of COMPAQ Computer Corporation.

dBASE, dBASE II, dBASE III, and dBASE III Plus are registered trademarks of Ashton-Tate Corporation.

IBM is a registered trademark and IBM PC XT, IBM Writing Assistant, and PS/2 are trademarks of International Business Machines Corporation.

LaserJet is a registered trademark of Hewlett-Packard Co.

Microsoft and MS-DOS are registered trademarks of Microsoft Corporation.

NetWare is a registered trademark of Novell, Inc.

PFS, PFS:FILE, PFS:GRAPH, PFS:REPORT, and PFS:WRITE are registered trademarks of Software Publishing Corporation.

PostScript is a registered trademark of Adobe Systems Incorporated.

Q&A is a trademark of Symantec Corporation.

R:base is a registered trademark of Microrim, Inc.

SmartKey is a trademark of Software Research Technologies.

WordPerfect is a registered trademark of WordPerfect Corporation.

WordStar is a registered trademark of MicroPro International Corporation.

Z80 is a registered trademark of Zilog, Inc.

# Introduction

## *What Is Q&A and What Can It Do for You?*

Q&A™ is an easy-to-use data filing program that combines word processing, report generation, and artificial intelligence in a tightly integrated package. The first microcomputer to use artificial-intelligence technology, Q&A is suitable for a wide range of business and personal applications.

Q&A's Intelligent Assistant, a natural-language processor, responds to queries in English. The program's integrated design automatically uses data from the File module in the Write and Report modules. Q&A is consistent; similar menus and screens appear in each module, so the user is always on familiar ground.

### *The Evolution of Q&A*

Because it was the first integrated program on the market to provide user-friendly interface and artificial-intelligence capabilities, Q&A has a lead on the software industry. The makers of Q&A used knowledge gleaned from tests and competitors' programs to develop a highly functional and competitive product. Q&A was first introduced in 1985 with Version 1.0. It was a flexible and powerful program, but as is common with any software, the program has evolved.

Version 1.1, released in January, 1986, added features and enhancements, including a Spell module to help check spelling in Write documents, an extended and more flexible search and replace capability, and the capacity to draw double lines and mix double and single lines.

Version 2.0, released in September, 1986, was an upgraded edition of Version 1.1. The system became easier to use on dual diskette systems, and overall program speed was increased. Users could print text in columns from the Write module and could print mailing labels directly from Write. File no longer accepted blank forms, preventing accidental entry of empty forms in files. Report became more flexible, and this version expanded macro and report-formatting capabilities. Import and export capabilities were greatly enhanced. Version 2.0 could integrate worksheet and graph files into Q&A documents and read Lotus® 1-2-3® worksheets into Q&A databases. The Intelligent Assistant ran four times faster and corrected Version 1.1's database recovery problems.

In early 1988, the company released Version 3.0. Available commands and functions have been expanded, and an external LOOKUP feature has been added to permit linking of external files to the current file. This addition moves Q&A toward a relational database that can provide significant improvements to the program.

Version 3.0 supports networking for multi-user access and uses the PostScript® printing standard. More date and time functions were added, and additions were made to the Report and Write modules. The Intelligent Assistant and Write modules are faster than in Version 2.0. The program is now available on 3.5-inch diskettes.

## *A Hardware History*

The personal computer was conceived in 1974 by Intel Corporation, not as the I/O box, monitor, and keyboard now used but as a silicon chip containing electronic circuits powerful enough to run applications previously performed on room-sized mainframe computers. Called the 8008 microprocessor, the chip, less than one-inch square, was soon used by hobbyists in the first homemade personal computers.

About the same time, a more powerful chip was developed by MOS Technologies (later acquired by Commodore® Business Machines). This chip, the 6502, was used in the early generation of microcomputers when computer kits weren't user friendly. Kit computers usually had flashing lights and switches used by creators to program machines. Therefore, the first personal computers were used only by people who could build and program computers.

The Apple® I arrived on the scene in 1977, thanks to developers Steve Wozniak and Steve Jobs. Originally sold as a kit, the Apple I sold 500 units before being upgraded to the Apple II. Unlike its predecessors, the Apple II was preassembled and included a disk drive and disk operating system.

Tandy®/Radio Shack® joined the market with the Z80® chip and TRS-80 computer, and a new generation of computing began. Each of these computers had expansion slots so that users could attach printers, additional disk drives, and modems. Nontechnical people with no knowledge of mainframes or programming languages could join the microcomputer revolution.

The IBM® Personal Computer, which used the 8088 microprocessor, was introduced in 1981. The IBM PC quickly dominated the market, setting the standard for computers that followed. As the need for more powerful computers arose, researchers worked on a nonremovable disk that could store larger amounts of information and increase the computer's execution speed. IBM responded in early 1983 by introducing the IBM PC XT™—the first mass-market personal computer with a hard disk drive. The hard disk and expanded memory capacity allowed developers to create complex programs such as Q&A.

In the industry's quest for faster and more powerful machines, the IBM Personal Computer AT was introduced in 1984. This microcomputer was the first computer to have Intel's 80286 microprocessor, which was three to five time faster than the 8088 of the IBM PC.

Another advance was made when COMPAQ® introduced the COMPAQ DeskPro 386™ in the fall of 1986. This computer was one of the first on the market with the 80386 microprocessor, which is up to 18 times faster than the 80286. Computer hardware technology has taken the fast track in recent years, and software development has followed a similar trail.

Today, high performance microcomputers using 80286 and 80386 chips are commonplace. IBM's PS/2™ line, computers from COMPAQ and other vendors have brought minicomputer performance to the desktop. Increasingly powerful and functional software is evolving with the development of hardware platforms to support them.

## The Software Story

The need for an easy-to-use programming language was discovered soon after the Apple microcomputer was introduced. A programming language called BASIC (Beginner's All-purpose Symbolic Instruction Code) was included with the new computers. Because BASIC was much easier to use than machine or assembly language, users could write their own programs.

Developers soon came out with "canned" software, programs written to answer specific needs such as spreadsheet or accounting applications. The first software program to make it big was VisiCalc®, a spreadsheet applications program introduced in 1978. During the next five years, VisiCalc sold more than 500,000 copies, making it the most popular software program of its time.

As software needs were recognized and answered, programs were developed for different applications. Word-processing programs threatened to make typewriters obsolete; data management programs began to replace metal file cabinets and manila file folders. Researchers worked on developing a microcomputer alternative to minicomputer and mainframe database systems.

In 1979, Software Publishing introduced the Personal Filing System (PFS®:FILE), a program used to store, sort, and retrieve data. Because PFS:FILE has limited report capabilities, PFS:REPORT was soon introduced. The programs were slow, and storage space was limited, but they were the first to use menu selections instead of a complex command structure. PFS:FILE is considered the forerunner of Q&A.

Each program improved its predecessor—software developers took what they learned from previous successes and failures and streamlined products. Software became more powerful; it could perform more tasks in less time. Software for microcomputers was easier to use than their mainframe counterparts, but one problem remained: the more powerful the program, the more the user had to learn. If the user needed more than one powerful program, the microcomputer was no longer as easy to use as advertisements promised.

As software evolved, software designers created different types of programs. If your office used VisiCalc for accounting, PFS:FILE for personnel files, and WordStar® for writing letters and reports, you had to use three separate programs. Integrated software was introduced to solve the compatibility problem.

1-2-3, the first integrated software program, combined graphics and data management capabilities in a strong spreadsheet environment. The data management aspect of 1-2-3 is its well-known weakness, however—a fact that makes compatibility with Q&A an attractive aspect of both programs.

The designers of Q&A understood the need for an integrated program that would work easily with an existing spreadsheet program like 1-2-3. Going a step further, they made the program as easy to use as possible by including artificial intelligence; the Intelligent Assistant is a user-friendly interface that makes it possible to use the computer without having to learn the computer's language.

## *The Development of Artificial Intelligence*

You probably recognize the term *artificial intelligence*, but do you know what it means? If your computer is artificially intelligent, it can't think, but it can make decisions when given necessary information.

Artificial intelligence was designed so that you can communicate with the computer in your own language. Instead of learning command sequences or selecting menu options, you can use Q&A's artificial intelligence to interpret and respond to sentence-style requests. Artificial intelligence also enables Q&A to "learn" about your database and provides a way of asking questions so that you can build on the base of knowledge programmed into the Intelligent Assistant.

In the mid-1970s, Gary Hendrix and a team of researchers developed the first artificial-intelligence program for the U.S. government. An improved version of the program appeared in 1978. The program was powerful, but the software was slow, could be run only on a million-dollar computer, and could be operated only by people trained in computational linguistics.

Hendrix also developed a natural-language technology that could be used in a database for less-experienced users. In 1982, he and coworker Norman Haas founded Symantec Corporation and began creating prototype English systems for personal computers. Q&A was introduced in 1985; it was the first microcomputer program that could adapt to any database, "learn" about the database, understand requests in the English language, and be used by people with varying degrees of expertise.

## A Note on the Versions of Q&A

As this book is written, Version 3.0 is the current release of Q&A and provides significant enhancements over previous versions. Q&A is a rich and dynamic product that has undergone several significant enhancements during its life. If you are using an earlier version of Q&A, you may want to upgrade to the latest release. Refer to your user's manual for details.

## Upgrading: Getting the Latest Features

If you are happy with the product you have, the expense of upgrading to a later software release may not seem warranted, but there are good reasons for upgrading.

Obviously, you receive new documentation and all upgrades and additions to the software. Any minor bugs or problems probably have been fixed. So one advantage to upgrading is that you always have all the latest features available in a given software package. The advantage to vendors is that they have to support only a single software version, because all customers are using the latest release of the product.

If your application is a casual one and you are satisfied with the operation of the software version you have, you may see little reason to upgrade. However, popular software products tend to gather third-party support that provides additional functionality. Add-on products and training guides usually are designed around the latest software version and will be upgraded to reflect changes in the target product.

Finally, as a software package gains popularity, users frequently wish to exchange design information, software templates, and even data files. If everybody is using the same version of the software, this process is much easier.

If you keep your software up-to-date, you will get better service from the software and the company that supports it.

## About This Book

*Using Q&A,* 2nd Edition, will help you get the most out of Symantec's software. Like the product it describes, this book is dynamic. As the first edition was being prepared for publishing in 1986, Symantec released an updated version of its software, and the original text had to be modified to reflect these changes.

Again in 1988, Symantec released an enhanced Q&A. In the second edition of this book, Q&A is covered from the perspective of Version 3.0. Earlier versions are fully compatible with Version 3.0, but if you are using an earlier release of the software, some of the advanced functions won't work. The text shows you where earlier releases of the software are not compatible with the current version, so no matter which release of Q&A you have, *Using Q&A,* 2nd Edition, will be a valuable addition to your reference library.

## Conventions Used in This Book

Q&A is an integrated, microcomputer-based, software application that includes facilities for creating data files to manage most kinds of information and for manipulating that information with reporting, word processing, and artificial-intelligent querying.

For convenience, and to conform to microcomputer-industry conventions, the term *database* is used to refer to the Q&A software and the pool of information files it creates and maintains.

In this book, the term *File* means the group of programs within Q&A that perform data management functions. *Write* is the word processor and its associated formatting and output functions, and *Report* is the database reporting tool. Generally, the *Intelligent Assistant* is referred to as the IA.

## Who Should Use This Book?

If you own Q&A, you should own this book. *Using Q&A,* 2nd Edition, is not meant to replace the program documentation; the manual provided in the package serves as a useful reference tool. The Instruction Manual divides the information about each module into sections in two books, so you can easily look up information on a specific area. *Using Q&A,* 2nd Edition, is an applications-oriented guide that teaches you how to use Q&A through examples and tutorial-style text.

Whether you are a first-time user or an old hand at composing data filing programs, *Using Q&A,* 2nd Edition, introduces you to the unique features of the Intelligent Assistant and shows you how to streamline your applications to minimize time and effort. If you currently use 1-2-3, Symphony®, PFS:FILE, the IBM Filing Assistant®, or any of the dBASE® products, you can learn how to import files into Q&A by reading Chapter 20.

If you're still trying to decide whether to buy Q&A, *Using Q&A,* 2nd Edition, will help you investigate the program's full range of capabilities. By reading through sample applications and procedures, you will see how easy it is to create and use a Q&A data system. You then can decide for yourself whether Q&A answers your business needs.

## How Do You Use This Book?

*Using Q&A,* 2nd Edition, will help you learn to use this innovative program to your best advantage. We demonstrate, through examples and discussions, how to create, customize, and implement a Q&A system.

We view this book as a direct-access reference. Although you certainly can begin with Chapter 1 and read through to the end, we anticipate that most readers will select portions of interest and go directly to them.

If you need additional help installing the software, refer to Appendix A. Once Q&A is installed, each section of this book should stand alone to provide quick reference information or detailed step-by-step procedures.

Notice the "Quick Start" Chapters 4, 9, and 14. These sections are designed to teach you quickly how to use software features. The material following each chapter expands on the Quick Start topics, providing increasingly detailed information as you are ready.

## What Is in This Book?

This book is divided into parts that reflect the various Q&A modules and applications. If you plan to use the data-filing features of Q&A, we recommend you read *Using Q&A,* 2nd Edition, in the order presented. If word processing is what you're after, however, you may want to start reading in Part III, "Using Q&A Write." Remember that before you can use the Intelligent Assistant feature or print reports, you must create a data file in the File module.

### Part I

The information in Part I focuses on teaching you the basics of Q&A. Chapter 1, "A Quick Tour of Q&A," introduces you to Q&A's features and provides some detail on individual Q&A modules. You also will learn when to use Q&A. This chapter can be a general Q&A reference as you read the remainder of the book.

Chapter 2, "Database Concepts," introduces you to database design and terminology that will help you understand other material in this book. Database design philosophy is introduced.

Chapter 3, "Q&A Basics," shows you how to start and end a Q&A session and provides additional detail on specific program features, such as the menu system, on-line help, the tutorial, and error messages.

## Part II

From the Quick Start chapter through customizing and printing a document, Part II focuses on Q&A File. Chapter 4, ''Q&A File Quick Start,'' is the first of several Quick Start sessions that provide detailed instructions for Q&A procedures. The Quick Start chapters are a good place to start when you are trying new operations and a good memory refresher for later in your experience.

Chapter 5, ''Setting Up a File,'' guides you through the Q&A File design process, providing step-by-step instructions and offering suggestions on how to get the most from Q&A File. You will learn the procedures for designing, formatting, and selecting options for a data entry form as well as ways to modify and redesign the data file.

Chapter 6, ''Using File,'' discusses ways to enter data and build the database file. In this chapter, you will learn to edit forms, add information, search and update forms, copy files, and delete information from the database.

Chapter 7, ''Customizing and Programming a File,'' teaches you how to make data manipulation easy by using Q&A custom features. You also will learn how to use calculation and programming statements to have Q&A File perform tasks automatically.

Chapter 8, ''Printing from File,'' explains how to move your data file information from disk to paper. We provide step-by-step procedures for creating print specifications, including Q&A's special features, such as printing mailing labels.

## Part III

In Part III, detailed instructions are given for using Q&A Write. Chapter 9, ''Q&A Write Quick Start,'' shows you how to use the Write module. Use this chapter when you first start experimenting with Q&A Write and refer to it often to refresh your memory.

Chapter 10, ''Creating a Write Document,'' explains Write's capabilities and guides you through the steps to produce a document. Editing, moving, copying, deleting, and formatting are just a few of the topics discussed in this chapter.

Chapter 11, ''Enhancing a Write Document,'' discusses text formatting, including tabs, margins, and fonts. We also show you how to customize Write features and how to use special operations, such as WordStar control characters and Q&A math functions.

Chapter 12, ''Merging Documents with Q&A Write,'' teaches you to use Write to merge data from the Q&A File module with documents such as form letters, memos, and reports. This chapter also includes the procedures necessary for merging ASCII documents into Write documents.

Chapter 13, ''Printing a Write Document,'' details printing procedures within Write. The print menus are explained along with special print operations, including PostScript and other font operations.

## Part IV

Using Q&A Report is detailed in Part IV. Chapter 14, "Q&A Report Quick Start," is an initial introduction to Q&A's report features. Use this chapter to familiarize yourself with the basic operations and as a reference chapter.

Chapter 15, "Creating a Report," expands on the information in Chapter 14. In this chapter, you learn about the various features of this module so that you can create formatted reports with custom features.

Chapter 16, "Printing a Report," shows you in detail how to use the print features of the Report module. Menus, print specification changes, and report previewing are a few of the topics.

## Part V

Part V focuses on understanding and using the Q&A Intelligent Assistant. Chapter 17, "Understanding the Intelligent Assistant," introduces you to the concept of this natural-language interface and teaches you to enter queries and requests that will be understood by the Intelligent Assistant.

Chapter 18, "Using the Intelligent Assistant," shows you how to expand the Intelligent Assistant's programmed "knowledge." You learn to teach the Intelligent Assistant facts and relationships that pertain to your particular database.

## Part VI

Part VI shows you how to get the most from Q&A by introducing advanced applications such as networking. Chapter 19, "Creating and Using Q&A Macros," teaches you to use macros to streamline your data management and data entry tasks. You learn to record often-used sequences to execute a series of commands with one keystroke.

Chapter 20, "Importing and Exporting Data in Q&A," walks you through the processes of importing and exporting data from popular programs such as 1-2-3, Symphony, PFS:FILE, IBM Filing Assistant, and various dBASE products.

Chapter 21, "Networking: Using Q&A in a Multi-User Environment," shows how to design files for shared access, discusses general network terms and concepts, and provides information on some specific types of networks.

Appendix A, "Installing Q&A," shows you how to prepare the software for operation with diskette or hard disk systems. Printer installation specifics also are provided.

## *What Is Not in This Book*

*Using Q&A,* 2nd Edition, will not replace the Symantec user's manual. *Using Q&A,* 2nd Edition, is a reference and tutorial guide designed to supplement the material supplied with the software.

This book is not a tutorial on database structures and design, although we include some information in this area.

You will find many examples to illustrate Q&A features, but we do not show you how to create extensive applications, like a comprehensive inventory and billing system. However, you can use the concepts illustrated to help you design such applications on your own.

This book is not a programming text. We show you how to customize Q&A applications with standard software features at the beginner and intermediate levels, but we do not try to cover extremely complex and advanced programming procedures.

Whether you're a die-hard database user who needs a sophisticated data management tool or a novice who needs nurturing, the chapters that follow will introduce you to the power and unique capabilities of Q&A.

# Part I

# Learning the Basics of Q&A

Includes

A Quick Tour of Q&A
Database Concepts
Q&A Basics

Chapter

1

# A Quick Tour of Q&A

If you think of the phrase "question and answer" when you see the name Q&A®, you already are aware of a major feature of the Q&A program. Q&A is defined as a sophisticated data manager, report writer, and word processor, but a special element called the Intelligent Assistant (IA) makes using the program as easy as entering a question and receiving an answer.

Unlike many other database programs, Q&A gives you the option of changing, querying, sorting, or reporting database information by simply typing English sentences and phrases. The type of answer that you receive depends on your application. Whether you want the Intelligent Assistant to sort a list of company names or display a financial report, you simply enter the question and Q&A supplies the answer. You can use the Intelligent Assistant to change, query, or sort the data in a database that you created in the File module. And you don't have to remember multiple menu commands and function keys.

Sound easy? It is. But even when you use the individual modules (File, Write, and Report) instead of the Intelligent Assistant, you don't need to be a computer specialist to perform data-management tasks, create documents, and print reports. Q&A makes data management, word processing, and report writing easy; the program includes similar screen layouts, function keys, and command menu systems in each of the three modules so that you know where you are in the program no matter which module you use most.

In this chapter, you will learn to think of Q&A as an information-management tool and will learn what the makers of Q&A had in mind when they designed the program. The range of Q&A capabilities and features is introduced in this chapter. And references to other sections point you toward more detailed information on the topics covered here.

## *Deciding Where and When To Use Q&A*

Different users respond differently to the issues of where and when to use a feature-rich program like Q&A. As an example, suppose that someone asks, ''What do you do with a car?'' Your answer can be simple: ''I drive it to work.'' On the other hand, you might reply, ''I use it for work, vacations, racing, and customizing.'' Or you may use a car for more activities, depending on your needs and experience. The answer, however, is based on your basic understanding of what an automobile is and on your experience in applying that understanding. This same concept applies to Q&A.

If you have used other computer-based information-management software, you can appreciate the value of a product such as Q&A. Q&A provides a nonthreatening, quick-to-learn user interface that also includes powerful and versatile features. If this is your first experience with such a product, you may need guidance. Either way, you will find that Q&A can solve many—if not most— of your data-management requirements.

At the low end of the applications scale, you may want to use Q&A File to maintain a simple name-and-address file of family members or business contacts. The Write module offers sophisticated word-processing features, but Write works just fine as a simple electronic typewriter to help make your letter- and memo-typing tasks easier.

At the high end of the applications scale, you can use the integrated features of the Q&A package for a comprehensive patient-tracking, appointments-scheduling, and medical-billing system. You can design an inventory, purchase order, and billing system for a wholesale business. And you can use Q&A as a card-catalog reference system for a personal, corporate, or public library.

Consider using Q&A as a travel-expense tracker and report writer. Use Q&A for project management and scheduling, and for preparing form letters for advertising, surveys, and billing. Use some of the IA features for statistical analysis of survey results or employee performance. Q&A is an excellent tool for you to use to maintain organization membership records, such as those for a church.

Although Q&A basically is not designed for textual databases, the IA component can help you keep short notes and ideas so that you can find random thoughts later.

Q&A is an information tool. To say ''use your imagination'' in applying this tool seems trite, but most users do just that after making most software purchases. These customers usually have one or two specific needs in mind or are responding to an intuitive belief that they should use such a tool. After the software is installed and the initial applications are in place, users begin thinking in terms of computer-based solutions to business and personal-information handling needs. And then each application builds on what was accomplished previously.

Accept Q&A as a tool in much the same way that you accept a screwdriver, wheel-barrow, food processor, or microwave oven. Each of these tools has one or more obvious applications, but new opportunities present themselves as the tools become comfortable in your hands.

At the same time, be cognizant of the design parameters of each tool that you use. You don't use a screwdriver as a hammer or a chisel. Although a screwdriver might serve the purpose, the results probably wouldn't be satisfactory.

The same applications concept applies to a software tool. Q&A is a microcomputer-based product with excellent and powerful features. However, the program is not intended for on-line transaction processing where millions of records must be manipulated in real time. Q&A doesn't serve well for highly customized applications where the user must be insulated from the database by applications-specific menus and procedures. Don't use Q&A for linked applications that require a database back-end called from conventional programming languages.

Q&A will not be your only database program if you intend to construct a true database of information for networked applications, if you expect the number of entries to be large, and if you want maximum flexibility in applying the data. However, if you truly are serious about database applications, Q&A *will* be one of your data-management software packages.

A number of applications do not require relational structure. And many applications in an office or even in a programming shop need to be brought on-line quickly, perhaps by the end user. Q&A can be an excellent choice for these applications.

Don't limit your horizons unnecessarily by your own preconceived notions or by the limitations suggested in this book. Be reasonable but be creative. Then you will get the most out of any software tool.

## Understanding the Design Philosophy of Q&A

One big headache that you often get when using many new software programs is caused by the "setup and discovery" stage. You spend time mulling over the documentation, designing the forms and fields that you will use, and experimenting with the various features of the program. Often, by trial and error, you discover that the setup stage is more complex than you originally thought.

The makers of Q&A designed the program to require a minimum amount of time needed for you to set up and discover. With Q&A, you can set up a file, enter data, and produce a report from the Intelligent Assistant in minutes. You don't need to learn complicated programming languages or sophisticated menu structures. Whether you want to use the Intelligent Assistant or the File, Write, and Report modules, you can learn how to use Q&A by just sitting down and getting to work.

In designing Q&A, the makers also considered the need for easy integration. Because Q&A is meant to be used for a variety of applications, the three separate modules (File, Write, and Report) were designed to be used together (see fig. 1.1). The data from File, for example, can be incorporated into a letter that you compose in Write or into a printout from Report. You can move quickly from one module to another without switching from program to program, as you would with individual programs. For business users, this "seamless" integration is an important selling point; major stand-alone programs such as WordStar® or dBASE III® often are difficult or impossible to integrate. And depending on your application and the size of your database, some data-management tasks may be faster with Q&A than they would be with a more powerful database program.

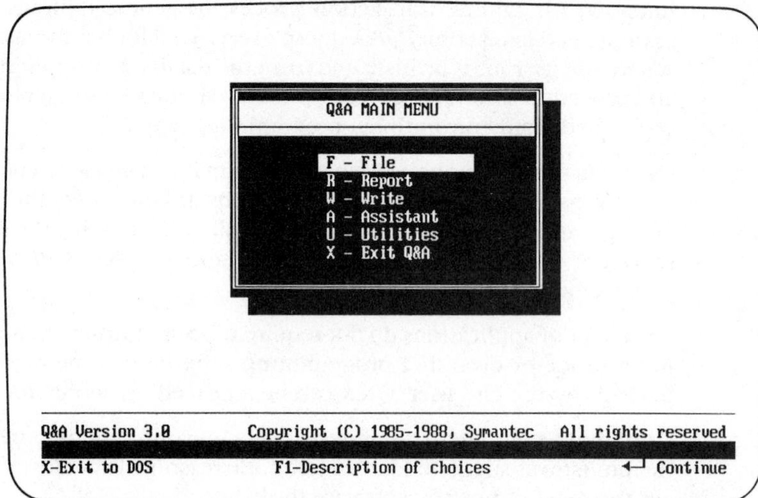


**Fig. 1.1**
*The Q&A Main menu.*

Q&A also offers an import/export feature that transfers data with a minimum of user effort. Importing and exporting data from other programs such as 1-2-3®, PFS:FILE®, or the IBM® Filing Assistant is almost as easy as copying a file. Similarly, you can import data from the dBASE® products into a Q&A file with just a few simple keystrokes. If you currently use any of these database programs, or if you use 1-2-3 for your spreadsheet needs, you can begin building your Q&A data system right away. (For more information on Q&A's import/export capabilities, see Chapter 20.)

Because Q&A is used in many different environments, the program must be flexible enough to meet the needs of persons with varying degrees of computer experience. In a small business, for example, the person responsible for designing database applications requires a package with the range of capabilities available in powerful programs like dBASE or R:base®. At the same time, Q&A must be easy to use so that an employee with no previous computer experience can enter data and produce reports.

Q&A can be used by people who are familiar with programming and applications as well as by people who have no computer experience. Creating a database form in File is as simple as entering text in the Write module. And when you design a report, you can use the database form that you created in File. Although the focus of Q&A is on front-end, easy-to-use features, don't be fooled; Q&A is powerful enough to perform a wide range of data-management, word-processing, and report-generating tasks.

# *Looking Inside Q&A*

Before you begin exploring the capabilities of Q&A, you need to investigate the Q&A package. When you open the package, you find seven 5.25-inch disks (four program disks, a dictionary disk, one tutorial disk, and one sample disk). The software is available optionally on a 3.5-inch format; in this case, you find only four disks. A swap form is included so that you can exchange the disks you have for the ones you want, directly from Symantec. Currently, Symantec doesn't charge for this service.

You also have two main spiral-bound manuals, a number of compact quick-reference guides, and order forms for Symantec and third-party support products such as keyboard templates.

The Q&A disks contain all the programs that you need to create, change, sort, and query database files; to design and print reports; and to enter and edit word-processing text. Table 1.1 gives you an overview of the Q&A program.

**Table 1.1**
**Q&A Version 3.0 Vital Statistics**

**Description**: A personal-computer program that integrates a file manager and report writer with artificial intelligence, a word processor, and a spelling checker.

**Package Contents**: Four program disks, a dictionary disk, a tutorial disk, a sample disk, quick-reference booklets and other references, and two spiral-bound instruction manuals.

**System Requirements**:

- An IBM PC, PC XT, Personal Computer AT, or other compatible personal computer
- Two 360K or larger disk drives (3.5-inch disks supported) or one disk drive and a hard disk (requires about 1M of storage)
- An 80-column color or monochrome monitor
- 512K RAM
- MS-DOS® or PC DOS Version 2.0 or above
- A printer

**Suggested Retail Price**: $349

**Availability**: Version 1.0, November, 1985; Version 2.0, October, 1986; Version 3.0, February, 1988.

**Table 1.1** — *Continued*

**Software Publisher**:

Symantec Corporation
10201 Torre Avenue
Cupertino, CA 95014
(408) 253-9600

**Module Overview**:

| | |
|---|---|
| *File* | Used to store, organize, and analyze information in database form |
| *Report* | Used to retrieve data from File to produce reports |
| *Write* | Used to create letters, memos, and reports |
| *Spell* | Used to find misspellings in Write documents and to offer alternative spellings from a 100,000-word vocabulary |
| *Intelligent Assistant* | A natural-language artificial-intelligence interface used to enter sentence-style requests for managing data and producing reports |

# Using Q&A File

The File module is probably the flagship portion of Q&A for most users. File is the data-storage module in which you create data files for names and addresses, inventory, personnel, accounting, or other information. Although other Q&A modules can use information from File for an integrated application, the File module also can stand alone. File is actually a series of complex programs that work together so that you can define the database, design data presentation screens, enter and edit information, and produce reports.

## File Structures and Capacities

Q&A File uses two basic file structures to store all the information about your data file. The DTF file stores the main database definition and information. The IDX file contains the database index information (see Chapter 3 for additional information on database and index concepts). Embedded in these files is additional information about your data, including search and report formats. Ordinarily, you will not need to know much more about how Q&A handles the information that you supply. If you move or copy a database from inside Q&A, the program knows to move or copy DTF and IDX files. If you use DOS to back up or move an application, however, you must remember to copy all files associated with the application.

Q&A can accept up to 16 million records per file. This storage capacity is so great that you probably will never face program limitations when you use File for personal or business data management. Table 1.2 lists the File module statistics.

**Table 1.2**
**File Module Statistics**

| *Item* | *Capacity* |
|---|---|
| Records | 16 million |
| Record size | 16,780 characters |
| Pages per form | 10 |
| Fields per record | 2,182 |
| Fields per page | 218 |
| Characters per field | 1,678 |
| Indexed fields | 115 |
| Lookup table size | 64K characters |
| Data types | 7 |
| Decimal accuracy | 15 digits |
| File size | 256M |
| File report width | 1,000 characters |
| File report columns | 50 |
| Sort limits | Up to 512 levels, ascending or descending |

## *File versus Other Databases*

Some notable differences exist between Q&A File and other popular database programs. For one thing, Q&A has more capacity than many other database programs. In addition, the Intelligent Assistant sets Q&A apart from the majority of offerings.

With Version 3.0 of Q&A File, you can relate multiple external files to the current application through the File and Report modules. For example, you can have a name-and-address file that includes a company ID but no more information on that company. A separate company file can store the detailed company information, including the address and main telephone number. However, you cannot construct logical views of the database that are independent of the physical structure of the file that is currently displayed.

You can construct a report that combines information from both files, and you can use the company-ID file as a lookup source to fill in information in the CONTACTS file. But the external file information must reside in a field on a displayed form.

Packages with full programming support give you access to screen design in such a way that you can construct custom display screens by combining information from multiple files; then you can write the information directly to the screen wherever you want. With Q&A, however, information retrieved from a linked file can be placed only on a database form.

This limitation is minor and probably will not cause problems for most Q&A users, if they understand the design philosophy of the product before applying it.

Other differences are in Q&A's favor. The modules contain user-oriented features that are available in a relatively limited number of higher performance products.

The reporting capabilities of Q&A, for example, are extremely easy to use. Even inexperienced users can retrieve the information they need with minimal training. The menu and on-line help systems keep the learning time to a minimum. And Q&A is powerful enough that experienced database users will find its features useful.

Q&A also is an integrated product, providing word processing and merging facilities in addition to the basic database functions. The macro features permit you to construct complicated command sequences that you can execute later with a simple key sequence.

## *File Screen-Design Features*

Among the strengths of the File module is its capability to custom-design data input and update screens. The procedure is as simple as using Q&A File's built-in word processor to place the field names and record labels where you want them on-screen. This easy-to-use feature permits you to specify a basic database structure without having to learn much beyond how to access the menu and how to use simple editing procedures (see Chapter 5 for more detailed information on designing File databases).

## *File Reporting Features*

Q&A includes a separate and versatile Report module, but File also can produce printed or on-screen reports directly. A Print menu selection from within the File module accesses these reporting facilities.

Use File's reporting features to design output for preprinted forms (Symantec calls this technique *coordinate* printing) or to custom-design a tabular report (*free-form* printing).

As with most Q&A operations, you will use QBE (Query By Example) or QBF (Query By Form) procedures to design the reports. You are presented with the screen form designed when the database was created, and you enter information into individual fields to construct the report. See Chapter 8 for additional information on printing from the File module.

# Using Q&A Write

Like File, Q&A Write is a collection of sophisticated programs that you can use to perform full-screen editing, text formatting, printing, report writing, and data-merging functions. Although Write's word-processing functions are not nearly as diverse as Microsoft® Word's or WordPerfect®'s, Write is a versatile package that can provide all the power most word-processing users will ever need. The following section introduces you to the Write module's capabilities. For additional details, see Part III of this book, "Using Q&A Write."

## Write Features

Write is a full-featured word processor with some useful enhancements that result from close integration with the File database module.

The usual editing features are supported, including search and replace operations, block operations, and bold, underline, and other font selections. And Write has an integrated spelling checker. In addition, Write supports row and column math with an interesting twist: you can place the results of a math operation anywhere in the document.

Write's mailmerge features are particularly strong. With the mailmerge feature, for example, you can write letters, mailing labels, invoices, memos, and other customized material that will use information (in a fill-in-the-blank fashion) from a File database during printing. The printing specification is as simple as surrounding the proper File field labels with asterisks inside the Write document. To print a different name and address at the top of each letter, for example, you can place the following header at the top of the letter:

```
*First Name* *Last Name*
*Title*
*Address*
*City*, *State* *Zip*

Dear *First Name*,
```

In addition to supporting merges with File, the Q&A Write module also can import 1-2-3 worksheets or named ranges from within worksheets. The Write module can insert bit-mapped images or 1-2-3 PIC files into a document, and Write supports document joins at printing. The Write module supports data import and export with other text processors as well.

With Version 3.0, Write's printing features are significantly enhanced. The program now supports about 100 printers, PostScript® output specifications, and versatile font selection and management. You now can print up to nine fonts on a single page.

Write provides an almost WYSIWYG (What You See Is What You Get) screen display, although you don't see accurate representations of proportional spacing typefaces.

An on-screen ruler shows your location in the document, and a horizontal menu is displayed continuously at the bottom of the screen.

Table 1.3 lists the Write module specifications.

**Table 1.3**
**Write Module Specifications**

| *Item* | *Capacity* |
|---|---|
| Document size | 80 pages (with 640K RAM) |
| Document width | 250 characters |
| Header/Footer | 18 lines total |
| Spelling checker | 100,000 words |
| Thesaurus | Optional |
| Laser printers | HP LaserJet®, Apple LaserWriter®, others |
| Columns | Up to eight columns (printout only) |
| Line drawing | Single or double lines |
| Math | Column/row total, average, count, multiply, divide |

## *Write versus Other Word Processors*

Q&A Write is a full-featured word processor and will serve for many, if not all, of your text-editing operations. Support for PostScript and bit-mapped files increases Write's functionality with laser technology and other modern printers. The Write module's close integration with the File module offsets some of the program's limitations. Together, File and Write are much more powerful than Write would be as a stand-alone word processor.

Write, however, is not designed for true electronic publishing, nor will Write serve in word-processing operations that require very large documents. Because Write documents are stored entirely in RAM, the maximum document size is about 80 pages with 640K of memory. You can, of course, use the join feature to print combined files for larger documents (see Chapter 13 for more information on using the join feature).

Write does not support such formatting enhancements as automatic-list preparation (indexes and tables of contents), parallel columns, split screens, simultaneous editing of multiple documents, footnotes, or sorting (you can print multiple snaking columns, but you cannot display them as such on-screen).

Many users find that Write is the only word processor they ever need. Others don't use Write at all and prefer a separate word processor. Some users apply Write for operations that benefit from the File connection and apply a stand-alone product for word-processing-only functions. As with any software product, you should assess your needs carefully before deciding on a single product.

### *Write Reporting Features*

The ultimate reason for maintaining any computer-based data is so that you can access that data in a useful form. Write's reporting features are versatile and functional. For example, with the mailing-label print routine, you easily can print labels from a File database by using Write's mailmerge facility.

The standard document print routine includes many formatting and merging functions that you can use to add additional flexibility to Write reporting. Also included is a routine you can use to print an address on an envelope from information in a letter document. By combining this routine with embedded printer-control codes, you can use a dual-bin printer to prepare letters and envelopes simultaneously.

You can select single or multiple copies of a document as it is printed. Right-margin justification is supported. And you can print a document in multiple columns. Print queues, special fonts, and document merge are among the other supported print operations.

PostScript print command support provides a wide range of output options. Write supports font descriptions for several popular laser printers. You also can load additional font descriptions from the Symantec bulletin board, and you can design your own font description files.

Chapter 13 provides detailed information on formatting and printing Write documents.

## *Using Q&A Report*

Report is another of the integrated modules of the Q&A package. Report supplements the output features of the File module by providing extensive preprogrammed capabilities. With Report, for example, control breaks are automatic. A control break occurs when data in one of the report fields changes. Suppose that you are listing names and addresses, sorted by city. Without control-break capability, a program must repeat the city with each record. Q&A, however, can print the city the first time it appears and then show blanks in that column as long as the city does not change:

| *CITY* | *NAME* | *SALESMAN* | *TELEPHONE* |
|---|---|---|---|
| Atlanta | Franklyn McCormic | SJ | 404-552-7722 |
| | Likado Tango | JJ | 404-526-6677 |
| | Jordan Wills | JJ | 404-723-5511 |
| Boston | Martha Eden | SJ | 617-426-5645 |
| | John Thomas | SJ | 617-584-2323 |

Report uses Query By Form (QBF) for easy report generation. Therefore, the report process uses the record forms with which you already are familiar because you designed the record forms during database design. For the simplest report, just specify which records you want to retrieve and the order in which you want the fields to appear. Q&A does the rest.

Flexible sorting capabilities let you arrange data in just about any way. In fact, you probably can sort every field in the report, if you need to, and you can choose ascending or descending order for individual fields. Report can produce listings up to 1,000 characters wide, assuming that your printer can support that number. You can send the printer special control codes from within Report, and you have good control over character and line spacing. Table 1.4 lists the Report module specifications.

**Table 1.4**
**Report Module Specifications**

| *Item* | *Capacity* |
|---|---|
| Columns | 50 |
| Width | 1,000 characters |
| Sort levels | 50 |
| Derived columns | 16 |
| Invisible columns | 49 |
| Saved formats | 100 per database file |

You can find more detailed information on Report in Part IV, ''Using Q&A Report.''

## *Using the Intelligent Assistant*

The idea of an English-language query came when the first computer drew power. But faster CPUs, larger disks, and huge memory were needed to make the idea possible. When Q&A first was released, the program was the only microcomputer database product to include this kind of artificial-intelligence query. The concept is so popular that a number of database programs now have some kind of conversational query capability.

The Q&A IA probably will not replace conventional reporting with the Report module, but the IA is an excellent supplement. In addition, the IA can provide database tools to people who can benefit from database access but do not want to be involved in the design process.

Because you can "teach" the Intelligent Assistant to recognize various words and phrases relating to your database, you can query, change, and add data by entering simple English phrases and sentences. After you have designed a database with File, you can rely entirely on the IA for your data-management needs, bypassing the program's command menu completely. For example, if you enter the request *Display the Chicago leads*, the Intelligent Assistant retrieves the appropriate records from the File module and displays the records in a columnar report (see fig. 1.2). You then can opt to print the report or ask another question.

```
Display the Chicago leads.

           Name                       COMPANY              Telephone
-----------------------------   -------------------   ------------
Simons Fred Associate Dean      Univ. of Michigan     517-486-3388
Jackson Ted General Manager     Bay City Laboratory   616-483-5847

SLSLEAD.DTF
******************************* END OF REPORT ********************************
Esc-Cancel   F2-Reprint   { →←↑↓ }-Scroll   Shift F9-Redesign   F10-Continue
```

**Fig. 1.2**
*The results of a simple request.*

The IA has a built-in vocabulary that enables it to recognize standard queries without any training from you. The IA can respond to date, time, and math questions, for example, without additional training. When you start the IA with each database, the IA first scans the file to learn about field names and database contents. Beyond that, you must spend some time training the IA about the terms you will use in asking questions. You can teach the IA synonyms for the information in your database, and you can add new vocabulary to its basic knowledge. This process can be time-consuming, depending on how large and complicated your database is, but the rewards can be great.

The IA is an excellent tool for ad hoc queries as a supplement to stored, macro-driven conventional reports. Table 1.5 lists the IA specifications.

For additional information about the Q&A IA, see Chapters 17 and 18 in Part V, "Using the Intelligent Assistant."

**Table 1.5**
**Intelligent Assistant Specifications**

| *Item* | *Capacity* |
| --- | --- |
| Built-in vocabulary | 450 words |
| User-defined vocabulary | Unlimited (up to disk capacity) |
| Sort levels | 50 |
| Intrinsic queries | Math, time, and date questions |

# Learning about Other Q&A Features

Q&A has a number of additional features in addition to those already mentioned. The next sections introduce you to these features.

## Integrated Features

As an integrated product, Q&A performs more than one software function, and the functions are tied together closely. Mailmerge is one example of this integration. You can select database information to be included in printed Write documents. This information can include not only names and addresses for letters but also invoice and billing information, inventory and personnel data, or anything else you have stored in a File database.

Data integration in Q&A flows the other way too. When you design a database file screen, use QBF searching, and enter or edit database information, you are using Write-compatible editing functions. In addition, the menu structures across Q&A modules are consistent, enhancing the integrated feel of the product and reducing learning time.

## Macros

A *macro* is a single command that combines a sequence of software functions. Suppose, for example, that you want to enter new information into the CONTACTS file. The sequence of functions that you must perform follow: first you select File from the Main menu and then select Add Data from the File menu; next you specify the name of the file to edit. This process can be reduced to a two-key combination. You can create a macro labeled Alt-E (for Edit) that automatically enters the File module and calls up a blank form from the CONTACTS file. Up to six macros can be installed on the Q&A Main menu to become part of the on-screen menu structure. However, you can define many more macros that can be accessed directly from the keyboard.

To define a keyboard macro, press Shift-F2 to display the Macro menu box from within any Q&A screen. Choose Define Macro and enter the key combination that you want to use for this macro identifier. A flashing block appears in the lower right corner of the screen to remind you that a macro definition is in process.

From that point, everything you type is saved in a special macro file to be played back when you enter the specified Alt-key combination. After you enter all the keystrokes for this particular macro, press Shift-F2 again to turn off the macro recorder. You then are asked which file to use to store the macro (accept the default QAMACRO.ASC).

You can do about anything that you want with macros, but one caution needs to be mentioned: don't use special key combinations that Q&A already uses for other operations. The software warns you if you try.

## *Multi-User Applications*

One interesting aspect of the evolution of powerful desktop computers is the trend toward connecting computers in Local Area Networks (LANs). This trend is particularly interesting because early microcomputer users generally purchased their machines in a rebellion of sorts against restrictions imposed by minicomputer and mainframe connections. As individual users began developing databases of information and applications, they have returned to central server connections for information sharing.

Symantec responded to this trend with the release of Q&A Version 3.0, which includes some multi-user features. Q&A is compatible with virtually any popular network products, including those from 3Com®, Novell, and IBM.

Software for a multi-user environment has to be different because, just as with physical matter, two pieces of database information cannot be at the same place at the same time. If two or more users access the same record, update it, and then try to save it back to disk, somebody gets short-circuited. Only the last version of the record to be saved is retained.

In addition, when more than one user has access to the information in a database, some security mechanisms must be implemented to limit access to authorized users. Some data files may exist that everyone should have access to; but sensitive company data, such as payroll information, obviously should be limited in distribution.

Q&A handles these problems by providing password-controlled access and by providing information-sharing features, called *locking*.

In Q&A and other shared products, certain facilities of the software are locked as soon as one user gains access to them. Other users may be able to access information, but they cannot update the information. As soon as the first user releases the record being examined, the next user in the queue can recall the record and update it.

Multi-user operation obviously opens up application possibilities; multi-user operation also imposes some user restrictions. For additional information on getting the most out of Q&A's multi-user features, see Chapter 21.

## Chapter Summary

This chapter was designed to introduce you to the features of Q&A. You learned about general software capabilities and some ways to apply Q&A. And you were introduced to the Q&A design philosophy.

The information in this chapter should help you start thinking about Q&A as a data-management tool for your individual needs. Refer to specific chapters for more detailed information on each Q&A topic.

Chapter

2

# Database Concepts

The term *database* means different things to different computer users. If you ask a minicomputer or mainframe user to describe a database, you probably will get a different answer than you will from most microcomputer users. The microcomputer world's *database* has become such a pervasive part of our computer jargon, however, that we will hold to that definition: a program that allows a user to store and retrieve information in an orderly fashion from a floppy or hard disk.

Generally, a microcomputer database program includes all the user-interface logic required to design files, add new information, edit existing data, and create reports. Modern database software usually consists of at least two distinctly separate entities. One is the data storage and retrieval logic—sometimes called a database engine—and the other is the support software, which presents user menus, displays input and edit screens, supports input and edit operations, and writes reports.

Information in a database can be quite diverse. A database may contain many different files for individual names and addresses, company names and addresses, inventory records, employee information, accounts receivable, accounts payable, a check register, a general ledger, sales-lead tracking, project management, and much more.

Physically, each class of information is stored in a separate file. Logically, information from any or all of these files can be linked to show relationships and form comparisons. These views are independent of the physical structure of the database. For example, you can combine data from the individual names and addresses file, the company names and addresses file, and the sales-lead tracking file so that on the screen, the information appears to be coming from a single file.

Storing the various types of information in different files provides flexibility in database design and operations. Combining selected pieces of information in an orderly way on-screen makes the data more useful to the user. Various files in a database system also can be distributed to many computers and storage devices, which are linked by some kind of networking system.

With Release 3.0 of Q&A, this microcomputer package moved another step closer to a conventional database management system (DBMS) by providing network support and rudimentary file linking through the @XLOOKUP function (see Chapter 7 for information on @XLOOKUP).

# Database Structures

Text editors and word-processing applications store and retrieve random information in blocks perhaps thousands of characters long. When you retrieve the information from a disk, you pull the data into your computer's memory as one large block. Although you can search for specific characters or word patterns in these files, output options are rather limited. Without a great deal of manual work, your only option is to print all or a portion of the file in the order in which the data is stored.

Most database applications, on the other hand, break up the data into smaller, more manageable units called fields and records. The data is stored together in a large file, but you can retrieve the units one at a time or in groups, sort the units, relate them in various ways, and print them in almost any order you choose.

Databases nearly always include three logical structures: fields, records, and files.

## Database Fields

A database *field* is the smallest piece of information the user identifies. A field consists of at least two components: the field label and the field data. Other field information, such as data attributes, also may be part of the field description. As the name suggests, the *field label* describes the contents of the field. The *field* is the smallest unit of the database. The *field data* is the piece of information you want to store and track as an individual unit. *Attribute data* defines the type of information each field can hold: text, numbers, dates, money amounts.

Common field labels are

Name
Company
Address
City
Invoice No.
Account No.
Description
Purchase Order No.

In most database systems, field labels and attributes are stored only once for each file description. This label and attribute information forms an overlay to describe, or define, raw data as it is entered and retrieved. Consider the following items of raw data:

PF432-688-Y
Idler Retainer Ring
Franklyn Engine Concepts
880615
B-423567-00015
12

16B
33
166-C
66
20
183
244

Although some of this information can be deciphered, you have no way to know for sure what some of these numbers mean without field labels and attributes. When Q&A combines this raw data with separate label and attribute overlays, the user is presented with

| | |
|---|---|
| Part No: | PF432-668-Y |
| Description: | Idler Retainer Ring |
| Manufacturer: | Franklyn Engine Concepts |
| Date of Mfg: | 06/15/1988 |
| Serial No: | B-423567-00015 |
| Quality Ctrl Chk: | 12 |
| Lot: | 16B |
| Warehouse: | 33 |
| Bin: | 166-C |
| Qty in Stock: | 66 |
| Reorder Qty: | 20 |
| Wholesale Cost: | $1.83 |
| Retail Price: | $2.44 |

In Q&A, you specify field labels on an editor screen by typing each label followed by a colon to separate the label from the field contents. A greater-than sign (>) marks the end of the field:

```
   Last Name:                 >
  First Name:              >
       Title:                          >
  Company ID:             >
        Keys:                                    >
```

This collection of fields describes a database record. This subject is covered fully in Part II of this book.

## Database Records

A *record* is composed of all the fields that refer to a single item. A complete name and address is one record. The part number, description, price, and other data that describes a unique inventory part form one record. Figure 2.1 shows a sample contacts database record showing field labels and field contents (data).

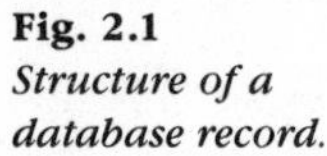

**Fig. 2.1**
*Structure of a database record.*

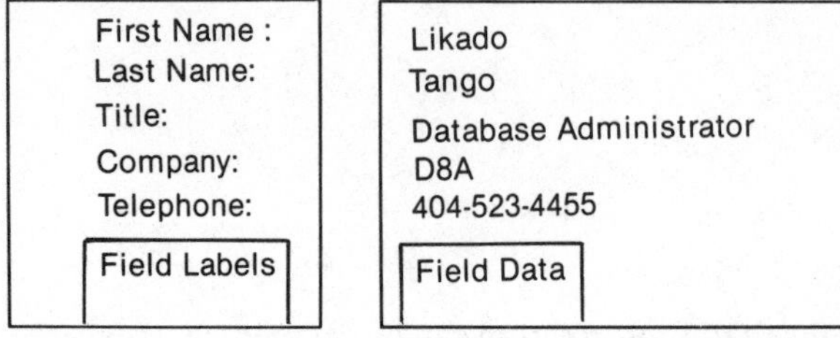


## *Database Files*

*File* is a term with which most computer users are at least slightly familiar. Although many kinds of files exist, the two most common basic types are program files and data files. *Program files* store the instructions that make the computer perform word-processing, database management, graphics, communications, printing, and other functions. *Data files* store the information you provide for these programs to use.

A *database data file* consists of all the records about a specific topic. Usually, but not always, a database contains separate files for inventory, names and addresses, accounting, and the like. The inventory file contains only inventory records, the company file contains only company records, and so on.

In some database programs, data files also hold other information besides just data records. Somewhere in the file may be information that describes how reports will be structured, for example, and, as mentioned earlier, field attribute information may be part of the file information.

Just as individual fields combine to form a database record, all the records in a group form a database file (see fig. 2.2).

**Fig. 2.2**
*The field, record, and file relationship.*

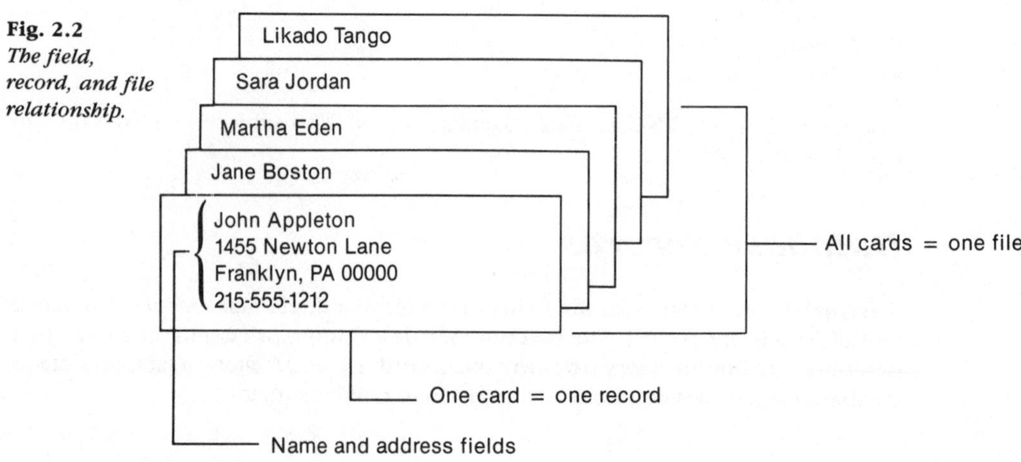

# Database Types

Among the many database structures in use today are hierarchical, extended network, relational, and flat files. Within these basic structures are many implementations. Today's microcomputer users most commonly use flat file and relational databases. *Flat files* are stand-alone data structures that cannot be connected to any other file. *Relational files* may include structures that are similar to flat files, but relational files can be related to each other in various ways.

## Flat Files

A flat file stands alone. It may contain all the field and record information described in the preceding paragraphs, but the database management software that supports the file is not capable of tying information from one file to information in another file. For many applications, flat file storage is sufficient. A simple name and address application used to track individuals and their companies, perhaps to print telephone directories or Rolodex® cards, may require nothing more sophisticated than a flat file.

Obviously, you can create many flat files with the same software, but you can't link information in different files with a program that supports only flat file structures.

The advantage of this type of program is its simplicity. It is usually menu driven, requires little time to learn, is probably storage efficient, and is low in cost.

The disadvantage is that repetitious data must be stored more than once. Suppose that your name and address file has only 300 individual companies but 1,000 individuals. That factor means that each company name and address is being stored, on the average, at least three times.

Not only is this structure wasteful of storage space, the structure cannot be modified without rewriting the entire file. To add a field of information, for example, you have to change the basic structure of the file.

## Relational Files

The actual data structures in a relational system are more efficient than structures in flat files. The difference is in the supporting software and other features that permit information in individual files to be linked. This operation is sometimes called a *join*.

To continue the name and address example, with a relational system, you build separate name and company files. The name file contains the individual's name, company ID, and whatever other information about that person you want. The company file contains the company ID, company name, address, telephone number, and any other information you need about the company.

The two files are linked through the common Company ID field. A relational program looks at the company identifier in the name file, then finds a matching entry in the company file. Assuming that the entry operator has not made an error, you can find out detailed information about the company for which this individual works (see fig. 2.3).

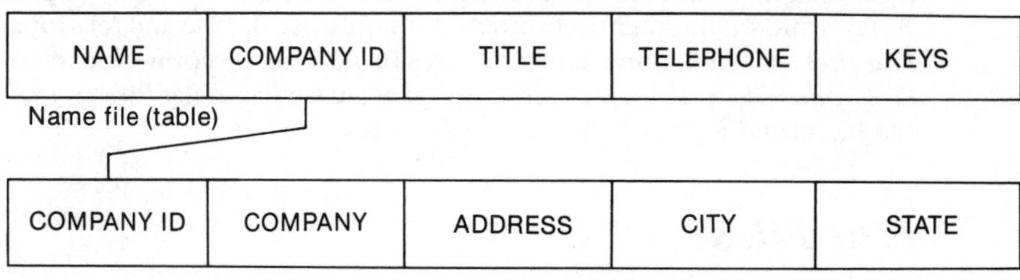


**Fig. 2.3** *Sample relational file join.*

With a relational structure you store the company information only once. Records about employees for each company can be stored in the name file. Storage space is conserved because the company data does not have to be repeated with each employee record.

In addition, if you discover, after the basic name and company files have been in use for a while, that you need to track additional information about individuals or their companies, you don't necessarily have to redesign either file.

You can add a transaction file, for example, to track each contact you make with individuals or companies. As long as you include a company ID in the file structure, the new transaction file can be linked to companies; with a unique Name or Contact Number field you can track transactions against individuals in the name file.

The main disadvantage of relational database programs is the increased complexity. The software is harder to program, so the user must learn more about the database structure in order to apply the software successfully. Nevertheless, the trend toward relational databases is clear in the database industry. Increasingly, databases for microcomputers, minicomputers, and mainframes use some form of relational structure. In addition, user friendly front ends—software that presents menus, graphics screens, on-line help, and other user aids—are designed for easy application development. As a result, just about anybody can use these new products.

Q&A File falls somewhere between true relational and flat files. With the @XLOOKUP command introduced in Version 3.0, File can link the current active file with information stored in other files. As a result, you can easily include additional data in the active file or in printed reports. You can maintain separate name and company files, as suggested, and then merge information from the two files to print a comprehensive contacts directory, complete with both company and name information.

See Chapter 7, "Customizing and Programming a File," for more information on @XLOOKUP and its associated commands and functions.

# Field Data Types

Most people think of data as being of two types: text and numbers. On the surface, this concept seems very simple: numbers are numbers and text is anything that isn't numbers. That distinction is partially true, but most computer programs divide data types beyond these two.

In Q&A File, for example, you can assign to each field one of seven data types: text, number, money, date, hours, yes/no (logical), and keywords. (Q&A also refers to these types as information types.) Within several of these field types, you have formatting options, which control the way the data is displayed and printed. This feature helps ensure that proper information is entered into each field and can make searching for data more precise.

## Text Type

Text fields contain alphanumeric data, which is precisely what the name implies. Alphanumeric data is information that includes both numbers and text. Text, however, is broader in definition than just the letters of the alphabet. In alphanumeric data types, special non-numeric characters that are not strictly alphabetic also are allowed: hyphens, for example, or slash marks (/), percent signs (%), asterisks (*), tildes (~), and anything else that appears on the standard computer keyboard. Depending on the application, alphanumeric also may include graphics characters, such as line draw characters (⊢), happy faces, or other symbols.

Q&A's *text* data type includes such nonalphabetic characters as dashes, parentheses, equal signs, and commercial at signs (@). Q&A text fields also can store graphics symbols.

The text data type is used for names, descriptions, cities, and states. Although the fact may seem strange, you probably will use the text data type for ZIP codes because the hyphen (-) commonly used to separate the first five and the last four numbers in some ZIP codes is not a numeric character. You can enter the ZIP code in a numeric ZIP field, but Q&A asks every time whether you are sure that this entry is a valid number. For the same reason, telephone numbers are considered text, whether you use the 123-456-7890 or the (123)456-7890 form. The hyphens and parentheses in these examples disqualify them for treatment as numbers, leaving them as text.

## Number and Money Types

Basic numeric data is a little simpler. It includes the digits from 0 to 9, in any combination, perhaps preceded by a negative sign or other indicator to show a below-zero value.

Any database field that contains only numerical values, such as price, quantity sold, number in stock, and total sales to date, should be entered as numbers because you can perform mathematical calculations on *number* data type fields. Text fields, on the other hand, cannot be used in any math calculations.

When you designate a field as the *money* data type, numeric values entered into the field are displayed with a dollar sign and two decimal places. The number 12.50, for example, becomes $12.50, and 12 becomes $12.00 in a Q&A money type field.

You also can specify certain global formats that change the way numeric data is displayed. A global format is one that applies to all fields in the database as opposed to only one specific field. You can have field-level as well as global formats in Q&A. For example, you can have numbers shown with a comma instead of a decimal point (12,50 instead of 12.50).

In money type fields, you can change the currency symbol to something other than a dollar sign, and you can specify how many decimal places should appear after the decimal point or comma. When you make some of these changes, you must also modify the operation of other features, such as the formats for some programming statements used to customize database forms. For example, if you replace the U.S. decimal point with a European comma, you must replace the comma separator in multistatement program lines with a semicolon.

One of Q&A's strengths is its capability to handle automatically other data types, including date, hours, yes/no (logical), and keywords.

## *Date Type*

Q&A supports 20 different formats for date type fields (see table 2.1). You choose a global date format by choosing the number beside the format you want. When you designate a field as a date type field, you must enter the date in one of these 20 formats. The on-screen display automatically changes to display the date in the format you have specified as the global default.

**Table 2.1**
**Q&A Date Formats**

Date: 1 2 3 4 5 6 7 8 9 10 11 12 13 14 15 16 17 18 19 20

| | | | |
|---|---|---|---|
| 1 - Mar 19, 1988 | 6 - 19/3/1988 | 11 - March 19, 1988 | 16 - 03-19-1988 |
| 2 - 19 Mar 1988 | 7 - 03/19/88 | 12 - 19 March 1988 | 17 - 19.03.88 |
| 3 - 3/19/88 | 8 - 19/03/88 | 13 - 3-19-88 | 18 - 19.03.1988 |
| 4 - 19/3/88 | 9 - 03/19/1988 | 14 - 3-19-1988 | 19 - 1988-03-19 |
| 5 - 3/19/1988 | 10 - 19/03/1988 | 15 - 03-19-88 | 20 - 1988/03/19 |

Unless you change the default, dates are displayed in the form mmm dd, yyyy. If you enter a date such as 05.24.88 or 24.05.88 or 05/24/88—or any of the other supported date formats—Q&A displays May 24, 1988. If you enter information that does not conform to Q&A's supported date formats, you are asked to confirm the information. Then you can leave the entry the way it is or change it to an accepted format.

## *Hours Type*

Hours (time) formatting in Q&A is similar to date formatting. Three hours formats are supported. You can enter data in any of the formats, and Q&A displays the information accordingly. An improper entry brings a prompt for verification from Q&A.

Q&A supports both 12- and 24-hour time formats, using either a colon or a period to separate hours and minutes. For example, you can use 13:42 or 13.42 in a time field. If you specify a 12-hour format, Q&A adds the am identifier to numbers below 12 and the pm format to numbers above 12. If you enter 13:42, for instance, Q&A displays 1:42 pm.

## *Yes/No (Logical) Type*

At times, you need to enter a simple yes or no answer to a field prompt. Some examples of the questions a logical field can answer are

Is this an active record?
Discount applied?
Follow-up call made?
Payment received?
Full-time employee?

You can design a text field and enter Y or N, or you can specify a yes/no (also called logical or Boolean) field. Logical fields have a length of one, and they work in a yes/no, 0/1, or true/false manner. You can enter data in a Yes field as Y(es), (T)rue, or 1 (logical true). Lowercase letters also work.

The advantage of using a logical data type is that you can perform certain logical operations (AND, OR, NOT) which may be helpful in producing reports from the data in the field.

## *Keywords Type*

The *keywords* data type is not a common structure. The keywords type permits you to enter text information in a field with the words or topics separated by semicolons. Then you can conduct database searches and produce reports based on information in the keyword field. For example, in your contacts file you may want to enter random words to typify each contact:

Advertising;Computers;Storage;Workstations

When you specify a keyword search, Q&A looks for the specified word pattern in that field in every record. You can search for more than one entry in a keyword field.

# Database Design Concepts

Designing a database is a little like programming an application. The difference in products like Q&A is that the job of specifying the database structure is much easier than with a conventional programming language.

Moreover, with Q&A you aren't stuck with the initial design. You can easily modify an existing data file if you discover, after bringing it on-line, that changes have to be made.

Nevertheless, some basic database design principles can make your job easier, reduce the number of later modifications, and produce reports that better satisfy your data management requirements.

Everybody has a different approach to any task, and you should use procedures that work for you. However, keep these basic design principles in mind as you work through database design:

- Design the output first.
- Identify the field labels.
- Select reasonable field lengths.
- Design a workable entry screen.
- Automate processes.

## Design the Output First

The best place to start a database design is to spend some time designing the output. After all, the reason for storing data on a computer in the first place is to look at the information in some specific way. If you start the design by deciding what output you want, you are sure to put into the database the information you need to get the reports you need.

Try to be imaginative at this stage. You probably are building the database for one or two specific reasons, but a general rule of computer use is that your information needs expand with your capability to process information. That is, you can do things with a computer that were impossible or too cumbersome to do by hand. Likewise, an easy-to-use product such as Q&A can make possible things that were too difficult or time-consuming with most programming languages. For these reasons, try to imagine applications that you haven't identified before.

## Identify the Field Labels

Once you know how the output from the database should look, you are ready to specify the field labels. Use Q&A's Write module or another word processor as a scratch pad to help you identify which fields should appear in each database record.

Experiment with field labels. Don't necessarily use the first label that comes to mind. Remember that you want to be as descriptive as possible, but you don't want to end up with unwieldy labels, either. Although a label like *Date of Last Contact* is certainly descriptive and Q&A supports such labels, they take up a great deal of room on reports. The label *Contacted* with a date type field serves the same purpose.

Consider issues such as whether you will need to sort the information by, say, a last name. If you think this need might ever occur, you need separate last name and first name fields. If you enter names in one long field, producing reports sorted by last name will be difficult—or impossible.

Will it be important to you to know when each record was entered or when it was last updated? If so, include one or more date fields so that you can track this information. Q&A supports auto-type entry, so you can enter new dates automatically as forms are entered and updated.

Will you probably include foreign addresses in your database? Remember that Canadian and other foreign addresses aren't formatted precisely like those in the U.S. A two-digit state field is of little use in entering these addresses, for example. How will you enter foreign addresses? Collect several examples to see what information you need to include. Ask some of the contacts themselves how they format their name and address files on their own computers. Add extra fields to cover unforeseen contingencies.

## Select Reasonable Field Lengths

Give some thought to how long each field should be. You need fields that are long enough to take the longest entry you regularly have. If you make fields too long, however, you waste disk and screen space.

With some information, the field length is obvious. ZIP codes, for example, require nine or ten spaces, depending on whether or not you use a hyphen to separate the last four digits from the first five. You should use no more than two characters for state entries (but remember to add fields for foreign addresses if you require them). The post office prefers the two-letter state abbreviations, most people recognize them, and they save storage and screen space.

Name, company, and address fields are a little more difficult. The best answer here is to experiment with representative entries of your own in order to find out how large these fields should be. A length of 25 to 35 characters seems to be a good average for such fields. You probably won't find many entries that exceed the upper limit of that range. The few that do can be abbreviated in some way to make them fit.

If you separate first name and last name fields to give more flexibility in sorting and report generation, experiment with reasonable lengths for both fields.

## Design a Workable Entry Screen

Q&A is particularly suited to good screen design because you use a full-screen editor to tell the software what the database will look like. Don't hesitate to redo this input/update screen several times.

Think about the sequence in which you normally enter the data into the database. What is the source of this information? In what order is the data presented to you or your operator? For example, using a Last Name, First Name, Company, Title sequence may be difficult if the source document lists First Name, then Last Name, then Title, and Company.

Isolate fields that are rarely updated, for example, social security numbers, part numbers, employee start dates, or birth dates. You can put these fields together on the right side of the screen and enclose them in a box. Once the information is entered, you may not have to open these fields again. The best practice is not to have to step through these fields each time you want to make a simple change to another database field.

## Automate Database Processes

Q&A File is a powerful data management tool that provides a number of end-user programming features to make database maintenance easier. Study the customizing and programming sections of this book and of the Q&A manual to learn how to reduce or eliminate redundant effort.

Consider the Ditto command, for one thing. This useful Q&A tool copies information from the preceding form to the current form so that you enter certain information only once. Suppose that you are working with payroll information grouped by department. You do not need to re-enter the department ID or number until it changes. The Ditto command carries over the department information from the preceding form, and you have to type new data in this field only when you process the first employee from the next department.

Likewise, why type the city and state every time when you are entering similar address records? Particularly if you are working with regional data, such as an employee file, it should be fairly simple to identify the major cities and towns where your employees reside. Enter the cities, along with the ZIP codes for these locations, into a Q&A lookup table. Then during record entry, you enter only the ZIP code. Q&A looks up the city and state and inserts them into the proper fields of the database. If you are dealing with a large number of records, the extra time spent building the ZIP code lookup table can be returned many times during data entry.

See Chapter 7 for more information about using lookup tables and customizing and programming a Q&A File database.

## *Chapter Summary*

Some basic database terms and concepts have been introduced in this chapter. You will see these terms in many other places throughout this book. We have defined a database, discussed some of the different database structures, and presented the concept of data types.

You also have been given a very brief introduction to database design concepts. These ideas are expanded in later sections of this book.

If this chapter should leave you with one basic idea, it is that Q&A is a versatile, user-friendly package. You should approach Q&A accordingly: use your imagination, experiment, test, redo, redesign. Your approach to getting the most out of Q&A database design should be a hands-on approach from the beginning.

Chapter

3

# Getting Started

Now that you understand the concepts and principles of databases, you are ready to begin using Q&A. In this chapter, you find, first, a detailed explanation of how to begin the program and how to exit safely without losing data. You also learn about the Q&A keyboard, the screen displays, and the menu system. The chapter also shows you how to get help from Q&A. You learn the basics of entering and editing text and of working with database and document files.

## *Starting and Ending a Q&A Session*

After the installation is complete (see Appendix A for details on installation), you are ready to use Q&A. How you start the program depends on the computer system you use—floppy disk or hard disk.

### *Starting with a Hard Disk System*

To start Q&A with a hard disk system, follow these steps:

1. Turn on the computer.
2. If prompted by DOS, fill in the date and time. If your system has a clock/calendar, the system automatically fills in the date and time.
3. At the DOS prompt (C> in most cases), change to the directory in which you installed Q&A. Type

   CD\QA

   or

   CD*directory name*

   If you have installed Q&A in the root directory, disregard this step.

4. Type *QA* to start the program. A large QA is displayed while the program is being loaded; then the Q&A Main menu screen is displayed (see fig. 3.1).

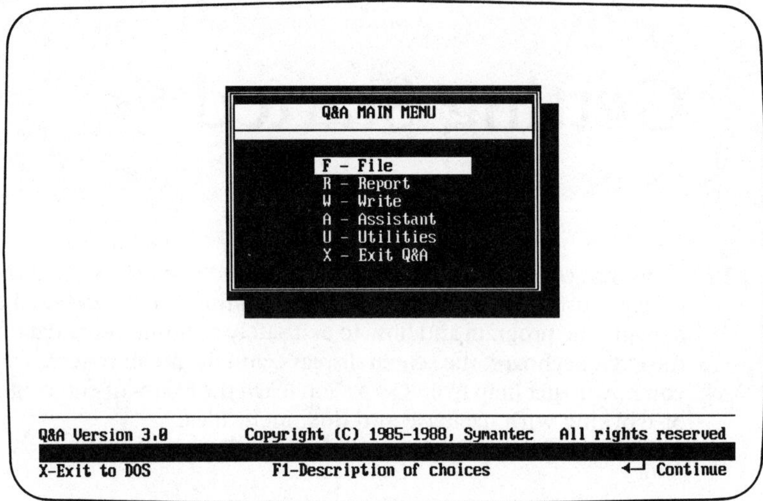


**Fig. 3.1**
*The Q&A Main menu.*

## Starting with a Floppy Disk System

To start using Q&A on a floppy disk system, begin with the computer off.

1. Insert a backup Q&A Startup disk into drive A and turn on the power.
2. Fill in the date and time as prompted. If your system has a clock/calendar, the system automatically fills in the date and time.
3. At the A prompt (A>), start Q&A by typing *QA* and pressing Enter. A large QA is displayed while the program is being loaded; then the menu in figure 3.1 is displayed. This menu is the starting and exiting point of the program.

## Exiting Q&A

You have more than one way to exit Q&A, depending on where you want to be when you exit. The important thing to remember is to protect your data so that it isn't destroyed when you exit.

To leave Q&A and return to DOS, move to the Q&A Main menu (which you can reach in most cases just by pressing the Esc Key several times); then choose X (for Exit Q&A).

You also can exit from the Main menu by pressing the number 6. When the DOS prompt is displayed, you can start another program or quit by turning off the computer.

Do not turn off the computer while you are working on a document or database file in any Q&A module. If you do, you may lose important information.

Do not, under any circumstances, turn off the power or reboot your computer when you are at any point in the program other than the following menus:

- Q&A Main menu
- File menu
- Report menu
- Write menu
- Intelligent Assistant menu
- Utilities menu

If you turn off your computer from any other place, you risk destruction of some or all of the file you are working in. (Note: If you are using Version 1.0, you may safely shut down at the Main menu only.) If you are careful about how you shut down, your data should be safe; as an additional safeguard, though, you should make regular backups of database and document files. For help with this procedure, refer to your DOS manual. If a file becomes damaged, select Recover Database from the Utilities menu. Some data may be lost, but the file will be restored so that you can access it.

## *Using the Q&A Tutor*

Using the Q&A Tutor, provided by the makers of the package, is an effective and easy way for you to learn the basics of Q&A. The tutorial program gives you a guided tour through the Q&A program with instructions and examples that help you begin to master Q&A. The tutorial uses the Q&A program, but as you can see from figures 3.2 and 3.3, some screens have been changed. As an aid to understanding, on-screen prompts offer explanatory messages and working examples.

To use the tutorial on a hard disk system,

1. Start from the DOS C prompt. If you are in Q&A, exit the program and return to DOS.
2. If the Q&A subdirectory is not the current subdirectory, change to the Q&A subdirectory by typing *cd\(subdirectory name)* and pressing Enter.
3. Copy the contents of the tutorial disk (Disk 5) to the Q&A subdirectory of the hard disk. (If you did this as part of step 5 of the section "Install-

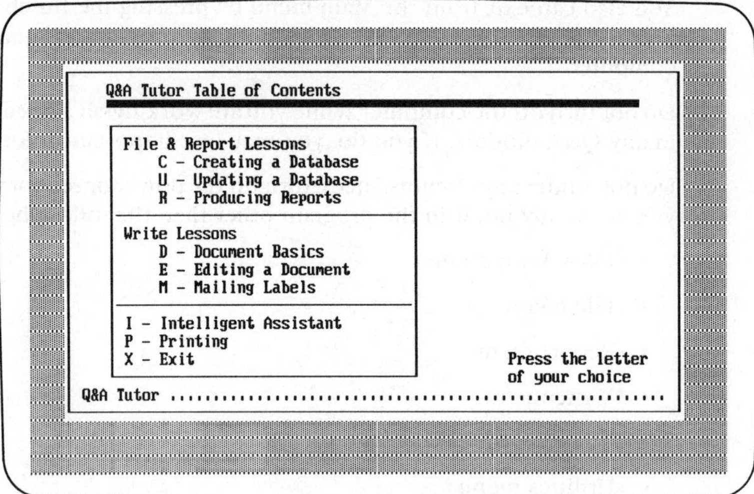


**Fig. 3.2**
*The Tutor's Main menu.*

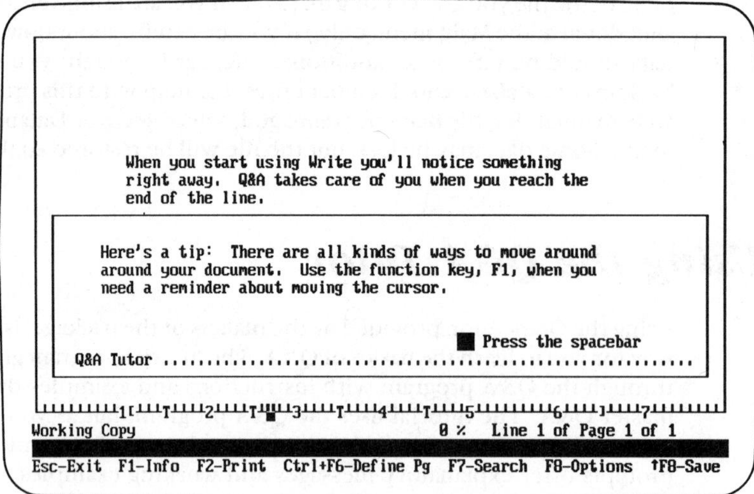


**Fig. 3.3**
*How the tutorial displays a lesson on using Write.*

ing Q&A in a Hard Disk System," skip to step 4.) Refer to the DOS manual for instructions on how to use the COPY command.

4. Start the tutorial from the Q&A subdirectory by typing *qatutor* and pressing Enter. The tutorial begins. Follow the on-screen instructions.

To use the tutorial on a floppy disk system,

1. Start from the DOS A prompt. If you are in Q&A, exit the program and return to DOS.

2. Insert Q&A Disk 1 into drive A.
3. Insert the tutorial disk (Disk 5) into drive B.
4. From the A prompt, type *qatutor* and press Enter. The tutorial begins, providing instructions to continue through the program.

# Understanding the Q&A Keyboard and Screen

The three most commonly used keyboards on IBM and IBM-compatible personal computers are shown in figure 3.4. The keyboards are divided into three sections: the alphanumeric keyboard in the center, the numeric keypad on the right, and the function key section on the left or across the top. The Enhanced Keyboard, which is used by the IBM Personal System/2™ family of computers and some AT-compatible computers, also has a separate group of cursor-movement keys.

## The Alphanumeric Keys

Most of the keys in the alphanumeric section at the center of the keyboard are the same ones you find on a typewriter, and they maintain their customary functions in Q&A. As table 3.1 illustrates, however, several keys (Esc, Tab, Shift, and Alt) on the alphanumeric keyboard take on new functions or are different from typewriter keys. As you become accustomed to these keys, you will find them helpful and easy to use.

**Table 3.1**
**Alphanumeric Key Operations in Q&A**

| *Key* | *Function* |
|---|---|
| Enter | Accepts an entry and continues; moves the cursor to the start of the next line |
| Esc | Cancels the current operation; exits the current screen and returns to the menu; leaves the current menu and moves to the preceding menu |
| Tab | Jumps cursor to next tab stop in document; jumps cursor to start of next field in database form |
| Shift-Tab | Jumps cursor to start of preceding field in database form (reverse tab) |
| Alt | Used simultaneously with function keys for special functions (see table 3.2) |

**Table 3.1 — *Continued***

| *Key* | *Function* |
|---|---|
| Shift | Used simultaneously with other keys: Changes the central section of the keyboard to uppercase letters and characters; activates a temporary Num Lock allowing numbers to be entered by using the numeric keypad on the right of the keyboard |
| Backspace | Erases the characters to the left of the cursor |

**Fig. 3.4**
***The three personal computer keyboards.***

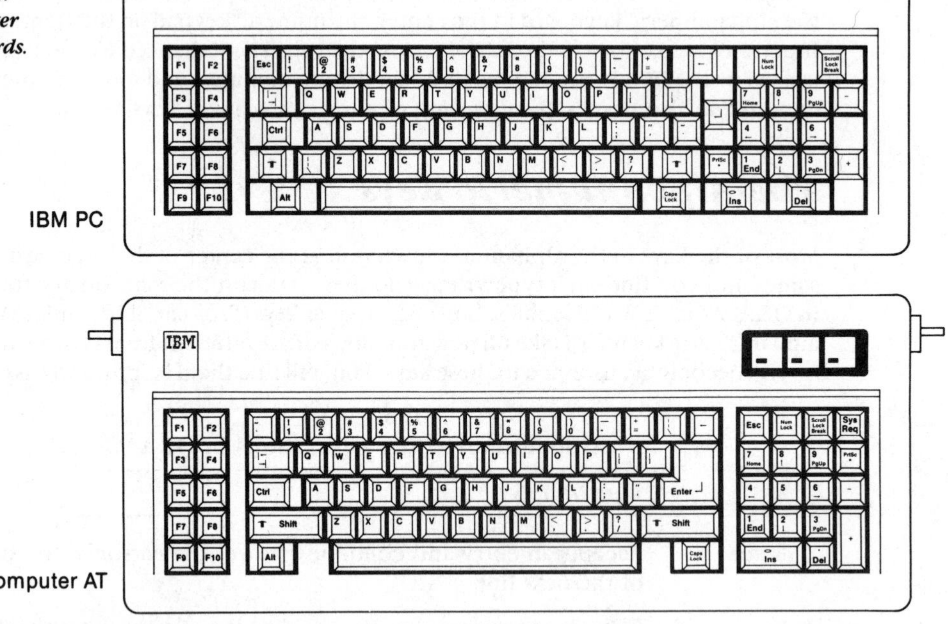


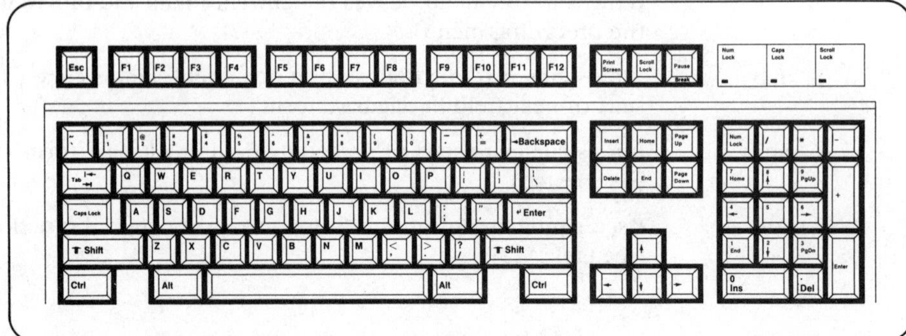

Enhanced Keyboard

## *The Function Keys*

The function keys F1 through F10 are used for special situations in Q&A. Notice the difference in location of the function keys on the two types of keyboard; the keys are on the far left of the PC and AT keyboards but across the top of the Enhanced Keyboard. The Enhanced Keyboard also has two more function keys, F11 and F12. Q&A, like many current programs, does not use these keys.

The function keys are explained in table 3.2. Notice that most keys have multiple actions, activated when the key is pressed with the Shift, Ctrl, or Alt key. Although Q&A is well-designed for continuity across the modules, some function keys perform different operations in different modules.

**Table 3.2**
**The Function Keys in Q&A**

| *Key* | *Action in Write* | *Action in File* | *Action in Report* |
|---|---|---|---|
| F1 | Get help screen | Get help screen | Get help screen |
| Shift-F1 | Check spelling in document | | |
| Ctrl-F1 | Check spelling of word | | |
| F2 | Print document | Print current form | |
| Shift-F2 | Use macros | Use macros | |
| Ctrl-F2 | Print text block | Print to end of stack | |
| F3 | Delete block | Delete current form or Clear Spec | Clear Spec |
| Ctrl-F3 | Document Specs | | |
| F4 | Delete to end of word | Delete to end of word | Delete to end of word |
| Shift-F4 | Delete line | Delete to end of field | Delete to end of field |
| Ctrl-F4 | Delete to end of line | | |
| F5 | Copy block | Ditto field (copy value) | |
| Shift-F5 | Move block | Ditto form | |
| Ctrl-F5 | Copy block to file | Insert system date | Insert system date |
| Alt-F5 | Move block to file | Insert system time | Insert system time |

**Table 3.2 — *Continued***

| *Key* | *Action in Write* | *Action in File* | *Action in Report* |
|---|---|---|---|
| F6 | Set temporary margins | Switch between table and form view or expand field | Expand field |
| Shift-F6 | Enhance text | | |
| Ctrl-F6 | Define page | GoTo Add Forms (from Edit) | |
| Alt-F6 | Hyphenate | | |
| F7 | Search and replace | Search (retrieve spec) | |
| Shift-F7 | Restore text/make multiple copies | | |
| Ctrl-F7 | GoTo Page/Line | | Logical (Boolean OR across fields) |
| Alt-F7 | List fields | | |
| F8 | Options menu | Calc | Derived columns |
| Shift-F8 | Save document | Set Manual/Auto Calc | |
| Ctrl-F8 | Export document | Reset @Number | |
| F9 | Scroll screen up | Save form and get preceding form | Go back to preceding operation |
| Shift-F9 | Scroll screen down | GoTo Customize Specs | |
| Ctrl-F9 | Make font assignments | | |
| Alt-F9 | Calculate | | |
| F10 | Continue | Save form and get next form | Continue |
| Shift-F10 | | Save form and exit | |

The use of each function key is more completely explained as it is introduced in the appropriate chapter, but some general aids and guides are given here.

Q&A provides two references and reminders of what the keys do: a key assignment line and a key usage help screen. The key assignment line appears at the bottom of the screen and identifies the functions of keys in the current situation (see fig. 3.5). The key usage help screen is displayed at data entry points in the program when you press the help function key, F1 (see fig. 3.6). Note that F1 is the help key throughout Q&A, even though the bottom-of-screen prompt for F1 changes with different modules. An optional function-key template can be purchased to fit over the function keys of the IBM PC, providing an instant guide to the function of the keys in Q&A.

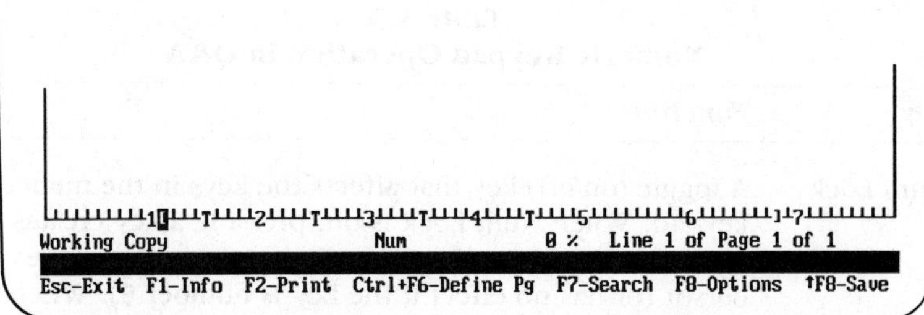


**Fig. 3.5**
*Function-key assignments.*

| | | | |
|---|---|---|---|
| F1 | Ctrl F1 Check spelling (word)<br>Shift F1 Check spelling (doc)<br>F1 Info | F2 | Ctrl F2 Print text block<br>Shift F2 Use macros<br>F2 Print document |
| F3 | Ctrl F3 Document statistics<br>F3 Delete block | F4 | Ctrl F4 Delete to end of line<br>Shift F4 Delete line (Ctrl Y)<br>F4 Delete word (Ctrl T) |
| F5 | Alt F5 Move block to file<br>Ctrl F5 Copy block to file<br>Shift F5 Move block<br>F5 Copy block | F6 | Alt F6 Hyphenate<br>Ctrl F6 Define Page<br>Shift F6 Enhance text<br>F6 Set temporary margins |
| F7 | Alt F7 List fields<br>Ctrl F7 Go to page/line<br>Shift F7 Restore text<br>F7 Search & Replace | F8 | Ctrl F8 Export document<br>Shift F8 Save document<br>F8 Options Menu |
| F9 | Alt F9 Calculate<br>Ctrl F9 Make font assignments<br>Shift F9 Scroll screen down<br>F9 Scroll screen up | F10 | F10 Continue |

Esc-Cancel →PgDn-More←

**Fig. 3.6**
*The key usage help screen in Write.*

## *The Numeric Keypad*

You use the numeric keypad, situated on the right side of the keyboard, mostly for cursor movement; the keypad holds the arrow keys, the Home key, the End key, and the PgUp and PgDn keys. These and other cursor-movement keys are described in detail in "The Cursor-Movement Keys." Table 3.3 explains the operation of the numeric-keypad keys that are not used for cursor movement.

On the IBM PC and AT keyboards, this numeric keypad has to do double duty. It functions as both a numeric-entry pad and as a cursor-movement pad. The Enhanced Keyboard duplicates this functionality for those who want it but also provides separate cursor-movement keys in the keypad section between the numeric keypad and the alphanumeric keypad.

**Table 3.3**
**Numeric Keypad Operation in Q&A**

| *Key* | *Function* |
|---|---|
| Num Lock | A toggle (on/off) key that affects the keys in the numeric keypad. When Num Lock is on, pressing a key creates a number; when Num Lock is off, pressing a key moves the cursor (or has no effect if the key is number 5). When the Num Lock key is on in Write, Q&A displays `Num` on the status line of the screen. |
| Del | Deletes the character highlighted by the cursor |
| Scroll Lock/ Break | Not used by Q&A |
| Ins | A toggle key that changes the typing mode from Overwrite to Insert. When Ins is on, entered characters are inserted at the cursor location; when Ins is off, entered characters replace existing characters. The Backspace key changes behavior in Insert mode; in Overwrite mode, the key replaces characters with blank spaces without affecting the rest of the line, but in Insert mode, the key deletes characters to the left of the cursor and shifts the remainder of the line to the left. |

To use the numeric keypad to enter numbers, you can do one of two things: (1) You can press the Num Lock key to turn on numbers before entering the numbers and press the key again to turn off numbers. (2) You can hold down the Shift key while you press the number keys.

If you press a cursor-movement key and a number typed, the Num Lock key is on. Press the Num Lock key to turn it off; then use the cursor-movement keys.

## *The Cursor-Movement Keys*

To move around the screen and from screen to screen, use the cursor-movement keys. If you use the arrow keys on the numeric keypad, make certain that Num Lock is disengaged.

The cursor-movement keys can be used alone or with the Tab and Ctrl keys. Generally, the cursor-movement keys are consistent from one module to the next, as can be seen in tables 3.4 and 3.5. This consistency makes learning to use the keys easy.

**Table 3.4**
**Cursor-Movement Keys in Q&A**

| *Key* | *Movement in a Write Document* | *Movement during Form Design* | *Movement within a Form* |
|---|---|---|---|
| ↑ | Up one line | Up one line | Up one line |
| ↓ | Down one line | Down one line | Down one line |
| → | Next character to right | Next character to right | Next character to right |
| Ctrl-→ | Next word to right | Next word to right | Next word to right |
| ← | Next character to left | Next character to left | Next character to left |
| Ctrl-← | Next word to left | Next word to left | Next word to left |
| PgUp | 1st character of preceding screen | 1st character of preceding page | 1st character of preceding page |
| Ctrl-PgUp | 1st character of preceding page | | |
| PgDn | 1st character of next screen | 1st character of next page | Next page |
| Ctrl-PgDn | 1st character of next page | | |
| Tab | Next tab stop to right | Next tab stop to right | Next field |
| Shift-Tab | Next tab stop to left | Next tab stop to left | Preceding field |
| F9 | Scroll up | | |
| Shift-F9 | Scroll down | | |

**Table 3.5**
**The Home and End Keys in Q&A**

| *Key* | *Movement in a Write Document* | *Movement during Form Design* | *Movement within a Form* |
|---|---|---|---|
| Home | *Move to* | *Move to* | *Move to* |
| 1st press | 1st character of line | 1st character of line | 1st character of field |
| 2nd press | 1st character of screen of current page | 1st character of page | 1st character of first field |
| 3rd press | 1st character of page | 1st character of form | 1st character of first field of form |
| 4th press | 1st character of document | | |
| Ctrl-Home | 1st character of document | | 1st form in database stack |
| End | | | |
| 1st press | Last character of line | Last character of line | Last character of current field |
| 2nd press | Last character of screen of current page | Last character of page | Last character of last field |
| 3rd press | Last character of page | Last character of form | Last character of last field of form |
| 4th press | Last character of document | | |
| Ctrl-End | Last character of document | | Last form in database stack |

Q&A uses certain keys to move the cursor in relation to the markings on the ruler line, which appears in the Write module and at the bottom of the File form design screen. The following keys make moving back and forth on the ruler easier:

| *Key* | *Cursor moves to* |
|---|---|
| Home | First space to the right of the left margin |
| End | First space to the left of the right margin |
| Ctrl-← | Five spaces to the left |
| Ctrl-→ | Five spaces to the right |

| | |
|---|---|
| Tab | Next tab marker to the right |
| Shift-Tab | Closest tab marker to the left |

## *The Q&A Screen Display*

Q&A's screen display places all program information on the bottom four lines, leaving the remainder of the screen available for you to use. Figure 3.7 shows this information on the Q&A File design screen; figure 3.8 shows how Write displays function key assignments. (The screens displayed while you are working in the Intelligent Assistant, however, vary in layout; see Chapters 17 and 18 for examples.) On the left side of the status line is the file name of the database or document you are using. Q&A also displays the cursor position, the current form or page, and the total number of forms or pages.

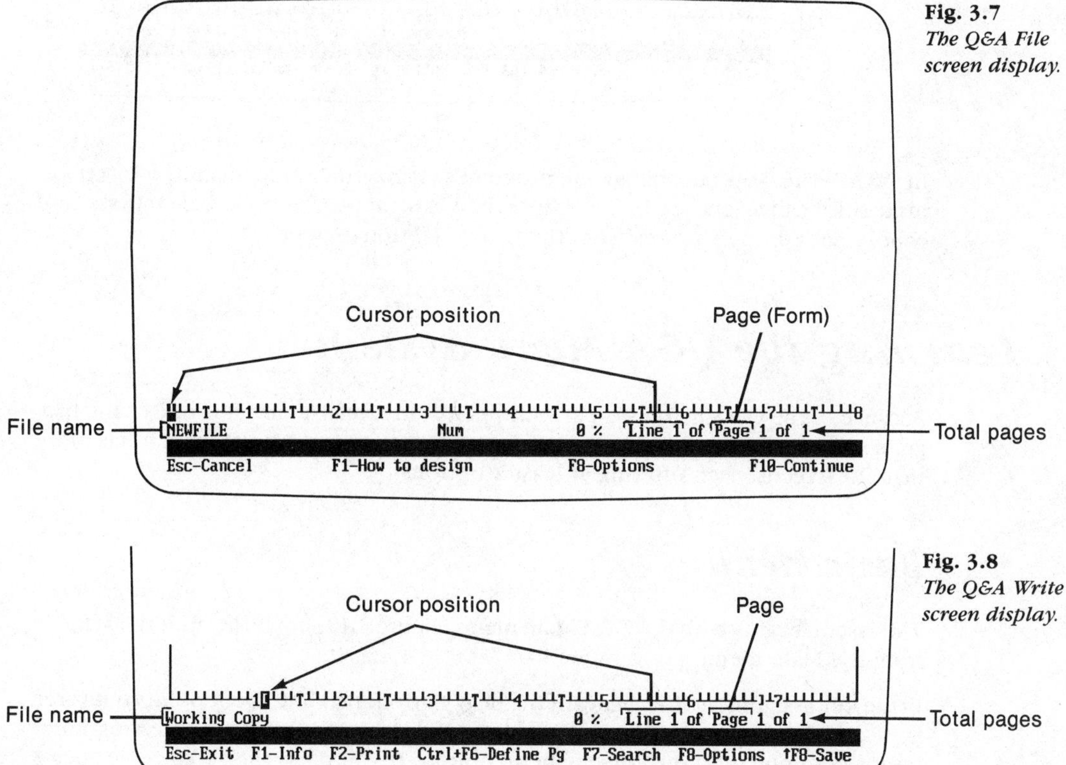


**Fig. 3.7**
*The Q&A File screen display.*

**Fig. 3.8**
*The Q&A Write screen display.*

The status line also shows information about the status of the toggle keys. Q&A has three of these on/off keys: Caps Lock, Num Lock, and Ins. On the status line in figure 3.9, the toggle-key indicators show that the three keys are on. When the Caps Lock key is on, all alphanumeric keys create uppercase characters. When the Num Lock key is on, all keypad number keys produce numbers rather than move the cursor. When the Ins key is on, characters to the right of the cursor move to the right as you enter new text. Notice also that when you are in the Insert mode, the cursor shape changes from a single thin horizontal line to a solid rectangular box. In Overwrite mode (no `Ins` indicator on the status line), new characters type over or replace existing characters.

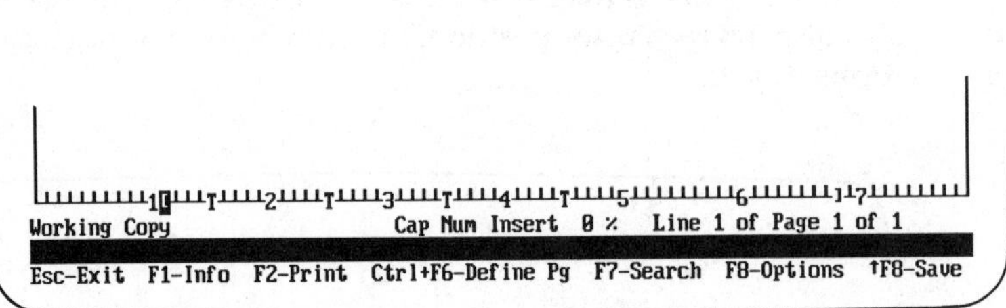


**Fig. 3.9**
*The on-off key indicators on the status line.*

In Q&A Write, you can change the program's Overwrite mode default to Insert. To make this change, choose Utilities from the Write menu, select Global Options, and choose Set Editing Options from the Global Options screen.

# Learning the Q&A Menu System

Because of the Q&A menu system's simplicity and consistency, it is one of the program's strongest features. The menu system is easy to use even though it has more than 20 screens, each offering at least 2 options.

## Basic Menus

The system begins with the Q&A Main menu. Figure 3.10 shows the options available from the Main menu.

In the key assignment line, beneath the heavy horizontal line, Q&A points out three keys as helpful or necessary. You can press X to leave the program. Pressing Enter means continue with the chosen menu option. If you press the F1 key, you access the Main menu help screen, which explains five menu options and displays a caution notice about safeguarding your data (see fig. 3.11). Press Esc to return to the Main

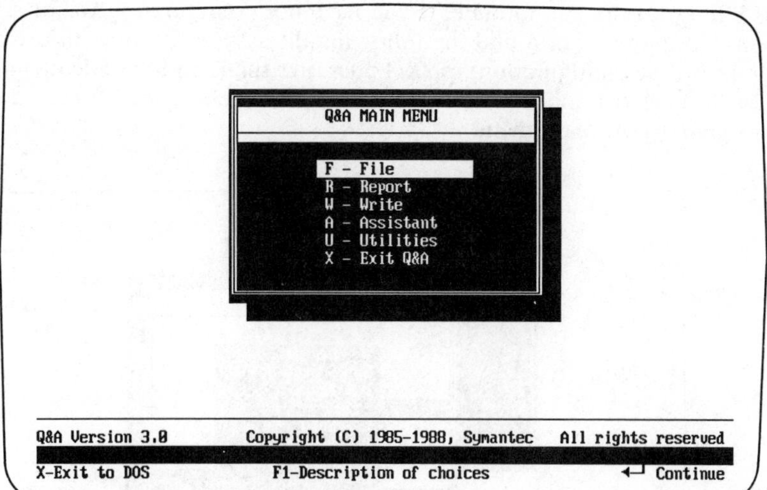


**Fig. 3.10**
*The Q&A Main menu.*

menu. The special keys highlighted on the key assignment line will be different for each menu or Q&A screen you access. (Help screens are fully explained in a following section.)

| CHOICE | DESCRIPTION | VOLUME |
|---|---|---|
| File | Create, fill out, and work with forms of information. | 1 |
| Report | Take information from your forms, sort and arrange it, print results in a table. | 1 |
| Write | Write and print documents. | 2 |
| Assistant | Teach your Intelligent Assistant (IA) about your forms then ask questions, generate reports, or change information using ordinary English. | 1 |
| Utilities | Set-up your printer, import/export data from other programs, DOS file facilities, etc. | 2 |

CAUTION: Sudden loss or interruption of power can damage a data file. Never turn your machine off or reboot the system UNLESS you are at one of the main Q&A menus. If a power loss does occur, however, you can probably recover the file (see pg. U-65). Make frequent backups (pg. F-187).

Esc-Cancel

**Fig. 3.11**
*The Q&A Main menu help screen.*

You select a menu option by typing the single letter at the beginning of the option and then pressing the Enter key. Use a lowercase or an uppercase letter—it doesn't matter. For most options, the single letter is also the first letter of the menu choice, for example, F for File and R for Report.

Press F to go to the File module. If you have not configured Q&A for single-key response (see Appendix A and the following discussion for more information on single-keystroke configuration), press Enter after the F, and the File menu appears (see fig. 3.12). Notice, in the key assignment line, that pressing the Esc key now returns the program to the Main menu.

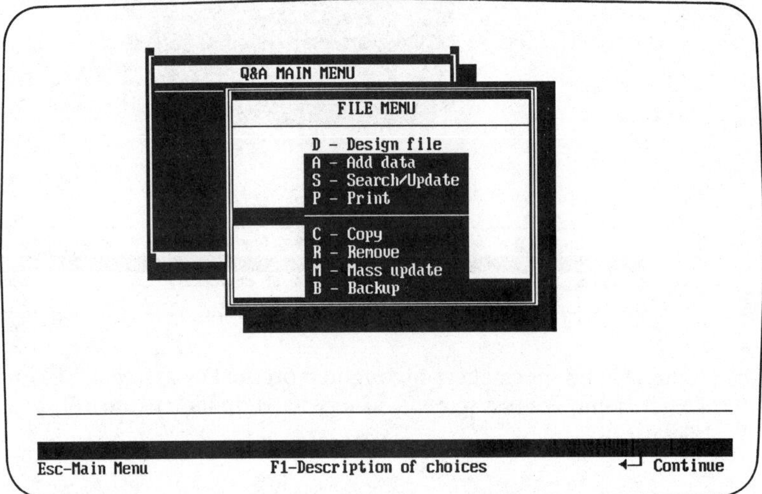


**Fig. 3.12**
*The File menu.*

Q&A also uses single-key menu selection. As easy as it is to choose a menu option by typing a single letter and pressing Enter, Q&A provides an easier and quicker way—just pressing a number.

Imagine a number in front of each option; start with 1 at the top left option and number consecutively from top to bottom and left to right. The following list is how the Main menu would be numbered according to that scheme:

(1) F - File
(2) R - Report
(3) W - Write
(4) A - Assistant
(5) U - Utilities
(6) X - Exit Q&A

To select a menu option, press its imaginary number—no need to press Enter.

Every menu can be numbered according to the same imaginary scheme and can therefore provide the same ease of choice.

You also can configure Q&A to respond instantly to the first letter in the menu choice without your having to press Enter. Select Utilities from the main Q&A menu; then choose Set Global Defaults. Specify Yes under Automatic Execution. In this mode, when you press F, for example, the File menu appears immediately. You don't have to press Enter.

## *Menu Paths*

This book at times refers to a series of menu selections as a menu path. The path usually starts from the Main menu with the menu selections separated by backslashes (\). For example, the path taken to the File Set Initial Values function is

File\Design File\Customize a File\Type File Name\Set Initial Values

Menu paths are quick ways to show how to get to a particular function.

**Table 3.6**
**The Q&A Main Menu and Its Following Menus**

Q&A Main Menu

| F-File | R-Report | W-Write | A-Assistant | U-Utilities | X-Exit Q&A |
|---|---|---|---|---|---|
| *File menu* | *Report menu* | *Write menu* | *Assistant menu* | *Utilities menu* | |
| D-Design File | D-Design/ Redesign a Report | T-Type/ Edit | G-Get Acquainted | I-Import Data | |
| A-Add Data | P-Print a Report | D-Define Page | T-Teach Me about Your Database | E-Export Data | |
| S-Search/ Update | S-Set Global Options | P-Print | A-Ask Me To Do Something | P-Install Printer | |
| P-Print | R-Rename/ Delete/ Copy | C-Clear | | D-DOS File Facilities | |
| C-Copy | | G-Get | | S-Set Global Defaults | |
| R-Remove | | S-Save | R-Recover Database | | |
| M-Mass update | | U-Utilities | | | |
| B-Backup | | M-Mailing Labels | | | |

# *Getting Help from Q&A*

Once you have become familiar with the Q&A keyboard, screen, and menu system, you may be able to begin using Q&A without further instruction. This ability is possible because of the thorough Q&A help screens.

Q&A provides context-sensitive help. You can reach a help screen from virtually every point in the program, just by pressing the F1 key. The help screen displays instructions specific to the functions available from the current screen. In most cases, the F1 key is a toggle switch: press it once and the help screen appears; press F1 again and the screen disappears. The Esc key provides an alternative exit from a help screen. In addition to context-sensitive and concurrent help screens, Q&A File has a custom help capability so that you can create personalized help screens.

Depending on where you are in the program when you press F1, Q&A presents four different help screens: menu, feature, concurrent, or two-level. Each screen offers a different kind of assistance.

### *Menu Help Screens*

When you are at a menu, pressing F1 displays an explanation of that menu's options. For example, when you press F1 at the Write menu, you see the Q&A Write menu help screen illustrated in figure 3.13. Note that the screen refers you to the page in the *Q&A Instruction Manual* where you can find more information about that menu option. Press Esc to return to the Write menu.

**Fig. 3.13**
*The Write menu help screen.*

| CHOICE | DESCRIPTION | VOLUME 2, PAGE: |
|---|---|---|
| Type/Edit | Edit the current document (the "working copy"). | W-11 |
| Define page | Set page size, margins, characters per inch, etc. | W-73 |
| Print | Choose print options, then print the document. | W-79 |
| Clear | Clear the current document from memory, and start a new one. | W-95 |
| Get | Get a document from disk: make it the current one. | W-97 |
| Save | Save the current document to disk. | W-101 |
| Utilities | Set global options: modify font file: export to ASCII: rename/delete/copy a document: list files: set editing options: change Print and Define Page screen defaults. | W-157 |
| Mailing labels | Create/edit and print mailing labels | W-119 |

Esc-Cancel

### *Context-Sensitive Help Screens*

Whatever you are doing in Q&A, you press F1 to display a help screen that has instructions specific to your environment: context-sensitive help. Suppose that you are adding data to a file form. To get help, press F1; Q&A displays the screen illustrated in figure 3.14. This help screen outlines the steps for adding or updating a form and lists function keys that are especially useful.

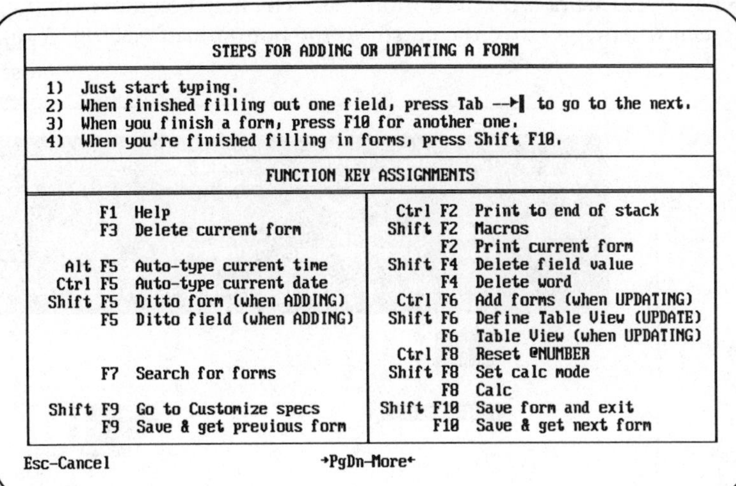


**Fig. 3.14**
*The help screen for adding or updating a File form.*

### *Concurrent Help Screens*

One of Q&A's many innovations is the use of concurrent help screens, which are displayed simultaneously with your work. In figure 3.15, the box in the lower half of the screen is a help screen; the top half is the file form. With a concurrent help screen, you can work on one half of the screen and keep the instructions displayed on the other half.

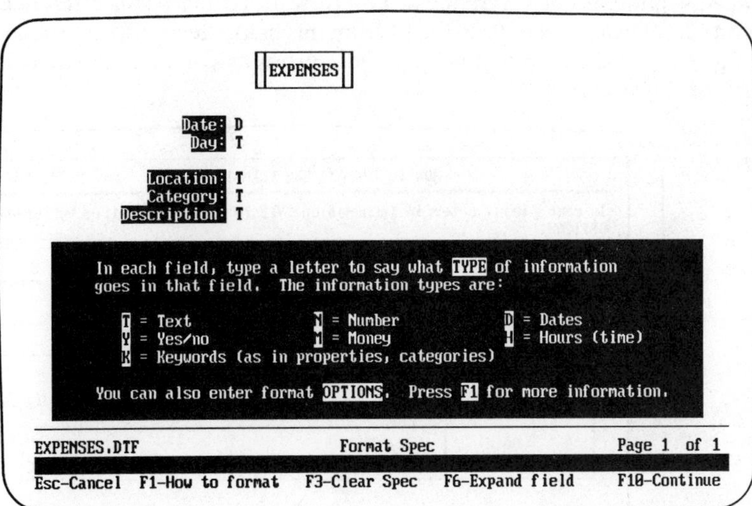


**Fig. 3.15**
*A concurrent help screen on the lower part of the screen.*

But what if your work is on the bottom half? The help box moves to the top half of the screen when you move the cursor to the bottom half (see fig. 3.16).

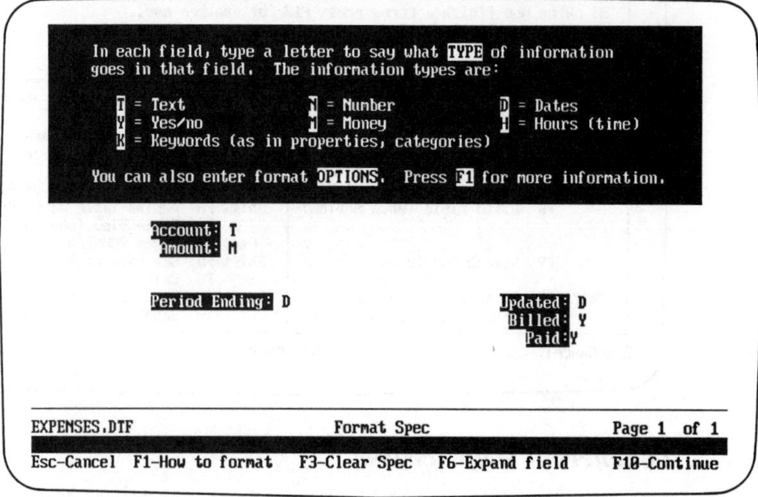
In each field, type a letter to say what TYPE of information goes in that field. The information types are:
T = Text
N = Number
D = Dates
Y = Yes/no
M = Money
H = Hours (time)
K = Keywords (as in properties, categories)
You can also enter format OPTIONS. Press F1 for more information.
Account: T
Amount: M
Period Ending: D
Updated: D
Billed: Y
Paid: Y
EXPENSES.DTF
Format Spec
Page 1 of 1
Esc-Cancel F1-How to format F3-Clear Spec F6-Expand field F10-Continue

**Fig. 3.16** *A concurrent help screen on the top part of the screen.*

### *Two-Level Help Screens*

If the program feature or operation is complex, or if all the instructions cannot fit on one screen, Q&A provides a two-level help screen. Look again at figure 3.16; notice the key assignment line reference to F1—How To Format. This reference indicates a second-level help screen. Pressing F1 from this help screen displays the second level (see fig. 3.17). If the help text is long, Q&A prompts you to press the PgDn key for additional information.

HOW TO FORMAT: THE FORMAT SPEC pg. F-22, 107

In each field, enter an information TYPE followed optionally by format OPTIONS:

| TYPE | MEANING | FORMAT OPTIONS |
|---|---|---|
| T<br>K<br>Y | Text<br>Keyword<br>Yes/No | JR = Justify Right U = Uppercase<br>JC = Justify Center<br>JL = Justify Left |
| N<br>M | Number<br>Money | JR, JL, JC<br>0-7 = # of decimal digits (for N only)<br>C = insert commas |
| D<br>H | Date<br>Time | JR, JL, JC |

Examples: N,2,JR,C = This field contains numbers, and they should have two decimal digits, be right justified, with commas.
T,U = This field contains text, in uppercase.

Esc-Cancel

**Fig. 3.17** *A second-level help screen.*

### *Custom Help Screens*

A custom help screen is one that is created by the user rather than by Q&A programmers. You can create custom help screens when you first design a file or after you determine where help is needed. A custom help screen can be created for each field in a database, although the possibility that every field will need one is unlikely.

Each screen can instruct the user about what information should be entered in the field. Figure 3.18, for example, shows a help screen listing the acceptable entries for the Category field of the database. Custom help screens also can help users by displaying reference material, documenting the field's formula, providing reminders for database users, or holding any other information or instructions you choose.

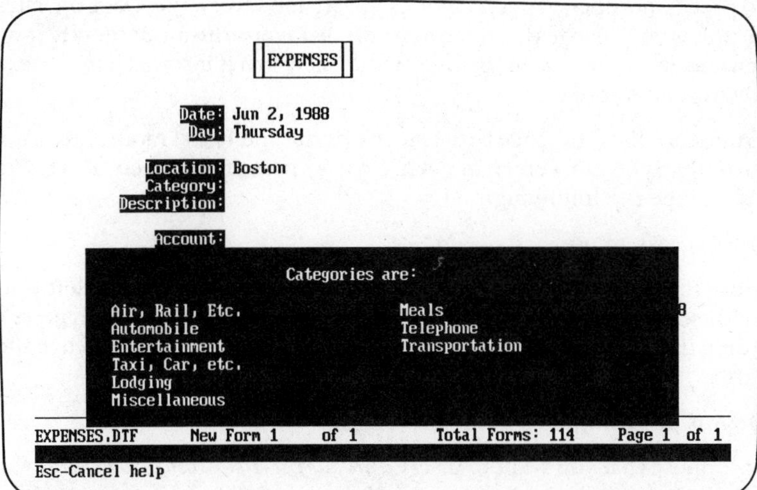


**Fig. 3.18** *A custom help screen.*

Custom help screens for a File database help everyone who uses the database. For people designing the database, custom help screens can facilitate the training of new users. For people using the database, custom help screens can be an aid in learning to use the database faster and getting work done sooner—because help is available, as needed, at the press of a key. See Chapter 7 for information on how to create custom help screens.

# *Entering and Editing Text in Q&A*

A major reason for Q&A's ease of use is the availability of most of the word-processing functions in all modules: File, Report, Intelligent Assistant, and Write. The word-processing functions work the same in all the modules. You use Q&A's word-processing functions to enter and edit text.

## *Entering Text*

To enter text in any Q&A module, move the cursor to the appropriate screen location and type the text. If you have questions about what the function keys do, press F1 to display the key usage help screen.

Q&A uses wordwrap; when the entered text continues beyond the end of a line, the sentence wraps around to continue on the next line. Allowing text to wrap to the next line keeps text connected from line to line. This feature is important for editing and formatting the text. To stop wordwrap, press Enter at the end of each line; this procedure disconnects the lines so that you can enter information that must remain on separate lines, as in tables or addresses.

Word processors operate in two modes: Insert and Overwrite. Q&A operates in Overwrite unless you change the mode to Insert. In Overwrite mode, new text writes over any characters on the screen. In Insert mode, new text is inserted into the text; existing text is pushed to the right.

To experience the difference between Overwrite and Insert modes, go from the Main menu to the Type/Edit screen in Q&A Write by pressing W; then, at the Write menu, select T. Type the following:

Q&A is easy to use.

Suppose that you want to change *easy to use* to *powerful*. Use the left-arrow key to move the cursor to the first letter of *easy*. Type *powerful.* and then press the space bar three times to delete the remaining letters and period. The sentence should look like this:

Q&A is powerful.

Now suppose that you want to insert *and easy to use* after *powerful*. Switch to the Insert mode by pressing the Ins key. Note that the cursor changes from the thin horizontal line to a rectangle, which is the insert cursor. Move the cursor to highlight the period after *powerful*. Press the space bar once and type

and easy to use

The sentence should look like this:

Q&A is powerful and easy to use.

The Ins key is a toggle switch. To return to the Overwrite mode from the Insert mode, press Ins again.

## *Marking and Deleting Text*

You can delete unwanted text one character at a time or in a block of characters: single words, groups of words, sentences, paragraphs, or any size block.

To delete a character, position the cursor under the character to be deleted and press the Del key, or position the cursor to the right of the character to be deleted and press the Backspace key. To delete the character you just typed, press the Backspace key.

To delete a word, move the cursor to the word's first letter and press F4 once—the word and the space after it are deleted. Positioning the cursor on any other letter of the word deletes from the cursor to the end of the word but does not delete the space that follows the word.

To delete a line, position the cursor anywhere in the line and press Shift-F4. In Q&A File, Shift-F4 deletes an entire field line.

To delete a block of words—including phrases, sentences, and paragraphs—move the cursor to the first character to be deleted and press F3; Q&A marks the spot. Next, move the cursor to the end of the block to be deleted. As you move the cursor, Q&A highlights the area to be deleted. When the highlighted area contains the material you want to delete, press F10. Press Esc to abandon the operation.

Suppose that you want to delete the middle sentence of the following paragraph:

> Seven salesmen went to Dallas. Six made their quotas. One did not return.

Move the cursor to the first letter of the second sentence and press F3 once. Next, move the cursor to the end of the sentence by holding down the Ctrl key and pressing the right-arrow key until the entire sentence is highlighted; then press F10. The sentence is deleted, but two extra spaces remain. The spaces can be deleted by pressing the Del key twice. You also can include the trailing spaces in the marked block by highlighting them with the right-arrow key while you are highlighting the sentence.

A quick way to get to the end of the sentence when you are marking a block is to press the period key after you press F3. Q&A immediately marks the text between the position where F3 is pressed and the first period the program finds after that position. In fact, you can mark large blocks of text easily by first positioning the cursor at the beginning of the block you want to mark, pressing F3, and then typing the last character in the block. Q&A highlights all the text from the beginning of the block to the first occurrence of the next character you type after pressing F3. Press F3 and Enter to mark the end of a paragraph.

## *Recovering Deleted Text: Shift-F7*

If you delete text by mistake, you can recover it by pressing Shift-F7. However, you must use Shift-F7 before you delete, copy, or move another block of text. Q&A retains in memory up to one page of text deleted in a block operation; only text that has been stored in a special section of blocked-text RAM can be recovered with Shift-F7. If the block of text being deleted is larger than Q&A can store and recover, the program issues a warning before the block is deleted.

Shift-F7 recovers only text deleted by F3. Text deleted by using the Del or Backspace key cannot be recovered.

## *Responding to Error Messages*

An error message may appear on your screen from time to time, as a warning that an operation is incorrect. An error message tells you when you enter an invalid retrieve specification in Q&A File (see fig. 3.19) or relays information that the program has its own trouble, such as a file not found (see fig. 3.20). In either of these cases, the problem is probably an incorrect data entry. Correcting the problem may be as simple as re-entering the information and trying the operation again.

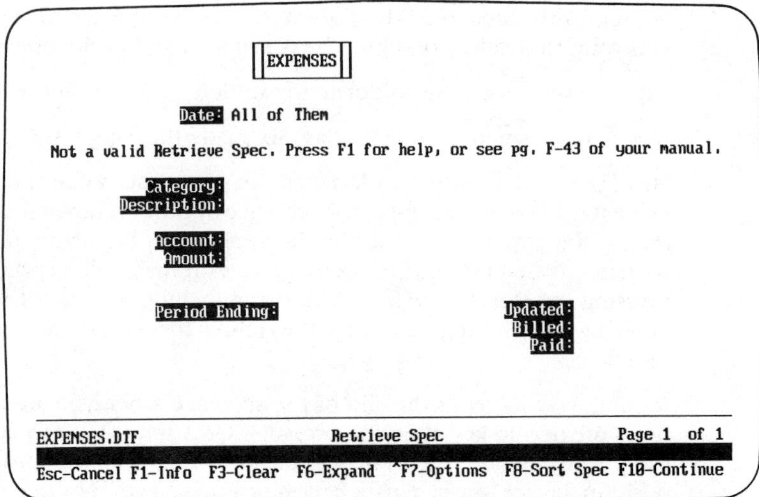


**Fig. 3.19**
*An error message for operator error.*

If a program problem causes the error message, you should take immediate steps to save your data:

1. Read the message carefully and follow any instructions it contains.
2. Refer to the "Error Messages" appendix at the end of the *Q&A Instruction Manual.*
3. Unless otherwise directed, try to save your document or database. Depending on the error condition, saving may or may not be possible. If you can save your work, use a new file name so that the old file is not erased—it may be the only good file to survive if a program malfunction has damaged the active file.

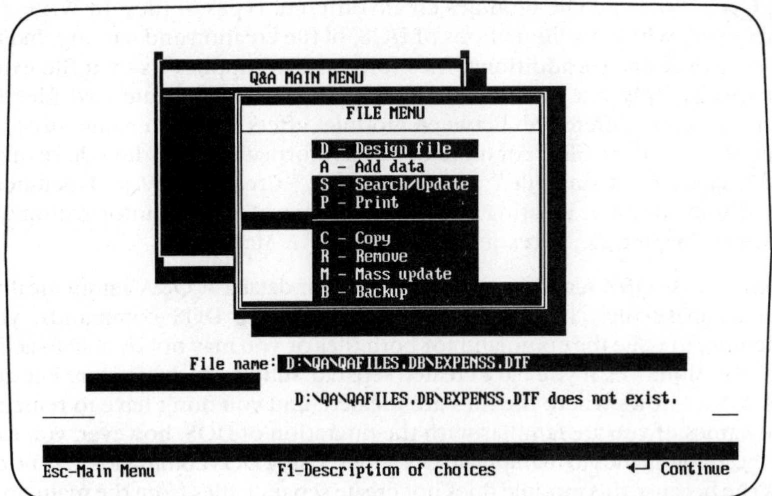


**Fig. 3.20** *An error message for a program problem.*

4. If an error reference number is displayed, write it down and save it for future reference. Discuss the problem with a Symantec user-support representative; these representatives often have current information for solving and avoiding problems.

If you find no explanation of the message in the appendix, you may have an undocumented error. Do the following:

1. Make a screen printout by turning on your printer and pressing PrtSc (or Print Scrn on Enhanced Keyboards); this step prints a record of the error message and the contents of the screen.
2. Make a record of the steps you took before the message was displayed.
3. Contact a Symantec user-support representative (the telephone number is in your Q&A manual) and supply the reference number shown on the screen.

In the rare instance where the problem resides in the Q&A program itself, the solution may be more difficult. Q&A has been extensively tested, and I have had no problems, but every program has the potential for occasional failure.

# *Working with Document and Database Files*

This section introduces you to the Q&A processes used to name, rename, save, copy, and delete Q&A documents and database files. You can perform all these functions in DOS by using the appropriate commands, but using the Q&A operations may be easier because of the way Q&A creates and handles files.

The Q&A Write and File modules create different types of files. In Write, you have full control, within the limitations of DOS, of file creation and naming. In File, Q&A automatically creates additional files for you and supplies its own file extensions. You specify only one file name; but the program may create two files for each database. These differences between modules affect how you name, store, retrieve, copy, and delete the files. For more detailed information regarding these operations, read Chapter 6, "Using File," and Chapter 10, "Creating a Write Document." You may at some point be creating and storing macros. For more information on macro files, see Chapter 19, "Creating and Using Q&A Macros."

When you use Q&A functions to work with your database, Q&A automatically adjusts both database files. If you use the corresponding DOS commands, you must remember to issue the command for both files or you may not be able to access your database. Moreover, if you have created separate subdirectories to store File and Write files, Q&A knows where the files are located, and you don't have to remember the path names. If you are familiar with the operation of DOS, however, you can freely use these commands to manipulate Q&A files. Using DOS commands may be desirable in Write because this module does not create separate files from the main document.

## *Naming a File*

Q&A file names follow DOS naming conventions—up to eight characters in length, followed by a period (.) and a three-character extension. The format for a Q&A file name is

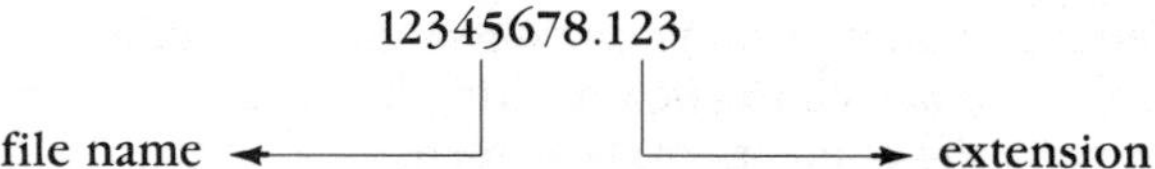


You can name Q&A document files according to this rule (although document files do not require an extension), but database files always have the extension DTF. This fact means that when you name a database file, you supply a name of up to eight characters, but the program supplies the extension.

No matter what type of file you create in Q&A, you control the eight-character name. Whether you control the three-character extension depends on the file type. The possible Q&A files and their extensions are

| *Type of File* | *Extensions* |
|---|---|
| Database file | DTF (for the data file)<br>IDX (for the index) |
| Document file | Your choice. Q&A does not add extensions to document file names |
| Macro file | ASC (Q&A's default) or your choice |

The Q&A Report module works differently. When you create a report for a specific database file, Q&A asks you to name that report. The report name you assign is stored in the database file. To access the report, you must retrieve the database file and then specify the report name. Remember that a single database file can have many different reports, each with its own name.

### *Naming a Document File*

Because you can designate the entire file name with Write documents, you can use the extension to help you identify the file. The following list shows some examples of document file names:

| *File type* | *Extension* | *Example* |
|---|---|---|
| Letters | LET | XMAS_88.LET |
| Reports | RPT | SALESOCT.RPT |
| Memos | MEM | STAFF.MEM |
| Documents | DOC | LEGAL.DOC |

### *Naming a Database File*

When you name a database file, you can use only the eight characters up to the period. The extension (DTF or IDX) is assigned by Q&A after you have defined the structure of the file.

Q&A File creates two files for each database you design: a data file and an index file. The data file name is given the DTF extension; IDX is assigned to the index. For example, if you create a database named CUSTOMER, Q&A creates two files: CUSTOMER.DTF and CUSTOMER.IDX. (You can enter any combination of upper- and lowercase, but Q&A displays the file names in uppercase only.) If you use Q&A utilities operations (instead of DOS commands) to rename, copy, and delete database files, you don't need to worry about the double file system; Q&A makes sure that both files are included in the operation.

### *File-Naming Tips*

Although an eight-character name doesn't give you much room to identify fully the contents of a file, you can use a few naming "tricks" to help you recognize the file later. For example, you can

- Use abbreviations (SALESRPT)
- Insert an underline character to separate words (SALES_RPT)
- Include a date in the name (SALE1015)
- Use the version number of the file (REPORTV2)

With a little imagination, you can come up with a variety of ways to pack information into eight-character file names.

### Naming a Database Report

When you design a report format for printing information from a database, you give the format a name. A report name can be up to 30 characters long.

Report formats are saved with the name you specify, but they are not saved the same way as document and database files. Because of this difference, reports can be accessed only through the Q&A Report module—not from DOS.

## Saving a File

When you are working on a database or document file, you can easily forget to save your work. Even though Q&A reminds you to save your files, until a file has been saved to disk, you risk data loss from a power failure or operator error. To avoid losing valuable time and effort, be sure to save your work regularly.

When a document is saved in Q&A Write, all contents and formatting characteristics of the document are saved in a single file. For a more detailed explanation of saving a document, see Chapter 10, ''Creating a Write Document.''

Remember to exit the database by pressing Esc or F10 and going through the menu sequence to the Main menu; never turn off your computer while your database is on the screen. Failure to follow the correct exit procedure may result in the loss of your IDX file, without which you cannot access your database. In some situations, Q&A's Recover function may be able to retrieve your database (see the section ''Exiting Q&A'' in this chapter).

## Listing Q&A Files

You can see a list of your Q&A files in many different ways. A list of document files can be reached from within Q&A Write, and a list of database files can be reached from within any of the other Q&A modules, including the IA. You also can list your files directly from the DOS File Facilities option of the Utilities menu. Press L for List Files and press Enter. You then can list your document files, your database files, or any other data and program files in your Q&A directory or other disk or directory. Type the appropriate path and press Enter; Q&A displays the list of files.

## *Using Q&A Function Keys for File Operations*

This section explains some basic Q&A operations for renaming, copying, and deleting your Q&A files. Subsequent chapters explain in detail the operations available for working with documents, databases, reports, and macros.

Whenever you have a list of your document or database files on-screen, you have several options available through the function keys: F1 gets you a help screen; F3 deletes files; F5 copies files; F7 searches for a file name, and F8 renames files. These options are available in all Q&A modules.

The F3 (Delete) key lets you delete specified files from a displayed list. When you press F3, Q&A displays the warning screen shown in figure 3.21. If you are sure that you want to delete the file, choose Yes and press Enter. The file is deleted.

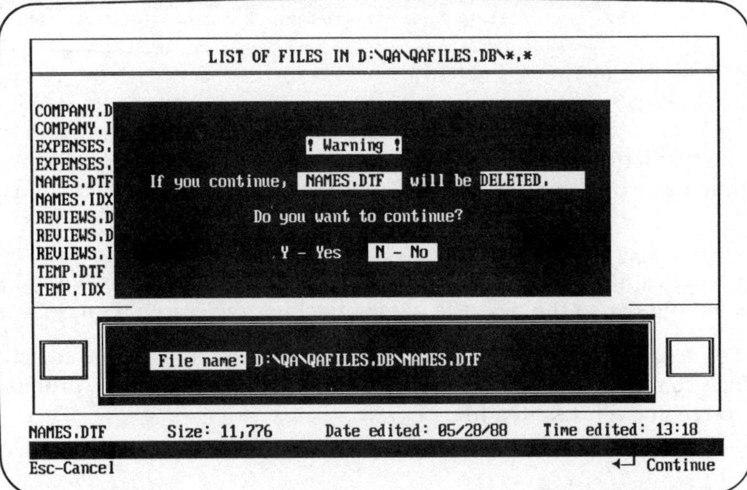


**Fig. 3.21**
*Q&A's warning when you are about to delete a file.*

Remember that once a file is deleted, Q&A may not be able to bring the file back. Third-party utility programs may be capable of restoring a crucial file for you; but these programs are successful only if the areas the file occupied on the disk have not been subsequently overwritten by other files. So be careful when you delete files. A good rule of operation is always to make current file backups before conducting rename, delete, and copy operations.

The F5 (Copy) key lets you copy specified files. If you have the list of files on your screen, you can use the arrow keys to select the file you want copied. When you press F5, you see the Copy To prompt (see fig. 3.22). Type the name of the file you want the file copied to and press Enter; the file is copied.

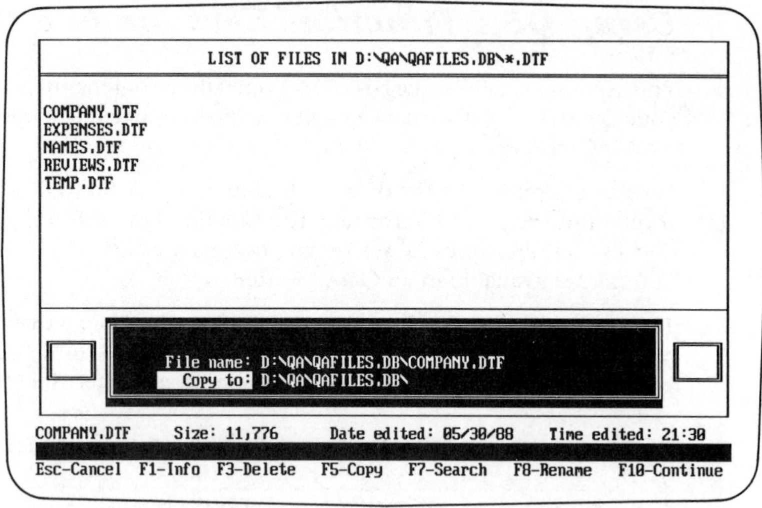


**Fig. 3.22**
*The List of Files screen showing the Copy To prompt.*

The F7 key allows you to search through a large directory by typing on the prompt line the first letter (or first few letters) of a group of file names. Type two periods after the letter or letters and press F7. Suppose, for example, that you type

SLS..

Q&A moves a highlight cursor to the first file name that begins with SLS. You can press F7 to move to the next file name matching the search request.

The F8 (Rename) key lets you rename specified files from a displayed list. Highlight the file you want to rename and press F8. Q&A shows a Rename To prompt, allowing you to rename the selected file.

## Using Wild Cards in File Operations

You can use the DOS wild cards in referring to file names, except when using the special delete, copy, search, and rename function keys. The wild-card characters are the question mark (?) and asterisk (*). You use the question mark as a replacement for any single keyboard character. For example, suppose that you want to see a list of files. Type the following on the prompt line:

SALES-MO.?88

Q&A displays all file names with any character in the position where the question mark appears. For example, the program retrieves such file names as

SALES-MO.188
SALES-MO.288

SALES-MO.X88
SALES-M0.%88

The asterisk wild-card character (*) lets you list, copy, rename, and delete multiple files with a single command; the asterisk represents a group of characters in the file names. If you type

GR*.TXT

you can list, copy, or erase all files ending with a TXT extension and beginning with the letters *GR*. For example, if you are erasing files, you would delete such files as

GROSS.TXT
GRANT723.TXT
GROVER.TXT

All these files disappear in response to the single delete command.

### Renaming a File

Two different methods can be used to rename Q&A database files:

- Change the name with Q&A's DOS File Facilities Rename command in the Utilities menu
- Rename from the List of Files screen with F8 (Rename). Display this screen by pressing Enter any time File asks for a file name.

When a database file is renamed, all report formats for that database are automatically transferred to the new name.

Q&A has four different methods for renaming document files. You can

- Change the name with Q&A's DOS File Facilities Rename command under the Utilities selection on the Main menu
- Rename from the List of Files screen with F8 (Rename). Access this screen by pressing Enter when Write asks for a file name.
- Choose the Utilities option from the Write menu and then select Rename a Document.
- Save the file under a different name (See Chapter 10, ''Creating a Write Document,'' for a complete discussion of this procedure.)

## *Copying a File*

By copying an existing database file, you can save yourself from creating and designing a new form, as well as entering identical data. Your options for copying a Q&A database file are

- Use Q&A's DOS File Facilities Copy command from the Utilities menu, which you select from the Main menu.
- Copy the file at the List of Files screen by using F5 (Copy). Display a list of files by pressing Enter when File asks for a file name. If a file name already is displayed, press space to remove the name and Enter to display the file list.
- Use the File menu's Copy option (See Chapter 6, "Using File," for a detailed explanation of this procedure.)

When a database file is copied with F5, the report formats also are copied automatically.

The three methods of copying a document file are similar to the methods of copying a database file.

- Use Q&A's DOS File Facilities Copy command, which you select from the Utilities menu. The Utility menu is one of the choices on the Q&A Main menu.
- Copy the file at the List of Files screen by using F5 (Copy). Display a list of files by pressing Enter when Write asks for a file name.
- Choose the Utilities option from the Write menu, and then select Copy a Document.

When you choose the Copy a Document option, you simply type at the prompt the name of the file you are copying to; then press Enter. The file is copied.

## *Deleting a File*

When you delete a database file using Q&A's facilities, both the DTF and IDX files are deleted. If you use the DOS delete (DEL or ERASE) command to delete the file, you must delete files individually. To delete database files, you can

- Use Q&A's DOS File Facilities Delete command, which you select from the Utilities menu under the Q&A Main menu.
- Delete the file at the List of Files screen by using F3 (Delete). Display a list of files by pressing Enter when Q&A asks for a file name.

You have three methods of deleting document files. The methods are

- Use Q&A's DOS File Facilities Delete command, which is chosen from the Utilities selection on the Q&A Main menu.

- Delete the file at the List of Files screen by using F3 (Delete). Display a list of document files by pressing Enter when Q&A asks for a document file name.
- Choose the Utilities option from the Write menu, and then select Delete a Document

When you choose the Delete a Document option, you use the arrow keys to select the document to be deleted; then press Enter. Q&A displays a warning screen. If you are sure that you want to delete the document, choose Yes and press Enter. The document is deleted.

## *Chapter Summary*

This chapter provides information important to you as you begin to use Q&A. You have learned how to begin the program and exit it safely, how to use the Q&A keyboard and the menu system, and how to get help from Q&A. The basics of entering and editing text are illustrated, and you have learned some fundamental procedures for working with database and document files. The information provided in this chapter is enough for you to begin to work with Q&A and provides a solid foundation for the detailed information that appears in the following chapters.

# Part II

# Using Q&A File

Includes

Q&A File Quick Start
Setting Up a File
Using File
Customizing and Programming a File
Printing from File

Chapter 4

# Q&A File Quick Start

Developing and using a database with Q&A is both quick and easy to do. You will work in the part of the Q&A program called the File module to design and store a database. In this chapter you will learn how to design a database, customize it for easy data entry, and use search methods for retrieving and sorting data.

To complete the database process, you need to understand some basic database terms. A *database* is an electronic filing system that stores data and enables you to retrieve that data in a variety of ways. With a Q&A database you can print reports based on the data, and merge the data with information located in Q&A's Write module.

Imagine a database as a filing cabinet. The database is the actual cabinet that holds the files. Each file within that filing cabinet is called a *form* (or *record*), and the categories of information contained within those files are called *fields*. A field consists of two parts. The first part describes what kind of data is stored in the field and is called a *field label*. The second part of a field is the actual data. You can retrieve data from any database field and sort the data in a logical manner for you to use.

## Designing a Database

To understand how useful and easy a database is to work with, you will build a database for a household inventory system. Let's assume that your insurance agent has requested that you keep an inventory of all covered items in your home worth more than $25.00. Your agent will use this inventory to determine whether your coverage is adequate and also to list possessions in case of fire or theft.

First, you will design the database to hold the information.

1. Select File from the Q&A Main menu.
2. Select Design File from the File menu.
3. Select Design a New File from the Design menu.

You will notice as you work through the system that the menu progression is displayed on the monitor. This menu progression lets you know exactly where you are in the system and which menus you used to get to your current location.

After you select Design a New File, Q&A prompts you for the name of the file you will design. The prompt for the file name includes the *drive path*, the route the computer takes to get to your file. The path begins with the drive you currently are in (C for a hard disk, and A or B for a floppy disk system). The next set of characters indicates the *directory* (the area) that holds the Q&A program. The name of that directory varies depending on how the program was copied into your computer's memory. Following the software directory should be a subdirectory separating your database files from your word-processing files. These subdirectories are set using the Utilities module on the Q&A Main menu. The file name follows the database subdirectory. The steps of the drive path are separated with backslashes (\).

4. Type the data file name *house* (see fig. 4.1).

**Fig. 4.1**
*Specifying the drive path for the file.*

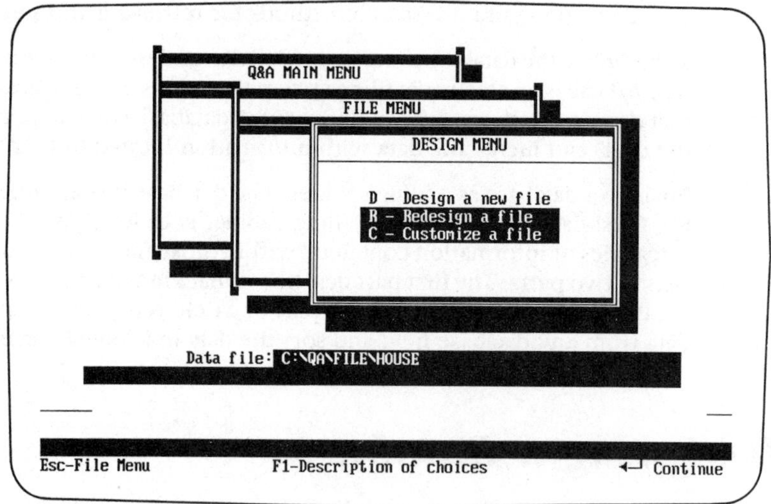


5. Press the Enter key. Q&A adds the extension DTF to the file name, indicating that this file is a database file.

A Q&A database file consists of two separate files. One file holds the data and has the file extension DTF. The other file consists of the index files, the form design and reports, and other files associated with the database. This file has the extension IDX. When you use the File module, Q&A combines the IDX and DTF files to form your database. When you make copies of the database using DOS, you should be sure to copy both files.

You now should see an almost empty screen; this is Q&A's *File form design screen* (see fig. 4.2). Near the bottom of the design screen is a *ruler line*, which shows the cursor location and tab settings. Three lines of information are displayed below the ruler line. The ***status line*** contains the file name, the percentage of memory the file occupies, and the line and page location of the cursor. The *message line*, usually blank, displays Q&A's messages when needed. The ***key assignment line*** lists frequently used function keys that you can use with this screen. The keys listed vary according to the screen. Not all the available function keys are displayed in the key assignment line—only those used most often. The following function keys are listed on the file form design screen:

| | |
|---|---|
| Esc (Cancel) | Cancel the database design process and return to the File menu |
| F1 (How to design) | Access on-screen help and reference specific pages in the instruction manual for more detail |
| F8 (Options) | Access options such as setting tabs, centering or uncentering lines, and drawing lines |
| F10 (Continue) | Continue the current process and proceed to the next step |

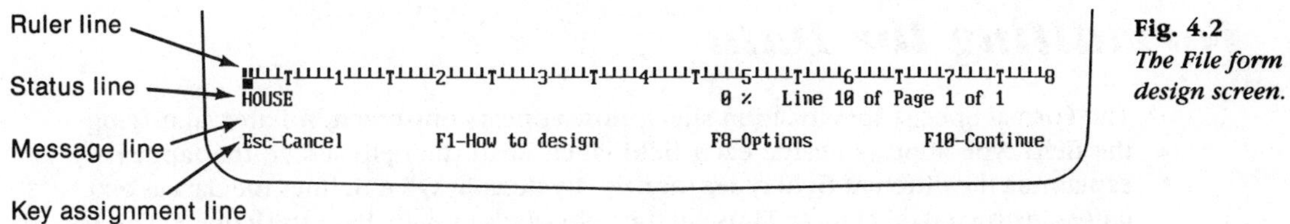


**Fig. 4.2** *The File form design screen.*

You will type a title and the field labels on the File form design screen.

6. With the cursor located in the upper left corner of the File form design screen, type the title *HOUSEHOLD INVENTORY*. Press the Enter key to move to the next line.

7. Type the following field labels as shown, following each name with a colon (:), indicating the end of the label and the beginning of the data. After each colon, press the Enter key to move to the next line.

   Item:
   Quantity:
   Location:
   Date of Purchase:
   Amount of Purchase:
   Serial Number:
   Description:
   Item Number:

   Your screen should look like figure 4.3.

8. Press F10 (Continue) to save your design and proceed to the next step.

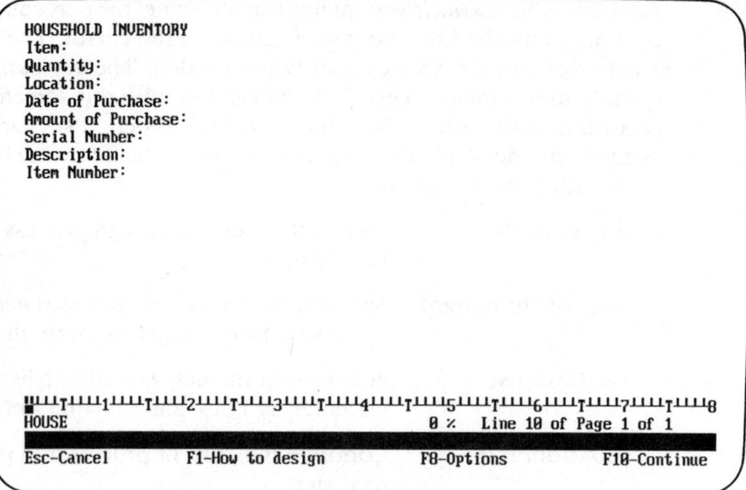


**Fig. 4.3** *Entering the field labels.*

# *Formatting the Data*

The Format Spec, a specification sheet, now appears on-screen. A letter signifying the field type appears beside each field label. Read the help screen that appears, explaining the different field types for data. By default, Q&A defines the data as text unless instructed otherwise. Thus, all the field labels initially have the letter *T*. Three fields in your database use other types of data: keyword, date, and money data. Therefore, you will modify these three fields.

1. Use the up- or down-arrow keys to move your cursor to the following fields, and type over the *T* to reflect the following data types:

   Location: K
   Date of Purchase: D
   Amount of Purchase: M

   Figure 4.4 shows how your screen should look.

2. Press F10 to continue to the next step.

The Global Format Options screen now appears. Use this screen to format the field types you chose on the Format Spec. You can format currency, time, and date displays for your database with this screen. You will change the date settings.

3. Use the arrow keys to move the cursor to setting number 11 in the Date section of the Global Format Options screen (see fig. 4.5). Setting 11 displays the date as Month dd, yyyy: for example, April 25, 1988.

4. Press F10 (Continue) to save the design and formats and return to the File menu.

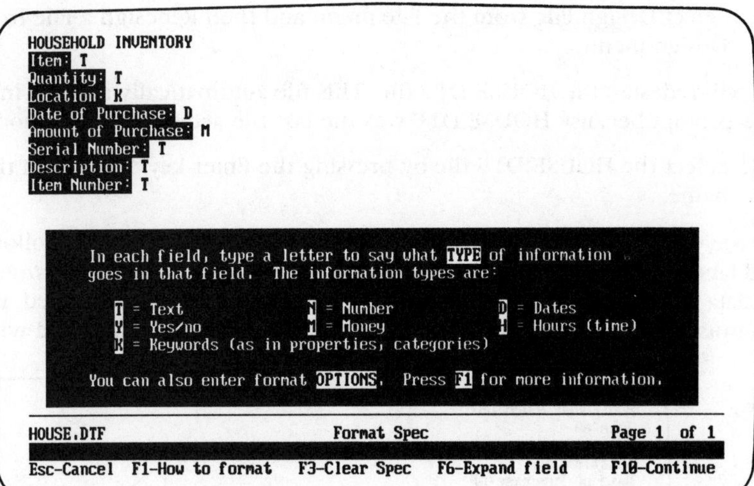

HOUSEHOLD INVENTORY
Item: T
Quantity: T
Location: K
Date of Purchase: D
Amount of Purchase: M
Serial Number: T
Description: T
Item Number: T
In each field, type a letter to say what TYPE of information goes in that field. The information types are:
T = Text
N = Number
D = Dates
Y = Yes/no
M = Money
H = Hours (time)
K = Keywords (as in properties, categories)
You can also enter format OPTIONS. Press F1 for more information.
HOUSE.DTF
Format Spec
Page 1 of 1
Esc-Cancel
F1-How to format
F3-Clear Spec
F6-Expand field
F10-Continue


**Fig. 4.4** *Changing the data type for three fields.*

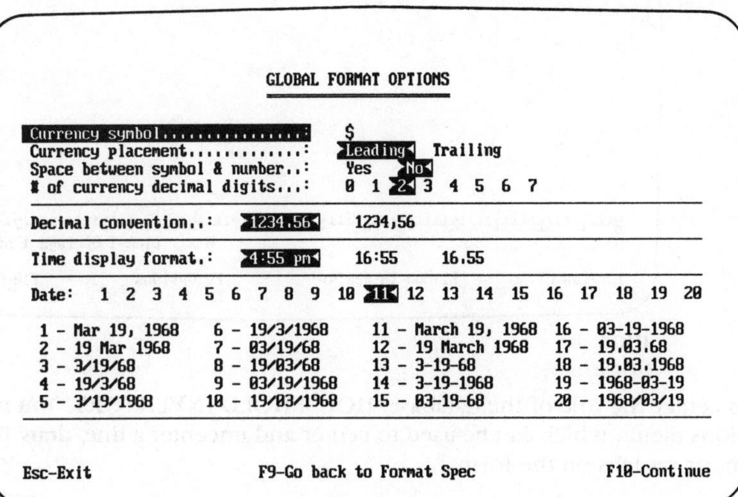

GLOBAL FORMAT OPTIONS
Currency symbol.................: $
Currency placement............: Leading Trailing
Space between symbol & number..: Yes No
# of currency decimal digits...: 0 1 2 3 4 5 6 7
Decimal convention..: 1234.56 1234,56
Time display format.: 4:55 pm 16:55 16.55
Date: 1 2 3 4 5 6 7 8 9 10 11 12 13 14 15 16 17 18 19 20
1 - Mar 19, 1968
2 - 19 Mar 1968
3 - 3/19/68
4 - 19/3/68
5 - 3/19/1968
6 - 19/3/1968
7 - 03/19/68
8 - 19/03/68
9 - 03/19/1968
10 - 19/03/1968
11 - March 19, 1968
12 - 19 March 1968
13 - 3-19-68
14 - 3-19-1968
15 - 03-19-68
16 - 03-19-1968
17 - 19.03.68
18 - 19.03.1968
19 - 1968-03-19
20 - 1968/03/19
Esc-Exit
F9-Go back to Format Spec
F10-Continue


**Fig. 4.5** *The Global Format Options screen.*

**Your design has been saved and is ready to accept data. Before you enter data, however, let's enhance the design to make the data more attractive.**

# *Redesigning Your Database*

The redesign process is similar to the design process. You will see the same screens with a few modifications.

1. Select Design File from the File menu and then Redesign a File from the Design menu.

You will redesign the HOUSE.DTF file. This file automatically appears in the `Data file` prompt because HOUSE.DTF was the last file accessed in this module.

2. Select the HOUSE.DTF file by pressing the Enter key to confirm the name.

The file you just designed appears on-screen but with one difference. Following each field label are two letters (see fig. 4.6). These characters, called *field tags*, connect the data to the field on the form. Any time a field is moved or changed, these field tags must accompany the field, or the data associated with that field will be lost.

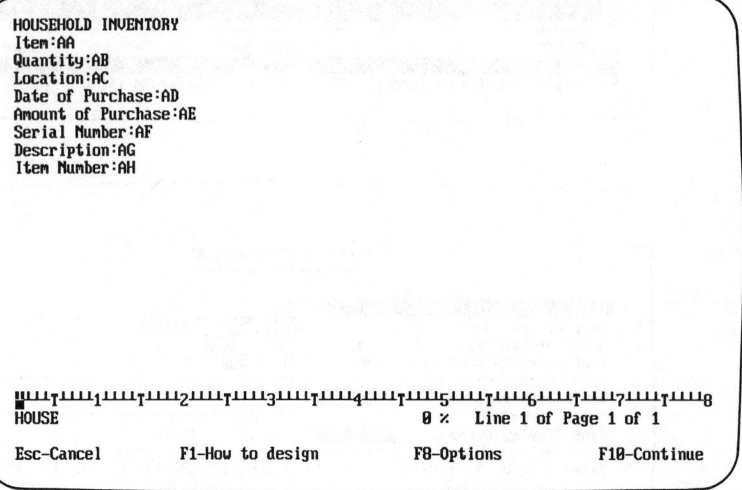


**Fig. 4.6**
*The field tags for the database fields.*

Let's center the title of the database, HOUSEHOLD INVENTORY. You will use the Options menu, which can be used to center and uncenter a line, draw lines on the form, or set tabs on the form.

3. Move your cursor beneath the *H* in *HOUSEHOLD*, if needed.
4. Press F8 (Options) to display the Options menu, and select Center Line from that menu. The title *HOUSEHOLD INVENTORY* moves to the center of the screen.
5. Press F10 (Continue) once to save the design, once to save the Format Spec, once more to save the global format options, and once again to return to the File menu.

## Customizing Your Database

Customizing provides you the ability to fine-tune your database and tailor it to fit your individual needs.

1. Select Design File from the File menu and then Customize a File from the Design menu to call up the Customize menu. When the file name HOUSE appears in the prompt, press the Enter key.

You will use three of the features displayed on the Customize menu. First, you will specify the Amount of Purchase field to display entries with commas. Then, you will instruct Q&A to display today's date and number the forms sequentially. Last, you will develop a lookup table and program Q&A, allowing you to fill the Location field (designating the room where the article is located) by typing just the first letter of that location.

2. Select Format Values from the Customize menu, and press F1 (How to format) to review the help screen associated with this feature. Press Esc (Cancel) to clear the help screen.
3. Using the arrow keys, move the cursor to the Amount of Purchase field and insert a comma and the letter *C* after the letter *M* (as in *M,C*). The field will display entries with commas.
4. Press F10 once to get to the Global Format Options screen and once again to save the change and return to the Customize menu.
5. From the Customize menu, select Set Initial Values, and press F1 (How to set initial values) to see the help screen at the bottom of the form.
6. Move your cursor to the Date of Purchase field and type *@DATE*. This function automatically enters the current date.
7. Move your cursor to the Item Number field and type *@NUMBER*. This function enters sequential numbers (x + 1). Compare your Initial Values Spec with figure 4.7.
8. Press F10 to save the changes and return to the Customize menu.

When you set initial values for a field, remember that you can override these values simply by typing over the data that appears.

9. From the Customize menu, select Edit Lookup Table. A lookup table appears.

*Lookup tables* are used to enter repetitive values in fields. They "look up" the key characters (which you enter as data in a field), match those characters in a table, and insert the appropriate information from the table into the field. Lookup tables offer two advantages: they ensure consistency of data, and they assist data entry by reducing the number of keystrokes needed to enter repetitive, frequently entered data.

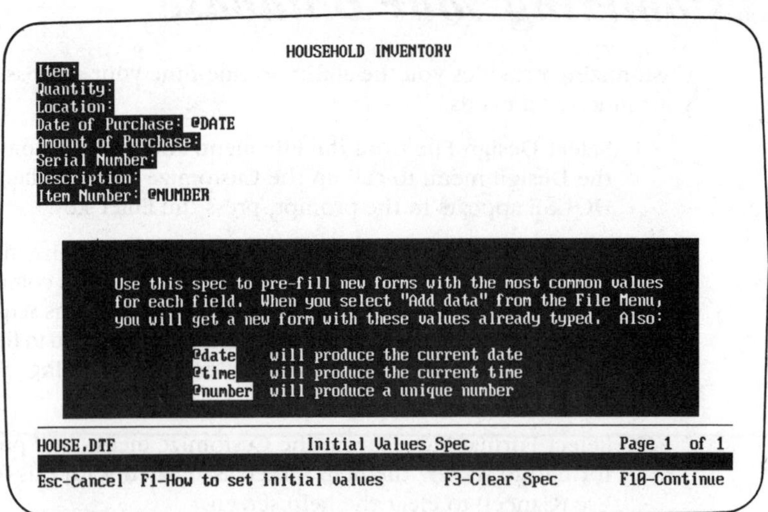
HOUSEHOLD INVENTORY
Item:
Quantity:
Location:
Date of Purchase: @DATE
Amount of Purchase:
Serial Number:
Description:
Item Number: @NUMBER
Use this spec to pre-fill new forms with the most common values for each field. When you select "Add data" from the File Menu, you will get a new form with these values already typed. Also:
@date will produce the current date
@time will produce the current time
@number will produce a unique number
HOUSE.DTF
Initial Values Spec
Page 1 of 1
Esc-Cancel F1-How to set initial values F3-Clear Spec F10-Continue

**Fig. 4.7** *Modifying Date of Purchase and Item Number.*

You will see a lookup table consisting of five columns. The first column is the Key column and will contain the key the program will try to match. Columns one through four will contain data that will be inserted after a match is found.

10. Type the following information in the table (you use only the Key column and column 1 for this exercise):

| *Key* | *1* |
|---|---|
| K | Kitchen |
| D | Den |
| L | Living Room |

Figure 4.8 shows your screen.

11. Press F10 to save your table and return to the Customize menu.

When the lookup table is completed, you can begin the second step of using the table: programming the form. Programming tells the form that data is stored in a lookup table and needs to be inserted into a field on the form.

12. Select Program Form from the Customize menu, and review the help screen associated with this feature. This help screen is several pages long; press Enter to continue. When you have read about LOOKUP, press Esc to clear the help screen.

13. Move your cursor to the Location field and type the following:

    >#1: Lookup (#1,1,#1)

This program tells Q&A to insert in this spot data from column 1 of the lookup table. The program is made of several components, each telling Q&A to perform a separate step:

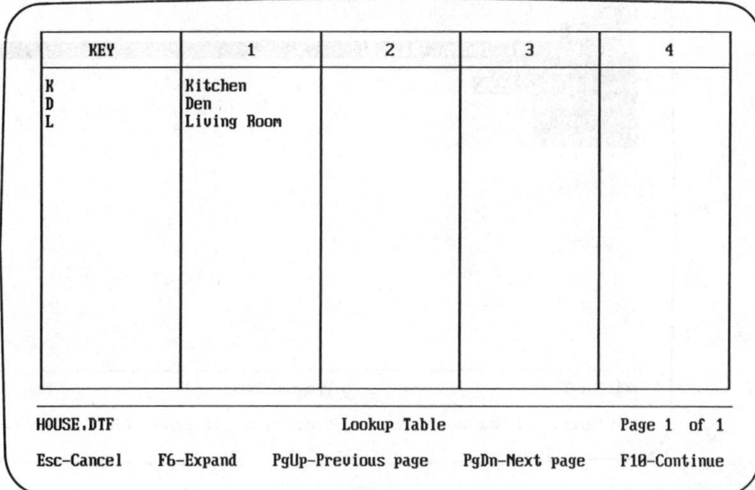


**Fig. 4.8**
*The lookup table for the database.*

| | |
|---|---|
| > | Executes this program when the cursor leaves this field |
| #1: | Identifies the field numerically |
| Lookup | A lookup table will be used for this program |
| (#1 | The key that matches the table is in field #1 (the Location field) |
| 1 | The data to go in the field resides in column 1 of that Key in the lookup table |
| #1) | Data from column 1 will be inserted into field #1 |

The Program Spec should look like figure 4.9.

14. Press F10 to save this program and return to the Customize menu.
15. Press Esc twice to return to the File menu.

# Adding Data to Your Database

Now that you have done all this work to build a database, let's enter some information and see whether the database works.

1. Select Add Data from the File menu for the file HOUSE.DTF.

You now have on your screen a blank entry form ready to receive data. Notice that today's date is entered in the Date of Purchase field and the Item Number field is numbered 1. These values are added automatically as a result of Q&A's @DATE and @NUMBER functions.

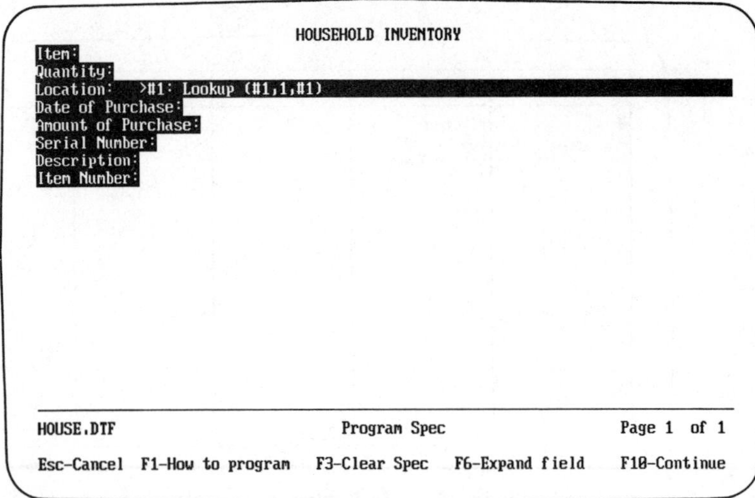
HOUSEHOLD INVENTORY
Item:
Quantity:
Location: >#1: Lookup (#1,1,#1)
Date of Purchase:
Amount of Purchase:
Serial Number:
Description:
Item Number:

HOUSE.DTF Program Spec Page 1 of 1
Esc-Cancel F1-How to program F3-Clear Spec F6-Expand field F10-Continue

**Fig. 4.9** *Adding a program to the Location field.*

You are going to fill out several forms. After you type the data into the forms, you will save the form by pressing F10 (Continue).

2. Fill out one form with the following information:

   Item: Radio
   Quantity: 1
   Location: D (for den)
   Date of Purchase: June 3, 1988 (already entered)
   Amount of Purchase: $79.95
   Serial Number: HSR260XFM
   Description: AM/FM portable radio
   Item Number: 1 (already entered)

   Figure 4.10 shows how your form should look.

3. Press F10 to save this form and display a new blank form.

You can keep track of your database with the information Q&A supplies at the bottom of the screen. You can see that you are in the database HOUSE.DTF; you are looking at new form 2 of 2 (you have one new form, and the second new form is ready to accept data); 1 form is saved; and you are on page 1 of 1. You can press F9 to view the forms already entered.

When you add new forms to your database, press F5 to copy data that was entered in that particular field on the preceding form. Pressing Shift-F5 copies the entire preceding form to this form.

4. Fill out at least three more forms with one more item located in the den and two items located in the kitchen. For items in the kitchen type *K*, the symbol you entered in the lookup table for the kitchen, in the Location field.

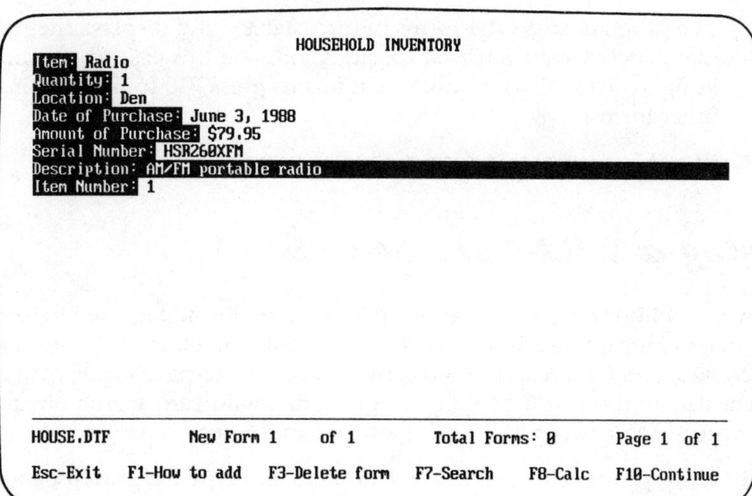
HOUSEHOLD INVENTORY

Item: Radio
Quantity: 1
Location: Den
Date of Purchase: June 3, 1988
Amount of Purchase: $79.95
Serial Number: HSR260XFM
Description: AM/FM portable radio
Item Number: 1

HOUSE.DTF New Form 1 of 1 Total Forms: 0 Page 1 of 1

Esc-Exit F1-How to add F3-Delete form F7-Search F8-Calc F10-Continue

**Fig. 4.10** *Entering the first form into the database.*

# *Retrieving Information from Your Database*

The Search/Update function retrieves data already entered into the database, allowing you to update that information if you choose and arrange it in the order you want. Search/Update can be accessed in two ways. It is on the File menu. Or if you already have selected Add Data from the File menu, you can simply press F7 (Search) to select it.

1. Select Search/Update by pressing F7 (Search).

   A Retrieve Spec replaces the data on the screen. The Retrieve Spec looks like a new form for adding data, but some new function keys are listed on the key assignment line.

2. Press F1 (Info) to see the first help screen. After reading that screen, press F1 again to see more retrieval parameters. Press Esc to remove the help screens and return to the Retrieve Spec.

You can search any database field for data by moving the cursor to that field and entering the correct parameters. When entering search parameters, you can type them in uppercase or lowercase; Q&A will retrieve all forms matching the search parameters regardless of capitalization. Start your search by looking for items that are located in the den.

3. Move your cursor to the Location field, type *den*, and press F10 (Continue).

The program scans the forms in the database and displays the first form that matches your retrieval specifications—in this case, the form shown in figure 4.10. To view additional forms, press F10 to page through the other forms.

4. Press F7 (Search) to return to the Retrieve Spec.

## *Using a Wild-Card Search*

Now you will retrieve the forms of items that are located in the kitchen. If you're in a hurry or are not sure how to spell ***kitchen***, you can retrieve this information easily by doing a *wild-card* search. Wild-card searches can retrieve forms with slightly different data in the specified field. To perform a wild-card search on any group of characters, enter two periods (..) anywhere in the search parameter.

1. Move your cursor to the Location field and type the search parameter as follows:

   Location: ki..

2. Press F10 (Continue) to start the search. In this file, only kitchen starts with ***ki***. Therefore, forms for items located in the kitchen appear on-screen.

## *Sorting Retrieved Forms*

When searching large databases, you sometimes will want to list the data in some order: alphabetically or from the highest to lowest item number. You can perform this sorting by using the F8 function key.

1. Press F7 (Search) from any form on your screen to return to the Retrieve Spec. Notice that the preceding search parameters appear on the Retrieve Spec.
2. From the Retrieve Spec, press F8 (Sort Spec) to display the Sort Spec screen. Press F1 (How to sort) to review Sort Spec instructions.
3. Move your cursor to the Amount of Purchase field and type *1 AS*, indicating sort level 1 (or first sort to be done) in ascending sort order (low to high). Your Sort Spec should look like figure 4.11.
4. Press F10 to start the sort.

Q&A scans the database for forms and sorts the retrieved forms in the appropriate order. The first form, for the least expensive item, will appear on-screen. Press F10 to view the other forms in order of increasing price.

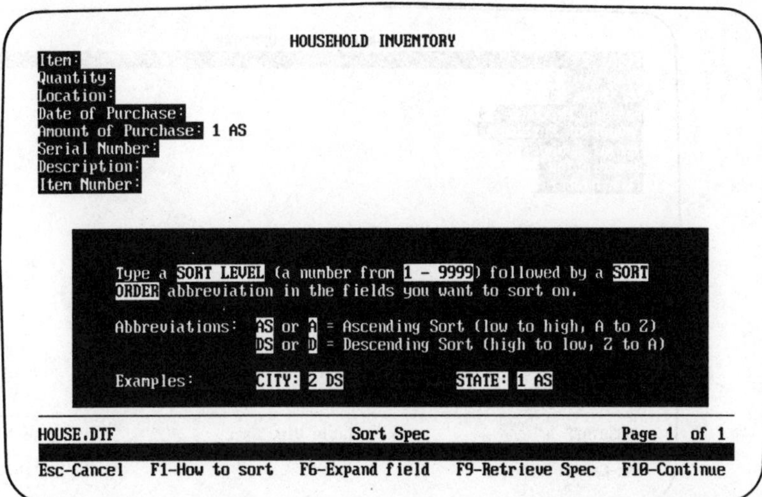


**Fig. 4.11**
*Specifying to sort the retrieved forms by purchase amount.*

## Viewing a Table of Retrieved Forms

Instead of paging through the forms one by one, you can construct a table that will show you the forms. This table is different from the lookup table in that it is used for display only and not for data entry. The F6 (Table) key controls this table.

1. Press F6 (Table) from the current form, displaying a table with the forms. This table has five columns, for the first five fields of your entry form.

You can change the display to see other data in the table.

2. Press Shift-F6 from the table view screen. A Table View Spec appears, as shown in figure 4.12. As you can see, the first five fields are numbered 1 through 5.

Let's assume that you want to display the serial numbers also. You cannot increase or decrease the number of columns displayed, but you can change the fields displayed in those columns by renumbering the fields.

3. Move the cursor to the Location field and press the space bar, deleting the number 3.

4. Move the cursor to the Serial Number field, type *3* in that field, and press F10 (Table View). You have changed the table view. Figure 4.13 shows the new table display.

5. Return to the Retrieve Spec by pressing F7.

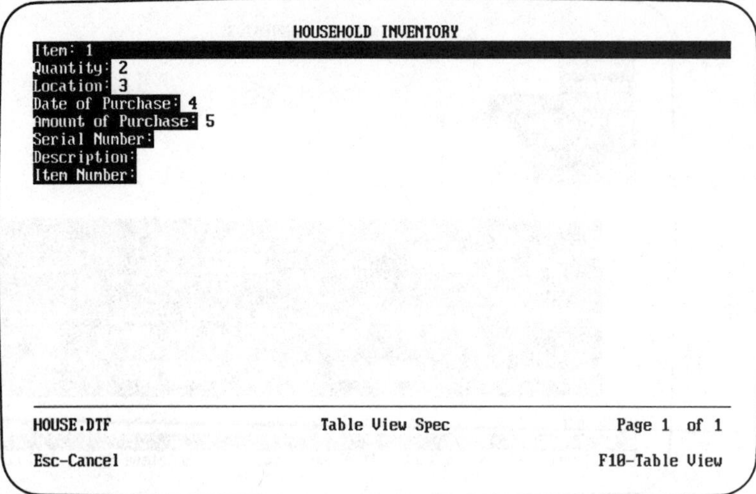


**Fig. 4.12**
*The column assignments of the fields in the table.*

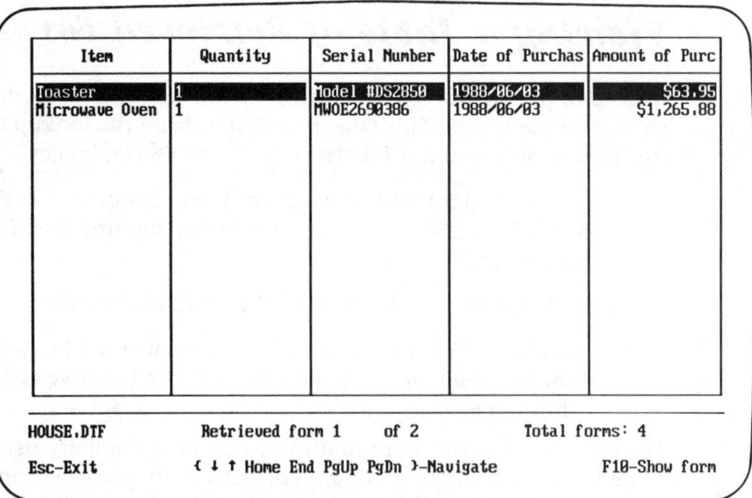


**Fig. 4.13**
*The revised table of forms.*

## *Using Keywords To Search*

One other way to search a database is by using keywords. *Keywords* are words that are used to classify types of data consistently. You can use these classifications as criteria for searching and retrieving information. For instance, the keyword *Den* classifies items located in the den rather than in the family room. If you searched for *Family Room*, you would not get the same search results. You can enter multiple keywords in a keyword field, separating them with semicolons (;). When searching keyword fields, you can request that one or more criteria be met for Q&A to retrieve forms. The ability to use multiple keywords for searching is a definite advantage over search methods you used earlier. Keyword searches only apply to keyword fields. You have one keyword field in your database: the Location field.

1. Move your cursor to the Location field and type the keywords as follows:

   Location: den;kit..

2. Press F10 (Continue).

Q&A selects all items located in the den or the kitchen. If you add an ampersand (&) at the beginning of this search (&den;kit..), items must be located in *both* the kitchen and den to be retrieved.

3. Return to the File menu by pressing the Esc key.

# Printing Information from Your Database

Reports containing database information can be generated in several ways in Q&A. You can print an individual form by pressing F2 while the form is displayed on-screen, or you can print information from a group of forms by selecting the Print command from the File menu. (A third method of printing data is discussed for the Report module in Chapter 14.)

1. Select Print from the File menu for HOUSE.DTF.
2. Select Design/Redesign a Spec from the Print menu.

   A list of print specs for this database appears. Because you just created this database, no print specs should be associated with the database, and therefore no specs are listed on-screen.

3. Type *INVENTORY* at the `Enter name` prompt to name your print spec, and press the Enter key.

   A Retrieve Spec appears. You want to retrieve all forms in the database, and you want them to be sorted. If you are not sure how to perform these operations, press F1 (Info) to display the help screen. Do not press F10 until asked to do so.

4. Press F8 (Sort Spec), type *1 AS* to indicate Location as the sort level in ascending sort order, and press F10 to continue to the Fields Spec. The Fields Spec tells Q&A where you want each field to be printed and in what sequence.
5. Press F1 (How to print fields) and review the three help screens.
6. Clear the help screens by pressing the Esc key until the Fields Spec reappears.

You will use Style #1 (Free-form) for your report.

7. Type the following information in the Fields Spec to arrange the printing of data:

| | |
|---|---|
| Item: 3X | Third field to print followed by a return |
| Quantity: 2+ | Second field to print followed by a space |
| Location: 6X | Sixth field to print followed by a return |
| Date of Purchase: 7+,5 | Seventh field to print followed by five spaces |
| Amount of Purchase: 8X | Eighth field to print followed by a return |
| Serial Number: 5X | Fifth field to print followed by a return |
| Description: 4+,2 | Fourth field to print followed by two spaces |
| Item Number: 1X | First field to print followed by a return |

8. Press F10 to continue to the next screen, File Print Options. This screen allows you to change the settings that determine how the report will print.

9. Use the arrow keys to change the Print To setting from `PtrA` to `SCREEN`. (To print a report on paper, you would select the appropriate printer according to your computer configuration.) Also, verify that the setting for Print Field Labels? is No, as in figure 4.14.

**Fig. 4.14**
*The File Print Options screen.*

```
                         FILE PRINT OPTIONS

Print to.....:    PtrA   PtrB   PtrC   PtrD   PtrE   DISK   SCREEN

Type of paper feed...........:   Manual  Continuous  Bin1   Bin2   Bin3
Printer offset...............:   0
Printer control codes........:
Print field labels?..........:   Yes  No
Number of copies.............:   1
Number of forms per page.....:   1
Number of labels across......:   1  2  3  4  5  6  7  8

HOUSE.DTF                Print Options for INVENTORY
Print to screen with page size adjusted to fit the screen.
Esc-Cancel         F8-Define Page          F9-Go back           F10-Continue
```

10. Press F8 (Define Page). The Define Page screen determines page width, length, and margins; characters per inch; and *headers* and *footers* (the text that repeats on consecutive pages).

11. Use the arrow keys to move to the Page Definition options, and set the options as follows:

Page Width : 240    Page Length..: 66
Left Margin: 0    Right Margin : 240
Top Margin : 3    Bottom Margin: 3
Characters Per Inch: 10

HEADER
1: HOUSEHOLD INVENTORY as of @Date

Your screen should look like fig. 4.15.

```
                         DEFINE PAGE

          Page width : 240        Page length..: 66

          Left margin: 0          Right margin : 240

          Top margin : 3          Bottom margin: 3

          Characters per inch:   10  12  15  17

───────────────────────────── HEADER ─────────────────────────────
1: HOUSEHOLD INVENTORY As of @Date
2:
3:
───────────────────────────── FOOTER ─────────────────────────────
1:
2:
3:
──────────────────────────────────────────────────────────────────
HOUSE.DTF                  Define page for INVENTORY

Esc-Cancel              F9-Go Back to Print Options       F10-Continue
```

**Fig. 4.15**
*Adding settings to the Define Page screen.*

12. After making these changes, press F9 (Go Back to Print Options) to return to the File Print Options screen, and press F10 to continue.

    A notice appears on-screen, telling you that your print specs have been saved and asking whether you want to print the forms now.

13. Respond Yes and press the Enter key. The report will be printed on-screen as shown in figure 4.16.

If you want to change something in the report, you can redesign the report by pressing Shift-F9 (Redesign).

To print a report that has already been designed and saved, use the Print Forms command from the Print menu. This command allows you to bypass the design process and immediately print the report. With this command, you also can make *temporary* changes to a report before printing. These changes will not be saved. To make permanent changes to a report, you must go through the Design/Redesign process.

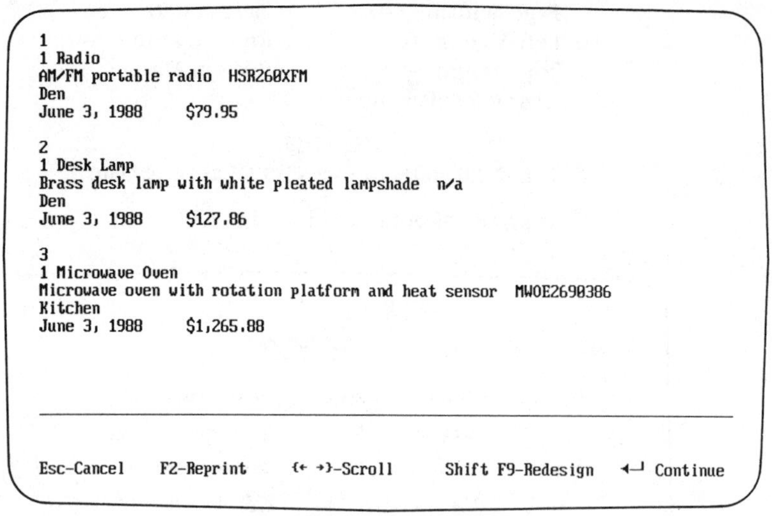

**Fig. 4.16**
*The database report printed on-screen.*

```
1
1 Radio
AM/FM portable radio  HSR260XFM
Den
June 3, 1988      $79.95

2
1 Desk Lamp
Brass desk lamp with white pleated lampshade  n/a
Den
June 3, 1988      $127.86

3
1 Microwave Oven
Microwave oven with rotation platform and heat sensor  MWOE2698386
Kitchen
June 3, 1988      $1,265.88

Esc-Cancel    F2-Reprint    {← →}-Scroll    Shift F9-Redesign   ←┘ Continue
```

# Chapter Summary

In designing this database, you have learned to center, customize, format, set initial values, do sequential numbering and dating, enter data, and search for data using several methods. You also have learned how to use lookup tables to minimize data entry and program forms.

Now you can modify your database to meet your particular needs and applications. Continuing with the scenario of the insurance reporting requirements, you can satisfy these requirements easily by printing a report for your agent to keep on file. You can keep a current inventory of items, updating the inventory as needed. In case of fire or theft, this inventory will be easily accessible. As your needs change, you will be able to change the database easily to fit that particular application. Before you go to the Write quick start (Chapter 9), you will want to look at Chapters 5 through 8, to learn more about the Q&A File module. Chapter 5 begins with setting up a file.

Chapter

5

# Setting Up a File

One of the most important steps in data management is setting up your file. File setup in Q&A involves several levels of file design. You must decide which fields to include in each file and how large each field should be. (Refer to Chapter 2, "Database Concepts," for help with database definitions and terms.) You must define any relationships among the fields, create an entry form (the end-user view of the data file), and define reports for the data. In Q&A, most of these processes are done at the same time, when you create the database screen form. (File\Design File\Design a New File is the path to this process from the Main menu.) You can design ad hoc reports from within the File module or use the additional reporting functions in the Report module. These separate processes are covered in later chapters.

The design of your file form determines how well your data can be organized and retrieved. A well-designed form helps other users learn to use your database. If you organize your file form so that the data can be entered in a logical order, you can save time and effort when you use the file.

The designers of Q&A understood the importance of setting up a file and designing workable input, edit, and report forms. With Q&A, you can design forms to suit your taste and fit the way you work. In addition, after you have designed one form, you can use that form to create other forms. With Q&A, you have the choice of setting up a file that is as basic or as complicated as you like. To help with using the design after it is created, you can build your own custom help screens that give detailed instructions for operations on individual fields.

This chapter guides you through the Q&A File design process, providing step-by-step instructions and offering suggestions on how to get the most from Q&A File. The topics discussed in this chapter include

- Laying out a file form
- Setting field lengths and formats
- Formatting the form
- Formatting the information

- Choosing global file format options
- Adding to the file form
- Redesigning a file form

## *What You Can Do with Q&A File*

We all use databases in some way every day. Recipe boxes, filing cabinets, and phone books are like computerized databases in that they all store information. At the most basic level, Q&A File is the same as a recipe box or a file folder of expense receipts: a place to store information.

Using Q&A File is easy: you design a file and its entry form (as one operation), enter the data, and save the file. As you use Q&A File, the program quickly becomes more than just a "shoe box" of information. When you need to retrieve information from the database, Q&A can find, display, and print the data with just a few simple keystrokes. You can produce regular reports from new information in a file even though you design the report form only once. Because Q&A stores the report specifications, you can recall reports by name at any time.

You can use Q&A to store simple or relatively complex databases, including lists, personal records, expense reports, card catalogs, inventory records, customer lists, contract proposals, address lists, and personalized mailings.

Analyzing data is Q&A's forte, especially with the capabilities of the Intelligent Assistant. You can, for example, ask the Intelligent Assistant, "Which customers in Colorado have May orders greater than their April orders?" Q&A can give you the answer.

Remember, however, that the key to successful data retrieval is good file design. You can't find information you didn't put into the file in the first place, and you won't get information into the database if your database tool is difficult or inefficient to use—or simply lacks storage locations for critical data.

## *Creating the File Form*

Before you start designing a file in Q&A File, you should spend some time with Q&A Write or a pad and pencil to determine informally how your database reports will appear and what information you need to capture. (Chapter 2 provides some hints on beginning file design.) If data management programs are new to you, you may want to write the reports and the entry forms by hand first (see fig. 5.1). By designing the entry form by hand, you can plan how you want the fields to appear on the form, and you can be sure to include all the fields you need for your application. You also should have a good idea about the length in characters of each field and the general order in which you will enter information most often.

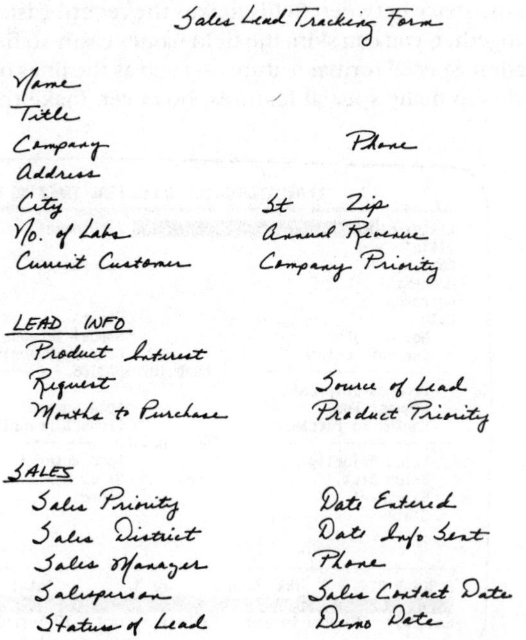

**Fig. 5.1**
*Planning the file form.*

Sales Lead Tracking Form

Name
Title
Company | Phone
Address
City | St | Zip
No. of Labs | Annual Revenue
Current Customer | Company Priority

LEAD INFO
Product Interest
Request | Source of Lead
Months to Purchase | Product Priority

SALES
Sales Priority | Date Entered
Sales District | Date Info Sent
Sales Manager | Phone
Salesperson | Sales Contact Date
Status of Lead | Demo Date

The sketched form in figure 5.1 is for a sales-lead tracking file for a wholesaler of medical laboratory testing equipment. The basis for the file is a contacts' name-and-address list, which also includes other information about sales and leads for each client.

The form is organized so that related fields appear together. The most important fields (the fields that will be used most often in sort operations) appear at the top of the form; the remainder of the fields are organized in two categories: sales-lead information and sales-action information.

The next step is to bring this preliminary database design into Q&A File and design the entry form on-screen. The entry form is essentially a list of field labels with space beside each label for the user to enter the field contents. A File entry form is a picture of the database record. The form establishes how the database will appear to users for data entry, editing, and report generation.

The following sections cover preliminary planning and the steps for creating your entry form.

## Planning a File Form

Whether you are creating a form that only you or many people will use, take the time to make the form attractive. The form in figure 5.2 is designed so the fields are not crowded; the space between fields makes the record easier to read. Because similar fields are together, you can skim the field names easily to find the one you need. Used in moderation, special format features— such as the lines on this form—can enhance the record. Too many special features, however, make the form look cluttered.

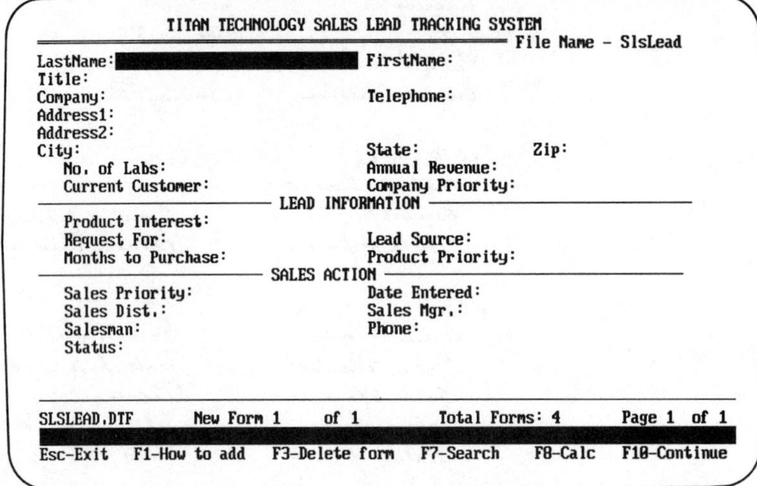
TITAN TECHNOLOGY SALES LEAD TRACKING SYSTEM
File Name - SlsLead
LastName: FirstName:
Title:
Company: Telephone:
Address1:
Address2:
City: State: Zip:
No. of Labs: Annual Revenue:
Current Customer: Company Priority:
LEAD INFORMATION
Product Interest:
Request For: Lead Source:
Months to Purchase: Product Priority:
SALES ACTION
Sales Priority: Date Entered:
Sales Dist.: Sales Mgr.:
Salesman: Phone:
Status:
SLSLEAD.DTF New Form 1 of 1 Total Forms: 4 Page 1 of 1
Esc-Exit F1-How to add F3-Delete form F7-Search F8-Calc F10-Continue

**Fig. 5.2**
*A Q&A File form on-screen.*

You want a database file to include everything required to produce the reports and queries you need. When you are laying out a form, though, you can easily get carried away. As you think of all the information you want to include, the form may grow to monstrous size. Remember that someone will have to enter all the information, and that someone may be you. To keep the form simple, include only necessary fields, and if possible, put all the fields on one page.

Before you design the form, you can determine the type of form you will need by answering a few questions about the application.

## How Will the Form Be Used?

When you set up the form, consider how the form will be used. Are you creating the form for a one-time project or an on-going process? For example, if the form will be used to develop a mailing-and-attendance list for your company's twentieth-anniversary banquet, the form should be easy to create and you won't need to spend too much time on design details. If, on the other hand, you are building a system to track maintenance and repairs for a fleet of delivery trucks, the form design will be more complex and used for a longer time. In this case, you need to create the form so that it can be used for regular report generation and analysis procedures and can be adapted for a variety of other uses.

Data analysis and reporting capabilities are two major strengths of Q&A File. The way you design the form has a great impact on the ease, flexibility, and speed with which the program analyzes data and generates reports.

### *Who Will Use the Form?*

You also should consider who will use the form. If you are the only user, you can design it any way you choose. If other people will be using it, however, the form design must be easily understood.

You can do several things to help other people use the form more easily:

- Make the labels clear and complete. If you use abbreviations or shorthand phrases, other users may not be able to interpret them. For example, if you have a field for the street name, and you abbreviate the label as ST, that field could be mistaken for the state field.
- Make the field names unique and indicative of the type of information to be entered in the field.
- Describe the information intended for a field by using a Q&A custom help screen (see Chapter 7).
- Be sure that the file name reflects the content or purpose of the file.

After you have designed the form on paper, you are ready to make the design with Q&A File. Don't worry about making mistakes; Q&A has a built-in safety net that gives you the option of redesigning your form at any stage without data loss.

## *Entering the Form Design*

One major strength of Q&A is the full-screen editor you use to create data file forms. To design a form in Q&A File, first select File from the Main menu. (You also can press 1, or if you have configured Q&A for single-keystroke entry, you can press F. Use the Utility menu to change this configuration. See Chapter 3 for more information.) The File menu is then displayed. Next, you select Design File to display the Design menu.

After you select the Design a New File option, Q&A prompts you to enter a file name. The name of the file can be up to eight characters long; the first character must be a letter or number. You don't need to enter an extension with the file name; Q&A File automatically adds the DTF extension. For the sales lead example, the file name is SLSLEAD. When you press Enter, Q&A displays the File form design screen. The cursor appears as a blinking rectangle in the top left corner of the screen. You move the cursor by pressing the cursor-movement keys.

To help you type the form design, several lines of information are displayed at the bottom of the Q&A form design screen (see fig. 5.3). The first of these lines is the ruler line. The ruler is divided into 10 characters per inch (pica character spacing).

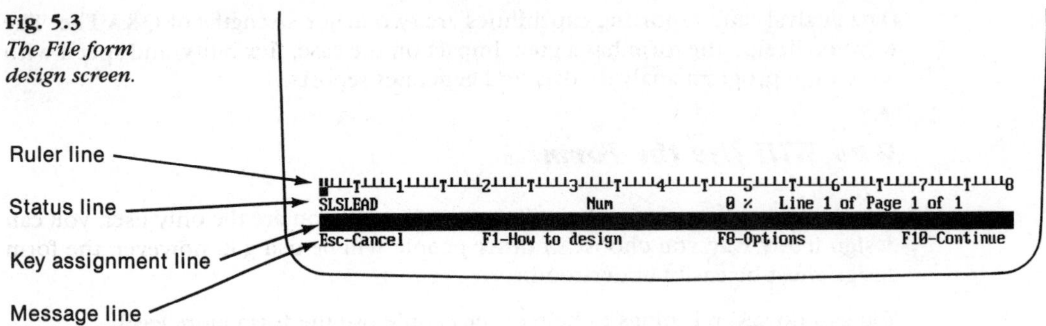


**Fig. 5.3** *The File form design screen.*

As you move the cursor on the screen, the rectangular bar on the ruler line moves to correspond with the cursor position. Tab stops also appear on the ruler line. Q&A has preset tabs every inch, but you can move the tabs to the positions you choose by using the Options screen (F8) from the form design screen. From the Options menu, you can choose to set tabs, center a line, uncenter a line, and draw.

The status line, just below the ruler line, displays information about your file. The file name is displayed on the far left side of the screen. The percentage of RAM memory used by the file is shown below the 5-inch point on the ruler. Initially, `0%` is displayed because nothing has been placed in the file.

The line location of the cursor is also indicated on the status line, along with the number of the page and the total number of pages in the form. When you begin designing the form, the cursor is on the first line of the first page, and the form has only one page. The display in the status line, therefore, is `Line 1 of Page 1 of 1`. When you move the cursor to a different line, the display changes to show the current cursor position.

The key assignment line lists some of the function keys available when you are designing a form. Remember that you can press F1 to display help screens whenever you need assistance.

Because Q&A File is integrated with the Q&A Write word processor, entering a form design is as easy as typing. The form design has three parts: the heading, the field labels, and space for field data. As you enter the items, remember that the editing capabilities of Write are available to help you insert, copy, move, and delete text. You can cancel the design procedure at any time by pressing Esc.

## *Entering a Heading*

Before you enter fields on the form, you may want to add a heading at the top of the first page of the form. The heading may include the name of the file, the date the file was created, the name of the person who created the file, and specifics about the file, such as company file number and security code. You can make the heading as complicated or as simple as you like, but remember that someone has to look at the form during data entry. Don't try to get so much information in the heading that the screen is cluttered or difficult to use. The heading appears on-screen but is not printed automatically on reports. You have to add the heading when you design the print specifications for the report. (See Chapter 8 for more information on printing File reports.)

To enter a heading, you simply type the text. Be careful not to use a colon (:) in the heading, however; during file design, Q&A reads any text followed by a colon as a field label.

The heading used in the sales lead example is a simple one (see fig. 5.4). As you can see, the name of the system is centered at the top of the form, and the file name is displayed on the right side of the screen. The double rule under the form heading is produced with the Draw command from the Options screen (F8).

```
                 TITAN TECHNOLOGY SALES LEAD TRACKING SYSTEM
================================================== File Name -- SlsLead
LastName:                          FirstName:
Title:
Company:                           Telephone:
Address1:
Address2:

SLSLEAD.DTF    New Form 1    of 1    Total Forms: 4    Page 1 of 1
Esc-Exit  F1-How to add  F3-Delete form  F7-Search  F8-Calc  F10-Continue
```

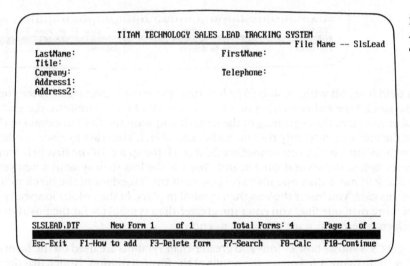

**Fig. 5.4** *A File form with a heading.*

## *Entering Field Labels*

To enter field names, move the cursor to the place where you want the first field to begin and type the label (refer to fig. 5.2 for the labels). End the field label with a colon. Figure 5.5 shows a partially completed form. Notice that this form design is an earlier one than fig. 5.4. The field specifications are different, and the double rule has not been added at this point.

## *Creating Information Blanks*

Q&A File leaves space for field data next to each field name. You determine the size of the blank, of course, according to the space you need for the information. A field that accepts a true or false value, for example, requires less space than a field with comment lines. The amount of space can range from two characters to an entire screen.

**Fig. 5.5**
*Creating information blanks.*

```
                 TITAN TECHNOLOGY SALES LEAD TRACKING SYSTEM
                                                   File Name:SlsLead
LastName:                                FirstName:

Title:

Company:                                 Telephone:

Address<
                                                                       >


Status:

                                                                       >



SLSLEAD                        Num     Insert  0 %   Line 17 of Page 1 of 1

Esc-Cancel         F1-How to design         F8-Options          F10-Continue
```

A field is set off with a colon (:) or less-than and greater-than signs. After you enter the label, type either a colon or a less-than symbol (<) to indicate the end of the label and mark the beginning of the field. If you want the field to extend to the end of the line, you need only the colon after the label. If you want to place another field on that same line, just enter another field label; the space for the first field stops one space before the second label begins. You use the less-than symbol when you have a blank of more than one line, and you want the left edges of the blank to line up. In this case, you insert the less-than symbol in place of the colon. To specify a field of more than one line, you enter the greater-than symbol (>) at the position on the screen where you want the blank to end.

Figure 5.5 shows how colons and greater-than symbols are used on the form design screen. In figure 5.6, you see the results of the form definition. Notice that the colons are visible but the greater-than signs are not. Q&A supplies the lines for the information, and the blank for the address field is highlighted as the current cursor position. This figure shows how multiple-line fields are handled in Q&A.

## *Formatting the Form*

The Q&A Write formatting options (Set Tabs, Center Line, Uncenter Line, and Draw) are also available when you design a form. You access the Options menu by pressing F8. To choose an option, type the first letter of the option.

### *Setting Tabs*

You arrange the fields during the form-design process by using the Set Tabs option. The tab stops remain set for the form-design process and subsequent redesign operations but not for data entry.

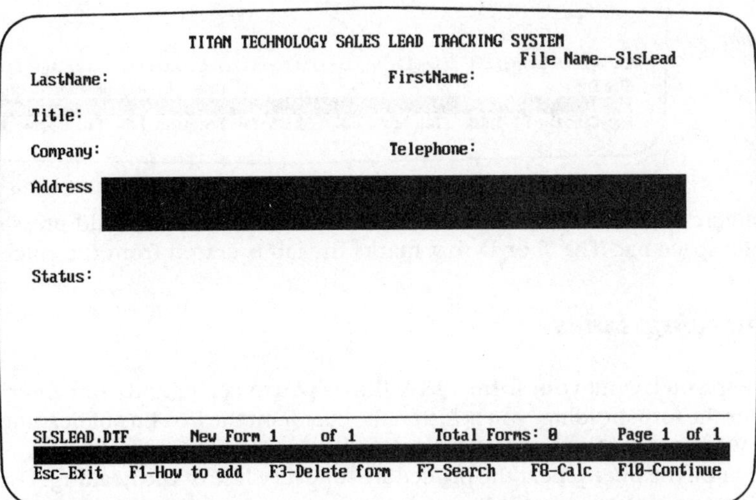


**Fig. 5.6.** *Results of the form definition.*

By selecting Set Tabs, you can delete existing tab stops and add new tab stops. Two types of tabs can be set: text tabs (T) align field labels flush left, and decimal tabs (D) align field labels flush right. When you begin typing above a text tab, the first character appears above the tab and the other characters are displayed to the right of the tab. When you use a decimal tab, the characters appear one space to the left of the decimal tab and move to the left until you type a period.

If you want to change the tab settings on your form, press F8 to display the Options menu. Then press S (for Set Tabs). Q&A displays a ruler line, and the cursor appears on the ruler as a rectangular box. Notice that the ruler line has several preset text tab stops. You can move to the point on the ruler where you want to edit the tab stops by using the following keys:

| *Key* | *Cursor movement* |
|---|---|
| Home | First space to the right of the left margin |
| End | First space to the left of the right margin |
| Ctrl-(←) | Five spaces to the left |
| Ctrl-(→) | Five spaces to the right |
| Tab | Next tab marker to the right |
| Shift-Tab | Next tab marker to the left |

To insert a tab stop, move to the position on the ruler where you want to add the tab stop; then press T for a text tab or D for a decimal tab. In figure 5.7, for example, a text tab was added in column 42 and a decimal tab in column 68. When you save the file, the new tab stop settings are also saved.

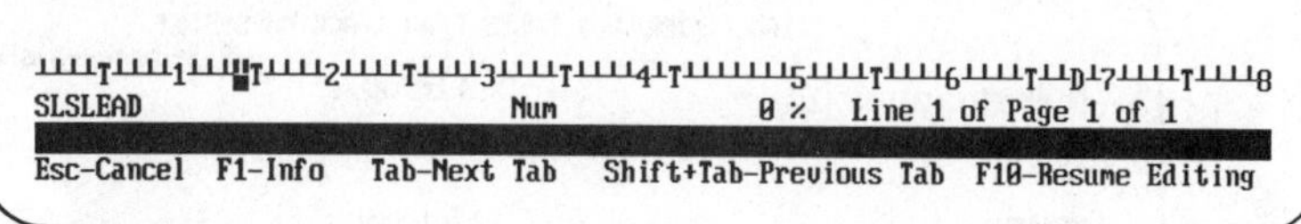


**Fig. 5.7**
*Text and decimal tabs.*

To delete a tab, move the cursor to the tab you want to delete and press either Del or the space bar. The T or D that marks the tab is erased from the ruler.

### *Centering Lines*

To help you lay out your form, Q&A allows you to center and "uncenter" lines. To center the form heading, you position the cursor on the first line of heading and press F8. When the Options menu is displayed, select C (for Center Line). Q&A centers all text on the line. Repeat the procedure for every line of the heading. Use the same option to center a line as it is entered. When you begin typing, the characters you enter are centered on the line and the cursor is kept in the center of the screen.

When you uncenter a line, you move it back to normal left-margin alignment. To uncenter a line, move the cursor into the centered line, press F8 to bring up the Options menu and select U for Uncenter Line. The line is realigned at the left margin.

### *Drawing Lines and Boxes*

The Draw feature of Q&A File allows you to enhance your form design by adding lines, boxes, and illustrations. Lines and boxes are often used to group related information so that the form is easier to understand. Ambitious users can create logos and other complex illustrations with the Draw feature.

The Draw feature was used in the sales lead file form (again see fig. 5.2). A double line separates the heading from the body of the form, and each category of information is set off by a single line.

To use Draw mode of Q&A File, place the cursor where you want the drawing to begin and press F8. When the Options menu is displayed, select Draw; then use the cursor keys to draw the lines. When you move the cursor, Q&A draws a single line; when you press the Shift key and move the cursor, the program draws a double line. You also can draw double lines by pressing the NumLock key and moving the cursor with the cursor-movement keys on the numeric keypad. The number keys 1, 3, 7, and 9 on the numeric keypad draw single diagonal lines. Press F10 to return to Editing mode.

You erase a line in Draw mode by pressing F8 (Erase) and moving the cursor over the lines you want to erase. When you press F8 in Draw mode, you can use any cursor-movement key to erase a line. You also can erase a line by pressing the Backspace key over those keystrokes without choosing the Erase mode. When you are ready to stop erasing and resume drawing, press F8 to return to Draw mode.

After the line is drawn and you exit Draw mode, the cursor can pass through the line without affecting it. If a space to the left of a line is deleted or inserted, however, the line changes positions.

## *Formatting the Information: The Format Spec*

After you design the form, you need to fill out a format specification form to tell Q&A how the fields should be formatted. On the Format Spec screen, you enter the type of information that will be included in each field and specify the data format options and global format options for each field (see fig. 5.8).

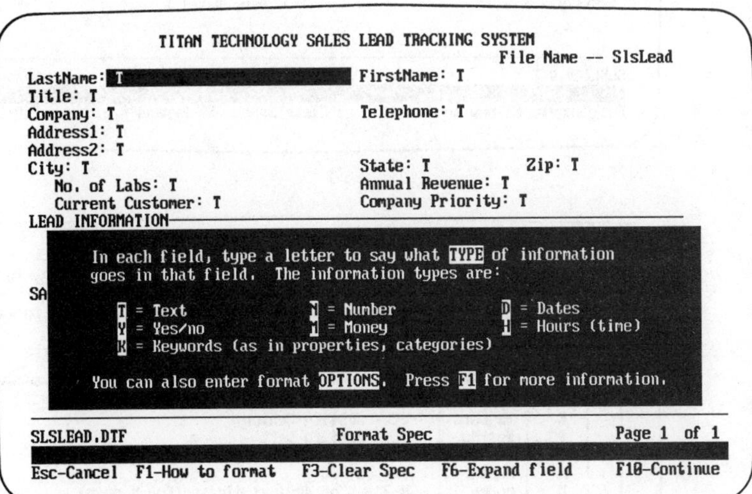


**Fig. 5.8**
*The Format Spec screen.*

### *Specifying Field Type*

The first step in filling out the Format Spec is specifying the type of information that will be entered in each field. Initially, each field is listed as a text field (T), but you can change the specification to match your field types. (See Chapter 2, "Database Concepts," for a discussion of data types.)

Depending on the field type, you enter the first letter of one of the following choices: text, numeric, yes/no, money, date, hour, or keyword. Move the cursor from field to field by pressing the cursor keys, Tab, or Shift-Tab. As you move the cursor to the bottom half of the screen, the help window moves to the top; so the instructions are always visible. Figure 5.9 shows the completed Format Spec screen for the sales-lead form. You can press F1 to display a second help screen, which lists the information types and data format options (see fig. 5.10).

**Fig. 5.9**
*The completed Format Spec.*

```
                    TITAN TECHNOLOGY SALES LEAD TRACKING SYSTEM
                                                         File Name -- SlsLead
LastName: T                            FirstName: T
Title: T
Company: T                             Telephone: T
Address1: T
Address2: T
City: T                                State: T,U          Zip: T
   No. of Labs: N,C                    Annual Revenue: M,C
   Current Customer: Y,U               Company Priority: N
LEAD INFORMATION-----------------------------------------------------
   Product Interest: K
   Request For: K                      Lead Source: K
   Months to Purchase: N               Product Priority: N
SALES ACTION----------------------------DATES------------------------
   Sales Priority: N,1                 Date Entered: D
   Sales Dist.: T                     Date Info Sent: D
   Salesman: T                         Sales Contact: D
   Status: K                               Demo Date: D

SLSLEAD.DTF                       Format Spec                  Page 1  of 1
Esc-Cancel  F1-How to format   F3-Clear Spec   F6-Expand field    F10-Continue
```

**Fig. 5.10**
*Format options help screen.*

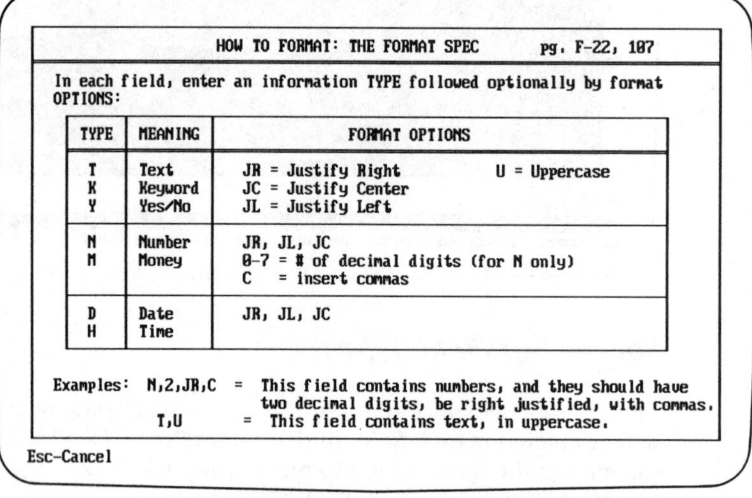

HOW TO FORMAT: THE FORMAT SPEC    pg. F-22, 107

In each field, enter an information TYPE followed optionally by format OPTIONS:

| TYPE | MEANING | FORMAT OPTIONS |
|---|---|---|
| T<br>K<br>Y | Text<br>Keyword<br>Yes/No | JR = Justify Right    U = Uppercase<br>JC = Justify Center<br>JL = Justify Left |
| N<br>M | Number<br>Money | JR, JL, JC<br>0-7 = # of decimal digits (for N only)<br>C = insert commas |
| D<br>H | Date<br>Time | JR, JL, JC |

Examples: N,2,JR,C = This field contains numbers, and they should have two decimal digits, be right justified, with commas.
T,U = This field contains text, in uppercase.

Esc-Cancel

A text field stores information that requires no special formatting features, although some are available. Fields that store both alphanumeric and numeric information—such as addresses, telephone numbers, serial numbers, or Social Security numbers—are defined as text fields. Although we may generally think of some of these entries as numeric entries, they sometimes include non-numeric data. A telephone number, for example, can be entered as (123)456-7890; a Social Security number usually includes hyphens. Nine-digit ZIP codes frequently include a hyphen between the first group of five numbers and the last four numbers. ZIP codes beginning with zero probably will not sort as expected unless they are entered in a text field. Numeric fields store numbers only; for example, you use numeric fields to store ages, quantities, and other strictly numeric data. The No. of Labs field in figure 5.9 has been designated a numeric field. Only numbers, minus and plus signs, commas, and decimal points are accepted in a numeric field. As an added feature, Q&A can use numeric fields for mathematical operations.

A yes/no field is shown in figure 5.9 as the Current Customer field. This type of field is used to store the answers to such questions as "Is this a preferred customer?" or "Is this customer on the mailing list?" Q&A accepts as an affirmative answer yes, Y, true, T, or 1; negative values can be no, N, false, F, or 0.

Numbers typed in a money field are formatted in the dollars-and-cents form—for example, $46,300.01. Q&A inserts the dollar sign and commas. You can change the currency symbol to the pound sign if you wish. Calculations can be made in money fields, as they can in numeric fields.

When you specify D in a field on the Format Spec screen, Q&A recognizes the field as a date field. The Date Entered field in figure 5.9 is an example of a date field. Q&A's default date display is in the form mmm dd, yyyy, but you can change the format to any of 20 different options available from the Global Format Options screen, which appears after you identify field types (see the "Choosing Global Options" section later in this chapter).

An hour field displays the time in either 12- or 24-hour format. In the 12-hour format, Q&A displays the time in the form hh:mm am/pm, such as `10:42 am` or `6:40 pm`. The program can correctly interpret time entered in a 24-hour format; that is, when you enter *22:05* but have chosen 12-hour format, Q&A displays the time as `10:05 pm`.

The date and hour information types are especially helpful when used with Q&A File advanced programming features and the Intelligent Assistant. For example, using advanced programming techniques, you can have Q&A notify you when a certain number of days has passed or alert you when a particular time has arrived.

Keyword fields are a special Q&A feature that programs like dBASE III Plus and PFS:FILE don't possess. Keywords give you the freedom to enter text values in more than one way.

You can set up a keyword field so that Q&A recognizes a set of entries for the field. For example, the sales lead sources are recorded in the Lead Source field in the database. Leads have been gained from several sources in this case, so you can designate several keywords to be accepted as entries in the field. For this example, the keywords ***Reference***, ***Adv***, ***Mailing***, ***Salesman***, and ***Other*** have been used. You can use these keywords to sort the file, produce reports, and analyze the lead-generating techniques. (For more information on specifying keywords, see Chapter 7.)

You can specify a keyword field on a Format Spec by typing *K* in the field. In figure 5.9, the Product Interest, Request For, Lead Source, and Status fields are keyword fields. You enter keywords by choosing the Restrict Values option from the Customize menu; you then type the keywords in the fields of the Restrict Spec, placing semicolons (;) between keywords. The specification for the preceding example appears as

Lead Source: Reference;Adv;Mailing;Salesman;Other

Remember to make your designations consistent; Q&A does not recognize different spellings of the same keyword. For example, if you enter Reference as the keyword and later ask for References from that field, Q&A cannot process your request.

## *Selecting Data Format Options*

Data field format specifications—Justify, Uppercase, Decimal Digits, and Commas—are entered in the field space of the Format Spec, following the code for information type (again see figs. 5.9 and 5.10).

When you specify U in a field, all text entered in that blank is displayed in uppercase letters. For example, even if you enter a value in the State field as *ca*, the value appears as CA if you have marked the field as uppercase.

You can specify up to seven decimal digits for your numeric fields, although you probably will use only two or three decimal digits for most of your fields. Figure 5.9 shows that the Sales Priority field is set to display values to one decimal place.

The comma specification causes commas to be inserted in numbers containing four or more whole digits. When entering multiple specs in a field, separate the specs by using commas and no spaces. The Annual Revenue field in figure 5.9 shows you how to specify comma insertion.

You also can select the justification for your fields. If you choose Justify Left (JL), the values in the field are aligned with the left edge of the field. Justify Center (JC) centers the values in the field, and Justify Right (JR) causes the values to be aligned with the right edge of the blank.

Table 5.1 shows which data format specifications can be used with the different information types.

**Table 5.1**
**Using Data Formats with Information Types**

| *Information Type* | *Justify Right* | *Justify Center* | *Justify Left* | *Uppercase* | *Decimal Digits* | *Insert Commas* |
|---|---|---|---|---|---|---|
| Text | Yes | Yes | Yes | Yes | | |
| Keyword | Yes | Yes | Yes | Yes | | |
| Yes/No | Yes | Yes | Yes | Yes | | |
| Number | Yes | Yes | Yes | | Yes | Yes |
| Money | Yes | Yes | Yes | | | Yes |
| Date | Yes | Yes | Yes | | | |
| Time | Yes | Yes | Yes | | | |

Figure 5.11 shows how the data in the record is displayed after the Format Spec is saved.

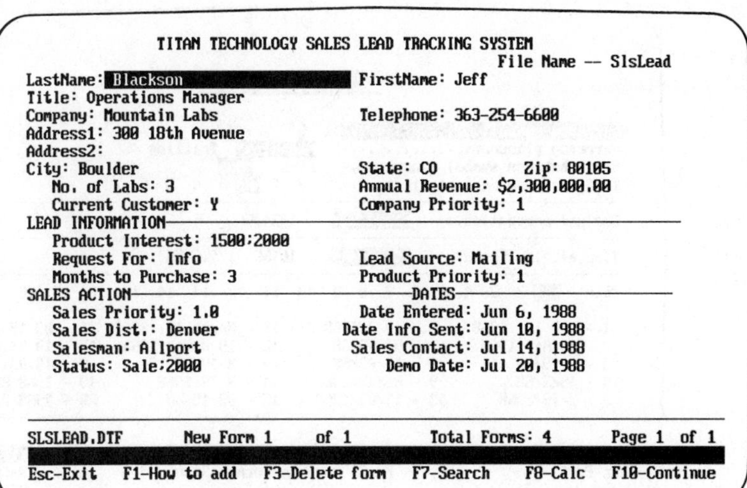

TITAN TECHNOLOGY SALES LEAD TRACKING SYSTEM
File Name — SlsLead
LastName: Blackson FirstName: Jeff
Title: Operations Manager
Company: Mountain Labs Telephone: 363-254-6600
Address1: 300 18th Avenue
Address2:
City: Boulder State: CO Zip: 80105
No. of Labs: 3 Annual Revenue: $2,300,000.00
Current Customer: Y Company Priority: 1
LEAD INFORMATION
Product Interest: 1500;2000
Request For: Info Lead Source: Mailing
Months to Purchase: 3 Product Priority: 1
SALES ACTION DATES
Sales Priority: 1.0 Date Entered: Jun 6, 1988
Sales Dist.: Denver Date Info Sent: Jun 10, 1988
Salesman: Allport Sales Contact: Jul 14, 1988
Status: Sale;2000 Demo Date: Jul 20, 1988

SLSLEAD.DTF New Form 1 of 1 Total Forms: 4 Page 1 of 1

Esc-Exit F1-How to add F3-Delete form F7-Search F8-Calc F10-Continue

**Fig. 5.11** *Results of data formats.*

### Choosing Global Format Options

If any information type has been specified as number, money, time, or date, the Global Format Options screen is displayed as the final formatting step (see fig. 5.12). On this screen, you specify the global formats for currency, decimals, time, and date. Notice that 20 options are available for date format. By selecting Global, you are telling Q&A to use the specified format every time the program encounters data in that type of field in the current file. For example, if you change the currency symbol from the dollar sign to the pound sign on the Global Format Options menu, Q&A displays the pound sign as the currency symbol in every money field in the file both on-screen and in printouts.

To select a global format option, use the Tab, Enter, or cursor keys to highlight a format option. When you have made your selections and saved the specifications, press F10 to continue.

## Redesigning a File Form

You may think of ways to improve a form after you have used it for a while. Perhaps your original design includes fields that you don't use, or maybe you want to change the order of the fields. In Q&A you can change the form quickly without danger of data loss—whether you want to make a top-to-bottom overhaul or only a slight adjustment. You can delete fields, insert fields, change field lengths, or select different formats.

Most important, you can make design changes even after you have entered data into the file; Q&A accepts the changes and adjusts the data to fit the new design. If you

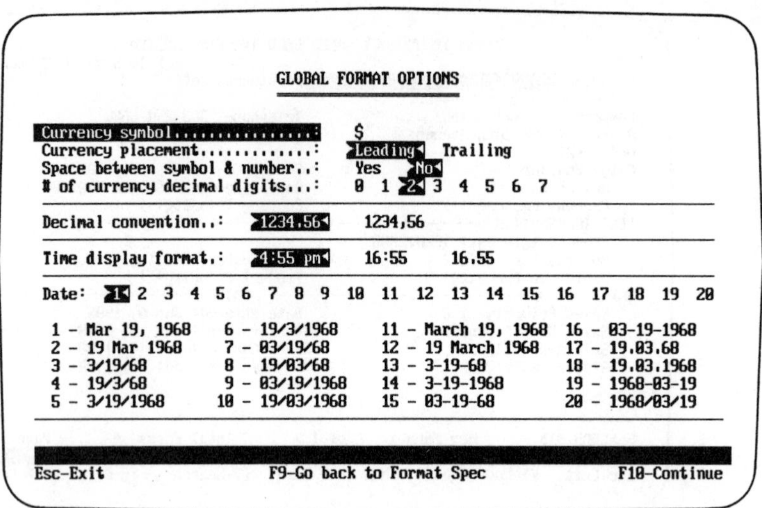

GLOBAL FORMAT OPTIONS
Currency symbol................: $
Currency placement.............: Leading Trailing
Space between symbol & number..: Yes No
# of currency decimal digits...: 0 1 2 3 4 5 6 7
Decimal convention..: 1234.56 1234,56
Time display format.: 4:55 pm 16:55 16.55
Date: 1 2 3 4 5 6 7 8 9 10 11 12 13 14 15 16 17 18 19 20
1 - Mar 19, 1968
2 - 19 Mar 1968
3 - 3/19/68
4 - 19/3/68
5 - 3/19/1968
6 - 19/3/1968
7 - 03/19/68
8 - 19/03/68
9 - 03/19/1968
10 - 19/03/1968
11 - March 19, 1968
12 - 19 March 1968
13 - 3-19-68
14 - 3-19-1968
15 - 03-19-68
16 - 03-19-1968
17 - 19.03.68
18 - 19.03.1968
19 - 1968-03-19
20 - 1968/03/19
Esc-Exit
F9-Go back to Format Spec
F10-Continue


**Fig. 5.12** *The Global Format Options screen.*

have ever lost data in another program while trying to change the design of a database form, you will appreciate this Q&A feature.

Be sure to make a backup copy of the entire file before you redesign a database; if you decide that you like your original form better than the redesigned version, you have the original on disk.

## *Modifying the Form*

With Q&A you can edit the file form more extensively and more easily than you can with many programs. Because File is linked with Q&A's built-in word processor, almost all the editing features are available while you work on the form.

For example, suppose that you need to redesign the sales lead example introduced in this chapter. The original form is shown in figure 5.13. The redesigned form is shown in figure 5.14. The form has been redesigned so that the LEAD INFORMATION and SALES ACTION headings are centered. Also, several of the date fields in the SALES ACTION section have been deleted.

The process for redesigning a form begins at the Design menu. First, select Redesign a File. Q&A prompts you to enter the name of the database file. You can type a file name, or you can select a database. First, press the space bar to erase the line, if necessary; press Enter to display a list of databases; move the highlight cursor over the desired file name, and then press Enter again to select the database you want. If a default file name is displayed and you want to enter a new name, just type it. Q&A erases the displayed file name when you type the first character.

In this example, the database selected is SLSLEAD. Each field has an identifying code supplied by Q&A (see fig. 5.15). Don't alter the codes on the form; the code for each

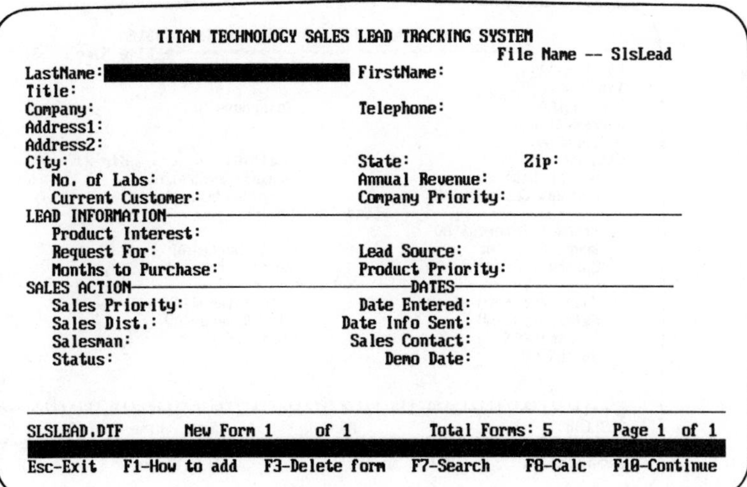

```
                 TITAN TECHNOLOGY SALES LEAD TRACKING SYSTEM
                                                  File Name -- SlsLead
LastName:                          FirstName:
Title:
Company:                           Telephone:
Address1:
Address2:
City:                              State:            Zip:
   No. of Labs:                    Annual Revenue:
   Current Customer:               Company Priority:
LEAD INFORMATION--------------------------------------------------------
   Product Interest:
   Request For:                    Lead Source:
   Months to Purchase:             Product Priority:
SALES ACTION-------------------------------DATES------------------------
   Sales Priority:                 Date Entered:
   Sales Dist.:                  Date Info Sent:
   Salesman:                      Sales Contact:
   Status:                            Demo Date:

SLSLEAD.DTF      New Form 1     of 1       Total Forms: 5      Page 1  of 1

Esc-Exit  F1-How to add  F3-Delete form  F7-Search   F8-Calc  F10-Continue
```

**Fig. 5.13**
*The original file form.*

```
                 TITAN TECHNOLOGY SALES LEAD TRACKING SYSTEM
==================================================File Name -- SlsLead
LastName:                          FirstName:
Title:
Company:                           Telephone:
Address1:
Address2:
City:                              State:            Zip:
   No. of Labs:                    Annual Revenue:
   Current Customer:               Company Priority:
---------------------------LEAD INFORMATION----------------------------
   Product Interest:
   Request For:                    Lead Source:
   Months to Purchase:             Product Priority:
------------------------------SALES ACTION-----------------------------
   Sales Priority:                 Date Entered: Jul 27, 1988
   Sales Dist.:                   Sales Manager:
   Salesman:                      Phone:
   Status:

SLSLEAD.DTF      New Form 1     of 1       Total Forms: 15     Page 1  of 1

Esc-Exit  F1-How to add  F3-Delete form  F7-Search   F8-Calc  F10-Continue
```

**Fig. 5.14**
*The redesigned file form.*

field must stay where the code was placed by the program. The codes, also called field tags, are used to identify your data and to reorganize the data when the form is redesigned. If you change a code, Q&A may be unable to process your request.

If you accidentally delete a code, you can type the code as it appeared on-screen or press Esc to cancel editing. When you add fields to the form, Q&A assigns codes to the new fields.

When the database form is displayed, you are ready to make the changes to the form.

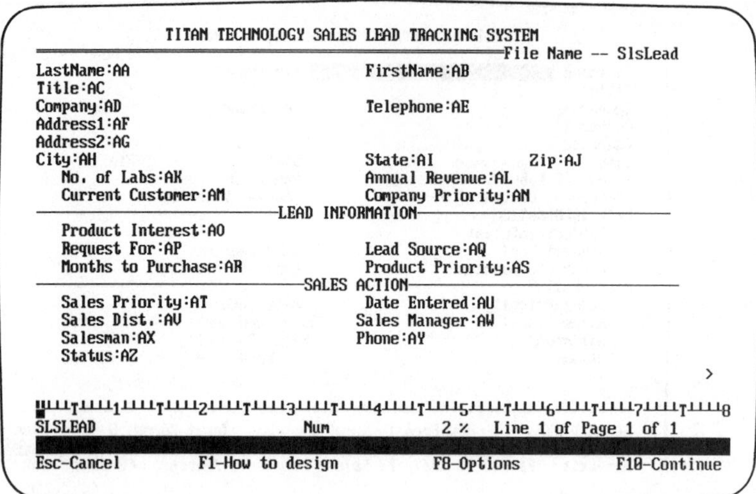


**Fig. 5.15**
*Q&A field identification codes.*

## *Changing Field Lengths*

After you have designed your file form, you may find that you have allotted too much space to some fields and not enough space to others. Changing the length of a field is easy, but be careful—you can lose part of your data in the process if a field is shortened.

***Note:*** Before you change field length, you may want to go to the Customize menu and select Change Palette. This method allows you to choose a palette that displays field lengths with highlights or lines, so that the fields are easier to see and change.

To change the length, simply add or delete spaces between the beginning and end of the field. Remember that colons (:) and greater-than and less-than signs (< >) mark the area of the field. When you shorten a field, Q&A displays a warning screen telling you that you may lose data. You can cancel the process or continue.

If you plan to shorten a field, first use Search/Update to read through the forms and check the length of the data in that field. If no data extends to the end of the field, shortening the field has little or no effect. If the data fills the field, however, shortening the field may destroy some important information.

## *Adding a Field*

You can add a field anywhere on the form. The field can be added on a new page or on a form page that has other fields. Use the PgUp and PgDn keys to move from page to page.

You may want to press the Ins key to change Q&A into Insert mode before you add a field so that you won't type over existing fields. If you want to insert a line for the new field, move the cursor to the place you want the line inserted. When you press Enter, the program inserts a new line at the cursor position, and all lines below the cursor move down one line. If a field is on the last line of the page, the field is moved to the top of the next page. Then, to add the new field, simply move the cursor to the place you want the field to be, and start typing.

### *Deleting a Field*

When you delete a field, make sure that you remove the entire field—label, colon, greater-than and less-than signs, and code. To delete a field, you can use the F4 key, the backspace key, or the Del key.

***Note:*** This occasion is the only time you should alter a code.

If your form includes calculated fields, and you delete a field that is referenced in the calculation formula, the program may display a warning screen. To correct the error, you can first re-enter the field, next select the Program Form option from the Customize menu, and then replace the programming statement. Another way to correct the problem is to change the calculation formula. After selecting Customize a File, choose Program Form and modify the formula so that it no longer references the deleted field.

### *Moving a Field*

After you begin using your file form, you may want to change the order of the fields. With Q&A, you can move and copy fields, even after data has been entered.

You can move a field in one of two ways: by copying the field and deleting the original or by moving the original. The copy-and- delete procedure is safer because if power is interrupted or a disk error occurs during the copy procedure, you still have the original intact.

Be careful when you use the Move and Copy commands. When the field is inserted in the new location, any other fields on the line shift to the right. This movement could upset the layout. You can avoid disruption by making room at the new location for the field you're about to move, perhaps by inserting an empty line.

To move a field, select Design File and then Redesign a File. When the screen appears for redesigning your form, you position the cursor on the first character of the field label you want to move. Press Shift-F5 to select Move; the cursor becomes a full-character highlight. Use the right-arrow key to highlight the entire field to be moved; make sure that you include the code and the greater-than symbol if the field has one. If, for example, you want the Title field above the LastName field, you highlight that field. To complete the selection, press F10. When you move the cursor to the new field location and press F10 again, the field is moved (see fig. 5.16).

To copy a field and delete the original, move the cursor to the first character of the field label and press F5 to select Copy; the cursor becomes a full-character highlight.

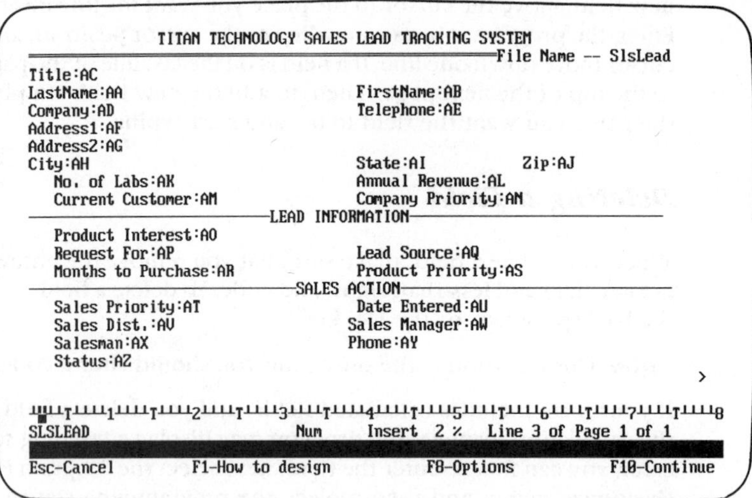
TITAN TECHNOLOGY SALES LEAD TRACKING SYSTEM
File Name -- SlsLead
Title:AC
LastName:AA FirstName:AB
Company:AD Telephone:AE
Address1:AF
Address2:AG
City:AH State:AI Zip:AJ
No. of Labs:AK Annual Revenue:AL
Current Customer:AM Company Priority:AN
LEAD INFORMATION
Product Interest:AO
Request For:AP Lead Source:AQ
Months to Purchase:AR Product Priority:AS
SALES ACTION
Sales Priority:AT Date Entered:AU
Sales Dist.:AV Sales Manager:AW
Salesman:AX Phone:AY
Status:AZ
SLSLEAD Num Insert 2 % Line 3 of Page 1 of 1
Esc-Cancel F1-How to design F8-Options F10-Continue

**Fig. 5.16**
*Moving a field.*

Use the right- arrow key to highlight the material to be copied; make sure that you include the greater-than symbol if one has been used. Press F10 to complete the selection process. When you move the cursor to the new field location and press F10 again, the field is copied. You then return to the original field and delete it by moving the cursor to the first character in the field name and pressing Del as many times as required or by pressing Shift-F4 to erase the entire line.

If you forget to delete the original, Q&A catches your mistake. When you press F10 to continue, Q&A checks the form; if the form has a duplicate field, the program moves the cursor to the copied field and displays the following warning:

```
You have a duplicate field code at the cursor. Codes must be unique.
```

## Changing Information Types and Formats

After you have moved, copied, inserted, or deleted fields, you may want to reformat some of them. You can reach the Format Spec screen by pressing F10 at the completion of your changes. You then enter format codes and information types for new fields or change the format codes and information type of edited fields. When you press F10 again, the File menu is displayed.

Q&A reorganizes the file. This process is part of Q&A's internal housekeeping. Depending on the size of the database and the number of changes you have made, the program may take some time to complete the task.

## *Chapter Summary*

The design of your file form is an important part of your database. With Q&A File, you can design a form as basic or as complex as you need. This chapter has explained the steps required to get your form up and running; the next chapter teaches you how to enter and edit information with Q&A File.

If you are designing a form that will be used by other people or if you want to try out Q&A's programming features before you begin to enter information into your file, you may want to read Chapter 7, "Customizing and Programming a File," before you begin Chapter 6.

Chapter 6

# Using File

After you have designed and formatted your file form, you can begin entering data. For details about designing and formatting files, see Chapter 5. As you use your form, you will find that planning and preparation have saved you considerable time and effort.

If the file form you have designed uses mostly text fields and does not require automatic calculation and entry of numeric, date, or time data, you are ready to use your form by following the directions in this chapter. If, however, your database fields use automatic calculations or require features customized to help other users, you may want to read Chapter 7, "Customizing and Programming a File," before you read this chapter. Chapter 7 explains programming techniques for streamlining the use of your form. This chapter explains the procedures used for

- Entering and adding information
- Retrieving and updating forms
- Copying information
- Using custom help screens
- Displaying forms in a table
- Locating forms
- Deleting information from the database

## Adding and Editing Information in File

Entering information in Q&A File is just as easy as in Q&A Write. The sales lead example used in the preceding chapter is continued here to help illustrate these operations.

You must open a file before you can add and edit information. To begin, select Add Data from the File menu by typing *A* or *2*. Q&A then prompts you for a file name.

You must specify a file before you can add or edit information. Type the name of the file, or press Enter to display a list of data files. After you select a file name, the entry form for that file is displayed. You may now add information, change information, and print a single form.

The number of the current form and the total number of forms in the database are displayed on the status line (see fig. 6.2). The number of new forms during a single add session is incremented with each new form. Figure 6.1 shows the first new form of this session. When you add a second form, the status line will change to show

```
New Form 2   of 2   Total Forms: 19   Page 1 of 1
```

The `Page 1 of 1` notation means that your form has only one page and that one page is displayed. If you were on the second page of a four-part form, the Page notation would show `Page 2 of 4`.

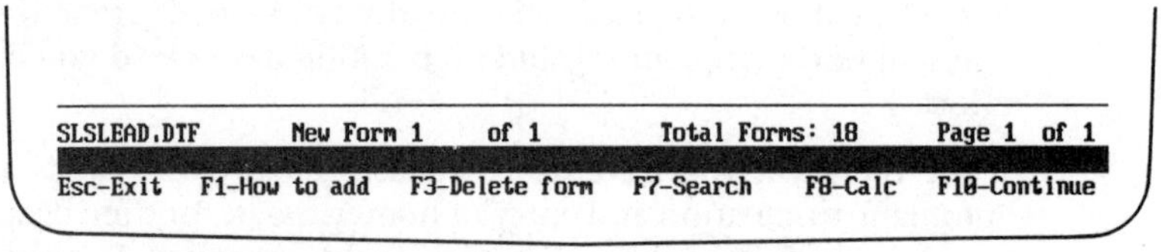

```
SLSLEAD.DTF        New Form 1     of 1          Total Forms: 18         Page 1  of 1
Esc-Exit   F1-How to add   F3-Delete form   F7-Search     F8-Calc    F10-Continue
```

**Fig. 6.1**
*The File status line.*

## *Using Special Keys for Entering Data and Moving through Forms*

You can use various special keys to help make entering data in your form easier. When the file form is displayed, the cursor is positioned in the first field. You simply type the information for that field. If you make mistakes typing, correct them by using the Q&A editing keys. (See "Editing Forms" in this chapter for a list of editing keys.)

When you finish entering data in the first field, press Enter or Tab to move the cursor to the next field. When you want to move to a preceding field, press Shift-Tab. When you finish entering data in all the fields on the first page of the form, you can move to the next page by pressing the PgDn key. Press PgUp to move to a preceding page.

When you have entered data in all the fields on the form, you have several options: you can press F10 to save the form and display a new one (you use this procedure when you need to fill in more than one form); you can press Shift-F10 to save the form and return to the File menu; or you can press F2 to print a quick copy of the form. (For more about printing a file, see Chapter 8.)

After you have entered and saved more than one form, you can press F9 to move back through preceding forms. F10 is used to scroll forward through the forms. The procedure is similar to paging though paper forms in a file folder, but Q&A makes the process faster and easier.

## *Entering Data into a Form*

When you enter information into Q&A File, the program checks to make sure that the information corresponds to the types you specified when you designed the form.

### *Entering Different Data Types*

As you already know, certain types of information should be entered in certain fields. For example, numbers go in numeric fields, and dates go in date fields unless you have a good reason for overriding these restrictions.

Q&A File alerts you to mismatches so that you can correct them. Mismatches are explained in the following sections, and some additional information is given about information types and date fields. Refer also to Chapter 2, ''Database Concepts,'' for additional information about Q&A data types.

Q&A File declares a mismatch for two reasons:

- The wrong type of information is entered into a file.
- The information doesn't conform to the restricted value.

For example, if you have specified that a field is a date field, but you enter alphanumeric text, Q&A notifies you that a possible mismatch has occurred. The restricted value feature of Q&A lets you program individual fields for specific values or ranges of values. If information outside these limits is entered, a mismatch occurs. See Chapters 4 and 7 for more information on entering restricted values.

Text fields accept any information, but other field types are more discriminating. If any characters other than numbers, commas, periods, plus or minus signs, and currency symbols are entered into number and money fields, Q&A does not accept the entry.

Q&A checks the information type when you try to leave date, time, and yes/no fields. If you have entered mismatched information, the cursor remains in the field, and an error message is displayed. You can change the entry, or you can accept it by pressing Enter and proceeding to the next field. In figure 6.2 an attempt was made to enter the text phrase *DON'T KNOW* in the Current Customer field. Because the Current Customer field is a yes/no field, File displays a message to alert you.

You can correct this problem in one of two ways: erase the mismatched information and enter the correct information, or accept the mismatch by pressing Enter. The information is entered if you accept the mismatch, and the cursor moves to the next field. (For this illustration, we have shown this field with a length of several characters. Normally, a yes/no field has a length of one.)

Notice that Q&A leaves the user in control. Many database products flatly refuse to accept information that does not match the specified type for a particular field—and for some excellent reasons. If your application depends heavily on consistent

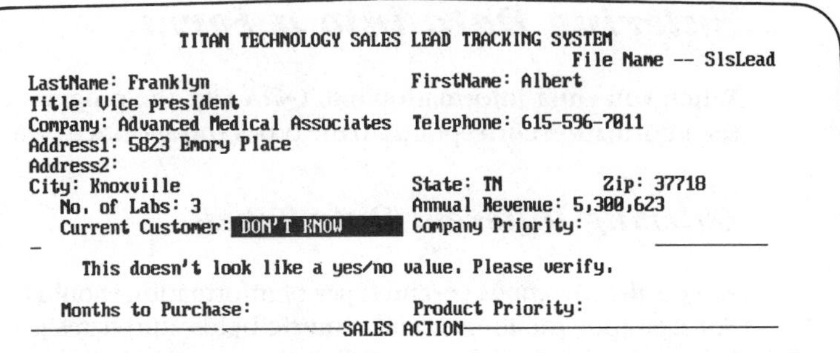
TITAN TECHNOLOGY SALES LEAD TRACKING SYSTEM
File Name -- SlsLead
LastName: Franklyn FirstName: Albert
Title: Vice president
Company: Advanced Medical Associates Telephone: 615-596-7011
Address1: 5823 Emory Place
Address2:
City: Knoxville State: TN Zip: 37718
No. of Labs: 3 Annual Revenue: 5,300,623
Current Customer: DON'T KNOW Company Priority:

This doesn't look like a yes/no value. Please verify.

Months to Purchase: Product Priority:
SALES ACTION

**Fig. 6.2** *Warning messages for the wrong data type.*

information in certain fields across the database (and most successful applications do), you want to avoid mismatched data in the database.

Although you can enter incorrect information, you also can enter data that helps you find forms with missing information. Suppose that you do not know the date of some occurrence when you are entering information for a specific record. A blank date field means that the event has not occurred or has not been scheduled, so you enter something like *unknown* instead of leaving the field blank. Q&A tells you that *unknown* is not a valid date, but you can enter it anyway. Later you can search for *unknown* to enter the correct date. In the meantime, you won't get invalid data in your reports because of a wrong interpretation of a blank date field.

In many situations, being strictly confined to the format or data restrictions designed into a database may be inconvenient. You must consider the question carefully, however, when Q&A asks whether you are sure that you want to enter the nonconforming data. If the entry is a typo or other mistake instead of a planned deviation from the specs, you want to correct the data instead of accepting it.

You have two options to ensure that entered information adheres to the programmed database restrictions. One is to create carefully designed custom help for these critical fields and instruct any data entry personnel to use custom help when Q&A returns data errors.

The other option is to program the form so that improper data simply cannot be entered. This approach is restrictive, but necessary in some applications. For example, if several different people are entering data and you want to make sure that all fields are filled consistently, you may need to restrict entry to specific data types or ranges of data. Such restrictions should be accompanied by custom help screens so that the operator doesn't get locked into one field, unable to decide what acceptable data to enter and unable to continue because the program restricts a continue or exit until certain data conditions are met.

On the other hand, at times, the sensible procedure is to enter what seems like wrong information to the database rules you have established. Consider an accounting database. Assume that you have imposed restrictions on account numbers during transaction entry so that expense entries are entered with account numbers between 800 and 999 only, income accounts are entered in accounts 600 to 799, and so on. (See the next section on restricted fields for more information on this concept.) To get a list of income transactions, you request all entries with account numbers between 600 and 799.

If you make a deposit and credit it to an expense account, Q&A warns you of the apparent error. However, you could use this reverse type of entry to account, in a simple way, for expenses for which you were reimbursed from your company. Here is a case where the restrictions trap is well-intentioned, but without a way to override the restriction, you are forced into a more complicated form design.

## *Entering Data into Restricted Fields*

When you customize your data entry form (see Chapter 7), you may choose to restrict some fields. Restricting fields affects the way data is entered into those fields. Restricted fields are designed to monitor and limit the data added to a field. This type of field is especially useful when you are using certain keywords.

Restricted fields accept specific words or phrases and alert you when unacceptable information is entered into the field. For example, in figure 6.3 *Phone* has been entered into the Lead Source field. However, the Lead Source field has been restricted to one of five specific words:

Mail
Telephone
Reference
Adv
Other

The word *Phone* is not one of the restricted values. In addition to demonstrating how Q&A handles information outside specified restricted ranges, this example also shows how easily you can be inconsistent in data entry.

Good database design includes planning for many data entry situations and handling them by programming if possible. Q&A is flexible enough to let you specify *telephone* or *phone* in this field so that you have more choices during data entry. You can even program the field to change the data entry to the preferred form if the operator enters something close to what is desired. Generally, the procedure for forcing operators to enter certain data, bypassing Q&A's built-in capability to accept information outside specified ranges, involves using a simple IF...THEN statement:

```
>#5: IF #5<10 OR #5>100 THEN GOTO #5
```

When you have this statement in a numeric or money field, you cannot exit the field if the value entered is less than 10 or greater than 100. When an incorrect value is entered and you press Enter, the cursor returns to the beginning of the field, and Q&A waits for you to enter data within the specified range. You can press Esc to exit the form, or you can press F10 to store the form and move to the next one. If you press Esc, the information already entered is not saved. If you press F10, data entered up to this point is saved, and a new form is presented. The greater-than symbol (>) at

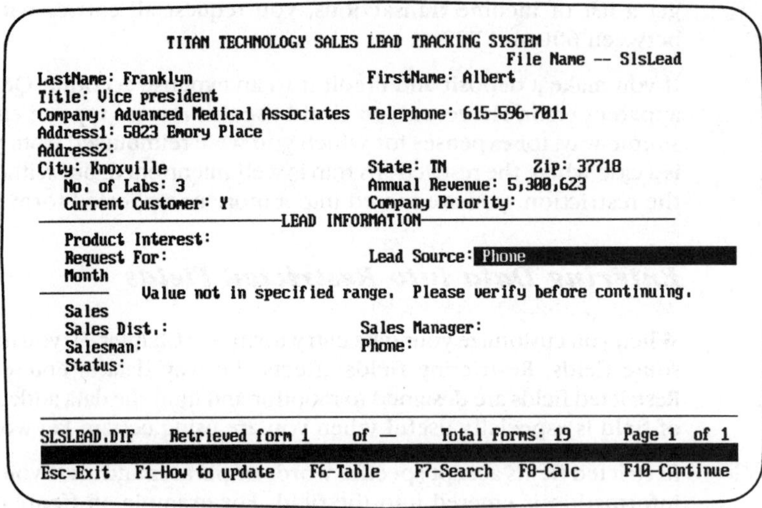


**Fig. 6.3** *Warning for unacceptable data in a restricted field.*

the beginning of the programming statement tells Q&A to evaluate this statement when you attempt to exit the field. See Chapter 7 for more information on programming a form.

## *Entering Data into Date Fields*

Q&A Version 3 offers 20 different date formats, as you can see in the following list (Version 1 accepted only 6 formats):

Mar 19, 1988 March 19, 1988
19 Mar 1988 19 March 1988
3/19/88 3-19-88
19/3/88 3-19-1988
3/19/1988 03-19-88
19/3/1988 03-19-1988
03/19/88 19.03.88
19/03/88 19.03.1988
03/19/1988 1988-03-19
19/03/1988 1988/03/19

You select a format from the Global Format Options screen when you design the form. This screen is presented automatically when you exit the Format Spec screen during form design.

When dates are entered in the forms, Q&A displays the dates in the selected format. If the form is later redesigned with a different date format, the dates in previously entered forms may not be displayed properly or may not fit the new format. If the information blank is too short for the format, the date may be cut off. For example, the longest date format requires 18 spaces (September 19, 1988), and the shortest format takes 8 spaces (12/19/88).

Once you have specified a date format, date information is stored in that format in the file. You can enter the date information in almost any way you choose, however. For example, you may want the date stored in the format mmm dd, yyyy, but you prefer entering dates in the form mm/dd/yy. When you exit the date field, Q&A reformats the date to conform to the specified format. If the year is the same as the year in the computer's system date, you need not enter the year as part of the date. Q&A assumes that you mean the current year.

## *Copying Entered Data from One Form to the Next*

If you are entering the same information into certain fields of consecutive forms of your database, you can use the Ditto key (F5) to copy the data from one form to the same fields in the next form. Q&A File remembers the data you enter in one form when you move to the next. When you display a new form, you can move to a field and press the Ditto key (F5); Q&A copies the data from the same field on the preceding form.

The Ditto feature is great when you're entering the same information into several consecutive forms. In figure 6.3, a sales lead from Knoxville, TN, was entered. The next lead in the database is also from Knoxville, so instead of typing the information again, you can press F5 to copy the data from the City field on the last form (see fig. 6.4).

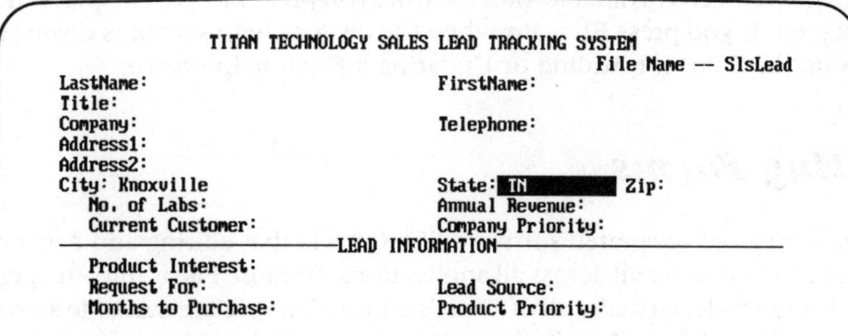
```
                TITAN TECHNOLOGY SALES LEAD TRACKING SYSTEM
                                                  File Name -- SlsLead
LastName:                              FirstName:
Title:
Company:                               Telephone:
Address1:
Address2:
City: Knoxville                        State: TN          Zip:
   No. of Labs:                        Annual Revenue:
   Current Customer:                   Company Priority:
-----------------------LEAD INFORMATION--------------------------
   Product Interest:
   Request For:                        Lead Source:
   Months to Purchase:                 Product Priority:
```

**Fig. 6.4**
*Using the Ditto key to enter information.*

## *Displaying Custom Help Screens*

As you enter and edit forms, you can use custom help screens to give you specific instructions, display restricted information about particular fields, or serve as reminders about codes and abbreviations. For example, suppose that a custom help screen has been designed for the Lead Source field in the Sales Lead Tracking System. This field is restricted to one of only five words. If you can't remember the words to use, you can press F1 to display the custom help screen. The screen is displayed as an overlay so that you can see the help information while you enter the correct value into the field (see fig. 6.5).

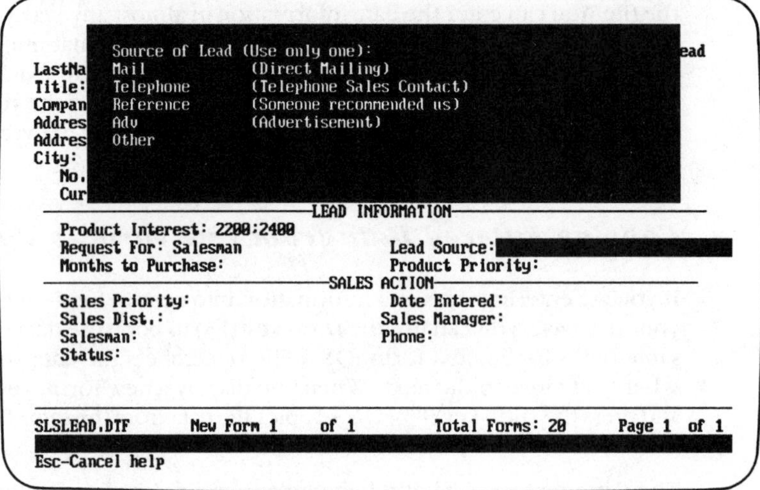


**Fig. 6.5**
*A custom help screen.*

The procedure for creating custom help screens is explained in Chapter 7, "Customizing and Programming a File."

Pressing F1 during data entry displays the Adding/Updating Forms help screen. If a custom help screen is available, the first time you press F1, Q&A displays the custom help screen. If you press F1 again when the custom help screen is displayed, Q&A brings up the Steps for Adding or Updating a Form help screen.

## *Editing Forms*

One advantage of integrated software like Q&A is that editing and data entry procedures can be consistent across all applications. Because File is fully integrated with Write, for example, virtually all of Write's editing features are available as you design an entry form and enter data. Table 6.1 lists the special editing and cursor-movement keys you can use to add and edit forms. Refer to Chapter 10 for details on Q&A editing procedures.

**Table 6.1.**
**Editing Keys Used in Q&A File**

| *Key* | *Function* |
|---|---|
| Enter, Tab | Moves cursor to next field |
| Shift-Tab | Moves cursor to previous field |
| ↓ | Moves cursor down one field |
| ↑ | Moves cursor up one field |
| → | Moves cursor to right |
| ← | Moves cursor to left |
| F4 | Erases data from cursor to end of field |
| Shift-F4 | Erases contents of current line |
| Ins | Turns on insert mode |

## *Entering Special Characters into a Field*

At times, you may want to enter special characters, such as superscript or subscript numbers, in a specific field. During File and Report print operations, you can send to your printer control codes to turn on font or other characteristics for each form or report. You must, however, control field-level printing during data entry.

To use special characters in Q&A, insert ASCII codes where you want the characters to appear. The codes either turn on a specific printer characteristic or display a character that is not on your keyboard.

An ASCII (American Standard Code for Information Interchange) code is the numeric representation of a character or symbol. The letter A is represented by the decimal number 65, for example. All standard character and graphics symbols can be represented by numbers. Refer to your computer operations manual, printer manual, or display adapter instructions for a list of character and graphics symbols and their numeric equivalents.

Many people, particularly those in technical and scientific fields, use superscript and subscript characters in day-to-day database use. Superscript and subscript characters may not appear as raised or lowered characters on your screen, however, depending on your computer system. For example, the IBM monochrome adapter and display does not show raised and lowered letters. The characters are printed as raised and lowered characters only when the printer is capable of supporting the features. To find out whether your system can produce superscript or subscript characters, consult your computer and printer manuals.

You turn on superscript with some commonly used printers by pressing Alt and typing *244* on the numeric keypad. (Don't use the number keys across the top of the keyboard.) Then type the characters you want to appear as superscript. To disable the superscript feature, press Alt and type *245*. Note that these instructions may not control superscript printing for your particular printer. Consult your printer manual to determine the proper codes.

An example of coding for superscript is shown in figure 6.6. The special character symbols before the *v* and after the *e* in *vice* indicate where the codes have been entered. When the form is printed, the codes will not appear.

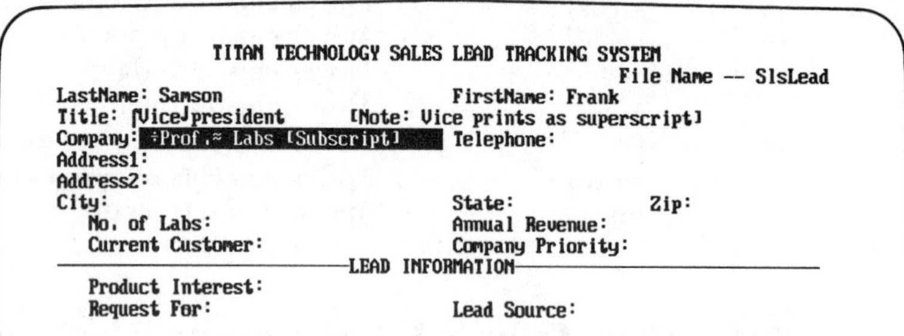

```
TITAN TECHNOLOGY SALES LEAD TRACKING SYSTEM
                                              File Name -- SlsLead
LastName: Samson                     FirstName: Frank
Title: Vicepresident        [Note: Vice prints as superscript]
Company: Prof. Labs [Subscript]      Telephone:
Address1:
Address2:
City:                                State:           Zip:
   No. of Labs:                      Annual Revenue:
   Current Customer:                 Company Priority:
---------------------------LEAD INFORMATION---------------------------
   Product Interest:
   Request For:                      Lead Source:
```

**Fig. 6.6** *Using the superscript and subscript features.*

With many printers, you turn on the subscript feature by pressing Alt and typing *246*. Again, be sure to use the numeric keypad. After you type the information you want to appear as a subscript, turn off subscript by pressing Alt and typing *247*. In figure 6.7, the noncharacter subscript code used to turn on the feature appears before the first *p* in *Prof*; the ending code is after the period. The codes will not appear on the printout. Again, the particular code for your printer may differ from these examples. Consult your printer manual for details.

With ASCII codes, you can enter virtually any character or symbol into a File database. A musical note (♪) is Alt-270, for example; the symbol pi ($\pi$) is Alt-227; a plus-or-minus sign ($\pm$) is Alt-241. Use caution with this technique, however. Some display-monitor combinations won't display the characters properly, and your printer may not be capable of handling some characters.

## *Calculating in Forms*

One of the more advanced features of Q&A File is the program's capacity to perform mathematical calculations. Chances are, whether you need to calculate a simple equation or a complex financial report, at some time you will need to use the calculation features of Q&A. In an inventory application, for example, you can calculate the selling price of items based on the wholesale price and a standard percentage markup. Or you can use Q&A's calculation feature to compute late charges, interest owed, or sales taxes. These calculations reduce the amount of keyboard data entry required.

Chapter 7 gives a detailed explanation of how to add calculation and programming statements to your form; this section gives only a brief overview of setting calculation modes and solving one kind of calculation error that may take place after the statements have been entered.

If your form contains arithmetic formulas or program statements, Q&A can calculate the fields manually or automatically. Q&A's default is manual calculation; you have to press the Calc key (F8) each time you want to calculate a field. If you want to change the setting to automatic recalculation, press Shift-F8. Q&A then displays the calculation menu across the bottom of the screen (see fig. 6.7).

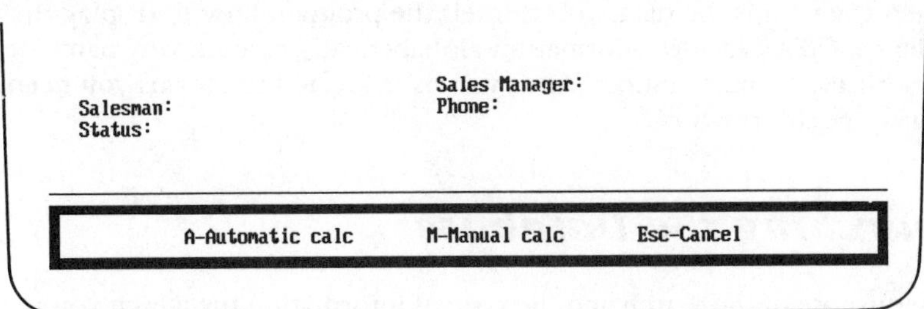


**Fig. 6.7** *The menu of calculation settings.*

Select A to choose automatic recalculation. In automatic mode, Q&A calculates a field's program statement as soon as the cursor is moved out of that field. The process takes time and can slow your data entry. If you have already chosen the Automatic Calc setting and want to return to Manual Calc, press M.

During the calculation process, if the result of a calculation is too large for the specified field length, Q&A displays asterisks. You can eliminate the asterisks and display the number by redesigning the form so that the field can accept a number that large. Another way to solve the asterisk problem is to change the format of the field so that fewer digits are displayed after the decimal point. (Chapter 5 includes more information on redesigning a file and formatting values.)

One type of calculation error to watch for is the divide-by-zero calculation. Q&A displays an ERR message in the field when a calc statement issues a divide-by-zero calculation. Fields that refer to the ERR field interpret the ERR as a zero value. If the divide-by-zero calculation is an error in the program statement, change the statement by selecting the Program Form option from the Customize a File menu.

Once you have entered the Program Form routine, you can edit any programming statements with standard Q&A editing commands. Study any formulas to make sure that they have no explicit errors. A common mistake is a formula that references another field which is not programmed to accept only data within a specified range. The correction for this problem is to include a program statement in the referenced field to force the operator to enter data within a range that is valid for the formula.

# Retrieving and Updating Forms

Similar to a paper-filing system, an electronic database is used most often to search for and update information. With Q&A's searching capability, you can easily find forms by searching for information in any field. For example, you can use Q&A to locate the customers who are covered by the Knoxville district sales office or to display a list of all the parts supplied by a certain company.

When Q&A finds the data, you can tell the program how to display the data. For instance, Q&A can sort information alphabetically by company name or list parts numerically by part number. After you have located the forms you need, you can update the information.

## Searching the Database

The purpose of the search and the type of information for which you're searching do not affect the search procedure; it is the same every time.

Suppose, for example, that you need to find the sales lead forms for the Knoxville sales district. To find the forms, you first select Search/Update from the File menu. Q&A then prompts you for a file name. Enter the file name (SLSLEAD) and press Enter. The Retrieve Spec for the sales lead file is then displayed (see fig. 6.8).

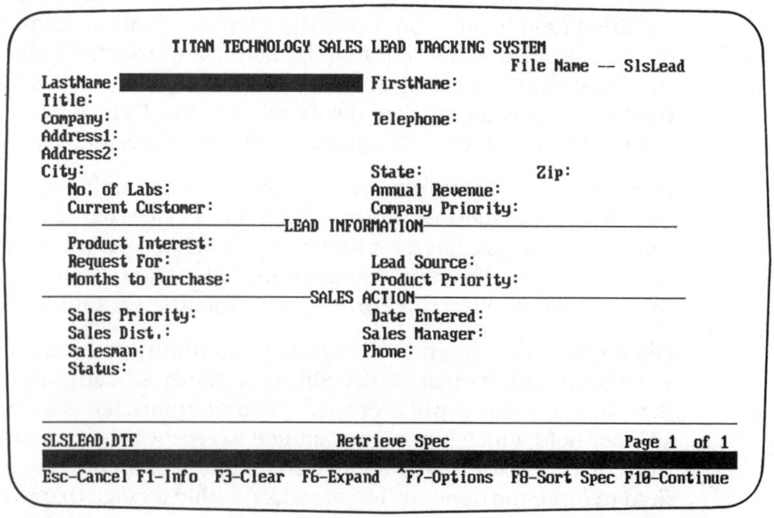

**Fig. 6.8**
*Retrieve Spec for the sales lead file.*

```
                 TITAN TECHNOLOGY SALES LEAD TRACKING SYSTEM
                                                  File Name -- SlsLead
LastName:                            FirstName:
Title:
Company:                             Telephone:
Address1:
Address2:
City:                                State:              Zip:
   No. of Labs:                      Annual Revenue:
   Current Customer:                 Company Priority:
--------------------------LEAD INFORMATION-----------------------------
   Product Interest:
   Request For:                      Lead Source:
   Months to Purchase:               Product Priority:
------------------------------SALES ACTION-----------------------------
   Sales Priority:                   Date Entered:
   Sales Dist.:                      Sales Manager:
   Salesman:                         Phone:
   Status:

SLSLEAD.DTF                    Retrieve Spec                  Page 1 of 1

Esc-Cancel F1-Info F3-Clear F6-Expand ^F7-Options F8-Sort Spec F10-Continue
```

Q&A's search procedure is sometimes called Query by Example (QBE) or Query by Form (QBF). Instead of entering commands (LOCATE FOR SALES DIST. = KNOXVILLE, for example), you type the information for which you want Q&A to search in the fields you want searched. Simply move the cursor to the field you want to use in the search and enter the search data. You can use any combination of upper- and lowercase letters; Q&A retrieves forms even when the case you type in the Retrieve Spec is different from the original. In this example, Knoxville is entered in the Sales Dist. field (see fig. 6.9). If you want the retrieved fields to be sorted, you have the option of accessing the Sort Spec (which is discussed later in this chapter).

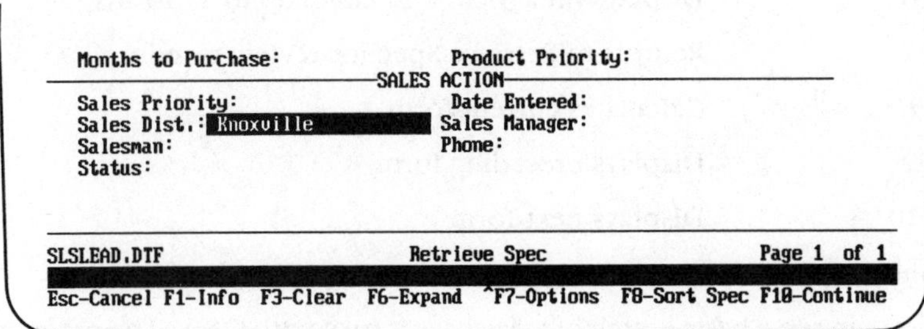
Months to Purchase: Product Priority:
SALES ACTION
Sales Priority: Date Entered:
Sales Dist.: Knoxville Sales Manager:
Salesman: Phone:
Status:
SLSLEAD.DTF Retrieve Spec Page 1 of 1
Esc-Cancel F1-Info F3-Clear F6-Expand ^F7-Options F8-Sort Spec F10-Continue

**Fig. 6.9**
*Filling in the Retrieve Spec.*

For now, complete the Retrieve Spec as shown in figure 6.9, and press F10 to start the search procedure. Q&A searches the database, retrieves the forms that match the Retrieve Spec, and displays the first of the forms (see fig. 6.10).

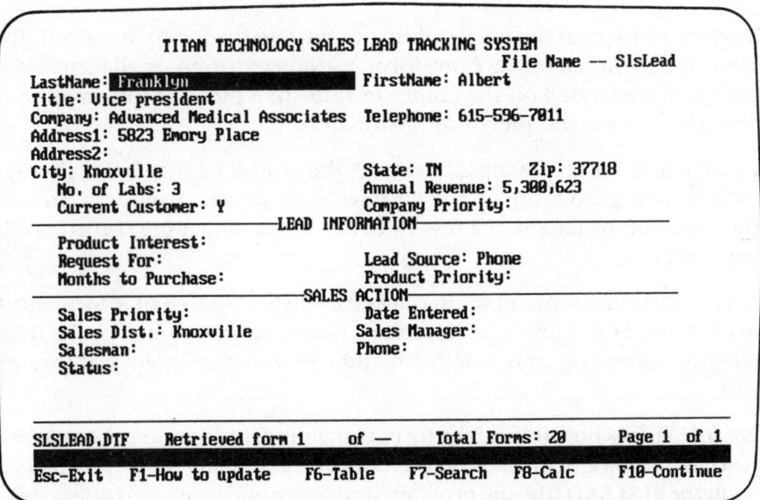
TITAN TECHNOLOGY SALES LEAD TRACKING SYSTEM
File Name — SlsLead
LastName: Franklyn FirstName: Albert
Title: Vice president
Company: Advanced Medical Associates Telephone: 615-596-7011
Address1: 5823 Emory Place
Address2:
City: Knoxville State: TN Zip: 37718
No. of Labs: 3 Annual Revenue: 5,300,623
Current Customer: Y Company Priority:
LEAD INFORMATION
Product Interest:
Request For: Lead Source: Phone
Months to Purchase: Product Priority:
SALES ACTION
Sales Priority: Date Entered:
Sales Dist.: Knoxville Sales Manager:
Salesman: Phone:
Status:
SLSLEAD.DTF Retrieved form 1 of — Total Forms: 20 Page 1 of 1
Esc-Exit F1-How to update F6-Table F7-Search F8-Calc F10-Continue

**Fig. 6.10**
*The form found as a result of the search operation.*

When the form has been found and displayed, you can make any changes you want. You use the function keys to perform a variety of operations, as shown in the following list:

| *Key* | *Function* |
|---|---|
| F1 | Displays help screen |
| F2 | Prints current form |
| F3 | Deletes current form |
| F6 | Displays (in a 5-column table) up to 17 forms |
| F7 | Returns to Retrieve Spec for review or edit |
| F8 | Calculates current form |
| F9 | Displays preceding form |
| F10 | Displays next form |
| Shift-F10 | Saves changed form |

As you can see, a basic search of a database is easy with Q&A. The program also has the flexibility to retrieve forms for more complicated applications, as explained in the following section.

## *Retrieving Forms*

Q&A gives you a great deal of flexibility in finding the forms you need. By using the Retrieve Spec, you can retrieve one form, a group of forms, or all forms. You can elect to retrieve forms based on the common value of a piece of information, a range of information, or several pieces of information.

The procedure for retrieving all forms is the easiest of the three: simply press F10 without entering anything on the Retrieve Spec screen. You then can look through all the forms in the database. Press F9 to show the preceding record or F10 to show the next record.

To retrieve one form, you enter in the Retrieve Spec a piece of information only that form contains. For example, a customer's name, a part number, or the title of a book is likely to appear on only one form and can therefore help you locate a specific record.

Figure 6.11 shows how to find the form containing information about Mountain Labs. As you can see, Mountain Labs is entered in the Company field. When Q&A searches through the SLSLEAD file, the program finds only one form containing this company; therefore, only that form is retrieved (see fig. 6.12).

At times, you may need to specify more than one value on a Retrieve Spec. For example, suppose that you need to see all sales leads that have three or more laboratories and have annual revenues greater than $5 million. To specify these searches, you enter *>=3* in the No. of Labs field and *>5000000* in the Annual Revenue field (see fig. 6.13). When Q&A searches the file, the program selects only the forms that meet the criteria (see fig. 6.14).

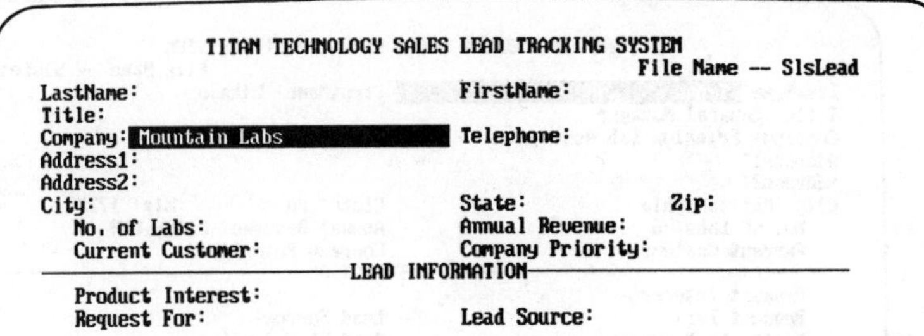

```
TITAN TECHNOLOGY SALES LEAD TRACKING SYSTEM
                                      File Name -- SlsLead
LastName:                           FirstName:
Title:
Company: Mountain Labs              Telephone:
Address1:
Address2:
City:                               State:          Zip:
  No. of Labs:                      Annual Revenue:
  Current Customer:                 Company Priority:
─────────────────────LEAD INFORMATION──────────────────────
  Product Interest:
  Request For:                      Lead Source:
```

**Fig. 6.11**
*The SlSLEAD file with Retrieve specification.*

```
TITAN TECHNOLOGY SALES LEAD TRACKING SYSTEM
                                      File Name -- SlsLead
LastName: Blackson                  FirstName: Jeff
Title: Operations Manager
Company: Mountain Labs              Telephone: 363-254-6600
Address1: 300 18th Avenue
Address2:
City: Boulder                       State: CO       Zip: 80105
  No. of Labs: 3                    Annual Revenue:
  Current Customer: Y               Company Priority: 1
─────────────────────LEAD INFORMATION──────────────────────
  Product Interest: 1500;2000
  Request For: Info                 Lead Source: Mailing
  Months to Purchase: 3             Product Priority: 1
────────────────────────SALES ACTION───────────────────────
  Sales Priority: 1.0               Date Entered: Jun 6, 1988
  Sales Dist.: Denver              Sales Manager:
  Salesman: Allport                Phone:
  Status: Sale;2000

───────────────────────────────────────────────────────────
SLSLEAD.DTF    Retrieved form 1    of —    Total Forms: 20    Page 1 of 1

Esc-Exit  F1-How to update    F6-Table   F7-Search  F8-Calc    F10-Continue
```

**Fig. 6.12**
*The form found as a result of the search.*

```
TITAN TECHNOLOGY SALES LEAD TRACKING SYSTEM
                                      File Name -- SlsLead
LastName:                           FirstName:
Title:
Company:                            Telephone:
Address1:
Address2:
City:                               State:          Zip:
  No. of Labs: >=3                  Annual Revenue: >5000000
  Current Customer:                 Company Priority:
─────────────────────LEAD INFORMATION──────────────────────
  Product Interest:
  Request For:                      Lead Source:
```

**Fig. 6.13**
*Retrieving forms based on more than one value.*

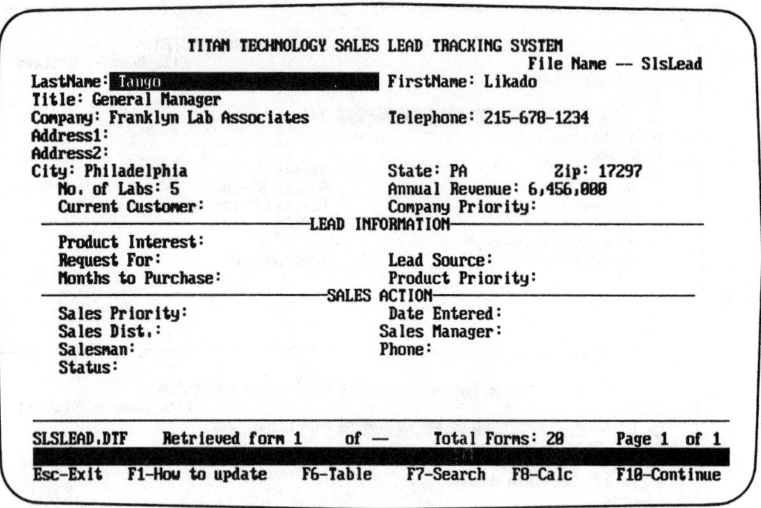
TITAN TECHNOLOGY SALES LEAD TRACKING SYSTEM
File Name — SlsLead
LastName: Tango FirstName: Likado
Title: General Manager
Company: Franklyn Lab Associates Telephone: 215-678-1234
Address1:
Address2:
City: Philadelphia State: PA Zip: 17297
No. of Labs: 5 Annual Revenue: 6,456,000
Current Customer: Company Priority:
LEAD INFORMATION
Product Interest:
Request For: Lead Source:
Months to Purchase: Product Priority:
SALES ACTION
Sales Priority: Date Entered:
Sales Dist.: Sales Manager:
Salesman: Phone:
Status:

SLSLEAD.DTF Retrieved form 1 of — Total Forms: 20 Page 1 of 1
Esc-Exit F1-How to update F6-Table F7-Search F8-Calc F10-Continue

**Fig. 6.14**
*The form retrieved as a result of the search.*

A useful thing to know: If you suspect mismatched data in one or more date fields of forms you want to find (text instead of a date, for example), precede the search specification with a right (closing) bracket (]). This code tells Q&A to search for this information even though a data type mismatch occurs.

## *Using Ranges To Retrieve Forms*

Although you frequently will need to find and display individual forms that meet certain criteria, you probably will use Q&A most often to display a group of forms that share a common value. When you retrieve forms, you can enter a specific item in a Retrieve Spec, as previously explained, or you can enter a range that is common to a group. For example, you can have Q&A display the records for sales prospects with ZIP codes between and including 94086 and 95997 by entering

> =94086..< =95997

in the Zip field of the Retrieve Spec form.

When you tell Q&A to retrieve a group of forms that have values within a range, the range type can be specified as money, numeric, text, keyword, date, or time. With Q&A, you also have the option of selecting a range that includes all types of information.

In figure 6.15, you see an example of a numeric range. The search criterion has been entered in the Annual Revenue field; all records that have in this field entries between $5 million and $10 million will be retrieved. A numeric range is specified by separating the low and high figures by two dots. Note the difference in searching a numeric range and a text range. The ZIP code search example is for a text-formatted field. If the ZIP code field were formatted as numeric, the search criteria would be simpler:

94086..95997. However, ZIP code values with numeric formatting limit you because you cannot enter the four-digit extension common with some ZIP codes without getting a Q&A error message.

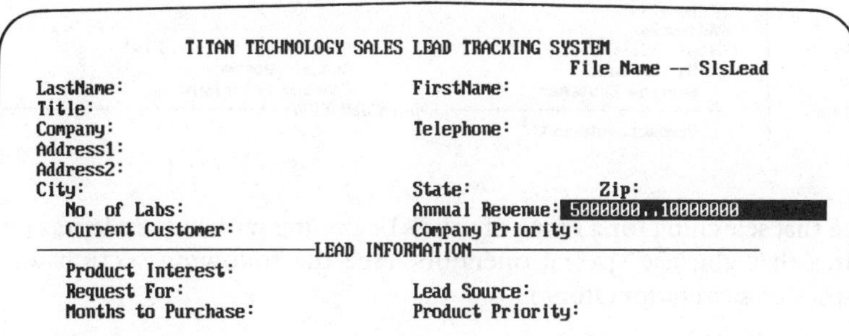


**Fig. 6.15**
*Retrieving on a numerical range.*

Using a keyword range, you can specify the retrieval of all sales leads that have the value Mail or Telephone in the Lead Source field (see fig. 6.16). Separate multiple keyword specifications with semicolons (;).

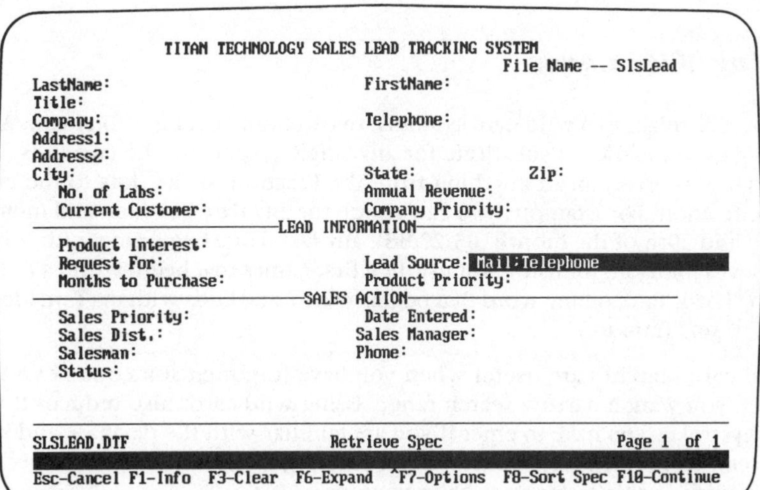


**Fig. 6.16**
*Retrieving on a keyword range.*

Another example of a range is an alphabetical range. You can, for example, retrieve all sales leads that have in the Company field names beginning with the letters A through M. Specify *A.. <N* (see fig. 6.17). Separate the alphabetical range with two dots. This example demonstrates the use of the less-than conditional operator (<) to mean "letters before N." You also could specify A..M and get the same results.

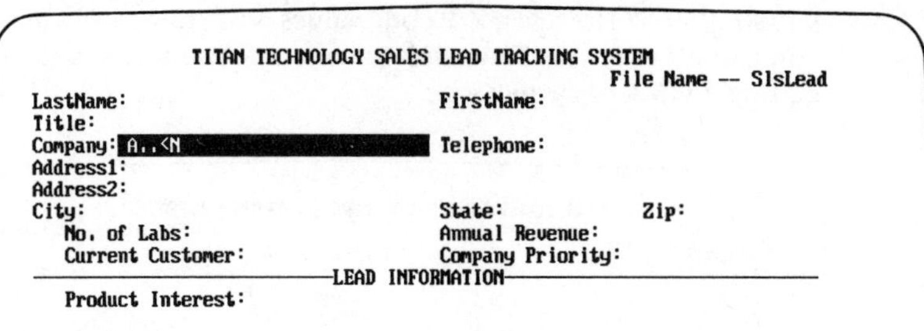


**Fig. 6.17**
*Retrieving on an alphabetical range.*

Notice that searching for a range of values beginning with certain letters or numbers requires that you use special operators. (See the following section for lists and examples of search operators.)

Q&A gives you considerable freedom in developing your own retrieval specifications. Use your imagination. You won't damage the program or your database. If you go beyond the limitations of the program, Q&A displays a warning message and asks whether you want to check or change your specifications. Select Yes if you want to try again, and you will be returned to the Retrieve Spec screen. Select No if you want to return to the File menu.

## *Using Wild Cards*

Q&A recognizes two wild-card symbols: two dots and the question mark. As in DOS, the question mark is a substitute for any single character. The two dots (similar to the DOS asterisk) mean anything from the location of the dots to the end of the specification. For example, you can search for any date between and including the 20th and 29th of the month (05/2?/88); any last name beginning with *John* (John.. retrieves Johnson, Johnston, Johnstone); first names that begin with *T* (T.. finds Ted, Tom, Thad, Tad); or any word that begins with *T* and ends with *m* (T..m locates Tom, tam, tram, Transam).

Wild-card searches are useful when you have forgotten someone's exact name or when you want a narrow search range. Using wild cards also reduces the number of keystrokes you have to enter if you are familiar with the database and know that you can get predictable results without entering the complete search spec. Think of wild cards in this instance as abbreviations.

If you want to use wild cards in your retrieval specifications, you can use the following formats:

| *Wild Card* | *Meaning* | *Example* |
|---|---|---|
| X.. | Begins with X | b.. |
| ..X | Ends with X | ..a |
| X..Y | Begins with X and ends with Y | b..a |

| *Wild Card* | *Meaning* | *Example* |
|---|---|---|
| ..X.. | Includes X | ..n.. |
| ? | Any character | ? |
| ..X..Y..Z | Includes X and Y and Z | ..b..n..a |

The following list shows how you can use wild-card operators to search for keywords:

| *Use the operator* | *To find* |
|---|---|
| a? | At, am, an |
| ..a.. | Bat, transamerica, aardvark |
| ???d | Find, fond, toad |
| ..e | Ape, mandate, George |
| ?i.. | City, hide |
| ..i?? | Mention, bring, write |
| h..n | Horn, Hohenzollern |
| P.. j.. | Peggy Johnson |

Q&A's range of options for retrieving data is impressive, particularly when compared with retrieval options in other databases. Q&A has another advantage over many database packages: Q&A doesn't require that you program the special conditions for retrieving data; you can enter the specifications directly on the Retrieve Spec screen.

## *Using Retrieval Operators*

The Retrieve Spec recognizes a range of symbols, called retrieval (or conditional) operators. You can enter these operators to specify the forms you want to retrieve. The following text explains the retrieval operators available with Q&A. Remember, however, that in the following lists, *X* represents any field value—not a literal X.

**Operators for Equal or Null Values.** Use the following operators to locate equal or null values in a field:

| *Operator* | *Meaning* | *Example* | *Explanation* |
|---|---|---|---|
| X | Equal to X | Denver | Finds exact match only |
| =X | Equal to X | =Denver | Finds exact match only |
| /X | Not X | /Denver | Finds everything except X |
| = | Empty | = | Finds empty fields; no value |
| /= | Not empty | /= | Finds any field with data |

**Operators for Greater- or Less-Than Values.** The operators in the following list can be used to find values that are greater or less than a specification:

| *Operator* | *Meaning* | *Example* |
|---|---|---|
| >X | Greater than X | >2000 |
| <X | Less than X | <2000 |
| > =X | Greater than or equal to X | > =2000 |
| < =X | Less than or equal to X | < =2000 |
| >X..<Y | Greater than X and less than Y | >2000..<4000 |
| X..<Y | Greater than or equal to X and less than Y (numeric fields only) | 2000..<4000 |
| > =X..<Y | Greater than or equal to X and less than Y (text fields) | > =2000..<4000 |
| >X..< =Y | Greater than X and less than or equal to Y | >2000..< =4000 |

**Operators for And, Or, and Range of Values.** The operators in this list can be used to specify either/or conditions or to determine a range of values in a field:

| *Operator* | *Meaning* | *Example* |
|---|---|---|
| X;Y;Z | X or Y or Z | Chicago;New York |
| &X;Y;Z | X and Y and Z | &Chicago;Atlanta;New York |

The & symbol can be used only in keyword fields, but x;y;z works in all fields.

**Operators for Minimum and Maximum Values.** Use the following operators to retrieve the highest or lowest values in a field:

| *Operator* | *Meaning* | *Example* |
|---|---|---|
| MAX n | Retrieve *n* highest values | MAX5 |
| MIN n | Retrieve *n* lowest values | MIN8 |

Only one each of these specifications can be used on a Retrieve Spec. On text fields, MAX returns the highest alphabetical characters; MIN finds the lowest. These operators cannot be used on keyword fields.

## *Sorting Forms before Retrieving*

Q&A retrieves forms in the order they were entered. Often, however, you will want to sort the forms in some different order. Q&A has the capability of sorting the forms on one or more fields in ascending or descending alphabetical or numerical order.

When more than one field is being sorted, the first field sorted is the primary sort, and the other fields are the secondary sorts. The order in which fields are sorted makes a big difference as to how the sort turns out.

For example, when the State field is the primary sort and the City field is the secondary sort, the forms are sorted in the following order:

| *Form* | *State* | *City* |
|---|---|---|
| 1 | Alaska | Fairbanks |
| 2 | Alaska | Nome |
| 3 | Colorado | Colorado Springs |
| 4 | Colorado | Denver |
| 5 | North Carolina | Charlotte |

When the City field is the primary sort and the State field is the secondary sort, the cities are sorted first, and then the states are sorted within the cities. The resulting order

| *Form* | *City* | *State* |
|---|---|---|
| 1 | Charlotte | North Carolina |
| 2 | Colorado Springs | Colorado |
| 3 | Denver | Colorado |
| 4 | Fairbanks | Alaska |
| 5 | Nome | Alaska |

Suppose that you want the sales leads retrieved by the alphanumeric search in figure 6.17 to be sorted in alphabetical order. From the Retrieve Spec screen, press F8; Q&A displays the file form in the Sort Spec screen. You then move the cursor to the Company field and type *1* in the field you want to be sorted first. If you want another field sorted (the State field, for example), you enter *2* in that field. You can sort all the fields on a form if you like, and you can have up to 512 different sort levels, probably more sorting flexibility than you will ever need.

After you specify sort order, indicate how you want the field to be sorted: ascending or descending. Use AS to specify an ascending sort or DS to specify a descending sort.

Figure 6.18 shows how the Company and State fields are coded to specify sort order. The Company field is the primary sort and will be sorted in ascending order. The State field is the secondary sort and also will be sorted in ascending order.

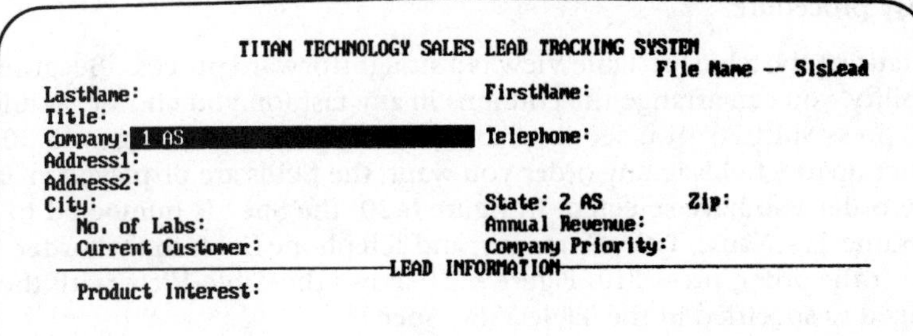

```
                 TITAN TECHNOLOGY SALES LEAD TRACKING SYSTEM
                                                  File Name — SlsLead
LastName:                                  FirstName:
Title:
Company: 1 AS                              Telephone:
Address1:
Address2:
City:                                      State: 2 AS        Zip:
  No. of Labs:                             Annual Revenue:
  Current Customer:                        Company Priority:
──────────────────────────LEAD INFORMATION────────────────────────
  Product Interest:
```

**Fig. 6.18** *Filling in the Sort Spec.*

Press F10 when you are finished with the Sort Spec. Q&A then retrieves the specified forms and displays them in the sort order you have indicated.

## Viewing Forms in a Table

Q&A displays forms one at a time in Search/Update mode. To display data from multiple forms simultaneously in a table, press F6 after you have entered the Sort Spec and pressed F10. You can display up to 17 forms at once in Table View (see fig. 6.19). Each row in the table displays the first five fields in a form.

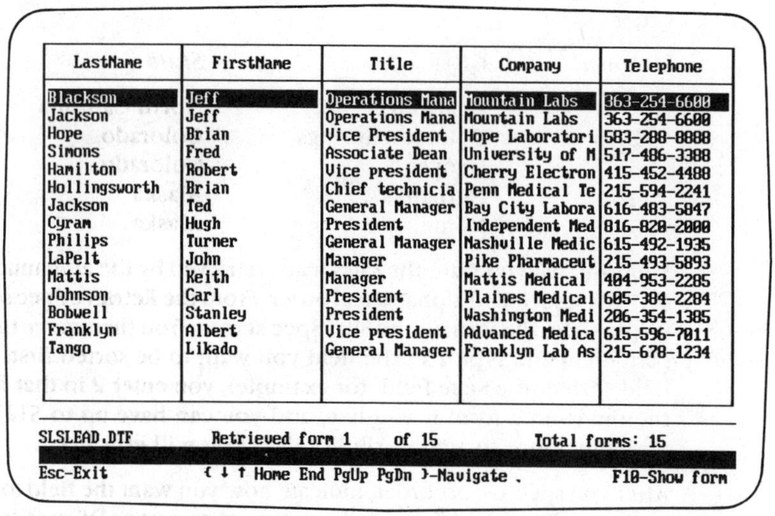

**Fig. 6.19**
*The Table View of a database.*

| LastName | FirstName | Title | Company | Telephone |
|---|---|---|---|---|
| Blackson | Jeff | Operations Mana | Mountain Labs | 363-254-6600 |
| Jackson | Jeff | Operations Mana | Mountain Labs | 363-254-6600 |
| Hope | Brian | Vice President | Hope Laboratori | 583-288-8888 |
| Simons | Fred | Associate Dean | University of M | 517-486-3388 |
| Hamilton | Robert | Vice president | Cherry Electron | 415-452-4488 |
| Hollingsworth | Brian | Chief technicia | Penn Medical Te | 215-594-2241 |
| Jackson | Ted | General Manager | Bay City Labora | 616-483-5847 |
| Cyram | Hugh | President | Independent Med | 816-828-2000 |
| Philips | Turner | General Manager | Nashville Medic | 615-492-1935 |
| LaPelt | John | Manager | Pike Pharmaceut | 215-493-5893 |
| Mattis | Keith | Manager | Mattis Medical | 404-953-2285 |
| Johnson | Carl | President | Plaines Medical | 605-384-2284 |
| Bobwell | Stanley | President | Washington Medi | 206-354-1385 |
| Franklyn | Albert | Vice president | Advanced Medica | 615-596-7011 |
| Tango | Likado | General Manager | Franklyn Lab As | 215-678-1234 |

SLSLEAD.DTF Retrieved form 1 of 15 Total forms: 15

Esc-Exit ← ↓ ↑ Home End PgUp PgDn →-Navigate . F10-Show form

When you are in Table View mode, you can scroll the display of forms by pressing the up- and down-arrow keys. If you want to display an entire form, highlight the first field of the form and press F10. Press F6 to return to Table View after you finish examining the form. The Table View feature makes looking through forms selectively an easy procedure.

Configuring the table for Table View is a straightforward process. Because of Q&A's flexibility, you can arrange the columns in any fashion you choose. While in Form View, press Shift-F6. You see the Table View Spec shown in figure 6.20. You can number up to 5 fields in any order you want; the fields are displayed in Table View in the order you have selected. In figure 6.20, the Spec is numbered to show the FirstName, LastName, Title, Company, and Telephone fields in that order. Once you have set the order, press F10. Figure 6.21 shows the Table View with the columns arranged as specified in the Table View Spec.

If you number fewer than five fields in the Table View Spec, only the numbered columns are always displayed when you choose Table View. You can display one more

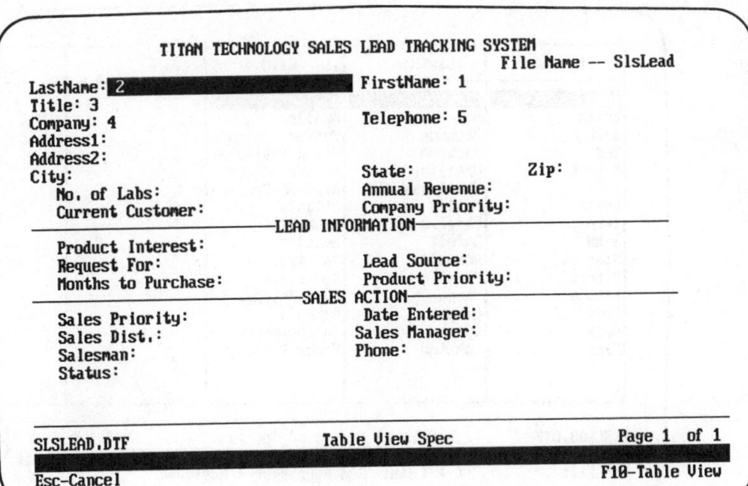

TITAN TECHNOLOGY SALES LEAD TRACKING SYSTEM
File Name -- SlsLead
LastName: 2
FirstName: 1
Title: 3
Company: 4
Telephone: 5
Address1:
Address2:
City:
State:
Zip:
No. of Labs:
Annual Revenue:
Current Customer:
Company Priority:
LEAD INFORMATION
Product Interest:
Request For:
Lead Source:
Months to Purchase:
Product Priority:
SALES ACTION
Sales Priority:
Date Entered:
Sales Dist.:
Sales Manager:
Salesman:
Phone:
Status:
SLSLEAD.DTF
Table View Spec
Page 1 of 1
Esc-Cancel
F10-Table View


**Fig. 6.20**
*Numbering fields on the Table View Spec.*

| FirstName | LastName | Title | Company | Telephone |
|---|---|---|---|---|
| Jeff | Blackson | Operations Mana | Mountain Labs | 363-254-6600 |
| Jeff | Jackson | Operations Mana | Mountain Labs | 363-254-6600 |
| Brian | Hope | Vice President | Hope Laboratori | 583-288-8888 |
| Fred | Simons | Associate Dean | University of M | 517-486-3388 |
| Robert | Hamilton | Vice president | Cherry Electron | 415-452-4488 |
| Brian | Hollingsworth | Chief technicia | Penn Medical Te | 215-594-2241 |
| Ted | Jackson | General Manager | Bay City Labora | 616-483-5847 |
| Hugh | Cyram | President | Independent Med | 816-820-2000 |
| Turner | Philips | General Manager | Nashville Medic | 615-492-1935 |
| John | LaPelt | Manager | Pike Pharmaceut | 215-493-5893 |
| Keith | Mattis | Manager | Mattis Medical | 404-953-2285 |
| Carl | Johnson | President | Plaines Medical | 605-384-2284 |
| Stanley | Bobwell | President | Washington Medi | 206-354-1385 |
| Albert | Franklyn | Vice president | Advanced Medica | 615-596-7011 |
| Likado | Tango | General Manager | Franklyn Lab As | 215-670-1234 |

SLSLEAD.DTF    Retrieved form 1    of 15    Total forms: 15
Esc-Exit    ← ↓ ↑ Home End PgUp PgDn →-Navigate    F10-Show form

**Fig. 6.21**
*The Table View as specified on the Table View Spec.*

field as the last column in the table by highlighting that field before you choose Table View. No matter how many fields are numbered in the Table View Spec, any field (other than the numbered fields) highlighted before you choose Table View becomes the final column in the display. If five fields are numbered, the highlighted field replaces the fifth column.

Figure 6.22 shows a Table View for which the FirstName and LastName fields are numbered 1 and 2 on the Table View Spec. Those fields always are displayed as columns 1 and 2 when F6 is pressed in Form View. In this case, however, the highlighter was first moved to the City field to select City as the last column in the table.

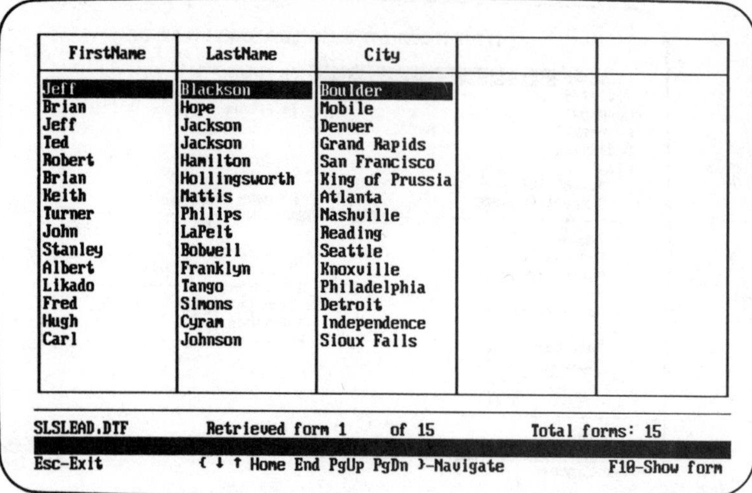

| FirstName | LastName | City | | |
|---|---|---|---|---|
| Jeff | Blackson | Boulder | | |
| Brian | Hope | Mobile | | |
| Jeff | Jackson | Denver | | |
| Ted | Jackson | Grand Rapids | | |
| Robert | Hamilton | San Francisco | | |
| Brian | Hollingsworth | King of Prussia | | |
| Keith | Mattis | Atlanta | | |
| Turner | Philips | Nashville | | |
| John | LaPelt | Reading | | |
| Stanley | Bobwell | Seattle | | |
| Albert | Franklyn | Knoxville | | |
| Likado | Tango | Philadelphia | | |
| Fred | Simons | Detroit | | |
| Hugh | Cyram | Independence | | |
| Carl | Johnson | Sioux Falls | | |



**Fig. 6.22** *Displaying the City field as the final column.*

When using Search/Update, you can edit the form's information blanks and change or add information. The same editing keys and functions are available as when you are adding and editing information. (See Chapter 10 for a description of editing keys and procedures.) When you have completed editing a form, press F10 to save the form and display the next one.

## *Mass Updating Forms*

Suppose that you have an inventory database that contains 250 records, and you need to update the Price field to reflect a three percent price increase. The task would be time-consuming if you had to update each form individually. With Q&A's Mass Update command, you can update all the forms at once.

Using Mass Update is a three-step process. After you select Mass Update from the File menu and indicate which database file you want to update, you use the Retrieve Spec to select the group of forms to be updated. If you want to update all forms, simply press F10. Q&A displays an Update Spec screen so that you can enter the information for changing or adding data. You have the option of confirming each field to be updated. After you confirm the fields, the forms are updated.

### *Retrieving Forms for a Mass Update*

The sales lead example illustrates the mass-update procedure. The procedure is useful, let's say, in a campaign to increase sales.

Suppose that the Sales VP has designated certain sales leads as "hot" leads and plans to offer bonuses if the leads are sold. The boss considers "hot" leads to be the companies that meet two criteria:

- The company has more than three laboratories.
- The company has promised to buy within two months.

Your task is to locate and update the records for these companies. The first step is to retrieve the forms to be updated. Select the Mass Update option from the File menu. After you enter the file name and press Enter, the Retrieve Spec screen is displayed.

If all the forms will be updated, you can press F10; Q&A retrieves them all. For this example, however, you need to enter retrieve specifications. Move the cursor to the No. of Labs field and type > =*3*. This entry tells Q&A that you want to retrieve the leads which have three or more laboratories (see fig. 6.23).

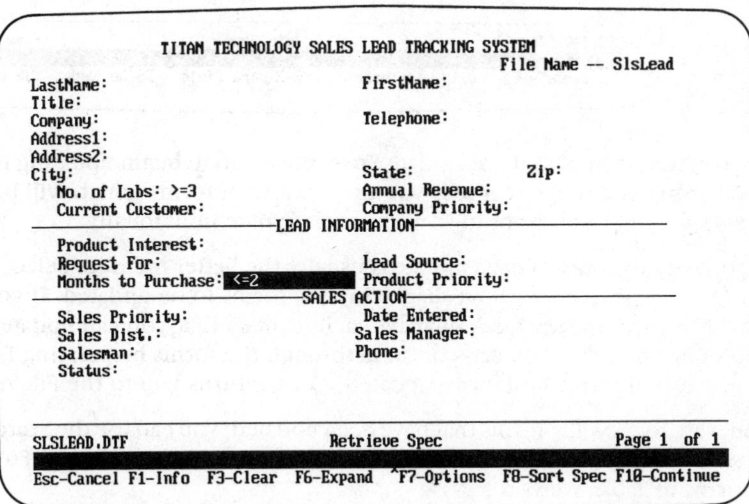


**Fig. 6.23**
*Filling in the Mass Update Retrieve Spec.*

Next, enter < =*2* in the Months to Purchase field. Q&A then retrieves the companies that have promised to make purchases within two months. When you press F10, Q&A finds the forms that meet both specifications and displays the Update Spec screen.

## *Using the Update Spec for Mass Update*

The Update Spec screen is used to update the fields. To enter the update specifications, move the cursor to the Sales Priority field and type

#1="Hot"

The pound sign and a number must be entered in every field that is to be updated or involved in calculations for the update. The pound sign indicates that a field number follows. Field numbers usually are sequential, but you may want to leave room between numbers for additions. An equal sign follows the number. Be sure to enter in quotation marks the text that is to be used in the update (see fig. 6.24). If you plan to use calculations in the update, use the format discussed in the section "Using Calc Statements" in Chapter 7. If, for example, you want to update a field that calculates sales commissions from sales, you change the calculation by following the rules used for entering calculations in the Program Spec, accessed through the Program Form option from Q&A's Customize a File menu.

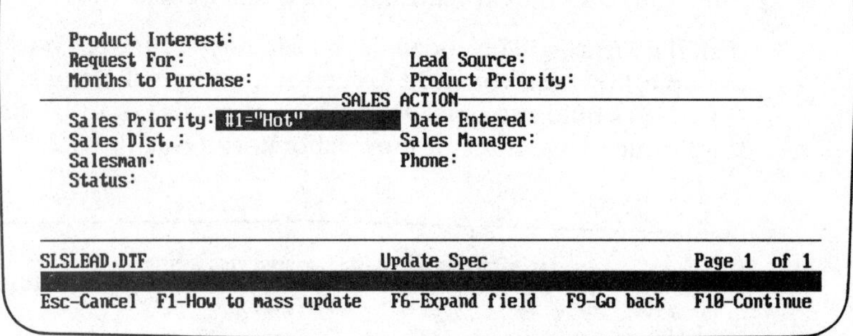


**Fig. 6.24** *Filling in the Mass Update Spec.*

After you have completed the Update Spec, press F10 to begin updating the forms. Q&A displays a message that tells you the number of forms which will be updated and asks whether you want to confirm each update individually.

Selecting Yes to confirm each update is usually the better method. Select No if you want Q&A to proceed without displaying the forms to be updated. If you choose to confirm each update, Q&A displays each form so that you can update the form by pressing Shift-F10. You can continue through the forms by pressing F10. When all the selected forms have been updated, Q&A returns you to the File menu.

If you want to view the forms that have been updated, you can use the Search/Update option to retrieve them, move the cursor to the updated field, and press F6 to display the forms in Table View.

## Copying Files

The File Copy command performs several functions:

- Copies a file design
- Copies a file design and IA information about the file
- Copies a file design and all or selected records
- Copies a file design and IA information and records

The Copy command helps you get extra benefits from your completed work—the file you designed, formatted, and customized, and the data you entered to build the database.

## Copying File Designs and Forms

Unlike some database products, Q&A makes designing file structure and designing forms to display file information a single operation. When you specify field labels and field widths, you also are designing a form to present (view) the data during entry or retrieval.

With Copy, you can copy a file design (including the display form), give the design a new file name, make slight alterations, and have a new database—all in far less time than designing a new database takes.

### Copying Form Designs

Remember that the form design includes the format of the form but not the data. You copy the form design of a customer list, for example, to create a new customer file containing some of the same fields and formats. You do not copy the data; you use the copied form design to build a new database.

To copy a form design, you first select Copy from the File menu. Q&A prompts you for a file name. After you enter the file name and press Enter, Q&A displays the Copy menu.

Select Copy Design Only by pressing D and then pressing Enter. You are again prompted for a file name. Be sure to enter a name that is not used by another file; then press Enter. Q&A then displays a message stating that the design is being copied and may take several minutes, depending on the length and complexity of the file design. When Q&A has completed the copy, the Copy menu is displayed again.

### Copying a Design with Intelligent Assistant Information

If you copy a design only, you do not copy any of the database information that you have taught the Intelligent Assistant. As you will learn in Chapters 17 and 18, you can teach the Intelligent Assistant a great deal about your database—information about the fields, adjectives and verbs used with the fields, and ways to analyze the data and produce reports. If you copy the design only, IA information is not available to the copied form.

Q&A allows you to copy the Intelligent Assistant information along with the file design. From the Copy menu, select the Copy Design with the IA Info option by pressing I. The procedure is the same as with the Copy Design Only option, but the Intelligent Assistant information is copied also. If you used the original design with the IA and want also to use the copied design with the Intelligent Assistant, choose the second option on the Copy menu.

## *Copying Selected Records from Database to Database*

The Copy command also can be used to duplicate and transfer whole or partial records from one database to another. This capability can be a significant time-saver. In the sales lead example, you will need to transfer the company data from the sales lead file to the customer file when sales lead companies become customers. Using the Copy command is much faster than entering all the data by hand.

Two files are involved in a copy operation: the *source file* and the *destination file*. Q&A copies the data *from* the current source file *to* the destination file and places the copied records at the end of the destination database. This method means that your destination database must have at least a record (form) design (which could be copied from an existing database), although data does not need to be entered in any of the records.

In the sales lead application, prospects are tracked until a piece of equipment is sold; then the company becomes a customer, and the information must be copied to the customer file. Figure 6.25 shows the customer list file form.

**Fig. 6.25**
*The destination file: the customer list.*

```
                     TITAN TECHNOLOGY CUSTOMER LIST
                                                  File Name -- CustList
LastName:                          FirstName:
Title:
Company:                           Telephone:
Address1:
Address2:
City:                              State:              Zip:

   No. of Labs:                    Annual Revenue:
   Products in Use:
   Sales Dist:                     Salesman:
   Status:

   Notes:



CUSTLIST.DTF                    Retrieve Spec                  Page 1 of 1

Esc-Cancel F1-Info F3-Clear F6-Expand ^F7-Options F8-Sort Spec F10-Continue
```

With the Copy Selected Forms option, you can copy data from database to database by copying all the data in selected records, by copying data from specified fields in all records, and by copying data from specified fields in selected records. All three copy operations can be accomplished by making slight variations in the same procedure.

To copy information from one database to another, first select Copy from the File menu. Q&A then prompts you for the file name of the source database. After you enter the source file name (SLSLEAD), press Enter; Q&A displays the Copy menu.

Choose the Copy Selected Forms option by pressing S; Q&A then prompts you for the destination database. Enter the name of the file to which the data will be copied (CUSTLIST), and press Enter. The Retrieve Spec for the source file is displayed.

You then can enter the specifications for the Retrieve Spec (see fig. 6.26). For this example, you want to copy the leads that have Status fields including the keyword Sale, which indicates that equipment has been sold to those leads. To specify this choice on the Retrieve Spec, you enter *Sale* in the Status field information blank. If you want all these forms copied, you don't need to enter any other criteria on the Retrieve Spec. At this point, you can press F8 to access the Sort Spec. In the example, the forms do not need to be sorted in any particular order.

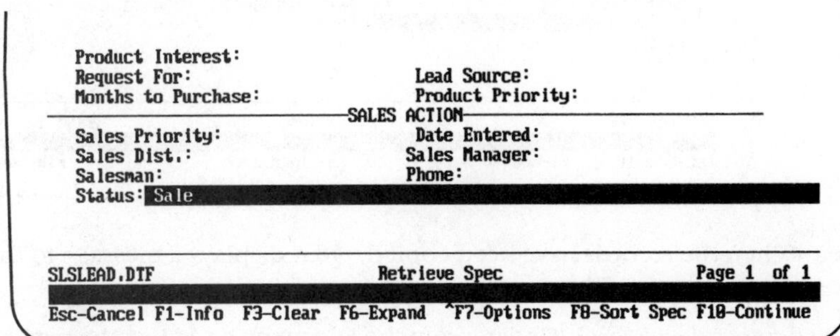


**Fig. 6.26** *Filling in the Retrieve Spec for copying selected forms.*

When you have entered all the necessary specifications, press F10. Q&A displays the source database on the Merge Spec screen. If you prefer, you can skip filling out the Merge Spec. This omission causes the data in the first source field to be copied to the first destination field, the second to the second, and so on. You can use this procedure when you have two databases with identical record designs.

If you want to copy only part of the database, or if you want to copy information from a database that has a different record structure, you use the Merge Spec to specify the destination fields. Figure 6.27 shows the Merge Spec with specifications entered.

To use the Merge Spec, move the cursor to the source field that stores the data you want copied to the first field on the destination form. Type *1*. In this example, the first field on the destination form (LastName) happens to be the same as the first field on the source form. Q&A numbers the forms from left to to right and from top to bottom.

Next, move the cursor to the source field for the second field and type *2*. Repeat the procedure until you have specified destination fields for all the source fields on your Merge Spec.

Note that the first 12 fields in these two files are in the same numerical positions. Field 13 in the customer list doesn't exist in the sales lead file. Sales Lead and Salesman fields in the sales lead file fall in positions 14 and 15 in the new customer file.

When you have completed the Merge Spec, press F10. Q&A begins the merge procedure, displaying the source and destination databases in turn as each record is

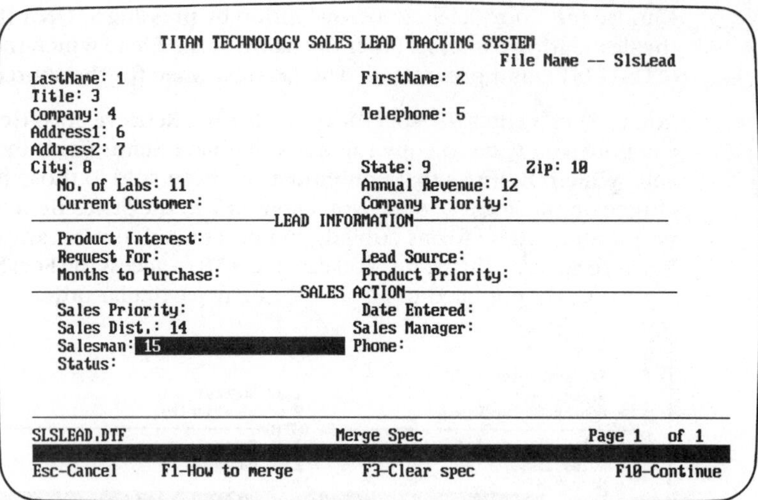

TITAN TECHNOLOGY SALES LEAD TRACKING SYSTEM
File Name — SlsLead
LastName: 1 FirstName: 2
Title: 3
Company: 4 Telephone: 5
Address1: 6
Address2: 7
City: 8 State: 9 Zip: 10
No. of Labs: 11 Annual Revenue: 12
Current Customer: Company Priority:
LEAD INFORMATION
Product Interest:
Request For: Lead Source:
Months to Purchase: Product Priority:
SALES ACTION
Sales Priority: Date Entered:
Sales Dist.: 14 Sales Manager:
Salesman: 15 Phone:
Status:

SLSLEAD.DTF Merge Spec Page 1 of 1
Esc-Cancel F1-How to merge F3-Clear spec F10-Continue

**Fig. 6.27**
*Filling in the Merge Spec.*

copied. When the records have been copied, Q&A displays a message to that effect and returns you to the File menu.

As a final step, select Search/Update from the File menu and view the new customer list file. This database has been created automatically by Q&A, requiring almost no time or effort on your part (see fig. 6.28).

TITAN TECHNOLOGY CUSTOMER LIST
File Name — CustList
LastName: Blackson FirstName: Jeff
Title: Operations Manager
Company: Mountain Labs Telephone: 363-254-6600
Address1: 300 10th Avenue
Address2:
City: Boulder State: CO Zip: 80105
No. of Labs: 3 Annual Revenue: 5370667
Products in Use:
Sales Dist: Denver Salesman: Allport
Status:
Notes:

CUSTLIST.DTF Retrieved form 1 of — Total Forms: 16 Page 1 of 1
Esc-Exit F1-How to update F6-Table F7-Search F8-Calc F10-Continue

**Fig. 6.28**
*The destination database with copied data.*

***Note:*** When Q&A copies data from one database field to another, the program pays no attention to labels, information types, or formats. Suppose that you tell Q&A to merge source field #1 with destination field #5, but you should specify #4 as the destination. This error results in strange data in the destination file. Check labels, information types, and formats for the proper match if you get strange results after the data has been copied to the destination fields. If any factors don't match, redesign the destination form.

# *Deleting Data and Removing Forms from a File*

With Q&A, you can delete data from a field, and you can remove forms from a file. Begin by making a backup copy of the file. To delete the contents of a field on the current form, position the cursor in the field and press Shift- F4. If you want to delete the current form, press F3. Q&A displays a window with a warning message asking whether you want to delete the form permanently. Make a selection in response to the prompt; then press Enter.

When you want to remove a group of forms from a file, you have two options. Using the Remove command is fast but risky because you aren't asked to double-check the forms that have been selected. The use of the Remove command has one restriction: all the forms must contain one or more pieces of information that are common to those forms only. If you use the Search command, however, you can press F3 to delete the form after you check it. This method is the slower but safer of the two methods.

## *Using the Remove Command*

The Remove command makes deleting forms easy. Be careful, however; once you remove a form, it is gone forever. To delete forms with Remove, you simply retrieve the forms and confirm that you want them removed.

For example, suppose that you want to remove from the sales lead file the forms that have been copied to the customer list file. Each of these forms has the keyword Sale in the Status field. To remove these forms, select Remove from the File menu, choose a file from the list of data files, and press Enter. Q&A responds by displaying the Retrieve Spec.

Move the cursor to the field containing the information that appears in all the forms to be removed. In this case, the common field is the Status field. Next, fill in the Retrieve Spec by typing the data that is common to these forms.

If the field is a keyword field and you are entering several keywords, separate them with semicolons (;). Be sure to press F1 to display an on-screen explanation of how to retrieve the forms. Press F1 again for a table of the symbols available for your retrieval operation. Press Esc to return to the form, or press F10 to accept the Retrieve Spec and continue.

When Q&A displays the warning message asking you to confirm the removal of the forms, make your selection and press Enter. Each form appears briefly on the screen just before that form is removed. After the forms have been removed, Q&A returns you to the File menu.

### Removing Forms Manually

If you choose to remove the forms by using the Search option and pressing F3 (Delete Form), you must first retrieve the forms you want and then manually delete them.

From the File menu, select the Search/Update option. Then enter a file name, and press Enter. Q&A displays the file form in the Retrieve Spec. Move the cursor to the field that has the information which is common to the forms to be removed (the Status field, in this case).

Specify the common data items by typing them in the correct fields on the Retrieve Spec. If the field is a keyword field and you are entering several keywords, separate them with semicolons (;). Press F10 to save the Retrieve Spec and continue.

Q&A searches through the database, retrieves the forms that meet the retrieval specifications, and displays the first form that meets the criteria. When the form is displayed, you can delete it by pressing F3. Q&A asks for verification that you want to delete the form. After you make your selection, press Enter.

If you select Yes, Q&A removes the form from the database and displays the next form. You have to continue pressing F3, selecting Yes, and pressing Enter until all the forms are removed from the database. Q&A then returns you to the File menu.

## Chapter Summary

Once you have designed your Q&A database, using database files is easy for you and other users responsible for entering and updating information. This chapter has introduced you to the commands and operations for using Q&A files. The Add Data command from the File menu is available for adding new forms to your database; Search/Update permits you to retrieve, sort, and change information in existing forms; the Mass Update command makes changing and adding information in a group of forms or the whole database easy; and the Copy command allows you to copy form designs and data.

The next chapter shows you how to customize and program File forms.

Chapter

7

# Customizing and Programming a File

The custom design features of Q&A File give you the opportunity to personalize your file with features that can save considerable time and work. The features are optional; if you are building a simple database, you may not need to use many or any of them. On the other hand, you will benefit from Q&A's options for customizing a file if your database requires calculating numeric data from different fields or requires automatic entry of numbers, dates, and times. Custom file features also are an advantage when other users will be entering data; through the options described in this chapter, you can change the way fields and data are highlighted on the screen, design custom help screens, and program your database so that it accepts only certain ranges of data. Q&A's customizing and programming features help you and others work efficiently and easily.

This chapter explains how to customize a file with Q&A. In the following sections, you learn how to make data manipulation easy by adding custom features to your file form. The second part of this chapter explains a more advanced method of customizing your file: programming. With Q&A's programming features, you can program your form to perform certain tasks automatically. This capability takes Q&A far beyond many data management programs available today.

## *Customizing a Form*

Before you can add custom features to a form, you need to call up a file. From the Design File menu, select Customize a File. Next, type the name of the file that you want to use. If you don't remember the name, you can list all available files by pressing the space bar to erase the default name and pressing Enter. Then the Customize menu is displayed (see fig. 7.1).

For some of the customizing and programming examples in this chapter, a Veterinary Clinic file will be used; the file tracks the pet owner's name and address and the pet's

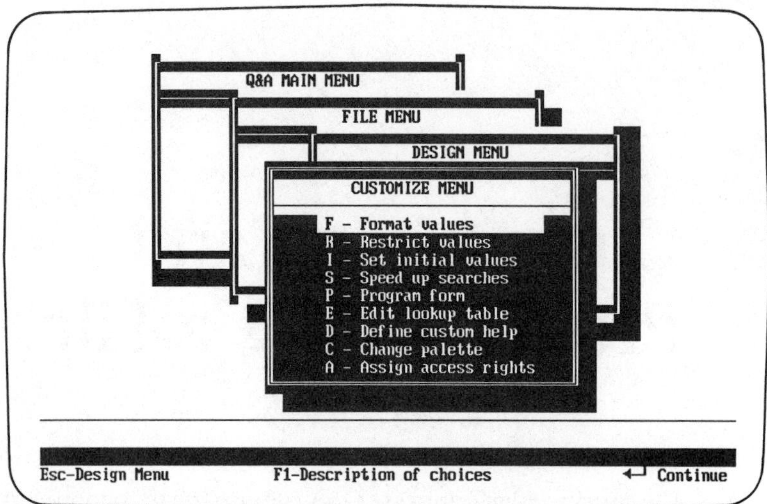


**Fig. 7.1** *The Customize menu.*

treatment history. This Veterinary Clinic file uses basic features that can be useful in many applications, including date arithmetic, money calculations, and services descriptions. You will customize and program this file and learn some possibilities for your own file enhancement. Examples from the previous Sales Lead Tracking file also will be used.

## Enhancing Your Original Form

Even though a straightforward form to record only the names, addresses, and phone numbers of clients may be easy to create, the form can be difficult to use when you are entering information or when you want to review information already entered. Nine options from the Customize menu allow you to format values, restrict values, set initial values, speed up searches, program a form, edit a lookup table, define custom help, change the video display of your form, and assign access rights. Whether you want to improve the appearance of the form or have Q&A perform complex calculations for you, this section explains how you can build on your original form to minimize your time and effort.

### Changing a File's Palette

When you customize your file, you may want to begin by improving the video display of the form. By changing the file's palette (the way the form appears on-screen), you can select the different formats in which your form is displayed.

Q&A offers seven palettes. Each palette has different combinations of reverse video, underline, highlighting, color, and cursor display. (The underline capability appears only on monochrome monitors.)

To specify a palette, select Change Palette from the Customize menu. The current form is displayed. Use the F8 key to step forward through the available palettes and the F6 key to move backward from palette to palette. As you change the palettes, the status line indicates which palette is displayed (see fig. 7.2). When a particular palette is shown on the screen, you can try out the palette by moving from field to field and entering data. The entries you make on this screen are erased when you leave the palette; the entries are for testing only. When the palette you want to use is displayed, press F10 to select it. Each time you use the file form after that, the palette you selected is displayed.

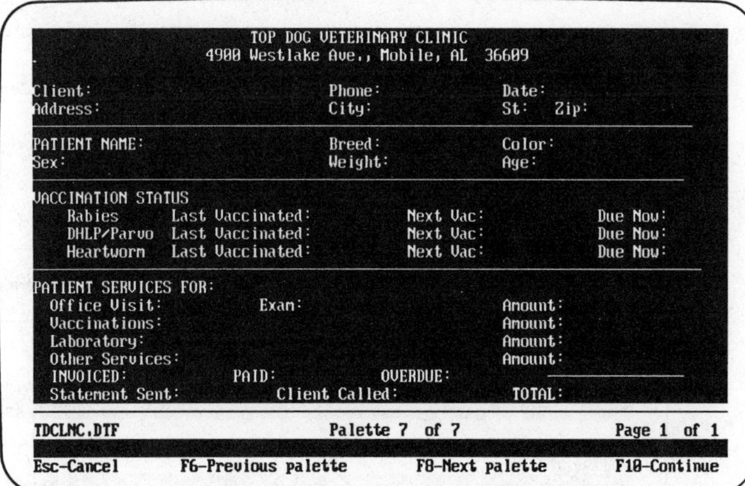

TOP DOG VETERINARY CLINIC
4900 Westlake Ave., Mobile, AL 36609

Client: Phone: Date:
Address: City: St: Zip:

PATIENT NAME: Breed: Color:
Sex: Weight: Age:

VACCINATION STATUS
Rabies Last Vaccinated: Next Vac: Due Now:
DHLP/Parvo Last Vaccinated: Next Vac: Due Now:
Heartworm Last Vaccinated: Next Vac: Due Now:

PATIENT SERVICES FOR:
Office Visit: Exam: Amount:
Vaccinations: Amount:
Laboratory: Amount:
Other Services: Amount:
INVOICED: PAID: OVERDUE:
Statement Sent: Client Called: TOTAL:

TDCLNC.DTF Palette 7 of 7 Page 1 of 1
Esc-Cancel F6-Previous palette F8-Next palette F10-Continue

**Fig. 7.2** *Changing the palette.*

After you have determined how you want the overall form to look, you can decide how to format individual data fields.

## *Formatting Field Information*

The Format Values option from the Customize menu lets you change field formatting on an existing file. By specifying information types, data formats, and global format options, you can make sure that data is entered in the correct format for each field (see Chapter 5 for more information on formatting).

When you select Format Values, Q&A displays the Format Spec screen. You can use this screen to change a field type (text, number, dates, yes/no, money, hours, and keywords) and to enter special format options for justification, case, and decimal place. For more information on data types, see Chapter 2.

## *Restricting Field Values*

One of the best features of Q&A's customizing capabilities is the Restrict Values option. By using this feature, you can limit the data that is entered in a field, thereby cutting down on data-entry errors and entry time. You simply tell Q&A what type of information to accept in a field, and the program alerts you when an incorrect entry is made.

Figure 7.3 shows that the Product Interest keyword field is restricted to five entries: 700, 1500, 2000, 2400, and Other. These values are entered on the Restrict Spec screen.

**Fig. 7.3** *Entering restricted values.*

```
                 TITAN TECHNOLOGY SALES LEAD TRACKING SYSTEM
                                                 File Name -- SlsLead
LastName:                               FirstName:
Title:
Company:                                Telephone:
Address1:
Address2:
City:                                   State:          Zip:
   No. of Labs:                         Annual Revenue:
   Current Customer:                    Company Priority:
─────────────────────────────LEAD INFORMATION─────────────────────────
   Product Interest: 700;1500;2000;2400;Other
   Request For: Info;Salesman;Demo;O→ Lead Source: Mail;Telephone;Reference;Adv→
   Months to Purchase:                  Product Priority:
─────────────────────────────SALES ACTION─────────────────────────────
   Sales Priority:                      Date Entered:
   Sales Dist.:                        Sales Manager:
   Salesman:                           Phone:
   Status: Sale;Postpone;700;1500;2000;2400;Other;Brock;Am Lab;Med Sci

SLSLEAD.DTF                        Restrict Spec                  Page 1  of 1

Esc-Cancel   F1-How to restrict values    F6-Expand field         F10-Continue
```

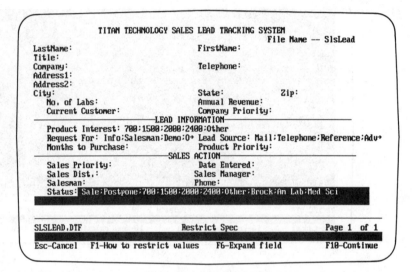

To enter a restricted value, select Restrict Values from the Customize menu. When the Restrict Spec is displayed, move the cursor to the field that you want to restrict and enter the restricted values. Separate individual values with a semicolon. After you finish, press F10 to return to the Customize menu.

The Restrict Values option doesn't prevent you from entering other information into the field; Q&A just displays a warning message that the data you entered is not one of the restricted values.

When a warning appears, you have two options: you can change the value to meet the restrictions or press Enter to cause Q&A to accept the value.

If certain fields in your database should not be left blank, you can specify these fields as required fields. To do this, type the following in the field information blank:

/=

When you enter information on the form, if you try to bypass a required field without making an entry, Q&A displays the prompt `This field requires a value. Please verify before continuing.` As with a restricted range specification, Q&A will not force you to place something in this field. If you simply press Enter after the warning, you can leave the field blank and go on to the next field.

If you specify several restricted values on a form, you may have trouble remembering which values are restricted in which fields. To help you remember the restricted values you have specified, you can create a custom help screen.

### *Creating a Custom Help Screen*

In addition to the program's built-in help screens, Q&A gives you the option of defining your own custom help screens. This capability is particularly useful when the form is to be used by other people. A custom help screen can provide users with additional instructions and reminders about their data-entry tasks. For example, you can design a custom help screen to give instructions for entering data in a specific field or to remind users of restricted values that have been defined. A custom help screen can be defined for each field on the form, and each screen can store six lines of up to 60 characters each.

To create a custom help screen, select Define Custom Help from the Customize menu. Q&A then displays your file form and the Help Spec. The cursor highlights the first field, indicating that a displayed help screen applies to that field.

Next, move the cursor by pressing F8 for the next field or F6 for the previous field. When the cursor is highlighting the appropriate field, type the text that you want to appear on the help screen. If you want to move to another field after you finish defining the first help screen, press either F8 or F6. When you have written all the help screens that you need, press F10 to save the screens. Then the Customize menu is displayed. You can return to the Help Spec at any time to create new help screens.

When you are adding or updating data, you can display a custom help screen by moving the cursor to the field and pressing F1 (see fig. 7.4). If you press F1 again, the Q&A help screen is displayed. If no custom help screen has been assigned, the program immediately displays the Q&A help screen. Pressing Esc causes the custom help screen to be removed from the display.

## *Customizing a File for Easy Data Entry and Manipulation*

Many Q&A customization features were designed to make your job easier. By setting initial values in a field, you lessen your data-entry tasks. With Q&A's Speed-up Spec, you can streamline the search procedures to save you valuable time. This section explains how you can use each of these features.

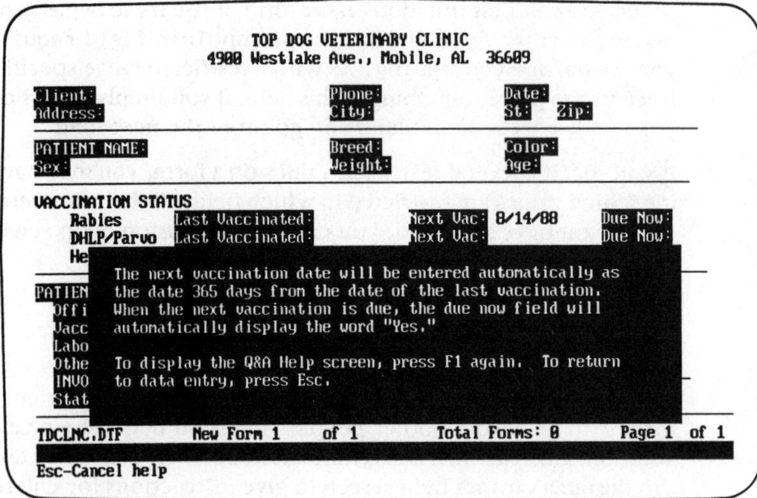
TOP DOG VETERINARY CLINIC
4900 Westlake Ave., Mobile, AL 36609
Client:
Address:
Phone:
City:
Date:
St:
Zip:
PATIENT NAME:
Sex:
Breed:
Weight:
Color:
Age:
VACCINATION STATUS
Rabies
DHLP/Parvo
Last Vaccinated:
Last Vaccinated:
Next Vac: 8/14/88
Next Vac:
Due Now:
Due Now:
The next vaccination date will be entered automatically as the date 365 days from the date of the last vaccination. When the next vaccination is due, the due now field will automatically display the word "Yes."
To display the Q&A Help screen, press F1 again. To return to data entry, press Esc.
TDCLNC.DTF
New Form 1
of 1
Total Forms: 0
Page 1 of 1
Esc-Cancel help

**Fig. 7.4** *Displaying a custom help screen.*

## *Setting Initial Field Values*

One way to reduce your data-entry time is to have Q&A enter the data for you. By using the Set Initial Values option from the Customize menu, you can have Q&A enter preset values into any fields you want.

You use the Initial Values Spec to enter the information into the fields. When you add a form to the file, the value is entered automatically in the field. You type the information once, and it appears on every form. For example, in the Sales Lead form, an initial value has been entered in the Date Entered field (see fig. 7.5). In figure 7.6, you can see that the date has been entered automatically.

To enter an initial value, select Set Initial Values from the Customize menu. Next, move the cursor to the field you want and enter the values. Press F10 to return to the Customize menu.

When you enter data, if the initial value is not what you want, move the cursor to the field and press F4 to delete the information. You then can enter the correct information.

## *Speeding Search Procedures*

By using Q&A's Speed-up Spec, you can decrease dramatically the time used by the program to search for records. You also can use this spec to verify that a field has a unique value.

A speedup search is Q&A terminology for a search through indexed fields. You create an index by extracting a field or fields from the records in a data file and storing this

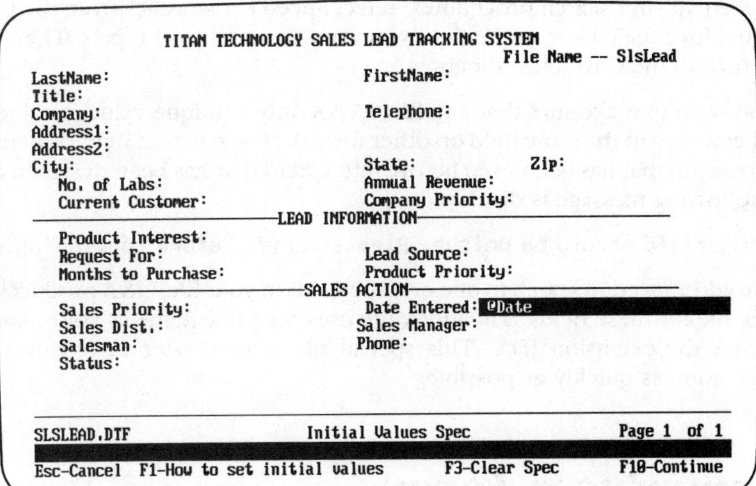

```
TITAN TECHNOLOGY SALES LEAD TRACKING SYSTEM
                                        File Name -- SlsLead
LastName:                       FirstName:
Title:
Company:                        Telephone:
Address1:
Address2:
City:                           State:          Zip:
  No. of Labs:                  Annual Revenue:
  Current Customer:             Company Priority:
-----------------------LEAD INFORMATION-----------------------
  Product Interest:
  Request For:                  Lead Source:
  Months to Purchase:           Product Priority:
-------------------------SALES ACTION-------------------------
  Sales Priority:               Date Entered: @Date
  Sales Dist.:                  Sales Manager:
  Salesman:                     Phone:
  Status:

SLSLEAD.DTF              Initial Values Spec          Page 1  of 1

Esc-Cancel  F1-How to set initial values     F3-Clear Spec   F10-Continue
```

**Fig. 7.5** *Entering an initial value.*

```
TITAN TECHNOLOGY SALES LEAD TRACKING SYSTEM
                                        File Name -- SlsLead
LastName:                       FirstName:
Title:
Company:                        Telephone:
Address1:
Address2:
City:                           State:          Zip:
  No. of Labs:                  Annual Revenue:
  Current Customer:             Company Priority:
-----------------------LEAD INFORMATION-----------------------
  Product Interest:
  Request For:                  Lead Source:
  Months to Purchase:           Product Priority:
-------------------------SALES ACTION-------------------------
  Sales Priority:               Date Entered: Jun 19, 1988
  Sales Dist.:                  Sales Manager:
  Salesman:                     Phone:
  Status:

SLSLEAD.DTF      New Form 1    of 1     Total Forms: 15    Page 1  of 1

Esc-Exit  F1-How to add  F3-Delete form  F7-Search  F8-Calc  F10-Continue
```

**Fig. 7.6** *The initial value entered automatically.*

information in a separate location. Then when you retrieve records by searching these fields, the software only has to search a portion of the record, reducing the time required to find the information you requested.

***Note***: Q&A suggests that you limit speedup search fields to only the minimum required to conserve time and storage space. Each time you update a record or add a new record, the speedup search field information must be extracted and stored in the proper place in the index. This procedure requires additional time and storage space.

To speed up your search procedures, select Speed Up Searches from the Customize menu. Move the cursor to the field you want to search and type *s*. Then press F10 to return to the Customize menu.

If you want to make sure that a field accepts only a unique value (a value that has not been used in the same field on other forms), type *u* in that field. When you type information that has been used before into a field that has been designated unique, the following message is displayed:

```
This field should be unique. Please verify before continuing.
```

If you add a speedup search to one or more fields in your file, Q&A produces a special index file for these fields. The index file uses the same name as your main file but attaches the extension IDX. This special file is used later to retrieve specified information as quickly as possible.

# Programming a Form

Programming is one of Q&A's most powerful customization features. You can program your form to provide user assistance, automate data entry, and perform other work- and time-saving tasks. By using the Program Form option from the Customize menu, you can write programming statements to perform calculations and to handle routine data-entry procedures.

Depending on the application, programming statements can be fairly simple or highly complex. The statements can involve no more than a simple addition, subtraction, multiplication, or division of values from your database fields. But you also can use more complex statements to test conditions, look up values from a lookup table or from a separate file, or automate the movement of the cursor from one field to another. Depending on the elements they contain, programming statements are grouped roughly into four categories of complexity: calculation statements, conditionals, functions, and table and forms control commands.

The simplest programming statements are calculations that consist of mathematical and logical operators used in combination with numerical values and code numbers that reference values in fields. For example, the programming statement #9=(#3*#5)/10 tells Q&A to multiply the value in field #3 by the value in field #5, divide the result by 10, and enter the result in field #9.

Simple programming statements like this one are used to calculate sales commissions, discount rates, and other data-dependent totals. Notice that each field involved in the calculation is given a number. These numbers are arbitrary designations and do not necessarily relate to the position of the field within the record. You can, however, number the fields sequentially. Or you can select numbers that designate the order of calculation you desire or use other numbering schemes that fit your application.

More complex programming statements can use commands for testing conditions and performing operations based on the existence of certain values. Suppose, for example, that you want Q&A to indicate in the Overdue field (which you have labeled #15) when payment is overdue on a customer account. If field #10 equals the current date and field #5 equals the date of last payment or when the obligation was made, you can use the following conditional operation in a programming statement:

IF #10=#5+30 THEN #15="Yes"

A set of functions is available for use in programming statements. *Functions* are programming tools that usually combine many operations into a single statement or command. In procedural languages, a single function may call a program subroutine that contains hundreds of lines of code.

In Q&A, each programming function is preceded by the commercial at sign (@). For example, you can enter current dates and times automatically with the @DATE and @TIME functions (#5=@DATE+30). Other types of @functions include mathematical functions (@SUM, for example), text functions (@LEFT(x,n), which extracts the leftmost n characters of the text string x, for example), and a function for numbering forms sequentially (@NUMBER, for example).

Three other types of special commands can be used in programming statements. First, a lookup command returns values from a lookup table that you have created; XLOOKUP returns values from an external file. Second, less-than (<) and greater-than (>) symbols can be used at the beginning of a programming statement to control when the statement is executed: either when the cursor moves into the field (<) or when the cursor leaves the field (>). The final programming commands are ones that move the cursor within a form (GOTO, CNEXT, and CHOME, for example). Programming statements that contain cursor-movement commands must begin with either a less-than (<) or a greater-than (>) symbol.

In the following sections, you are given examples of programming statements that show how you can use all the elements available for your special applications.

## *Entering Program Statements*

You program a form by writing programming statements, which are entered on a Program Spec screen. The Program Spec form is displayed when you select the Program Form option from the Customize menu. You then can specify whatever programming statements you need to perform your calculations and automate your data-entry tasks.

For example, on the form shown in figure 7.7, most of the data is entered into fields automatically by programming statements. Very little data entry is necessary. The data in the Phone and Address fields is retrieved from a lookup table by a programming statement (Note: You also can use XLOOKUP to retrieve information from an external file). The Amount field total is figured and inserted by a statement using a calculation formula.

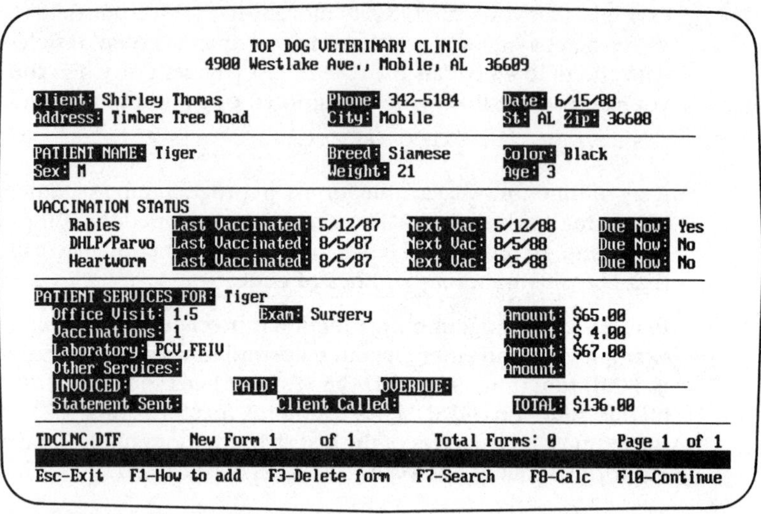
TOP DOG VETERINARY CLINIC
4900 Westlake Ave., Mobile, AL 36609

Client: Shirley Thomas  Phone: 342-5184  Date: 6/15/88
Address: Timber Tree Road  City: Mobile  St: AL Zip: 36608

PATIENT NAME: Tiger  Breed: Siamese  Color: Black
Sex: M  Weight: 21  Age: 3

VACCINATION STATUS
Rabies  Last Vaccinated: 5/12/87  Next Vac: 5/12/88  Due Now: Yes
DHLP/Parvo  Last Vaccinated: 8/5/87  Next Vac: 8/5/88  Due Now: No
Heartworm  Last Vaccinated: 8/5/87  Next Vac: 8/5/88  Due Now: No

PATIENT SERVICES FOR: Tiger
Office Visit: 1.5  Exam: Surgery  Amount: $65.00
Vaccinations: 1  Amount: $ 4.00
Laboratory: PCV,FEIV  Amount: $67.00
Other Services:  Amount:
INVOICED:  PAID:  OVERDUE:
Statement Sent:  Client Called:  TOTAL: $136.00

TDCLNC.DTF  New Form 1 of 1  Total Forms: 0  Page 1 of 1

Esc-Exit  F1-How to add  F3-Delete form  F7-Search  F8-Calc  F10-Continue

**Fig. 7.7** *Data entered by programming statements.*

Don't worry if you don't understand how the automatic data entry occurred in figure 7.7. The rest of this chapter explains in detail how programming statements are written and used in file forms.

## *Writing Programming Statements*

The format of a programming statement is simple. Each statement contains a field ID number, a colon (:) or an equal sign (=), and the statement formula. (If the statement contains a cursor-movement command, the statement also must begin with a greater-than [>] or a less-than [<] symbol.)

The field ID number includes a pound sign (#) and an integer; the ID number identifies the field for use in programming statements. Numerical field IDs must be used for any field that contains a programming statement or for any fields that are referenced by a programming statement. The field ID numbers are arbitrary, and a relationship doesn't necessarily exist between these numbers and the field position on the form. You have to number only the fields that will be used or referenced in a program statement; for best results, however, give each field a field ID number, even though you may not plan to use it (see fig. 7.8). Numbering each field gives you flexibility in modifying programming specifications later and reduces confusion that might occur as program complexity grows with nonsequential field assignments. Also, you may want to leave some numbers between these sequential field IDs to give you room to add additional fields later.

For example, suppose that you have only three fields referenced by calculation statements; instead of numbering the fields 1, 2, and 3, you can use the ID numbers 3, 6, and 9 or 5, 10, and 15. That way, when you add other fields later, you can insert

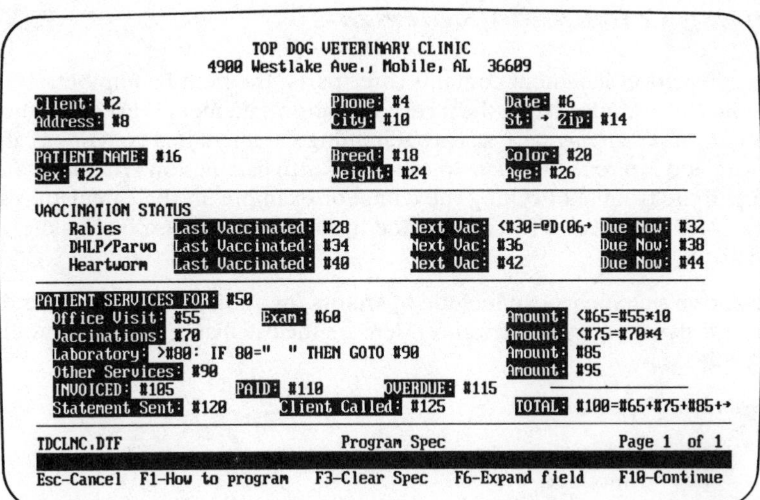


**Fig. 7.8** *Entering field ID numbers.*

the fields without having to renumber. BASIC programmers frequently use this technique when numbering program lines. By using this technique, you leave room between sequential numbers to add more program statements without having to renumber the whole program.

The colon (:) separates the field ID from the statement that follows. The statement can be a cursor-movement command, a lookup command, a calculation that depends on logical conditions being met, or a highly complex logical statement using text and mathematical functions.

The equal sign (=) following the field ID indicates that a calculation will be made and the result entered into the field. For example, suppose that a field contains the programming statement #42=#37+22. The field ID #42 labels the field in which the statement is entered; Q&A adds the value in the field labeled #37 to 22 and enters the result in field #42.

The sections that follow show you how to use Q&A's variety of programming statements.

## *Using Calculations in Programming Statements*

For a basic form, you may have included fields that store text items (Client and Address fields, for example) and fields for numeric entries (such as charges for services). Q&A can perform tasks beyond simple data-recording processes, however. You can include calculations in programming statements so that Q&A automatically computes and enters the results whenever you add or update a form.

## *Writing Calculation Statements*

Each calculation statement contains three parts: the field ID number, an equal sign (=), and the formula. (Note: the term calculation statement is used for convenience. A *calculation statement* is just a programming statement that contains a calculation.) You can add references to data in other fields in calculation statements in order to save you the trouble of typing the data. For example, in the calculation statement #6=#4+14, Q&A adds 14 to the value in field #4 and then inserts the value into field #6.

Calculation statements can include operators for adding, subtracting, and dividing data, and also for comparing values. Here are the calculation operators available with Q&A File:

| *Operator* | *Definition* |
|---|---|
| + | Add |
| – | Subtract |
| * | Multiply |
| / | Divide |
| = | Equal to |
| < | Less than |
| > | Greater than |
| <= | Less than or equal to |
| >= | Greater than or equal to |
| <> | Not equal to |

When you write calculation statements, you can use either upper- or lowercase letters. If the statement you are writing is too long to fit within the field width, press F6 to display the Long Value line at the bottom of the screen (see fig. 7.9). You can enter up to 69 characters on the line. After you press Enter, the first part of the statement is displayed in the field, along with a right arrow indicating that the statement extends beyond the field. If you are entering the calculation statement on a field that has multiple lines, however, the statement can occupy the entire field, including multiple lines.

You can include spaces in a calculation statement to make the statement more readable. Spaces are not necessary to make the calculation work, however. If you have a long statement, you may want to delete the spaces and condense the line.

The following examples illustrate how you use field IDs and operators in writing calculation statements:

| *When you enter* | *Q&A will* |
|---|---|
| #8=#2+#6 | Add the contents of fields #2 and #6 and place the results in field #8 |
| #9=#5/27 | Divide the contents of field #5 by 27 and put the result in field #9 |

| *When you enter* | *Q&A will* |
|---|---|
| #10 = #3 | Copy the content of field #3 in field #10 |

An example of a multiplication calculation statement is illustrated in the first Amount field of figure 7.10. Field #65 contains the statement #65 = #55 * 45, which means "field #65 is equal to field #55 multiplied by 45."

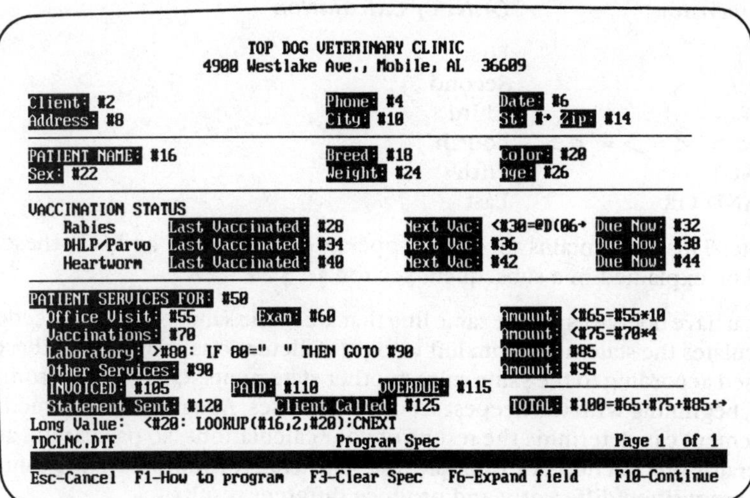


**Fig. 7.9**
*The Long Value cursor line.*

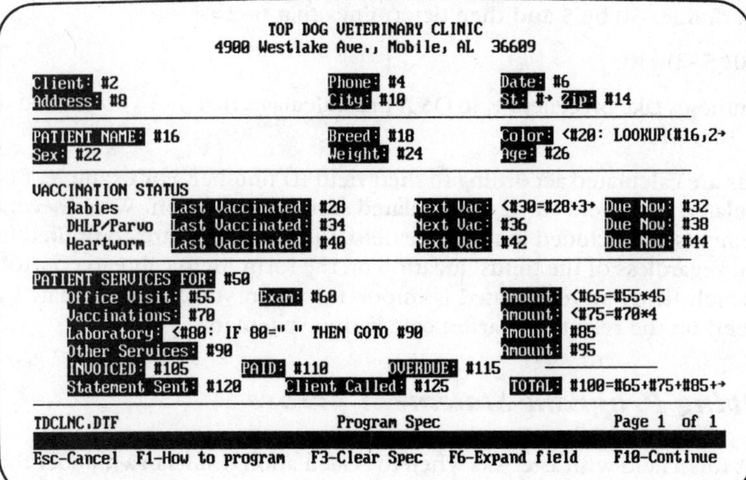


**Fig. 7.10**
*A multiplication calculation statement.*

## *Understanding the Order of Calculation in Programming Statements*

Q&A calculates the operations in programming statements in a particular order. The order is called the order of precedence. The following list shows the order of precedence in Q&A calculations:

| *Operator* | *Order of Calculation* |
|---|---|
| ( ) | First |
| * / | Second |
| + − | Third |
| < > <= >= <> | Fourth |
| NOT | Fifth |
| AND OR | Last |

(Note: This list contains the logical operators NOT, AND, and OR; these operators will be explained in a subsequent section.)

If you have operators on the same line that are in the same order of precedence, Q&A calculates the statement from left to right. Calculations inside parentheses are processed according to the same rules as other statements. Q&A works from the inside out, beginning with the deepest set of parentheses. As a result, the structure of your statement can determine the results of your calculations; so pay careful attention to operator precedence. For example, the following formulas have the same numbers but are written differently and produce different results:

30/5−2=4

Q&A divides 30 by 5 and then determines that 6−2=4.

30/(5−2)=10

Parentheses take precedence, so Q&A first calculates that 5−2=3 and then determines that 30/3=10.

Fields are calculated according to their field ID number. For example, field ID #1 is calculated first, field ID #2 is calculated second, and so on. When several separate statements are included in the same field, the statements are computed from left to right, regardless of the fields' location on the form. Being able to control the order in which fields are calculated is important when you have calculated fields that depend on the results of earlier calculation statements.

## *Solving Program-Statement Errors*

Q&A fills a field with asterisks when the calculation results in a number that is longer than the field length. The asterisks are read as a zero value by calculation statements referring to the field. To solve the problem, you can redesign the form so that the field is long enough to accommodate the number. Or you can shorten the number by deleting insignificant digits after the decimal. You also can use the Format Values option from the Customize menu to reduce the number of decimal places displayed.

If you have a calculation statement that divides by zero, Q&A displays an error message in the field containing the calculation statement. Other fields that reference that particular field read the error message as a zero value.

Q&A offers you a great deal of flexibility in writing programming statements, and a wide variety of statements is possible. If you aren't sure whether you can write a statement in a certain way, try it. Q&A may display the error message `Not a valid Program Spec`, but you can correct the problem. Simply use the cursor-movement and editing keys to change the statement and then press Enter. Q&A reevaluates the statement. If no error message is displayed, you can enter data and see whether the form works the way you had planned.

Q&A doesn't accept the Program Spec if you enter something incorrectly. An error message appears, and the program shows you where the error is by positioning the cursor under the first incorrect character.

## *Applying a Sample Calculation Statement*

In the Veterinary database, a calculation statement can be used to calculate the date of the next vaccination for each animal. You do this procedure by adding one year—365 days—to the date in the Last Vaccinated field. Therefore, the calculation statement for the Next Vac field (#30) is #30=#28+365 (see fig. 7.11).

This statement says, "Add the number in field #28 to 365 and put the sum in field #30." Figure 7.12 shows the result of the calculation.

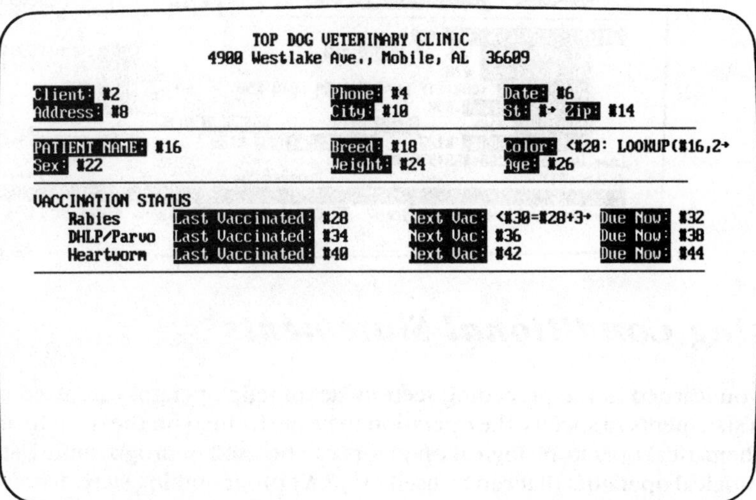


**Fig. 7.11**
*The Next Vac calculation statement.*

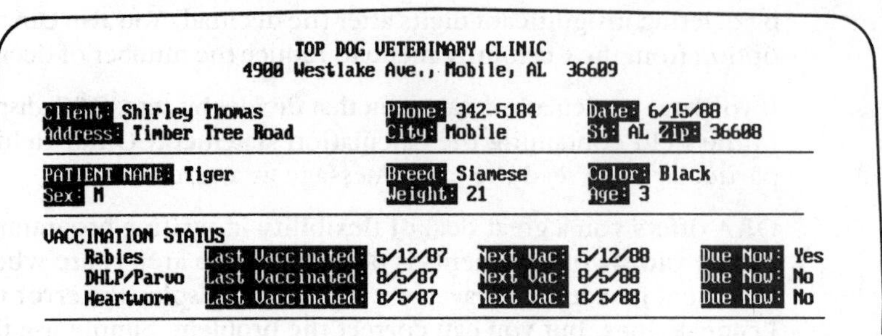


**Fig. 7.12**
*The result of the calculation.*

The first Amount field stores the dollar amount due for the office visit. The calculation is based on the amount of time spent on the office visit (in hours) multiplied by the doctor's hourly fee. The Amount calculation statement in the Long Value line in figure 7.13 shows that the doctor's hourly fee is $45. Therefore, the Amount calculation statement is #65=#55*45.

This calculation statement says, "Multiply the number in field #55 by 45 and put the result in field #65." Figure 7.14 shows the result of the calculation.

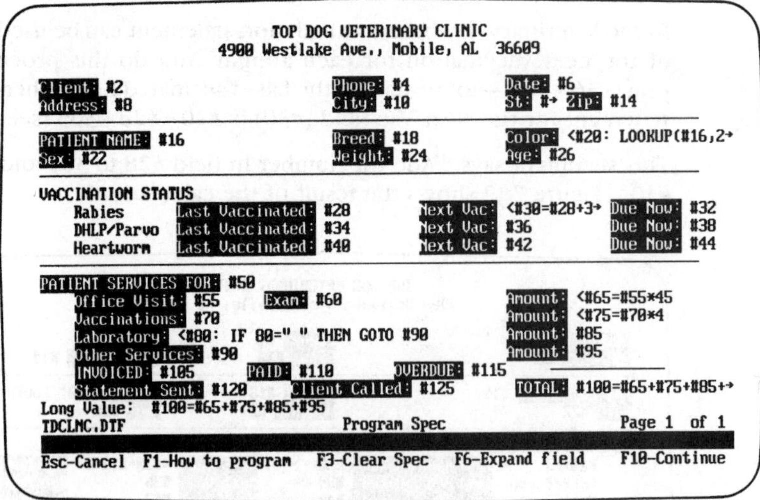


**Fig. 7.13**
*The Amount calculation statement.*

## *Using Conditional Statements*

As you learned in the preceding section, arithmetic operators are used in calculation statements to specify the operation to be performed on the data. In addition to mathematical operators, logical operators can be used in programming statements. The logical operators that can be used in Q&A's programming statements are shown in the following list:

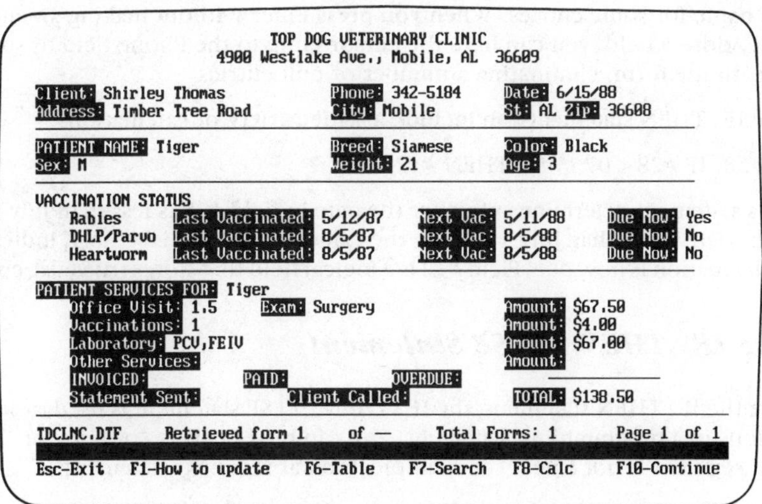
TOP DOG VETERINARY CLINIC
4900 Westlake Ave., Mobile, AL 36609

Client: Shirley Thomas Phone: 342-5184 Date: 6/15/88
Address: Timber Tree Road City: Mobile St: AL Zip: 36608

PATIENT NAME: Tiger Breed: Siamese Color: Black
Sex: M Weight: 21 Age: 3

VACCINATION STATUS
Rabies Last Vaccinated: 5/12/87 Next Vac: 5/11/88 Due Now: Yes
DHLP/Parvo Last Vaccinated: 8/5/87 Next Vac: 8/5/88 Due Now: No
Heartworm Last Vaccinated: 8/5/87 Next Vac: 8/5/88 Due Now: No

PATIENT SERVICES FOR: Tiger
Office Visit: 1.5 Exam: Surgery Amount: $67.50
Vaccinations: 1 Amount: $4.00
Laboratory: PCV,FEIV Amount: $67.00
Other Services: Amount:
INVOICED: PAID: OVERDUE:
Statement Sent: Client Called: TOTAL: $138.50

TDCLNC.DTF Retrieved form 1 of — Total Forms: 1 Page 1 of 1
Esc-Exit F1-How to update F6-Table F7-Search F8-Calc F10-Continue

**Fig. 7.14** *The result of the Amount calculation statement.*

| *Logical Operator* | *Description* |
|---|---|
| IF..THEN | IF the first segment is true, THEN do the second segment. |
| IF..THEN...ELSE | IF the first segment is true, THEN do the second segment, ELSE do the third segment. |
| AND | Both the first AND second segments must be true for the third segment to occur. |
| OR | Either the first segment OR the second segment must be true for the third segment to occur. |
| NOT | NOT excludes the segment that follows from being a true condition and also negates the segment that follows by reversing its meaning. |

## *The IF..THEN Statement*

The IF..THEN statement is used when you need to make a programming statement conditional. For example, suppose that you want the cursor to move to field #90 if field #80 is empty; you enter the following programming statement:

```
#80: IF #80=" " THEN GOTO #90
```

Calculations such as this one can save keystrokes during data entry. In this example (refer to fig. 7.8), if no laboratory services are entered in field #80, the cursor skips the amount for that service. You can save even more time if a large number of fields are to be skipped. Suppose that you are entering names and addresses and have only the name for some entries. When you press Enter without making an entry in the first Address field, you can have the cursor jump to the Phone field or somewhere else on the form, eliminating a number of null entries.

The IF..THEN statement can include a wide variety of calculations:

```
#28: IF #28<07.15.88 THEN #32="Y"
```

This statement determines whether the date in field #28 is less than July 15, 1988. If the date is less than July 15, 1988, the value of field #32 is set to *Y*, indicating that a vaccination is now due. Field #32 is a logical field that stores true/false conditions.

### *The IF...THEN...ELSE Statement*

Like the IF..THEN statement, the IF..THEN...ELSE statement is used to set up conditions in a programming statement. You can read ELSE as "or else" or "but if the first segment is not true." For example, look at this next statement:

```
#32: IF #30>(#28+365) THEN #32="Yes" ELSE #32="No"
```

This statement says, "If field #30 is greater than field #28 plus 365, then enter the word *Yes* in field #32; or else enter the word *No* in field #32." This statement is another way you can have the program compute whether a vaccination is due.

### *The AND Statement*

When you use the AND statement, both the first and second segments must be true before the third segment is executed. For example, look at the following programming statement:

```
#65: IF #60<>" " AND #55>=1 THEN #65=(#55*10)+(#60*15)
```

This statement says, "If field #60 is not blank and field #55 holds a value of at least 1, then field #65 is equal to the sum of field #55 times 10 and field #60 times 15." Both conditions must be true for the calculation to be conducted.

### *The OR Statement*

The OR statement is used when you want either the first or the second segment to be true before the third segment is executed. An example of the OR statement follows:

```
#65: IF #60<>" " OR #55>=1 THEN #65=(#55*10)+(#60*15)
```

This statement says, "If field #60 is not blank or field #55 holds a value of at least 1, then field #65 is equal to the sum of field #55 times 10 and field #60 times 15." In this example, the calculation is carried out if either of the conditions is true.

### The NOT Statement

The NOT statement actually serves two purposes. In an IF...THEN statement, you can use NOT to exclude the truth of a value in a program statement or to search for a false condition. The following statement inserts a logical Y in field #115 if the value in field #110 is less than the amount due in #100 and the invoiced date in field #105 is more than a month old:

```
#115: IF #110 NOT>=#100 AND @DATE-#105 NOT<=30 THEN #115="Y"
```

NOT is used to indicate a false condition also. For example, the following statement determines whether the value in #80 is blank. If the value is not blank, the cursor is moved to field #85; otherwise, the cursor jumps to field #90:

```
#80: IF #80 NOT " " THEN GOTO #85 ELSE GOTO #90
```

## Using Functions in Programming Statements

You can use functions to perform certain calculations, return certain text values, or perform other data-entry tasks. Functions save you the time and effort of writing calculation formulas or complex programming statements. When a function is used as part of a programming statement, the value returned by the function is used in the programming statement when the statement is executed. Functions offer you shortcuts when you're writing programming statements. Functions take the following form:

```
@function(argument)
```

The @ sign tells Q&A that the following word or words form a function. The function itself is the word that triggers a preprogrammed series of operations, and the argument enclosed within parentheses provides the data that the function will use to perform its calculations. Generally, an argument can be a constant, a field ID, or another calculation that returns a usable value.

### Mathematical Functions

Q&A offers mathematical functions to perform many calculations for you. If you have used spreadsheet programs, you may recognize some of the functions discussed in this section. These functions are similar to BASIC and 1-2-3 commands that perform similar operations.

Table 7.1 lists the mathematical functions available with Q&A.

**Table 7.1**
**Mathematical Functions**

| *Function* | *Example* | *Meaning* |
|---|---|---|
| @ABS(x) | @ABS(#15) | Returns the absolute value of the value in field #15 (strips signs so that @ABS(–10)=10) |
| @ASC(x) | @ASC(#15) | Returns the ASCII decimal value of the first character in field #15. @ASC(''Apple'') is 65 |
| @AVG(fields) | @AVG(#1,#4,#5,#9) | Returns the average of values in listed fields |
| | @AVG(#1..#9) | Returns the average of fields 1 through 9 |
| @EXP(x,y) | @EXP(#15,#16) | Raises x to the power of y. For x=4 and y=2, @EXP(x,y)=16 |
| @INT(x) | @INT(#15) | Returns the integer of the value in field #15 (INT (10.45)=10) |
| @MAX(fields) | @MAX(#1,#4,#5,#9) | Returns the largest value in listed fields |
| | @MAX(#1..#9) | Returns the maximum value in range of fields 1 through 9 |
| @MIN(fields) | @MIN(#1,#4,#5,#9) | Returns the lowest value in the listed fields |
| | @MIN(#1..#9) | Returns the lowest value in range of fields 1 through 9 |
| @NUM(x) | @NUM(#15) | Returns the numerical value of x. Converts text fields to numbers by extracting numerical content. Text characters are removed and numbers concatenated. For #15=IN322, @NUM(#15)=322. For x=3IN22, @NUM(x)=322 |
| @ROUND(x,y) | @ROUND(#15,16) | Rounds x to y number of decimal places. For x=10.45678 and y=2, @ROUND(x,y)=10.46 |
| @SGN(x) | @SGN(#15) | Returns the sign of x. If x is a negative value, @SGN(x)=–1. If x is a positive number, @SGN(x)=1. For x=0, @SGN(x)=0. |

**Table 7.1** — *Continued*

| *Function* | *Example* | *Meaning* |
|---|---|---|
| @SQRT(x) | @SQRT(#15) | Returns the square root of the value in field #15. For #15=144, @SQRT(#15)=12 |
| @STD(fields) | @STD(#2,#4,#6,#8) | Calculates the standard deviation of the values in the field list. Measures how much individual items in a list vary from the average of all members. For #2=17, #4=28, #6=20, and #8=21, @STD(#2,#4,#6,#8)=4.03. Standard deviation is the square root of variance. One rule of thumb is that about 68 percent of all data points will be within one standard deviation of the average of all points |
| @SUM(fields) | @SUM(#1,#4,#5,#9) | Adds the values in fields 1, 4, 5, and 9 and returns the total |
| | @SUM(#1..#9) | Adds the values in fields 1 through 9 and returns the total |
| @VAR(fields) | @VAR(#2,#4,#6,#8) | Returns the variance of the values in the listed fields. Like standard deviation, variance measures how far individual data items vary from the average of all items. For #2=17, #4=28, #6=20, #8=21, @VAR(#2,#4,#6,#8)=16.25 |

## *Text Functions*

In addition to the mathematical functions, Q&A provides a variety of text functions. You can use these functions to find a particular part of a text string, to extract portions of the string, or to delete selected text strings. Table 7.2 lists the text functions available with Q&A.

**Table 7.2**
**Text-String Functions**

| *Function* | *Example* | *Meaning* |
|---|---|---|
| @CHR(x) | @CHR(#15) | Returns the character equivalent of the value in field #15. For #15 = 261, @CHR(#15) = . For #15 = 65, @CHR(#15) = A |
| @DEL(x,y,z) | @DEL(#9,8,5) | From the fifth character position (z), eight characters (in the text string *Old English Sheepdog* the word *English* and a space) are deleted. The string *Old Sheepdog* is returned |
| @DITTO(fields) | @DITTO(#1,#2) | Carries values from the preceding form to the current form. Useful during data entry of city, state, and other repetitive information |
| @FILENAME | @FILENAME | Returns the current file name. Can be used to insert name of file that provides source data for names and addresses, financial information, and other data. Can provide audit trail of data file changes |
| @HELP(x) | @HELP(#15) | Displays user-defined help screen for specified field. Useful during programming of a form to display help for certain fields as operator prompt |
| @INSTR(x,y) | @INSTR(#9,5) | Finds the position of the string *English* in the text string *Old English Sheepdog*. The string appears in the fifth character position, so the value 5 is returned |
| @LEFT(x,y) | @LEFT(#9,3) | Returns three characters (y) from the text string (x). From *Old English Sheepdog*, the word *Old* is returned |
| @LEN(x) | @LEN(#15) | Returns length of field x. For field #15 = Old English Sheepdog, |

Table 7.2 — *Continued*

| *Function* | *Example* | *Meaning* |
|---|---|---|
| | | @LEN(#15)=20. Note that spaces count as characters |
| @MID(x,y,z) | @MID(#9,5,7) | Returns seven characters (z) from text string (x) starting at the fifth character position (y). The word *English* is returned |
| @MSG(x) | @MSG(#15) | Displays contents of field x on message line at the bottom of screen. Useful for operator prompting, establishing custom screens, etc. |
| @RIGHT(x,y) | @RIGHT(#9,5) | Returns five characters (y) from the right side of text string (x). The string *Sheep* is returned from the text string *Old English Sheepdog* |
| @STR(x) | @STR(#15) | Converts a number to a string (text) value. Useful for including numbers in string manipulations |
| @TEXT(x,y) | @TEXT(5,#15) | Repeats character y a total of x times. If #15 holds a plus sign, then @TEXT(5,#15)= + + + + + |
| @WIDTH(x) | @WIDTH(#15) | Returns width of field x. This is the numerical value that represents the total number of characters that field can hold, not the length of the string stored in field x |

## *The @DATE and @TIME Functions*

Q&A has a number of built-in functions for date and time computations. The most common of these functions are the @DATE and @TIME functions.

### *@DATE*

The @DATE function computes past and future dates by adding and subtracting whole numbers. You can use @DATE, for example, to alert you when the time comes to do something. For example, if you need to renew some office equipment you are renting, you can use the following @DATE statement:

#60: IF #15>@DATE+345 THEN #60="Time to renew"

This statement says, "If field #15 is greater than today's date plus 345 (days), then field #60 should read *Time to renew.*"

The @DATE function is used frequently for date-stamping forms. If you want the current date entered automatically when you first enter information on a form, simply select Program Form from the Customize menu and move the cursor to the date field; then, supposing that the field is #5, enter the following statement:

#5: IF #5=" " THEN #5=@DATE

This statement says, "If field #5 is empty, then field #5 should equal the current date." This statement causes the current date to be entered in all forms that have an empty date field.

### @TIME

The time function is @TIME, which computes past and future time when numbers in time format (00:00) are added or subtracted. The @TIME function works like the @DATE function, except @TIME computes shorter periods. The @TIME function can be useful in a multiuser environment where records get frequent updates. @TIME not only can report on the time of the last record change but, like @DATE, can alert the operator if updates are too close together or too far apart when combined with some programming logic. The programming logic would be the same as for @DATE.

Sometimes, working with individual portions of a composite date is convenient. Examples include the day of the month, the year, the day, the name of the day, or the name of the month. Q&A File includes four functions that extract these values from a conventional date. These functions are discussed next.

### @DOM

If you have selected a date format of May 28, 1988, you may want to display the day of the month separately. Or you may need to extract the value of the day for use in other calculations, such as the number of days between two dates. The @DOM function returns the numerical value of the day of a date:

@DOM(date)

You usually will use @DOM to compute the day of a date stored in another field:

@DOM(#22)

For the date May 28, 1988, this function returns the number 28.

### *@MONTH*

The @MONTH function is similar to @DOM except that @MONTH returns the numerical value for the month of a date. For example,

@MONTH(#22)

returns the number 5 if field #22 contains the date May 28, 1988.

### *@YEAR*

You can isolate the year in a date for further calculations by using the @YEAR function:

@YEAR(#22)

If field #22 contains the date May 28, 1988, this function returns the number 1988.

### *@DOW$*

The @DOW$ function is convenient for automatically entering the day of the week as a word. You can use a conventional date field as the source, and @DOW$ computes the day of the week:

@DOW$(#22)

If field #22 contains the date May 28, 1988, this function returns *Saturday.*

### *@MONTH$*

This function works like @DOW$ except that @MONTH$ computes the name of the month. This function can be useful if you have selected a date format that is all numbers, such as 05/28/88. If field #22 contains this date,

@MONTH$(#22)

returns the month *May.*

### *@D*

Q&A's @DATE function can compute date arithmetic, as described previously. At times, you may find that employing a date constant in your calculations is useful. You know that tax returns always are due on April 15 (unless you have established another tax year), for example, and you might want to use this date in some calculation. Or you may want to base all date calculations around the beginning of your fiscal year or the date on which your business was established.

The @D function uses a fixed date for its computations. The generic form of the function is @D(date).

If date=June 15, 1988, the statement

```
#30=@D(June 15, 1988)+60
```

stores 8/14/88 (60 days after June 15) in field #30.

Symantec recommends that you spell out dates in this format or use the yyyy/mm/dd format for the greatest accuracy with this function.

### *@T*

The @T function works like the @D function but provides a time constant for calculations. The generic format is @T(time).

If time=3:00 pm, the statement

```
#10=@T(3:00 pm)+#5
```

adds the value of field #5 to 3:00 pm and stores the result in field #10.

If field #5 contains 3 (for three hours), #10 is set to 6 p.m. Note that you can use 12-hour or 24-hour time formats (3:00 pm = 15:00; 6:00 pm = 18:00). But if you use 12-hour formats, you must type *am* and *pm* in the format; otherwise, Q&A automatically uses *am*.

### *@USERID*

For password-protected databases, @USERID returns the identification of the current user. You can place the user ID in a database field with the following statement:

```
#10=@USERID
```

This function can be useful in managing database maintenance by showing the last user who updated specific information and providing a record of file entries.

## *The @ADD and @UPDATE Functions*

You can use the @ADD or @UPDATE functions to instruct Q&A to take action depending on whether forms are being added or updated. @ADD returns a True value when records are being added to the database; @UPDATE returns a True value when records are being updated. Because True/False values are returned by these functions, @ADD and @UPDATE work well in IF...THEN expressions. For example, consider the following statement:

```
#15: IF @ADD THEN #15=@DATE
```

This statement says, "If forms are being added, then field #15 should equal the current date." These functions can be a great help in making decisions based on programming needs.

### The @NUMBER Function

The @NUMBER function enters sequential numbers (x+1) in a field. This function can be used when you need to make sure that a different number is entered in each field. @NUMBER says, "The preceding number plus one."

When your form has fields for purchase-order numbers, ticket numbers, or any sequentially numbered set of items, your job can be made easier with the @NUMBER function.

## Financial Functions

Like many spreadsheet programs, Q&A includes functions for financial calculations. Four such functions are compound growth rate, future value of an annuity, payment on a loan, and present value of an annuity.

Although you can construct formulas to calculate these figures from other Q&A math functions, having functions to do these tasks reduces programming time and probably will produce more accurate and consistent results. Some financial formulas can be rather complicated.

All of Q&A's financial functions can accept as arguments any number, a field designator, or other formulas that result in numbers. This feature lets you play some what-if calculation games with Q&A financial functions.

### Compound Growth Rate

This function computes the percentage growth rate of an investment, given the present value, the future value, and the life (how long you want the investment to last).

The generic form of this function is CGR(pv,fv,t). Note that pv = present value, fv = future value, and t = term or life.

Suppose that you have $5,000 to invest now, and you want to double your money in 10 years. What interest rate will you have to find to make this plan happen? Select the field where you want the value to appear and enter the following function:

```
#1=@CGR(5000,10000,10)
```

When the value is calculated, the number 0.0717734625 should appear in field #1, which means that your planned investment would have to earn a compound interest rate of 7.18 percent to double in 10 years.

You can use File format features to restrict the number of decimal places that are displayed as the result of such a calculation. For more readable output, select Format Values from the Customize menu and specify two decimal places by typing *n2* in the field where the @CGR function appears.

To display in a percentage format, multiply the result by 100:

#1=@CGR(5000,10000,10)*100

Now field #1 will display `7.18` rather than `0.07`.

### *Future Value of an Investment*

Q&A's @FV function can tell you how much a regular investment will be worth at the end of a specified time if you know the interest rate. The generic form of this function is @FV(pmt,in,t). Note that pmt=payment, in=periodic interest, and t=term.

Assume that you can invest $1,500 a year for five years at an interest rate of 7.5 percent. How much money will you have at the end of five years?

Enter the @FV function #1=@FV(1500,.075,5) in the field you have designated #1 (or enter the function in any other field by changing the #1 to another number). The result is $8,712.59.

Notice that the interest must be entered as *.075* rather than *7.5*. Also, the interest is the periodic rate, which means 7.5 percent per year in this example. If the payments were to be made monthly, the periodic rate would be (7.5)/12.

As with all Q&A financial functions, you can use field designators rather than numerical values for the arguments:

@FV(#6,#7,#8)

The results are based on end-of-period calculations. In other words, the regular payments are made on the last day of the period.

### *Payment on a Loan*

Sometimes, showing the payment on a loan in a Q&A File field is useful. The intrinsic @PMT function can do that for you. The generic form of the function is @PMT(pv,in,t). Note that pv=present value or principal, in=periodic interest, and t=term.

If the present value (principal) on a loan is $50,000, at an annual interest rate of 12.5 percent, you can pay off the obligation in 30 years at a monthly rate of $533.63:

@PMT(50000,(12.5/100)/12,30*12)

In this example,

pv = 50,000
in = 0.0104 per month
t = 360 months

Entering the formula as shown is convenient so that you have a record of how the numbers were derived. The interest rate 0.0104 wouldn't mean much after some time passes, whereas 12.5 is probably the way you think of interest. (12.5/100 returns the annual interest rate of 0.125. That figure is divided by 12 months to derive the monthly rate.) Also, you usually think of paying off a loan in a matter of years, not months, unless the loan is a small amount; so the term is shown as 30 years times 12 months per year.

As with other File financial functions, you can use field numbers for the values in @PMT calculations:

```
@PMT(#1,(#2)/12,#3*12)
```

Again, the calculations are based on payments that occur at the end of the period.

### Present Value of an Investment

Computing present value is a way of determining how much money you can afford to borrow if you know the interest rate the lending institution is charging, you know how long you want to make payments, and you have determined the amount of the monthly payment you can afford.

The generic form of the present value function is @PV(pmt,in,t). Note that pmt=payment, in=periodic interest, t=term.

Suppose that you want to buy a new car and are willing to pay for it during a five-year span. The bank is charging you 10.5 percent for the privilege, and you calculate that you can afford $225 per month. With the @PMT function, you can determine how much you can afford to spend:

```
@PV(225,(10.5/100)/12,5*60)
```

The result is $10,468.09, after any downpayment. As in the previous examples, enter the full values (10.5 for interest) and calculate the working value. This practice makes debugging or modifying form calculations easier. You also can use field numbers in place of numeric literals. This function uses end-of-period calculations.

## Using LOOKUP: Statements, Functions, and Tables

Among Q&A's more powerful programming tools are the lookup features. With LOOKUP, you can search a table that is part of the current application. You can search for matching information and automatically enter data in a form field based on data found in the table. You can program a form to accept a ZIP code from the keyboard, for example, and then look up the city and state from a table and insert this data into a record.

With Version 3.0 and later, you also can use an external file to store lookup information, eliminating the size limitations of the RAM-resident table and enabling the linking of multiple files with a single application. An *external file* is a standard Q&A database that is separate from the one you are currently using. While the LOOKUP command uses a RAM-resident table that is part of the database you are using, Version 3.0's XLOOKUP accesses a second data file to find the information it needs.

These lookup capabilities are divided between internal and external features, and programming statements and functions exist in both of these areas.

Statements form complete programming instructions, telling Q&A what information to find in a lookup table, what data to retrieve from the table, and where to put it on the displayed form.

Functions, on the other hand, do not specify where the retrieved data should reside. You have to supply additional programming logic for this information, but functions are more versatile because you can include them in derived columns in reports.

## Internal LOOKUP

Internal LOOKUP commands use a table that is actually part of the database you are currently accessing. This internal table contains one compare (or key) column and four data columns. When you use one of Q&A's internal lookup features, the software scans the key column for a specified value and then selects information from one of the data columns that is linked to the key. The data selected from the table can be placed in any of the fields on the current form, used in calculations, or applied in any way that other field data might be used.

### The Lookup Table

Before you can use internal LOOKUP in your form, you need to know how to create a lookup table. A lookup table can be used to store information you enter often, such as phone numbers and addresses of regular customers (see fig. 7.15). When you use the LOOKUP command, Q&A searches the lookup table for the information and enters it on the form.

Figure 7.16 shows how LOOKUP is used on the Veterinary Clinic form. When you enter the client's name, the LOOKUP command in the Phone field retrieves the phone number from the lookup table and enters the data into the form automatically (see fig. 7.17). The street address also is entered from the lookup table. The CNEXT command in both these fields moves the cursor to the next field as soon as the information is retrieved and placed in the field. Notice that the City, St, and Zip fields are filled in automatically by the Set Initial Values procedure. The less-than sign (<)

| KEY | 1 | 2 | 3 | 4 |
|---|---|---|---|---|
| Harlan Tompkins | 342-3485 | 519 Juba Road | | |
| Shirley Thomas | 342-5184 | Timber Tree Rd. | | |
| Joe Crocker | 342-2727 | 2542 14th Ave. | | |
| Joe Carlton | 342-5968 | 1927 Lyle St. | | |
| Tyler Johnson | 342-5811 | 1934 Lyle St. | | |
| PATIENT NAME | BREED | COLOR | SEX | WEIGHT |
| Sheba | Cocker | Brown | F | 38 |
| Blackie | Lab | Black | M | 75 |
| Charlie | Am Husky | White | M | 78 |
| Bimbo | Cocker | Brown | M | 36 |
| Tiger | Siamese | Black | M | 15 |
| Cat | Mix Cat | Black/White | F | 12 |
| Fluffy | Mix Cat | Brown | F | 18 |
| King | Gd. Ret. | Gold | M | 64 |
| Princess | Mix Cat | Black | F | 18 |
| Sandy | Terrier | Brown | M | 17 |
| Potzie | Siamese | White | F | 14 |

TDCLNC.DTF Lookup Table Page 1 of 1

Esc-Cancel F6-Expand PgUp-Previous page PgDn-Next page F10-Continue

**Fig. 7.15** *A sample lookup table.*

tells Q&A to fill in the value as soon as the cursor enters the field. The CNEXT command moves the cursor to the next field as soon as the value is entered.

In this example, then, the operator never types the telephone number, the street address, the city, the state, or the ZIP code. This type of forms programming assumes that all clients live in the same city and have the same ZIP code. This type works for an application with a small area of coverage but probably will not be universally acceptable. See the section on the XLOOKUP command for a way to enter the entire address automatically, regardless of where the client resides.

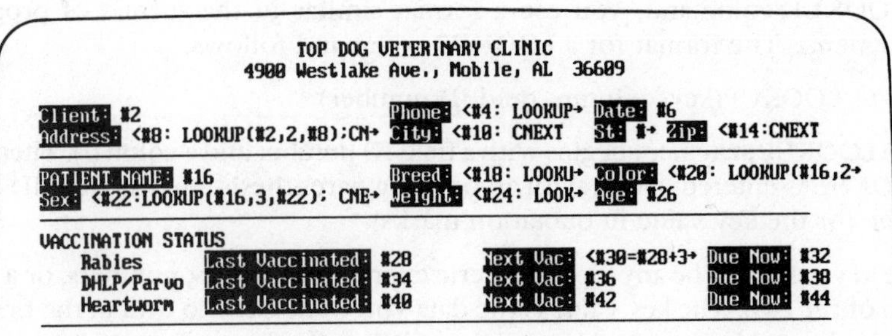
TOP DOG VETERINARY CLINIC
4900 Westlake Ave., Mobile, AL 36609

Client: #2 Phone: <#4: LOOKUP→ Date: #6
Address: <#8: LOOKUP(#2,2,#8);CN→ City: <#10: CNEXT St: #→ Zip: <#14:CNEXT

PATIENT NAME: #16 Breed: <#18: LOOKU→ Color: <#20: LOOKUP(#16,2→
Sex: <#22:LOOKUP(#16,3,#22); CNE→ Weight: <#24: LOOK→ Age: #26

VACCINATION STATUS
Rabies Last Vaccinated: #28 Next Vac: <#30=#28+3→ Due Now: #32
DHLP/Parvo Last Vaccinated: #34 Next Vac: #36 Due Now: #38
Heartworm Last Vaccinated: #40 Next Vac: #42 Due Now: #44

**Fig. 7.16** *Using LOOKUP commands.*

To fill in a lookup table, select Edit Lookup Table from the Customize menu. When the blank table is displayed, use the Tab key to change columns and the cursor keys to select the row you want to edit. Type the data and move the cursor to the next entry location. You may want to enter column headings for each group of information so that the form will be clear to others who may use the file. Be sure to use column headings that will not be used as key values, to prevent Q&A from finding a heading during a lookup procedure and mistaking the heading for a key value. If this mishap would occur, improper data would be returned.

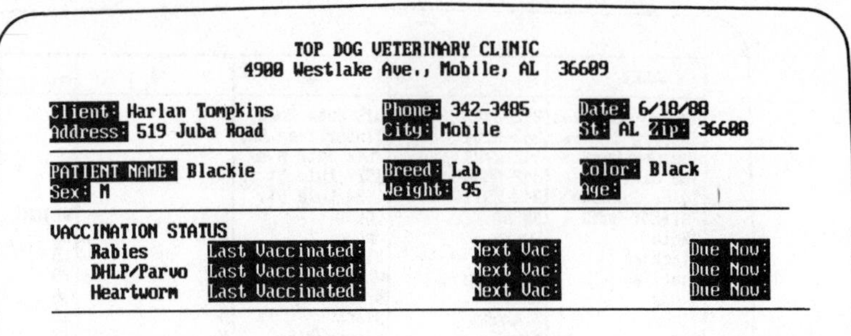


**Fig. 7.17** *The results returned by LOOKUP commands.*

If you want to change something on a lookup table, move to the location you want to edit and press F4 to delete a word or Shift-F4 to delete the entire location. Then type the new data.

A lookup table can store up to 64,000 characters, depending on the available RAM in your machine. A computer with 512K of RAM can store a lookup table with 600 100-character lines. Each item in a lookup table can be up to 240 characters, making the maximum line length 1,200 characters.

When you enter data in the columns of a lookup table, confine each column to one set of information. For example, if the key value is a client name, you could use column 1 for phone numbers, column 2 for addresses, column 3 for cities, etc. You can enter any type of information: text, numbers, dates, and times.

### *The LOOKUP Statement*

The LOOKUP statement acts like a complete programming statement. When you write a LOOKUP command, you use a format similar to the format of programming statements. The format for a LOOKUP command follows:

*#n*: LOOKUP(key, column, field ID number)

The LOOKUP statement begins with a field ID number and a colon (:). Then the word *LOOKUP* is entered, along with an opening parenthesis and the field ID of the key value (or the key value in quotation marks).

The key value can be any alphanumeric expression: words, numbers, or a combination of the two. The key value is the data you want Q&A to find in the first column of a lookup table. A typical key value is a ZIP code, for example. Q&A uses the ZIP-code key to scan a lookup table until a matching value is found. The program then returns the city and state associated with the specified ZIP-code key. Be careful to enter the key value exactly as it appears in the lookup table, or Q&A will not be able to locate the data. If the key value appears more than once, Q&A uses the first one listed.

Next, enter a comma after the key value and specify the number of the column that contains the data to be retrieved. Finally, enter the field ID of the field in which Q&A

will enter the data and end the statement with a closing parenthesis. For example, the following statement searches the lookup table for the key value stored in field #2, retrieves the data associated with it in column 1 of the lookup table, and stores the retrieved information in field #4:

#4: LOOKUP(#2,1,#4)

Suppose that field #2 holds a ZIP code, for example, and the list in column 1 of the LOOKUP table stores city names; then if field #2 holds *37918*, this program statement will store *Knoxville* in field #4.

### *The LOOKUPR Statement*

The LOOKUPR statement, like the other internal LOOKUP commands, uses the table resident with the data file. Unlike the LOOKUP statement, however, LOOKUPR does not have to find an exact match. If you specify a key value that LOOKUPR cannot locate, this statement returns the next lowest value in the table.

The statement takes the following general form:

*#n*: LOOKUPR(key, column, field ID #)

The key is the value to search for in the lookup table key column, and the column is a number (1 through 4) that specifies which lookup table column holds the data to be retrieved.

Suppose that you are working with the following accounting system: account numbers from 0 to 50 are cash accounts, numbers from 51 to 100 are checking accounts, numbers from 600 to 799 are income accounts, and numbers from 800 to 999 are expense accounts. As you write reports about transactions against these accounts, you may want to show the account type on the data-entry screen. If the lookup table appeared like the one in table 7.3, then as detailed transactions are entered, the appropriate category would be entered automatically in the appropriate place in the form. Now suppose that the LOOKUPR statement contained these values:

LOOKUPR(823,1,#33)

Field #33 would be loaded with expenses from the lookup table.

As with other Q&A statements, you can use formulas and field IDs for some or all of the arguments to LOOKUPR. Suppose, for example, that you are tracking inventory with Q&A. If your part-numbering scheme includes a pointer to warehouse location, you can use a formula to extract this information from the complete part number, look up the location in the table, and place it in the Location field on the displayed form.

Consider a part number such as 1052-E4662-GE and assume that the first four digits, 1052, show the warehouse location according to the lookup table in table 7.4. If the part number is entered in field #10, and the location is entered in field #12, then the following LOOKUPR statement fills in field #12 automatically:

**Table 7.3**
**Sample Lookup Table for LOOKUPR**

| KEY | 1 | 2 |
|---|---|---|
| ACCOUNT NUMBER | TYPE ACCOUNT | |
| 1 | Cash | |
| 51 | Checking | |
| 600 | Income | |
| 800 | Expense | |

```
LOOKUPR(@left(4,#10),1,#12)
```

The string function @left removes the left four digits to use in the LOOKUPR statement, performs the lookup, and returns *Aisle 4, East* from the table for field #12.

**Table 7.4**
**Sample Lookup Table for LOOKUPR**

| KEY | 1 | 2 |
|---|---|---|
| LOCATION NUMBER | WAREHOUSE LOC. | |
| 1000 | Aisle 4, East | |
| 2000 | Aisle 5, East | |
| 3000 | Aisle 1, West | |
| 4000 | Aisle 2, West | |

### *The @LOOKUP Function*

The @LOOKUP function works like the LOOKUP statement except that the @LOOKUP function does not include a target field for data retrieved from the lookup table. In addition, functions can be used in derived columns in the Report module (see Chapter 15 for more information on Report).

The generic form for @LOOKUP is *#n* = @LOOKUP(key, column). Key is the value to search for in the lookup table key column, and column is the lookup table data column from which information will be retrieved.

Notice that you specify where to place the information that is found by including @LOOKUP as part of a calculation formula. The preceding example shows the function used in the target field. You also can load another field, as this example shows:

#5: #10 = @LOOKUP(key,column)

In other situations, the @LOOKUP function operates like the LOOKUP statement.

### *The @LOOKUPR Function*

The @LOOKUPR function performs the same operations as the LOOKUPR statement except that you must include the function in a calculation formula to tell Q&A where to place the information it finds in the lookup table.

The general form of the command is *#n* = @LOOKUPR(key,column). Key is the compare value for the lookup table's key column, and column is the table's data column from which information that is found will be retrieved.

## *The External LOOKUP Commands*

The external LOOKUP commands (entered on the Program Spec screen) added to Q&A with Release 3.0 increase the power and flexibility of this database program. With external LOOKUP, you are not limited to the form and size of the internal lookup table.

The external commands use another Q&A data file as the source of retrieved information. Otherwise, the functions are similar.

The external LOOKUP features offer relational-like functions for Q&A File; these features link key fields across multiple files. Consider the Veterinary Clinic example from the previous discussion of the internal LOOKUP statement. The internal table is a limiting factor in this application because not enough table fields are available to permit you to store the full address and telephone number.

With external LOOKUP, however, you can build a separate name and address database and load the treatment record from this separate file.

### *The External LOOKUP File*

The external functions depend on all the linked files being indexed on the same fields. (The speedup search must be set for the same fields. Select Speed Up Searches from the Customize menu.) Figure 7.18 shows a portion of the name and address file (NAD.DTF) and a portion of the veterinary service file (TDCLNC.DTF). The two files are linked through the indexed CLIENT field.

For this example, the clinic file is the primary file and the name and address file is the external file. The primary file is always the one receiving the information; the external file is always the one supplying the information.

You can link to TDCLNC a third file that holds records of treatment for each patient, for example. In this case, the common link is the indexed PATIENT NAME field. You can tie together virtually as many files in this manner as you need. Once the link

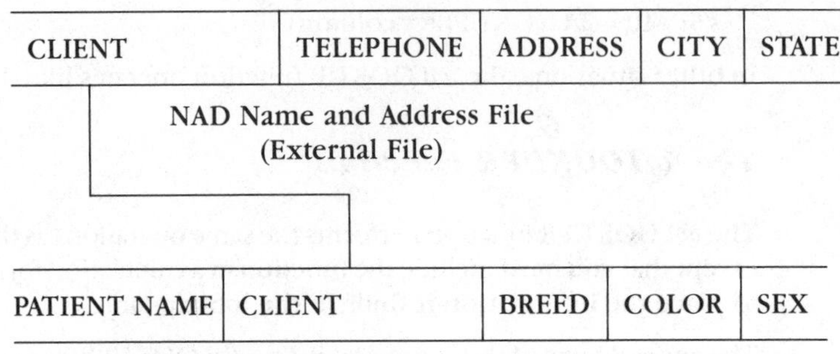


**Fig. 7.18** *Sample XLOOKUP file join.*

is made, you can use external LOOKUP commands to fill in fields in the TDCLNC file and to construct reports on the data with the Report module.

### *The XLOOKUP Statement*

The XLOOKUP statement functions almost identically to LOOKUP, discussed previously, except that you are using the external data file as the reference table instead of the internal lookup table.

The generic form of this statement follows:

```
XLOOKUP(''fn'',key#,''xkey'',''xdat'',loc#)
```

Note:

fn = the external file name

key# = the number of the key field in the primary file

xkey = the name of the external key field that will link to key# in the primary file

xdat = the name of the field from which data will be extracted from the external file

loc# = the field number in the primary file where information from xdat should be placed

Notice that each of the named arguments in this statement is enclosed in quotation marks; the number designations do not take quotation marks.

If you use the files in figure 7.18, for example, the statement might take this form:

```
<#8: XLOOKUP("NAD",#1,"CLIENT","ADDRESS",#8)
```

This statement uses the information in field #1 of the NAD file to find a corresponding record in the CLIENT file. The information in the CLIENT ADDRESS field is copied into field #8 of the NAD file. Such a statement can load addresses into the NAD file automatically.

In this example, the primary field names and the external field names for client and address are the same. (Figure 7.18 does not show the entire files. See figure 7.16 to see the complete client record.) However, you could use CLIENT in the veterinary services file and NAME in the NAD file and use ADDRESS in one file and STREET in the other, as long as matching data was in the two files for Q&A to find. The less-than sign at the beginning of this program statement tells Q&A to conduct the lookup procedure as soon as the cursor enters field #8.

### *The XLOOKUPR Statement*

The XLOOKUPR statement is identical to the LOOKUPR statement except that, like XLOOKUP, XLOOKUPR uses an external file for the reference table. The rules for using this statement are the same as for XLOOKUP and LOOKUPR.

The general format for this statement follows:

XLOOKUPR(“fn”,key#,“xkey”,“xdat”,loc#)

Note:

fn = the external file name

key# = the number of the key field in the primary file

xkey = the name of the external key field that will link to key# in the primary file

xdat = the name of the field from which data will be extracted from the external file

loc# = the field number in the primary file where information from xdat should be placed

For an example of how to use XLOOKUPR, refer to the previous section on LOOKUPR.

### *The @XLOOKUP Function*

Q&A functions add a level of flexibility that is lacking in program statements, although the user has the responsibility of writing more of the logic to make the functions work.

The @XLOOKUP function has this general structure:

@XLOOKUP(“fn”,key#,“xkey”,“xdat”)

Note:

fn = the external file name

key# = the number of the key field in the primary file

xkey = the name of the external key field that will link to key# in the primary file

xdat = the name of the field from which data will be extracted from the external file

As with other Q&A functions, you must specify where the retrieved data will be placed in the primary form. If you use the previous Veterinary Clinic example, the function syntax might be the following:

#8=@XLOOKUP("NAD",#1,"CLIENT","ADDRESS")

### *The @XLOOKUPR Function*

This function is similar to @LOOKUPR except that @XLOOKUPR uses an external File database as the source of information. The general format for this function follows:

@XLOOKUPR("fn",key#,"xkey","xdat")

Note:

fn = the external file name

key# = the number of the key field in the primary file

xkey = the name of the external key field that will link to key# in the primary file

xdat = the name of the field from which data will be extracted from the external file

## *Executing Programming Statements*

Q&A executes the statements entered on the Program Spec whenever you add or update data on the form. Formulas are calculated and values are returned at that time. You have the option of selecting either manual or automatic calculation. Q&A's default setting is manual calculation, which means that in order to carry out the calculations, you must press the calculation key (F8). You also can use the less-than (<) or greater-than (>) symbols at the beginning of programming statements to override the standard rules of execution.

If the calculation is based on data in a specific field, that is entered from the keyboard, you probably will specify that the calculation will occur when the cursor exits the field. If, on the other hand, you don't want the data-entry person to add information to a field, or even to have to make a decision about entering data into a field, then you will calculate the value when the cursor enters the field.

## Using Automatic Calculation

You can have Q&A calculate the forms automatically by pressing Shift-F8 and typing *a*, while in either the Add Data or Search/Update option of the File menu. In Automatic mode, all programming statements are computed when the cursor is moved from any field that has been changed. Even if you have not changed every field on the form, each field that has a calculation statement is recalculated. That process can take quite a bit of time in a form with a dozen or more statements. Q&A remains in Automatic mode until you press Shift-F8 and press M while in either the Add Data or Search/Update option.

## Overriding Standard Execution Rules

If a programming statement begins with either a greater-than or a less-than symbol, Q&A overrides the standard rules of execution. The less-than symbol causes the statement to be executed when the cursor enters the field; the greater-than symbol tells Q&A to execute the statement when the cursor is moved out of the field. Remember, however, that if you use the less-than symbol, the statement will be executed before the typist can enter data. The typist will not be able to change the data that Q&A enters. The following examples show the effect of the greater-than and less-than symbols.

| *Formula* | *How To Read the Formula* |
|---|---|
| <#6: #6=#4+14 | When the cursor enters field #6, 14 is added to the value in field #4 and the result is entered automatically in field #6. |
| <#4: LOOKUP(#2,1,#4) | When the cursor enters field #4, data is retrieved from the lookup table and entered automatically in field #4. |
| >#6: GOTO #8 | After exiting field #6, the cursor moves to field #8. |
| >#12: CHOME | After exiting field #12, the cursor moves to the first field on the form. |
| <#27: IF #6>(#22+245) THEN #27="Yes" ELSE #27="No" | If field #6 is greater than field #22 plus 245, field #27 displays *Yes*. If #6 is less than field #22 plus 245, #27 displays *No*. This statement is executed when the cursor enters the field. |
| >#17: IF #35>=(@DATE+ #30) THEN #40= "Past Due" | If field #35 is equal to or greater than the current date plus the value in field #30, field #40 will state *Past Due*. This statement is executed when the cursor exits the field. |

CHOME and GOTO are cursor-movement commands that are explained in the next section. Whenever cursor-movement commands are included in a programming statement, the statement must begin with a greater-than or a less-than symbol.

## *Moving the Cursor in a Program Statement*

In Q&A, you use the Tab key or the Enter key to move the cursor from field to field. You can automate cursor movement by including the following words in your programming statements:

| *Word* | *Moves the cursor to the* |
|---|---|
| GOTO | Specified field |
| CNEXT | Next field |
| CPREV | Previous field |
| CHOME | First field |
| CEND | Last field |
| PGDN | Next page |
| PGUP | Previous page |

When a cursor-movement command is used, the program statements in the form move the cursor as though you were using the Tab or Enter keys. All the cursor moves happen within the same form; you cannot use cursor-movement commands to move from form to form.

Remember that programming statements containing any one of these cursor-movement commands do not execute according to the standard rules. Statements that contain cursor-movement commands must begin with either a greater-than or a less-than symbol; the statements will execute as explained in the preceding section.

If you want Q&A to execute the programming statement and then move the cursor, place the cursor-movement word as the last item in the statement. Separate the statement and the cursor-movement word with a semicolon. For example, the following statement can be used at the end of a page:

```
<#50: IF @DATE>#30 THEN #50=15; PGDN
```

You can enter the movement word in the middle of a statement such as this:

```
<#120: IF #100>40000 THEN CNEXT ELSE #120=5
```

In this example, CNEXT is executed only if #100 is greater than 40,000.

You usually will include only one cursor-movement word in a program statement because you probably want to exit the current field immediately or leave the cursor there for keyboard entry. However, you can use more than one cursor-movement word. For example, you can add a cursor-movement command at the end of the preceding statement. The command will be executed if the ELSE segment is used.

```
<#120: IF #100>40000 THEN CNEXT ELSE #120=5; GOTO #140
```

If #100 is greater than 40,000, CNEXT is executed and the cursor moves to the next field. If #100 is less than 40,000, the ELSE segment causes field #120 to be given a value of 5, and the cursor is moved to field #140.

If you do use more than one cursor-movement command in a statement, be careful. An infinite loop can be created by cursor-movement words: statement 1 moves the cursor to statement 2, which moves the cursor back to statement 1, which moves the cursor to statement 2. To interrupt an infinite loop, press Esc. Then select the Program Form option from the Customize menu and correct the error in the program statements.

When you have program statements in several consecutive fields, Q&A can insert initial values or enter data from a lookup table faster than the fields can be displayed on-screen. Simply use CNEXT at the end of each statement, as shown in figure 7.19. The fields Phone, Date, Address, City, St, and Zip are entered automatically as soon as you type the client name.

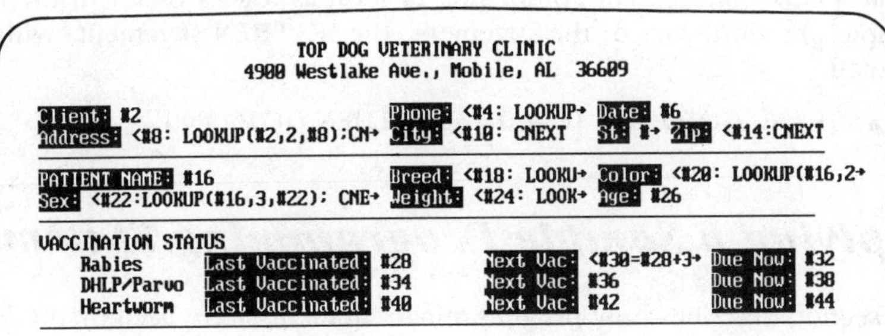


**Fig. 7.19**
*Using CNEXT in programming statements.*

## *Writing Multiple Statements*

If you need to perform several tasks at once, you can enter multiple programming statements in one field. This capability is especially helpful when the timing of data entry is important or when the other fields on the form cannot store more information.

The format for multiple statements requires that the statements be separated by a semicolon so that Q&A knows where one statement ends and another begins. For example, the following line has three statements:

```
<#65: #60=#5/15; IF #5>7 THEN #70="No"; IF #70="No" THEN
GOTO #75
```

Because you can increase the number of statements when you use IF...THEN and IF...THEN...ELSE, you can execute a number of tasks with a single IF statement. The conditional statements must be set off by BEGIN and END; or the statements must be set off by braces ({ and }), where { replaces BEGIN and } replaces END. For example, consider the following statement:

```
IF statement THEN BEGIN statement 1; statement 2 END ELSE BEGIN
statement a; statement b END
```

This statement says, "If the first statement is true, then do statement 1, statement 2, and other statements that follow; or else do statement a, statement b, and other statements that follow." As you can see, one IF statement can do a considerable amount of work.

Here is another example of a multiple IF statement:

```
<#140: IF #70>21500 THEN BEGIN #140="No"; #145=10000; GOTO
#150 END ELSE BEGIN #140="Yes"; #145=15000; CEND END
```

This statement says, "If field #70 is greater than 21,500, then make field #140 read *No* and field #145 read *10,000* and go to field #150; but if #70 is less than 21,500, then make #140 read *Yes* and #145 read *15,000* and go to the last field."

Be careful if you use cursor-movement commands in multiple statements; Q&A executes cursor-movement commands as soon as it sees them. In the following example, the third part of the statement, the IF...THEN statement, will never be executed.

```
<#50=#16; GOTO #60; IF #60="No" THEN GOTO #90
```

## Applying a Sample Programming Statement

This section describes how programming statements were used by the Veterinary Clinic employees to automate the operation of the database form.

The LOOKUP command is used in four fields that provide patient information: Breed, Color, Sex, and Weight (see fig. 7.19). When the patient name is entered, the cursor moves through these fields (because of the GOTO and CNEXT commands) and the client information is retrieved and entered automatically (see fig. 7.20). The name of the patient also is copied in the Patient Services For field because of the formula #50=#16.

The Due Now field contains a formula that displays a *Yes* or *No* value. The formula determines whether the current date is greater than the Next Vac date plus 365 (days). If the date value is greater, the vaccination is due and *Yes* is entered in the field. If the value is not greater than 365, *No* is entered in the Due Now field (see fig. 7.21). The following statement is used to accomplish this:

```
<#32: IF #6>(#28+365) THEN {#32="Yes"} ELSE {#32="No"};
CNEXT
```

After the formula is calculated and the result is placed in the field, the cursor is moved to the next field with the CNEXT command (see fig. 7.22).

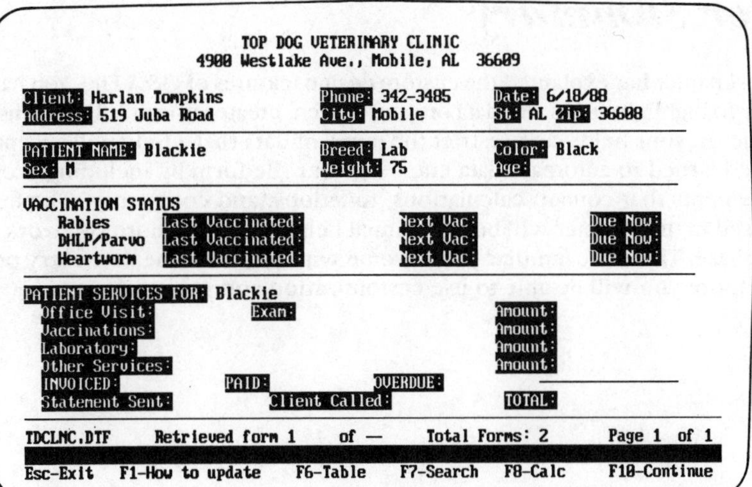


**Fig. 7.20** *Client data entered with LOOKUP commands.*

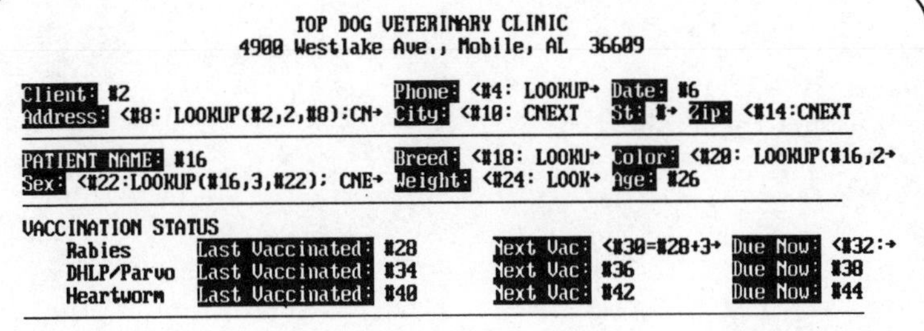


**Fig. 7.21** *Using the IF...THEN...ELSE statement.*

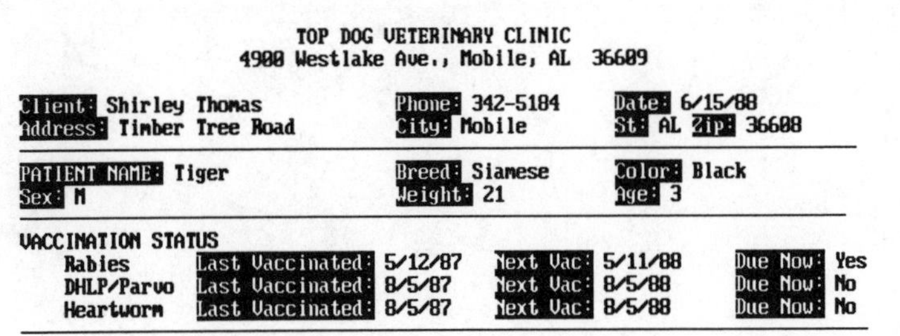


**Fig. 7.22** *Results of the IF...THEN...ELSE statement.*

# *Chapter Summary*

This chapter has explained the custom design features of Q&A File. You have learned how to highlight fields and data on your screen, create custom help screens, set initial values in your fields, and restrict the range of data that a field will accept. You also have learned to automate data entry on your file form by including programming statements that contain calculations, functions, and commands. The features discussed in this chapter will be a continual help to you the more you work with your database. The more familiar you become with your routine data-entry procedures, the more you will be able to use customization and programming.

Chapter

8

# Printing from File

Q&A File stores information and displays records in the form you want. Frequently, you need a printed copy of the records in your database. You can print the entire database or just one record. You may, for instance, want to print all the records pertaining to a certain company, person, or product. With Q&A, printing any number of records is easy.

When you print from Q&A File, you have several options. You can

- Use the DOS PrtSc, or Print Screen, facility to print a single record displayed on the screen
- Print a single record with a Q&A print utility within File
- Create a print specification—called a Print Spec—to print elaborate customized reports

A Print Spec is a list of instructions that tell Q&A which fields to print in what order. Designing a Print Spec involves filling in a series of specification screens. You can save the completed Print Spec for use again later, and you can modify the saved specification in order to change the report before you print again.

You also can generate reports from Q&A files from within the separate Report module. The printing features in the Report module are more flexible. See Chapter 16 for details on using the printing features of Report. The Write module also has separate report capabilities. Details on these features are in Chapter 13.

This chapter explains how to use all the printing options in Q&A File.

## *Printing One Complete Form*

You will sometimes want only a quick copy of the displayed record. The DOS Print Screen feature is a simple way to make a quick copy. Use a Retrieve Spec (discussed in Chapter 6) to display the record you want to print and press the PrtSc, or Print Scrn, key. The screen contents are sent to your printer. Note that the entire screen is printed with this method. In addition to the retrieved record and field names, your printout includes any on-screen Q&A prompts, messages, and function-key assignments. If the current form is longer than one page, you must scroll and print again until you get a printout of the entire form.

If you want to print information from a single record or from a few selected records without the Q&A messages, simply press F2 and then F10 to accept the default print specs. If your printer is installed correctly, the contents of the current record are printed with field names. If you need help installing your printer, refer to Appendix A, "Installing Q&A," for more information.

***Note:*** Any lines or boxes on your screen may not appear properly on your printout, depending on your printer's capabilities.

If you don't press F10 after you press F2, you can make changes to the File Print Options screen, which is slightly different from the one in the Write module. This screen does not prompt you to specify pages to print, because in File you print records, not documents.

If you plan to print a record from a database, the Print Field Labels option on the File Print Options screen is important. Unless you have changed the Global Default screen setting for this option, the default is No, in which case no labels appear when you print a record. You get a printout of "bare" data, and, depending on how many fields and different field types you have defined, it may be impossible to tell which labels go with which data (see fig. 8.1). To change the setting, select Yes to the Print Field Labels line.

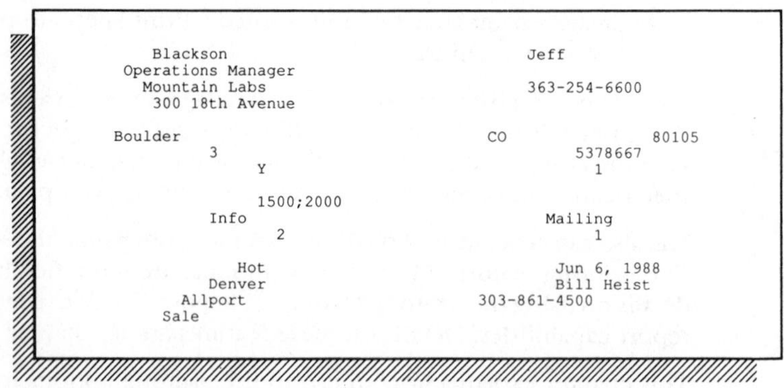

```
     Blackson                                 Jeff
  Operations Manager
    Mountain Labs                             363-254-6600
     300 18th Avenue

Boulder                                 CO                 80105
          3                                      5378667
               Y                                    1

               1500;2000
          Info                                 Mailing
                    2                               1

             Hot                                 Jun 6, 1988
          Denver                                 Bill Heist
      Allport                           303-861-4500
    Sale
```

**Fig. 8.1**
*A form printed without field labels.*

The same record printed with labels appears in figure 8.2. As you can see, the labels make the information easier to read and understand.

If you are printing mailing labels or envelopes, however, you won't want the labels to appear. In this case, set the Print Field Labels option to No.

```
                    TITAN TECHNOLOGY SALES LEAD TRACKING SYSTEM
                                                      File Name -- SlsLead
LastName: Blackson                           FirstName: Jeff
Title: Operations Manager
Company: Mountain Labs                       Telephone: 363-254-6600
Address1: 300 18th Avenue
Address2:
City: Boulder                                State: CO           Zip: 80105
   No. of Labs: 3                            Annual Revenue: 5378667
   Current Customer: Y                       Company Priority: 1
-----------------------------LEAD INFORMATION-----------------------------
   Product Interest: 1500;2000
   Request For: Info                         Lead Source: Mailing
   Months to Purchase: 2                     Product Priority: 1
-------------------------------SALES ACTION-------------------------------
   Sales Priority: Hot                       Date Entered: Jun 6, 1988
   Sales Dist.: Denver                      Sales Manager: Bill Heist
   Salesman: Allport                        Phone: 303-861-4500
   Status: Sale
```

**Fig. 8.2**
***A printout with fields identified by labels.***

# *Creating and Using Print Specs*

Printouts would be terribly boring if we always had to print the same fields on the same forms in the same typeface. Fortunately, most software packages have some flexibility for printing forms. Q&A is no exception. Through the use of Print Specs, you can pull specific data from a database to print mailing labels or fill in preprinted forms.

Before you can print from the Print menu, you must first create a Print Spec to tell Q&A how you want the data to be printed. Print Specs can be saved and used again; you also can copy an existing Print Spec or modify it to create a new one. By using the Retrieve and Sort Specs, you designate which records to print and in what order. This section explains how to create and use Print Specs; a later section discusses how to use the specs you have already defined.

## *Designing a Print Spec*

To begin creating a Print Spec, select Print from the File menu. After you have chosen a database, the Print menu is displayed, and you can choose from one of four possibilities: design or redesign a Print Spec; start printing right away using a new or old Print Spec; set global options; or rename, delete, or copy a Print Spec.

Select Design/Redesign a Spec from the Print menu. If you have already designed other print specifications, Q&A displays a list of Print Spec names and prompts you to choose a name. If you haven't created any other Print Specs, the list is blank, but Q&A still requests a name. Enter a name that will help you identify the Print Spec you are creating. Print Spec names can be up to 31 characters long, and the names do not necessarily have to conform to DOS file naming conventions. A name and address reference list, for example, could be called NAD Quick Reference. A more detailed report might be named Detailed Name/Address List.

***Note:*** Print Specs are not DOS files, so Print Specs do not appear on a DOS file directory listing. Print specifications are stored within the database.

The following sections explain the Retrieve and Sort Spec screens used from within the File module to select and sort the data for printouts.

## *Using Retrieve Specs*

After you name the Print Spec, the Retrieve Spec screen is displayed so that you can specify which records to select for printing (see fig. 8.3). For example, you can specify all records from a specific state by typing the state name in the State field on the Retrieve Spec screen. You can select records with annual sales above a certain figure or within date ranges in a similar way. Once you have entered the retrieve specifications, Q&A scans the database, selecting the records that meet your selection criteria and rejecting the records that do not fit within the specifications.

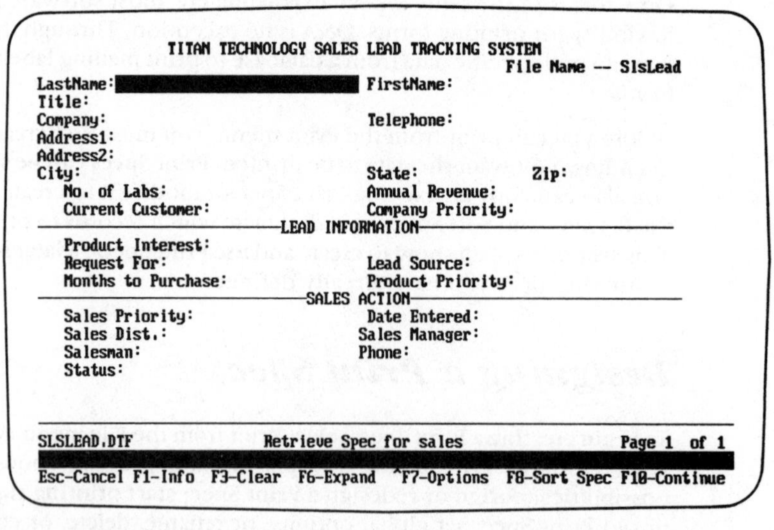

```
                 TITAN TECHNOLOGY SALES LEAD TRACKING SYSTEM
                                                        File Name -- SlsLead
LastName:                             FirstName:
Title:
Company:                              Telephone:
Address1:
Address2:
City:                                 State:              Zip:
   No. of Labs:                       Annual Revenue:
   Current Customer:                  Company Priority:
-------------------------LEAD INFORMATION------------------------------
   Product Interest:
   Request For:                       Lead Source:
   Months to Purchase:                Product Priority:
----------------------------SALES ACTION-------------------------------
   Sales Priority:                    Date Entered:
   Sales Dist.:                       Sales Manager:
   Salesman:                          Phone:
   Status:

SLSLEAD.DTF            Retrieve Spec for sales                Page 1 of 1

Esc-Cancel F1-Info  F3-Clear  F6-Expand  ^F7-Options  F8-Sort Spec F10-Continue
```

**Fig. 8.3**
*The Retrieve Spec screen.*

Notice that this Retrieve Spec screen is the same as the Retrieve Spec you fill out when you select Search/Update from the File menu. For example, if you want to print fliers for your Illinois customers only, you enter the letters *IL* in the State field. You can make the set of retrieved records as selective as you like. Suppose that the mailing is for a short-term special price offering, and you want to send it to only the customers who have said they plan to purchase something within two months. You can make that specification by placing *L*=2 in the Months to Purchase field. The next section shows how to sort information within the fields.

## *Using the Sort Spec Screen*

If you want the displayed accounts to be sorted in a particular order, such as alphabetically by last name, in ZIP code order, or by state name, press F8 to call up the Sort Spec screen (see fig. 8.4). This screen is identical to the Retrieve Spec screen, with the exception of the name (Sort Spec) at the bottom of the screen. You then can specify the sorting order by entering numbers between 1 and 999 in the fields you want to sort. Q&A recognizes the field with the number 1 as the primary sort.

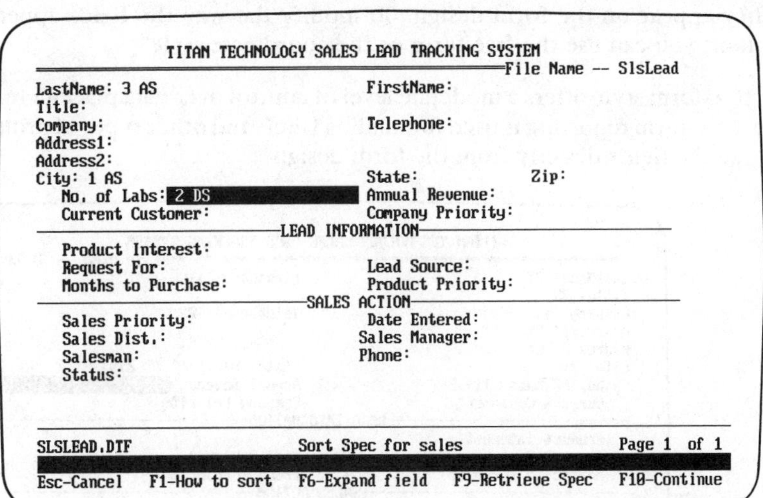


**Fig. 8.4** *The Sort Spec screen.*

Suppose that you want to sort by city within the state of Illinois (or any other state you specify in the State field). Enter a 1 in the City field. If your secondary sort is to be by the number of labs, type *2* in that field. After the numbers in the Sort Spec fields, enter *AS* or *DS* to indicate an ascending sort or a descending sort, respectively. In this example, a primary ascending sort by city arranges the records for the cities in the state alphabetically, starting with the letter A. The field entry is

1 AS

The secondary descending sort by number of labs ranks all the accounts in each city by showing the records with the most labs first. In the Number of Labs field, you type

2 DS

You probably want a third sort, by the customer's last name. This sort should be an ascending sort so that the customers in a particular city with credit limits of $5,000, for example, are listed alphabetically within the $5,000 group for that city. In the LastName field of the Sort Spec screen, you enter

3 AS

You also can enter the sort specs without spaces between the field number and the AS or DS specification, or you can use a comma between the two items (1AS or 1,AS).

When you're finished with the Sort Spec, press F10 to continue to the Fields Spec screen. Again, the only difference is in the name displayed at the bottom of the screen. The next section explains how to use the Fields Spec screen.

## *Setting Field Specs: Free-Form or Coordinate*

The Fields Spec screen is used to tell Q&A where to print the fields on the page (see fig. 8.5). If you press F10 when the Fields Spec screen is displayed, all fields are printed as they appear on the form design. To modify the way the fields appear on the printout, you can use the free-form or the coordinate style.

The free-form style offers a moderate level of control over data placement on printouts. Free-form reporting is used for mailing labels and other types of printouts that can use the fields directly from the form design.

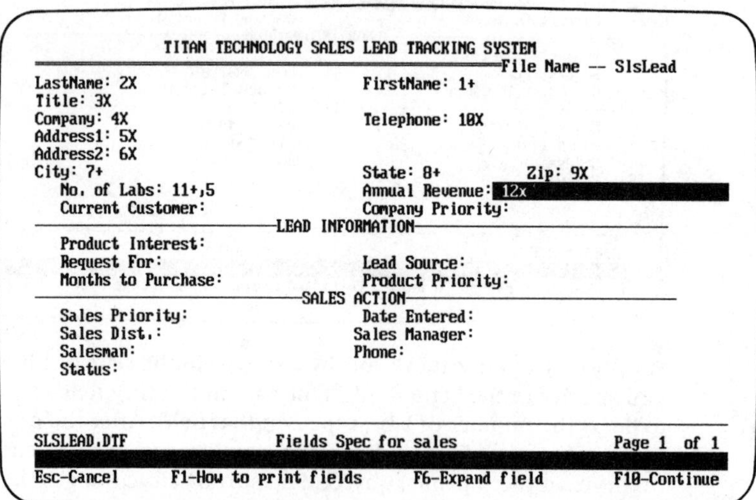


**Fig. 8.5.** *The Fields Spec screen.*

You print free-form fields by placing either an *X* (upper- or lowercase) or + (plus sign) in the fields you want to print. An X tells Q&A to print the field and move down one line; a + causes the program to print the field, skip a space, and print the next field. You also can specify how many lines should follow an X field and how many spaces should follow a + field. The following examples show how Q&A interprets these symbols:

| *If you enter* | *Q&A prints* |
|---|---|
| 1X,3 | That field first and moves the cursor down three lines |
| 2+,3 | That field second and moves the cursor right three spaces |

Although Q&A Write includes a mailing-label routine that provides easy flexible mailing-label preparation, you can prepare labels and similar special reports with

File's free-form printing. For example, if you have a file that includes names and addresses, you can number the fields and set carriage returns to construct mailing labels. The field locations on the form can be in any order. When you number the fields during free-form printing, you tell Q&A how actually to print the information.

The free-form printing style is basically line oriented because it lets you specify where data prints only in relation to the preceding printed field. When you specify 6X, for example, you are telling Q&A to print this field sixth in line and to follow the information with a carriage return. Where field number 6 actually is printed depends on where field number 5 is printed (see fig. 8.6).

The coordinate style can be used to generate custom-designed reports and to transfer information to preprinted forms. In the coordinate style, you specify field length and the exact printing location of the fields by row and column coordinates. Unlike free-form printing, coordinate printing is page oriented because you can print any field

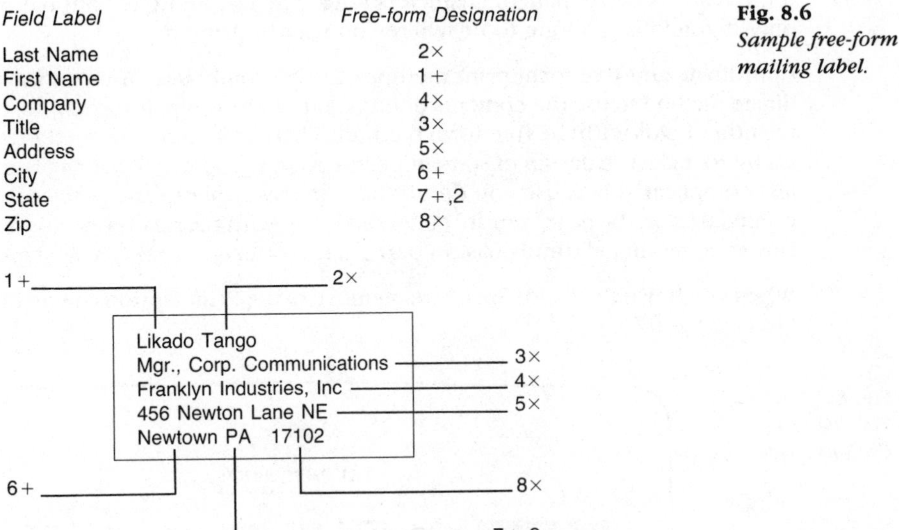


**Fig. 8.6** *Sample free-form mailing label.*

in the record anywhere on the page regardless of where other fields are printed. Coordinate printing is particularly useful if you are printing File output in preprinted forms and you need to have the data fit precisely in a predetermined location. You can print only one form per page with coordinate style.

The concept of coordinates assigns a unique designation to every possible printing position on the page. Two numbers are required to define any point on the page: one for the horizontal position and another for the vertical position. You can think of coordinates like a spreadsheet's rows and columns or the coordinate positions on an XY graph. The first printing position on the upper left corner of the page is equivalent to the A1 spreadsheet location or the intersection of the X and Y axes on a graph.

This first position is designated in Q&A by the numbers 1,1, for the first row in the first column. Some other printing and screen graphics programs designate this first position as 0,0. Q&A makes understanding the concept easier by using a designation more in line with the way people think.

From this home position you can define any other page position by increasing the row and column numbers the proper amount. The approximate center position on the first printing line of an 8.5-inch page, for example, is 1,40. Notice that the first number is for the row, the second number is for the character column. The center printing position on the 20th printing line is 20,40. Q&A will accept these specs separated by a comma or a space.

To construct coordinate reports, you enter two or three numbers (column number, line number, and field length), separated by commas, in the fields you want to print. For example, suppose that you enter *4,6,10* in the Company field. The company name from each record will be printed starting at column 6, line 4 and will be truncated if the name is more than 10 characters long. The last figure is optional; you use it only if a field is too long to fit where you want it printed.

Coordinate and free-form print methods can be combined. You can use the coordinate method to use the contents of one field as a heading, for example; then print the other fields with the free-form method. This combination of methods might be useful to make the design of some reports easier. Free-form reporting is sometimes less complicated because you do not have to worry about the precise location of printed data on the page. You are concerned only with the relative positions of fields. However, mixing methods has no particular advantage from Q&A's standpoint.

When you finish the Fields Spec screen, move to the Print Options menu by pressing F10 (see fig. 8.7).

**Fig. 8.7**
***The File Print Options screen.***

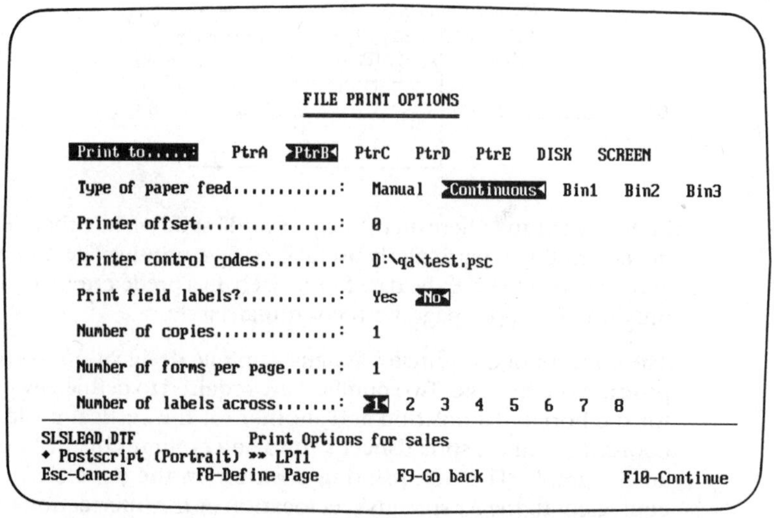

```
                         FILE PRINT OPTIONS

Print to.....:     PtrA  ►PtrB◄  PtrC  PtrD  PtrE  DISK  SCREEN

Type of paper feed...........:  Manual  ►Continuous◄  Bin1  Bin2  Bin3

Printer offset...............:  0

Printer control codes........:  D:\qa\test.psc

Print field labels?..........:  Yes ►No◄

Number of copies.............:  1

Number of forms per page.....:  1

Number of labels across......:  ►1◄ 2  3  4  5  6  7  8

SLSLEAD.DTF              Print Options for sales
◆ Postscript (Portrait) »» LPT1
Esc-Cancel         F8-Define Page        F9-Go back            F10-Continue
```

### *Selecting Print Spec Options*

The File Print Options screen gives you an opportunity to change some of the report output options. You can choose among five printers, a disk file, and the screen. You also can enter printer offset and printer control codes from this screen. The Printer Offset option lets you choose the default left margin for printed material. The default is 0, but you may need to change this setting to account for special paper sizes or to allow for operational peculiarities of your printer. The Printer Control Codes option allows you to send special instructions to your printer to control font selection or other features. You can turn on compressed print, for example, or send PostScript commands directly to the printer by entering the proper codes in this field.

After you specify the number of copies you want to print, you need to enter the number of forms you want on each printed page. Q&A's default for this setting is 1. If you are printing the contents of only a few fields from a small database and your printed page is mostly blank, you may want to change this option.

One full database screen covers 21 printed lines. If each record from your database uses only one screen, you may want to set your printer page length at 66 (on the Define Page screen) and the number of forms per printed page option to 3. You will get three records on each page and save paper. Of course, you may have good reason to print only one record per page and leave the rest blank. If you need to sort the printed records, if you need to distribute parts to different locations, if you are putting the printouts into a notebook, or if you need to make hand-written notes on each record, leave one record per page.

When you have completed your choices from the File Print Options screen, you can press F8 to call up the Define Page screen in order to format the appearance of page contents.

## *Enhancing the Printout with Define Page*

When the Define Page screen is displayed, you can change margins, page width, page length, and characters per inch. You also have an opportunity to set headers and footers from this screen (see fig. 8.8). The default for this screen is a page width of 85 characters and a length of 66 lines. The right margin is set for 85 characters.

### *Changing Defaults*

You change the default settings on the Define Page screen by highlighting the options you want to change and typing the new setting in the space after that option. You can enter the new settings in inches or as the number of rows or columns. For example, if you want to specify dimensions in inches, you add the inch mark (") after each number.

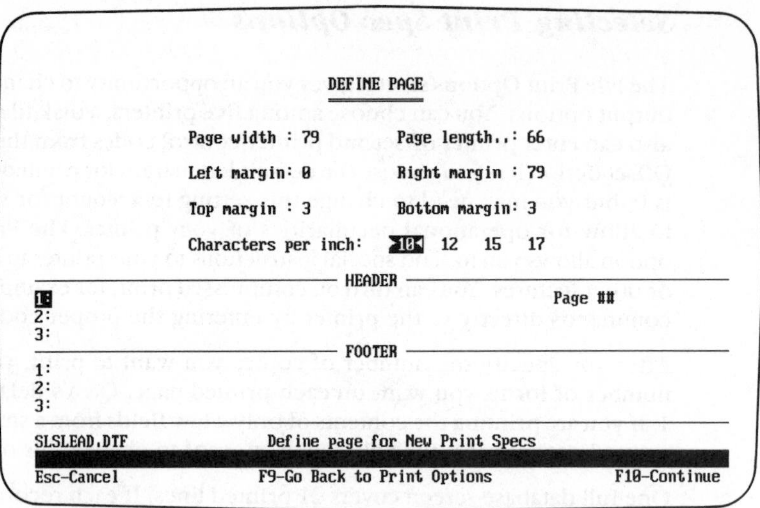


**Fig. 8.8**
*The Define Page screen.*

You also can change pitch (the number of characters per inch) with the Define Page screen. Ten characters per inch is used most often, but 12-pitch, which corresponds to a typewriter's elite type, is popular also. The third option, 15-pitch, may cause characters to overlap on some daisy-wheel or laser printers, unless you change the print wheel or font cartridge. The final option is 17-pitch, which produces condensed type on most dot-matrix printers. Some printers respond properly to this command only if they are set to print in draft mode.

## Using Headers and Footers

You can use the Define Page option to customize your printouts by adding headers and footers to pages before printing. The procedure is simple. Just tab down to where the word `HEADER` is displayed. Position the cursor on the line below the word and type the text you want to appear at the top of each page of your printout. Handle bottom-of-page information in the same way by typing footer text below the `FOOTER` prompt. You may use the three available lines in the header and footer areas for anything you want. You can use one line or all three.

If you want the pages to be numbered automatically, place a pound sign (#) at the position on the line where you want the number to appear. If you put two pound signs together on a line in a header (*page ##*, for example), Q&A prints a pound sign with the page number. At the top of the third page, for example, you see

page #3

In other words, when two pound signs are next to each other in a header or footer, the program interprets the first sign literally and computes and enters a page number to replace the second pound sign.

Through the settings on the Define Page screen, you can have Q&A read the date and time from the system clock and enter them in a header or footer. Just type *@DATE(n)* where you want the date to appear and *@TIME(n)* where the time is to be displayed. The *n* stands for the date or time format. For @DATE, the *n* can be a number from 1 to 20; for @TIME, the *n* can be a number from 1 to 3 (see Chapter 2 for details).

You can separate the header and footer lines into three segments by using exclamation points (!) between the sections. For example, if you enter

@DATE(1) ! WEEKLY REPORT ! Page #

Q&A prints the footer as

August 12, 1988 WEEKLY REPORT Page 6

Everything before the first exclamation point is left-justified, the section following the first exclamation point is centered, and the section after the second exclamation point is right-justified. Remember that Q&A treats spaces as characters, so any spaces in the information formatted with the exclamation point will be included in the formatting. Unnecessary spaces may throw off centering and justification. Without the second exclamation point, everything to the right of the first exclamation point is centered.

In the following header, all the data will be right-justified because the header command is preceded by two exclamation points:

!! @DATE @TIME Page ##

As a result, the header is printed as

August 12, 1988 5:43 pm Page #6

### *Saving Your Print Spec and Printing*

After you finish designing and customizing your Print Spec, you can save the choices by pressing F10 from the Print Options screen or the Define Page screen. At this point, you can print your information from the specifications you have entered, or you can return to the Print menu without printing. In either case, the Print Spec you have just designed is saved to disk, and you can print the spec later if you desire. If you print, the Print menu is displayed after the printing is complete.

## *Using Existing Print Specs*

So far in this section, you have learned to design and use a Print Spec to specify how a printed report will appear. After the Spec is created, you can rename it, copy it, delete it, or design a new one. You also can make temporary changes to the Print Spec.

To use an existing Print Spec, select P from the File menu. Type a file name or erase the name that appears, if any, and press Enter to display a list of file names. You then move the highlighting to the database you want and press Enter. When the Print menu appears, select P for Print Forms. A list of existing Print Spec names is displayed. Using the cursor keys, highlight the Spec you want to use and press Enter again.

Before the printing begins, a screen message asks whether you want to make any temporary changes to the design before you print. You can use this opportunity to modify the Retrieve Spec, for example, or to select a printer different from the one specified when the Print Spec was designed. If you choose to make temporary changes by selecting Y and pressing Enter, each specification screen used in designing a Print Spec is displayed.

When you elect to make temporary changes to a Print Spec, you are led through a series of screens identical to those you have seen before. On the Retrieve Spec, you specify the forms to be printed. If you want to enter sort specifications, you go to the Sort Spec screen by pressing F8. Then, from either the Retrieve or the Sort Spec, you can press F10 to get to the Fields Spec. After you have specified the field arrangement on the Fields Spec screen, press F10 to access the Print Options screen. You then can press F8 if you want to go to the Define Page options. Then, from either Print Options or Define Page, you can press F10 to start the printing process.

If you select N and press Enter, the printing process begins. While the document is being printed, you may see that you need to change some of the specifications. To make changes, press Shift-F9 and the printing will stop. Instead of going through all the specification screens, you can access directly the screen you want to change. The direct access menu is shown in figure 8.9. Press F2, choose the screen you want to edit, make the changes, and press F10 to start the printing from the beginning of the print job.

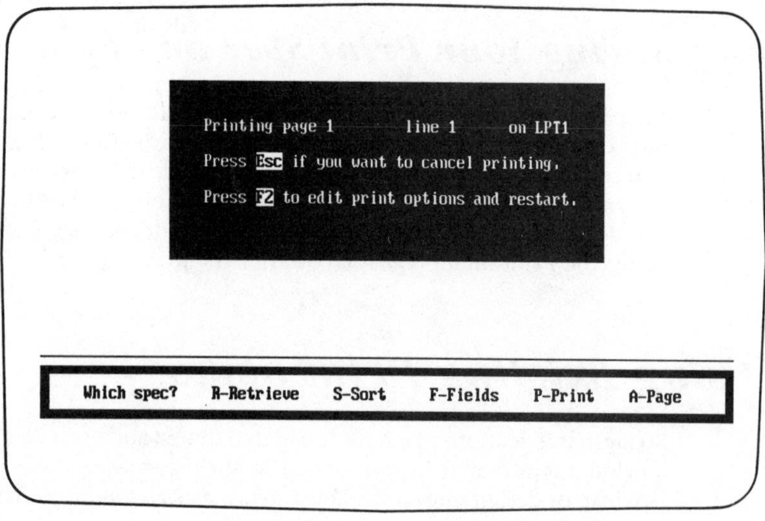

Printing page 1 line 1 on LPT1
Press Esc if you want to cancel printing.
Press F2 to edit print options and restart.
Which spec? R-Retrieve S-Sort F-Fields P-Print A-Page


**Fig. 8.9** *The direct access menu.*

### Renaming and Copying a Print Spec

In addition to creating a new Print Spec or modifying an existing one, you can rename or copy a print specification. The Rename/Delete/Copy menu accesses these options.

When you select Rename a Print Spec or Copy a Print Spec, you are asked for the name of the Print Spec. Press Enter to see a list of defined print specifications if you can't remember the name of the Spec you want. Use the cursor keys to highlight the name of the Print Spec you want and press Enter. If you are using the Rename command, you are prompted for the new name. If you have selected Copy, you are asked for the name of the specification to which you are copying.

### Deleting Print Specs

If you choose to delete a Print Spec, a different prompt is displayed. After you enter a Print Spec name, Q&A asks for confirmation before the spec is deleted.

Because Print Specs are stored within the database and are not DOS files, no disk utility can restore the erased specification. If you accidentally delete a Print Spec, you can't get it back; you will have to create the specification again. If you are sure that you want to delete, select Y and press Enter. The Print Spec is deleted.

## Using Special Printing Procedures

Q&A provides several advanced printing features. You can choose from among several fonts to change the entire look of your printed document. You also can use the PostScript command language. Other commands give you increased control over your printer.

### Selecting and Using Different Fonts

With Q&A Version 3.0, Symantec recognized the rising popularity of laser printers. The software now includes special files so that you can use the multiple font capabilities of laser printers.

A font, sometimes called a typeface, is a group of letters, numbers, and symbols of a particular style and size. When you change fonts, you change the size of the characters, their weight, perhaps the pitch, and certainly the overall general appearance.

Type falls into four main classes: roman, sans serif, script, and black letter. Within each class can be several hundred fonts, one for each set of characters of a particular typeface, size, and style. Some common font names are Gothic, Courier, Helvetica, and Times Roman.

Character size is measured in points, each point being 1/72nd of an inch tall. In traditional set type, sizes range from 4-point to 144-point. Most newspapers use 8- or 9-point type. This book is set in 9.5-point type. A large newspaper headline may be 72-point type, or one inch tall.

Type weight is the relative darkness or lightness of the characters. In mechanical computer printers, such as dot-matrix or daisy-wheel devices, darker weight is usually achieved by hitting the paper harder and more often for each letter, sometimes with the paper offset slightly from the original position. Laser printer mechanisms achieve the same results by depositing more material at the print position instead of making multiple passes.

Using multiple fonts with Q&A requires one of Q&A's font support files, and a printer with its own internal or cartridge fonts. Q&A does not supply actual fonts to the printer—only the instructions to use the fonts built into or downloaded to the printer. To change fonts at the printer level, you usually must plug in one or more electronic cartridges that store the various typefaces. Some printers support downloadable fonts. In this case, you transfer the soft font information from a floppy or hard disk, through the printer port, to the printer. If your printer uses downloadable fonts, you must load the fonts from DOS—outside Q&A—before you can use Q&A's font support. Most printers of this type have diskette-based utility software to help you with this procedure. Refer to your printer manual for detailed instructions.

## *Printing with PostScript Command Files*

Different printers use different instructions to select characters and graphics. One standard instruction set that is available on many printers is PostScript, a printer-control command language used to define font and page characteristics. Because PostScript has become a printing standard, the number of printer-control languages any software or hardware manufacturer must support has been reduced. By supporting PostScript, software can output information to any PostScript-compatible printer, and the number of printers that support PostScript is growing rapidly.

If you have a PostScript printer, such as a QMS PS-810 or a NEC LC-890, specify PostScript fonts for your File reports on the File Print Options screen (again see fig. 8.7). On the Printer Control Codes line, you type the name of a file that store special printer features, such as PostScript procedures or font definitions. During printing, the File print routine sends the specified control file to the printer at the beginning of each form.

An important function of PostScript support in Q&A is to reduce the number of special control files needed for a broad range of printers. Your printer may have a control language of its own; but if your printer also supports PostScript, as many do, you can use the PostScript file for almost all printer operations. Although Q&A supports many printers, with PostScript you can change printers without changing the printer definitions file.

Such computer industry standards are making life in a heterogeneous hardware and software environment much easier for users of these products.

### *Using Other Printer Commands*

If your printer does not support PostScript, you can send the command sequences directly from the File print routine. Use the Printer Control Codes line from the File Print Options screen. Instead of specifying a file name for Q&A to send to the printer (as you do to send a PostScript command file), enter a command that specifies a printer-resident font name, the point size, weight, and other features. Q&A calls this line the On Code, and it has the format:

!Font Points (Ln In Sn)

The exclamation point at the beginning of the line differentiates the printer command line from a PostScript command file name. *Font* is the name of any font your printer recognizes and *Points* is the font size in 1/72nd-inch intervals. If you enter *4* for *Points*, the font is four points high, or 4/72nds of an inch. A one-inch-high font is specified as 72. To enter this point size, type *!Font 72*. The range of possible values for *Points* depends on your printer.

The parameters in parentheses are optional and can be used to set

Ln Line spacing, where *n* is the number of points between lines. The default value for Ln is L12, which provides the standard 6 lines per inch (72/12 = 6).

In Control for accented characters in the IBM character set. If you accept the default (I1), Q&A matches the IBM character set where possible. If your printer does not support PostScript fonts, use I0.

Sn Symbol table selection. Q&A automatically matches the IBM character set as closely as possible. Standard PostScript characters are switched with others to match the IBM set. To disable this feature, enter S0.

## *Creating Specific Applications*

As suggested in earlier sections of this chapter, File's print features support a variety of specialized printing features, including printing labels and filling in other printed forms. Although most stick-on labels are called mailing labels, you can use them to print labels for inventory items or for other functions. This section gives you two specific applications for these special printing features accessible from within File.

## Mailing Labels

You can use File's free-form printing option to design a print specification for mailing labels and other special forms. Before you design a mailing label spec in File, however, investigate the possibility of doing the job from the Write module. Q&A Write includes some features for preparing mailing labels from data in File, and these features could save you time. See Chapter 13 for more information for printing mailing labels from Write.

Free-form printing from File can support label formats from one-up (one label horizontally across the page) to eight-up (eight labels across the page). The label becomes a custom-size form, as if you were printing on a very small piece of paper. Change print options defaults item on the File Print Global Options screen. The last selection on the screen is Number of Labels Across, and you can select from 1 through 8.

The first step in designing a label Print Spec is to determine the size of your labels. How many lines at standard line spacing (6 lines per inch) will the label hold? How many characters will fit across the label? Information from the label supplier should give you these figures.

Next, decide which fields should appear on the label and in what order. Refer to the previous section on changing the order of printed fields in free-form printing. The previous information on sorting also applies to label printing.

To print labels from a File database, define a Print Spec for labels by placing X's and +'s, as explained earlier, into the appropriate fields on the Fields Spec screen. For example, to print standard mailing labels from a name and address file, use the free-form style and mark the fields as shown in figure 8.10. Particularly when you have different fields for first and last names, you will want to specify field order, as shown.

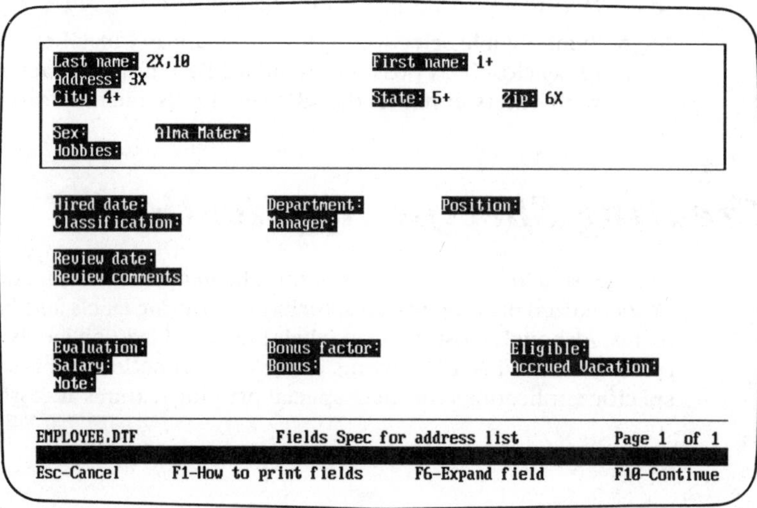


**Fig. 8.10** *Free-form printing of mailing labels.*

If the combined first and last name, the address field, or other label information will be longer than the width of the label, you can truncate some fields by placing at the end of that field's Print Spec a number that tells Q&A how many characters to print. The field width specification follows the spacing instructions. The sample in figure 8.10 shows the first name field shortened to 10 characters to make room for the long last name field.

## *Preprinted Forms*

Q&A's coordinate printing, mentioned earlier in this chapter, lets you specify precisely where File fields will be printed. You make this specification by placing coordinate numbers in the fields you want to print.

You can use coordinate printing in Q&A to print File information on preprinted forms. This capability is useful in preparing purchase orders, invoices, and other lists from the File database. The only limitation is that you can print only one record per page. Q&A has no provision for looping on fields to allow you, for example, to print a page header with information from the first record, and then fill in sequential lines with subsequent records.

You can, however, fill in forms such as employee evaluations or single-sheet product descriptions from a File database. Suppose that you are using the inventory and product description file shown in figure 8.11. This data file tracks some of the usual inventory information and, in addition, carries product specifications that might be useful in a reference catalog for an outside sales force or counter sales.

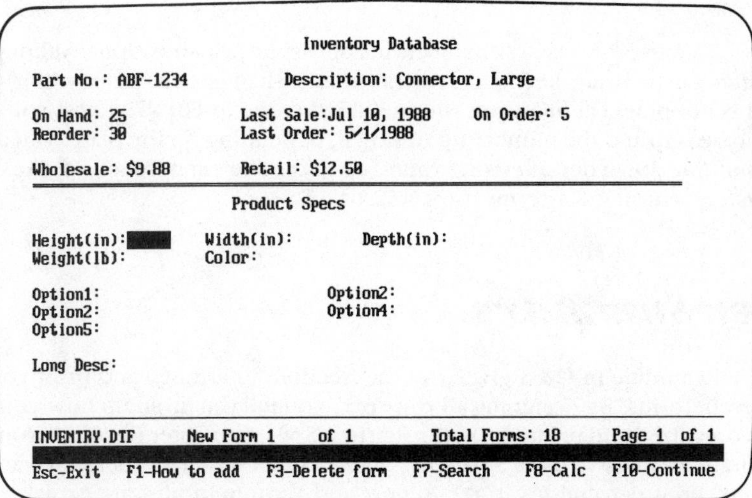


**Fig. 8.11** *The inventory database record.*

You have forms printed on colored paper to present the basic information of company name and address, telephone numbers, and any advertising copy you want. The remainder of the form is used for information about individual products. As the database changes, you print replacement catalog sheets for the sales force and single-sheet summary forms to mail to prospective clients for information and advertising.

If you are using preprinted forms as opposed to custom-designed forms, you should ask your supplier for a forms programming, or forms coordinate, sheet. A forms coordinate sheet is a reproduction of the form with print coordinates shown for each piece of information. Most suppliers have these sheets, which can greatly reduce your forms setup time.

If you don't have a forms coordinate sheet, you can make one from graph paper. Use paper with an even number of squares per inch. If you use paper that has 10 squares per inch and a font that prints 10 characters per inch, for instance, you can convert the number of squares directly to print positions.

First, in your File database, number the fields that will be printed on the form. Next, use a ruler to determine the coordinates on the preprinted form. Measure from the left side to get the column position and from the top to get the row number. If you find that one print position, for example, is 4.5 inches from the top and 5.25 inches from the left side, you now have the print coordinates in inches:

Row = 4.50 inches
Column = 5.25 inches

In Q&A format, these coordinates are expressed as 4.50,5.25. Q&A, however, does not use inches to position the print head on the page; the program uses print positions. Standard characters print 10 per inch, so these coordinates in Q&A are expressed as 45,52.5.

Oops! Q&A uses only whole numbers in coordinate print positions. Although today's printers can be controlled in increments smaller than one character width, this precision is not practical in a print routine like the one in File. The best you can do in this case is round the number up or down, depending on the blank you are filling. If rounding down doesn't work, round up to the nearest number. So, to express this measurement in Q&A terms use 45,52 or 45,53.

## Chapter Summary

The File module of Q&A gives you the freedom to arrange and print your data in different forms. By designing a Print Spec, you tell the program how you want the data organized and printed. On the Retrieve Spec, you enter the fields you want the program to find. With the Sort Spec, you tell Q&A in what order you want the data sorted. Print capabilities in the Report and Write modules are explained later in this book.

The next chapter introduces you to the Write module with some Quick Start hints.

# Part III

# Using Q&A Write

Includes

Q&A Write Quick Start
Creating a Write Document
Enhancing a Write Document
Merging Documents with Q&A Write
Printing a Write Document

Chapter 9

# Q&A Write Quick Start

Q&A's word-processing module is Write. Write is easy to use and offers many word-processing features:

- Search and replace text
- Check spelling
- Use mailmerge (with the File module)
- Use headers and footers
- Enhance characters by making them italic, boldface, or underlined
- Perform calculations within a document

Many related capabilities are available as well. The Write module contains a full set of help screens that you can access when creating documents by pressing F1 (Info). When you're editing and creating documents, the wordwrap feature is used. And you can edit documents by using the Insert key to add text or by using the ''strikeover'' feature to type over existing text.

In this quick start chapter you will learn how to create, save, format, edit, print, and retrieve documents in Write. You will apply many of Write's most essential capabilities to two documents you will create.

## *Creating a New Document*

You access the Write module from the Q&A Main menu the same way as the File module.

1. From the Q&A Main menu, select Write. The Write menu, which has eight options, is displayed.

To create a new document, follow these steps:

2. Select Type/Edit from the Write menu.

A screen appears that closely resembles the file form design screen in the File module. The file name displayed in the lower left corner is `Working Copy`, and several new function keys are listed on the key assignment line.

3. Press F1 (Info) and review the function key assignments. Press Esc (Exit) to return to the blank screen.

You will start by typing a letter to your insurance agent, reporting a loss due to a fire in your den.

4. Move your cursor to the upper left corner of the screen and type the following letter. Press the Enter key only to separate paragraphs and address lines. Don't worry about spelling errors, because you will correct them later:

   National Fire Insurance Company Pte. Ltd.
   2345 Flame Street
   Timber, Colorado 12345

   Dear Sirs:

   I would like to submit a claim against my homeowner's insurance policy for a radio damaged in an electrical fire. The radio was totally destroyed and cannot be repaired. Because I have no deductible amount to be satisfied on this claim, I am submitting the information on the radio along with a copy of the fire department's report on the fire.

   Thank you for your prompt attention.

## *Adding a Signature Block*

Letters usually have a signature block at the bottom for the writer's name and signature. Before you add a signature block, you must add a tab setting to the document, using the Options menu.

1. From any location in the document, press F8 (Options) to view the Options menu. This menu is used for headers, footers, tabs, centering, insertions, page breaks, and lines and boxes.
2. Select Set Tabs from the Options menu. The cursor disappears from the document section of the screen and reappears on the ruler line.
3. Using the left- and right-arrow keys, move the cursor to a position slightly more than halfway across the ruler line, type *t* for a standard tab, and press F10 to return to your document. A *T* appears on the ruler line to mark the tab setting.

You can set a decimal tab by following the same procedure but typing *d* rather than *t*. Now you can add the signature block two lines below the last paragraph of your document.

4. Press Enter twice if needed, to create a blank line after the last paragraph of the letter.

5. Press the Tab key to move across the page to the tab you just set, and type

   *Sincerely,*

6. Press Enter three times to create two blank lines, press the Tab key to move beneath *Sincerely,* and type your name. Figure 9.1 illustrates how your screen should look.

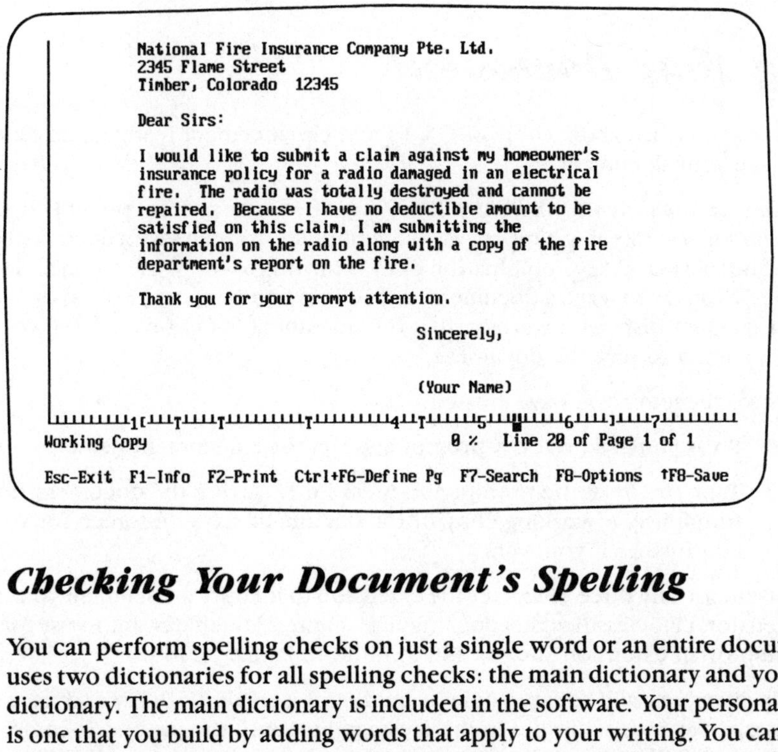

```
National Fire Insurance Company Pte. Ltd.
2345 Flame Street
Timber, Colorado  12345

Dear Sirs:

I would like to submit a claim against my homeowner's
insurance policy for a radio damaged in an electrical
fire.  The radio was totally destroyed and cannot be
repaired.  Because I have no deductible amount to be
satisfied on this claim, I am submitting the
information on the radio along with a copy of the fire
department's report on the fire.

Thank you for your prompt attention.

                              Sincerely,


                              (Your Name)

Working Copy                               0 %  Line 20 of Page 1 of 1

Esc-Exit  F1-Info  F2-Print  Ctrl+F6-Define Pg  F7-Search  F8-Options  ↑F8-Save
```

**Fig. 9.1** *Adding a signature block to your letter.*

## *Checking Your Document's Spelling*

You can perform spelling checks on just a single word or an entire document. Q&A uses two dictionaries for all spelling checks: the main dictionary and your personal dictionary. The main dictionary is included in the software. Your personal dictionary is one that you build by adding words that apply to your writing. You can add words like customer names or terms that are unique to your industry or trade.

1. Press Ctrl-Home to move your cursor to the top left corner of the document, and press Shift-F1 to invoke the spelling checker.

   Q&A then checks the document for spelling errors (the message `Checking...` appears above the key assignment line). When Q&A finds an unknown word, the spelling menu appears. You can choose any of the following options (notice that you can add any word to your personal dictionary):

List Possible Spellings

Ignore Word & Continue

Add to Dictionary & Continue

Add to Dictionary & Stop

Edit Word & Recheck

2. Proceed through the document, using the spelling menu as needed. A message on the message line tells you when the spelling check is complete, and your cursor returns to its original location.

## *Saving Your Document*

Before you learn about some of Q&A's text-enhancement features, take a moment to save your document.

*Save your documents frequently.* By saving often, you prevent possibly losing your document if something happens to your computer. You can save a document by using the Shift-F8 (Save) key combination or by returning to the Write menu and selecting Save. If you try to leave a document and go into another part of the system without saving, Q&A displays a warning that the document is not saved and gives you the opportunity to save the document.

To save the letter you have created,

1. Press Shift-F8 (Save). A prompt appears for a document name.
2. Type *fire.ltr* at the prompt and press Enter, saving the document for future use. A working copy of the document stays on-screen for you to edit further if you want.

You can use any three-character file extension to identify a document you save. The extension LTR classifies this document as a letter. You may want to use MMO for a memo or an extension such as 188 to indicate January 1988.

This document will be saved quickly because it is small. With larger documents, the message `Saving...` flashes in the message line until the process is complete. The document will be saved for future use, but a working copy of it will still be on your screen for your editing. Each time you save the document, Q&A will remember the document name and fill it in. You don't need to change the name unless you want to save another copy of the document under a new name.

## *Enhancing Text for Emphasis*

By using the Shift-F6 key combination, you can do many things to improve the appearance of your letter: make text boldface, underlined, or italic; use subscript, postscript, and strikeout; select fonts; or switch settings back to regular type.

To make text boldface, follow this procedure:

1. Move your cursor to the start of the second sentence in your letter (*The radio was . . .*), and press Shift-F6 to display the enhance text menu.
2. Select Bold from that menu. A message appears on the message line, instructing you to select the text and press F10.
3. Use the arrow keys to highlight the entire sentence, and press F10. The portion of highlighted text is displayed in a different shade depending on your particular monitor (the text doesn't appear highlighted in the figures). When printed, this portion reflects the enhancement that you requested.

## *Using Search and Replace*

Now you will use Write's search and replace capacity. Instead of referring to the damaged item as a *radio*, you will refer to it as an *AM/FM radio*. You don't have to go through the letter and retype each occurrence of *radio* manually; Q&A will do the work for you.

1. From any location in the document, press F7 (Search). A search/replace box appears over your document. This dialog box has three fields: Search For, Replace With, and Method.
2. At the Search For field, type *a radio* and press Enter.
3. At the Replace With field, type *an AM/FM radio* and press the Enter key.
4. At the Method field, select the Manual option and press F10 to begin the search. Q&A will stop at each occurrence of *a radio* for you to approve the replacement.
5. Follow the prompt that appears on the message line for each occurrence of the phrase. Press F10 to replace and continue, F7 to search again, or Esc to cancel the operation.

   Figure 9.2 illustrates how your screen should look. Each occurrence of *a radio* is now *an AM/FM radio*.

**Fig. 9.2**
*Replacing a term with another term.*

```
National Fire Insurance Company Pte. Ltd.
2345 Flame Street
Timber, Colorado 12345

Dear Sirs:

I would like to submit a claim against my homeowner's
insurance policy for an AM/FM radio damaged in an
electrical fire. The radio was totally destroyed and
cannot be repaired. Because I have no deductible
amount to be satisfied on this claim, I am submitting
the information on the radio along with a copy of the
fire department's report on the fire.

Thank you for your prompt attention.

                                    Sincerely,

FIRE.LTR       Bold                   0 %   Line 9 of Page 1 of 1
Esc-Exit F1-Info F2-Print Ctrl+F6-Define Pg F7-Search F8-Options ↑F8-Save
```

## Setting Temporary Margins

Before you have a chance to mail the letter, you discover that damage also was done to the electrical wiring in the outlet. Your electrician estimates that the rewiring will cost $275.00. You need to add this claim to the letter. To emphasize the estimate, the text will be indented. When starting this process, check that you are in the Insert mode: `Insert` will be displayed in the status line. If the indicator isn't present, press the Ins key on the numeric keypad to activate this feature.

1. Move your cursor to the end of the first paragraph and press the Enter key twice to create a new paragraph.
2. Add the following paragraph:

   The following electrical work must be completed to repair damaged wiring:

3. Press Enter and continue typing the information on the estimate:

   Replacement of the outlet and adjoining wiring and testing of the circuit. Estimate $275.00 including parts and labor.

Now you will indent the estimate ten spaces from both the left and right margins.

4. Use the arrow keys to position your cursor on the *R* in *Replacement*. Press the space bar ten times to move the line ten spaces to the right.
5. Press F6, displaying the Set Temporary Margin menu along the bottom of the screen, and select Left from that menu. The paragraph moves ten spaces to the right, and a greater-than sign (>) appears on the ruler line, indicating a temporary left margin.

Now you will set the right margin.

6. Position your cursor ten spaces to the left of the right margin, which is indicated with a closing bracket (]). If you are going to split a word, move your cursor a few spaces to the left to avoid doing so.

7. Press F6 to display the Set Temporary Margin menu again, and select Right from that menu. The paragraph moves in from the right margin as you indicated, and a less-than sign (<) appears on the ruler line, as in figure 9.3.

```
National Fire Insurance Company Pte. Ltd.
2345 Flame Street
Timber, Colorado 12345

Dear Sirs:

I would like to submit a claim against my homeowner's
insurance policy for an AM/FM radio damaged in an
electrical fire. The radio was totally destroyed and
cannot be repaired. Because I have no deductible
amount to be satisfied on this claim, I am submitting
the information on the radio along with a copy of the
fire department's report on the fire.

The following electrical work must be completed to
repair damaged wiring:
            Replacement of the outlet and
            adjoining wiring and testing
            of the circuit. Estimate
            $275.00 including parts and
            labor.

FIRE.LTR                              Insert 0 %   Line 20 of Page 1 of 1

Esc-Exit  F1-Info  F2-Print  Ctrl+F6-Define Pg  F7-Search  F8-Options  ↑F8-Save
```

**Fig. 9.3**
*Temporary margins appear on the ruler line.*

To clear the temporary margins when you are through with them, choose Clear from the Set Temporary Margin menu.

## *Deleting a Line*

After reading the letter, you decide that the last sentence doesn't fit the tone you want to convey. Perhaps something milder would be appropriate. Deleting is easy in Write.

1. Move your cursor to the last sentence of the letter before the signature block (the sentence that reads, *Thank you for your prompt attention*).

2. Press Shift-F4 to delete that line.

The line, and thus the entire sentence, is deleted. If you want to delete only a word, you press F4, without the Shift key. Now let's add more information and replace the sentence.

## *Calculating within a Document*

Just to make sure that the insurance company knows the exact amount you are expecting, include a small table with a calculation. Q&A can perform several calculations within documents: total, average, count, multiply, and divide. You will total a column of numbers.

1. Type the following (with the Insert mode active):

   The total amount of my claim is as follows:
   AM/FM radio $ 79.95
   Electrical 275.00

2. To total these figures, move your cursor to the last *0* in *275.00* and press Alt-F9. The Calculation menu appears across the bottom of the screen.

3. Select Total from the Calculation menu. A message appears asking you to position your cursor where you want the result to appear and to press F10.

4. Position your cursor on the line directly below the *2* in *275.00*, and press F10. Q&A inserts the total of the two numbers.

Now you need a line to separate the two figures from the total.

5. Position your cursor on the *2* in *275.00*, and press Shift-F6 to display the enhance text menu.

6. Select Underline and move your cursor to highlight the entire amount of *275.00*.

7. Press F10 to underline the amount. On some screens the enhancement appears as reverse or brightened text (the text doesn't appear brighter in the figures). However, the amount will print underlined on paper.

Now add the final sentence to the letter.

8. Move your cursor one space past *354.95*, and press Enter twice to create a blank line for separation.

9. Type the following sentence:

   I appreciate any help you can give me to expedite my claim.

10. Press Enter to create a blank line beneath the sentence, and reposition the signature block so that *Sincerely* is even with the tab you set. Your letter should now look like figure 9.4.

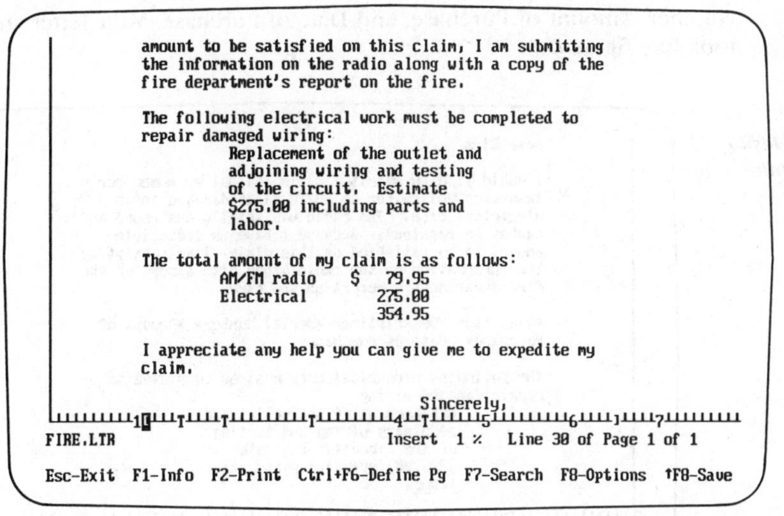

```
amount to be satisfied on this claim, I am submitting
the information on the radio along with a copy of the
fire department's report on the fire.

The following electrical work must be completed to
repair damaged wiring:
          Replacement of the outlet and
          adjoining wiring and testing
          of the circuit. Estimate
          $275.00 including parts and
          labor.

The total amount of my claim is as follows:
          AM/FM radio     $   79.95
          Electrical          275.00
                              354.95

I appreciate any help you can give me to expedite my
claim.

                              Sincerely,
FIRE.LTR                      Insert  1 %    Line 30 of Page 1 of 1

Esc-Exit  F1-Info  F2-Print  Ctrl+F6-Define Pg  F7-Search  F8-Options  ↑F8-Save
```

**Fig. 9.4** *Inserting a calculated total and a new closing sentence.*

# *Merging Information from the File Module*

The last step you will perform before printing the letter is *mailmerge*, the process of copying information from File into Write. With mailmerge you can insert directly into documents information that already exists in the File module. You entered information about the radio into a database called HOUSE.DTF. To import that information directly into the letter when printing, you first need to determine where you want the information to appear (it should be positioned between the first and second paragraphs). Then you need to insert the fields to be imported into the document.

1. Move your cursor to the end of the last sentence in the first paragraph.
2. Immediately following *fire*, press the Enter key twice to create two blank lines, and then press Alt-F7.
3. When Q&A asks for the name of the database that holds the information to be merged, type *house* and press Enter. (If you are unsure of the database name, you can press Enter at this prompt for a list of available databases.)

   On the right side of the screen, a menu appears listing field names within the HOUSE.DTF database.
4. Use the arrow keys to highlight the field name Quantity and press Enter. The field name will be copied into the document complete with asterisks necessary to complete the merge.
5. Repeat this process, separating each field by pressing the space bar once. Copy the following fields in this order: Description, Serial

Number, Amount of Purchase, and Date of Purchase. Your letter should look like figure 9.5.

**Fig. 9.5**
*Entering fields to be merged into your letter.*

```
Dear Sirs:

I would like to submit a claim against my homeowner's
insurance policy for an AM/FM radio damaged in an
electrical fire. The radio was totally destroyed and
cannot be repaired. Because I have no deductible
amount to be satisfied on this claim, I am submitting
the information on the radio along with a copy of the
fire department's report on the fire.

*Quantity* *Description* *Serial Number* *Amount of
Purchase* *Date of Purchase*

The following electrical work must be completed to
repair damaged wiring:
          Replacement of the outlet and
          adjoining wiring and testing
          of the circuit. Estimate
          $275.00 including parts and
          labor.

FIRE.LTR                          Insert 1 %  Line 16 of Page 1 of 1

Esc-Exit F1-Info F2-Print Ctrl+F6-Define Pg F7-Search F8-Options ↑F8-Save
```

# Printing Your Document

Now you will print the letter to see what it looks like. You use the Print Options screen to specify what you want printed and how.

1. Press F2 (Print) from any location in the document to begin the print operation. The first screen you see is the Print Options screen.

2. Insert a blank formatted floppy disk in drive A.

3. Change the Print To setting to DISK, and check for the following settings on the Print Options screen:

   From Page . . . . . . . . . : 1    To Page . . . : 1
   Number of copies . . . : 1    Print Offset: 0
   Line Spacing . . . . . . . : Single
   Justify . . . . . . . . . . . . : No
   Print to . . . . . . . . . . . : DISK
   Type of Paper Feed . . : Continuous
   Number of Columns . : 1
   Printer Control Codes: (blank)
   Name of Merge File . : C:\QA\FILE\HOUSE.DTF

   Q&A remembers the merge file from the mailmerge operation.

Now you should check the Define Page screen to be sure that margins, width, length, and headers (when used) are specified.

4. Press Ctrl-F6 (Define Pg), and check for the following settings on the Define Page screen that appears:

   Left Margin: 10 — Right Margin .: 68
   Top Margin: 6 — Bottom Margin: 6
   Page Width: 78 — Page Length . .: 66
   Characters Per Inch: 10
   Begin Header/Footer on Page # . . . :1
   Begin Page Numbering with Page #:1

5. Press F2 to return to the Print Options screen.

6. Press F10 (Continue), displaying the Disk Print menu. Documents that are printed to disk are automatically converted into a standardized code that can be read by other computers and software programs.

7. From the Disk Print menu select IBM ASCII Format, and press Enter. Write displays a prompt for the file name.

8. Type *a:fire.ltr* at the prompt and press Enter. A Retrieve Spec appears. You want to specify which form you want merged with the letter.

9. In the Item field of the Retrieve Spec, type *radio* (see fig. 9.6).

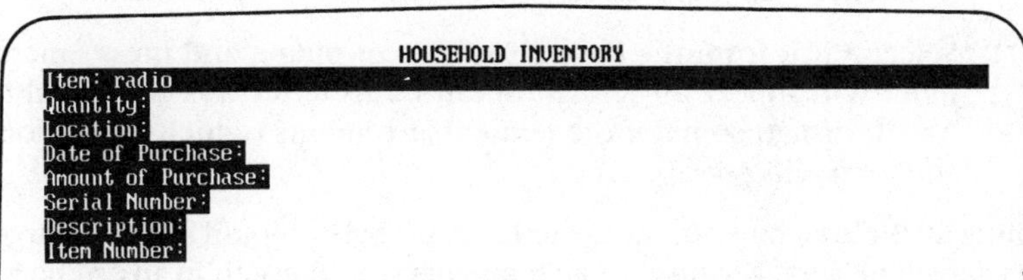


**Fig. 9.6** *Entering the form to merge into the letter.*

Because the printing process will be quick, let's preview what will happen after you press F10 (Continue). Q&A will go into the database HOUSE.DTF and scan the forms to retrieve the form for *radio*. When Q&A retrieves this form, the form will flash momentarily on your screen. A message will appear on the message line indicating that Q&A is preparing to print the document. Then a block will appear, telling you which line and page are currently printing. The light on the front of drive A should be on, showing that the disk is in use and the document is being saved to it. When the process is finished, Q&A will return you to your document.

10. Press F10 (Continue) and watch the printing process.

11. After printing is completed, save your document and then press Esc (Exit) to return to the Write menu. Figure 9.7 illustrates how the final letter looks with the mailmerge fields completed.

If you want to retrieve the final letter from your disk to review it,

12. Choose Get from the Write menu.

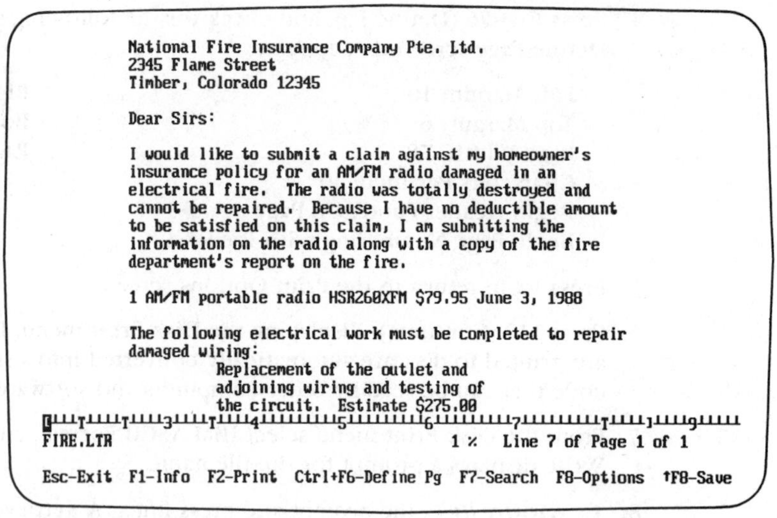

**Fig. 9.7** *Your letter printed on-screen.*

```
National Fire Insurance Company Pte. Ltd.
2345 Flame Street
Timber, Colorado 12345

Dear Sirs:

I would like to submit a claim against my homeowner's
insurance policy for an AM/FM radio damaged in an
electrical fire. The radio was totally destroyed and
cannot be repaired. Because I have no deductible amount
to be satisfied on this claim, I am submitting the
information on the radio along with a copy of the fire
department's report on the fire.

1 AM/FM portable radio HSR260XFM $79.95 June 3, 1988

The following electrical work must be completed to repair
damaged wiring:
              Replacement of the outlet and
              adjoining wiring and testing of
              the circuit. Estimate $275.00
FIRE.LTR                                    1 %   Line 7 of Page 1 of 1

Esc-Exit  F1-Info  F2-Print  Ctrl+F6-Define Pg  F7-Search  F8-Options  ↑F8-Save
```

13. At the document name prompt, change the document name to *a:fire.ltr* and press Enter. Q&A recognizes that the document is in a different format and displays the Import Document menu.
14. Select ASCII from the Import Document menu, and press Enter. The letter will appear on-screen. Because this letter was converted to ASCII format, some of the text enhancements (which ASCII doesn't support) will not appear.

Mailing all the attachments with your letter probably would require a large envelope with a mailing label, because the attachments would not fit in an ordinary envelope. To generate mailing labels, you use the Mailing Labels command from the Write menu, the Mailing Label Print Options screen, and a Retrieve Spec. However, the specific steps you must take vary depending on your hardware configuration. For more information on mailing labels, see Chapter 13.

## Creating Another Document

There are a few more features that you should practice using the information you have developed. Your electrician has requested a similar letter to authorize the required electrical repair. This letter can use the same text but needs to be addressed to Shocky's Speedy Electrical Repair Service. Shocky's also requires a copy of the letter to send to the insurance company, as verification that the claim has been filed for payment.

## *Copying Text*

You will copy a portion of the insurance company's letter into a new document; add the electrical company's name, address, and salutation; and add a closing.

1. Select Type/Edit from the Write menu to return to your letter.
2. Move the cursor to the beginning of the third paragraph in the letter (*The following electrical work* . . .).

You can press F1 (Info) to find which function key copies a block to a file (Ctrl-F5). You can see from the help screen that two copy features are available. With F5 you can copy a block of text to another location in the same document. To copy a block of text into a new file or document, you use Ctrl-F5. Press Esc to clear the help screen.

3. Press Ctrl-F5. A message appears on the message line, asking you to select the text you want to copy.
4. Using the arrow keys, highlight the paragraph starting *The following electrical work* . . . and including the next paragraph, containing the estimate information (see fig. 9.8).
5. Press F10 to continue. A prompt asks you for the file name to which to copy the block of text.
6. Enter the file name. Call the letter *electric.ltr*. Press the Enter key to save the text to the new document file.

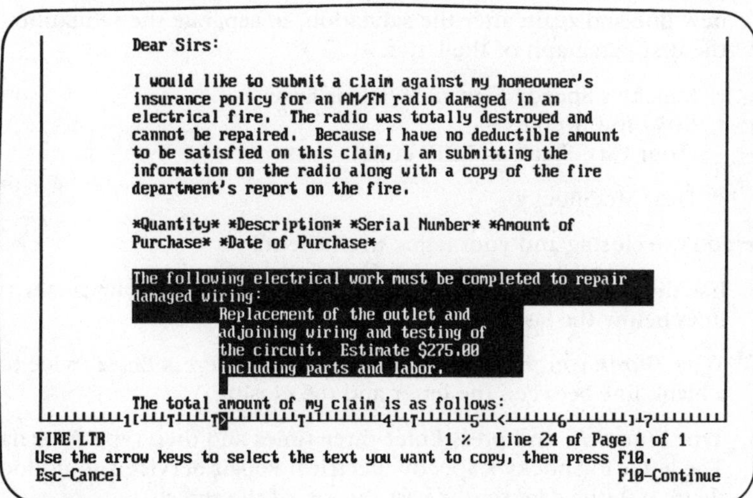


**Fig. 9.8** *Selecting the text to copy.*

Moving text is done the same way as copying text. You can move text within a document or into a new document just as you did with the copy function except that you use Shift-F5 and Alt-F5.

## *Adding Text*

The selected information is now copied into a new document. You will edit the letter to reflect the electrical company information.

1. Press Esc to return to the Write menu.

2. Select Get from the Write menu for the document ELECTRIC.LTR, and press Enter. The new document appears on your screen.

The letter still needs a date, address, and salutation and requires a closing and your name.

Your cursor should be located in the top left corner of your screen. Be sure that you are in Insert mode (if not, press the Ins key on the numeric keypad to activate Insert).

3. Press Enter once to create a blank line. Press the up-arrow key to move your cursor to the first space of the blank line.

Just to make this exercise a bit different, let's not use the same format as used for FIRE.LTR. Instead of having the closing and signature area to the right of center on the page, you will format it left-aligned on the page.

4. Type today's date. Press the Enter key four times to insert four blank spaces between the date and the beginning of the address.

Now you will add the name, address, and salutation to the letter.

5. Enter the name and address as shown, pressing the Enter key for each new line and again after the salutation, to separate the salutation from the first paragraph of the letter:

   Shocky's Speedy Electrical Repair Service
   9054 Jolt Avenue
   (Your City, State, and ZIP code)

   Dear Mr. Shocky:

Now add the closing and your name to this letter.

6. Use the down-arrow key and the Enter key to move your cursor two lines below the last sentence of the letter.

7. Type *Thank you for your help in this matter.* Press Enter twice to make a blank line between the letter and the closing.

8. Type *Sincerely,* and press Enter three times and then type your name. The letter to Shocky's Speedy Electrical Repair Service should look like figure 9.9 (the date scrolls past the top of the screen).

```
Shocky's Speedy Electrical Repair Service
9054 Jolt Avenue
(Your City, State and Zip Code)

Dear Mr. Shocky:

The following electrical work must be completed to repair damaged
wiring:

          Replacement of the outlet and adjoining
          wiring and testing of the circuit.  Estimate
          $275.00 including parts and labor.

Thank you for your help in this matter.

Sincerely,


(Your Name)
[LLLLTLLLLTLL█LLLL3LLLLTLLLL4LLLLLLLLL5LLLLLLLLL6LLLLLLLLL7LLLLLLLLLTLLLL]LLLL9LLLLL
ELECTRIC.LTR                         Insert  0 %   Line 21 of Page 1 of 1

Esc-Exit  F1-Info  F2-Print  Ctrl+F6-Define Pg  F7-Search  F8-Options  ↑F8-Save
```

**Fig. 9.9** *Your electrical company letter.*

## *Indicating a New Page on Your Document*

As you remember, Shocky's requires a copy of the letter to send to the insurance company. To do this, you need to add the insurance letter as a second page to this letter and reference it as an attachment. The Options menu is used for this purpose.

First, you need to indicate that the current letter is page one and that you will be adding a second page to this document:

1. Move your cursor one line below your name.
2. Select F8 (Options).
3. Select Newpage from the Options menu and press Enter.

You are on page two. Press the up-arrow key once to view the preceding page. A character that resembles a reverse double *L* is on the left margin at the bottom of the page. This *page break character* tells the program that a second page will follow.

## *Inserting a Document*

Now let's add the second page to the document:

1. Move your cursor to the beginning of page two by pressing the down-arrow key.

Because you addressed the first letter to the insurance company, you can insert that entire document on page two of the Shocky's letter.

2. Press F8 (Options).
3. Select Insert Document from the Options menu, and press Enter. A prompt will ask for the name of the document to be inserted. Check that the drive path displayed in the prompt is correct.
4. Type the name of the letter: *fire.ltr*. Press Enter. The letter to the insurance company appears at the top of page two of your new document.

## *Using Headers and Footers in Your Document*

You have one more step to finish the letter: adding a header so that Mr. Shocky will know this is an attachment. A *header* (or *footer*) is a block of text that will print at the top (or bottom) of the pages of a document. You can use the Define Page screen to specify that the header or footer begin printing on any page in the document.

1. Press F8 (Options) and select Edit Header from the Options menu. Several blank lines and a double line appear at the top of the letter. This header editing area will hold the header text.
2. Type *Attachment A* and press Enter. Your header should look like figure 9.10.

**Fig. 9.10** *Adding a header to the second page of your letter.*

```
Attachment A

National Fire Insurance Company Pte. Ltd.
2345 Flame Street
Timber, Colorado 12345

Dear Sirs:

I would like to submit a claim against my homeowner's insurance policy
for an AM/FM radio damaged in an electrical fire.  The radio was
totally destroyed and cannot be repaired.  Because I have no
deductible amount to be satisfied on this claim, I am submitting the
information on the radio along with a copy of the fire department's
report on the fire.

*Quantity* *Description* *Serial Number* *Amount of Purchase* *Date of
ELECTRIC.LTR                              Insert  2 %   Line 2 Header

F1-Info          Shift+F6-Enhance        F8-Options          F10-Exit Header
```

3. Press F10 to exit the header and return to the body of the document.

   Headers now will appear on the document when it is printed. The header should start on page two because page one is not an attachment. The starting page number is specified on the Define Page screen you viewed earlier. You need to check this screen to verify the setting.

4. Press Ctrl-F6 (Define Pg) to see the Define Page screen.
5. Adjust your settings to match the following settings, if needed:

   Left Margin: 10 Right Margin .: 68
   Top Margin: 6 Bottom Margin: 6
   Page Width: 78 Page Length . .: 66
   Characters Per Inch: 10
   Begin Header/Footer on Page # . . . : 2
   Begin Page Numbering with Page #: 1

6. Press F10 to return to your document, and save the document using Shift-F8.
7. Press Esc to return to the Q&A Write menu.

## *Retrieving a Document That Has Been Saved*

If you decide to edit your letter to the National Fire Insurance Company and select Type/Edit, you will return to your ELECTRIC.LTR document. If you select Clear, you will only get a blank screen. To retrieve documents that have been saved, you use the Get command on the Write menu.

1. Select Get from the Write menu.
2. When prompted for the name of the file, type *fire.ltr* and press Enter. Q&A will retrieve the document FIRE.LTR from disk and will display the document on-screen for further editing.

   If you can't remember the name of a document, press Enter at the `Document` prompt, and Q&A will show you a list of all the files in the logged disk or subdirectory. Move the cursor to choose the correct file, and press Enter to retrieve the file to the editing screen.

If you want to leave Write, press Shift-F8 to save the file and press Esc until you reach the Main menu.

## *Chapter Summary*

Your quick start session has showed how to create new documents and enhance them through the use of text enhancement such as boldface and options such as headers. You printed a letter to disk and merged information residing in a database in the File module. You can set tabs, check spelling, and use temporary margins when needed. Now you have the basic tools to combine both the File module and the Write module into a comprehensive database/word-processing package capable of sharing information between the modules easily.

Chapter 14 introduces you to the Q&A Report module. Before you jump to that quick start chapter, however, you will want to learn about the range of Write's capabilities. Chapters 10–13 explain more about Write, including creating documents, formatting and enhancing text, and printing in Write.

Chapter

10

# Creating a Write Document

Q&A Write is an easy-to-use word processor that has all the features you need for producing memos, letters, reports, and other professional documents. If you have experience with other word-processing programs, you will find that Q&A outperforms many of them. If you have used WordStar®, learning Q&A Write will be easy because of the similarities in the Ctrl-key commands. In addition to a complete tool box for word-processing features, Q&A Write includes an integrated spelling checker and supports the PostScript printer definition language.

Because Q&A Write keeps the current document in RAM (random-access memory), the program is exceptionally fast. However, the size of your document is limited by the size of your computer's memory. If you use the preset page format, a typical page of your text will contain about 528 6-character words, or 3,168 characters. Based on a standard 66-line page, the maximum document sizes for the standard memory sizes are as follows:

512K RAM   50-page document
640K RAM   80-page document

These limits apply if memory is not also being used by memory-resident programs, print spoolers, RAM disks, or other memory utilities.

This chapter explains all of Q&A Write's capabilities, from basic to advanced, and gives you tips for using them. The chapter begins with the basic operations for entering and editing text, including moving, copying, and deleting text. The chapter also explains how to add headers and footers, format the entire document page, and search text automatically for something you want to find or change. Finally, you will learn how to use the spelling checker and how to count the number of words in the document. When you have finished this chapter, you will have a thorough understanding of how to produce a finished document. (See Chapter 11 for information on formatting text and Chapter 13 for information on printing Write documents.)

# Starting the Writing Process

To start, select Write from the Q&A Main menu. Q&A will display the Write menu shown in figure 10.1.

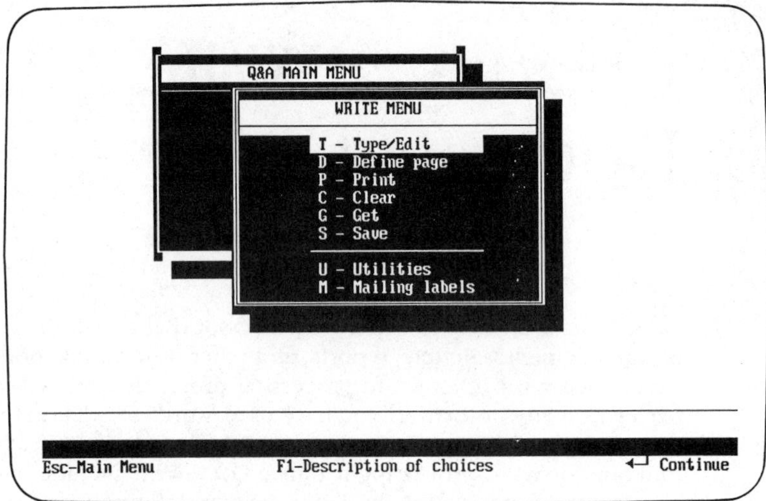


**Fig. 10.1** *Selecting Type/Edit from the Write menu.*

For an explanation of each Write menu option, press F1 to view the Q&A Write help screen. The page numbers listed on the help screen (W-11, for example) indicate where to find more information in the *Q&A Instruction Manual.* Press Esc (Cancel) to return to the Write menu.

To begin using Write, select the Type/Edit command. You don't have to press Enter if you have configured Q&A for single-key entry. (See the installation information in Appendix A.) Another way to enter commands is to use single-key number selection: instead of pressing a letter and the Enter key, you press a number that corresponds to the option. The order of menu options is numbered from upper left (1) to lower right. Using this method, you press 1 to select the Type/Edit option. You are now ready to begin a document by entering and editing text.

# Entering and Editing Text

A sales lead memo (see fig. 10.2) will serve to illustrate how to prepare a document with Q&A Write, beginning with entering and editing text. Some writers enter the entire document before they format the text; others prefer to format the text as they enter it. As you work with Write, you will choose which method you prefer. In this example, you will enter and edit the document first. You will format it later, in Chapter 11.

```
TO:              District Sales Managers

DATE:            June 30, 1988

FROM:            Steven Hill, Marketing Support Manager

SUBJECT:         JUNE SALES LEADS

Enclosed are the sales lead forms received during June from
prospects in your sales district.  Also included is a report
that summarizes the sales leads by city, sales
priority, company, and customer request.

We are implementing a new sales tracking system that will
give you a means to keep track of sales leads and follow
up.  This should help each of you unify your sales force
and make sure that each lead is pursued effectively.  A
Q&A disk is enclosed that contains the sales leads for
your district. Please copy these leads into your file, and
maintain them in the following manner:

    1. When each lead is assigned, enter the name of the
       Sales Person.
    2. Enter the date when the first sales contact was
       made with the sales lead.
    3. Record the date of the demonstration.
    4. Enter the status of the sale after the demonstration in
       one of the following forms:

          Sale (Model Number)     a sale was made

          Postpone                the purchase decision
                                  was delayed

          Competitor (select one) the prospect bought from a
                                  competitor

          Brock
          Med Sci
          Am Lab

          Other

At the end of the month, please send me a copy of this report
and the updated forms (on disk).  I will then prepare an
analysis of your district's sales activity and effectiveness.
We will be discussing this new system more fully at our next
district meeting.
```

**Fig. 10.2** *A memo: your first writing project.*

As you can see from figure 10.3, the editing screen is similar to a typewriter page. The top portion of the screen looks like a sheet of paper; the bottom of the screen holds a ruler line indicating the location of the left ([) and right (]) margins, the tab stops (*T*), and the cursor. (For a detailed description of the Write Type/Edit screen, see Chapter 3.)

As you enter and edit text, you will need to move the cursor within the screen and around the document. Whenever you need help, press F1 (Info) to see the key usage help screen, which lists the actions related to the function keys. Return to the Type/Edit screen by pressing the Esc key.

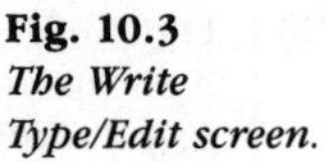

**Fig. 10.3**
*The Write Type/Edit screen.*

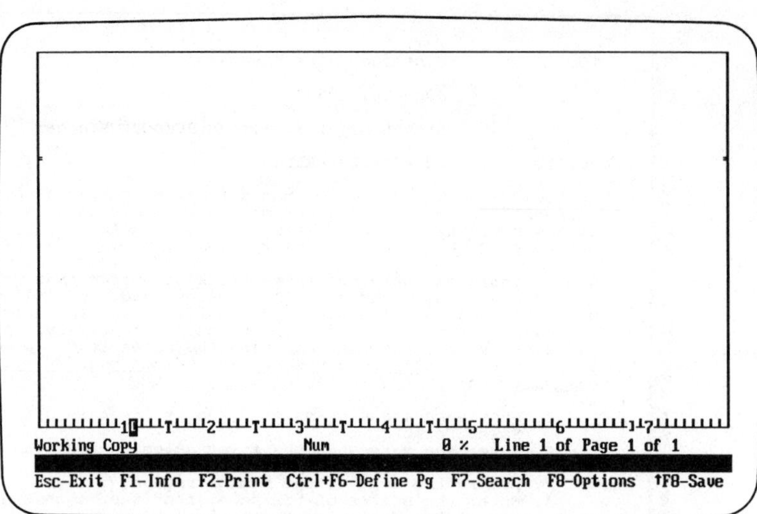


## *Entering Text*

To enter text with Q&A Write, you simply type it. Q&A Write has more power and more options than a typewriter, but entering text is similar in most respects. However, if you are new to microcomputing, you should recognize the distinct differences between the typewriter keyboard and the computer keyboard. The following example will help you understand the special features of keys and the screen when you use Write. Let's begin the sample memo by entering the date and the TO and FROM information. Enter the date by typing *June 15, 1988*; then press Enter twice to move the cursor down two lines.

Begin to enter the memo's address line by typing *TO:*. To make uppercase letters, you can type while holding down the Shift key or after toggling on the Caps Lock key. When you press the Caps Locks key once, the indicator `Cap` appears in the status line to show that the key is on. Your Caps Lock key also may have a light to indicate when it is on. However, although the letters *T* and *O* appear in uppercase, you must press the Shift key while pressing the semicolon/colon key to enter a colon. Be sure to toggle off the Caps Lock key by pressing it again. The `Cap` indicator will disappear from the status line.

Press the tab key twice to move the cursor to the second tab stop (the second *T* on the ruler line), and type *District Sales Managers*.

Press the Enter key twice to move the cursor down two lines. To enter the FROM line, type *FROM:* and press the tab key once; then type *Steven Hill, Marketing Support Manager*. Press the Enter key twice to move the cursor down two more lines.

Press the Caps Lock key and type *SUBJECT:* (remembering to press the Shift key for the colon). Press the tab key once and type *JUNE SALES LEADS*. Toggle off the Caps Lock key and press the Enter key twice.

Enter the first paragraph of the memo as it appears in figure 10.4. Do not press Enter at the end of each line; Q&A Write uses wordwrap, which automatically wraps the end of one line to the beginning of the next as you type.

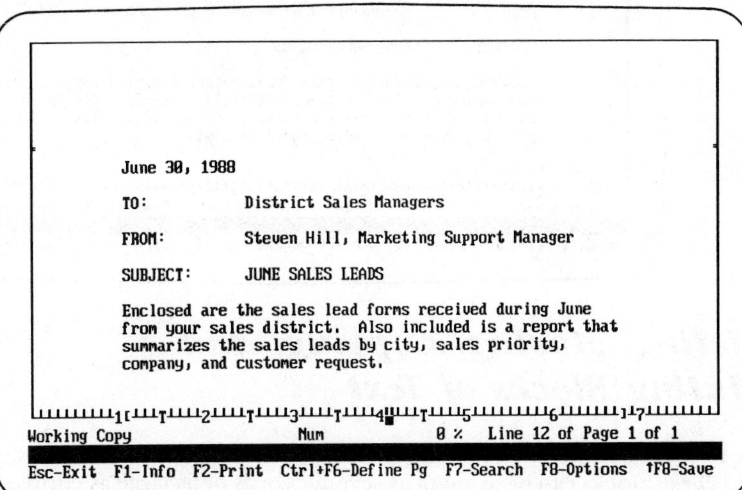

```
June 30, 1988

TO:           District Sales Managers

FROM:         Steven Hill, Marketing Support Manager

SUBJECT:      JUNE SALES LEADS

Enclosed are the sales lead forms received during June
from your sales district. Also included is a report that
summarizes the sales leads by city, sales priority,
company, and customer request.

Working Copy              Num          0 %  Line 12 of Page 1 of 1
Esc-Exit  F1-Info  F2-Print  Ctrl+F6-Define Pg  F7-Search  F8-Options  ↑F8-Save
```

**Fig. 10.4** *Entering the first paragraph.*

## *Inserting Text*

Whenever you want to edit text by deleting or inserting characters, you can use one of two modes: Overwrite or Insert. In Overwrite mode (Q&A's default mode), you can change characters or add spaces directly over the text where the cursor is positioned. In Insert mode (accessed by pressing the Ins key on the numeric keypad), you can delete or insert any character or a space at the cursor position. With the typing mode set to Insert, you can type information anywhere in the text without erasing the text already there.

Notice in the memo's first paragraph that you can improve the phrase *from your sales district* by inserting the words *prospects in* after the word *from*. To insert the new text, move the cursor to the first letter of the word *your* by pressing the up-arrow key once and then pressing Ctrl-left arrow nine times. Press the Ins key once to change to Insert mode. (Notice the word `Insert` on the status line, indicating that Insert mode is on.) Type *prospects in* and press the space bar once. Finally, press the Ins key to turn off Insert mode. Your screen should look like figure 10.5.

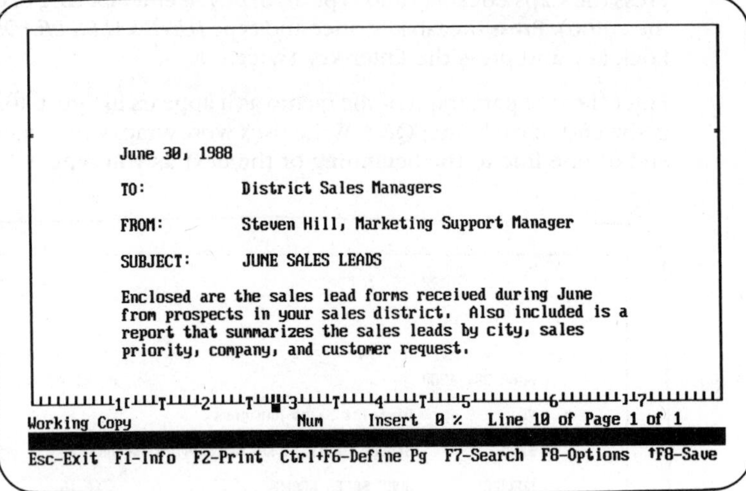


**Fig. 10.5** *Inserting words in a paragraph.*

## *Deleting, Moving, Copying, and Printing Blocks of Text*

You can work with blocks of text for four Write operations: Delete, Move, Copy, and Print. These blocks can be as small as several words or as large as entire paragraphs or pages. Before you work with a block, you first select it. The "pivot character," central to the selection process, is the character at which the cursor is located when you start the block selection operation. This technique is a fast and flexible way to edit a document.

To select and work on a block of text,

1. Position the cursor at one end of the text block; this location becomes the pivot character.
2. Press F3 to delete, F5 to copy, Shift-F5 to move, or Ctrl-F2 to print a block.
3. Select the text block by moving the cursor to the other end of the block, using one of three methods: the cursor-movement keys; the character keys; or the Delete, Move, and Copy function keys (explained in this section). The text is highlighted as you select it.
4. Complete the procedure for the specified operation, as explained in the following sections.

As mentioned in step 3, three methods are available for marking a block of text. First, you can use the standard cursor-movement keys (the arrow keys, Home, End, PgDn, and PgUp) for selecting a text block.

Second, you also can use character keys to select a text block. If you press a character key, such as *d* or the period (.), Write moves from the pivot character through the document until it finds the next occurrence of that character. All characters between the pivot and final characters will be highlighted.

If you position the character at the beginning of a paragraph, press F5 to begin the Copy operation, and then type *y*. Write highlights all characters to the first *y* (in *your*). If you type *y* again, the highlight continues to the next *y* (in *city*). If, instead, you want to select the entire paragraph, press Enter or the period (.) key twice (see fig. 10.6).

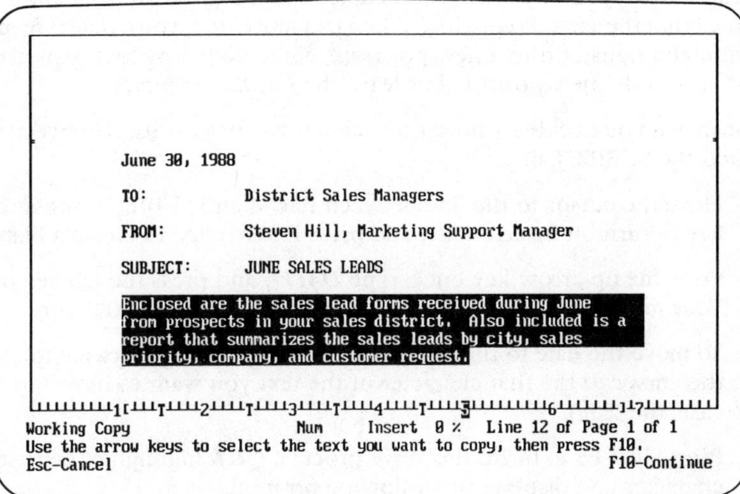


**Fig. 10.6**
*Selecting a paragraph.*

You can type any character or combination of characters to move the cursor through the document. Press the space bar to select the next word. Press Enter to select the rest of the paragraph. To cancel a selection, press Esc.

Third, to select a block of text quickly, you can use the F3, F5, or Shift-F5 function keys (Delete, Copy, or Move, respectively). The number of times you press one of these keys determines what happens:

| *Pressing the Key* | *Gives This Result* |
|---|---|
| Once | Activates the function (Delete, Copy, or Move) |
| Twice | Selects and highlights the entire word in which the cursor is located; highlights the preceding word if the cursor is located in the single space between words or on the end-of-sentence period |
| Three times | Selects and highlights the entire sentence |

| | |
|---|---|
| Four times | Selects and highlights the entire paragraph |
| Five times | Selects and highlights the entire document |

Q&A displays a message indicating what you have selected. Complete the selected operation by pressing F10 according to the procedures explained in the following sections. The following sections explain the two most common operations for many users: moving text and copying text.

## *Moving Text*

You can move text easily within a document by using the Shift-F5 key. Notice that moving is not the same as copying. When you move text, you delete it from its initial position and transfer it to a new position. When you copy text, you make a copy of the text in the new position but leave the initial text intact.

Suppose that you decide to move the memo's date to a position between the FROM line and the SUBJECT line.

1. Move the cursor to the line between FROM and SUBJECT, press the Ins key to turn on Insert mode, and press Enter twice to create a blank line.
2. Press the up-arrow key once, type *DATE:*, and press the tab key once. Your memo, ready for the move, now has an empty DATE line.
3. To move the date to the new line, press the Home key twice to move the cursor to the first character of the text you want to move (in this case, the date).
4. Press Shift-F5 to begin the Move process. Q&A highlights the first character and displays the following prompt:

   ```
   Use the arrow keys to select the text you want to move, then
   press F10.
   ```

5. Select the date by pressing the right-arrow key until the entire line is highlighted. To select a line using a single keystroke, press the End key. Then press F10 to confirm that the highlighted text is to be moved. (If you find that the text you have highlighted is not what you want moved, press Esc and repeat steps 1–3.) When you press F10, Q&A displays the prompt:

   ```
   Move the cursor to the place you want the text moved, then
   press F10.
   ```

6. Move the cursor to where you want to move the highlighted text. To move the cursor in the memo, press the down-arrow key six times and the right-arrow key once. Then press F10. The date will appear to the right of the cursor (see fig. 10.7).

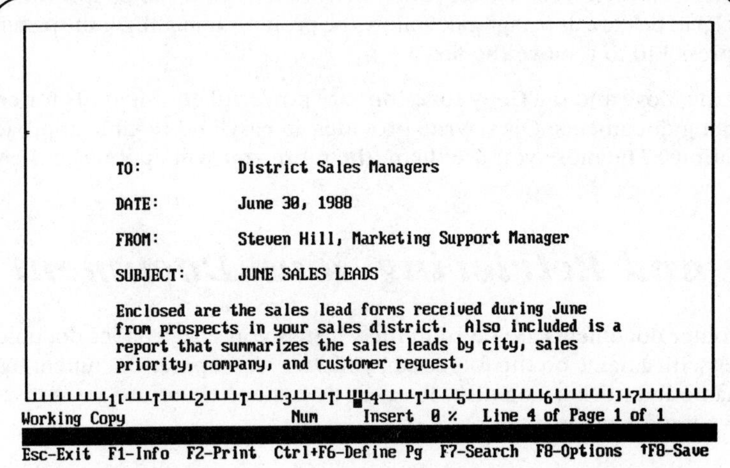


**Fig. 10.7**
*Moving the date.*

Remember that text can be selected for the Move process by any of the three methods described in this section and then moved by pressing F10 as described in this section.

## *Copying Text*

Copying is similar to moving: you press F5, select the text to be copied, and move to where you want to copy the text. Remember that when you copy text, the text remains in the initial location and is reproduced in the new location.

Suppose that you want to copy the first paragraph in the memo:

1. Move the cursor to the first character of the paragraph.
2. Press F5, the Copy function key. Q&A tells you to select the text to be copied and to then press F10.
3. Highlight the paragraph by moving the cursor to the end of the paragraph (remember to include the period). Q&A offers several ways to do this. An easy way is simply to press the period key after Block mode is turned on; Q&A will move the cursor to the next period. You also can press End once to highlight the first line, press the down-arrow key three times to highlight the entire paragraph, and then press F10. Or you can press F5 four times to highlight the paragraph before pressing F10.
4. Use the down-arrow key to move the cursor down two lines to where you want the copied paragraph to begin; then press F10. Notice that the copied paragraph starts where the cursor is positioned, rather than at the beginning of the line as the original did.

You can now review the Delete function by deleting the paragraph you just copied. Press F3 to delete this paragraph. Follow the prompts to highlight the paragraph again, and press F10 to remove the text.

Both the Move and the Copy functions are powerful editing tools for creating and changing documents. Q&A Write provides an easy and flexible approach to these operations. The more you use them, the more you will appreciate them.

# *Saving and Retrieving Your Document*

Computer documents are saved in files. Just as you save a paper document in a file folder with a name on the folder tab, you save a computer document by giving it a file name and storing it on disk. To save a document, therefore, you must know how to give it a file name.

## *Naming Document Files*

Q&A Write file names must adhere to the rules of DOS: a limit of eight characters plus a three-character file extension. A period is used between the root file name and the extension, but no other punctuation or special characters are allowed. Unlike the Q&A File module, Q&A Write allows you to add your own file extension. You can take advantage of this feature by using the extension to indicate what kind of document the file contains. For example, you can use LET for letters and MEM for memos. You also can use extensions to identify the category of a document: for example, SLS for sales and CUS for customers. You can develop an extension system that best suits your documents.

Documents often evolve through several revisions. To indicate which version of a document a file contains, you can include a number in your file names. For instance, you could call the first version of the sales lead memo SLSLEAD1.MEM, and the second version SLSLEAD2.MEM. This numbering system helps you to keep track of a document from first draft to final copy.

You can use this numbering system in other ways as well. For files that refer to specific months, use two digits (01 through 12) to identify the month. For example, you can use SLSTOT10.RPT as the file name for the October Sales Totals report. If documents refer to the quarters of a year, you can use Q1, Q2, Q3, and Q4 in the file name, as in FINRPT.Q1, the file name of the financial report for the first quarter.

An eight-digit file name is limiting. By using the extension and numbering systems, you can increase significantly the program's file-naming capability.

## *Saving a Document*

Write includes two ways to save Write documents: the menu method and the function-key method. The function-key method uses Shift-F8 and is a quick way to save a current document. The menu method uses the Write menu's Save option. To use this method, press the Esc key to return to the Write menu, select Save, and enter a new document name.

To save the memo using the menu,

1. Press Esc to leave the Type/Edit screen.
2. Choose Save from the Write menu. A prompt appears, asking for the file name.
3. Enter a document name. Type *SLSLEAD.MEM* (you can use either uppercase or lowercase) and press Enter. Q&A will save the document to the default drive and directory.

   If you already have saved the document, Q&A shows you its file name. If you want to save the document to a different file name, you can do one of three things:

   - Edit the file name and then press Enter to save the document.
   - Erase the existing file name (not the existing file) by pressing the space bar once. Then type another file name (new or existing) and press Enter to save the document.
   - Erase the existing file name by pressing the space bar once. Then press Enter to display the list of document names, move the cursor to the name of the file to which you want to save the document, and save it by pressing Enter again.

Notice that Q&A automatically adds the default drive and directory to the file name. If you set a different drive and directory, the document will be saved and its file named accordingly. After saving the document, Q&A returns to the Write menu.

Use the function-key method (Shift-F8) as a shortcut for saving both new and existing documents. To safeguard against a sudden power outage or equipment failure, use this method frequently when you work. Shift-F8 is available only from the Type/Edit screen. When you save a document using Shift-F8, Q&A returns you to the editing screen after the save. Thus, you can continue working with minimal interruption. To save an existing document with Shift-F8,

1. Press Shift-F8 at any point in Type/Edit. Q&A will display a box over the document containing the document's file name.
2. Name the document. Simply press Enter to confirm the current file name, or edit the file name.

### *Clearing the Type/Edit Screen*

If you want to erase everything on the Type/Edit screen, press the Esc key to return to the Write menu. Then select Clear and press Enter. If the entire contents of the Type/Edit screen have been saved already, Q&A will erase whatever was on-screen and return you to a clear screen. The saved document will remain on disk; only the RAM-resident version is cleared in this process.

If the Type/Edit screen contains text that has not been saved, the Q&A displays a warning screen when you attempt to clear the screen. To prevent erasing unsaved text, press Enter. To continue the erasing process, choose Yes and then press Enter.

***Caution:*** Using the Clear option permanently erases all unsaved text on the Type/Edit screen. However, any information previously saved to disk remains intact.

### *Retrieving a Document File*

Retrieving a previously saved document, such as the sales lead memo, is easy with Q&A. From the Write menu, select Get. Q&A will prompt you for the name of a document.

You can enter the document's name in one of two ways. You can type the name (including the extension) exactly as it was saved. You don't have to type the drive or directory unless they are different from the default drive and directory. To retrieve the sales lead memo using this method, type *SLSLEAD.MEM*. Remember that you can use either uppercase or lowercase letters.

The other way to enter a document's name is to press Enter to display the list of documents, move the cursor to the name of the document you want to retrieve, and press Enter again.

## *Formatting the Page*

You can format the document page in the same way you format the text in a Q&A Write document. You set the margins, page width and length, number of characters per inch, and the appearance of headers and footers from the Define Page screen, which is accessed from the Write menu. Most page format changes can be seen on-screen as well as in printouts.

To display the Define Page screen, with the document on the Type/Edit screen, you press the Esc key to go to the Write menu. Select the Define Page command and press Enter. Q&A will display the Define Page screen.

To set the page format, use the tab, up-arrow, and down-arrow keys to move the cursor to the setting you want to change. Type the new settings for all items except characters per inch (for this setting, use the space bar or the arrow keys to highlight your choice).

Accept the setting by pressing Enter. Press F10 to return to your document on the editing screen, and check the new page format.

You can change permanently the default page format so that Q&A will automatically use your preferred settings. See Chapter 11 for further information on defining page defaults and on the last two options of the Define Page screen.

## *Page Size and Margins*

The page size and margins determine the *document area*—the space available for text on the page. The preset page size and margins shown in figure 10.8 are based on an 8.5-by-11-inch page. Notice that the right margin, at column 68, is measured from the left edge of the page. New settings can be entered using the Define Page screen.

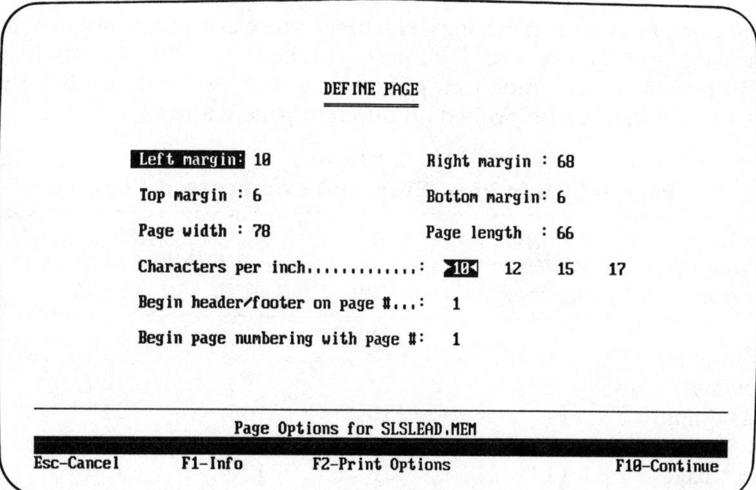


**Fig. 10.8**
*Preset page size and margins.*

The document area is ordinarily measured in columns and lines. Horizontal measurements are in columns, with each column equal to one character in the display and to one pica character when printed (pica print is 10 points per inch). Vertical measurements are in lines, usually with six lines equal to one inch.

As an alternative, you can enter the measurements in inches in the Define Page screen. You must add the inch symbol (") after the number of inches. Measurements of less than one inch must be indicated in decimals, not fractions. Q&A converts the inch measurements to lines and columns—for example:

| *Inches* | *Vertical Lines* | *Horizontal Columns (pica)* |
|---|---|---|
| 0″ | 0 | 0 |
| .5″ | 3 | 5 |
| 1″ | 6 | 10 |
| 1.5″ | 9 | 15 |

## *Characters Per Inch*

The width of characters is measured by the number of characters per inch (CPI). The CPI settings of 10, 12, 15, and 17 correspond to the standard measures for characters:

10 CPI Pica (Q&A's default value)
12 CPI Elite
15 CPI Compressed daisy-wheel printing
17 CPI Compressed dot-matrix printing

If your printer can print in varying CPI settings, you can take advantage of the capability by using the Characters Per Inch setting of the Define Page screen. Refer to your printer manual to determine your printer's capabilities. Table 10.1 lists the number of characters that can be printed on different page widths.

**Table 10.1**
**Page Width in Pica, Elite, and Compressed Characters**

| *Page Width* | *Page Width in Inches* | *Page Width in Columns* 10 CPI | *12 CPI* | *15 CPI* | *17 CPI* |
|---|---|---|---|---|---|
| Minimum | 1″ | 10 | 12 | 15 | 17 |
| Default | 7.8″ | 78 | 93 | 120 | 132 |
| Maximum | 14″ | 140 | 168 | 217 | 238 |
| 8.5″ page | 8.5″ | 85 | 102 | 128 | 145 |
| 11″ page | 11″ | 110 | 120 | 150 | 170 |

## *Changing Header and Footer Size*

Using the Top Margin and Bottom Margin settings in the Define Page screen, you can change the size of a header or footer that contains too many or too few lines. (See Chapter 11 for more on formatting headers and footers.)

The default setting for top and bottom margins is six lines. The ordinary measurement is in lines, with six lines equal to one inch, but you also can enter a new header or footer size in inches, adding the inch symbol (″) after the number of inches. Be sure to indicate a portion of an inch as a decimal, not as a fraction. Q&A converts the inch measurements to lines—for example:

| *Inches* | *Vertical Lines* |
|---|---|
| 0″ | 0 (Zero leaves no space) |
| .5″ | 3 |
| 1″ | 6 |
| 1.5″ | 9 |

To change the size of headers and footers, follow these steps:

1. From the Write menu, select Define Page. From the Type/Edit screen, press Ctrl-F6 (Define Pg). The Define Page screen appears.
2. Using the tab or the down-arrow key, move the cursor to Top Margin to change the header size, or to Bottom Margin to change the footer size.
3. Enter the appropriate number of lines or inches for the header or footer, and press Enter.
4. Press F10 to return to the Type/Edit screen.

## Searching, Replacing, and Deleting

Like most other word processors, Q&A Write possesses an effective search-and-replace function. Write takes only seconds to search for, find, and replace words and phrases. Write even can delete selected words and phrases automatically.

When you want to search for something, you need only tell Q&A the word or words you want found. If you want to replace the word or phrase, you also type the new word or phrase. To delete a word or phrase, you replace it with nothing, which removes the word or phrase.

If you enter all lowercase letters when you ask Q&A to search, the program will find the item in any combination of lower- and uppercase letters. If, however, you use uppercase letters when you enter the search item, what Q&A finds is limited, as follows:

| *Searching for* | *Q&A Finds* |
|---|---|
| senior manager | senior manager, Senior manager, Senior Manager, SENIOR MANAGER |
| Senior manager | Senior manager, Senior Manager, SENIOR MANAGER |
| Senior Manager | Senior Manager, SENIOR MANAGER |
| SENIOR MANAGER | SENIOR MANAGER |

You can begin a search anywhere in your document. Q&A will search to the end of the document and then go to the beginning of the document and search to the point at which the search began.

## *Searching for Text*

To search for text in Write, press F7 (Search). The sales lead memo is addressed to District Sales Managers and refers several times to *districts*. Suppose that the districts were changed to *areas*. You would want to change the memo accordingly. To find each instance of *district* quickly, follow these steps:

1. From the memo, press F7 (Search) to begin the search. Q&A displays the search window shown in figure 10.9.
2. At the Search For field, type the phrase you want Q&A to find and then press Enter. In this example, you type *district*. Q&A accepts up to 47 characters and spaces for a search.
3. Press F10 to begin the search, skipping the other two items in the search window. Q&A will find your phrase, highlight it, and await your next action.

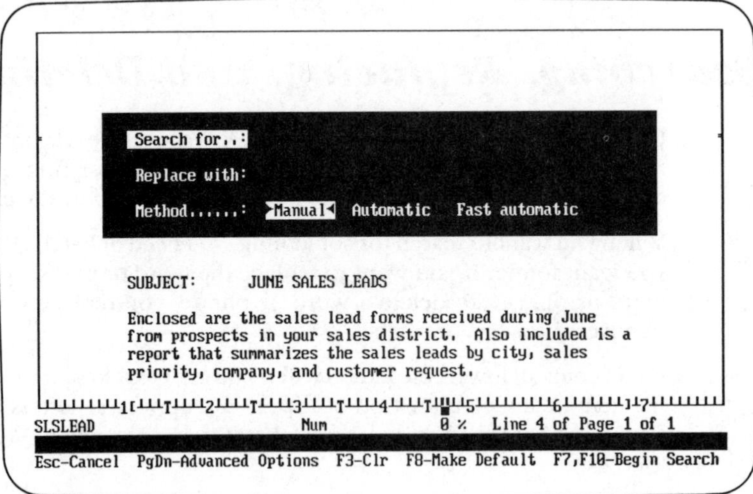


**Fig. 10.9**
*The search window.*

When Q&A finds the phrase you are searching for, you have three choices: edit the phrase, which cancels the search; press F7 or F10 (Begin Search) to search for the next appearance of the phrase; or press the Esc key to end the search.

If Q&A does not find the phrase, Q&A displays `(phrase) NOT FOUND` on the message line and ends the search.

Because the search window retains your entries after you finish a search, you can repeat the search without reentering your phrase. To search for another phrase, you can erase the previous phrase by typing over it or by pressing Shift-F4.

## *Searching with Wild Cards*

What do you do if you want to search for a word or phrase that you're not sure how to spell? With Q&A, you can use a portion of a word or phrase to do a wild-card search. Q&A has two wild-card characters:

| *Wild Card* | *Function* |
|---|---|
| ? (question mark) | Represents any single character |
| .. (two periods) | Represents any group of characters |

These characters can be used in almost any combination. Table 10.2 lists some sample search phrases; many others are possible. You can experiment with wild cards to find almost any phrase.

**Table 10.2**
**Sample Wild-Card Search Phrases**

| *Search Word or Phrase* | *Meaning* | *Examples* |
|---|---|---|
| a? | Any two-letter word beginning with *a* | at, Al |
| a.. | Any word beginning with *a* | ant, alpha |
| ..m | Any word ending with *m* | am, sam, beam |
| ???m | Any four-letter word ending with *m* | team, clam |
| ..i?? | Any word with *i* as its third-to-last character | Siam, location |
| Q.. W.. | Two words: the first beginning with *Q*, the second beginning with *W* | Q&A Write, quit working |

***Note:*** Using the search function, Q&A Write can count the words in your documents. This feature is good news for those who have to write 100 words of advertising copy, a 500-word paper, a 3,000-word speech, or who are being paid by the word! To count the words in your document, follow these steps:

1. With the cursor at the beginning of your document, press F7 (Search). Q&A displays the search window.
2. At the Search For field, type two dots (..).
3. Press Enter twice or the tab key twice to get to the Method field. Select Automatic and press F7 or F10 to begin the count. As it counts, Q&A displays the word `Counting...` on the message line. When the count is finished, the following phrase gives you the word count:

   ```
   Automatic search COMPLETED after (number of words) matches.
   ```

   The sales lead memo consists of 242 words.

## *Searching for and Replacing Text*

If you want Q&A to find one phrase and replace it with another, you must make some additional choices when you use the F7 key. Suppose, as in the preceding example, that you want to replace *district* with *area* in the sales lead memo.

1. From the memo, press F7 (Search) to begin the search. Q&A displays the search window (refer to fig. 10.9).
2. At the Search For field, type *district* (the phrase you want Q&A to find) and then press Enter. Q&A accepts as many as 47 characters and spaces.
3. At the Replace With field, type *area* (the phrase you want Q&A to insert). Type the phrase exactly as you want it to appear, using the appropriate uppercase and lowercase letters. Then press Enter.
4. Use the cursor-movement keys to highlight the method you want to use:
    - Manual search—Q&A flashes each change on the screen before it is made. You can look at the phrase each time it occurs and decide whether to replace it. Manual is the best choice if the phrase occurs in different contexts—you may want to retain the phrase in some contexts and replace it in others.
    - Automatic search—Q&A searches for and automatically replaces the phrase each time it occurs. Q&A updates the screen display as each change is made.
    - Fast Automatic search—Q&A does not update the screen after each change, speeding up the process. When the search and replace operation is complete, the current screen is updated.

    For this search and replace, select Manual and press F10 (Begin Search).
5. When Q&A finds the phrase, you can do one of four things:
    - Press F10 to replace the highlighted phrase, and then press F7 to continue the search or the Esc key to end the search.
    - Press F7 if you don't want to replace the current phrase but do want to search for the next occurrence of the phrase.
    - Edit the phrase, which cancels the search.
    - End the search by pressing the Esc key.

To make an automatic search, choose Automatic in the Method field of the search menu and press F10. Q&A will automatically search for a phrase, replace it, and report the number of replacements that have been made.

Q&A Write's sophisticated search-and-replace capability can find parts of words and arbitrary sequences of characters. For example, you can replace *ed* with *ing* at the end of a word, or change *1.– to 1.——*, or change other strings of characters:

| | | |
|---|---|---|
| pretended | to | pretending |
| 1. Type | to | 1. Type |
| C6H4(CO3)2 | to | C6H4(CH3)2 |

This capability is especially useful when you need to make one change in several different words or phrases. Using Write, you can make these changes in one pass through the document rather than several repeated passes.

The backslash (\) is the key to Write's extended search-and- replace capability. When you enter the backslash before and after the search characters and the replace characters, as in *ed*\ and *ing*\, Write understands that the phrases are partial words or arbitrary sequences of characters, which will not appear as whole, separate words.

To replace the *ed* with *ing*, use Write's extended search-and-replace capability. First, press F7 (Search); Write will display the search window. Press PgDn to display the advanced search options. Change the Type option from Whole Words to Text Pattern. Move the cursor back to the Search For prompt, type *ed*\, and press Enter. At the Replace With prompt, type *ing*\ and press F7 to begin. Use the Manual rather than the Automatic setting. Write will highlight all occurrences of the *ed*.

To replace the highlighted characters, press F10; then press F7 to continue the search. Continue to press F10 until all occurrences of *ed* have been found. If, instead of replacing the current syllable you want to search for its next appearance, press F7. You can edit the text at any time, but doing so will cancel the search. To stop an ongoing search, press the Esc key.

### *Searching for and Deleting Text*

If you want to delete a certain word or phrase throughout your document, Q&A's search capability can help you make the changes. For example, if attorney Flanders leaves the law firm of Kennedy, Flanders, and Wood, you will want to delete *, Flanders,* from all occurrences of the firm name in a document.

To search for and delete text, you follow the same steps you follow to delete text. However, at the Replace With field you type two dots (..), which are a symbol for *null replace*, and then press Enter. Q&A gives you the same options for this operation that it gives for the search-and-replace operation.

## *Using the Spelling Checker*

Some computer users say that a spelling checker is a luxury but not a necessity; others say that any feature that makes documents look professional is important. Whether luxury or necessity, the Write spelling checker is integrated, fast, and expandable, and can be a valuable work saver. The spelling checker rapidly scans your documents word-by-word looking for misspellings, repeated words (such as *hereby hereby*) and typing errors. You can check one word or the entire document.

Q&A uses two dictionaries to check spelling: the main dictionary and a personal dictionary. The main dictionary contains 100,000 words. The personal dictionary can be expanded to hold as many words as will fit on your storage disk (the number is virtually unlimited if you are using a hard disk).

To use the spelling checker, press Ctrl-Home to move the cursor to the start of the document. Then press Shift-F1 while your document is displayed on the Type/Edit screen. Q&A begins to check from the cursor to the end of the document and displays the word `Checking...` in the message line. To check one word only, position the cursor on or immediately after that word and press Ctrl-F1.

When Write performs a spelling check, the program highlights words that are not in the dictionaries (see fig. 10.10). The spelling menu is displayed in the center of the screen, offering five options. To choose an option in the spelling menu, press the appropriate letter and then press Enter.

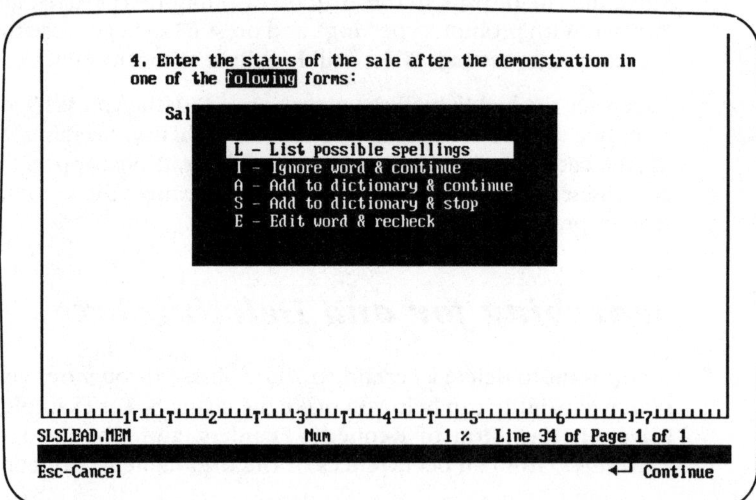


**Fig. 10.10**
*The spelling checker window.*

If you choose List Possible Spellings, Write displays another window containing as many as seven alternative spellings. If the correct spelling is on the list, select that word by pressing its number or by using the arrow keys to move the highlight to the word. When you press Enter, the selected word will instantly replace the misspelled word in your document.

If the correct spelling is not on the list, press the Esc key to return to the spelling menu. Choose Edit Word & Recheck, and a box requesting the correct spelling is displayed. Type the correct spelling of the word, and press F10. Q&A rechecks the word and places it in the document.

Choosing the Ignore Word & Continue option causes Write to skip over the highlighted word and continue the check. After you choose to ignore a word, that word is skipped for the remainder of the document search. You can use this option for words that are spelled correctly but you don't use often enough to add to the personal dictionary, such as street addresses, proper names, cities, and the like.

Choose Add to Dictionary & Continue to add the word to the personal dictionary and continue the spelling check. Use this option for frequently used words.

If you select Add to Dictionary & Stop, Write adds the word to the personal dictionary and ends the check.

## *Editing the Personal Dictionary*

You cannot edit the main dictionary (the QAMAIN.DCT file), but you can put special terms, personal names, geographical names, slang terms, or any words you choose into the QAPERS.DCT file. You can fill the personal dictionary with words you use that are not included in the main dictionary's 100,000 words.

You have three ways to enter words into the personal dictionary:

- While using the spelling checker in a normal document, select the Add to Dictionary & Continue or the Add to Dictionary & Stop option to add the new word to the personal dictionary automatically.
- Using method #1, have the spelling checker go through a particular document that contains many technical terms, or through a glossary, or even through another computer dictionary in ASCII file format.
- Load the QAPERS.DCT file (an ASCII file) and type words into the file as though you were typing them into a document. Choose these words carefully, however, so that you don't fill the system's storage space with words already in the main dictionary.

To edit the personal dictionary file, load the file by selecting Get from the Write menu. If you are using a hard disk, the QAPERS.DCT file is stored in the same path as your Q&A program files. To access the QAPERS.DCT file for editing, you may need to indicate the correct path with the file name. When you press Enter, Q&A displays the Import Document menu, which you use to select the file format. Choose ASCII as the file format and press Enter. Q&A displays the personal dictionary (see fig. 10.11).

Now you can edit the dictionary, adding and deleting words as you would in any document. However, there is one important difference: Words added to the personal dictionary *must be entered in alphabetical order, one word to a line.* You can use uppercase or lowercase, but be sure that the words you enter are spelled correctly!

## *Saving the Personal Dictionary*

To save the personal dictionary after you have edited it, follow these steps:

1. Press the Esc key to return to the Write menu.

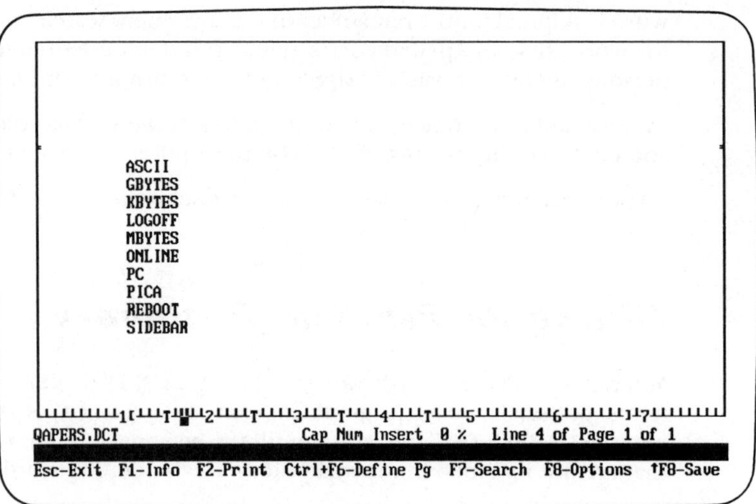


**Fig. 10.11**
*The personal dictionary.*

2. Select the Utilities command and press Enter.
3. Select Export to ASCII from the Write Utilities menu.
4. Select Standard ASCII from the ASCII Export menu. Q&A will display the file name QAPERS.DCT, along with any drive or path designation you have specified. Press Enter to save the personal dictionary to disk in ASCII format. (Note: The default edit mode of `ASCII with CR` should be selected from the Editing Options screen, available from the Global Options menu).

It is important to remember to use the Utilities menu's Export option to save the edited personal dictionary. *Do not* use the Save option.

# Chapter Summary

This chapter introduces Q&A Write's capabilities and shows how to produce a document. You learned how to use the search-and-replace function of Q&A Write, and you were shown how to use the spelling checker. After reading this chapter, you should be able to use the word-processing capabilities of Q&A Write to produce a document. Chapter 11 covers using Write's formatting capabilities, including formatting text, setting tabs and margins, and setting headers and footers. You use these features to produce a polished Write document.

Chapter 11

# Enhancing a Write Document

Chapter 10 covers the fundamental Write capabilities of creating and saving documents, and entering and searching for text. This chapter shows you how to enhance your Write document with special text features such as boldface, underline, tabs, margins, and line drawing. In addition, this chapter covers changing indentations and margins, enhancing headers and footers, and using Q&A Write's math functions.

## *Formatting Text*

Formatting improves your documents in several ways. Formatting adds style, emphasis, and clarity to your documents; it makes documents easy to read; and it gives documents a professional appearance.

Q&A Write offers the following formatting capabilities:

Text tabs and decimal tabs
Temporary margins and indentations
Boldface, italic, and underlined text
Superscript and subscript characters
Centered lines
Single- and double-line drawing

These formatting characteristics reside in the document file with the text. When you save a document, you save not only the text but all the formatting information as well.

As with most Q&A operations, setting document formats generally involves pressing a special key combination (Shift-F6, for example) that displays a menu of possible operations. You select the enhancement you want from the list, and then highlight the text you want to format. Most text enhancements can be specified for a single character, a word, or a block of text. Centering text, however, is line oriented. You must repeat the centering procedure for every line you want to center.

The following sections describe Write's formatting features in detail.

## *Using and Setting Tabs*

The Tab key moves the cursor to the left and right a preset number of spaces, according to tab stops set in the ruler line. Q&A Write documents contain two kinds of tab stops: text tabs (marked by a *T*) and decimal tabs (marked by a *D*). Both are set in the same way, but they affect text differently.

Figure 11.1 illustrates the default ruler line in a Q&A Write document: its four text tab stops are indicated by a *T* marker in the 15th, 25th, 35th, and 45th columns. These stops are relative to the left margin; if you change the left margin, the positions of the preset tab stops change.

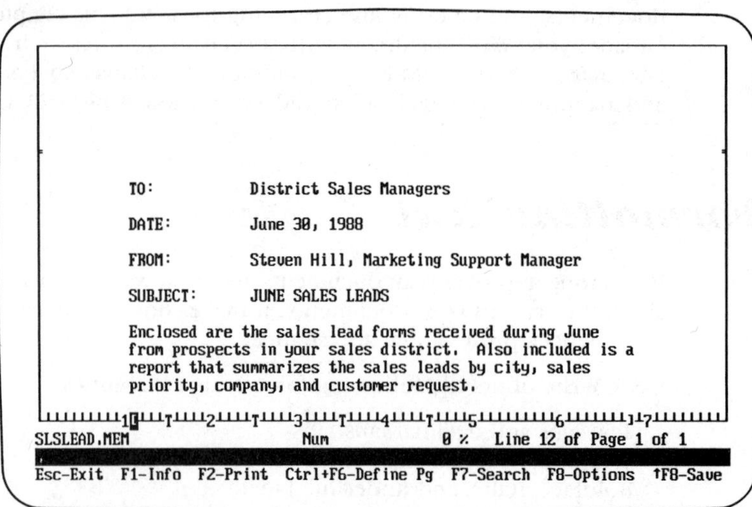

TO: District Sales Managers
DATE: June 30, 1988
FROM: Steven Hill, Marketing Support Manager
SUBJECT: JUNE SALES LEADS
Enclosed are the sales lead forms received during June
from prospects in your sales district. Also included is a
report that summarizes the sales leads by city, sales
priority, company, and customer request.
SLSLEAD.MEM Num 0 % Line 12 of Page 1 of 1
Esc-Exit F1-Info F2-Print Ctrl+F6-Define Pg F7-Search F8-Options ↑F8-Save


**Fig. 11.1**
*The ruler line tab stops.*

By selecting Set Tabs from the Options menu, you can delete and add text tab stops or decimal tab stops. You have complete control over the number and kind of tab stops in every document. The following sections explain how to use tab stops and how to add and delete them.

### *How To Use Tabs*

The Tab key is commonly used to indent the first line of a paragraph or to indent whole sections of text. This indentation is made by pressing the Tab key once. Each subsequent press of the Tab key will move the indent to the next tab stop. To tab to the left, press the Shift and Tab keys at the same time; the cursor will move to the first tab stop to the left.

Before you type a paragraph in a Write document, you can indent a line in either Overwrite or Insert mode. To indent previously entered text, however, you must use Insert mode; if you use Overwrite mode, you will move the cursor without changing the text.

To eliminate a tab indent, position the cursor on the first character of the line and move the character to the left margin by pressing the Backspace key repeatedly while in Insert mode.

*Text tabs* align text and numbers at the tab stop, proceeding from the stop to the right (see fig. 11.2). In this figure, one column is aligned with the left margin. Notice that the other three columns are aligned with three text tabs. To use a text tab stop, you type the first column, press the Tab key once to jump to the first tab stop, and then type the second column and press the Tab key again.

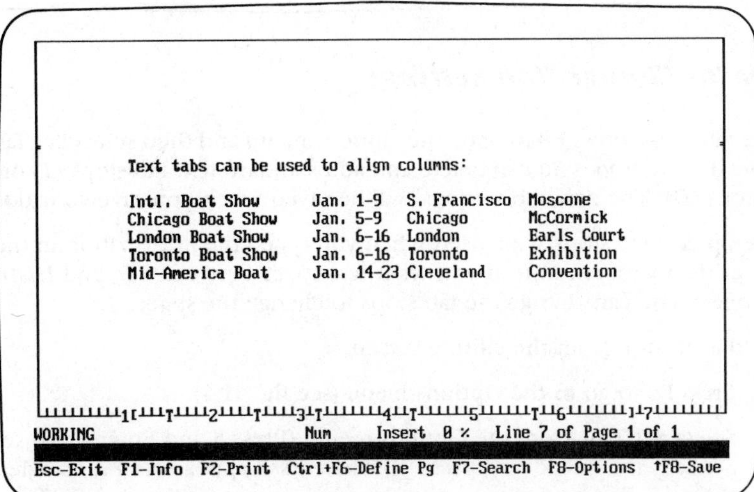


**Fig. 11.2**
*Text tabs align columnar text.*

Q&A Write's *decimal tabs* can make formatting a document with numbers easy. Decimal tabs are used to align numbers on the decimal point (see fig. 11.3). As figure 11.3 illustrates, a decimal tab is indicated by the *D* on the ruler line. You also can use decimal tabs as a convenient way to right-justify single lines of text for lists.

To use the decimal tab stop, press the Tab key to jump to the stop; then enter your information. Note that numbers and text appear to the left of the cursor until you enter a decimal point. By moving the cursor before or during the data-entry process, you cancel the decimal tab alignment. To right-justify a text list using decimal tabs, use the Tab key to move the cursor to the decimal tab, and enter the text (make sure that the text has no periods). The text moves to the left, ending at the decimal tab.

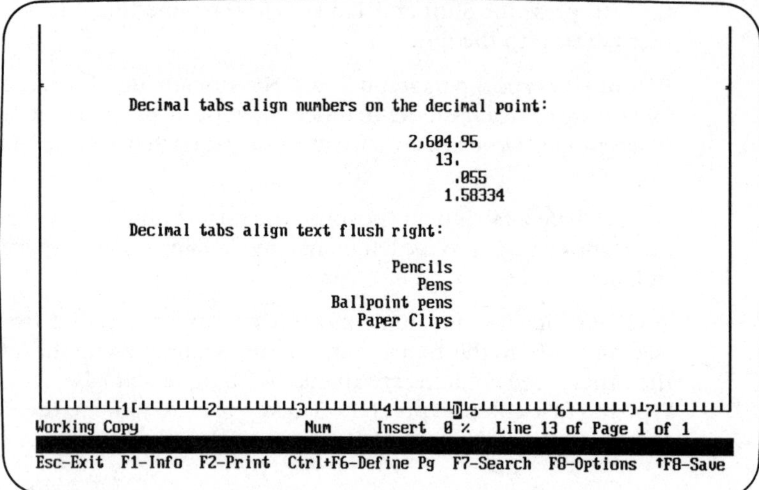


**Fig. 11.3**
*Decimal tabs align numbers and text.*

## *How To Change Tab Settings*

To set tab stops, press F8 to open the Options menu and then select Set Tabs. Using the Set Tabs option, you can delete and add standard text tab stops (*T*) or decimal tab stops (*D*). The new tab settings will be saved when you save your document.

Write's preset tab stops were used when you typed the information in the various lines of the memorandum. If you want less space between *TO:* and *District Sales Managers*, you can change the tab stops to change the space.

To add a tab stop from the editing screen,

1. Press F8 to go to the Options menu (see fig. 11.4).
2. Select Set Tabs from the Options menu. (Press S and Enter or, to select Set Tabs the quick way, press 3.) The cursor appears as a rectangle on the ruler line, and a new set of key assignments is listed at the bottom of the screen:

   Esc (Cancel)
   F1 (Info)
   Tab (Next Tab)
   Shift-Tab (Previous Tab)
   F10 (Resume Editing)

3. Move the cursor to the position where you want to set the new tab stop (column 21), and type *T*. A *T* will appear at the ruler line's 21st column, marking the tab setting. Press F10 or Enter to resume editing.

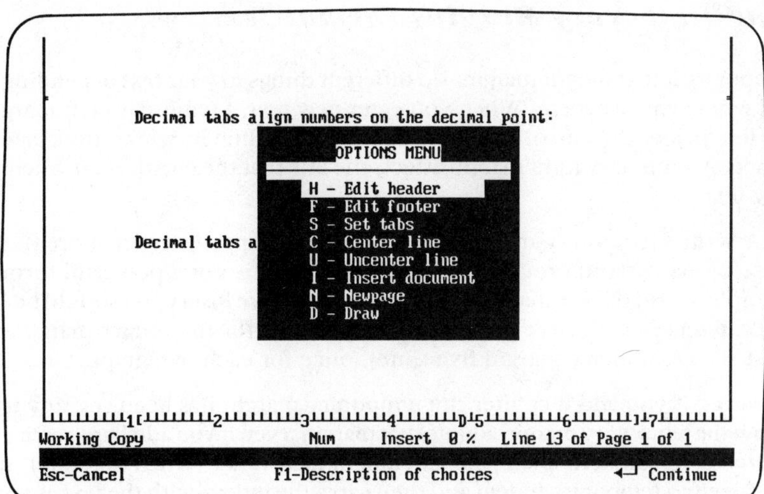


**Fig. 11.4** *The Options menu.*

Deleting a tab stop is similar to adding one. To delete a tab stop, select Set Tabs from the Options Menu, move the cursor to that tab stop, and press the Del key or the space bar to delete the tab stop from the ruler line. Press F10 or Enter to resume editing.

Moving back and forth on the ruler line is easy when you use these keys:

| *Key(s)* | *Cursor Moves To* |
|---|---|
| Home | First space to the right of the left margin |
| End | First space to the left of the right margin |
| Ctrl-← | Five spaces to the left |
| Ctrl-→ | Five spaces to the right |
| Tab | Next tab stop to the right |
| Shift-Tab | Next tab stop to the left |

## *Changing Temporary Margins and Indentations*

Left and right margins are displayed on-screen exactly as they appear when printed. Therefore, you are assured that the margins you set on-screen will remain the same when printed. Two methods are available for changing margins. You can change margins for the whole document by using the Define Page screen from the Write menu (see the "Formatting the Page" section in Chapter 10), or you can change margins temporarily for a part of your document.

## How Temporary Margins Format Text

Temporary left and right margins do different things to your text depending on when and where you use them. When you enter new text, a temporary left margin affects the line below the cursor but does not affect the line in which the cursor is positioned. A temporary right margin affects the line that the cursor is on when you enter new text.

Q&A Write's temporary-margin and indentation capabilities are more flexible than those of many word processors, but the program is not a powerful formatter. For example, if you decide that five paragraphs you have just typed should be indented, you cannot select the five paragraphs and then set the temporary margin once. You must set a temporary margin five times, once for each paragraph.

However, if you add text after the temporary margin has been set, any text added below the temporary margin adopts that margin, even if you add hard carriage returns. There is a lesson here: plan your document in advance (when possible) so that you can specify a temporary indent and then carry the indent with the text as you enter it.

## How To Set a Temporary Margin

You can change the left and right margins by using F6, the temporary margin key. Setting temporary margins is a three-step process in which you move the cursor where you want to set the margin, press F6, and then press L for the left margin or R for the right margin. Temporary margins can be set and cleared anywhere in your document, as often as you choose.

In the sales lead memo, the second paragraph is followed by a list of instructions that require a temporary margin. To prepare your memo, enter the second paragraph as it appears in figure 11.5; include the colon (:) at the end of the paragraph. Press Enter twice to move the cursor two lines below the second paragraph.

To set the temporary left margin,

1. Move the cursor to the memo's 16th column, the position at which you will place a temporary left margin.
2. Press F6. The Set Temporary Margin menu will appear at the bottom of the screen (see fig. 11.6). The menu offers three choices:
   - To create a left margin, choose Left. The Set Temporary Margin menu disappears and a greater-than sign (>) marks the margin in the ruler line.
   - To create a right margin, choose Right. The Set Temporary Margin menu disappears and a less-than sign (<) marks the margin in the ruler line.
   - To delete a temporary margin and restore the default margin settings, move the cursor into the paragraph you want to

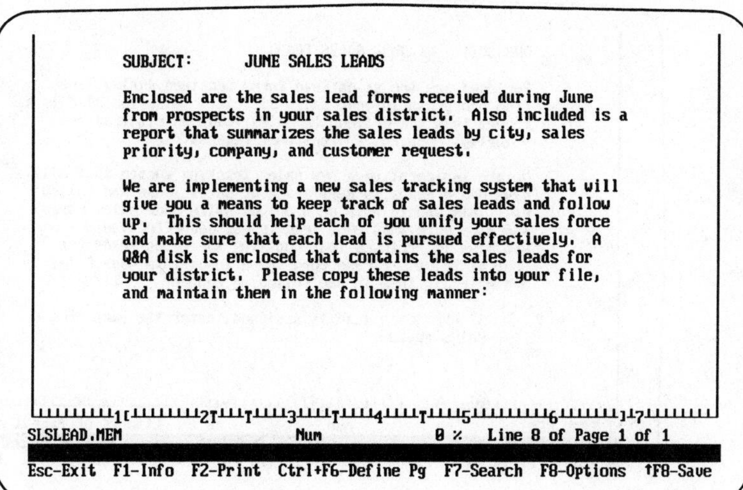


**Fig. 11.5** *Temporary margins in the memo.*

```
and maintain them in the following manner:

Set temporary margin:    L-Left    R-Right    C-Clear
```

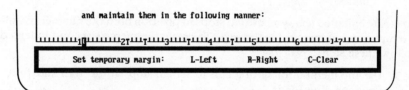

**Fig. 11.6** *The Set Temporary Margin menu.*

change and choose Clear. The temporary margin marker on the ruler line is deleted.

3. Select Left to set a temporary left margin for the memo's first numbered item.

After you set the temporary left margin at column 16, enter the first of the memo's numbered items (see fig. 11.7).

## *How To Indent Text*

Temporary margins are used most often to create a hanging indent format for numbered or bulleted text. A *bullet* is a special character, usually a small circle or dot, used to mark the beginning of elements in a list.

1. This text is an example of the hanging indent format used for numbered or bulleted paragraphs. All text "hangs" flush left, to the right of a number or bullet.

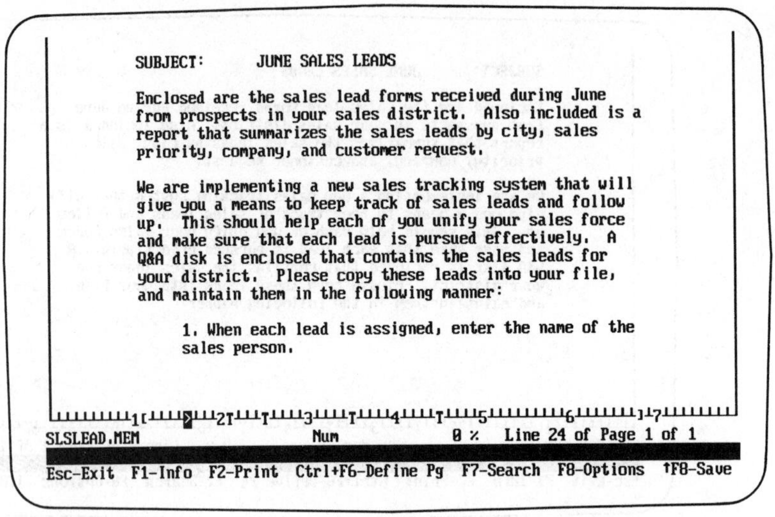

**Fig. 11.7** *Using a temporary margin to indent text.*

```
SUBJECT:      JUNE SALES LEADS

Enclosed are the sales lead forms received during June
from prospects in your sales district.  Also included is a
report that summarizes the sales leads by city, sales
priority, company, and customer request.

We are implementing a new sales tracking system that will
give you a means to keep track of sales leads and follow
up.  This should help each of you unify your sales force
and make sure that each lead is pursued effectively.  A
Q&A disk is enclosed that contains the sales leads for
your district.  Please copy these leads into your file,
and maintain them in the following manner:

      1. When each lead is assigned, enter the name of the
      sales person.

SLSLEAD.MEM                    Num        0 %  Line 24 of Page 1 of 1
Esc-Exit  F1-Info  F2-Print  Ctrl+F6-Define Pg  F7-Search  F8-Options  ↑F8-Save
```

- This text is an example of a hanging indent format using a bullet.

To create indented text, you use tab stops to position both the number or bullet and a temporary left margin for the text. To create the memo's second indented item, follow these steps:

1. Use the method for setting tabs to set tab stops at the 16th and 19th columns, if needed.
2. Press Enter to begin a new item.
3. Press the Tab key to move to the first tab stop (the 16th character on the ruler line).
4. Type *2.*, and press Tab.
5. Press F6 and select Left.
6. Type the text as shown in figure 11.8.

To enter another indented item, press Enter to begin a new item, press Shift-Tab to move the cursor to the left so that you can enter a number or a bullet, and then type the text.

Compare the numbered items in figure 11.8. Notice the difference between the normal format of item 1 and the hanging indent format of item 2, in which the number juts out. You can delete tabs when you are through using them, to keep the ruler line from being cluttered with too many tabs.

```
SUBJECT:        JUNE SALES LEADS

Enclosed are the sales lead forms received during June
from prospects in your sales district. Also included is a
report that summarizes the sales leads by city, sales
priority , company, and customer request.

We are implementing a new sales tracking system that will
give you a means to keep track of sales leads and follow
up. This should help each of you unify your sales force
and make sure that each lead is pursued effectively. A
Q&A disk is enclosed that contains the sales leads for
your district. Please copy these leads into your file,
and maintain them in the following manner:

     1. When each lead is assigned, enter the name of the
     sales person.
     2. Enter the date when the first sales contact was
        made with the sales lead.

SLSLEAD.MEM                Num     Insert  1 %   Line 19 of Page 1 of 1
Esc-Exit  F1-Info  F2-Print  Ctrl+F6-Define Pg  F7-Search  F8-Options  ↑F8-Save
```

**Fig. 11.8**
*Entering a hanging indent paragraph.*

## *Enhancing Text*

Q&A Write includes a full range of text enhancements: boldface, underline, italic, superscript, and subscript. You can enhance text as you enter it or afterward. In either case, you press Shift-F6 to select an option from the enhance text menu (see fig. 11.9).

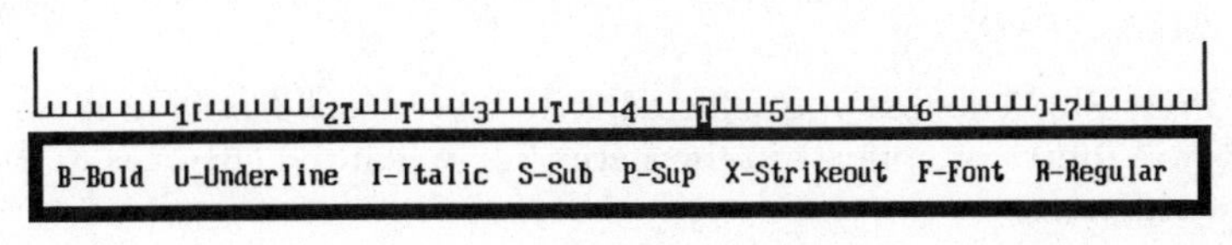


**Fig. 11.9**
*The enhance text menu.*

To enhance text as you type it,

1. Press Shift-F6 for the enhance text menu.
2. Choose an enhancement from the enhance text menu, shown in figure 11.9.
3. Press F10 to continue.
4. Press the Ins key to turn on Insert mode.
5. Enter the text.

You can use one of several methods to turn off the enhancement: press the Ins key to turn off Insert mode; press Enter to start a new line; return to the enhance text menu and select Regular; or press the right-arrow key.

To enhance text that has been entered, select an enhancement and then highlight the text to be enhanced. (You can use a macro to automate the procedure for turning on an enhancement. For information about macros, see Chapter 19.)

Your computer system will determine whether you see the enhancements on-screen or only on the printout. Most displays and printers will show boldface; underline will be visible on monochrome displays but will be shown as a change in color on most color displays.

You edit enhanced text as you would any other text. Characters added within enhanced text will also be enhanced.

## *Boldface Text*

Boldface text usually prints as especially dark text. In the example, let's boldface *JUNE SALES LEADS*. To boldface text that has been entered,

1. Move the cursor to the first character you want to boldface (the *J* of *JUNE*).
2. Press Shift-F6. Q&A displays the enhance text menu.
3. Choose Bold from the enhance text menu; the menu disappears, and Q&A prompts you to select the text to boldface.
4. Move the cursor to highlight the text you want to boldface: *JUNE SALES LEADS.*
5. Press F10. The text you selected is now boldface. Notice that the `Bold` indicator appears in the status line when the cursor is in the boldface text.

## *Underlined Text*

Underlining text that has already been entered requires a slightly different procedure. In the example, the memo's second paragraph asks district sales managers to copy and maintain their files. Because busy sales managers might not read the memo carefully, let's underline this sentence for emphasis:

> Please copy these leads into your file, and maintain them in the following manner:

To underline existing text,

1. Move the cursor to the first character you want to underline. (In the memo, that character is the *P* in *Please.*)

2. Press Shift-F6. Q&A displays the enhance text menu at the bottom of the screen.

3. Select Underline from the enhance text menu; the menu disappears, and Q&A prompts you to select the text to be underlined.

4. Move the cursor to highlight the text you want underlined.

5. Press F10. The text you selected will now print underlined. Notice that the status line includes the `Undl` indicator when the cursor is in the underlined text. How the underlined text appears on-screen depends on the type of display adapter and monitor you are using.

Underlining a blank line presents special problems. If you are creating a form, you may want such a line—for example,

Name_______________________________________________

Underlining cannot be used in completely empty spaces. The line may be displayed on your screen but probably will not print on your printer. To get around this obstacle, put an insignificant character (like a period) at the end of the underline.

You might try to use the Q&A Draw features (explained later in this chapter) to create an underlined blank space. The Draw line, however, is a midline that appears in the middle of the character space, whereas an underline appears under the character space. Compare the underline with the line created with Draw:

Name———————————————————————

## *Italic Text*

Q&A Write also supports italic text. You can use this enhancement if your printer supports italic type. Most printers support this feature. Refer to your printer manual for the specific codes necessary to initiate italic text with your printer. The standard IBM® monochrome and color graphic adapters do not display italic. Instead, italicized text is marked with boldface and the status line indicates `Ital` when the cursor is in the italic text.

You will italicize the term *sales person* in step 1 of the sales lead memo. To italicize text that has been entered previously,

1. Move the cursor to the first character you want to italicize. (In the sales leads memo, that character is the first *s* in *sales*.)

2. Press Shift-F6. Q&A displays the enhance text menu at the bottom of the screen.

3. Select Italic from the enhance text menu. The menu disappears, and Q&A prompts you to select the text to be italicized.

4. Move the cursor to highlight the text you want italicized (the words *sales person* in the memo).

5. Press F10. The text you selected is now italic. Notice that the status line includes the Ital indicator when the cursor is in the italic text.

## *Superscript and Subscript Text*

*Superscript* and *subscript* text is printed above or below the base printing line and usually is smaller than surrounding text. Documents that include scientific terms or footnotes may use superscript or subscript text. A superscript is frequently used to point to a footnote or other document note:

...is the smallest of the sub-atomic particles.[1]

Superscripts also are used in measurement or other special designations:

$ft^3$
$yd^2$

Subscripts display characters below the base printing line and are useful in scientific and engineering applications:

$H_2O$
...Enter the number $A5_{16}$ and press Enter.

As with other text enhancements, superscript and subscript may not be available for your printer. They almost certainly will not show up on your screen.

To superscript or subscript existing text,

1. Move the cursor to the first character you want to enhance.
2. Press Shift-F6. Q&A displays the enhance text menu at the bottom of the screen.
3. Choose Sup (superscript) or Sub (for subscript) from the enhance text menu. The menu disappears, and Q&A prompts you to select the text to be enhanced.
4. Move the cursor to highlight the text you want enhanced.
5. Press F10. The text you selected will now print as superscript or subscript (assuming that your printer supports the enhancement). Note that Q&A cannot display these special text enhancements on-screen.

The status line includes the Subs indicator when the cursor is in subscript text. If the cursor is in superscript text, the Sups indicator is displayed.

Return enhanced text to normal by following the procedure for creating enhanced text, except that you choose the Regular option from the enhance text menu.

## *Centering and Uncentering a Line*

Q&A Write offers an easy way to center text on a page. With the Center Line command from the Options menu, you can instantly center a line of text between the left and right margins. With the Uncenter Line command, you can quickly uncenter a centered line.

As with other formatting commands, Center Line can be used to center existing text or to center text as you enter it. Add the word *INSTRUCTIONS* at the left margin, between the first and second paragraphs of the memo. To center the word as shown in figure 11.10,

1. Move the cursor to the line you want to center.
2. Press F8 (Options).
3. Select Center Line from the Options menu. Q&A instantly moves the text to the center of the page.

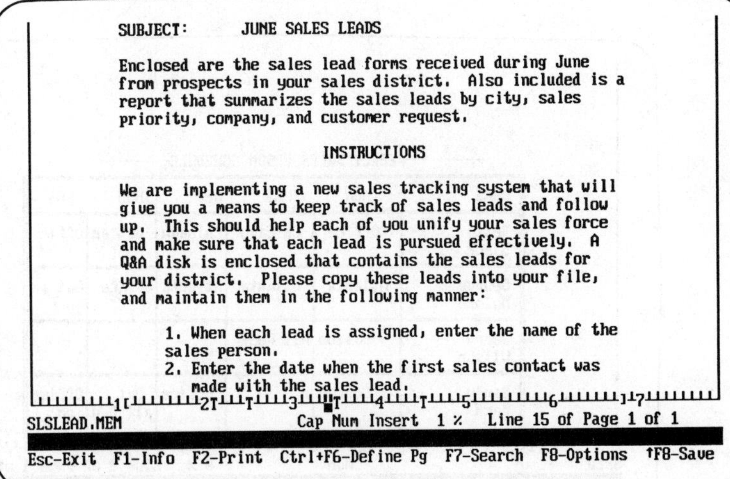
SUBJECT: JUNE SALES LEADS

Enclosed are the sales lead forms received during June from prospects in your sales district. Also included is a report that summarizes the sales leads by city, sales priority, company, and customer request.

INSTRUCTIONS

We are implementing a new sales tracking system that will give you a means to keep track of sales leads and follow up. This should help each of you unify your sales force and make sure that each lead is pursued effectively. A Q&A disk is enclosed that contains the sales leads for your district. Please copy these leads into your file, and maintain them in the following manner:

1. When each lead is assigned, enter the name of the sales person.
2. Enter the date when the first sales contact was made with the sales lead.

SLSLEAD.MEM Cap Num Insert 1 % Line 15 of Page 1 of 1

Esc-Exit F1-Info F2-Print Ctrl+F6-Define Pg F7-Search F8-Options ↑F8-Save

**Fig. 11.10**
*Centering a line.*

To uncenter the line: move the cursor to the centered line, press F8 (Options), and select Uncenter Line. Q&A moves the text to the left margin.

## *Drawing Lines and Boxes*

Q&A's drawing capability is a formatting feature that allows you easily to create single or double lines. Using the Draw feature's single and double lines, you can add lines, boxes, and even simple illustrations to your documents, reports, and forms. Figures 11.11 and 11.12 demonstrate some of the possibilities.

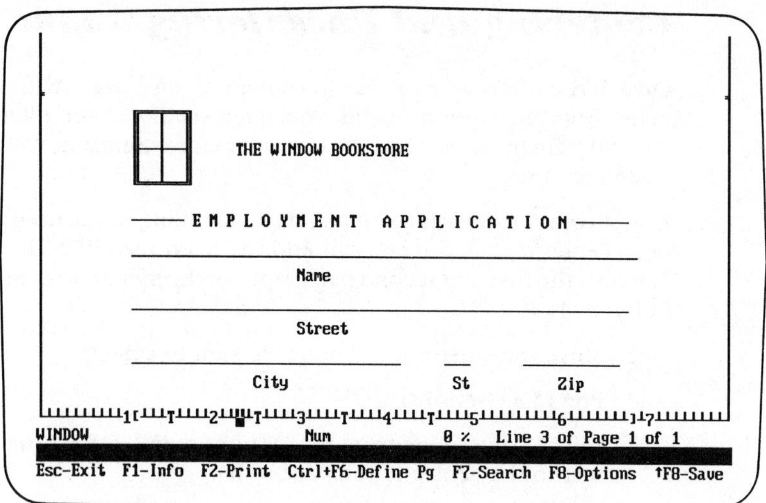


**Fig. 11.11** *Business forms created with Draw.*

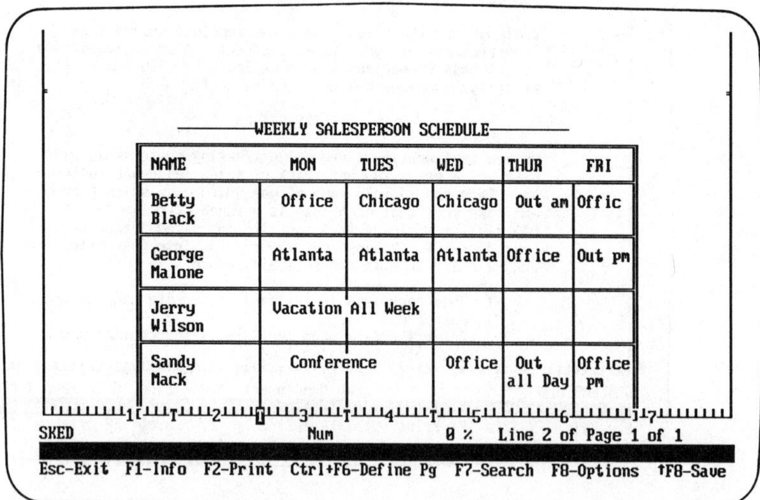


**Fig. 11.12** *Form created with Draw.*

To use the Draw feature, you first enter and edit the text, leaving room for the lines; then you draw the lines. You must work in this order because inserting and deleting characters can move sections of lines, leaving distorted illustrations. As you enter the text, imagine where you will put the lines. Be sure to leave enough space to ensure a pleasing layout.

You can use a line to box a section of a document (see fig. 11.13). To box the text, set temporary margins to indent the text and make room for the box. Next, center the *INSTRUCTIONS* heading, if needed. Then draw the box, using the cursor drawing keys shown in figure 11.14 to move the cursor and draw lines.

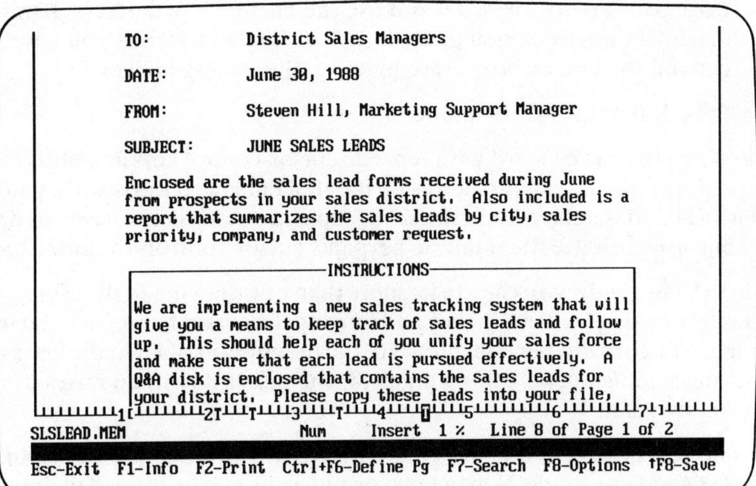

TO: District Sales Managers

DATE: June 30, 1988

FROM: Steven Hill, Marketing Support Manager

SUBJECT: JUNE SALES LEADS

Enclosed are the sales lead forms received during June from prospects in your sales district. Also included is a report that summarizes the sales leads by city, sales priority, company, and customer request.

INSTRUCTIONS

We are implementing a new sales tracking system that will give you a means to keep track of sales leads and follow up. This should help each of you unify your sales force and make sure that each lead is pursued effectively. A Q&A disk is enclosed that contains the sales leads for your district. Please copy these leads into your file,

SLSLEAD.MEM Num Insert 1 % Line 8 of Page 1 of 2

Esc-Exit F1-Info F2-Print Ctrl+F6-Define Pg F7-Search F8-Options ↑F8-Save

**Fig. 11.13** *Using the Drawing feature.*

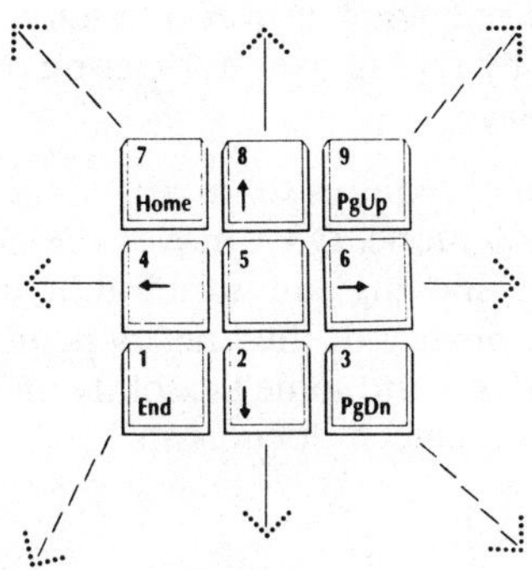


**Fig. 11.14** *The cursor drawing keys.*

To draw the box,

1. Place the cursor where you want to start drawing the corner of the box.

2. Press F8 (Options).

3. Select Draw from the Options menu. Q&A displays drawing instructions in the message line.

4. Draw single lines by pressing the cursor drawing keys to move the cursor. To draw double lines, hold down the Shift key and move the cursor or press Num Lock (the `Num` indicator appears) and then move the cursor. To erase part of a line while you are drawing it, use the

Backspace key, or press F8 and use the cursor drawing keys. (Draw diagonal lines by pressing the 1, 3, 7, and 9 keys.) Once you have entered the line or box, erase by using the Backspace key.

5. Press F10 to quit Draw mode.

***Note:*** If you have a keyboard with separate cursor-control keys as well as cursor controls on the numeric keypad (such as on the IBM Enhanced Keyboard), you will need to work a little differently. You can use the separate cursor-control keys to draw *single* lines, but you must use the numeric keypad's cursor controls to draw *double* lines.

While in Draw mode, you can create more than one drawing in the same document. Do this by pressing F6 (Pen Up) key and moving the cursor to the location of the next drawing. Notice that when you press F6, the description of F6 in the key assignment line changes to `Pen Down`. F6 is a toggle. If the pen is down, F6 raises it; if the pen is up, F6 lowers it.

If you make a mistake while drawing with Q&A, you can erase the error. Press F8 to put Q&A in Erase mode. Now when you move the cursor, instead of drawing you'll be erasing both lines and text—so be careful. When you are ready to begin drawing again, press F8 to return to Draw mode.

To quit drawing, press F10. Be careful with your drawing, however; after you return to Type/Edit mode, you can ruin the drawing by typing over it, deleting part of it, inserting new text, or moving a line out of place.

Drawing anything more than fairly simple shapes requires some real concentration and probably a little frustration. Even in Draw mode, Q&A moves the cursor by character spaces, so you may envision just the drawing you want but be unable to get the cursor to go there precisely. Also, the quality of the lines depends on the graphic capabilities of your printer. A little testing—and some flexibility on how the finished drawing should look—will result in enhanced documents.

## Starting a New Page

When you want to begin a section of a document on a new page, Q&A Write lets you insert a page break in the middle of a document. The text following the break will begin at the top of the next page. To start a new page, move the cursor to the line on which you want to start the next page, press F8 for the Options menu, and select Newpage.

To start the sales memo's INSTRUCTIONS box on a new page,

1. Position the cursor on what will be the first line of the new page.
2. Press F8 (Options).
3. Select Newpage from the Options menu, moving the box to the next page (see fig. 11.15).

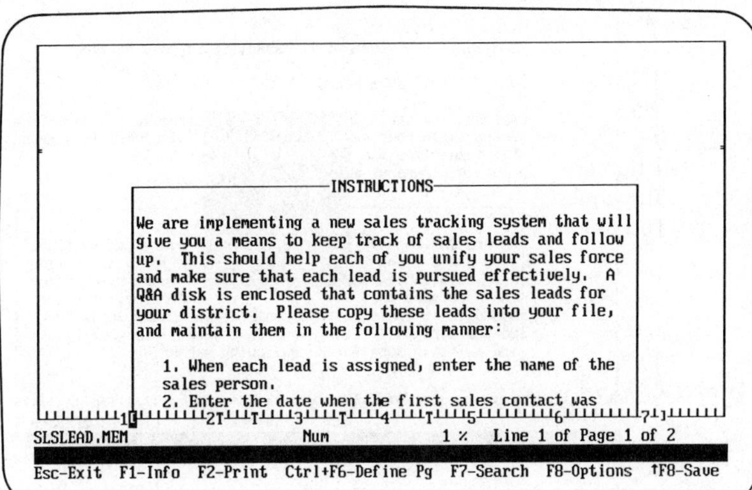
INSTRUCTIONS

We are implementing a new sales tracking system that will give you a means to keep track of sales leads and follow up. This should help each of you unify your sales force and make sure that each lead is pursued effectively. A Q&A disk is enclosed that contains the sales leads for your district. Please copy these leads into your file, and maintain them in the following manner:

1. When each lead is assigned, enter the name of the sales person.
2. Enter the date when the first sales contact was

SLSLEAD.MEM Num 1 % Line 1 of Page 1 of 2

Esc-Exit F1-Info F2-Print Ctrl+F6-Define Pg F7-Search F8-Options ↑F8-Save

**Fig. 11.15** *The new page with the text at the top.*

Q&A adds a page-break marker in column 1 of the last line of the preceding page. The marker looks like a reversed double *L*.

To delete a page break, position the cursor on the page-break marker and press the Del key.

## *Moving the Cursor to Another Page*

You can use Ctrl-F7, the GoTo key, to move to another page in your document or to move to a specific line on a page. When you press Ctrl-F7, a box is displayed (see fig. 11.16). The box prompts you to enter the number of the page you want to display; type the number and press Enter. Next, enter the line number and press F10. The cursor moves to the location you specified.

Pressing F5 copies the current page and line number into the GoTo box. You can use this feature as a page marker; when you move to a different location and press Ctrl-F7, the cursor position recorded when you pressed F5 is displayed.

## *Using Headers and Footers*

For reports, letters, and memos that are longer than a page, or for other types of long manuscripts, Q&A's header and footer capabilities offer the option of automatically entering titles, dates, page numbers, and so forth at the top or bottom of each page. A simple footer, for example, is a page number. Business letters of more than one page often have an identification header that starts on the second page. The header could include the addressee's name, the page number, and the date—for example,

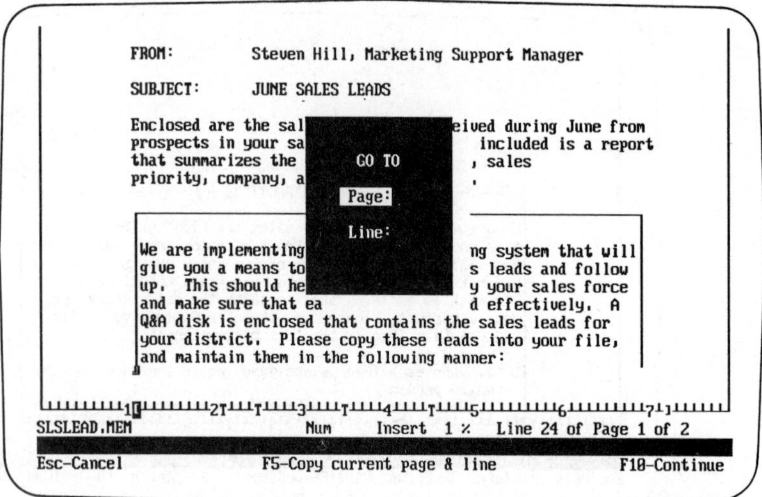


**Fig. 11.16**
*The GoTo box.*

Mr. Robert Woods — 2 — June 15, 1988

Headers, footers, or both can be added, edited, or deleted at any point in the document. Their starting page can be set in the Write menu's Define Page option. Once added, headers and footers appear on every page, beginning with their starting page.

## *Adding Headers and Footers*

The header at the top of page two of the sales memo displays the memo's subject and date. The footer at the bottom of page two is the page number—for example, *Page 2*.

To add a header,

1. Press F8 (Options).
2. Select Edit Header from the Options menu. Q&A displays the top of the page (see fig. 11.17). Notice that the cursor is in the header and that a double line separates the header from the rest of the page. Notice also that the key assignment line indicates that the enhance text menu and the Options menu are available for editing the header.
3. Type the information to be included in the header (see fig. 11.17). Remember that the top edge of the paper is indicated by the top border lines above the header.

To format the header, use the Enhance and Option features. The Options menu offers the Set Tabs, Center Line, Uncenter Line, and Draw commands. The enhance text menu offers Boldface, Underline, Italic, Subscript, and Superscript type. You also can

```
        June Sales Leads
        June 30, 1988


        TO:            District Sales Managers

        DATE:          June 30, 1988

        FROM:          Steven Hill, Marketing Support Manager

        SUBJECT:       JUNE SALES LEADS

        Enclosed are the sales lead forms received during June
        from prospects in your sales district.  Also included is a
        report that summarizes the sales leads by city, sales
SLSLEAD.MEM                              1 %   Line 1 Header
When finished, press F10 to return to main text.
F1-Info        Shift+F6-Enhance        F8-Options        F10-Exit Header
```

**Fig. 11.17** *The header editing area.*

enter print codes directly in the text (discussed in Chapter 13). After you have created the header, press F10 to return to Type/Edit mode.

The procedure for adding a footer is the same as that for adding a header, except that you select Edit Footer from the Options menu. Type *Page #* as the footer text.

To edit a header or footer, you select Edit Header or Edit Footer from the Options menu and then use the program's normal text-editing features.

## *Setting the Header and Footer Starting Points*

Set the starting point for a header and footer using two options in the Define Page screen:

Begin Header/Footer on Page #
Begin Page Numbering with Page #

When you set one, you ordinarily set the other as well. For example, because the memo's header will begin on page two, the footer containing the page number also will begin on page two.

To set the header and footer starting points,

1. From the Type/Edit screen, press the Esc key to return to the Write menu. The document will remain on-screen.

2. Select the Define Page command and press Enter. Q&A displays the Define Page screen.

3. Using the Tab or down-arrow keys, move the cursor to the `Begin Header/Footer on Page #` option.
4. Type *2* (the number of the page on which you want the header or footer to start) and press Enter.
5. Move the cursor to the `Begin Page Numbering with Page #` option.
6. Type *2* and press Enter.
7. Press F10 to return to the Type/Edit screen and the memo. Notice that the header and footer begin on page two rather than page one. Notice also that the page number on page two correctly states *2*.

## *Inserting Page Numbers in Headers and Footers*

Q&A Write can number your pages automatically. For example, the memo's footer reads *Page #*. Q&A Write reads the pound sign (*#*) as ''Put the page number here.'' The page number will appear wherever you enter the pound sign in a header or footer. If you want a header or footer to show a pound sign followed by the page number, enter *##*. This will be printed on page 7 as *#7*.

## *Adding Date and Time to Headers and Footers*

Headers and footers often include the date and time. Q&A uses the computer's current date and time; that is, the time and date you set when you turned on the computer. To include the date or time in a header or footer, use the following format:

*@DATE(n)*     *@TIME(n)*

The *n* is the display format number for the date and time. Twenty different formats are available for dates, and three formats for time. The following list shows all the available date and time formats:

| | | | |
|---|---|---|---|
| @DATE(1) | Sep 2, 1988 | @DATE(11) | September 2, 1988 |
| @DATE(2) | 2 Sep 1988 | @DATE(12) | 2 September 1988 |
| @DATE(3) | 9/2/88 | @DATE(13) | 9-2-88 |
| @DATE(4) | 2/9/88 | @DATE(14) | 2-9-88 |
| @DATE(5) | 9/2/1988 | @DATE(15) | 09-02-88 |
| @DATE(6) | 2/9/1988 | @DATE(16) | 09-02-1988 |
| @DATE(7) | 09/02/88 | @DATE(17) | 02.09.88 |
| @DATE(8) | 02/09/88 | @DATE(18) | 02.09.1988 |
| @DATE(9) | 09/02/1988 | @DATE(19) | 1988-09-02 |
| @DATE(10) | 02/09/1988 | @DATE(20) | 1988/09/02 |
| @TIME(1) | 11:39 am | @TIME(3) | 11.39 |
| @TIME(2) | 11:39 | | |

Although dates and times are used often within headers and footers, these features can be used anywhere in the document. If you are creating a form letter, for example, you could save considerable time by having Q&A insert the date and time for you.

# Customizing Global Options in Q&A Write

Q&A Write has values preset for a wide range of global settings that affect the editing of your document as well as its appearance on the screen and in printouts. These values include

Tab settings
Page formats
Header/footer settings
Print options

By changing these settings, you can customize the Write word processor to meet your own preferences and needs.

To change Write's global settings, select Utilities from the Write menu. Then select Set Global Options from the Write Utilities menu, calling up the Global Options menu. This menu includes three commands:

Set Editing Options
Change Print Defaults
Change Page Defaults

From the Global Options menu you can elect to change editing, printing, and page settings. The global options determine how Write is configured when you first load it. Of course, you can make changes inside Write for special treatment of any document, but you should establish global options so that Write is set up the way you want to use it most of the time.

Remember that none of the changes from the Global Options menu is retroactive. Changes apply only to newly created documents. Each document retains its own formatting specifications with it when it is saved.

## Setting Editing Options

To set the editing defaults, select Set Editing Options from the Global Options menu. The Editing Options screen will be displayed (see fig. 11.18).

Use the Default Editing Mode option to determine whether you will use Insert or Overwrite mode when you edit the document. The setting you choose depends on your personal preference. People often use Insert mode to keep them from accidentally typing over text they have entered.

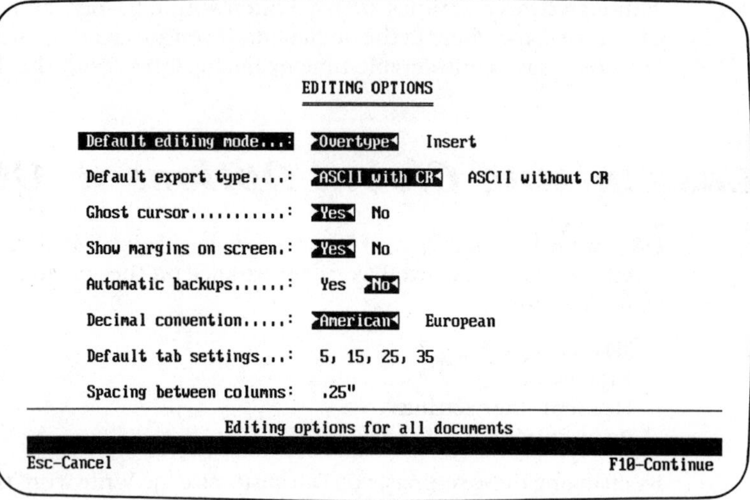
EDITING OPTIONS

Default editing mode...: Overtype Insert
Default export type....: ASCII with CR ASCII without CR
Ghost cursor...........: Yes No
Show margins on screen.: Yes No
Automatic backups......: Yes No
Decimal convention.....: American European
Default tab settings...: 5, 15, 25, 35
Spacing between columns: .25"

Editing options for all documents

Esc-Cancel F10-Continue

**Fig. 11.18** *The Editing Options screen.*

The Default Export Type setting is used to export files in ASCII format. The two options represent the types of ASCII files: with carriage returns or without. The ASCII with CR option places a carriage return-line feed at the end of every line. You would select this setting for exporting tables and charts, or for use in another editing system that does not support wordwrap. The ASCII without CR option places carriage return-line feed combinations only at paragraph breaks. Lines within paragraphs do not end in a carriage return, so another text processing package can perform its own wordwrap on the text. (For more information on exporting data to ASCII files, see Chapter 20.)

The Ghost Cursor option displays on the ruler line a cursor that corresponds to the cursor on the Type/Edit screen. The ghost cursor is like a shadow of the main cursor and helps you locate the exact typing position in the document by character position. You also can choose to turn off the margins display by setting the Show Margins on Screen setting to No. If you accept the Yes default, two brackets appear on the ruler line, indicating the right and left margins, and a screen border indicates page edges.

Another global option is the Automatic Backups selection. When you select Yes, a backup of your document is created each time you save the file. Before you can use this feature, you must have saved the file one time so that Q&A has a file name to work with. For example, with this option, if you have an existing document named LET1.DOC, and you edit and save it to disk, your disk will contain two files: LET1.DOC and LET1.BAK. This duplication is a major safety feature of Q&A: in case of data loss, you can simply rename the BAK file instead of recreating your entire document.

With the Decimal Convention setting, you can choose the European or American decimal system; the only difference is the decimal indicator. The European style uses the comma as the indicator (for example, 1,2), whereas the American style uses the period (for example, 1.2). You'll need to use this feature when you are setting decimal tabs or using row/column arithmetic.

With the Default Tab Settings, you can assign a ruler line location to each tab. For example, if you want to set tabs at five-character intervals beginning at the twenty-fifth character position and set a decimal tab at position 50, you would type

25, 30, 35, 40, 45, 50D

Because Write can print more than one column of text on a page, the Global Options screen has an option, Spacing between Columns, for setting the amount of space between columns. You can enter the setting in inches (.25"), centimeters (.95cm), or ruler line increments (7). These settings indicate how columns will print if you have specified multiple-column printing from the Print Options screen for a specific document. The default is one column, but you can specify up to eight columns. Display the Print Options screen by pressing F2 (Print) in the Type/Edit mode.

After you have made all the appropriate changes, press F10 to save the settings. These global settings will now apply to all new documents created in Write. If you don't want to save the settings, press Esc to return to the Global Options menu.

## *Changing Print Defaults*

From the Global Options menu (accessed by choosing Set Global Options from the Write Utilities menu), you also can change global print settings. When you select Change Print Defaults, the Print Options screen is displayed. This screen is the same Print Options screen you see when you print an individual document. The difference is that these settings are global in nature. (See Chapter 13 for more information on setting print options.)

After you make any necessary changes, press F10, and the new settings will apply to all new documents created in Write. If you want to abandon the changes, press Esc to return to the Global Options menu.

## *Changing Page Defaults*

Change Page Defaults is the third command on Write's Global Options menu. When you select this command, the Define Page screen is displayed. The screen is the same one displayed when you press Ctrl-F6 (Define Pg) in the Type/Edit mode. When entered through the Global Options menu, however, any changes apply to all new documents rather than just the document currently on-screen.

You can choose the defaults for the left, right, top, and bottom margins, and specify page length and width for new documents from this screen. The length and width settings indicate the paper size in characters or inches. To define margins in inches, use whole or fractional numbers followed by the inch sign ("). If you use character columns or number of lines, you must use whole numbers.

The left and right margins are shown as the brackets on the ruler line, and the top and bottom margins appear on the screen as equal signs (=). Other defaults include the characters per inch setting, header and footer designation, and page numbering system.

After you make the changes and save the settings, all new documents will have the same defaults. You can modify the defaults if necessary, which makes creating several different documents from one Write document an easy task. (See Chapter 10 for more information on the Define Page screen).

# *Using WordStar Control Characters in Q&A Write*

If you have used WordStar, you will feel at home with Q&A. Q&A Write incorporates the WordStar control characters listed in tables 11.1 and 11.2. You can add other WordStar commands by defining a macro and assigning it to the WordStar control-key combination. (For more information about macros, see Chapter 19.)

**Table 11.1**
**WordStar Cursor-Movement Keys**

| *Keys* | *Moves to* |
|---|---|
| Ctrl-A | Preceding word |
| Ctrl-S | Preceding character |
| Ctrl-D | Next character |
| Ctrl-F | Next word |
| Ctrl-E | Up one line |
| Ctrl-X | Down one line |
| Ctrl-R | First character of preceding screen (page up) |
| Ctrl-C | First character of next screen (page down) |
| Ctrl-I | Tab |
| Ctrl-M | Enter |

**Table 11.2**
**WordStar Editing Keys**

| *Keys* | *Function* |
|---|---|
| Ctrl-G | Delete character at cursor |
| Ctrl-T | Delete to end of word |
| Ctrl-N | Insert line |
| Ctrl-H | Backspace |
| Ctrl-Y | Delete line |
| Ctrl-V | Insert on/off |

## *Using Q&A's Math Functions*

If your document includes numbers, such as costs of individual items, travel expenses, quantities, and the like, you may need to use Q&A to perform calculations. You can perform calculations on numbers you type directly into a Write document or on numbers that are imported into a document from another program, such as 1-2-3® or Symphony®.

You can use the Alt-F9 key to calculate equations, but you must first position the cursor. To calculate a row of numbers, position the cursor *after* the last number in that row. To calculate a column of numbers, place the cursor *on* the last number in the column. When you press Alt-F9, the calculation menu appears, which includes five math functions: Total, Average, Count, Multiply, and Divide.

After you position the cursor and press Alt-F9, the numbers in the calculation are highlighted. Select the appropriate choice from the menu, position the cursor where you want the result of the calculation to appear, and press F10. Q&A is capable of performing calculations on rows or columns that contain only numbers (no text) as well as on rows or columns that have text and numbers together (see figs. 11.19 and 11.20).

```
Monthly sales have increase gradually with July sales at
$17,892, August at $18,900 and September at $19,200, totaling
```

**Fig. 11.19** *Calculating numbers interspersed with text.*

```
Monthly sales have increase gradually with July sales at
$17,892, August at $18,900 and September at $19,200, totaling
$55,992. As the table below indicates, sales for these three
months significantly increased over last years' for the same
three months.

                  1987 Sales          1988 Sales

July               12,245              17,892
August             12,568              18,900
September          13,798              19,200
                   ------              ------
                   38,611

Calculation:  T-Total  A-Average  C-Count  M-Multiply  D-Divide
```

**Fig. 11.20** *Calculating columns of numbers.*

To conduct calculations on columns of numbers,

1. Position the cursor at the end of the last number in the column you want calculated.
2. Press Alt-F9. The column will be highlighted.
3. Select the operation you want.
4. Move the cursor to the screen position where the result should be inserted, and press F10. The calculation will be conducted and the result placed at the cursor location.

If you change any of the numbers on which you have performed a calculation, you need to recalculate the values by repeating the Alt-F9 operation. Q&A Write does not automatically recalculate.

## *Using Apple Macintosh Documents with Write*

With Q&A Version 3.0, Symantec has addressed the growing trend toward heterogeneous computer environments. Rarely do all users in a business use the same machines and operating systems. For example, some people depend on the IBM PC or a clone, for the variety of software or for compatibility across a broad range of applications. Others use an Apple Macintosh™ for its excellent graphics support or friendly user interface.

Whatever the reason, users increasingly need to be able to share information among both similar and dissimilar machines. To answer this need, Q&A is compatible with a number of IBM PC-based networks, as well as Apple's AppleShare™ file server software. AppleShare support lets you attach an IBM PC running Q&A to an AppleShare file server and share files across the network with other PCs or Apple machines.

To use Q&A with an AppleShare file server, you need a special interface card for your PC. Your Apple dealer can supply more information. Once the hardware link is working, you can store Q&A programs and files on the AppleShare file server. You can run programs on your PC from the server and store Q&A Write or File data on the server, where other PC-based Q&A users can share the data and where Apple users can access files you have stored in an Apple-compatible format.

Currently, Q&A does not run directly on Apple machines, but Apple users can access Microsoft® Word, WordPerfect®, and other word-processing programs. As a Q&A user, you can save Q&A text files in Macintosh ASCII format for access by an Apple software program.

To export files to ASCII format, select Utilities from the Write menu and then choose Export to ASCII. The ASCII Export menu will be displayed, which includes three commands. The Standard ASCII command includes a carriage return-line feed combination at the end of every line. The Document ASCII command includes carriage returns and line feeds only at paragraph breaks. This command is designed for use with other text-processing software that can handle wordwrap. The third command, Macintosh ASCII, exports files with the Macintosh carriage return character, which is different from the one used by PC DOS or MS-DOS® computers.

## Chapter Summary

This chapter has demonstrated text enhancements and formatting. After reading this chapter and Chapter 10, you should be able to use the word-processing capabilities of Q&A Write to produce an edited and formatted document, ready to be printed.

Q&A Write compares favorably with other word processors in most of its functions and outshines the others in at least one function—a direct link to the mailing lists and other data in Q&A File. This integration helps you produce personalized mailings, reports with information from databases, and dozens of other mailmerge projects. The next chapter thoroughly explains how you can become the fastest "mailmerger" in your office.

Chapter

12

# Merging Documents with Q&A Write

You often begin your work by using only one document at a time. As the various segments of your work become related, however, you may need to combine the information from files originally created in Q&A and those created with other software programs. You may want to pull blocks of text from one document and insert them into another, add one document to another, or merge file data into a document. Q&A's power and flexibility can help you perform these operations.

This chapter explains how to move text from an existing Write document to a newly created Write document, how to import text from other programs and insert the text into a Write document, and how to use Q&A's mailmerge capability to merge File data into a Write document.

## *Moving Text from an Existing Write Document to a New Write Text File*

Write's built-in capacity to move blocks of text out of an existing document and into a newly created document can be used in many ways. You can extract from a memo pieces of information that you want to use again, for example. Or you can save only what you need from a long document, thus reducing disk storage space.

To move text out of a document and into a new text file, use the Alt-F5 command with the text-block selection process explained in Chapter 10. Note that this operation not only moves text to a new text file but also removes that text from the current document.

Suppose that you want to export the second paragraph in figure 12.1 to another file so that you can copy it into other documents.

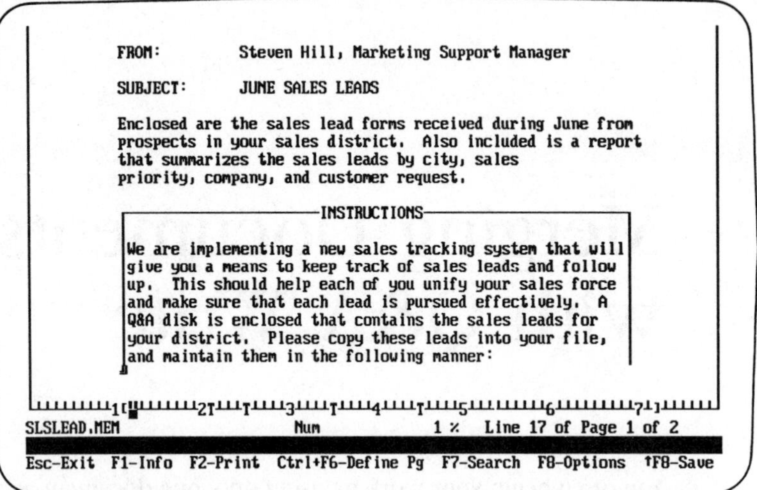


**Fig. 12.1**
*Moving text to a new document.*

The procedure for moving a block of text on-screen to another file consists of marking the block that you want to move and indicating the file name. First, move the cursor to the beginning of the text you want to move. Press Alt-F5 to begin the move operation. When Q&A prompts you to highlight the block you want to export, move the cursor to the end of the block (see fig. 12.2). (To highlight a block quickly, use the procedures described in the section "Deleting, Moving, Copying, and Printing Blocks of Text" in Chapter 10.)

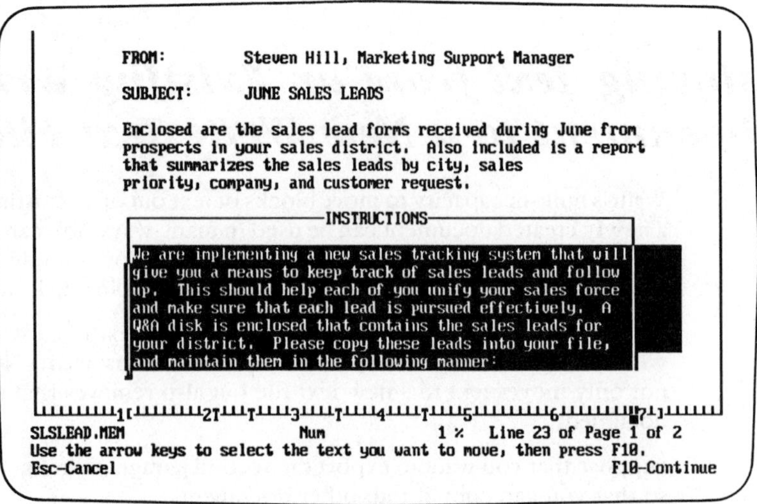


**Fig. 12.2**
*Highlighting the text to be moved.*

Next, press F10 to indicate where you want the block moved. When the prompt `Move to` appears, you can enter a file name either to create a new file for saving the block or to use an existing file. If you use the name of an existing file, all text currently in the file will be overwritten by the new block. If an existing file is going to be overwritten, Q&A alerts you and asks for confirmation to proceed with the operation. After you indicate the text file to which Q&A should move the block, Q&A removes it from the document on-screen and saves it to the file.

## Merging Q&A File Data into a Write Document

Mailmerge, an automated process in which Q&A File and Write are closely integrated, is an excellent example of Q&A's "appropriate integration" of database and word processor. In the *mailmerge* operation, Q&A automatically inserts data from a File database into a Write document and prints the document. Few programs perform mailmerge operations as effortlessly as Q&A.

With mailmerge, you can produce forms and automatically fill the forms with appropriate information. Such forms include contracts and other legal documents; personnel records; form letters; and tax, accounting, and business forms.

Before you can perform a merge operation, you must have a Q&A File database from which to retrieve data. Merging the File data into a Write document is a two-step process. First, using Write, you create a merge document (such as a letter or form) to which you add formatting instructions for the merged data. You then specify the proper print options and print the document. Wherever information is to be merged into the document, an asterisk precedes and follows the name of a database field. Q&A automatically merges the appropriate data from the file into the merge document.

The merge operation occurs when a document is printed. When you instruct Write to print with a merge operation, Q&A notes the database from which the merge information will be retrieved, looks through the document for merge specifications that indicate which fields to use in the merge, and retrieves that information from the database. Then Q&A inserts the information into the document and prints the document with the merged information.

Figures 12.3 and 12.4 show the Write documents and the File form involved in a mailmerge. Figure 12.3 shows a contract form before the merge.

The merge operation is based on field names in a File database. By enclosing field names in asterisks, you tell Write to go to a File database, look for the named field, and substitute the information found there for the field label in the Write document. These File specifications in a Write document form the merge spec. The merge spec tells Q&A Write which fields to use from the linked database and where to place the fields in the document.

The example in figure 12.3 uses field labels from the CONTRACT.DTF database shown in figure 12.4. Note that during the initial document design and preparation, you do not need to specify which database File will use during the merge. That information is supplied when the Write document is printed.

Write searches the CONTRACT.DTF database for the field label Software and inserts *Autobook* where the merge spec **Software** appears. Write finds the field label Version in the same record and substitutes *1.0* where the merge spec **version** appears in the Write document.

**Fig. 12.3** *A Write document with merge specifications.*

```
                    COPYRIGHT ASSIGNMENT
     The "Software" shall mean the computer program currently
referred to as *Software*, version *version*. The "Developer"
is *Developer*.  The "Publisher" is *Publisher*.

    For valuable consideration, the Developer, *Developer*,
hereby assigns, sells, transfers, sets over, and conveys to
the Publisher, *Publisher*, all right, title, and interest in
and to *software*, version *version*, including the undivided
copyrights, trade secret rights, and other proprietary rights,
therein now known or hereafter created throughout the world,
and further, including any and all claims, demands, and causes
of action, for infringement or otherwise, of the same, past,
present, and future, and all of the proceeds from the
foregoing accrued and unpaid and hereafter acruing.

COPYRITE                  Num     Insert  0 %   Line 15 of Page 1 of 1
Esc-Exit  F1-Info  F2-Print  Ctrl+F6-Define Pg  F7-Search  F8-Options  ↑F8-Save
```

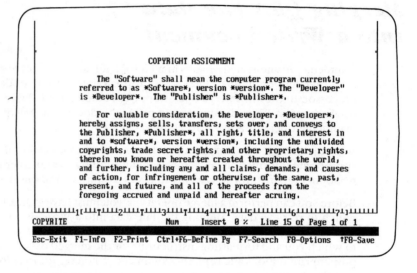

**Fig. 12.4** *The file form that is the source of merge data.*

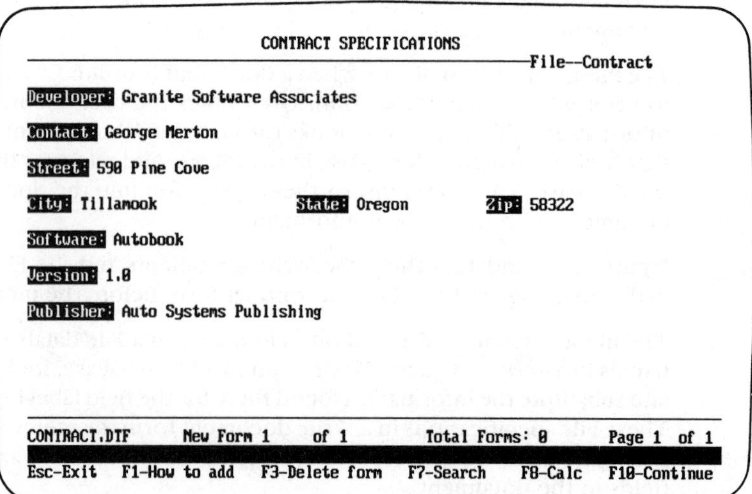

```
                    CONTRACT SPECIFICATIONS
                                                  File--Contract
Developer: Granite Software Associates

Contact: George Merton

Street: 590 Pine Cove

City: Tillamook              State: Oregon          Zip: 58322

Software: Autobook

Version: 1.0

Publisher: Auto Systems Publishing

CONTRACT.DTF     New Form 1     of 1       Total Forms: 0      Page 1  of 1
Esc-Exit  F1-How to add   F3-Delete form   F7-Search   F8-Calc   F10-Continue
```

In addition to using mailmerge with legal documents, you can use mailmerge to produce personalized mailings by inserting names, addresses, and other information into a form letter. With Q&A's mailmerge operation, you can address a single letter to one person or hundreds of letters to hundreds of people.

Figure 12.5 shows an example of a mailmerge letter from the sales lead tracking system. Data has been merged from the sales lead database form shown in figure 12.6.

Turner Philips
General Manager
Nashville Medical Technology
552 Thompson Lane
Nashville, TN 37204

Dear Mr. Philips:

Thank you for your interest in Titan Technology products. I have enclosed our sales catalog, along with flyers announcing our current sale items.

If you have any questions or would like to see a demonstration of our products, contact Mr. Gubin at our Cincinnati office. To place an order, call 1-800-456-1234.

We appreciate your interest in Titan Technology and look forward to working with you in the future.

**Fig. 12.5** *A personalized letter with merged file data.*

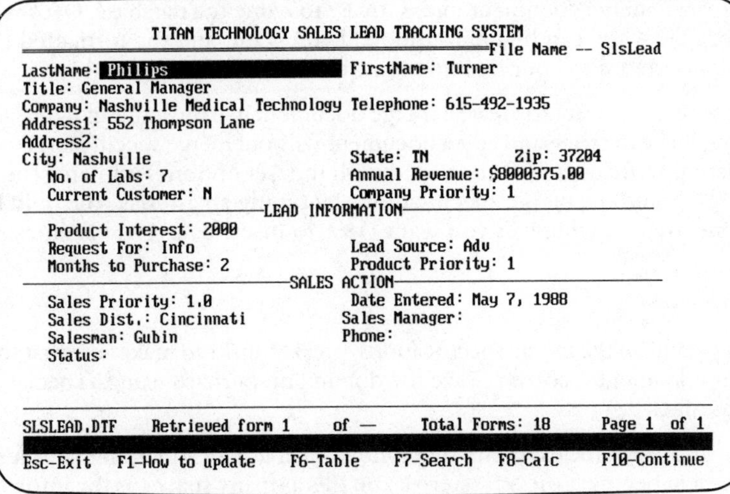

TITAN TECHNOLOGY SALES LEAD TRACKING SYSTEM
File Name -- SlsLead
LastName: Philips FirstName: Turner
Title: General Manager
Company: Nashville Medical Technology Telephone: 615-492-1935
Address1: 552 Thompson Lane
Address2:
City: Nashville State: TN Zip: 37204
No. of Labs: 7 Annual Revenue: $8000375.00
Current Customer: N Company Priority: 1
LEAD INFORMATION
Product Interest: 2000
Request For: Info Lead Source: Adv
Months to Purchase: 2 Product Priority: 1
SALES ACTION
Sales Priority: 1.0 Date Entered: May 7, 1988
Sales Dist.: Cincinnati Sales Manager:
Salesman: Gubin Phone:
Status:

SLSLEAD.DTF Retrieved form 1 of — Total Forms: 18 Page 1 of 1
Esc-Exit F1-How to update F6-Table F7-Search F8-Calc F10-Continue

**Fig. 12.6** *The file form from which merged data was retrieved.*

## *Creating and Formatting a Merge Document*

A merge spec can be located on a line of its own, within a paragraph, or wherever you want it.

You can see by comparing figures 12.5 and 12.7 that the length of the merged database information changes with the actual data found in the specified file. The entire first name found in the file will be inserted at the specified location, a space will be entered, and then the entire last name will be inserted. The name Joe Smith requires less space in the merged Write document than the name Franklyn McCormick.

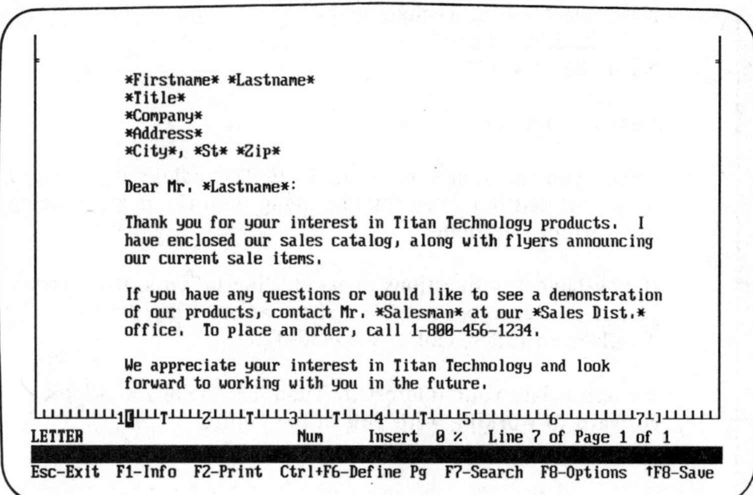

*Firstname* *Lastname*
*Title*
*Company*
*Address*
*City*, *St* *Zip*
Dear Mr. *Lastname*:
Thank you for your interest in Titan Technology products. I have enclosed our sales catalog, along with flyers announcing our current sale items.
If you have any questions or would like to see a demonstration of our products, contact Mr. *Salesman* at our *Sales Dist.* office. To place an order, call 1-800-456-1234.
We appreciate your interest in Titan Technology and look forward to working with you in the future.
LETTER Num Insert 0 % Line 7 of Page 1 of 1
Esc-Exit F1-Info F2-Print Ctrl+F6-Define Pg F7-Search F8-Options ↑F8-Save

**Fig. 12.7**
*A form letter in Write with merge specs.*

To prepare a merge document, press Alt-F7 to name the database. Q&A will display a list of fields. You can highlight the field you want, and the formatted field name will be inserted into your document at the cursor location.

Suppose that you want to create a merge document like the letter in figure 12.7. Begin by using Write to create and edit a document without merge specifications or by using an existing Write document retrieved with the Get option. Following the format in figure 12.7, add the merge specifications by typing an asterisk, the field label, and a second asterisk wherever you want Q&A to insert data. Here is an example:

```
*Name*
*Part No.*
```

When you finish the merge specifications, press Shift-F1 to make sure that the spelling in your document is correct. Save the document, perhaps using a special extension such as MRG.

As you will see in the examples that follow, database information that is merged into a document begins at the left asterisk and fills as many spaces as the information has characters. After the database information has been printed, printing of the document resumes in the first space to the right of the final asterisk. Note that the asterisks do not occupy spaces in the printout.

For example, the salutation with a merge spec

Dear *First Name*:

prints as

Dear Jeff:

The sentence with a merge spec

Thank you for your order of *Quantity* *Part*s and the payment in advance.

prints as

Thank you for your order of 2,500 bowling balls and the payment in advance.

Certain situations call for different formats, which you can control by using text and tabular formatting.

## *Using a Text Format*

If your database data has been entered on more than one line but you want the data to appear on one line in the merge document, use the Text command in the merge spec at the end of the field name.

For example, suppose that the database field is on two lines:

Address: 195 Greenbush St.
Minot, ND 58301

You can use the Text command to force the two lines into one line. The sentence with a merge spec

Your address is listed as *Address(T)*.

prints as

Your address is listed as 195 Greenbush St. Minot, ND 58301.

Note that the space between asterisks expands to fit the text being merged. By using a text format merge, you force the data fields into a wordwrap document.

## *Using a Tabular Format*

The widely used tabular format is invaluable for creating columns, formatting documents that will be printed on preprinted forms, and dozens of other needs.

To create a document field in which the text appears flush left or flush right, Q&A mailmerge uses the Left-Justify command (L) and Right-Justify command (R) with a pair of asterisks. The asterisks set the document's field length.

In the following examples, notice that when the Left- and Right-Justify commands are used, the space between the asterisks is no longer flexible; the space becomes a set width, determined by your merge spec.

### *Using the Left-Justify Tabular Format*

You can create a document field and position merged data on the field's left margin by combining the Left-Justify command and a pair of asterisks.

For example, the merge specs

```
*LastName(L)        * *FirstName(L) *
*Position(L)        * *Date Hired(L) *
```

will print as

```
Finklebinder        Jerome
Light-bulb tester   6/17/59
```

The data in the LastName field is merged in a flush-left format within the document field, starting at the position of the first asterisk.

Note that space is available for 20 characters between the asterisks in the first document field (the LastName field). When the merge data (the name, in this case) has fewer characters than the document field has spaces, Q&A fills with blank spaces the space between the end of the data and the second asterisk. If the merge data has more characters than the document field has spaces, however, the characters will overrun the field and be lost. Q&A truncates File data to fit into the space you specify in the Write tabular merge spec. Be sure, therefore, to make document fields wide enough for the data they will hold.

The left-justify tabular format has many uses. For example, the format can be used to create a merge document that automatically fills a form with data (see figs. 12.8 and 12.9). As you can see in figures 12.8 and 12.9, the asterisks are spaced to provide room for the form's information.

### *Using the Right-Justify Tabular Format*

When you use the Right-Justify command, the right-justify tabular format creates a document field between asterisks and positions the information at the right side of the field.

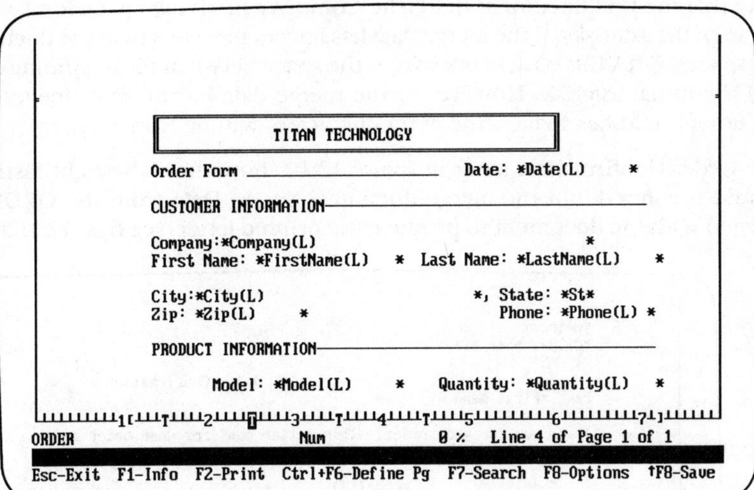

TITAN TECHNOLOGY
Order Form Date: *Date(L) *
CUSTOMER INFORMATION
Company:*Company(L) *
First Name: *FirstName(L) * Last Name: *LastName(L) *
City:*City(L) *, State: *St*
Zip: *Zip(L) * Phone: *Phone(L) *
PRODUCT INFORMATION
Model: *Model(L) * Quantity: *Quantity(L) *
ORDER Num 0 % Line 4 of Page 1 of 1
Esc-Exit F1-Info F2-Print Ctrl+F6-Define Pg F7-Search F8-Options ↑F8-Save


**Fig. 12.8** *Creating a document with left-justified tabular format.*

TITAN TECHNOLOGY

Order Form Date: July 5, 1988

CUSTOMER INFORMATION

Company: Northern Supply Company
First Name: Jack Last Name: Wilson

City: West Fargo State: ND
Zip: 52832 Phone: 701-292-3006

PRODUCT INFORMATION

Model: 1500 Quantity: 5

**Fig. 12.9** *The printed document with left-justified format.*

For example, the merge specs

| | |
|---|---|
| *Company(R) * | *Amount Due(R) * |
| *Credit Code(R) * | *Date Due(R) * |

print as

| | |
|---:|---:|
| Burns Medical | $55,142.00 |
| 5A | 10/1/86 |

The data in the fields is merged in a flush-right format that ends at the final asterisk's position.

Note that the first document field (the Company field) has space for 20 characters between the asterisks. If the merge data has fewer characters than the document field has spaces, Q&A fills with blank spaces the space between the beginning of the data and the initial asterisk. However, if the merge data has more characters than the document field has spaces, the extra characters will be truncated.

The Order Confirmation letter in figure 12.10 shows how the right-justify tabular format is entered into the merge document specs. Data from the ORDERS file is merged with the document to produce the printed letter (see figs. 12.11 and 12.12).

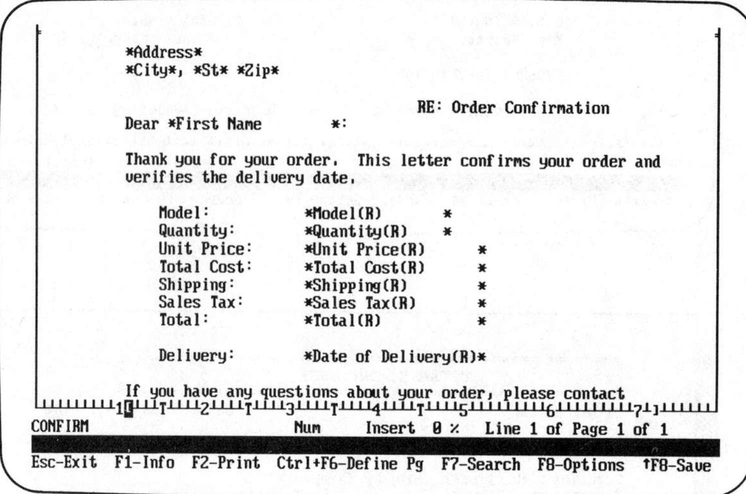

```
*Address*
*City*, *St* *Zip*

                                RE: Order Confirmation
Dear *First Name        *:

Thank you for your order. This letter confirms your order and
verifies the delivery date.

     Model:            *Model(R)       *
     Quantity:         *Quantity(R)    *
     Unit Price:       *Unit Price(R)       *
     Total Cost:       *Total Cost(R)       *
     Shipping:         *Shipping(R)         *
     Sales Tax:        *Sales Tax(R)        *
     Total:            *Total(R)            *

     Delivery:         *Date of Delivery(R)*

If you have any questions about your order, please contact
CONFIRM                  Num     Insert  0 %   Line 1 of Page 1 of 1
Esc-Exit  F1-Info  F2-Print  Ctrl+F6-Define Pg  F7-Search  F8-Options  ↑F8-Save
```

**Fig. 12.10** *Creating a document with right-justified tabular format.*

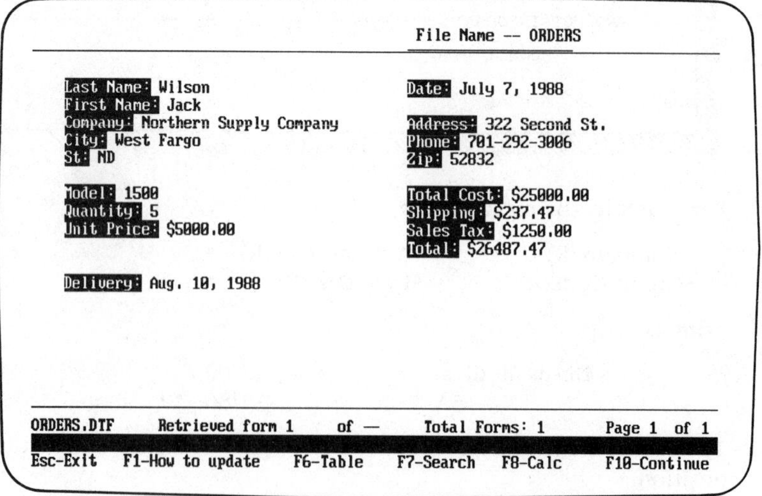

```
                                        File Name -- ORDERS

   Last Name: Wilson                    Date: July 7, 1988
   First Name: Jack
   Company: Northern Supply Company     Address: 322 Second St.
   City: West Fargo                     Phone: 701-292-3006
   St: ND                               Zip: 52832

   Model: 1500                          Total Cost: $25000.00
   Quantity: 5                          Shipping: $237.47
   Unit Price: $5000.00                 Sales Tax: $1250.00
                                        Total: $26487.47

   Delivery: Aug. 10, 1988

ORDERS.DTF    Retrieved form 1    of —     Total Forms: 1      Page 1  of 1
Esc-Exit  F1-How to update   F6-Table   F7-Search   F8-Calc    F10-Continue
```

**Fig. 12.11** *The file form that is the source of merge data.*

```
322 Second St.
West Fargo, ND 52832
                                   RE: Order Confirmation
Dear Jack:

Thank you for your order.  This letter confirms your order and
verifies the delivery date.

     Model:                         1500
     Quantity:                         5
     Unit Price:                $5000.00
     Total Cost:               $25000.00
     Shipping:                   $237.47
     Sales Tax:                 $1250.00
     Total:                    $26487.47

     Delivery:           Aug. 10, 1988

If you have any questions about your order, please contact
```

**Fig. 12.12** *The printed document with right-justified format.*

Notice that one serious limitation exists in the way Q&A handles merge specs in Write documents: you can place only one File record in each copy of the document, and each document can be linked to only one File database. You cannot, for example, pull a name and address from a client file and then set up a table in a document that loops through a transaction database, filling in sequential records until a control break is encountered. You would want to do this procedure to print monthly statements where a number of transactions has occurred against a single client record or to detail items in a bill of materials list. You can, however, maintain a database of clients with charge summaries and use the mailmerge features of Write to send simple statements or invoices. You might store such information as the following:

Customer name and address

Date of last purchase

Amount of last purchase

Date of last payment

Amount of last payment

Total purchases to date

Total payments to date

Amount due or credit

From this information, you can construct an invoice/statement form in Write to prepare automatic mailings to all your clients. Refer to the form in figure 12.9. By modifying this form to meet your individual needs, you easily can construct a statement or billing form.

## *Printing a Merge Document*

After you create and format a merge document, you instruct Q&A to print the document. First, set the print options, including the name of the database file from which the data will be retrieved. Next, using the Identifier Spec screen, match the database field labels with the document's merge specifications. Note that if your merge fields and database fields use the same names, the Identifier Spec is unnecessary and Q&A skips this step. Then you fill in the Retrieve Spec to determine the database forms from which the data will be retrieved.

To help you through this three-step merge-printing process, you will again use the Order Confirmation letter as an example.

### *Setting the Print Options*

The first step in printing a merge document is to set the print options. Set options to determine how many copies will be printed and to set the length of the document (if you want to print only page 9, for example, type *9* as the From Page and the To Page options on the Print Options screen). You establish whether the document will be single- or double-spaced and whether the text will be justified. You even can set an option to print an envelope. By setting the Print To option, you direct printing to a specific printer or to disk. You can set the print offset, the printer control codes, and the type of paper feed.

To set the print options for a merge document, begin by pressing F2 from the merge document. Q&A displays the Print Options menu. Set the print options as you normally would to print the document. Move the cursor to the Name of Merge File option and enter the name of the Q&A File database from which the merge data is to be retrieved. Complete the procedure by pressing F10.

Q&A displays the Identifier Spec screen if differences exist in your merge document field names and those used in the database itself.

### *Using the Identifier Spec*

The purpose of the Identifier Spec screen is to help you match the document merge specs with the database field labels. If all document merge specs match their database field labels, the Identifier Spec screen does not appear. You can press F10 to proceed to the Retrieve Spec screen.

If the merge specs and the field labels are different, you must match them so that Q&A can do the merge. For example, in the Order Confirmation letter, the labels and the specs differ:

Document merge spec: Date of Delivery
Database field label: Delivery

To match the label and the spec, type *Date of Delivery* in the Identifier Spec's Delivery field.

The way you fill in the Identifier Spec depends on whether you know which database field labels need substitute names. If you know which field labels do not match the merge specs, move the cursor to the appropriate database field, enter the substitute merge spec, and press F10. If you enter the substitute specs incorrectly or incompletely, Q&A displays the Identifier Spec warning screen.

Also, if you don't know which merge specs do not match the field labels, press F10 before you enter anything in the Identifier Spec screen. Q&A displays the Identifier Spec warning screen, which lists the merge specs that don't match the database field labels. (In this example, the spec *Date of Delivery* does not match.)

To match specs and labels after such a warning, press Esc and then enter the substitute merge spec into the Write document. (Substitute **Delivery** for **Date of Delivery**, for example.) Press F10 to continue. If you press F10 without entering the substitute merge spec, that merge spec is not merged when you print the document.

Under most circumstances, the Write document merge specs should use the same field labels that appear in the linked database file. However, you may want to write generic documents that can refer to more than one file and therefore to different field labels. In this case, choose a field label in the merge document that describes the type of data that will be substituted; then use the Identifier Spec screen to make the actual link just before you print the document.

## *Using the Retrieve Spec*

Use the Retrieve Spec to specify which forms are to be merged with the document. Fill out the spec as you would any Retrieve Spec in Q&A File. Remember that you can get help by pressing the F1-Help key. (To learn how to fill out a Retrieve Spec, see Chapter 6, "Using File.") You may want to specify an entire database or one form, as in the Order Confirmation letter.

Because the Order Confirmation letter will be sent to Mr. Turner Philips at Nashville Medical Labs, you will retrieve only the Philips form. To do so, enter *Philips* in the Last Name field (see fig. 12.13).

If you want to sort forms before the merge print begins, press F8. Q&A displays the Sort Spec screen. If you use the Sort Spec to sort forms alphabetically before you print them, the documents print in alphabetical order (for more information on the Sort Spec, see Chapter 6, "Using File"). If the mailing is large, you may want to sort by ZIP code instead, to help prepare the documents for the post office.

Press F10 to continue the printing process. Q&A will confirm the merge-print operation, displaying the name of the document and the number of database forms to be merged. If you want to start printing, press Enter; if not, press the Esc key.

Many ways are available to use Q&A Write's capacity to insert Write text files and Write-compatible files into a Write document. For example, you can create a separate

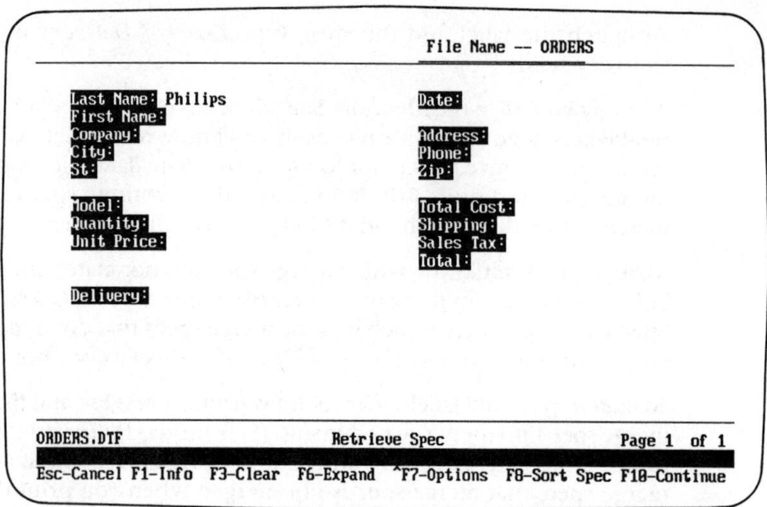


**Fig. 12.13** *Specifying a retrieval on the Retrieve Spec screen.*

report from portions of other reports, insert boilerplate paragraphs into contracts, and import tables and charts from other programs.

# *Importing Files To Insert into Write Documents*

The format of a document or file determines how it is inserted. Q&A Write automatically inserts other Write files and text files created with PFS:WRITE® or IBM's Writing Assistant. Files from WordStar ASCII files or 1-2-3 and Symphony files, however, go through Q&A's reformatting procedure before being imported to Write.

## *Inserting Q&A Write-Compatible Files*

Use the same process to import other Write files or files from PFS:WRITE or the IBM Writing Assistant program into a Write document.

Suppose that you want to incorporate a PFS:WRITE file into the middle of a document you are creating with Q&A Write. Begin by positioning the cursor where you want the text from the source file (PFS, in this case) to begin. Press F8 to access the Options menu and select Insert Document. When Q&A prompts you for the name of the file that you want to insert into your present text, type the file name and press Enter. (If the file you want to import is stored in the default directory, press Enter immediately after selecting Insert Document to display a complete list of files. If the file is not in the default directory, you must specify a path name so Q&A can find it.) After you press Enter, the new text appears in your current document.

## Inserting Files from Other Software Packages

Whenever you want to insert a file other than a Q&A Write, PFS:WRITE, or IBM Writing Assistant file, choose Insert Document from the Options menu to make one of four other selections: ASCII, Special ASCII, WordStar, or Lotus 1-2-3 or Symphony (see fig. 12.14).

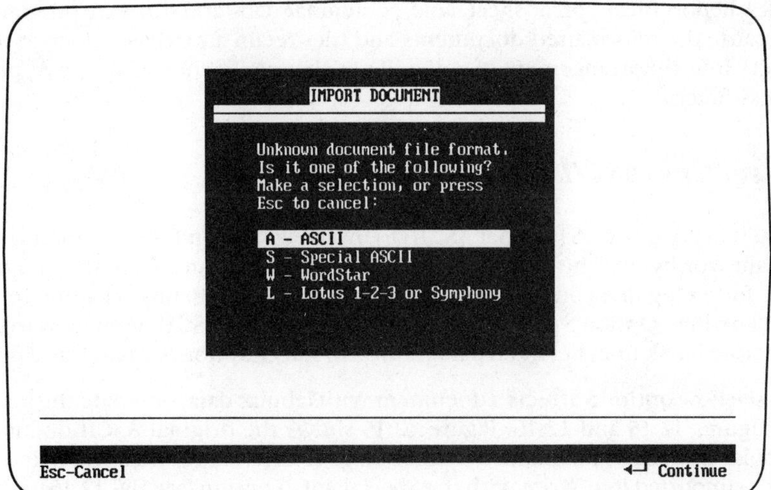


**Fig. 12.14** *The Import Document window.*

To insert any of these four types of files into a Q&A Write document, you follow the same initial procedure used for inserting Write, PFS, or IBM Writing Assistant files. The procedure changes, however, after you type the name of the file to insert. Because the format is different from the format for Write, PFS, and IBM Assistant files, Q&A displays the options shown in figure 12.14.

If the file you want inserted is in one of the four formats, Q&A automatically reformats the file and inserts it into your Write document, as explained in the following sections.

If the file is too big, Q&A displays this message: `!Problem! Not enough memory to complete your request.` (For more information, see Appendix F.) Press Enter to continue.

### Inserting WordStar Files

Because of Q&A's unique file format, WordStar files (and those of most other word processors) are not compatible with Write. To insert a WordStar file into a Write document, you must choose WordStar from the Import Document window (see fig. 12.14); press W and press Enter. Write automatically reformats the WordStar file, making it compatible with Q&A. Then the former WordStar document can be edited as though it were a Write document. If you need to keep this document in its original WordStar format, make a copy before using this Q&A reformat feature.

### *Inserting ASCII Files without Wordwrap*

Choose option A when you do not want wordwrap in the reformatted document. You will use option A (ASCII) frequently for such files as database reports (including Q&A Report files), spreadsheet tables, columnar data, and software program listings. Because the reformatted documents and files retain a carriage return at the end of every line, the arrangement of text will not change. To choose option A, press A and press Enter.

### *Inserting ASCII Files with Wordwrap*

You will use option S (Special ASCII) to insert wordwrap files in which you want to retain wordwrap. This option removes the carriage return from the end of a line if the following line contains text; the carriage return remains on a line followed by a blank line. Option S retains the original form of an ASCII document that has one or more blank lines between paragraphs. To select option S, press S and press Enter.

To see how option S affects a document with tabular data, compare the text samples in figures 12.15 and 12.16. Figure 12.15 shows the original ASCII document with tabular data that is maintained with carriage returns at the end of each line. After the file is imported into Write with the Special ASCII option (see fig. 12.16), the carriage returns have been removed and the tabular format has been lost.

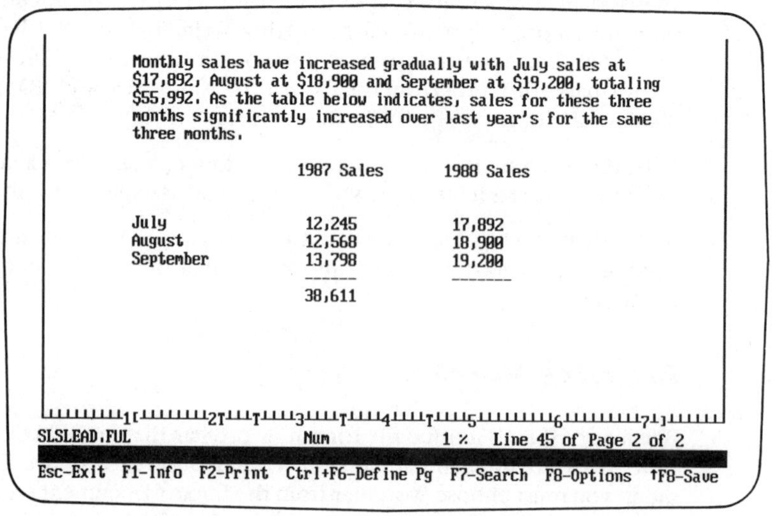

**Fig. 12.15**
*Text in an ASCII file.*

```
Monthly sales have increased gradually with July sales at
$17,892, August at $18,900 and September at $19,200, totaling
$55,992. As the table below indicates, sales for these three
months significantly increased over last year's for the same
three months.

                    1987 Sales          1988 Sales

July                  12,245              17,892
August                12,568              18,900
September             13,798              19,200
                      ------              -------
                      38,611

SLSLEAD.FUL                 Num          1 %   Line 45 of Page 2 of 2
Esc-Exit  F1-Info  F2-Print  Ctrl+F6-Define Pg  F7-Search  F8-Options  ↑F8-Save
```

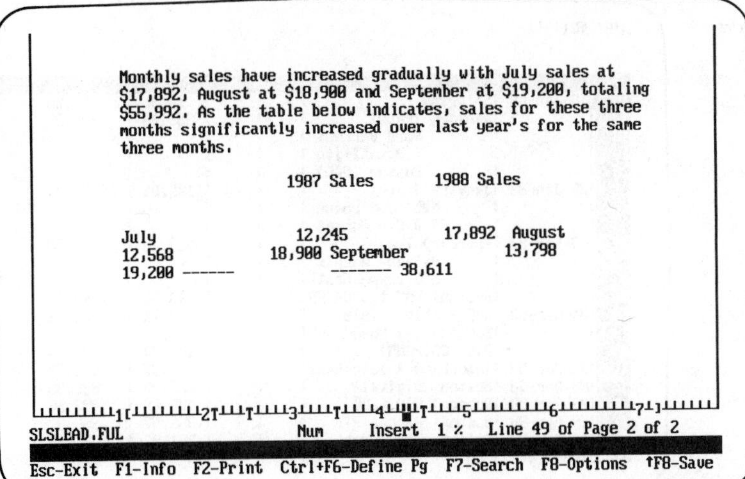


**Fig. 12.16** *Imported ASCII text after using the Special ASCII option.*

The Special ASCII format is useful if you want to format data that contains only text and you want Write to be able to conduct its own formatting. But if the original ASCII file contains information that should be presented in Write without changes, use the standard ASCII format instead.

## *Inserting 1-2-3 and Symphony Files*

The fourth option available for inserting files into a Write document allows you to import 1-2-3 and Symphony worksheet files. This option particularly benefits those who use 1-2-3 or Symphony for creating financial spreadsheets and want to import some or all of the numeric data into a Q&A document. Inserting 1-2-3 and Symphony files is similar to inserting ASCII or WordStar files. One exception, however, is that when you import 1-2-3 and Symphony files, you are not limited to inserting only the complete file; you can insert any part of the 1-2-3 or Symphony worksheet file.

Suppose, for example, that you want to insert the January and February travel expenses from a 1-2-3 worksheet containing expenses for the entire year (see fig. 12.17). To insert the information you need, you must import the range of the columns and rows from the worksheet in figure 12.17.

To insert these columns into a Q&A Write document, begin by moving the cursor to the location in your Write document where you want the first column inserted. With the cursor located where you want the insert to begin, press F8 (Options) and select Insert Document from the Options menu.

When the prompt box appears and asks for the file name of the worksheet you want to insert, type the file name or press Enter for a complete list of available file names. Remember that when you press Enter for a list of files, Q&A returns the files from the

**Fig. 12.17**
*Information on a 1-2-3 worksheet.*

```
A16: [W1] '|                                                        READY

    A  B          C                       E F  G  H  I  J       K    L       M
16  |18-Jan-88  |Shipping                 |    |     |  10.86 |    10.86 |
17  |           |January Travel           |    |     | 389.05 |   389.05 |
18  |           |          Word Perfect   |    |     |        |          |
19  |           |            Datability   |    |     |        |          |
20  |           |          Boston (DEC)   |    |     |        |          |
21  |28-Jan-88  |January Travel           |    |     |1100.81 |  1100.81 |
22  |           |        NYC--Ungermann   |    |     |        |          |
23  |           |          D.C.--Comnet   |    |     |        |          |
24  |19-Feb-88  |February Travel          |    |     | 843.28 |   843.28 |
25  |           |        Dallas: Usenix   |    |     |        |          |
26  |           |        NYC:Dexpo East   |    |     |        |          |
27  |           |Boston: VAXstation 80    |    |     |  43.56 |    43.56 |
28  |04-Mar-88  |NYC + Ship + Tele        |    |     | 253.71 |   253.71 |
29  |           |Boston: Vax 8800         |    |     |        |          |
30  |           |D.C. OSI/ANSI            |    |     | 137.30 |   137.30 |
31  |31-Mar-88  |Interface + Telephone    |    |     | 573.37 |   573.37 |
32  |09-Apr-88  |Boston: Digital          |    |     | 825.35 |   825.35 |
33  |29-Apr-88  |Boston: VAX 6200         |    |     | 495.66 |   495.66 |
34  |29-Apr-88  |Boston: Ancona+eln       |    |     | 356.97 |   356.97 |
35  |16-May-88  |Atlanta, Bos, Mob        |    |     | 791.93 |   791.93 |
04-Jul-88  07:12 AM                                          NUM
```

default drive and path; if your 1-2-3 or Symphony worksheet file is located in another drive and path, change the drive and path in the prompt box before pressing Enter.

After you select the worksheet file and press Enter, Q&A displays the Import Document menu, which indicates that the file format is unknown and asks you to select one of the conversion selections listed (see fig. 12.14). Select the fourth option, Lotus 1-2-3 or Symphony, to insert your worksheet or part of a worksheet.

After you select Lotus 1-2-3 or Symphony, Q&A displays a Define Range screen, which enables you to indicate specific columns and rows or a range name for the area of the worksheet you want to insert (see fig. 12.18). Notice that the third line of text in figure 12.18 indicates the complete data area in the worksheet from which you want to insert information. Figure 12.18 shows that the expenses worksheet covers the area from column A, row 1, to column R, row 55. If you want to insert all data from the worksheet, press F10. If you want to import only part of the worksheet, indicate the columns and rows or the range name of the area. In working with spreadsheets, use range names for any area you are likely to reference often. This process reduces the chance of errors when you specify the ranges manually during calculation, merge, or other operations.

To insert the merge range, move the cursor to the range section on the screen and type the name. Or press the PgDn and PgUp keys to select the range from available ranges in the spreadsheet. The merge range occupies cells A16 through M37. Press F10 to complete the procedure; Q&A will import the remaining columns of data (see fig. 12.19). Note that the 1-2-3 file uses a date-formatting function (@DATE(88,1,18)). The date fields are formatted in 1-2-3 to be displayed as 18-Jan-88, but Q&A interprets the dates as 1/18/88.

Once you have inserted data from a 1-2-3 or Symphony worksheet into your Write document, you can use all the Write commands and keys for editing or changing data.

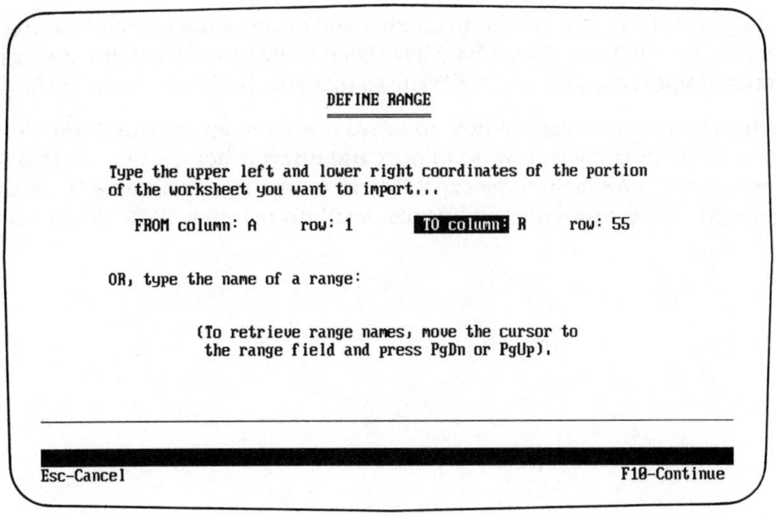

DEFINE RANGE

Type the upper left and lower right coordinates of the portion
of the worksheet you want to import...

FROM column: A row: 1 TO column: R row: 55

OR, type the name of a range:

(To retrieve range names, move the cursor to
the range field and press PgDn or PgUp).

Esc-Cancel F10-Continue

**Fig. 12.18**
*The Define Range screen for choosing 1-2-3 data.*

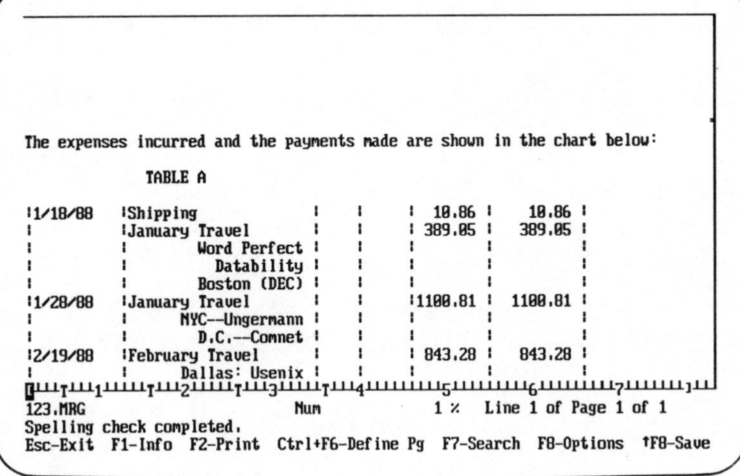


**Fig. 12.19**
*Data from a 1-2-3 worksheet inserted into a Write document.*

In particular, you can use Write's math calculation capability to total, average, count, multiply, and divide the numbers inserted from 1-2-3 or Symphony.

# *Chapter Summary*

The capacity to merge files from other modules or other programs is an important feature of Q&A Write. As your database system becomes more complex, you will need to move data from one module to another and to create documents by using data from existing documents or files. If you have been using other word-processing programs, you can import the files to Q&A Write so that you don't have to enter the data again.

In this chapter, you learned how to move text from an existing Write document to a new Write document, how to import and insert other documents into Write, and how to use Q&A's mailmerge capability to merge File data into a Write document. The next chapter provides additional detail on printing Write documents.

Chapter 13

# Printing a Write Document

One of Q&A's most impressive features is the capacity to retrieve, organize, and print data. Each of the Q&A modules has the capability of producing printouts. Whether you want a record from File, a letter from Write, a listing of survey results from Report, or a compiled columnar list from the Intelligent Assistant, Q&A makes printing easy.

Unlike other popular programs, Q&A has a print feature that does not apply "across the board." That is, instead of having one print procedure that applies to all features of the program, Q&A provides each module with its own procedure, complete with different menus and specification screens. Each module of Q&A has separate print options, so you don't have to leave the Main menu of any module in order to print. Although this feature may seem confusing at first, the logical structure of the separate print procedures will help you catch on quickly. This chapter introduces you to the print features in the Write module of Q&A.

## *Printing from Write*

When you're ready to make a printed copy of a document you have created with Write, you have several options. One option is to print the document as soon as you have entered it—without leaving Type/Edit mode. Plain and simple reports are easy to print with Q&A—ideal for interoffice memos and other short correspondence (see fig. 13.1). If you want a more elaborate printout, Q&A can accommodate you also by offering the easy-to-use Print Options settings and by accepting printer control codes for text enhancement (see fig. 13.2).

**Fig. 13.1**
*A plain memo printed with Q&A Write.*

```
TO:           District Sales Managers

DATE:         June 30, 1988

FROM:         Steven Hill, Marketing Support Manager

SUBJECT:      JUNE SALES LEADS

Enclosed are the sales lead forms received during June from
prospects in your sales district.  Also included is a report
that summarizes the sales leads by city, sales
priority, company, and customer request.

We are implementing a new sales tracking system that will
give you a means to keep track of sales leads and follow
up.  This should help each of you unify your sales force
and make sure that each lead is pursued effectively.  A
Q&A disk is enclosed that contains the sales leads for
your district. Please copy these leads into your file, and
maintain them in the following manner:

    1. When each lead is assigned, enter the name of the
       Sales Person.
    2. Enter the date when the first sales contact was
       made with the sales lead.
```

## *Printing from the Type/Edit Screen*

If you have just finished typing a document, you can order printing without leaving the Edit mode. For example, if your work is still on the screen, you can press F2 to print it. The Print Options screen, which is discussed later in this chapter, is then displayed. If Q&A is installed for your printer and the Print Options settings are correct, you can bypass the menu by pressing F10. Your document is printed instantly.

Q&A users often forget that they can print any portion of a document quickly without displaying the Print Options screen. All you do is press Ctrl-F2 and then highlight the block to be printed by using the cursor arrow keys. Once the block is marked, make sure that your printer is ready; then press F10. The block is printed immediately.

If you don't like the way the document is being printed from the Type/Edit screen, press Esc to cancel the operation. Q&A returns you to the Type/Edit screen. Printing stops if you press F2, and the Print Options screen is displayed again. You then can modify the settings on the Options menu and press F10. The printing starts again from the beginning of the file. If your printer has a buffer that stores input from your computer, however, printing does not stop immediately when you press F2. If the buffer is large, you may want to turn off the printer and reset the top of the form when you cancel printing in order to avoid printing large amounts of unwanted text.

TO: District Sales Managers

DATE: June 30, 1988

FROM: Steven Hill, Marketing Support Manager

SUBJECT: **JUNE SALES LEADS**

Enclosed are the sales lead forms received during June from prospects in your sales district. Also included is a report that summarizes the sales leads by city, sales priority, company, and customer request.

We are implementing a new sales tracking system that will give you a means to keep track of sales leads and follow up. This should help each of you unify your sales force and make sure that each lead is pursued effectively. A Q&A disk is enclosed that contains the sales leads for your district. Please copy these leads into your file, and maintain them in the following manner:

1. When each lead is assigned, enter the name of the *Sales Person*.
2. Enter the date when the first sales contact was made with the sales lead.
3. Record the date of the demonstration.
4. Enter the status of the sale after the demonstration in one of the following forms:

| | |
|---|---|
| Sale (Model Number) | a sale was made |
| Postpone | the purchase decision was delayed |
| Competitor (select one) | the prospect bought from a competitor |

Brock
Med Sci
Am Lab

Other

At the end of the month, please send me a copy of this report and the updated forms (on disk). I will then prepare an analysis of your district's sales activity and effectiveness. We will be discussing this new system more fully at our next district meeting.

**Fig. 13.2**
*A memo with text enhancements and formatting features.*

# *Printing from the Write Menu*

If you want to print a document from the Write menu, the document must be on the editing screen. To print the document, return to the Write menu, select the Print option, and press F10. Before you can print a file that you are not working on currently, you must load the file into memory by selecting the Get option from the Write menu.

Q&A displays the name of the most recently used file as the default in the document line. If you cannot remember the name of the file you want to print, press the space bar to clear the default name and press Enter. A list of available document files is displayed (see fig. 13.3).

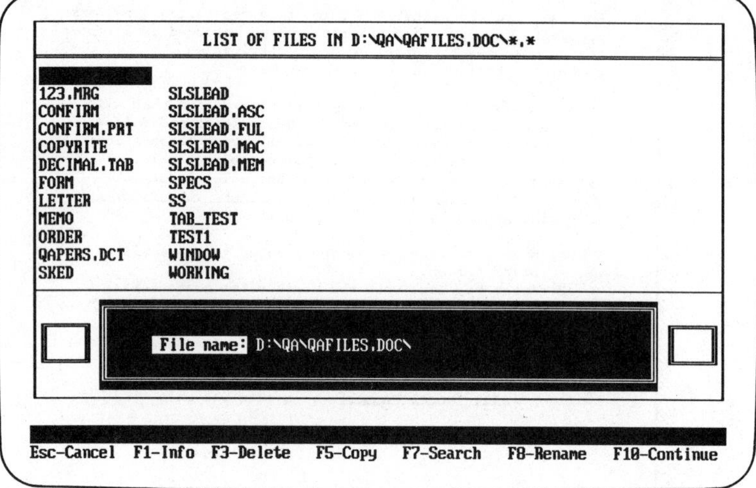


**Fig. 13.3**
*Pressing Enter to see a list of your files.*

Use the cursor keys to move the highlighting to the file you want and press Enter. The file is displayed on the Type/Edit screen. You then can press F2 to print, as explained in the preceding example.

## *Using the Print Options Screen*

As you can see, you have the option of changing Q&A's defaults or accepting them as they are. At times, however, you may not want to print every page of your document. You can change the default so that Q&A prints only the pages you want. In your office correspondence, you may be required to make three copies of every letter; you can set the default to take care of this task for you. If you find that you use a certain setting often, you may want to change that setting permanently. Even after you change a default permanently, you can modify the default at any time.

The Print Options screen gives you the chance to change the way your text is printed (see fig. 13.4). Before printing a document, you can arrange and enhance the printed text by adjusting line spacing, setting the justification, specifying the number of columns, and adding special print codes. You can control the printing by specifying the number of copies, printer ports, and merge files used. The changes you make at this point are good only during this session; when you leave the Write module, all your settings return to the Q&A default settings. You modify the default settings by specifying options on the Write Utilities menu. The following sections explain how you can use these features of Q&A to make your printouts more attractive.

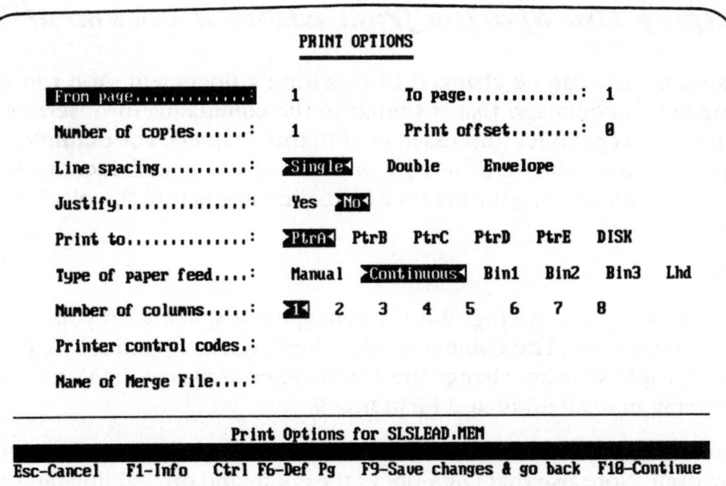
PRINT OPTIONS

From page..............: 1 To page.............: 1
Number of copies......: 1 Print offset........: 0
Line spacing..........: Single Double Envelope
Justify...............: Yes No
Print to..............: PtrA PtrB PtrC PtrD PtrE DISK
Type of paper feed....: Manual Continuous Bin1 Bin2 Bin3 Lhd
Number of columns.....: 1 2 3 4 5 6 7 8
Printer control codes.:
Name of Merge File....:

Print Options for SLSLEAD.MEM
Esc-Cancel F1-Info Ctrl F6-Def Pg F9-Save changes & go back F10-Continue

**Fig. 13.4** *Changing the default print options.*

## *Arranging the Text*

Different kinds of printouts deserve different text arrangements. For example, although you double-space the first draft of your monthly report, you may prefer single-spacing for the final draft. With the options on the Print Options screen, Q&A allows you to change the line spacing and justification of your text with just a few simple keystrokes. Remember, however, that the settings are good only for the current session.

### *Changing Line Spacing from the Print Options Screen*

Three line-spacing options are available; select one by typing the first letter of the option. Single- and double-spacing require no explanation, except the reminder that Q&A always shows you a document single-spaced on the screen. When the document is printed, the spacing you specified is provided.

The page designations on the Print Options screen do not change when you change the line spacing. For example, if you take a three-page, single-spaced document and select double-spaced printing, the number of pages in your printout actually is doubled, even though the number in the To Page option does not change to 6. Therefore, if you tell Q&A to print only the first page of the double-spaced document, the first two pages are printed.

The print options will respond to a change in page length. If you shorten the page length by one-third, for example, the total number of pages indicated is increased by a third.

## *Changing Line Spacing from within a Document*

Line spacing also can be changed from within a document. You can change line spacing with a command that is similar to the commands for inserting characters and changing type styles (discussed later in this chapter). For example, if you want a single-spaced section in the middle of your double-spaced document, embed the following command in your file on a blank line just before the place you want the change to occur:

```
*LS 1*
```

The *LS* stands for line spacing. You also can type *line spacing 1* if you find that phrase easier to remember. The command can be entered as uppercase or lowercase. To switch to triple-spacing, change the *1* in these examples to *3*. Q&A recognizes any line-spacing interval up to and including *9*.

Remember that this command, because it affects line spacing, must appear on a blank line by itself. Note also that Q&A obeys the command on that line but the line containing the command is not printed; the line is eliminated entirely from the printout.

## *Setting Text Justification for a Complete Document*

Most correspondence does not use justified text; usually a ragged-right margin is preferred for business use. *Justified* means that blank space is inserted between words so that each line extends to the right margin. Although a justified right margin gives the printout a pleasing appearance, many people consider this format to be the sign of a printed form letter (see fig. 13.5).

As you can see, as many as three spaces are between some words. This erratic spacing can make the paragraphs harder to read. Although the justification shows up on the printout, the Type/Edit screen does not show the extra spacing. To select justification, you set the Justify option to Yes on the Print Options screen. If you decide to use Q&A's justification feature, you may want to turn off the feature when you create a table. You probably will discover that lining up the columns in a table is almost impossible when justification is turned on. To turn off justification, set the Justify option to No.

Similar to popular word-processing programs, Q&A supports microjustification. In a microjustified document, small spaces are inserted between the characters, so the spacing effect is less noticeable. To see whether your printer can support microjustification, check your printer manual.

TO: District Sales Managers

DATE: June 30, 1988

FROM: Steven Hill, Marketing Support Manager

SUBJECT: **JUNE SALES LEADS**

Enclosed are the sales lead forms received during June from prospects in your sales district. Also included is a report that summarizes the sales leads by city, sales priority, company, and customer request.

We are implementing a new sales tracking system that will give you a means to keep track of sales leads and follow up. This should help each of you unify your sales force and make sure that each lead is pursued effectively. A Q&A disk is enclosed that contains the sales leads for your district. Please copy these leads into your file, and maintain them in the following manner:

1. When each lead is assigned, enter the name of the *Sales Person*.
2. Enter the date when the first sales contact was made with the sales lead.
3. Record the date of the demonstration.
4. Enter the status of the sale after the demonstration in one of the following forms:

| | |
|---|---|
| Sale (Model Number) | a sale was made |
| Postpone | the purchase decision was delayed |
| Competitor (select one) | the prospect bought from a competitor |

Brock
Med Sci
Am Lab

Other

At the end of the month, please send me a copy of this report and the updated forms (on disk). I will then prepare an analysis of your district's sales activity and effectiveness. We will be discussing this new system more fully at our next district meeting.

**Fig. 13.5** *Erratic spacing caused by right justification.*

## *Setting Text Justification for Part of a Document*

In some cases, you may want to justify only a section of the text within a document. With your file displayed in Type/Edit mode, instead of selecting justification from the menu, enter the following command just before the text you want to justify:

*Justify Yes*

This command can be abbreviated as follows:

*JY Y*

To end justification, move to the place you want the justification to stop and type the following:

*Justify No*

Here is the abbreviation for this command:

*JY N*

Figure 13.6 shows the file in Type/Edit mode with the opening and closing justification commands. Figure 13.7 shows the printout. As you can see, the commands that appear on the screen do not appear on the printed letter.

**Fig. 13.6**
*A memo printed with open and close justification commands.*

```
FROM:        Steven Hill, Marketing Support Manager

SUBJECT:     JUNE SALES LEADS

Enclosed are the sales lead forms received during June from
prospects in your sales district.  Also included is a report
that summarizes the sales leads by city, sales
priority, company, and customer request.
*Justify Yes*

We are implementing a new sales tracking system that will
give you a means to keep track of sales leads and follow
up.  This should help each of you unify your sales force
and make sure that each lead is pursued effectively.  A
Q&A disk is enclosed that contains the sales leads for
your district. Please copy these leads into your file, and
maintain them in the following manner:
*Justify No*

     1. When each lead is assigned, enter the name of the
SLSLEAD.MEM              Num    Insert  2 %   Line 23 of Page 1 of 1

Esc-Exit  F1-Info  F2-Print  Ctrl+F6-Define Pg  F7-Search  F8-Options  ↑F8-Save
```

## *Enhancing the Printout with Printer Control Codes*

If you use Q&A Write for business applications, your company may expect certain stylistic conventions for memos and reports. With Q&A, you can stylize your documents with different type size and text enhancements by inserting printer codes in the body, header, or footer of a document. If your printer produces near-letter-quality text when you use Double-strike mode, you can insert codes in your document so the printing is done that way. You also can use Q&A to print in Condensed mode, if your printer supports that mode. (Check your printer manual to see which effects are supported by your printer and what the codes are for those effects.)

| | |
|---|---|
| TO: | District Sales Managers |
| DATE: | June 30, 1988 |
| FROM: | Steven Hill, Marketing Support Manager |
| SUBJECT: | **JUNE SALES LEADS** |

Enclosed are the sales lead forms received during June from prospects in your sales district. Also included is a report that summarizes the sales leads by city, sales priority, company, and customer request.

We are implementing a new sales tracking system that will give you a means to keep track of sales leads and follow up. This should help each of you unify your sales force and make sure that each lead is pursued effectively. A Q&A disk is enclosed that contains the sales leads for your district. <u>Please copy these leads into your file, and maintain them in the following manner</u>:

1. When each lead is assigned, enter the name of the *Sales Person.*
2. Enter the date when the first sales contact was made with the sales lead
3. Record t

**Fig. 13.7**
*A memo printed with only the second paragraph justified.*

Q&A recognizes printer codes that are entered in ASCII code. For example, on an Epson printer, ESC 15 is the code for Condensed mode. The decimal equivalent of ESC is 27. Therefore, to print a Q&A document in Condensed mode, you enter the following code at the Printer Control Codes prompt:

27, 15

Most printer manufacturers supply ASCII control-code tables with their documentation because ASCII codes are commonly used to send controls to a printer. Sometimes, codes are shown as a combination of nonprintable control characters (such as ESC) and alphabetic characters (*ESC "E"*, for example). Use the ASCII conversion chart in your printer documentation to make the necessary conversion or enter the control sequences in Q&A in the way your printer documentation suggests.

The Printer Control Code prompt on the Print Options screen is helpful if you want to print an entire document in a different mode. But what if you want only a line or a few words printed in Condensed mode? Q&A allows you to insert printer control codes directly in your document so that you can enhance selective portions of your text.

Make sure that the document you want to enhance is loaded in the Type/Edit screen. To do this procedure, remember that you select Get from the Write menu and enter the file name. With the text on-screen, move to the place where you want the effect to start. You may want the code to begin in the middle of a word if only certain characters are to be affected.

Enter an asterisk (*) so that Q&A will know that the characters which follow are a command. Then type the word *Printer*—or just the letter *P*, if you prefer—and press the space bar. Next, enter the decimal ASCII equivalent code for the effect you want and end the command with another asterisk. For example, if you want to print expanded-width characters on an Epson printer, you can enter the following code:

    *P 27,14*

Then move to the place where you want the enhancement to end and enter the same command. If you want to use multiple codes, separate the numbers with commas. The codes make the screen look cluttered, but don't worry; the codes will not appear on your printout.

When you insert printer control codes directly in your text, Q&A does not readjust the text for printing. For example, if you insert the codes to print the company name in expanded type, you need to center the title manually. When you insert the codes, the title is moved to the right, and when the memo is printed, the title appears on paper in the same place it appears on-screen.

In figure 13.8, the code has been inserted in the first line of the memo so that the company name is printed in large letters. The ending code is not really necessary in this case because Epson's command for expanded printing is valid for only one line. After the coded line, the print type returns to normal. Figure 13.9 shows the printout of the memo.

**Fig. 13.8**
*The printer code that produces expanded characters.*

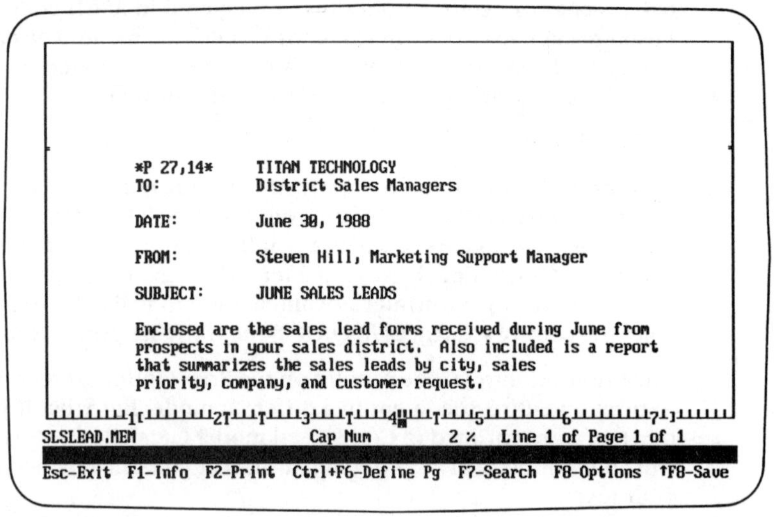

```
*P 27,14*          TITAN TECHNOLOGY
TO:                District Sales Managers

DATE:              June 30, 1988

FROM:              Steven Hill, Marketing Support Manager

SUBJECT:           JUNE SALES LEADS

Enclosed are the sales lead forms received during June from
prospects in your sales district.  Also included is a report
that summarizes the sales leads by city, sales
priority, company, and customer request.

SLSLEAD.MEM                  Cap Num        2 %   Line 1 of Page 1 of 1
Esc-Exit  F1-Info  F2-Print  Ctrl+F6-Define Pg  F7-Search  F8-Options  ↑F8-Save
```

Most printers can print more characters than the ones that appear on the keyboard. Q&A accepts special character codes that will cause these characters to be printed in your document. With a procedure similar to inserting printer control codes, you can print foreign money symbols, mathematical symbols, copyright notices, accent marks for foreign languages, and other special characters. If these characters are supported by your printer, you can insert them anywhere in a Q&A Write document (see your printer manual for the special character codes).

TITAN TECHNOLOGY

TO: District Sales Managers

DATE: June 30, 1988

FROM: Steven Hill, Marketing Support Manager

SUBJECT: **JUNE SALES LEADS**

Enclosed are the sales lead forms received during June from prospects in your sales district. Also included is a report that summarizes the sales leads by city, sales priority, company, and customer request.

We are implementing a new sales tracking system that will give you a means to keep track of sales leads and follow up. This should help each of you unify your sales force and make sure that each lead is pursued effectively. A Q&A disk is enclosed that contains the sales leads for your district. Please copy these leads into your file, and maintain them in the following manner:

1. When each lead is assigned, enter the name of the Sales Person.
2. Enter the date when the first sales contact was made with the sales lead.
3. Record the date of the demonstration.
4. Enter the status of the sale after the demonstration in one of the following forms:

Sale (Model Number) — a sale was made

Postpone — the purchase decision was delayed

Competitor (select one) — the prospect bought from a competitor

Brock
Med Sci
Am Lab

Other

At the end of the month, please send me a copy of this report and the updated forms (on disk). I will then prepare an analysis of your district's sales activity and effectiveness. We will be discussing this new system more fully at our next district meeting.

**Fig. 13.9** *Printout of text with expanded characters.*

One problem with embedding printer and special character codes in your text is that the file as it appears on-screen may be difficult to read. Because wordwrap is affected, you also may have trouble visualizing how the document will look on paper. In Chapter 19, you will learn how to create macros that help you differentiate the codes from the text and keep track of the codes you use most often.

## *Selecting Options for Printing*

After you select the options for formatting and enhancing the text, you are ready to print the document. Similar to other popular word processors, Q&A allows you to print partial or complete documents and make multiple copies of the same document with one keystroke. Options are provided in the Print Options menu so that you can make your printer pause for paper change or start printing from a different point on the page. By selecting different printer ports for different print jobs, you can use more than one installed printer with Q&A.

### *Designating the Page Range for Printing*

You may not always want to print a document from beginning to end. Suppose that you have modified pages 2 and 3 of a report; you can tell Q&A to print only those pages by specifying their page numbers in the From Page and To Page options of the Print Options menu. If you enter a *2* at the From Page prompt and a *3* at the To Page prompt, printing will start at the beginning of page 2 and continue to the end of page 3. If you want to print one page only, that page number should appear in both the From Page and To Page positions. If you don't specify a page number, Q&A will print the document from start to finish.

### *Printing Multiple Copies*

In some cases, you may need to print several copies of the same document. Perhaps you have a memo that should go to four different managers. You can enter a *4* at the Number of Copies prompt; when the document is printed, four copies will be produced automatically.

### *Using the Offset Option*

The Printer Offset option establishes the position from which the print head starts printing. The default value is zero, but you can change the setting by adjusting the left margin. To start the print head farther to the left, enter a minus sign (–) before the number of characters. For example, if you want the printing to begin three spaces to the left of the default setting, enter –3. Entering a plus sign (+) and a number, or just a number, shifts the printing that number of characters to the right.

### *Selecting the Printer Port*

You must specify which printer port you are using before you can send any data to the printer. If you have installed more than one printer, you can tell Q&A which printer to use for each job by redirecting the output to a different printer port. The default port is LPT1, which is the port most often used for parallel printers. If you choose the Disk option, a standard ASCII file is created for exporting data to another software program. The file includes the same margins and page breaks as the Q&A file, and headers and footers are preserved.

### *Selecting Paper Type*

An important choice to make is the setting for the type of paper you will use. Many computer users choose perforated paper rather than single-sheet paper; this choice allows users to print a document or report without having to insert sheets individually. To use this type of paper, select the Continuous option. If you plan to insert paper one sheet at a time, choose the Manual option.

The other four options (Bin1, Bin2, Bin3, and Lhd) are used when you have a sheet feeder on your printer. Each Bin setting corresponds to the bin of the sheet feeder from which the paper will be taken. Lhd is used to specify that the first sheet will be letterhead paper and the rest of the sheets will be standard bond paper. Lhd causes the first sheet to be taken from Bin1 and the remaining pages from Bin2.

### *Printing Columns*

Q&A has a word-processing feature that few other programs have: the capability of printing more than one column on a page. Up to eight columns, also called *newspaper columns*, can be printed on a page, depending on the width of your paper.

To print the text in a columnar format, move the cursor to the Number of Columns option and select the number of columns you want to print. You may want to set the Justify option to Yes so that your columns are displayed evenly.

## *Special Print Applications*

At some time, you may want Q&A Write to do more than just print reports and memos. Suppose that you are sending a mailing to all customers in Santa Cruz, California. You could address all the envelopes by hand, or you could delegate the responsibility. Why not have Q&A do it for you? Q&A can even insert another Write document into the one you want to print or merge data from another file into your printout. This section discusses these special print applications available with Q&A Write.

### *Merging Other Files with Write*

When you are creating a report, you can enhance your document by adding parts of a worksheet or graph. Files from PFS:GRAPH® or spreadsheets and graphs from 1-2-3 or Symphony can be incorporated into your Write document to help illustrate your discussion.

Specifying this feature is similar to specifying other merge features; type the word *spreadsheet*, the name of the file to import, and the range of the worksheet you want to include. For example, each of the following lines can import graphs or spreadsheets into your Write document:

*spreadsheet budget, A1-H19*
*ss budget, A1-H19*
*ss c:\data\123\budget, A1-H19*
*graph pie*

As with other merge commands, these lines must be enclosed within asterisks. When you are importing a range from a worksheet, you have the option of typing the word *spreadsheet* or entering the letters *ss*. The file name extension is not necessary. After the name of the file, type a comma and enter the range of the worksheet you want to import.

To import a graph, simply type *graph* and enter the graph name. If necessary, you can add the drive designation and path, but the file name extension is unnecessary.

## Printing a Merge Document

You may want to merge data from another file instead of incorporating the entire file by using the Join command (discussed later in this chapter). For example, if you want to pull names and addresses from files stored in a Q&A database, you can use the program's merge capability.

If you are working on the document you want to print, you can start the merge process by pressing F2. You also can press P to choose the Print option from the Write menu. The Print Options menu is then displayed. After setting all the defaults you want to use, move to the Name of Merge File prompt. Type the name of the file you want to use with the Write document and press F10.

### Using the Identifier Spec Screen in Merge Operations

When you have named the file to be merged and have pressed F10, a new screen, called the Identifier Spec, is displayed (see fig. 13.10). You will not see this screen anywhere else in Q&A. With this screen, you can identify the fields to be merged from the File database, using any names you want. The correct names are shown on the Identifier Spec screen, and you can type any substitute names you used in the document. Q&A then accepts those names as field merge specifications.

Notice that the line at the bottom of the screen shows that you can use F6 to expand a field. This option appears on other Q&A screens and permits you to type instructions or specifications that are longer than the space available on-screen. Even though the information on the display may be truncated, the entire entry in the field will remain intact.

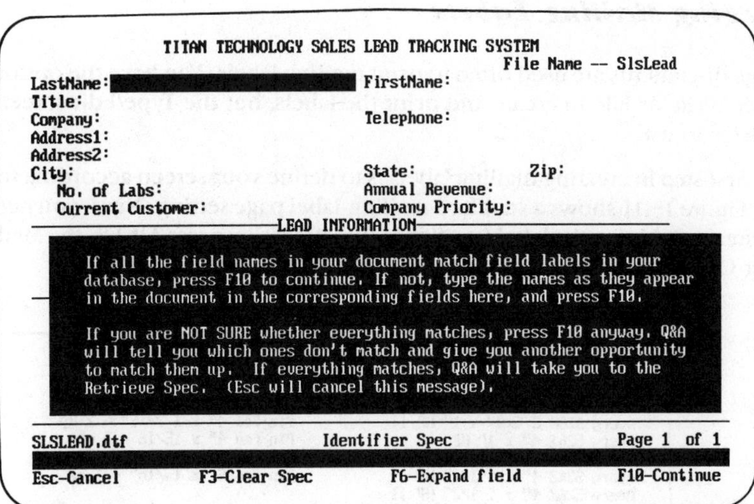


**Fig. 13.10** *The Identifier Spec.*

If you press F10 again, the Retrieve Spec screen will be displayed, unless you have included in your merge document field names that don't match the fields in your database. In that case, you will be confronted with a warning screen. You then can match the names by entering them on the Identifier Spec or press F10 to ignore the field names.

## *Using Retrieve and Sort Specs in Merge Operations*

The Retrieve Spec is used in merge operations to select certain items of information. You can use the Retrieve Spec, for example, to select customers in Chicago who should receive a special mailing.

Don't forget that you can press F1 to get a list of available retrieval specification symbols whenever the Retrieve Spec screen is displayed.

If you want to sort the forms before the merge printing, press F8 from the Retrieve Spec to display the Sort Spec screen (for more information on Sort Specs, see Chapter 6).

Press F10 to begin printing. If you have made a mistake in filling out the Retrieve Spec screen, you may get this warning message: `No forms were found that meet your retrieve request. Do you want to check or change your request?` If you select Yes, the Retrieve Spec is displayed again, and you can make any necessary changes.

## *Merging Mailing Labels*

Merge documents are used often to print mailing labels. You have the option of using either Write or File to create and print the labels, but the Type/Edit screen in Write is easier to use.

The first step in creating mailing labels is to define your screen according to the label size. Figure 13.11 shows a standard mailing-label page setting. Next, you need to type the merge fields for the label (see fig. 13.12). After you press Alt-F8, the Mailing Label Print Options screen is displayed.

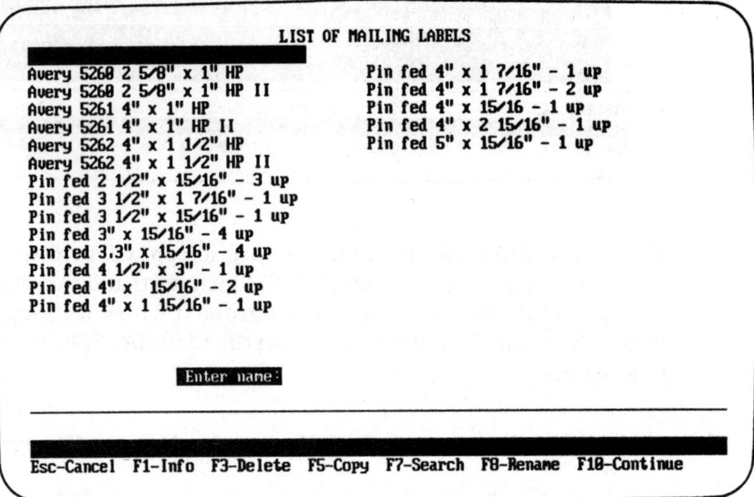


**Fig. 13.11** *Standard mailing-label page setting.*

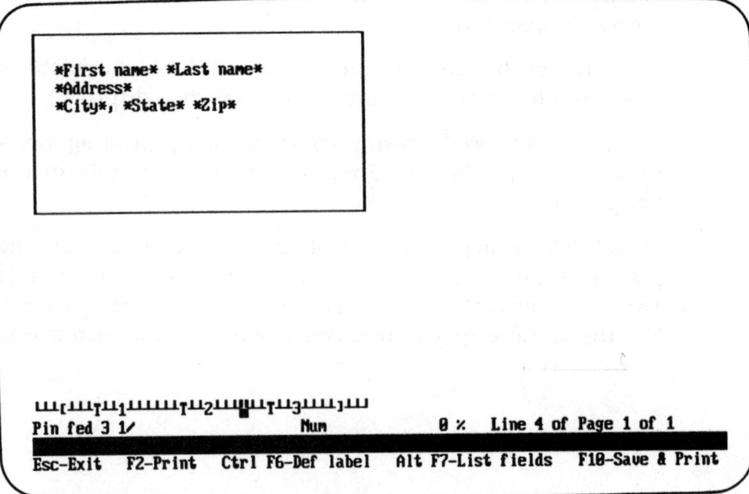


**Fig. 13.12** *Merge fields for mailing labels.*

Choose your print offset, printer port, and paper feed type. The type of paper feed you choose will depend on your application. If you are printing mailing labels, for example, you will want to choose continuous paper feed; if you are printing envelopes, you will need to use manual paper feed unless you have continuous-feed envelopes. You then specify the number of labels to be printed across one page, the special printer control options, and the name of the database to use for the mail merge print. When you press F10, printing begins.

## *Integrating Documents with the Join Command*

Suppose that you are writing a business letter to a sales manager and you want to incorporate in the letter a copy of a one-page table you have stored in a separate file. You can insert one Write document into another by using the Join command. If you are using files in an ASCII format, you can insert documents produced by other programs, such as PFS:REPORT®.

If the file you want to insert is in the current directory on the current drive, you can enter the following command at the point where you want the document added:

*Join *filename**

If you like, you can abbreviate *Join* by typing *J*. If the file is on another drive (D, for example), you enter the following:

*Join D:*filename**

## *Mass Printing with Queue*

Printing can be one of the most time-consuming aspects of computing. Because this process can waste valuable time, you may want to save all your printing to do at one time. Using Q&A's Queue command, you can organize all the print jobs into one file that you can print later.

To use the Queue command to consolidate your printing tasks, create a Write document by choosing Type/Edit from the Write menu. Enter the Queue command as follows, with the names of the files you want printed:

*queue letter1.doc*
*queue letter2.doc*
*queue letter3.doc*

After you have specified all the files you want to print, save the document under a name such as QUEUE.MRG and then print it. The page settings in the QUEUE.MRG file don't matter because the page settings are taken from each document listed with the Queue command.

## Nesting Fields

When you print a merge document, you can use nested fields to substitute different field names for different conditions. Suppose that the Title field in the sales lead database stores values such as President, Vice President, and Purchasing Agent. By using nested fields, you can send a letter to each of these people and change the third paragraph to include the correct title of each recipient.

To do this procedure, enter the following line in place of the third paragraph when you type the letter:

*join *Title**

Then type each of the different paragraphs you want to insert at this point; be sure to save each paragraph in a separate file named to match the title name (President, Vice President, etc.). When you merge print your document, the paragraph that corresponds to the Title field will be inserted in the correct place.

## Printing Envelopes

A special line-spacing option is available for envelopes. If you have a letter loaded in memory, you can have Q&A "pick up" the name and address from the letter. Simply type *e* (for envelope) on the Line Spacing option line of the Print Options screen. Then select the rest of the print options as appropriate. After you have chosen the print settings, press F10. You then are prompted to insert the envelope into your printer.

Q&A prints at a predetermined position on the envelope, so inserting the envelope correctly is important. The envelope should be inserted in the printer so that the top edge is under the print head. Printing will start 10 lines down from that position and 3.5 inches from the left margin.

How does Q&A know where the address is on the letter? Q&A ignores the indented material and assumes that the first line of copy at the left margin is the name of the person to whom the letter is addressed and that the lines immediately following are the address. If you prefer to use a flush-left format, Q&A can handle that, too. The program checks to see whether the first line is a date or a name. If the first line ends in two or more digits, the line is assumed to contain a date. The program skips that line and finds the first line that isn't indented. Q&A assumes that this line is the first line of the address and that the blank line following the address marks its end.

## *Chapter Summary*

Printing a document from Q&A Write is not a difficult process. Depending on the type of printout you want, you can print the on-screen document instantly by pressing F2 or tailor the printout by specifying print options from the Print Options screen.

Q&A's capacity to accept printer control codes allows you to change the print type in your document and to insert special character codes so that your printout can include any characters supported by your printer.

In the next chapter, you will learn how to use Q&A Report. To learn how to print from Q&A File, see Chapter 8. To learn how to print from Q&A Report, see Chapter 16.

# Part IV

# Using Q&A Report

Includes

Q&A Report Quick Start
Creating a Report
Printing a Report

Chapter 14

# Q&A Report Quick Start

Report is Q&A's module for converting your data in File into usable and easy-to-create reports. In addition to producing hard copy of data in File, the Report module also can perform calculations and generate derived columns, headers, footers, lookup functions, and unique column headings. The reports generated in this module follow the traditional columnar report format, rather than the free-form or coordinate styles available in File. As in the other modules, information on designing and printing these reports is at your fingertips if you press F1 (Info).

You will begin using Report by designing a basic report. After going through the design steps and printing a report, you will use some of the more advanced features to redesign the report.

## *Designing a Report*

Access the Report module from the Q&A Main menu the same way you access the File module.

1. Select Report from the Q&A Main menu.

   The Report menu appears. This menu has four selections: Design/Redesign a Report, Print a Report, Set Global Options, and Rename/Delete/Copy.

2. Select Design/Redesign a Report from the Report menu. Q&A asks you for the name of the database from which the report will be compiled.

3. Type *house.dtf*, or press the Enter key to view database names and choose HOUSE.DTF from that list.

If you were redesigning an existing report, at this point a menu listing all reports saved for the database HOUSE.DTF would be displayed; you could select the report to redesign by using the arrow keys. You will name this new report Inventory.

4. Type the report name *Inventory* and press Enter.

## *Retrieving Forms for Your Report*

Next, you need to retrieve the forms for this report. You will use the Retrieve Spec screen, the next screen that appears, to retrieve the forms.

1. Press F1 (How to retrieve) to review how to retrieve forms for the report.

For this report, you need to retrieve all the forms in the database.

2. Press F10 to indicate that all forms will be retrieved.

## *Determining Columns and Sorting Order*

Column/Sort Spec is the next screen that appears. You will use this screen to determine which fields will print in which columns and the sorting for each of those fields. This spec can become quite complex, depending on your requirements.

1. Press F1 (Info) to view the help screens (the screens are several pages long). Then press Esc (Cancel) to return to the Column/Sort Spec.
2. Enter the following specifications in the appropriate fields:

| | |
|---|---|
| Item: 3 | Third column to print |
| Quantity: 2 | Second column to print |
| Location: 1,AS | First column to print, in ascending order (A–Z) |
| Date of Purchase: 6 | Sixth column to print |
| Amount of Purchase: 7 | Seventh column to print |
| Serial Number: 5 | Fifth column to print |
| Description: 4 | Fourth column to print |
| Item Number: (blank) | This field will not be included |

   Your Column/Sort Spec should look like figure 14.1.

3. Press F10 (Continue) to save the specifications in the Column/Sort Spec and continue to the next step.

## *Entering Print Options for Your Report*

The Report Print Options screen appears next. Although similar to the File Print Options menu, this screen also allows you to print totals and justify text within the report. You will use this screen to determine which printer to use, the type of paper, the printer offset, any external printer codes, totals to be included, and the text

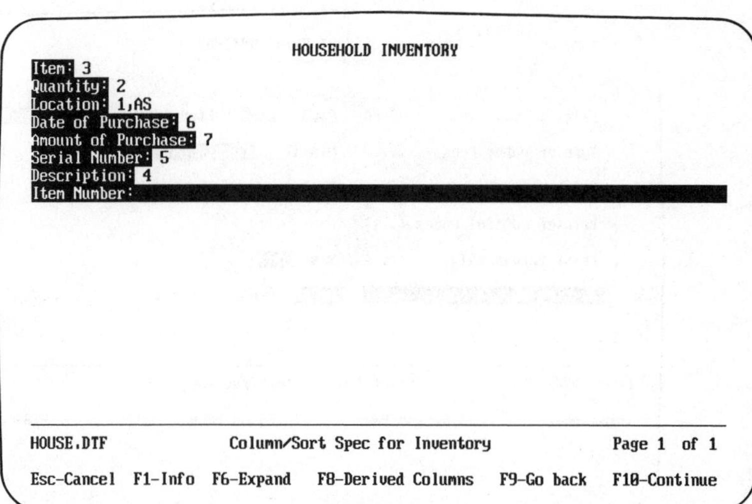

HOUSEHOLD INVENTORY
Item: 3
Quantity: 2
Location: 1,AS
Date of Purchase: 6
Amount of Purchase: 7
Serial Number: 5
Description: 4
Item Number:
HOUSE.DTF
Column/Sort Spec for Inventory
Page 1 of 1
Esc-Cancel F1-Info F6-Expand F8-Derived Columns F9-Go back F10-Continue


**Fig. 14.1** *Entering specifications in the Column/Sort Spec.*

justification for the report. You should verify the settings in the Report Print Options screen and change them if necessary:

Print to: SCREEN

Type of Paper Feed: Continuous

Printer Offset: 0 (To move the entire report five spaces to the right, you would enter 5.)

Printer Control Codes: (blank)

Print Totals Only: No

Justify Report Body: Left

Compare your Report Print Options screen with figure 14.2.

## *Defining the Page Options*

Before printing the report, you need to be sure that the Define Page settings are sufficient to print the entire report. You will print several columns, and they require extra space.

1. Press F8 (Define Page) to move to the Define Page screen.

The Define Page screen holds information about margins, page length, characters per inch, and any headers or footers to appear on the report. You will change some of these settings to allow for the extra width of the report. You also will set a header to display the current date at the top of the report and a footer to display the page number at the bottom of the report.

**Fig. 14.2** *Verifying the print options.*

```
                    REPORT PRINT OPTIONS

Print to..........:   PtrA  PtrB  PtrC  PtrD  PtrE  DISK  ►SCREEN◄
Type of paper feed........:  Manual  ►Continuous◄  Bin1  Bin2  Bin3
Printer offset............:  0
Printer control codes.....:
Print totals only.........:  Yes ►No◄
Justify report body.......:  ►Left◄  Center  Right

HOUSE.DTF              Print Options for Inventory
Esc-Cancel        F8-Define Page        F9-Go back             F10-Continue
```

2. Check the parameters on the Define Page screen, and change them if necessary to the following settings:

   Page Width: 240 Page Length: 66
   Left Margin: 5 Right Margin: 235
   Top Margin: 3 Bottom Margin: 3
   Characters Per Inch: 17

   HEADER

   1: Inventory Report As of @DATE(n)

   FOOTER

   1: Page #

   Your screen now should look like figure 14.3.

These parameters are chosen for specific reasons. The page width is 240 because that's the maximum width of a report. If you don't know the width needed, 240 is a good starting point. You then can decrease the width setting as needed. The right margin of 235 allows for a five-space margin if the entire width of 240 spaces is required. You are using 17 characters per inch to gain the benefit of condensed type. The width of the report will be minimized using smaller characters (possibly minimized enough to fit on a sheet of 8.5-inch-by-11-inch paper if needed), thus making the report more compact but still readable. However, because you are printing to the screen, you will not see a smaller type size on-screen.

The header will appear at the top of each printed page and will include today's date. Each page will be numbered at the bottom as specified in the footer. However, because you are printing to the screen, headers and footers will not appear.

**Fig. 14.3**
*Verifying the Define Page screen settings.*

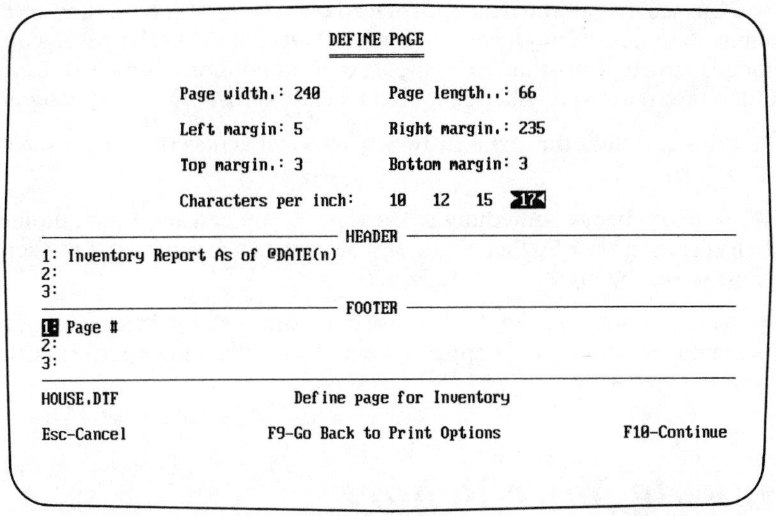

```
                         DEFINE PAGE

          Page width.: 240         Page length..: 66
          Left margin: 5           Right margin.: 235
          Top margin.: 3           Bottom margin: 3
          Characters per inch:     10   12   15   17

──────────────────────── HEADER ────────────────────────
1: Inventory Report As of @DATE(n)
2:
3:
──────────────────────── FOOTER ────────────────────────
1: Page #
2:
3:
─────────────────────────────────────────────────────────
HOUSE.DTF               Define page for Inventory

Esc-Cancel          F9-Go Back to Print Options      F10-Continue
```

3. Press F10 to save your design and continue. A notice appears, informing you that your design has been saved and asking whether you want to print the report.
4. Respond Yes and press Enter.

The final report is printed to your screen. Because your data is not identical to this HOUSE.DTF database, your field information will be different. The column headings and placement are shown in figure 14.4.

**Fig. 14.4**
*Printing your report on-screen.*

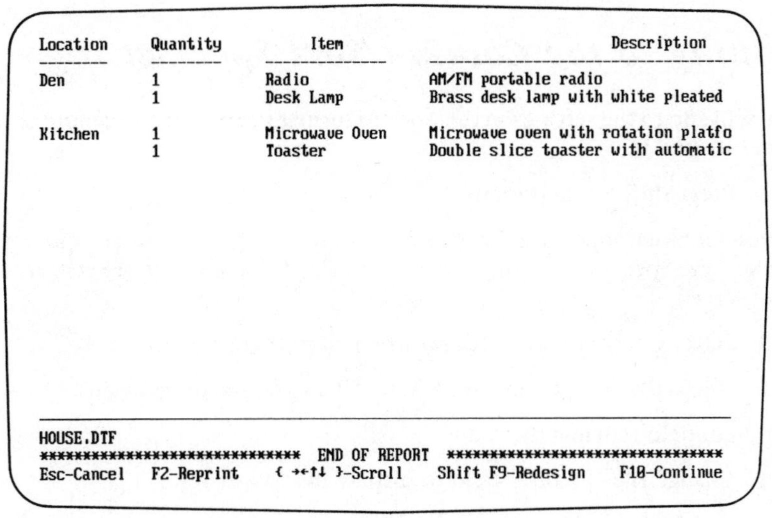

```
Location   Quantity      Item                      Description
--------   --------  --------------  ----------------------------------
Den        1         Radio           AM/FM portable radio
           1         Desk Lamp       Brass desk lamp with white pleated

Kitchen    1         Microwave Oven  Microwave oven with rotation platfo
           1         Toaster         Double slice toaster with automatic

──────────────────────────────────────────────────────────────────────
HOUSE.DTF
******************************** END OF REPORT ********************************
Esc-Cancel  F2-Reprint   ( →←↑↓ )-Scroll   Shift F9-Redesign   F10-Continue
```

As you can see, not all the data is displayed on-screen. You requested several more columns than Location, Quantity, Item, and Description. The other columns are included in the report—they are to the right of the columns displayed. To view these "hidden" columns, you will use the scroll feature shown on the key assignment line.

5. Press and hold the right-arrow key to scroll across the rest of the report.

If you want to change something in the report, you can access the design screens again by pressing Shift-F9 (Redesign), or you can change settings on the Report Print Options screen by pressing F2 (Reprint).

Now that you know how to design a basic report, let's explore some of the many ways to improve this report's appearance and have the report perform calculations for you.

## Redesigning Your Report

Once reports are saved, they stay with the database they reference until you delete the reports from memory. You can redesign saved reports at any time. One way to redesign a report is to select Design/Redesign a Report from the Report menu. Another way is to redesign a report after it appears on your screen. A good practice to follow is to print reports to the screen before printing them on paper. Then you can see what the report looks like before producing a printed copy, and you can make changes quickly. You will redesign the Inventory report by adjusting the Column/Sort Spec settings and by adding a new column that uses other columns in the report to make calculations.

### Adding to the Column/Sort Spec Settings

You will add to the settings in this spec to format the report to be more concise and easier to read.

1. Press Shift-F9 (Redesign).

A message block appears at the bottom of the screen, giving you the option to change the Retrieve Spec, the Column/Sort Spec, Derived Columns, Print Spec, or the Define Page screen.

2. Select Column/Sort. Q&A returns you to that screen.

Your settings for this spec are saved. You will use these settings again and adjust them.

The Item field remains the same.

3. Change the Quantity field to display the following:

   2,F(JC)

Each element of this program instructs Q&A to carry out a separate step:

| | |
|---|---|
| 2 | Second column to print |
| F | A format being specified |
| JC | The field to be center-justified |

The Location and Date of Purchase fields do not change.

4. Change the Amount of Purchase field as follows:

   7,ST,F(JR,C),H(12:Amount!of Purchase)

   Each element of this program gives an instruction to Q&A:

| | |
|---|---|
| 7 | Seventh field to print |
| ST | This field to have sub-totals |
| F | A format being specified |
| JR | The field to be right-justified |
| C | The field to have commas inserted |
| H | This heading to be changed |
| 12 | The heading to have 12 spaces |
| Amount! | The first line of the heading is "Amount." The exclamation mark (!) indicates that the heading will split and be continued on the next line. |
| of Purchase | The second line of the heading is "of Purchase" |

   The Serial Number field does not change.

5. Change the Description field as follows:

   4,H(40:)

   The elements in this program give Q&A three instructions:

| | |
|---|---|
| 4 | Fourth field to print |
| H | The heading to be changed |
| 40 | The heading to have 40 spaces |

The text of the heading doesn't change. Figure 14.5 shows the Column/Sort Spec.

If you had used all the space in a field into which you were entering the column/sort criteria, you could have expanded the length of that field temporarily to contain additional sorting criteria by pressing F6 (Expand). Pressing F6 expands to a maximum of 240 spaces the area that will accept sorting or programming criteria.

**Fig. 14.5**
*Revising the Column/Sort Spec.*

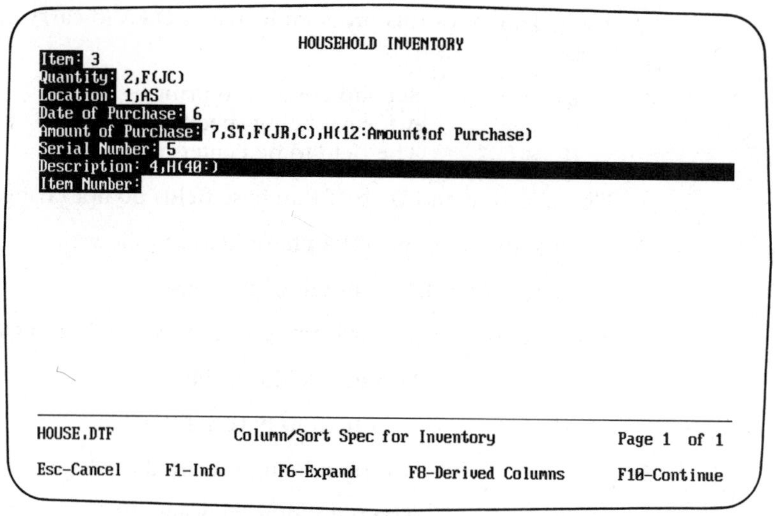

```
                         HOUSEHOLD INVENTORY
Item: 3
Quantity: 2,F(JC)
Location: 1,AS
Date of Purchase: 6
Amount of Purchase: 7,ST,F(JR,C),H(12:Amount!of Purchase)
Serial Number: 5
Description: 4,H(40:)
Item Number:

HOUSE.DTF          Column/Sort Spec for Inventory          Page 1 of 1
Esc-Cancel   F1-Info   F6-Expand   F8-Derived Columns   F10-Continue
```

## *Using a Derived Column*

A *derived column* is a column that does not exist in the database from which the Report module gets its data. The column is *derived* from data in other columns in the report and holds its own unique data. Many mathematical functions can be performed in a derived column, such as a total, average, count, minimum, and maximum.

The Inventory report would be better if you could determine a total value of all items included in your household inventory. This number does not exist in any field, but you can calculate the number and display it in a derived column.

1. From the Column/Sort Spec, press F8 (Derived Columns) to display the Derived Columns screen.

The Derived Columns screen consists of Heading, Formula, and Column Spec settings. Only four groups of settings are displayed on-screen, but up to 16 derived columns are available. In the bottom right of the screen you see `Page 1 of 4` on the message line. This screen is four pages long, and you can enter additional derived column data by pressing the PgDn key.

2. In the first group of settings on the Derived Columns screen, enter the following data:

| | |
|---|---|
| Heading: Total Value!of Inventory | The first line of the heading will be ''Total Value''; the second line will be ''of Inventory'' |
| Formula: #7 + #8 | The column will hold the totals of column #7 (Amount |

| | |
|---|---|
| | of Purchase) and column #8 (the derived Total column) |
| Column Spec: 8,T | The derived column will be column #8, and calculations will be totaled at the end of the report |

Figure 14.6 shows the Derived Columns screen with this information entered.

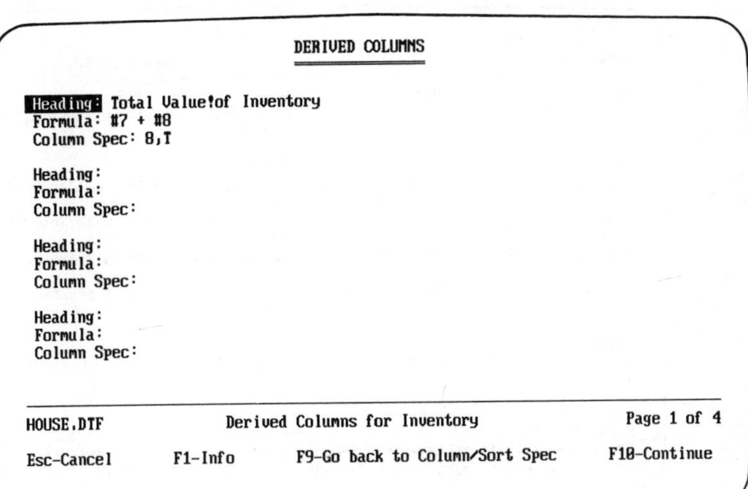


**Fig. 14.6**
*Entering settings for the derived column.*

3. Press F10 (Continue) to save the settings for the derived column.
4. Respond Yes when Q&A asks you whether you want to print the report. You are now ready to print the report. The new report appears on-screen.
5. Use the arrow keys to scroll across the report, verifying the changes you made:
    - Data in the Quantity column is centered.
    - The Description column is narrower, with the descriptions wrapping to a second or third line if needed.
    - The Amount of Purchase column heading is now two lines instead of one; the column is subtotaled, right-justified with commas, and twelve spaces wide.

- Total Value of Inventory is the last column, with subtotals calculated as items are added and a grand total as the last figure in the column.

Figures 14.7 and 14.8 show your Inventory report.

6. Press Esc to return to the Report menu.

**Fig. 14.7**
*The first screen of your final report.*

```
Location  Quantity      Item                      Description
--------  --------  --------------  ----------------------------------------
Den          1      Radio           AM/FM portable radio
Den          1      Desk Lamp       Brass desk lamp with white pleated
                                    lampshade

Total:
Kitchen      1      Microwave Oven  Microwave oven with rotation platform
                                    and heat sensor
Kitchen      1      Toaster         Double slice toaster with automatic
                                    cleaning
Kitchen      6      Serving Dishs   Crystal desert serving dishes with
                                    saucers
Kitchen      6      Spoons          Silver spoons to match crystal serving
                                    dishes

Total:
========  ========  ==============  ========================================
Total:

HOUSE.DTF
******************************  END OF REPORT  ******************************
Esc-Cancel   F2-Reprint    { →←↑↓ }-Scroll    Shift F9-Redesign    F10-Continue
```

**Fig. 14.8**
*The second screen of your final report.*

```
                                                    Amount      Total Value
               Serial Number  Date of Purchase   of Purchase   of Inventory
-------------  -------------  ----------------   -----------   ------------
               HSR260XFM      June 3, 1988           $79.95         $79.95
e pleated      n/a            June 3, 1988          $127.86        $207.81

                                                 -----------
                                                    $207.81
ion platform   MWOE2690386    June 3, 1988        $1,265.88      $1,473.69

 automatic     Model #DS2850  June 3, 1988           $63.95      $1,537.64

shes with                     June 9, 1988            $0.00      $1,537.64

ystal serving                 June 9, 1988            $0.00      $1,537.64

                                                 -----------
                                                  $1,329.83
=============  =============  ================   ===========   ============
                                                                 $6,374.37

HOUSE.DTF
******************************  END OF REPORT  ******************************
Esc-Cancel   F2-Reprint    { →←↑↓ }-Scroll    Shift F9-Redesign    F10-Continue
```

# *Printing Your Report without Making Permanent Changes*

You can print existing reports without going through all the steps you just completed. Reports that are saved in memory can be printed using the Print a Report command on the Report menu.

1. Select Print a Report from the Report menu. The program asks for the name of the database that contains the report.
2. Enter the name of the database. Type the file name *house.dtf* and press Enter. If you are not sure of the name, press the Enter key, and a list of the databases appears for you to select from. A list of reports in the HOUSE.DTF database, including Inventory, is displayed.
3. Use the arrow keys to select the Inventory report, and press Enter.

   A menu appears, asking you whether you want to make any temporary changes. Notice that any changes are *temporary* and will not be saved after you print the report. This feature is useful if you want to modify a report to meet a one-time requirement yet want to keep the original report unchanged. If you choose to make temporary changes, Q&A will take you back through all the screens used to design or redesign a report and offer you the opportunity to change the screens. You will not make any temporary changes now.
4. Respond No on this menu and press Enter. The report as you designed it is printed on your screen (refer to figs. 14.7 and 14.8).
5. Press Esc until you are at the Report menu.

# *Setting Global Options*

*Global options* are choices that affect column headings and widths, and format, print, and page definitions. These options automatically apply to all the current database's reports generated after these options are set. Reports created before you change any of these settings remain as originally designed and are not altered.

Select Set Global Options from the Report menu for the database HOUSE.DTF. The Global Options menu appears. This menu includes four commands:

Set Column Headings/Widths
Set Format Options
Set Print Options
Set Page Options

With the first command, Set Column Headings/Widths, you can change headings and column widths for all the reports that reference HOUSE.DTF. Perhaps you want the Item field to be called Object on all reports and to be centered. This formatting would be done from this screen. (The same format is used as with the Column/Sort Spec when you first designed the Inventory report.) Or maybe you would like the Amount of Purchase field always to be printed as a two-line heading. You would indicate that in the appropriate field; all future reports would reflect that specification.

The second command, Set Format Options, provides four formatting features. You can set the number of spaces between columns to a definite number, instead of letting the spacing vary according to the page width. In your Inventory report, most of the spaces between columns were five or six. To condense a report, you could reduce these spaces to three or four. Also, printing reports that require identical values to be repeated is indicated with this command. For example, in the Inventory report when the location of items was identical, the location was printed only once. But for a report containing last names, you would want to print all the last names—even identical ones. You also can use this command to fill blank values with zero; financial reports compiled from a database require zeros to be placed in all blank fields for effective calculation and presentation. The last item that can be changed is to skip column breaks. For large reports, for instance, you can specify not to leave a blank line after each column break.

The third command, Set Print Options, controls the Report Print Options menu that appears when you print a report. You have worked with these items already. One other useful setting is the type of paper feed. Depending on your printer, you might use either continuous paper or paper that is stored in bins, such as letterhead or second sheets to letterhead. This setting can be changed here. Another frequent change is the printer that is used. Large spreadsheets often are printed on a printer different from the printer used for letterhead. You could specify here the printer for a database that is used to generate wide reports.

The final selection, Set Page Options, displays the Define Page screen. You can specify consistent margins or characters-per-inch settings for a particular database, thus eliminating the need to check the Define Page screen when *queuing* (or arranging) reports to print. Most reports require page numbering, which you can set here; pages then would be automatically numbered on all reports or even dated with the current date.

Press Esc to accept the default settings until you return to the Q&A Main menu.

# Chapter Summary

In this quick start chapter you learned how to design a report to extract information from a database. You now can sort information, print the information in the proper sequence, and generate and print new data in a derived column. You can redesign previously saved reports and make permanent changes to those reports, or print a temporary report while preserving your original design. By using global options, you can format and define all future reports, thus saving valuable time by not editing standard formats every time you generate a report.

With the Report module you can retrieve the data in the File module in a form that is beneficial to both you and your organization. In the next two chapters, you will learn much more about Q&A's Report module, including more on the possibilities for creating, formatting, and printing reports.

[illegible] report while preserving your original design. By using global options, you [illegible] all future reports [illegible] every time you generate a report.

[illegible] you can [illegible] the data in the [illegible] Q&A [illegible] report.

Chapter 15

# Creating a Report

After you have created a database and entered data in the files, you need to be able to organize the data into a report for your analysis and for others to review. Q&A Report can pull information from the forms in File and print reports in a variety of ways.

Q&A Report lets you selectively print database records with user-specified column headings and sort order. Additionally, you can compute information that is not stored in the database for inclusion on the report.

The Report module is one of three ways of retrieving information from a Q&A File database. The other two ways are retrieving and printing records with print facilities inside the File module and using the Intelligent Assistant. For information on using the print facilities in the File module see Chapters 6 and 8.

You may prefer to use the Intelligent Assistant to produce ad hoc reports quickly and easily. The Intelligent Assistant's reporting features work best when you need a quick report that answers a specific question or one-time request. (For detailed information on using the IA to produce reports, see Chapters 17 and 18.)

When you need to design a report that will be used repeatedly, however, you will want to use the flexibility of Q&A Report, which allows you to customize column headings and widths, include derived columns, and add headers and footers. This chapter explains how to create and use this type of report.

## Reports Available with Q&A Report

Q&A Report produces several varieties of columnar, detailed, and summary reports by using the data entered in File. If you have used classic database design methods to build your files, you already have a good idea how you want the reports to appear, but you can use the flexible design features in the Report module to experiment with data presentation.

Figure 15.1 shows the Source of Leads report. The sales leads on this report are grouped by source: Advertising, Mailing, Phone, and Salesman. The rows of calculated subtotals show that Phone Sales produced the most leads during the reporting period. This information will be helpful in planning future sales promotions.

**Fig. 15.1**
*The Source of Leads report.*

| Source of Lead | Date Entered | State | Sales Priority | Product Interest | Request For | Status |
|---|---|---|---|---|---|---|
| Adv | Jun 15, 1988 | MO | Hot | 2500;1500 | Demo | Sale; 2500 |
| | Apr 16, 1988 | CA | 1.0 | 1500;2000 | Demo | Postpone |
| | Jul 27, 1988 | IN | 2.0 | 2500 | Salesman | Sale; 2500 |
| | May 7, 1988 | TN | 1.0 | 2000 | Info | Postpone |
| | Jul 1, 1988 | AL | 1.0 | 2500;1500 | Demo | No Decision |
| Count: | | 5 | | | | |
| Mail | Jun 2, 1988 | MI | 1.5 | 2000;1000 | Info | Postpone |
| | Jun 6, 1988 | CO | Hot | 1500;2000 | Info | Sale |
| | Jul 27, 1988 | IN | 1.0 | 2000 | Info | Follow up |
| Count: | | 3 | | | | |
| Phone | Jul 10, 1988 | TN | 1.0 | 2000;1200 | Info | Sale; 1200 |
| | Jul 15, 1988 | SD | Hot | 1200;2000 | Info | Follow up |
| | May 15, 1988 | GA | 1.5 | 2000;2500 | Salesman | No Decision |
| | Jul 29, 1988 | CO | 1.0 | 1000;1500 | Salesman | Follow up |
| | Jul 27, 1988 | IN | 2.0 | 1000 | Info | Follow up |
| | Jun 4, 1988 | PA | 1.0 | 1200;1500 | Demo | Postpone |
| Count: | | 6 | | | | |
| Salesman | Jul 5, 1988 | PA | 1.5 | 1200;1500 | Demo | Sale; 1500 |
| | Apr 28, 1988 | WA | 2.0 | 1500;2500 | Info | Sale; 1500 |
| | Jun 5, 1988 | MI | 1.5 | 1000;2000 | Salesman | Postpone |
| | Jul 20, 1988 | PA | 1.5 | 2000;1500 | Salesman | Sale; 2000 |
| Count: | | 4 | | | | |

The Sales District report, shown in figure 15.2, shows the leads divided according to sales districts. This type of report might be sent to the district sales managers. Subtotal and total counts are included in this report.

The Sales Leads Revenue per Lab report, shown in figure 15.3, is an analysis of the company's annual revenue. This report contains a special column (Revenue per Lab) that is calculated for this report only. Three of the columns have total, average, maximum, and minimum calculations. Marketing information of this type is helpful for long-range planning.

You can produce many different reports from a single database. Each can have its own format, calculations, and derived columns. This chapter explains how to design a report by using the different capabilities of Q&A Report.

# *Designing a Report*

Designing a report with the Report module is relatively easy. You should follow this basic procedure:

1. Specify which data file or files Report will use.

| Sales Dist. | Company | City | Request For | Product Interest | Sales Priority |
|---|---|---|---|---|---|
| Atlanta | Mattis Medical Laboratories | Atlanta | Salesman | 2000;2500 | 1.5 |
| Count: | 1 | | | | |
| Cincinnati | Nashville Medical Technology | Nashville | Info | 2000 | 1.0 |
| Count: | 1 | | | | |
| Denver | Mountain Labs | Denver | Salesman | 1000;1500 | 1.0 |
| | Mountain Labs | Boulder | Info | 1500;2000 | Hot |
| Count: | 2 | | | | |
| Detroit | University of Michigan | Detroit | Salesman | 1000;2000 | 1.5 |
| Count: | 1 | | | | |
| Indiana | Central Laboratories | | Info | 2000 | 1.0 |
| | Indiana Medical, Inc. | | Info | 1000 | 2.0 |
| | Hoosier Clinics, Inc. | | Salesman | 2500 | 2.0 |
| Count: | 3 | | | | |
| Knoxville | Advanced Medical Associates | Knoxville | Info | 2000;1200 | 1.0 |
| Count: | 1 | | | | |
| Los Angeles | Cherry Electronics, Inc. | San Francisco | Demo | 1500;2000 | 1.0 |
| Count: | 1 | | | | |
| Michigan | Bay City Laboratories | Grand Rapids | Info | 2000;1000 | 1.5 |
| Count: | 1 | | | | |
| Missouri | Independent Medical Labs | Independence | Demo | 2500;1500 | Hot |
| Count: | 1 | | | | |
| Mobile | Hope Laboratories, Inc. | Mobile | Demo | 2500;1500 | 1.0 |
| Count: | 1 | | | | |
| Philadelphia | Franklyn Lab Associates | Philadelphia | Demo | 1200;1500 | 1.5 |
| | Penn Medical Technology | King of Prussia | Demo | 1200;1500 | 1.0 |
| | Pike Pharmaceutical, Inc. | Reading | Salesman | 2000;1500 | 1.5 |
| Count: | 3 | | | | |
| Seattle | Washington Medical Labs, Inc | Seattle | Info | 1500;2500 | 2.0 |
| Count: | 1 | | | | |

**Fig. 15.2** *The Sales District report.*

2. Tell Report which records to print—the Retrieve Spec.
3. Choose the fields from each record to print.
4. Specify field and record order.

Although each of these basic steps may have several parts, if you remember the basics, the process is not difficult.

Think of a printed or on-screen report as a window into the database. Once you have the data you want to analyze stored on disk, you can look through the report window to view the data in many forms. This concept is particularly important if you are in a multi-user environment, because Q&A Report allows you to look at File information only at a suspended moment in time. All the reports you generate reflect how the database looks when you ask for the report. Other users may change information while your report is being prepared, but you won't see the changes unless you generate a later report. This capability allows Q&A to support simultaneous access by users.

**Fig. 15.3**
***The Sales Leads Revenue per Lab report.***

| Company | No. of Labs | Annual Revenue | Revenue Per lab | Sales Priority | Sales Dist. |
|---|---|---|---|---|---|
| Mountain Labs | 3 | $5378667.00 | $1,792,889.00 | Hot | Denver |
| Hope Laboratories, Inc. | 2 | $500000.00 | $250,000.00 | 1.0 | Mobile |
| Plaines Medical Associates | 4 | $750000.00 | $187,500.00 | Hot | South Dakota |
| Hoosier Clinics, Inc. | 3 | $100000.00 | $33,333.33 | 2.0 | Indiana |
| Central Laboratories | 1 | $50000.00 | $50,000.00 | 1.0 | Indiana |
| Indiana Medical, Inc. | 4 | $125000.00 | $31,250.00 | 2.0 | Indiana |
| Independent Medical Labs | 3 | $223500.00 | $74,500.00 | Hot | Missouri |
| Mountain Labs | 2 | $100210.00 | $50,105.00 | 1.0 | Denver |
| Advanced Medical Associates | 3 | $5300623.00 | $1,766,874.33 | 1.0 | Knoxville |
| Cherry Electronics, Inc. | 20 | $4000000.00 | $200,000.00 | 1.0 | Los Angeles |
| Nashville Medical Technology | 7 | $8000375.00 | $1,142,910.71 | 1.0 | Cincinnati |
| Franklyn Lab Associates | 5 | $6456000.00 | $1,291,200.00 | 1.5 | Philadelphia |
| Penn Medical Technology | 3 | $50000.00 | $16,666.67 | 1.0 | Philadelphia |
| Mattis Medical Laboratories | 5 | $1000210.00 | $200,042.00 | 1.5 | Atlanta |
| Washington Medical Labs, Inc | 6 | $200500.00 | $33,416.67 | 2.0 | Seattle |
| University of Michigan | 3 | $325000.00 | $108,333.33 | 1.5 | Detroit |
| Pike Pharmaceutical, Inc. | 1 | $210000.00 | $210,000.00 | 1.5 | Philadelphia |
| Bay City Laboratories | 1 | $150250.00 | $150,250.00 | 1.5 | Michigan |

To begin designing a report, select Report from the Q&A Main menu; the Report menu is then displayed. As you design your report, remember to use the Help key (F1) to display instructions for each step.

Two procedures can be used in designing a report form: sequential and direct. The *sequential procedure* goes through the design process step-by-step; the *direct procedure* takes you straight to the step you want. This section focuses on the sequential method. Later, you learn how to use the direct method to make changes to the report design.

To begin the design process, select Design/Redesign a Report from the Report menu. The program then prompts you for the name of the file that stores the data. Type the file name or press Enter to display a list of files. When you have found the file name you want, press Enter. If you have designed reports previously, a list of report names is displayed.

To design a new report, respond to the prompt at the bottom of the screen by typing a report name of up to 20 characters. After you press Enter, Report responds by displaying the Retrieve Spec screen, and you are ready to begin retrieving information for your report.

## *Retrieving File Information*

The Retrieve Spec is used to specify the forms that are to be included in your report. If the report you are creating will use all the forms in the file, simply leave the Retrieve Spec blank, and press F10 to continue.

When you want to use only a selected group of forms, you can specify the forms by entering retrieval operators on the Retrieve Spec. (For more information on using retrieval operators and specifying the forms you want to use, see Chapter 6, "Using File.")

When you retrieve a group of forms, you can have the program search for either a piece of information or a range of information. If you want to retrieve all sales leads from the New York sales district, for example, enter *New York* in the Sales Dist. field (see fig. 15.4). On the other hand, if you want to retrieve all sales leads that have between 1 and 10 labs, you enter the range specification of 1..10 in the No. of Labs field. To retrieve a range in a text field, use the format >1..<10.

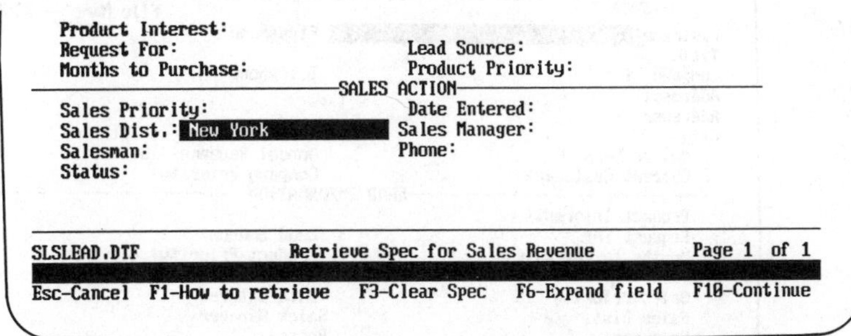


**Fig. 15.4** *Entering a retrieval spec.*

If you are not sure how information might have been entered with File, use Q&A's Sounds Like searching character, the tilde (~). Use the tilde at the beginning of a search spec when you are only guessing at the correct spelling or the correct choice among several possibilities.

Suppose that you want a list of the sales leads from the Hohenwald, Tennessee, office, and you suspect that different people have entered the office name in different ways. By specifying *~Hohenwald* in the Sales District field, you will retrieve records with such diverse spellings as Hoenwald, Hoenwaldt, and Hoinwald.

(Note that you can prevent this varied data entry problem by using lookup tables, external files, and custom help screens to enforce spelling compliance during data entry.)

You can use the Tab key, Return, and the cursor-movement keys to move the cursor from field to field in report screens. If you need more space when entering a retrieval specification, you can press F6 to expand the field length. If you want to erase the Retrieve Spec without saving it, you can press Esc to return to the Report menu. When all necessary specifications have been entered, press F10 to continue. The Column/Sort Spec screen is then displayed.

## Organizing Information for a Report

The simplest report you can create with the Report module consists of fields from your database file displayed in columnar form, but you can generate more complex reports. For example, you can create special columns—derived columns—that show the results of calculations using values from the original database forms. You also can create reports that are divided into categories based on information in keyword fields. The following sections teach you how to use features for organizing database information into a Q&A report.

### Selecting Fields for Columns

The next step in designing a report involves selecting and ordering the fields by using the Column/Sort Spec screen (see fig. 15.5).

**Fig. 15.5** *Selecting and ordering the file fields on the Column/Sort Spec screen.*

```
                    TITAN TECHNOLOGY SALES LEAD TRACKING SYSTEM
                                                     File Name -- SlsLead
LastName:                                  FirstName:
Title:
Company: 1                                 Telephone:
Address1:
Address2:
City:                                      State:              Zip:
   No. of Labs: 5                          Annual Revenue: 10
   Current Customer:                       Company Priority:
 --------------------------------LEAD INFORMATION----------------------------
   Product Interest:
   Request For:                            Lead Source:
   Months to Purchase:                     Product Priority:
 -----------------------------------SALES ACTION----------------------------
   Sales Priority: 15                      Date Entered:
   Sales Dist.: 20                        Sales Manager:
   Salesman:                              Phone:
   Status:

SLSLEAD.DTF           Column/Sort Spec for Sales Revenue          Page 1  of 1

Esc-Cancel  F1-Info  F6-Expand   F8-Derived Columns   F9-Go back   F10-Continue
```

When you organize a report, each field you select becomes a column in the report. You select the fields by numbering them, as shown in figure 15.5. Notice that the Column/Sort Spec in figure 15.5 does not show consecutive numbering. Numbering with increments larger than one allows columns to be added between the original columns without renumbering the fields. Figure 15.6 shows that the number you type in the field determines the column in which the field information will appear in the report.

To organize fields in report columns, move the cursor to the field that you want to appear in the left column of the report, and type 1. In figure 15.5, the Company field is designated as the left column. Continue entering numbers in the fields that you want to appear on the report. You may want to avoid numbering the fields consecutively to accommodate later insertions.

| Company | No. of Labs | Annual Revenue | Revenue Per lab | Sales Priority | Sales Dist. |
|---|---|---|---|---|---|
| Mountain Labs | 3 | $5378667.00 | $1,792,889.00 | Hot | Denver |
| Hope Laboratories, Inc. | 2 | $500000.00 | $250,000.00 | 1.0 | Mobile |
| Plaines Medical Associates | 4 | $750000.00 | $187,500.00 | Hot | South Dakota |
| Hoosier Clinics, Inc. | 3 | $100000.00 | $33,333.33 | 2.0 | Indiana |
| Central Laboratories | 1 | $50000.00 | $50,000.00 | 1.0 | Indiana |
| Indiana Medical, Inc. | 4 | $125000.00 | $31,250.00 | 2.0 | Indiana |
| Independent Medical Labs | 3 | $223500.00 | $74,500.00 | Hot | Missouri |
| Mountain Labs | 2 | $100210.00 | $50,105.00 | 1.0 | Denver |
| Advanced Medical Associates | 3 | $5300623.00 | $1,766,874.33 | 1.0 | Knoxville |
| Cherry Electronics, Inc. | 20 | $4000000.00 | $200,000.00 | 1.0 | Los Angeles |
| Nashville Medical Technology | 7 | $8000375.00 | $1,142,910.71 | 1.0 | Cincinnati |
| Franklyn Lab Associates | 5 | $6456000.00 | $1,291,200.00 | 1.5 | Philadelphia |
| Penn Medical Technology | 3 | $50000.00 | $16,666.67 | 1.0 | Philadelphia |
| Mattis Medical Laboratories | 5 | $1000210.00 | $200,042.00 | 1.5 | Atlanta |
| Washington Medical Labs, Inc | 6 | $200500.00 | $33,416.67 | 2.0 | Seattle |
| University of Michigan | 3 | $325000.00 | $108,333.33 | 1.5 | Detroit |
| Pike Pharmaceutical, Inc. | 1 | $210000.00 | $210,000.00 | 1.5 | Philadelphia |
| Bay City Laboratories | 1 | $150250.00 | $150,250.00 | 1.5 | Michigan |

**Fig. 15.6.** *File fields as they appear in the report.*

The number of columns you specify is not limited to the width of your printer's paper. With Q&A, you can set the page width up to 1,000 characters. Because most printers are limited to a width of 240 characters, a large report may be partitioned onto more than one page. Whenever the page width isn't enough for your report, you are prompted with the following menu:

C - Cancel Printing
T - Truncate report and continue
E - Edit options & reprint
S - Split report across pages

You select C to cancel the report so that you can redesign it to fit on the page. The second option, Truncate, continues with the report, but any data that does not fit on the standard page width is dropped. You also can choose E to make minor changes in the report design before trying to reprint, and you can specify S to generate a report split across two or more pages.

Now that you have specified the columns for the report, you can print a simple report to check what you have done. Press F10 to display the Report Print Options menu. You can send the report to the screen or the printer.

After you have organized the fields into columns, you can add derived columns to the report. The following section explains derived columns and shows how you can use them.

### *Adding Derived Columns*

Q&A Report has the capability of creating, or deriving, a column by calculating two or more existing columns in the report. As a result, your report can have columns displaying information that doesn't exist in the file itself. Each report can have up to 16 derived columns, which are calculated from file fields or other derived columns.

In the report in figure 15.6, the Revenue per Lab column is a derived column. To find the values in that column, Q&A divides the values in the Annual Revenue column by the numbers in the No. of Labs column.

To add a derived column to a report, press F8 from the Column/Sort Spec to display the Derived Columns screen (see fig. 15.7).

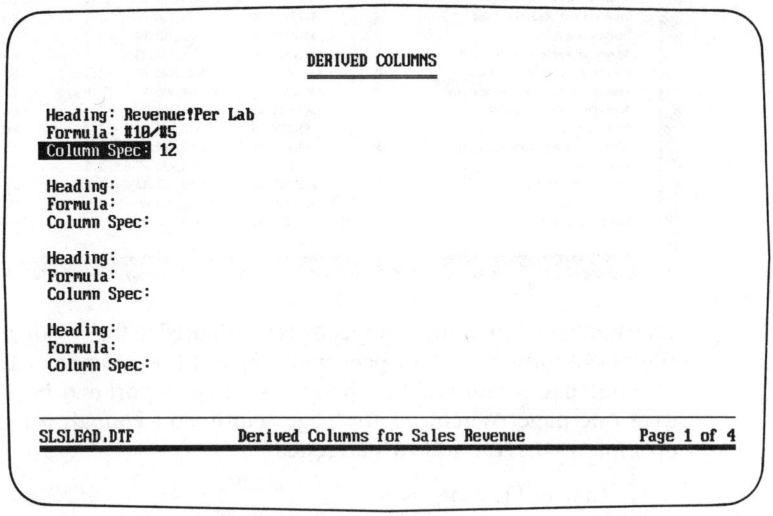

```
                         DERIVED COLUMNS

Heading: Revenue!Per Lab
Formula: #10/#5
Column Spec: 12

Heading:
Formula:
Column Spec:

Heading:
Formula:
Column Spec:

Heading:
Formula:
Column Spec:

SLSLEAD.DTF        Derived Columns for Sales Revenue        Page 1 of 4
```

**Fig. 15.7** *Filling in the Derived Columns spec.*

### *Entering a Derived Column Heading*

On the Derived Columns screen, you type the heading, formula and column location (see fig. 15.7). The first item that appears on the Derived Columns screen is the Heading prompt. A column heading can be on one line only, but headings that have more than one word look better divided into two or three lines (three lines is the maximum). Use an exclamation mark to indicate where you want the heading to break. For example, the entry Order!Minus!Discount will print as

```
  Order
  Minus
Discount
```

### *Entering a Derived Column Formula*

The line below the Heading prompt is the Formula prompt. On this line, you enter the formula used to create the derived column (again see fig. 15.7). A derived-column formula uses a combination of column numbers and arithmetic operators. The calculation order of the operators is

| | |
|---|---|
| ( ) | First |
| * / | Second |
| + – | Third |

The formulas for derived columns look like simple mathematical equations. For example, consider the following formulas:

| *Formula* | *Calculates* |
|---|---|
| #4 + #5 – #7 | Column 4 plus column 5 minus column 7 |
| #1 / (#3 + #5) | Column 1 divided by the sum of columns 3 and 5 |
| #2 + #3 + #5 + #6 | The sum of columns 2, 3, 5 and 6 |

The example in figure 15.7 computes the revenue per lab by dividing the total annual revenue by the number of labs. The heading is split into two lines with the exclamation mark between Revenue and Per Lab.

At the Column Spec prompt, type a number that indicates where the derived column should be located. In this example, the derived column is the new fourth column; it is given a number (12) between the third column (10) and the current fourth column (15). When the Derived Columns screen is complete, press F10 to return to the Report Print Options screen, or press F9 to go to the Column/Sort Spec.

Use derived columns when you want to display information that is not stored in the database. You can save storage space and data entry time by calculating information you need rather than entering and storing it with each record. You also can use constants as part of the derived column spec as well as references to columns.

## *Creating Self-Referencing Derived Columns*

Derived columns can reference themselves in Q&A Report formulas to produce running totals as shown in figures 15.8 and 15.9.

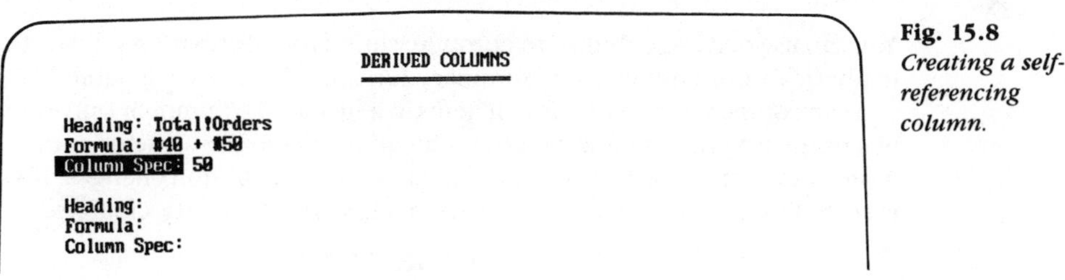


**Fig. 15.8**
*Creating a self-referencing column.*

In fig. 15.8, the formula in the derived Total Orders column adds column 40 (Total) to column 50 (derived Total Orders). You enter formulas like this the same way you enter formulas on a calculator: #40 + #50. The example in figure 15.9 shows how Report adds the number from the preceding row of the TOTAL ORDERS derived column to the current row of the Quantity column and puts the result in the current row of the TOTAL ORDERS column.

**Fig. 15.9**
*Total Orders in a self-referencing column.*

| Company | Model | Quantity | TOTAL ORDERS |
|---|---|---|---|
| Cherry Electronics | 1500 | 13 | 13 |
| Mountain Labs | | 10 | 23 |
| Northern Supply Company | | 5 | 28 |
| | Total: | 28 | |
| Plaines Medical Services | 2000 | 45 | 73 |
| Nashville Medical Technology | | 12 | 85 |
| Bay City Laboratory | | 8 | 93 |
| Arizona Medical Services | | 6 | 99 |
| Independent Medical Laboratory | | 5 | 104 |
| Hope Laboratories | | 2 | 106 |
| Washington Medical Labs | | 1 | 107 |
| | Total: | 79 | |
| Pike Pharmaceutical Co. | 2400 | 23 | 130 |
| Univ. of Michigan | | 4 | 134 |
| Penn Medical Labs | | 2 | 136 |
| Mattis Medical Labs | | 1 | 137 |
| | Total: | 30 | |

## *Using Summary Functions in Derived Columns*

You can use derived columns to compute summary information on data that appears in physical columns. Available summary functions are shown in table 15.1. Note that you can compute summaries for all items in a specified column, or only subsummaries by conducting the calculation after a break occurs in the same or another column. A break in a report occurs when the data in a sorted column changes. If your report is sorted by city, for example, a break occurs when the city changes.

**Table 15.1**
**Derived Column Summary Functions**

| *Function* | *Meaning* |
|---|---|
| @TOTAL(x) | Total of values in column x |
| @AVERAGE(x) | Average of values in column x |
| @COUNT(x) | Count of values in column x (how many different values listed in report) |
| MINIMUM(x) | Minimum of all values that appear in column x |

**Table 15.1 — *Continued***

| *Function* | *Meaning* |
|---|---|
| MAXIMUM(x) | Maximum of all values that appear in column x |
| @TOTAL(x,y) | Subtotal of values in column x on a break in column y |
| @AVERAGE(x,y) | Subaverage of values in column x on a break in column y |
| @COUNT(x,y) | Subcount of values in column x on a break in column y |
| @MINIMUM(x,y) | Subminimum of values in column x on a break in column y |
| @MAXIMUM(x,y) | Submaximum of values in column x on a break in column y |

### *Using LOOKUP Functions in Derived Columns*

Among Q&A's most powerful functions are LOOKUP and XLOOKUP, which allow you to use internal and external tables to store data associated with information in database forms. For example, you can store a short sales office ID code in the database and keep the office name and address in a File lookup table. This technique saves considerable storage space but gives you all the information on printed reports. You also can use the XLOOKUP function to store customer names and addresses in a separate File database for retrieval during report preparation. The LOOKUP functions in Report operate essentially the same as those for File. (See Chapter 7 for details on these functions.)

To use the XLOOKUP function in Report, select Derived Columns (F8) from the Column/Sort Spec screen and enter the appropriate function in the Formula position for the derived column. For example, to insert the company name in Report column 2 from an external file into a report, you could use the following formula, assuming that the company ID is in the primary file field #1:

```
Heading:Company Name
Formula:@XLOOKUP("Company",#1,"Company ID","Company Name")
Column Spec: 2
```

Remember that to use external data files in this way, you must have matching data in the primary and external files; the linked fields in both files must be indexed (set for speed-up searches), and the key-field data must be unique.

### *Making a Keyword Report*

A keyword report can be used to sort and format a report on one keyword field. Remember that a keyword field contains a variety of items separated by semicolons.

When you specify a keyword report type, Q&A knows that it will be dealing with multiple entries in this field and can search for the terms you specify.

This capability allows you to categorize report sections according to types of data in a keyword field (see fig. 15.10). Files without keywords also can be sorted and formatted, but you have to enter all the specifications.

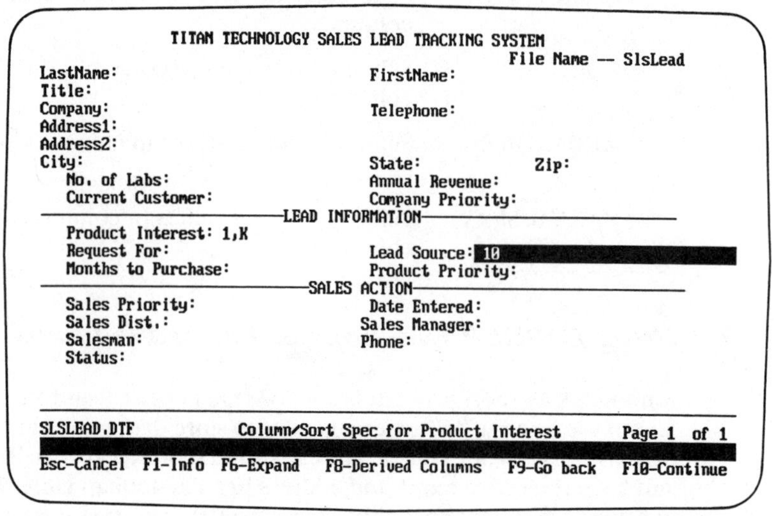

**Fig. 15.10**
*The Product Interest keyword report.*

```
                TITAN TECHNOLOGY SALES LEAD TRACKING SYSTEM
                                              File Name -- SlsLead
LastName:                             FirstName:
Title:
Company:                              Telephone:
Address1:
Address2:
City:                                 State:            Zip:
   No. of Labs:                       Annual Revenue:
   Current Customer:                  Company Priority:
--------------------------LEAD INFORMATION-----------------------
   Product Interest: 1,K
   Request For:                       Lead Source: 10
   Months to Purchase:                Product Priority:
-----------------------------SALES ACTION------------------------
   Sales Priority:                    Date Entered:
   Sales Dist.:                      Sales Manager:
   Salesman:                         Phone:
   Status:

SLSLEAD.DTF        Column/Sort Spec for Product Interest      Page 1  of 1
Esc-Cancel  F1-Info  F6-Expand   F8-Derived Columns   F9-Go back   F10-Continue
```

You specify a keyword report on the Column/Sort Spec. In figure 15.10, the Product Interest field shows the keyword report code (K). Figure 15.11 shows that the keyword fields—product model numbers—are automatically grouped and sorted in ascending order.

To produce a keyword report, you must organize the file fields into report columns, as explained previously. When you specify the column order, however, assign the lowest number to the keyword field, making it the left column.

After the column specification, type the letter K. Then add other columns and specifications to complete the report.

If you want to retrieve information based on a single keyword, that keyword must be entered in the appropriate field of the Retrieve Spec. For example, if the Product Interest Report in figure 15.11 is to include only the sales leads that have expressed interest in model 1500, the Product Interest field of the Retrieve Spec appears as

Product Interest: 1500

To retrieve information based on more than one keyword, several keywords must be entered in the appropriate field of the Retrieve Spec. For example, if the Product Interest Report is to include sales leads interested in both model 1500 and model 2000, the Product Interest field of the Retrieve Spec appears as

Product Interest: &1500;2000

The entry must begin with an ampersand (&), and the keywords must be separated by semicolons (;). Do not put any spaces between the semicolons and the keyword entries.

| Product Interest | Source of Lead | Company |
|---|---|---|
| 1000 | Phone | Mountain Labs |
| | Mail | Bay City Laboratories |
| | Salesman | University of Michigan |
| | Phone | Indiana Medical, Inc. |
| 1200 | Salesman | Franklyn Lab Associates |
| | Phone | Penn Medical Technology |
| | Phone | Advanced Medical Associates |
| | Phone | Plaines Medical Associates |
| 1500 | Salesman | Washington Medical Labs, Inc |
| | Phone | Mountain Labs |
| | Adv | Cherry Electronics, Inc. |
| | Salesman | Franklyn Lab Associates |
| | Adv | Hope Laboratories, Inc. |
| | Phone | Penn Medical Technology |
| | Adv | Independent Medical Labs |
| | Salesman | Pike Pharmaceutical, Inc. |
| | Mail | Mountain Labs |
| 2000 | Salesman | University of Michigan |
| | Salesman | Pike Pharmaceutical, Inc. |
| | Mail | Bay City Laboratories |
| | Phone | Mattis Medical Laboratories |
| | Adv | Cherry Electronics, Inc. |
| | Adv | Nashville Medical Technology |
| | Mail | Mountain Labs |
| | Phone | Advanced Medical Associates |
| | Phone | Plaines Medical Associates |
| | Mail | Central Laboratories |
| 2500 | Adv | Hoosier Clinics, Inc. |
| | Adv | Hope Laboratories, Inc. |
| | Adv | Independent Medical Labs |
| | Phone | Mattis Medical Laboratories |
| | Salesman | Washington Medical Labs, Inc |

**Fig. 15.11**
***Specifying the Product Interest keyword report.***

# *Formatting Report Columns*

After you have organized the file information into a columnar report, you need to add formatting instructions on the Column/Sort Spec. With Q&A Report, you can

- Sort up to 16 columns in ascending or descending order
- Format the contents of a column
- Remove column breaks
- Insert page breaks
- Repeat a category
- Make columns "invisible"

## Sorting Information

Although a maximum of two or three sort columns is common among some competing products, up to 16 column sorts, in ascending or descending order, can be specified with Q&A Report.

To specify a sorting order, you enter codes in either the Column/Sort Spec or the Derived Columns screen. If you want the column to be sorted in ascending order, enter the code *AS*; for a descending sort, enter *DS*. Entering the code for an ascending sort in the Lead Source field results in the forms being sorted in ascending order according to the first letter of the entry (see fig. 15.12). Note that the primary sort is the Product Interest field, which is the keyword field.

**Fig. 15.12**
*The result of the sort specifications.*

```
                TITAN TECHNOLOGY SALES LEAD TRACKING SYSTEM
                                                  File Name -- SlsLead
LastName:                                 FirstName:
Title:
Company:                                  Telephone:
Address1:
Address2:
City:                                     State:         Zip:
   No. of Labs:                           Annual Revenue:
   Current Customer:                      Company Priority:
-------------------------------LEAD INFORMATION--------------------------
   Product Interest: 1,K
   Request For:                           Lead Source: 10,AS
   Months to Purchase:                    Product Priority:
----------------------------------SALES ACTION---------------------------
   Sales Priority:                        Date Entered:
   Sales Dist.:                           Sales Manager:
   Salesman:                              Phone:
   Status:

SLSLEAD.DTF          Column/Sort Spec for Product Interest       Page 1 of 1

Esc-Cancel  F1-Info  F6-Expand   F8-Derived Columns   F9-Go back  F10-Continue
```

If you want to sort a derived column, press F8 to display the Derived Columns screen. Type the column number after the Column Spec prompt; then press the space bar, and type the correct code.

When all the sorting codes are entered, you can press F10 to print the report, or you can add other formatting specifications, as explained in the following sections.

## Formatting Column Contents

When a report is generated, Q&A's default format settings do a good job of formatting your data. For example, text appears left-justified, numbers are right-justified, and money is displayed in a currency format. The date and time appear as they are entered in the database.

Although the default settings are fine for basic formatting, you may want to make some changes when creating a custom report design. Table 15.2 shows all the options available for specifying column formats.

**Table 15.2**
**The Options for Specifying Column Format**

| *Symbol* | *Command* | *Meaning* |
|---|---|---|
| JR | Justify Right | All data in the column will be aligned on the right. This is the default for numbers and money. |
| JL | Justify Left | All data in the column will be aligned on the left. This is the default for text. |
| JC | Justify Center | All data in the column will be centered. |
| U | Uppercase | All text in the column will be uppercase. |
| C | Comma | Numbers print with commas. Money values print with commas and currency symbols by default. |
| WC | Without Comma | Money values print without commas. |
| Dx | Date format x | x is a number from 1 to 20, standing for one of 20 different date formats. |
| Hx | Hour format x | x is a number from 1 to 3, standing for one of 3 different time formats. |
| TR | Truncate | Truncate data that does not fit in the column width instead of continuing the data on the next line of the column. |
| M | Money | Treat a number as money. |
| Nx | Number format x | x is a number from 1 to 7, standing for up to 7 decimal places to a number. If x is not specified, Q&A determines how many decimal places to use based on its default. |
| T | Text | Treat a number as text. |

To specify column formats, type the word *Format* (or press F) in the correct field, and enter the code in parentheses. For example, to sort the first column in ascending order and display the values in uppercase letters centered in the column, you enter

1,AS,FORMAT(U,JC)

If you run out of room as you type the specifications, press the Expand Field key (F6).

## *Setting Column Headings and Widths*

The last step before printing is adjusting the column headings and widths. When you first design a report, Q&A uses the field labels as headings and determines column width based on data width. Report also centers the headings and spaces the columns.

To make adjustments for the fields you want to change, enter the column width and heading specifications on the Column/Sort screen (or after the Heading prompt on the Derived Columns screen, if you're printing a derived column). Be sure to separate the column width and the heading by entering a colon (:). Even if you don't indicate a new heading, a colon must follow the column width. For example, suppose that the field you are specifying is to be the first column, sorted in ascending order, assigned a column width of 6, and titled Labs. To make these settings, you enter

1,AS,HEADING(6:Labs)

Figure 15.13 illustrates a report before changes were made. The field names were used as column headings, the column widths are adapted to data or heading width, and the forms are not sorted.

**Fig. 15.13**
*A report before changes are made on the Column/Sort Spec screen.*

| Company | No. of Labs | Current Customer | Company Priority | Source of Lead |
|---|---|---|---|---|
| Mountain Labs | 3 | Y | 1 | Mail |
| Hope Laboratories, Inc. | 2 | N | 2 | Adv |
| Plaines Medical Associates | 4 | N | 1 | Phone |
| Hoosier Clinics, Inc. | 3 | Y | 3 | Adv |
| Central Laboratories | 1 | N | 2 | Mail |
| Indiana Medical, Inc. | 4 | N | 1 | Phone |
| Mountain Labs | 2 | N | 1 | Phone |
| Advanced Medical Associates | 3 | Y | 2 | Phone |
| Cherry Electronics, Inc. | 20 | Y | 1 | Adv |
| Nashville Medical Technology | 7 | N | 1 | Adv |
| Franklyn Lab Associates | 5 | N | 2 | Salesman |
| Penn Medical Technology | 3 | Y | 1 | Phone |
| Mattis Medical Laboratories | 5 | Y | 3 | Phone |
| Washington Medical Labs, Inc | 6 | Y | 3 | Salesman |
| University of Michigan | 3 | Y | 2 | Salesman |
| Pike Pharmaceutical, Inc. | 1 | Y | 1 | Salesman |
| Bay City Laboratories | 1 | Y | 1 | Mail |
| Independent Medical Labs | 3 | Y | 2 | Adv |

Figure 15.14 illustrates the report after changes have been made in the No. of Labs field. That field is now the first column with the heading Labs. The column width (6) is slightly larger than the heading width, and the forms are sorted in ascending order.

After you have made all the changes to the Column/Sort Spec, press F10 to display the Report Print Options screen. If you press F10 again, Q&A saves your design and asks whether you want to print the report.

| Labs | Company | Current Customer | Company Priority | Source of Lead |
|---|---|---|---|---|
| ------ | -------------------------- | -------- | -------- | -------- |
| 1 | Bay City Laboratories | Y | 1 | Mail |
| | Pike Pharmaceutical, Inc. | Y | 1 | Salesman |
| | Central Laboratories | N | 2 | Mail |
| 2 | Hope Laboratories, Inc. | N | 2 | Adv |
| | Mountain Labs | N | 1 | Phone |
| 3 | University of Michigan | Y | 2 | Salesman |
| | Penn Medical Technology | Y | 1 | Phone |
| | Mountain Labs | Y | 1 | Mail |
| | Independent Medical Labs | Y | 2 | Adv |
| | Advanced Medical Associates | Y | 2 | Phone |
| | Hoosier Clinics, Inc. | Y | 3 | Adv |
| 4 | Indiana Medical, Inc. | N | 1 | Phone |
| | Plaines Medical Associates | N | 1 | Phone |
| 5 | Franklyn Lab Associates | N | 2 | Salesman |
| | Mattis Medical Laboratories | Y | 3 | Phone |
| 6 | Washington Medical Labs, Inc | Y | 3 | Salesman |
| 7 | Nashville Medical Technology | N | 1 | Adv |
| 20 | Cherry Electronics, Inc. | Y | 1 | Adv |

**Fig. 15.14**
*The report after changes are made.*

## *Removing Column Breaks*

Q&A automatically inserts blank lines, called *column breaks,* when the value changes in a sorted column. For example, a blank line is inserted when the Company value in figure 15.11 changes. You can remove these column breaks by entering the cancel subcalculation code (CS).

Figure 15.15 shows the printout that results from placing the cancel subcalculation code in the Company field. Column breaks still appear in the Lead Source field. To eliminate these, add an additional CS code in the Lead Source field.

## *Inserting Page Breaks*

To make your form easier to read, you can designate column breaks that cause a new page to be printed every time a column break occurs. Just enter the page-break code (P) in the appropriate field. This code causes a new page to be started when values in the field change. The header and the column headings are reprinted at the top of each page.

## *Repeating Values*

When a sorted column is displayed in report form, the value in the sorted column is usually displayed only once. In the example in figure 15.15, Q&A displayed the value for the first entry only, even though the Product Interest model number 1000

**Fig. 15.15**
*A printout with fewer column breaks.*

| Product Interest | Source of Lead | Company |
|---|---|---|
| 1000 | Mail | Bay City Laboratories |
| | Phone | Indiana Medical, Inc. |
| | | Mountain Labs |
| | Salesman | University of Michigan |
| 1200 | Phone | Advanced Medical Associates |
| | | Penn Medical Technology |
| | | Plaines Medical Associates |
| | Salesman | Franklyn Lab Associates |
| 1500 | Adv | Cherry Electronics, Inc. |
| | | Hope Laboratories, Inc. |
| | | Independent Medical Labs |
| | Mail | Mountain Labs |
| | Phone | Mountain Labs |
| | | Penn Medical Technology |
| | Salesman | Franklyn Lab Associates |
| | | Pike Pharmaceutical, Inc. |
| | | Washington Medical Labs, Inc |
| 2000 | Adv | Cherry Electronics, Inc. |
| | | Nashville Medical Technology |
| | Mail | Bay City Laboratories |
| | | Central Laboratories |
| | | Mountain Labs |
| | Phone | Advanced Medical Associates |
| | | Mattis Medical Laboratories |
| | | Plaines Medical Associates |
| | Salesman | Pike Pharmaceutical, Inc. |
| | | University of Michigan |
| 2500 | Adv | Hoosier Clinics, Inc. |
| | | Hope Laboratories, Inc. |
| | | Independent Medical Labs |
| | Phone | Mattis Medical Laboratories |
| | Salesman | Washington Medical Labs, Inc |

applies to all companies. By entering the repeat value code (R) in the Column/Sort Spec, you can tell Q&A to print the value for each form.

In figure 15.16, the repeat value code has been entered in the Product Interest and the Lead Source fields. Figure 15.17 shows the effect of the codes.

## *Making a Column Invisible*

You may need to hide columns because they contain confidential information or because you need to reduce the width of a report. Even though these columns do not appear when displayed on-screen or when printed, you can still reference the columns in a formula that returns data in another column. These hidden, or invisible, columns can be used to produce a page break.

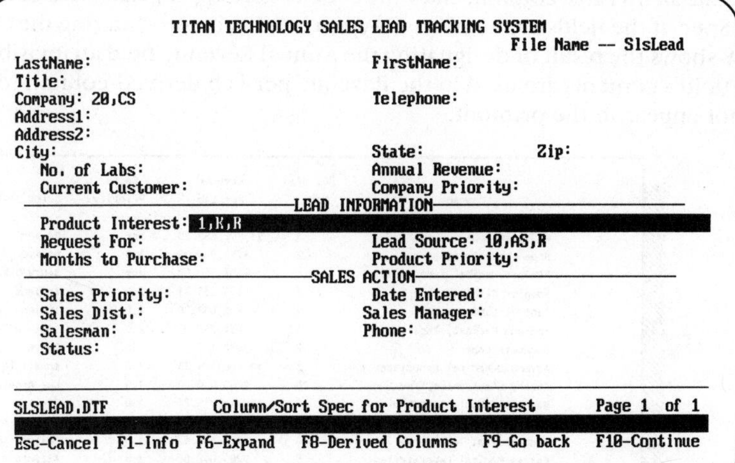

TITAN TECHNOLOGY SALES LEAD TRACKING SYSTEM
File Name — SlsLead
LastName:
FirstName:
Title:
Company: 20,CS
Telephone:
Address1:
Address2:
City:
State:
Zip:
No. of Labs:
Annual Revenue:
Current Customer:
Company Priority:
LEAD INFORMATION
Product Interest: 1,K,R
Request For:
Lead Source: 10,AS,R
Months to Purchase:
Product Priority:
SALES ACTION
Sales Priority:
Date Entered:
Sales Dist.:
Sales Manager:
Salesman:
Phone:
Status:
SLSLEAD.DTF
Column/Sort Spec for Product Interest
Page 1 of 1
Esc-Cancel F1-Info F6-Expand F8-Derived Columns F9-Go back F10-Continue


**Fig. 15.16** *Entering the repeat-values code.*

| Product Interest | Source of Lead | Company |
|---|---|---|
| 1000 | Mail | Bay City Laboratories |
| 1000 | Phone | Indiana Medical, Inc. |
| 1000 | | Mountain Labs |
| 1000 | Salesman | University of Michigan |
| 1200 | Phone | Advanced Medical Associates |
| 1200 | | Penn Medical Technology |
| 1200 | | Plaines Medical Associates |
| 1200 | Salesman | Franklyn Lab Associates |
| 1500 | Adv | Cherry Electronics, Inc. |
| 1500 | | Hope Laboratories, Inc. |
| 1500 | | Independent Medical Labs |
| 1500 | Mail | Mountain Labs |
| 1500 | Phone | Mountain Labs |
| 1500 | | Penn Medical Technology |
| 1500 | Salesman | Franklyn Lab Associates |
| 1500 | | Pike Pharmaceutical, Inc. |
| 1500 | | Washington Medical Labs, Inc |
| 2000 | Adv | Cherry Electronics, Inc. |
| 2000 | | Nashville Medical Technology |
| 2000 | Mail | Bay City Laboratories |
| 2000 | | Central Laboratories |
| 2000 | | Mountain Labs |
| 2000 | Phone | Advanced Medical Associates |
| 2000 | | Mattis Medical Laboratories |
| 2000 | | Plaines Medical Associates |
| 2000 | Salesman | Pike Pharmaceutical, Inc. |
| 2000 | | University of Michigan |

**Fig. 15.17** *Repeating values in a report.*

To create an invisible column, enter the code I in the appropriate field of the Column/Sort Spec. If the fields are numbered, type a comma before entering the code. Figure 15.18 shows the result of designating the Annual Revenue field an invisible column. The field's contents are used in the Revenue per Lab derived-column formula, but do not appear in the printout.

**Fig. 15.18**
*A report with an invisible column.*

| Company | No. of Labs | Revenue Per Lab | Sales Priority | Sales Dist. |
|---|---|---|---|---|
| Mountain Labs | 3 | $1,792,889.00 | Hot | Denver |
| Hope Laboratories, Inc. | 2 | $250,000.00 | 1.0 | Mobile |
| Plaines Medical Associates | 4 | $187,500.00 | Hot | South Dakota |
| Hoosier Clinics, Inc. | 3 | $33,333.33 | 2.0 | Indiana |
| Central Laboratories | 1 | $50,000.00 | 1.0 | Indiana |
| Indiana Medical, Inc. | 4 | $31,250.00 | 2.0 | Indiana |
| Mountain Labs | 2 | $50,105.00 | 1.0 | Denver |
| Advanced Medical Associates | 3 | $1,766,874.33 | 1.0 | Knoxville |
| Cherry Electronics, Inc. | 20 | $200,000.00 | 1.0 | Los Angeles |
| Nashville Medical Technology | 7 | $1,142,910.71 | 1.0 | Cincinnati |
| Franklyn Lab Associates | 5 | $1,291,200.00 | 1.5 | Philadelphia |
| Penn Medical Technology | 3 | $16,666.67 | 1.0 | Philadelphia |
| Mattis Medical Laboratories | 5 | $200,042.00 | 1.5 | Atlanta |
| Washington Medical Labs, Inc | 6 | $33,416.67 | 2.0 | Seattle |
| University of Michigan | 3 | $108,333.33 | 1.5 | Detroit |
| Pike Pharmaceutical, Inc. | 1 | $210,000.00 | 1.5 | Philadelphia |
| Bay City Laboratories | 1 | $150,250.00 | 1.5 | Michigan |
| Independent Medical Labs | 3 | $74,500.00 | Hot | Missouri |

## *Specifying Calculated Columns*

Calculations on text and numerical columns can be produced automatically with Report. By specifying the correct codes on either the Column/Sort Spec or the Derived Columns screen, you can

- Calculate all columns (text and numerical)
- Perform full-column and subcolumn calculations
- Perform more than one calculation on a column
- Combine calculations on various columns

To calculate a column, move the cursor to the correct field and type the calculation code (see table 15.3). Be sure to separate codes with a space or comma.

**Table 15.3**
**Calculation Operators**

| *Code* | *Calculation* |
|---|---|
| T | Totals numerical columns |
| A | Averages numerical columns |
| C | Counts numerical or text values |
| MIN | Finds minimum numerical values |

**Table 15.3 — *Continued***

| *Code* | *Calculation* |
|---|---|
| MAX | Finds maximum numerical values |
| ST | Subtotals numerical columns |
| SA | Subaverages numerical columns |
| SC | Subcounts numerical and text values |
| SMIN | Finds subminimum values in numerical columns |
| SMAX | Finds submaximum values in numerical columns |

The last five calculations are used to determine intermediate results. The answers for these calculations are displayed at column breaks.

## *Calculating the Entire Column*

When you perform a calculation on a column, every entry in that column is affected. Figure 15.19 shows that when you enter the Total code (T) in the No. of Labs and

| Product Interest | Company | No. of Labs | Annual Revenue | Revenue Per Lab |
|---|---|---|---|---|
| --------------- | -------------------------- | ----- | ------------- | ----------- |
| 1000 | University of Michigan | 3 | $325000.00 | $108,333.33 |
| | Bay City Laboratories | 1 | $150250.00 | $150,250.00 |
| | Mountain Labs | 2 | $100210.00 | $50,105.00 |
| | Indiana Medical, Inc. | 4 | $125000.00 | $31,250.00 |
| 1200 | Franklyn Lab Associates | 5 | $6456000.00 | $1,291,200.00 |
| | Advanced Medical Associates | 3 | $5300623.00 | $1,766,874.33 |
| | Penn Medical Technology | 3 | $50000.00 | $16,666.67 |
| | Plaines Medical Associates | 4 | $750000.00 | $187,500.00 |
| 1500 | Washington Medical Labs, Inc | 6 | $200500.00 | $33,416.67 |
| | Pike Pharmaceutical, Inc. | 1 | $210000.00 | $210,000.00 |
| | Penn Medical Technology | 3 | $50000.00 | $16,666.67 |
| | Independent Medical Labs | 3 | $223500.00 | $74,500.00 |
| | Franklyn Lab Associates | 5 | $6456000.00 | $1,291,200.00 |
| | Mountain Labs | 3 | $5378667.00 | $1,792,889.00 |
| | Cherry Electronics, Inc. | 20 | $4000000.00 | $200,000.00 |
| | Hope Laboratories, Inc. | 2 | $500000.00 | $250,000.00 |
| | Mountain Labs | 2 | $100210.00 | $50,105.00 |
| 2000 | Central Laboratories | 1 | $50000.00 | $50,000.00 |
| | Plaines Medical Associates | 4 | $750000.00 | $187,500.00 |
| | University of Michigan | 3 | $325000.00 | $108,333.33 |
| | Nashville Medical Technology | 7 | $8000375.00 | $1,142,910.71 |
| | Bay City Laboratories | 1 | $150250.00 | $150,250.00 |
| | Cherry Electronics, Inc. | 20 | $4000000.00 | $200,000.00 |
| | Mattis Medical Laboratories | 5 | $1000210.00 | $200,042.00 |
| | Advanced Medical Associates | 3 | $5300623.00 | $1,766,874.33 |
| | Mountain Labs | 3 | $5378667.00 | $1,792,889.00 |
| | Pike Pharmaceutical, Inc. | 1 | $210000.00 | $210,000.00 |
| 2500 | Independent Medical Labs | 3 | $223500.00 | $74,500.00 |
| | Washington Medical Labs, Inc | 6 | $200500.00 | $33,416.67 |
| | Hope Laboratories, Inc. | 2 | $500000.00 | $250,000.00 |
| | Hoosier Clinics, Inc. | 3 | $100000.00 | $33,333.33 |
| | Mattis Medical Laboratories | 5 | $1000210.00 | $200,042.00 |
| =============== | ========================== | ====== | ============= | ============ |
| Total: | | 137 | $57565295.00 | |

**Fig. 15.19** *Totals in entire-column calculations.*

Annual Revenue fields, the columns are added and the sum is displayed at the bottom of the column.

Note that Report prints a double line under the columns, the name of the calculation (Total) in the left column, and the result of the calculation. The result is printed in the same format as the column.

You also have the option of mixing and matching calculations and columns. In figure 15.20, the columns and their calculations include

| *Column* | *Calculation Performed* |
|---|---|
| Company | Count |
| No. of Lab | Total, Count, Average |
| Annual Revenue | Total, Average, Minimum, Maximum |

**Fig. 15.20**
*A variety of entire-column calculations.*

| Product Interest | Company | No. of Labs | Annual Revenue | Revenue Per Lab |
|---|---|---|---|---|
| 1000 | University of Michigan | 3.00 | $325000.00 | $108,333.33 |
| | Bay City Laboratories | 1.00 | $150250.00 | $150,250.00 |
| | Mountain Labs | 2.00 | $100210.00 | $50,105.00 |
| | Indiana Medical, Inc. | 4.00 | $125000.00 | $31,250.00 |
| 1200 | Franklyn Lab Associates | 5.00 | $6456000.00 | $1,291,200.00 |
| | Advanced Medical Associates | 3.00 | $5300623.00 | $1,766,874.33 |
| | Penn Medical Technology | 3.00 | $50000.00 | $16,666.67 |
| | Plaines Medical Associates | 4.00 | $750000.00 | $187,500.00 |
| 1500 | Washington Medical Labs, Inc | 6.00 | $200500.00 | $33,416.67 |
| | Pike Pharmaceutical, Inc. | 1.00 | $210000.00 | $210,000.00 |
| | Penn Medical Technology | 3.00 | $50000.00 | $16,666.67 |
| | Independent Medical Labs | 3.00 | $223500.00 | $74,500.00 |
| | Franklyn Lab Associates | 5.00 | $6456000.00 | $1,291,200.00 |
| | Mountain Labs | 3.00 | $5378667.00 | $1,792,889.00 |
| | Cherry Electronics, Inc. | 20.00 | $4000000.00 | $200,000.00 |
| | Hope Laboratories, Inc. | 2.00 | $500000.00 | $250,000.00 |
| | Mountain Labs | 2.00 | $100210.00 | $50,105.00 |
| 2000 | Central Laboratories | 1.00 | $50000.00 | $50,000.00 |
| | Plaines Medical Associates | 4.00 | $750000.00 | $187,500.00 |
| | University of Michigan | 3.00 | $325000.00 | $108,333.33 |
| | Nashville Medical Technology | 7.00 | $8000375.00 | $1,142,910.71 |
| | Bay City Laboratories | 1.00 | $150250.00 | $150,250.00 |
| | Cherry Electronics, Inc. | 20.00 | $4000000.00 | $200,000.00 |
| | Mattis Medical Laboratories | 5.00 | $1000210.00 | $200,042.00 |
| | Advanced Medical Associates | 3.00 | $5300623.00 | $1,766,874.33 |
| | Mountain Labs | 3.00 | $5378667.00 | $1,792,889.00 |
| | Pike Pharmaceutical, Inc. | 1.00 | $210000.00 | $210,000.00 |
| 2500 | Independent Medical Labs | 3.00 | $223500.00 | $74,500.00 |
| | Washington Medical Labs, Inc | 6.00 | $200500.00 | $33,416.67 |
| | Hope Laboratories, Inc. | 2.00 | $500000.00 | $250,000.00 |
| | Hoosier Clinics, Inc. | 3.00 | $100000.00 | $33,333.33 |
| | Mattis Medical Laboratories | 5.00 | $1000210.00 | $200,042.00 |
| ================ | ============================ | ====== | ============== | ============= |
| Total: | | 137.00 | $57565295.00 | |
| Average: | | 4.28 | $1798915.47 | |
| Count: | 32 | 32 | | |
| Maximum: | | | $8000375.00 | |
| Minimum: | | | $50000.00 | |

### Subcalculations in a Column

Report also produces subcalculations at the column breaks in a column. Enter your choice of the subcalculation codes listed in table 15.3.

The effect of a subcalculation is different from an entire column calculation, as in figures 15.21 and 15.22. The subcount calculations appear at every column break; the calculation name is repeated in the left column, and a line is drawn in the columns with a subcalculation.

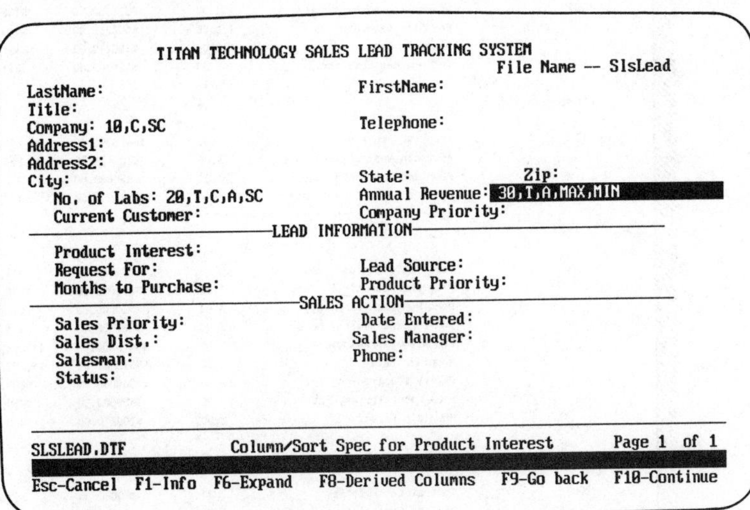

```
          TITAN TECHNOLOGY SALES LEAD TRACKING SYSTEM
                                        File Name -- SlsLead
LastName:                         FirstName:
Title:
Company: 10,C,SC                  Telephone:
Address1:
Address2:
City:                             State:        Zip:
  No. of Labs: 20,T,C,A,SC        Annual Revenue: 30,T,A,MAX,MIN
  Current Customer:               Company Priority:
--------------------------LEAD INFORMATION--------------------------
  Product Interest:
  Request For:                    Lead Source:
  Months to Purchase:             Product Priority:
----------------------------SALES ACTION----------------------------
  Sales Priority:                 Date Entered:
  Sales Dist.:                    Sales Manager:
  Salesman:                       Phone:
  Status:

SLSLEAD.DTF       Column/Sort Spec for Product Interest     Page 1 of 1

Esc-Cancel  F1-Info  F6-Expand  F8-Derived Columns  F9-Go back  F10-Continue
```

**Fig. 15.21** *Entering subcalculation codes.*

### Canceling Subcalculations

In some report designs, a subcalculation code can create too many column breaks and cause too many subcalculations (see fig. 15.23). This happens when a sorted column creates breaks every time the value in the column changes.

To eliminate this problem and make the form easier to read, cancel the subcalculation in the sorted column by entering the cancel subcalculation code (CS) in the Column/Sort Spec (see figs. 15.24 and 15.25).

## Breaking on Year, Month, or Day

If you want to organize your report by year, month, or day, you can use Q&A Report to divide the pages. To do this, you enter the codes

| *Code* | *Meaning* |
|---|---|
| YB | Yearly Break |
| MB | Monthly Break |
| DB | Daily Break |

For example, if you want a field to be displayed in the second column, sorted in descending order and divided by month and year, you enter

2,DS,MB,YB

**Fig. 15.22**
*A variety of subcalculations.*

| Product Interest | Company | No. of Labs | Annual Revenue | Revenue Per Lab |
|---|---|---|---|---|
| 1000 | University of Michigan | 3.00 | $325000.00 | $108,333.33 |
| | Bay City Laboratories | 1.00 | $150250.00 | $150,250.00 |
| | Mountain Labs | 2.00 | $100210.00 | $50,105.00 |
| | Indiana Medical, Inc. | 4.00 | $125000.00 | $31,250.00 |
| Count: | 4 | 4 | | |
| 1200 | Franklyn Lab Associates | 5.00 | $6456000.00 | $1,291,200.00 |
| | Advanced Medical Associates | 3.00 | $5300623.00 | $1,766,874.33 |
| | Penn Medical Technology | 3.00 | $50000.00 | $16,666.67 |
| | Plaines Medical Associates | 4.00 | $750000.00 | $187,500.00 |
| Count: | 4 | 4 | | |
| 1500 | Washington Medical Labs, Inc | 6.00 | $200500.00 | $33,416.67 |
| | Pike Pharmaceutical, Inc. | 1.00 | $210000.00 | $210,000.00 |
| | Penn Medical Technology | 3.00 | $50000.00 | $16,666.67 |
| | Independent Medical Labs | 3.00 | $223500.00 | $74,500.00 |
| | Franklyn Lab Associates | 5.00 | $6456000.00 | $1,291,200.00 |
| | Mountain Labs | 3.00 | $5378667.00 | $1,792,889.00 |
| | Cherry Electronics, Inc. | 20.00 | $4000000.00 | $200,000.00 |
| | Hope Laboratories, Inc. | 2.00 | $500000.00 | $250,000.00 |
| | Mountain Labs | 2.00 | $100210.00 | $50,105.00 |
| Count: | 9 | 9 | | |
| 2000 | Central Laboratories | 1.00 | $50000.00 | $50,000.00 |
| | Plaines Medical Associates | 4.00 | $750000.00 | $187,500.00 |
| | University of Michigan | 3.00 | $325000.00 | $108,333.33 |
| | Nashville Medical Technology | 7.00 | $8000375.00 | $1,142,910.71 |
| | Bay City Laboratories | 1.00 | $150250.00 | $150,250.00 |
| | Cherry Electronics, Inc. | 20.00 | $4000000.00 | $200,000.00 |
| | Mattis Medical Laboratories | 5.00 | $1000210.00 | $200,042.00 |
| | Advanced Medical Associates | 3.00 | $5300623.00 | $1,766,874.33 |
| | Mountain Labs | 3.00 | $5378667.00 | $1,792,889.00 |
| | Pike Pharmaceutical, Inc. | 1.00 | $210000.00 | $210,000.00 |
| Count: | 10 | 10 | | |
| 2500 | Independent Medical Labs | 3.00 | $223500.00 | $74,500.00 |
| | Washington Medical Labs, Inc | 6.00 | $200500.00 | $33,416.67 |
| | Hope Laboratories, Inc. | 2.00 | $500000.00 | $250,000.00 |
| | Hoosier Clinics, Inc. | 3.00 | $100000.00 | $33,333.33 |
| | Mattis Medical Laboratories | 5.00 | $1000210.00 | $200,042.00 |
| Count: | 5 | 5 | | |
| Total: | | 137.00 | $57565295.00 | |
| Average: | | 4.28 | $1798915.47 | |
| Count: | 32 | 32 | | |
| Maximum: | | | $8000375.00 | |
| Minimum: | | | $50000.00 | |

```
                   Source
Product Interest   of Lead     Company
----------------   -------     ---------------------------
1000               Mail        Bay City Laboratories
                               ---------------------------
                   Count:                                1

                   Phone       Indiana Medical, Inc.

                               Mountain Labs
                               ---------------------------
                   Count:                                2

                   Salesman    University of Michigan
                               ---------------------------
                   Count:                                1

                               ---------------------------
Count:                                                   4

1200               Phone       Advanced Medical Associates

                               Penn Medical Technology

                               Plaines Medical Associates
                               ---------------------------
                   Count:                                3

                   Salesman    Franklyn Lab Associates
                               ---------------------------
                   Count:                                1

                               ---------------------------
Count:                                                   4

1500               Adv         Cherry Electronics, Inc.

                               Hope Laboratories, Inc.

                               Independent Medical Labs
                               ---------------------------
                   Count:                                3

                   Mail        Mountain Labs
                               ---------------------------
                   Count:                                1

                   Phone       Mountain Labs

                               Penn Medical Technology
                               ---------------------------
                   Count:                                2

                   Salesman    Franklyn Lab Associates
```

**Fig. 15.23**
*A subcalculation on a sorted column.*

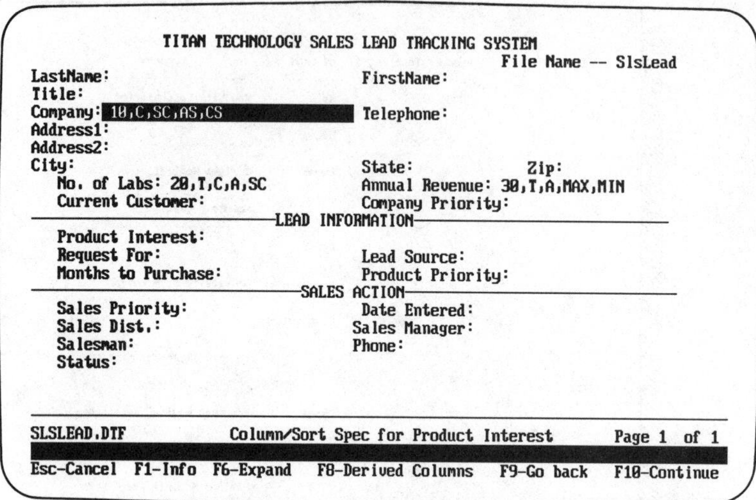


**Fig. 15.24**
*Entering the cancel subcalculation code.*

These levels of break control also function with @ functions such as @TOTAL. For additional detail, see the section on using summary functions in derived columns earlier in this chapter (see also table 15.1).

### *Breaking on Alphabetic Change*

You also can create a break when the first character of a sorted field changes. Unlike a break on field value, the alphabetic break occurs on only one letter. This feature is useful for printing lists such as telephone directories, bibliographies, or indexes.

To achieve an alphabetic break, insert the code AB in the appropriate field in the Column/Sort Spec screen. If field 1 is the last name field in a file, for example, you can cause a break whenever the first letter in the last names changes. Enter the code

1,AB

## *Redesigning a Report*

To edit the original design of an existing report, select Design/Redesign a Report from the menu, and enter the name of the file you want to edit. (If you don't remember the name, you can press Enter and select the file from the list of data files displayed.) Then follow the basic procedure for designing a report, as explained in the previous sections.

| Product Interest | Source of Lead | Company |
|---|---|---|
| 1000 | Mail | Bay City Laboratories |
| | Phone | Indiana Medical, Inc. |
| | | Mountain Labs |
| | Salesman | University of Michigan |
| Count: | | 4 |
| 1200 | Phone | Advanced Medical Associates |
| | | Penn Medical Technology |
| | | Plaines Medical Associates |
| | Salesman | Franklyn Lab Associates |
| Count: | | 4 |
| 1500 | Adv | Cherry Electronics, Inc. |
| | | Hope Laboratories, Inc. |
| | | Independent Medical Labs |
| | Mail | Mountain Labs |
| | Phone. | Mountain Labs |
| | | Penn Medical Technology |
| | Salesman | Franklyn Lab Associates |
| | | Pike Pharmaceutical, Inc. |
| | | Washington Medical Labs, Inc |
| Count: | | 9 |
| 2000 | Adv | Cherry Electronics, Inc. |
| | | Nashville Medical Technology |
| | Mail | Bay City Laboratories |
| | | Central Laboratories |
| | | Mountain Labs |
| | Phone | Advanced Medical Associates |
| | | Mattis Medical Laboratories |
| | | Plaines Medical Associates |
| | Salesman | Pike Pharmaceutical, Inc. |
| | | University of Michigan |
| Count: | | 10 |
| 2500 | Adv | Hoosier Clinics, Inc. |
| | | Hope Laboratories, Inc. |
| | | Independent Medical Labs |
| | Phone | Mattis Medical Laboratories |
| | Salesman | Washington Medical Labs, Inc |
| Count: | | 5 |

**Fig. 15.25** *A canceled subcalculation on a sorted column.*

# *Setting Global Options*

Up to this point, you have designed the report by entering specifications on a blank screen. If you use some of the same settings repeatedly, you can make them the default values to avoid entering the settings every time you enter report specifications. These default values are called global options.

Report's Global Options screen is displayed when you choose Set Global Options from the Report menu. From this menu, you also can set all default options except the options on the Retrieve Spec.

## Setting Global Default Column Widths and Headings

The first global default you can set is column widths and headings. By choosing C from the Global Options menu, you can display the Column Headings/Width Spec screen.

The Column Headings/Width Spec is similar to the Column/Sort Spec. You can move from field to field on this Spec screen to enter the column width and column heading separated by a colon (:), but you don't need to enclose the width and heading in parentheses or enter the word *heading*.

After you enter changes, press F10, and the Report Global Options screen is displayed. The new settings apply to all reports in the database, including reports generated by the Intelligent Assistant.

## Setting Global Format Options

To set the global format options for all report designs, select Set Format Options from the Report Global Options screen. After you press Enter, the screen in figure 15.26 is displayed.

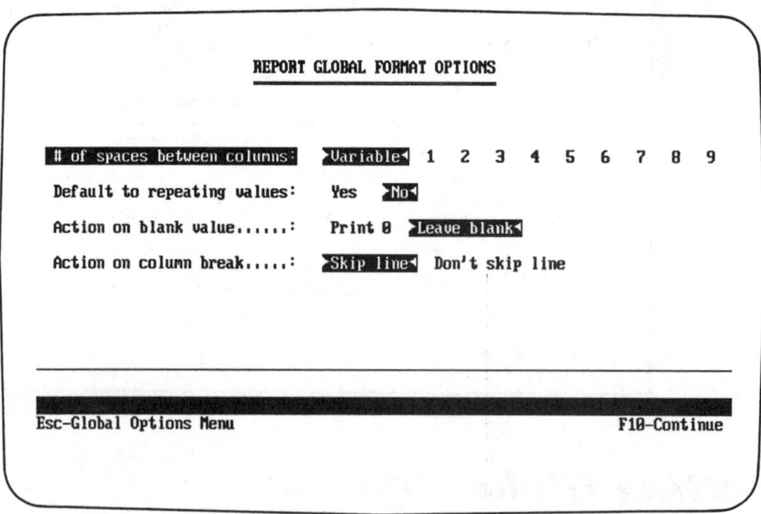

REPORT GLOBAL FORMAT OPTIONS
# of spaces between columns: Variable 1 2 3 4 5 6 7 8 9
Default to repeating values: Yes No
Action on blank value......: Print 0 Leave blank
Action on column break.....: Skip line Don't skip line
Esc-Global Options Menu
F10-Continue


**Fig. 15.26** *The Report Global Format Options screen.*

Use the up- and down-arrow keys to move through the options and the right- and left-arrow keys to set each choice. You can specify the number of spaces (up to 9) to be inserted between columns, or you can keep the variable setting so that Q&A makes the determination. The default value is 5 spaces, but the program may choose fewer if the area is limited.

Other settings on this screen are for repeating values, printing blank values, and inserting space between column breaks.

As previously explained, if a value is repeated in a column, Q&A prints only the value's first occurrence. With the global default options, however, you can have the program print the repeated values. Select Yes in the Default to Repeating Values field on the Repeat Global Format Options screen.

If a number or money field has no data, the Report module is preset to enter a zero (0) in that position. If you prefer a blank to a zero, select Leave Blank on the Action on Blank Value line.

You can elect not to skip a line after a column break by choosing Don't Skip Line on the Action on Column Break line. The default is set to skip one line at each column break.

## *Setting Global Page Options*

Your printer and the paper you use have particular characteristics that you need to specify. If you repeatedly use the same paper size, you can set a default value for your page settings. To do this, choose D for Set Page Options at the Global Options menu and make selections on the Define Page screen (see fig. 15.27).

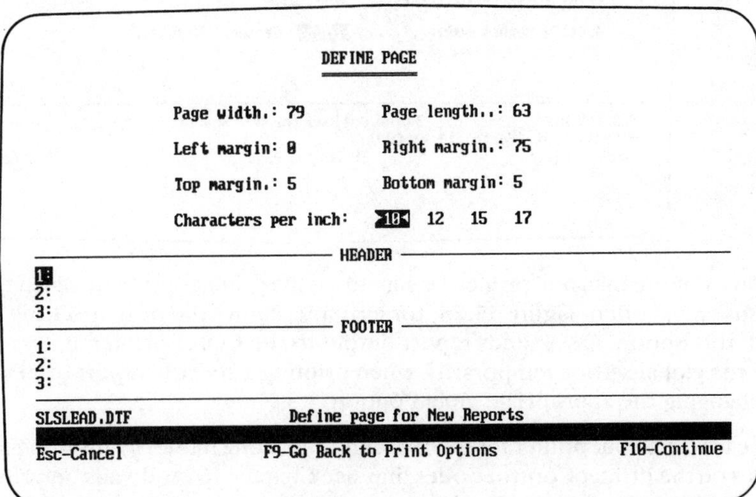


**Fig. 15.27** *The Define Page screen.*

Page width is the number of characters that can fit on one page of paper; page length is the number of lines on the page. The standard page length is 66 lines. You also can set the left and right margins for printing.

Although the number of lines allowed for top and bottom margins is fixed at three (three lines for the header and three lines for the footer), you can increase the margins. The Characters per Inch setting controls the number of printed characters per inch by determining the size of the characters. The choice you make for this option depends on your database and the reports you intend to produce.

## Setting Global Print Options

Before you print the report, press P to choose Set Print Options from the Global Options menu. You can use the Report Print Options screen to specify printer settings (see fig. 15.28). You need to specify the printer port and type of paper feed you will use. If you want to have the report printed to the screen as a default, you can specify this by selecting SCREEN after the Print To option. You also can specify printer offset and set printer control codes. The next-to-last option on this screen allows you to print the entire report or the calculated totals only, and the last option lets you left-justify, right-justify or center the report body.

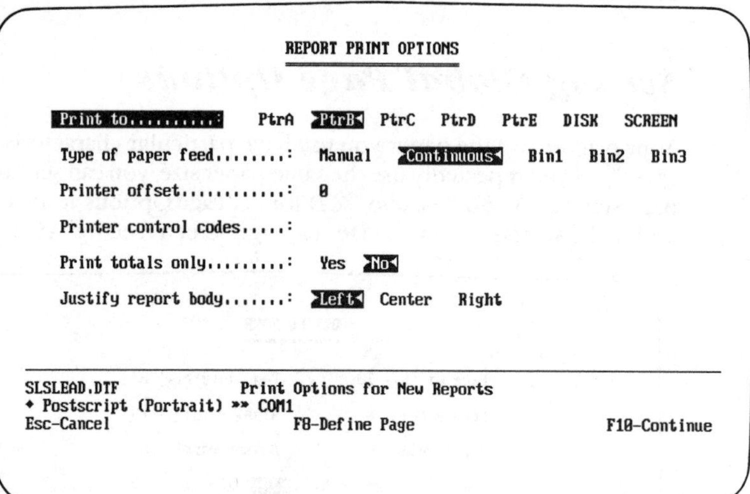

REPORT PRINT OPTIONS
Print to..........: PtrA PtrB PtrC PtrD PtrE DISK SCREEN
Type of paper feed........: Manual Continuous Bin1 Bin2 Bin3
Printer offset............: 0
Printer control codes.....:
Print totals only.........: Yes No
Justify report body.......: Left Center Right
SLSLEAD.DTF Print Options for New Reports
◆ Postscript (Portrait) » COM1
Esc-Cancel F8-Define Page F10-Continue


**Fig. 15.28** *The Report Print Options screen.*

If you use more than one printer, be sure to set the printer option to match the printer you use most often. Figure 15.28, for example, shows the printer setting as COM1. With this option, Q&A sends report output to the COM1 printer, unless you override the global setting temporarily when printing a specific report or permanently by changing the appropriate global option.

You can set up your printer for special fonts or printing modes by inserting the proper codes on the Printer Control Codes line. See Chapter 16 for details on printing your report after it has been defined.

# Renaming, Deleting, and Copying a Report

The Rename/Delete/Copy option in the Report menu can be used to manipulate existing reports. Rename changes only the report's name; Delete erases the report, and Copy duplicates the report. You can use Copy to create a report that is similar to an existing one. Just copy the report, and then redesign and rename it.

To rename a report, select Rename/Delete/Copy from the Report menu. When the File Name prompt is displayed, enter the name of the file or select it from the list of data files. The following options are then displayed:

R - Rename a Report
D - Delete a Report
C - Copy a Report

Note that a File Name prompt does not appear if you have been working with a file in the current Q&A session.

After you select Rename a Report, enter the name of the report you want to rename. At the Rename To prompt, press enter to see a list of the reports you have designed for the selected file or enter a new name of up to 20 characters. Report returns you to the Rename/Delete/Copy menu after you press Enter.

To delete a report, select the appropriate option, enter the name of the report, and press Enter. Q&A displays a warning message that asks you to confirm the operation. If you press Y, the report is deleted; if you press N, the operation is canceled.

Copying a report is similar. Select Copy a Report, and enter the name of the report you want to copy at the Copy From prompt. At the Copy To prompt, enter the name of the new report. If the report is to be copied to another drive, enter the drive specification, such as

A:New_Report

After you press Enter, you are returned to the Rename/Delete/Copy menu.

## Chapter Summary

After entering data in the File forms, you are ready to generate a report. Q&A Report can pull information from the forms in File to produce reports as basic or as complex as needed.

This chapter has explained how you can create a basic report and enhance it by adding column headings and widths, derived columns, and headers and footers. The next chapter introduces you to printing from the Report module.

Chapter

# 16

# Printing a Report

Printing a report is a natural extension of the report design process. To print a report from a database you created in the File module, you first design the report specifications and then send the output to the printer.

When you select Print a Report from the Report menu, you have several options, including one to make temporary changes to the report specifications before you print the report. If you want to make temporary changes to a report, you can modify and print it by using the Retrieve and Column/Sort Specs within the Print a Report option. The procedure is essentially the same as described in the preceding chapter under report design.

If you want to modify permanently the print settings for your report, you make changes from the Design/Redesign a Report option of the Report menu. You don't need to leave the Design Option screen before you print the report; after you make the modifications, the report can be printed. Because this section is devoted primarily to printing with Report, only a brief discussion of making permanent changes to your print settings is included. For a more detailed explanation, refer to Chapter 15, "Creating a Report."

## *Printing an Existing Report*

After you create a database to store and organize your information, you need to be able to combine the information in printed reports. You can use Q&A's Report module to arrange and print your data in a variety of ways. As discussed in Chapter 15, you can specify the records to be used in the report by using the Retrieve Spec, and tell Q&A how you want the data to be organized by using the Column/Sort Spec.

If you don't want to make any changes to the report before you print it, the print procedure from Report is a simple one. From the Main menu, select Report and then select Print a Report (see fig. 16.1). Q&A prompts you to select a database and the report you want to print. After you make the selections, Q&A asks whether you want to make any temporary changes (see fig. 16.2). When you select No, the report is sent to the printer.

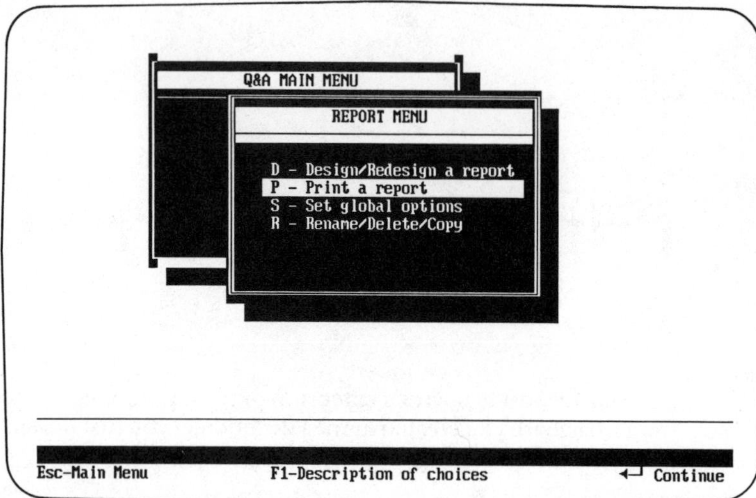


**Fig. 16.1**
*Choosing the Print a Report option.*

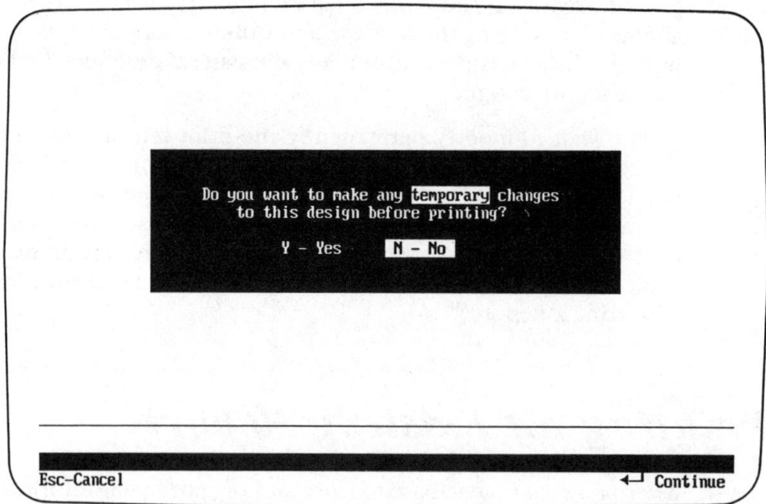


**Fig. 16.2**
*The screen prompt for temporary changes.*

# *Making Temporary Changes to an Existing Report*

At times you may want to make temporary changes to a report, print it, and then return the specifications to their original settings. For example, perhaps you want to invert the column order in a report or modify the Retrieve Specs for one printing.

If you want to make temporary changes to an existing report, first select Print a Report from the Report menu. After you select the database and the report name, Q&A asks whether you want to make temporary changes. In this case, select Yes.

## *Using the Retrieve Spec*

When you choose to make temporary changes, Q&A displays the Retrieve Spec. You can then select the forms to be pulled from the database. Suppose that you want to print a report of the Boston sales prospects that have an annual revenue over $2,000,000. On the Retrieve Spec screen, you enter *Boston* in the City field and >=*2000000* in the Annual Revenue field (see fig. 16.3). When you press F10, the Column/Sort Spec is displayed.

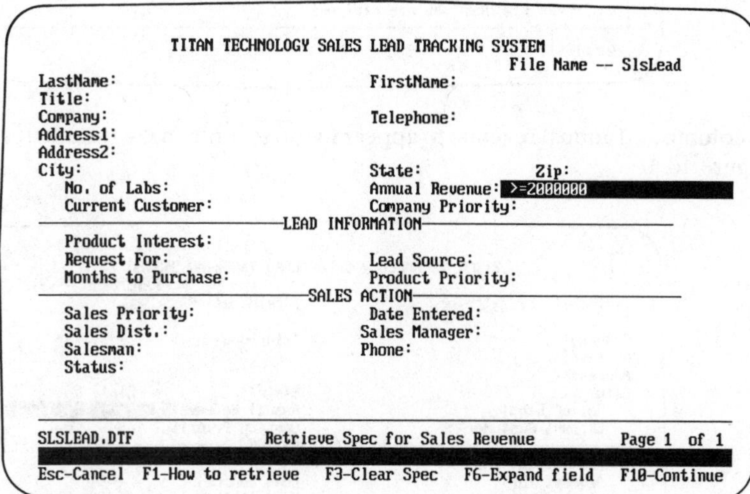


**Fig. 16.3**
*Using the Retrieve Spec.*

## *Using the Column/Sort Spec*

You use the Column/Sort Spec to tell Q&A which fields you want to print as columns on the report. At the same time, you can determine the sorting order for the records and specify which numeric fields you want to count, total, subtotal, or average. You also can change the column headings or column widths or justify the data within the column.

If you press F1 when the Column/Sort Spec is displayed, you see a brief reminder of how to fill out the screen. If you press F1 again, a detailed help screen appears (see fig. 16.4). By pressing PgDn, you can display a second screen of information.

Decide in what order you want Q&A to print the columns, and enter corresponding numbers in the fields. For example, if you want the company name to appear in the

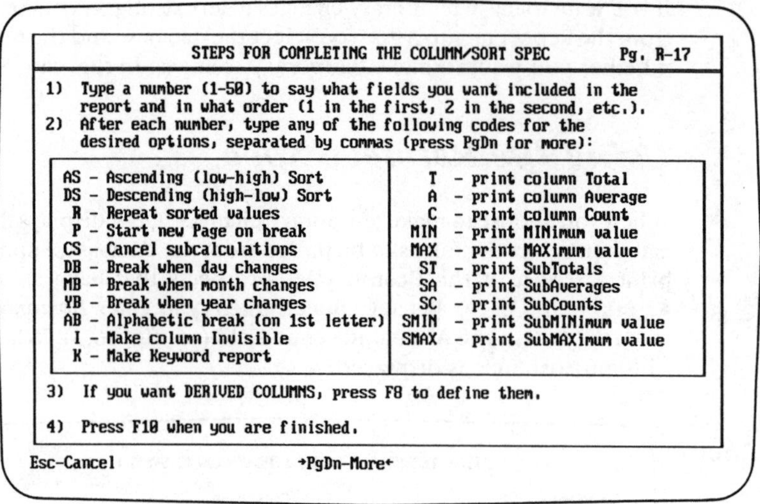

```
STEPS FOR COMPLETING THE COLUMN/SORT SPEC                      Pg. R-17

1)  Type a number (1-50) to say what fields you want included in the
    report and in what order (1 in the first, 2 in the second, etc.).
2)  After each number, type any of the following codes for the
    desired options, separated by commas (press PgDn for more):

  AS - Ascending (low-high) Sort               T    - print column Total
  DS - Descending (high-low) Sort              A    - print column Average
   R - Repeat sorted values                    C    - print column Count
   P - Start new Page on break                 MIN  - print MINimum value
  CS - Cancel subcalculations                  MAX  - print MAXimum value
  DB - Break when day changes                  ST   - print SubTotals
  MB - Break when month changes                SA   - print SubAverages
  YB - Break when year changes                 SC   - print SubCounts
  AB - Alphabetic break (on 1st letter)        SMIN - print SubMINimum value
   I - Make column Invisible                   SMAX - print SubMAXimum value
   K - Make Keyword report

3)  If you want DERIVED COLUMNS, press F8 to define them.

4)  Press F10 when you are finished.

Esc-Cancel                      →PgDn-More←
```

**Fig. 16.4** *A detailed help screen for completing the Column/Sort Spec.*

first column and annual revenue to appear in the second, make the entries as shown in figure 16.5.

```
              TITAN TECHNOLOGY SALES LEAD TRACKING SYSTEM
                                                 File Name -- SlsLead
LastName:                          FirstName:
Title:
Company: 1                         Telephone:
Address1:
Address2:
City:                              State:              Zip:
   No. of Labs:                    Annual Revenue: 2
   Current Customer:               Company Priority:
──────────────────────────────LEAD INFORMATION──────────────────────
   Product Interest:
   Request For:                    Lead Source:
   Months to Purchase:             Product Priority:
──────────────────────────────SALES ACTION──────────────────────────
   Sales Priority:                 Date Entered:
   Sales Dist.:                    Sales Manager:
   Salesman:                       Phone:
   Status:

SLSLEAD.DTF          Column/Sort Spec for Sales Revenue        Page 1  of 1

Esc-Cancel  F1-Info  F6-Expand  F8-Derived Columns  F9-Go back  F10-Continue
```

**Fig. 16.5** *Specifying the order of columns to be printed.*

You also have the option of arranging the data in ascending (AS) or descending (DS) order. If you enter an incorrect letter code in any field, Q&A displays the warning `Not a valid Column/Sort Spec` (see fig. 16.6). Before you can continue, you must correct the error by changing the letter code. Press F1 if you need help.

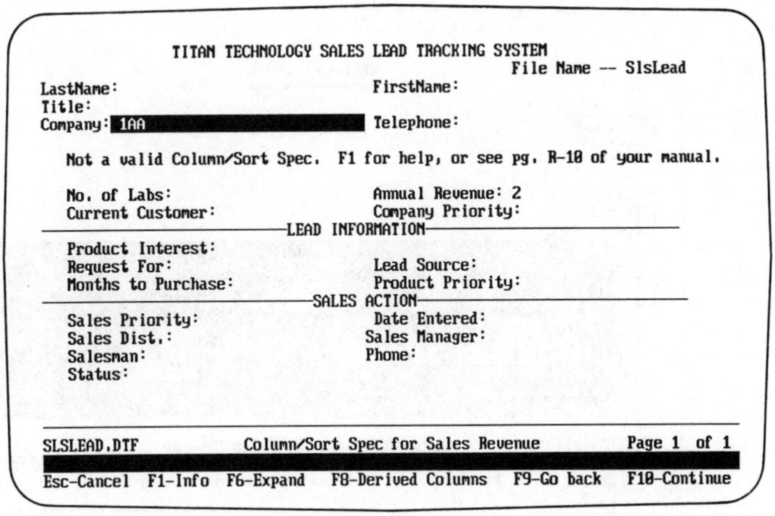

```
TITAN TECHNOLOGY SALES LEAD TRACKING SYSTEM
                                        File Name -- SlsLead
LastName:                          FirstName:
Title:
Company: 1AA                       Telephone:

  Not a valid Column/Sort Spec. F1 for help, or see pg. R-10 of your manual.

  No. of Labs:                     Annual Revenue: 2
  Current Customer:                Company Priority:
─────────────────LEAD INFORMATION─────────────────
  Product Interest:
  Request For:                     Lead Source:
  Months to Purchase:              Product Priority:
────────────────────SALES ACTION──────────────────
  Sales Priority:                  Date Entered:
  Sales Dist.:                     Sales Manager:
  Salesman:                        Phone:
  Status:

SLSLEAD.DTF        Column/Sort Spec for Sales Revenue        Page 1 of 1
Esc-Cancel F1-Info F6-Expand  F8-Derived Columns  F9-Go back  F10-Continue
```

**Fig. 16.6**
*A Column/Sort Spec screen with an error message.*

## *Using the Derived Columns Menu*

In some cases, you may need to produce a column that is not included in a field of your database. For example, if you have defined fields to store the number of sick days allotted to and the number of sick days used by each employee, you may want a field on the report that shows the number of remaining sick days. You can use the Derived Column menu to produce such a column. To design, redesign, or make temporary changes to a derived column, press F8 from the Column/Sort screen to display the Derived Columns screen.

Similar to the Column/Sort screen, the Derived Columns screen has context-sensitive help that you can access by pressing F1. When one of these help screens is superimposed on the Derived Columns menu, you can use the arrow keys to move the cursor so that you can see a different help screen appropriate for the adjacent line on the menu (see fig. 16.7). For example, if you move the cursor from Formula to Heading, a help screen on headings is displayed. (For a detailed account of how to use the Derived Columns menu, see Chapter 15.)

## *Using Print Options in Report*

When you press F10 from either the Column/Sort Spec or the Derived Columns menu, the Print Options screen appears. On this version of the menu (several versions exist, remember, throughout the different Q&A print procedures), you can elect to print only totals if you want to create a summary report (see fig. 16.8).

With the options on this screen, you also can decide how you want the report justified on the page. For example, if your page width is set at 132 characters, and your report

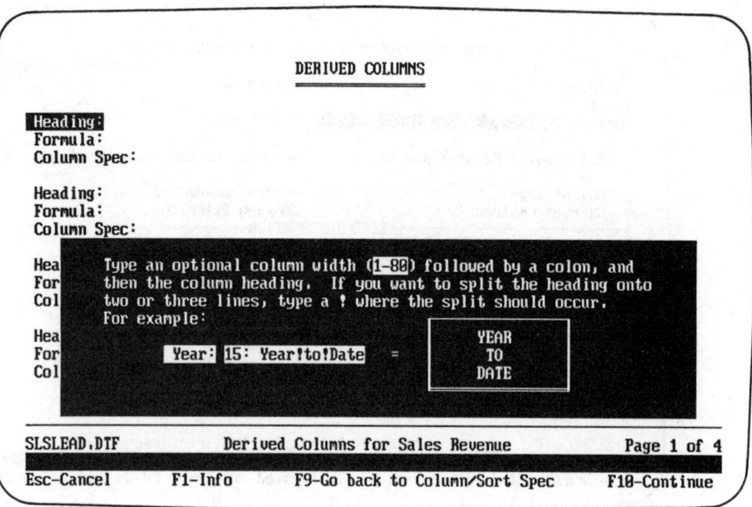


**Fig. 16.7**
*A help screen superimposed on the Derived Columns screen.*

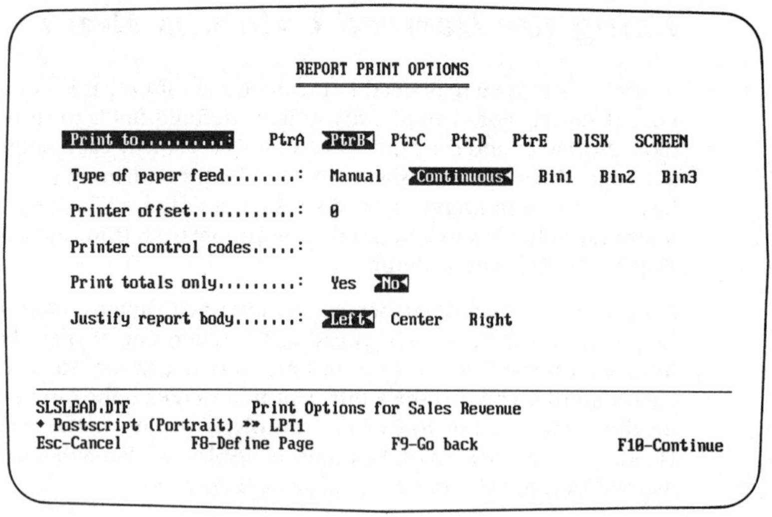

```
                    REPORT PRINT OPTIONS

Print to..........:   PtrA  PtrB  PtrC  PtrD  PtrE  DISK  SCREEN

Type of paper feed........:  Manual  Continuous  Bin1  Bin2  Bin3

Printer offset............:  0

Printer control codes.....:

Print totals only.........:  Yes  No

Justify report body.......:  Left  Center  Right

SLSLEAD.DTF              Print Options for Sales Revenue
◆ Postscript (Portrait) »» LPT1
Esc-Cancel        F8-Define Page        F9-Go back        F10-Continue
```

**Fig. 16.8**
*The Print Options screen in Report has a Print Totals Only option.*

is only 100 characters wide, you can choose to print the text centered or right-justified rather than on the left side of the page.

As another option, you can press F8 to access the Define Page menu. The following section explains how you can use this menu to enhance your printout.

### *Using the Define Page Menu*

Similar to screens in other modules, Report's Define Page screen allows you to arrange the text on your printout. By entering headers and footers and changing page length and margins, you can vary the way your report is printed. By widening the margins of your report, you can print more information on one page. You don't have to worry about making your reports too wide, however; Q&A automatically divides wide reports into more than one page.

When you are finished making all your temporary changes, press F10 to begin printing. While the report is printing, you can press F2 to cancel the operation and bring up the Print Options screen again. You can then make additional changes, if necessary. When you press F10 again, Q&A restarts the printing from the beginning of the file.

## *Making Permanent Changes to an Existing Report*

If you want to make permanent changes to the print specifications for your report, you can do so through the Design/Redesign a Report option of the Report menu. When you choose this option, you see the Retrieve and Column/Sort Specs, where you can make your adjustments. After you fill the Specs, Q&A displays the Print Options screen and asks whether you want to print the saved report. (For an in-depth discussion of creating Print Specs for Report, see Chapter 15.)

## *Printing a New Report*

The procedures for printing a new report and designing a report are similar. If you want to create a temporary report, you first select Print a Report from the Report menu. When the list of report names is displayed, just press Enter. Q&A displays each of the screens you enter when you design a report. The name `NEW` appears on the status line so that you know that the report is temporary (see fig. 16.9). After you print the report, Q&A returns you to the Report menu. The temporary report is not saved.

## *Selecting Fonts*

In Chapter 8 you learn how to select laser printer fonts when printing from within the File module. Q&A Report provides the same capabilities. From Report's Print Options screen, the last screen displayed before printing begins, you can enter

**Fig. 16.9**
*The Temporary Report screen.*

```
                TITAN TECHNOLOGY SALES LEAD TRACKING SYSTEM
                                                   File Name -- SlsLead
LastName:                          FirstName:
Title:
Company:                           Telephone:
Address1:
Address2:
City:                              State:            Zip:
  No. of Labs:                     Annual Revenue:
  Current Customer:                Company Priority:
-----------------------LEAD INFORMATION--------------------------
  Product Interest:
  Request For:                     Lead Source:
  Months to Purchase:              Product Priority:
-------------------------SALES ACTION----------------------------
  Sales Priority:                  Date Entered:
  Sales Dist.:                     Sales Manager:
  Salesman:                        Phone:
  Status:

SLSLEAD.DTF              Retrieve Spec for (NEW)              Page 1 of 1

Esc-Cancel  F1-How to retrieve   F3-Clear Spec   F6-Expand field   F10-Continue
```

PostScript file names or direct printer commands in the Printer Control Codes field. For a complete discussion of this procedure, see Chapter 8, "Printing a File."

If you are sending a PostScript control file to the printer, simply enter the full path name and file name. If you are sending direct printer control commands, precede the sequence with an exclamation mark (!). Use codes appropriate to your printer, in the following format:

!Font Points (Ln In Sn)

The exclamation point at the beginning of the line differentiates the printer command line from a PostScript command file name. The words and abbreviations in this example are variables that stand for text or numeric values. *Font* is the name of any font your printer recognizes, and *Points* is the font size in 1/72-inch intervals. For example, when the number 4 is substituted for the variable *Points*, the font is four points high, or 4/72 of an inch. A one-inch-high font is specified as 72. The range of possible values for Points depends on your printer.

The parameters in parentheses are optional and indicate the following settings:

*Ln* = Line spacing, where *n* is the number of points between lines. The default value for *n* is L12, which provides the standard 6 lines per inch (72/12 = 6).

*In* = Control for accented characters in the IBM character set. If you accept the default (I1), Q&A matches the IBM character set where possible. If your printer does not support PostScript fonts, set *In* at I0.

*Sn* = Symbol table selection. Q&A automatically matches the IBM character set as closely as possible. Standard PostScript characters are switched with others to match the IBM set. To disable this feature, set *Sn* at *S0*.

Q&A does not accept font commands for defined printers that do not support fonts, or for undefined printers. Even if you have a PostScript or other font-supporting printer defined, you must have it selected as the current printer on the Print Options screen. If you don't, an error is returned when you try to enter font commands on the Printer Control Codes line.

## Checking the Report before Printing

If you want to see before printing how your report will look, you can choose SCREEN from the Print To line of the Print Options screen. Q&A then displays the report on your monitor (without headers and footers) one screen at a time. You can use the cursor keys to scroll the report so that you can check it all. The End key takes you to the right edge of the report if it's too wide for one screen; the Home key returns you to the left edge. The PgUp and PgDn keys move you from the current screen to the preceding and next screens, respectively. Pressing either Enter or F10 also brings up the next screen.

When you are satisfied with the report, print the report by specifying the printer port on the Print Options screen. If you notice as the report prints that you should make additional changes, press Shift-F9. A direct access window then appears, and you can go directly to the spec that you need to change (see fig. 16.10). After making the changes, press F10; the report starts printing again from the beginning of the file.

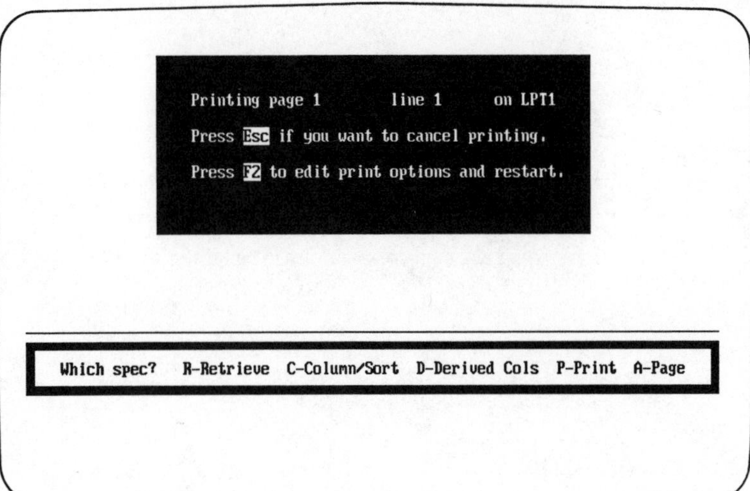
Printing page 1 line 1 on LPT1
Press Esc if you want to cancel printing.
Press F2 to edit print options and restart.
Which spec? R-Retrieve C-Column/Sort D-Derived Cols P-Print A-Page

**Fig. 16.10**
*The direct access screen.*

If the report is too wide for your page, a warning message displays before the report is printed. You can ignore the warning and proceed—Q&A will truncate the data that is beyond the edge of the page. Instead of losing that part of your printout, you can either return to the Print Options screen and correct the problem or cancel printing altogether.

## Chapter Summary

Printing from Report is quite simple. Although the Report module can perform complex tasks, by the time you are ready to print your information, the hard work is over.

In this chapter you learned how to use the Report menu to select reports to print and how to modify existing reports before you print them. By printing from Q&A's Report module, you can tailor your reports to display data in a variety of ways. You can permanently modify the print settings for your report by using the Design/Redesign a Report option of the Report menu. If you already have a Print Spec defined in File, you can simply select Print from the Report menu.

# Part V

# Using the Q&A Intelligent Assistant

Includes

Understanding the Intelligent Assistant

Using the Intelligent Assistant

Chapter

# 17

# Understanding the Intelligent Assistant

If you use Q&A Write, File, and Report, you have three powerful, easy-to-use tools for your small-business or departmental word-processing, data management, and reporting needs. Although you will benefit from your investment in Q&A by using the File and Report modules only, you will not be taking advantage of the feature that makes Q&A far more powerful and easier to use than many other programs that have integrated word-processing and database capabilities. Q&A's Intelligent Assistant (also referred to as the IA) is the feature that sets it apart from most other microcomputer applications programs available today.

The Intelligent Assistant uses a sophisticated artificial-intelligence technology, so you can communicate with Q&A by using your own language rather than the command menu system in File and Report. You can use English phrases and sentences to query a database that you created with File, produce reports, edit records, or add new records. Sentences also can be used to perform mathematical calculations or to ask for the date and time.

Once you begin to use the Intelligent Assistant, you will discover how it reduces the time spent on and complexity of many of your data-management and reporting applications. Before you can use the IA successfully, however, you need to learn its basics, experiment with its capabilities, and devise your own method for handling your data management and reporting needs.

In this and the following chapter, you will learn to experiment with and develop applications for the IA. This chapter gives you a conceptual introduction to the Intelligent Assistant and describes the general capabilities. You are encouraged to experiment as soon as you have learned the basics of Q&A File and have created your own database. The next chapter provides more details on how to use the IA's data management and report capabilities.

# *What Is the Intelligent Assistant?*

The IA is a language processor, or interpreter, and it has a built-in vocabulary of about 400 words. You can teach the IA new words, and the IA can learn new words that it finds in your database. With the Intelligent Assistant, you no longer have to communicate with Q&A through its own language, the command menu system in File and Report. Using the Intelligent Assistant is similar to asking a human assistant to locate, organize, change, analyze, or report information. If, for example, you had a file cabinet full of sales leads and wanted the leads for your company's Los Angeles office, you might ask your secretary or assistant, "Please bring me the file of Los Angeles sales leads." With the Intelligent Assistant, you make this request by typing *Display the Los Angeles forms.*

Q&A then displays all sales leads for the Los Angeles office. If you want to change a phone number in your database, you might ask your assistant, "Please change the phone number on Blackson's sales lead form." With the Intelligent Assistant, you simply type the following:

Change Blackson's phone number to "363-886-3980".

The English words, phrases, or sentences replace the sequence of command operations that would be executed if you used the File or Report modules without the Intelligent Assistant.

To answer your requests, the IA depends on built-in knowledge and on information it learns from your databases. Before you teach the IA about a database, it already knows the following:

- The time of day
- The current date
- How to conduct mathematical calculations
- About 400 words

After you teach the IA about your database, it also knows the following:

- Database field names
- Field contents and data types
- Field descriptions (which field contains locations, for example)
- Relationships between fields (the first-name and last-name fields combine to form a complete name, for example)
- Synonyms for field names and contents
- Additional vocabulary words that you teach it

## *Is the Intelligent Assistant for Advanced Users Only?*

The Intelligent Assistant is not for advanced users only. If you know how to use File to create a form and enter data into a database, you're ready to begin experimenting with Q&A's Intelligent Assistant. One of the best ways to sharpen your skills with the IA is to begin experimenting right away. By testing the capabilities of the Intelligent Assistant, you quickly will discover the powerful, easy-to-use qualities of this Q&A feature.

Just as you must give a new employee time to become familiar with your habits, you must allow the IA to "get to know" how to respond to your requests. The rest of this chapter helps you learn to experiment with the IA so that you can begin to use it for your own applications.

## *How To Experiment with the Intelligent Assistant*

Even before you begin, the Intelligent Assistant already has a limited amount of information. By using the Teach Me about Your Database option (subsequently referred to as the Teach option) on the Assistant menu, you can teach the IA more about the English commands and the methods you will use to request information.

If you want to bypass this option, you can move directly to the Ask Me To Do Something option (subsequently referred to as the Ask option) and request an action from Q&A. You can use the Intelligent Assistant for simple searching, sorting, changing, and reporting tasks. Because you will learn faster by experimenting immediately, try using the Ask option. The first time you use this option, the IA displays the procedure screen shown in figure 17.1. This initial step must be conducted the first time you use the IA with any data file.

Because all the file records you are working with must be scanned the first time you use the IA, this initial procedure takes longer when many records are in the database. If you plan to use the IA with a particular data file, do this start-up procedure before you have many records entered.

When you move directly to the Ask option without teaching Q&A about your database, the IA is capable of performing a number of simple operations on the forms available in your database. You must, however, phrase all your requests by using words that are found in the IA's built-in vocabulary or come from the field names and values in your database. For example, even before you use the Teach option, you can have the IA display telephone numbers from records with a field labeled Phone. At the IA prompt, just type the following:

Show me the phone numbers.

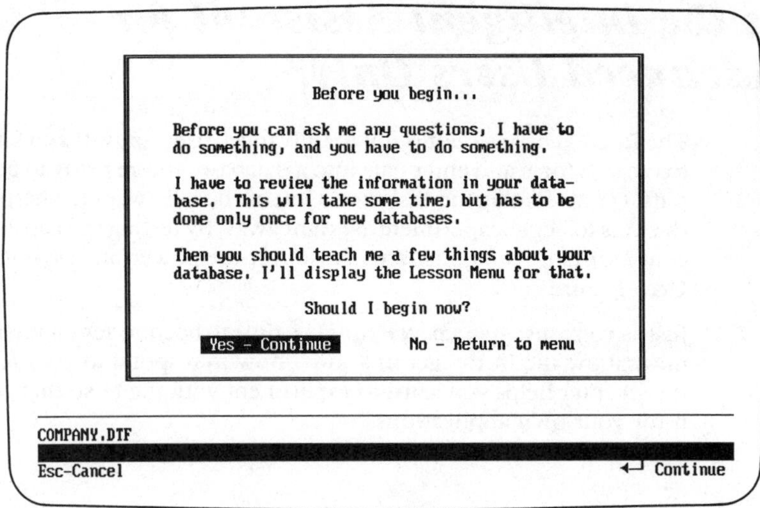

Before you begin...
Before you can ask me any questions, I have to do something, and you have to do something.
I have to review the information in your database. This will take some time, but has to be done only once for new databases.
Then you should teach me a few things about your database. I'll display the Lesson Menu for that.
Should I begin now?
Yes - Continue
No - Return to menu
COMPANY.DTF
Esc-Cancel
Continue


**Fig. 17.1** *The Intelligent Assistant initial procedures screen.*

Experimenting with the Intelligent Assistant in this manner helps you to discover the range of requests and responses allowed by the program. When you try to make more complicated requests, however, you will see how much help the Intelligent Assistant needs. A request for a sophisticated summary report, for example, may require much more information than is available in the built-in vocabulary and the database words. For complex applications, the Teach option is a necessary part of using the Intelligent Assistant.

Whenever you use the Ask option from the Assistant menu, the information can be displayed in the form it was originally entered (see fig. 17.2). You also have the option of requesting a summary report of the information on-screen (see fig. 17.3). How the information is displayed depends on how you ask the question and what you have told the IA about displaying the information it finds.

Part of teaching the IA about your database involves defining which fields will be used in reports. Once these fields have been specified, a request such as *Show me the phone numbers* will produce a columnar report that includes these fields.

Suppose that you are more specific and use the term *form* in your request: *Display forms where city=Boulder.* Then you would get a full-screen display of the record.

As you read through the rest of this chapter, you can experiment with the Intelligent Assistant by following these steps:

1. Create a simple practice database by using Q&A's File module. You can duplicate the database example used throughout this chapter or create your own.

2. Make sure that you make a backup of the database file by using either the Copy command from Q&A's File menu or the DOS COPY command (see Chapter 6 for directions on copying).

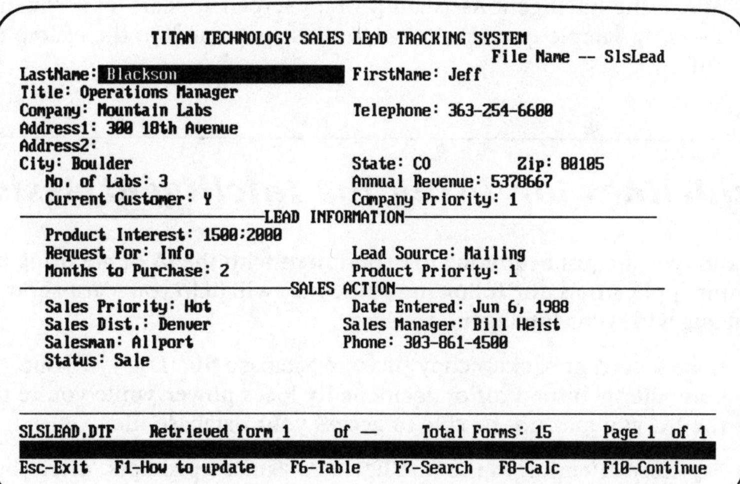

```
TITAN TECHNOLOGY SALES LEAD TRACKING SYSTEM
                                        File Name -- SlsLead
LastName: Blackson                 FirstName: Jeff
Title: Operations Manager
Company: Mountain Labs             Telephone: 363-254-6600
Address1: 300 18th Avenue
Address2:
City: Boulder                      State: CO         Zip: 80105
  No. of Labs: 3                   Annual Revenue: 5378667
  Current Customer: Y              Company Priority: 1
——————————————————LEAD INFORMATION——————————————————
  Product Interest: 1500;2000
  Request For: Info                Lead Source: Mailing
  Months to Purchase: 2            Product Priority: 1
———————————————————SALES ACTION—————————————————————
  Sales Priority: Hot              Date Entered: Jun 6, 1988
  Sales Dist.: Denver              Sales Manager: Bill Heist
  Salesman: Allport                Phone: 303-861-4500
  Status: Sale

SLSLEAD.DTF   Retrieved form 1   of —   Total Forms: 15   Page 1 of 1

Esc-Exit  F1-How to update  F6-Table  F7-Search  F8-Calc  F10-Continue
```

**Fig. 17.2** *Information in forms displayed by the Intelligent Assistant.*

```
Display the company, annual revenue, product interest, sorted according to
sales priority

Sales Priority       Company                          Annual Revenue   Product I
--------------       ------------------------------   --------------   ---------
                     Advanced Medical Associates        $5300623.00    2000;1200
                     Mountain Labs                      $100210.00     1000;1500

1.5                  Pike Pharmaceutical, Inc.          $210000.00     2000;1500
                     University of Michigan             $325000.00     1000;2000
                     Franklyn Lab Associates            $6456000.00    1200;1500
                     Mattis Medical Laboratories        $1000210.00    2000;2500
                     Bay City Laboratories              $150250.00     2000;1000

2.0                  Washington Medical Labs, Inc       $200500.00     1500;2500

Hot                  Independent Medical Labs           $223500.00     2500;1500
                     Plaines Medical Associates         $750000.00     1200;2000

SLSLEAD.DTF

Esc-Cancel   F2-Reprint   <→ ← ↓ ↑ PgUp PgDn>-Scroll   F10-Continue
```

**Fig. 17.3** *Summary reports displayed by the Intelligent Assistant.*

3. Enter the Intelligent Assistant module by selecting Assistant from Q&A's Main menu.
4. Select the Get Acquainted option from the Assistant menu.
5. Select the Ask Me To Do Something option from the Assistant menu and indicate the file name for the database you want the IA to use.
6. When the Before You Begin... screen appears (see fig. 17.1), press Enter to indicate that the Intelligent Assistant should analyze your database.

7. When the Intelligent Assistant prompt screen appears, experiment with entering sample queries similar to those presented in the examples that follow.

### *Guidelines for Using the Intelligent Assistant*

Whether you are just beginning to experiment with the IA or are using it regularly for your applications, the following guidelines will help you learn about and avoid problems with your Intelligent Assistant:

- Keep a current backup copy of your database file (DTF). If your computer is turned off or accidentally loses power while you're using the IA, you may not be able to access your database file.
- Pay close attention to the Intelligent Assistant's prompts. After you enter a request, if the prompts displayed indicate that the IA is unable to complete the task, don't proceed with the operation.
- Leave the Intelligent Assistant by pressing Esc from the IA menu to return to the Q&A Main menu.

# *File versus the Intelligent Assistant*

When you compare using File alone with using File with the Intelligent Assistant, you see the IA's power. Suppose that you want to ask the IA to display all sales leads for the Los Angeles office. The procedures you follow to complete this task by using the Intelligent Assistant and by using File are quite different.

## *Steps for Using File To Query a Database*

Data management capabilities are available through Q&A File even if you are not using the Intelligent Assistant. When you use File alone, however, even simple database searches or sorts can involve many steps. If you want to use File to search a sales lead database for the leads in the Los Angeles office, you first select the Search/Update option from the File menu. Q&A then displays the Retrieve Spec screen, and the cursor is positioned in the first field (see fig. 17.4).

To display all records for the Los Angeles sales district, move the cursor to the Sales Dist. field and type *Los Angeles*. With this specification entered as the data search, you are asking Q&A to display all Los Angeles records. When you press F10

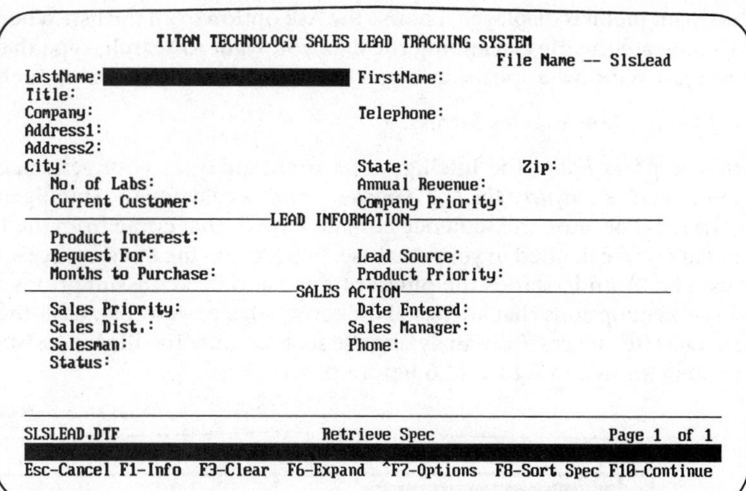
```
                 TITAN TECHNOLOGY SALES LEAD TRACKING SYSTEM
                                                   File Name -- SlsLead
LastName:                               FirstName:
Title:
Company:                                Telephone:
Address1:
Address2:
City:                                   State:         Zip:
   No. of Labs:                         Annual Revenue:
   Current Customer:                    Company Priority:
                  ------------LEAD INFORMATION------------
   Product Interest:
   Request For:                         Lead Source:
   Months to Purchase:                  Product Priority:
                  --------------SALES ACTION--------------
   Sales Priority:                      Date Entered:
   Sales Dist.:                         Sales Manager:
   Salesman:                            Phone:
   Status:

SLSLEAD.DTF                   Retrieve Spec                   Page 1 of 1
Esc-Cancel F1-Info  F3-Clear  F6-Expand  ^F7-Options  F8-Sort Spec F10-Continue
```

**Fig. 17.4** *The Retrieve Spec screen.*

(Continue), the first record with *Los Angeles* entered in the Sales Dist. field is displayed. Each time you press F10, the next record that matches the search is displayed (see fig. 17.5).

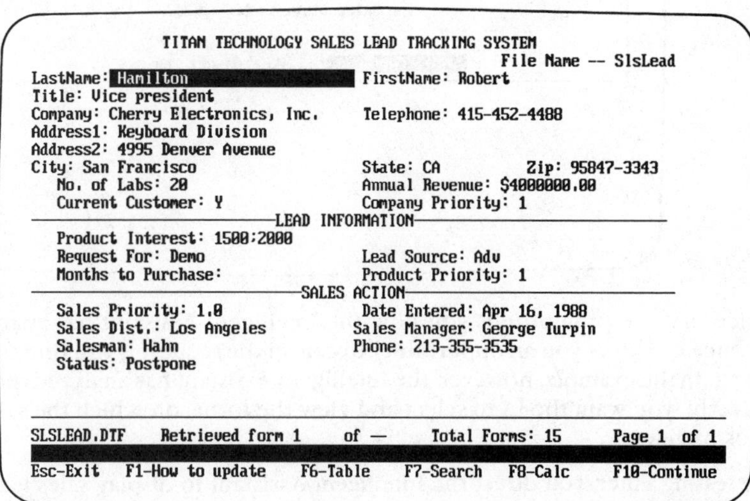
```
                 TITAN TECHNOLOGY SALES LEAD TRACKING SYSTEM
                                                   File Name -- SlsLead
LastName: Hamilton                      FirstName: Robert
Title: Vice president
Company: Cherry Electronics, Inc.       Telephone: 415-452-4488
Address1: Keyboard Division
Address2: 4995 Denver Avenue
City: San Francisco                     State: CA        Zip: 95847-3343
   No. of Labs: 20                      Annual Revenue: $4000000.00
   Current Customer: Y                  Company Priority: 1
                  ------------LEAD INFORMATION------------
   Product Interest: 1500;2000
   Request For: Demo                    Lead Source: Adv
   Months to Purchase:                  Product Priority: 1
                  --------------SALES ACTION--------------
   Sales Priority: 1.0                  Date Entered: Apr 16, 1988
   Sales Dist.: Los Angeles             Sales Manager: George Turpin
   Salesman: Hahn                       Phone: 213-355-3535
   Status: Postpone

SLSLEAD.DTF   Retrieved form 1    of —    Total Forms: 15    Page 1 of 1
Esc-Exit   F1-How to update   F6-Table   F7-Search   F8-Calc   F10-Continue
```

**Fig. 17.5** *The first form that meets the search criteria.*

## *Steps for Using the Intelligent Assistant To Query a Database*

You also can use the Intelligent Assistant to complete the search for sales leads from the Los Angeles office. Begin by selecting the IA from the Q&A Main menu. When the Assistant menu is displayed, choose the Ask option from the list. When Q&A asks you to indicate the file containing the data you want to search, type the file name. The request window appears, and you can type a simple sentence such as this:

Display the Los Angeles forms.

When you press Enter, the Intelligent Assistant analyzes your sentence. A simple sentence such as *Display the Los Angeles forms* is easy for the Intelligent Assistant to understand because the sentence contains words that come from the IA's built-in vocabulary or are defined in your database. In addition, the IA can process the request because the IA understands the plural of *form* and makes assumptions about your request—assumptions that are based on knowledge of your database and databases in general. After successfully analyzing the sentence, the Intelligent Assistant displays the prompt shown in figure 17.6 before proceeding.

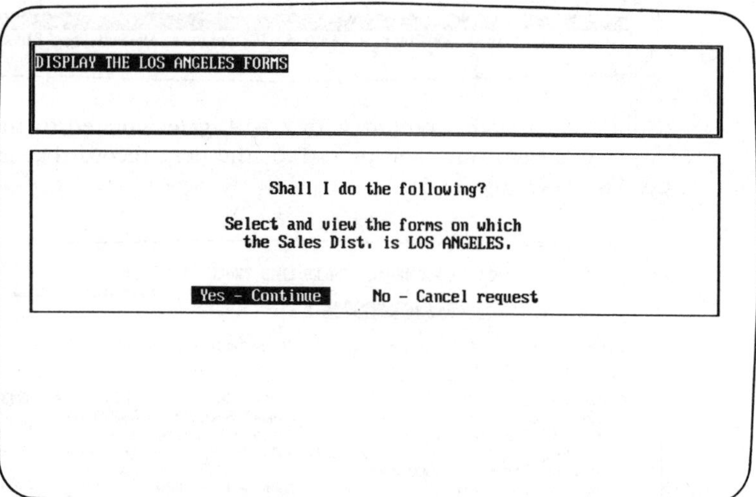
DISPLAY THE LOS ANGELES FORMS
Shall I do the following?
Select and view the forms on which the Sales Dist. is LOS ANGELES.
Yes - Continue
No - Cancel request

**Fig. 17.6** *The IA interpreting your request and asking for confirmation.*

Notice that the prompt tells you how the Intelligent Assistant has analyzed your sentence and gives you an opportunity to cancel the request if you find the analysis wrong. In the example, however, the Intelligent Assistant has analyzed the sentence correctly; you want the IA to select and view the forms on which the sales district is Los Angeles.

By pressing Enter, you direct the Intelligent Assistant to display sales leads for the Los Angeles sales district. Because Los Angeles is a value in only one field, the IA assumes that you want the search to be conducted on that field. The IA displays the same initial form that is displayed when you manually request the Los Angeles leads by using the Search/Update command, the Retrieve Spec, and the function keys in the File module.

After the Intelligent Assistant displays the first record that meets the Los Angeles sales-district criterion, you can press F10 (Continue) to display other records for Los

Angeles sales leads. When you have reviewed all records that meet the criterion, you either can display the records again or press Esc to return to the IA. When the Intelligent Assistant screen is displayed, you can enter other questions for sorting or searching for information in your database.

One of the Intelligent Assistant's most sophisticated features is its capacity to modify the database. For example, you can ask the IA to change the telephone number on one of your forms:

Change Blackson's telephone number to "363-886-3980".

After you press Enter, the Intelligent Assistant analyzes your request, asks you to confirm its interpretation, and searches the forms in the database for the specified record. When the IA displays the forms you want to change, you press Shift-F10 to change the data and save the modifications.

## *Chapter Summary*

This chapter gave you an introduction to the capabilities of Q&A's natural-language query facility: the Intelligent Assistant. The material provided in this chapter will help you get acquainted with IA features and guide you through initial experiments with using the Intelligent Assistant.

The next chapter offers additional help and more detailed information on applying the IA to your needs.

Chapter 18

# Using the Intelligent Assistant

Chapter 17 introduces the Intelligent Assistant and encourages you to learn how to use this unique Q&A feature by experimenting with it. The chapter also explains the range of capabilities and the way the IA processes your requests. In that chapter, you learned what the Intelligent Assistant can do even before you expand its knowledge of your database and applications. In this chapter, you learn how to apply the Intelligent Assistant to your particular database and reporting applications. You will learn how to use the IA most effectively by reading the information on

- Getting started with the IA
- Expanding the IA's knowledge
- Planning your requests
- Preparing the IA with Teach Me about Your Database
- Entering requests
- Updating the IA's knowledge
- Using macros to automate the IA

## *Getting Started with the Intelligent Assistant*

The Intelligent Assistant module is available through Q&A's Main menu. You select Assistant in the same way you select File, Report, or Write.After you choose the Assistant option, Q&A displays the Assistant menu. This menu provides three selections: Get Acquainted, Teach Me about Your Database, and Ask Me To Do Something. The Get Acquainted option provides a brief summary of the Intelligent Assistant's capabilities and makes recommendations on how to use the Intelligent Assistant. Use the Teach option to expand the Intelligent Assistant's vocabulary and teach relationships to the IA so that it can process your requests. Selecting the Ask option displays the prompt screen, where you enter your requests.

When you first select the Teach or the Ask option, the Intelligent Assistant asks for the name of the database file to use. If you press Enter at this prompt, Q&A displays a list of database (DTF) files from the default data drive or path (see fig. 18.1). If the database file you want is listed, move the cursor to that name and press Enter. If your file is on another drive or path, type the new drive or path name and press Enter. Q&A then displays the new list of DTF files.

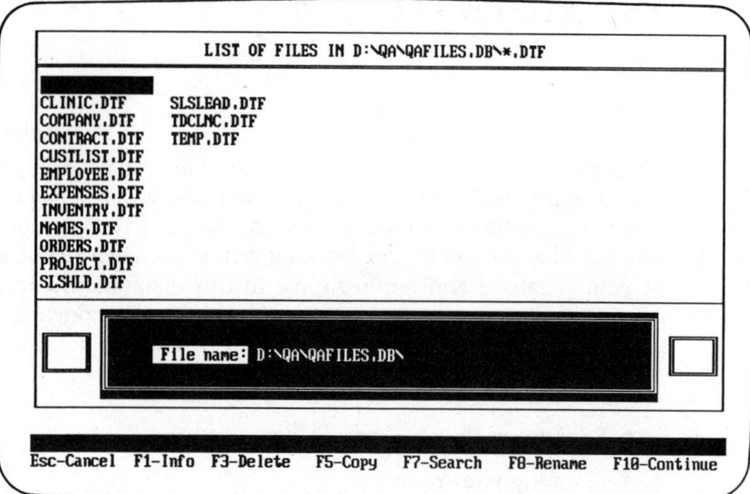


**Fig. 18.1**
*A list of the DTF files.*

The first time you use the Intelligent Assistant with your database, the IA analyzes the database before proceeding with the Teach or the Ask option. This analysis is necessary so that the IA can learn the field names, field type specifications, and information in each database form. After the Intelligent Assistant has analyzed your database, you can continue using the Teach or Ask option, as explained in the rest of this chapter.

The Q&A documentation recommends that you begin to use the Intelligent Assistant by working through the lessons available with the Teach option. We recommend, however, that you learn about the IA's capabilities by experimenting with it. This "hands-on" method gives you an immediate grasp of the IA's capabilities and helps you use the IA to meet your particular needs. This type of approach has one drawback: the experimenting can cause the IA to use disk space that may not be required once you learn how you will use this feature. You may want to create a temporary Q&A system for use while you learn about the IA, especially if you are operating on a network. Then you can delete the temporary files and implement the required IA features in your working Q&A system.

After you have experimented with the Intelligent Assistant enough to be comfortable with its features and operation, use the IA for your daily data management needs by following these basic steps:

1. Use a piece of paper or Q&A Write to make a list of requests you might enter.
2. Analyze your requests to determine what kind of assistance the IA needs so that it can understand your requests. Remember that you can teach the IA synonyms for field names, combine fields and give the combination a new name, and add words to the IA vocabulary. By studying the types of requests you are likely to give the IA, you can determine how to configure it for your application.
3. Prepare the IA for your requests by using some or all of the lessons available in the Teach option. The sample requests you have prepared can help you teach the IA what it needs to know to handle your application.
4. Enter requests for the IA to process.
5. Add to the Intelligent Assistant's knowledge as your needs grow. Remember to update the Intelligent Assistant's vocabulary and teach the IA about the relationships between your requests and the database to which your requests refer.

## *Why Use the Teach Option?*

You can use the Intelligent Assistant without expanding its built-in vocabulary or teaching it specific information about your database. Chapter 17 shows, for example, that as long as your questions contain words from the Intelligent Assistant's built-in vocabulary and the field names and values in your database, you can enter a wide range of requests. If a request contains a word the Intelligent Assistant doesn't recognize, however, the IA stops processing the request and prompts you to supply information about the unknown word. Depending on the word's context, the Intelligent Assistant may not be able to process the request.

The best way to make sure that the Intelligent Assistant can process most of your data management and reporting requests is to use the Teach option. Even though you can forgo that step and still use the IA to answer simple requests and produce reports, for more complicated tasks you need to teach the IA to recognize words that are unique to your database. When you use the Teach option to expand the Intelligent Assistant's information bank, you gain three important benefits:

1. You can substitute alternative field names so that you can enter the same request many different ways. For example, in the sales lead database, many field names consist of two or more words, such as the

No. of Labs, Annual Revenue, and Sales Manager fields (see fig. 18.2). To make queries easier, you can change these names to Labs, Revenue, and Manager and then use such questions as

Which leads have more than 10 labs?
Who is the manager in the Philadelphia district?
Which leads have revenue over $500,000?

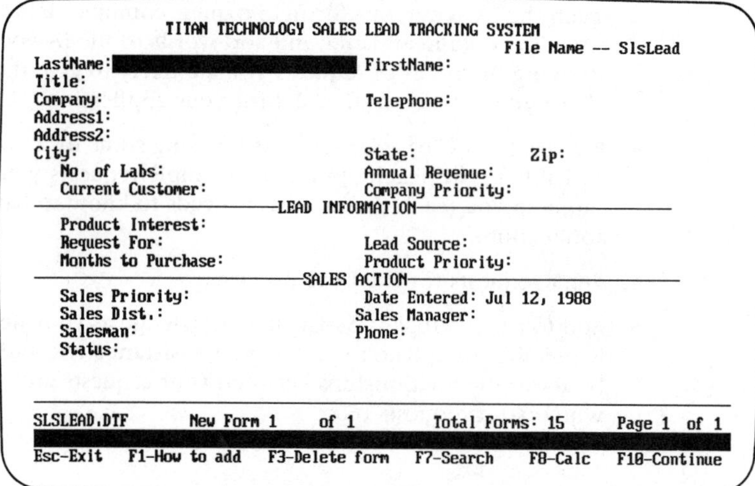
```
TITAN TECHNOLOGY SALES LEAD TRACKING SYSTEM
                                               File Name -- SlsLead
LastName:                        FirstName:
Title:
Company:                         Telephone:
Address1:
Address2:
City:                            State:              Zip:
  No. of Labs:                   Annual Revenue:
  Current Customer:              Company Priority:
----------------------LEAD INFORMATION----------------------
  Product Interest:
  Request For:                   Lead Source:
  Months to Purchase:            Product Priority:
------------------------SALES ACTION------------------------
  Sales Priority:                Date Entered: Jul 12, 1988
  Sales Dist.:                   Sales Manager:
  Salesman:                      Phone:
  Status:

SLSLEAD.DTF      New Form 1    of 1      Total Forms: 15    Page 1  of 1
Esc-Exit  F1-How to add  F3-Delete form  F7-Search  F8-Calc  F10-Continue
```

**Fig. 18.2**
*The sales lead database.*

Before you use the Teach option, if you enter a request that includes only a part of a field name, such as Labs or Revenue in the preceding example, the Intelligent Assistant cannot process your request without help. The Intelligent Assistant doesn't understand that *labs* is your alternative for No. of Labs, that *revenue* refers to Annual Revenue, or that *manager* means Sales Manager.

2. Teaching the IA about your database makes querying easier for others who use your database. Suppose that other people use the IA to prepare reports and to query, change, or sort your database. For example, you may ask your secretary to prepare a report listing annual revenues for all companies in the sales lead database. If you haven't taught the Intelligent Assistant the default field information to include in every report, the program responds to the request "List annual revenues" by displaying only a column of annual revenues—and no information as to what companies earn these revenues. Teaching the IA alternative words for fields and values also makes other users' tasks much easier. Then, when they query the IA, other users don't have to use the same words that you used to design the database.

3. The more the Intelligent Assistant knows about your database, the faster the IA can process your requests. Whenever the Intelligent Assistant encounters an ambiguous word or a word not included in the IA's vocabulary, processing stops. This delay can waste valuable time. For example, suppose that you ask the IA the following question before you have used the Teach option:

    Which companies requesting demonstrations on the 1500 are not current customers?

    The Intelligent Assistant pauses three times before it can process this request. First, the IA asks for clarification of the verb *requesting* because this word does not exist in either the Intelligent Assistant's built-in vocabulary or in the words available in your database (see fig. 18.3). Second, the IA asks for clarification of *demonstrations*. Although the database stores information indicating which sales leads have asked for product demonstrations, this information is entered in abbreviated form—as *demo*. Third, the Intelligent Assistant asks you to clarify the use of the number *1500* (see fig. 18.4). Because the IA recognizes 1500 as a number and also as a value in the Product Interest field, the IA needs to know how you have used the number in your request.

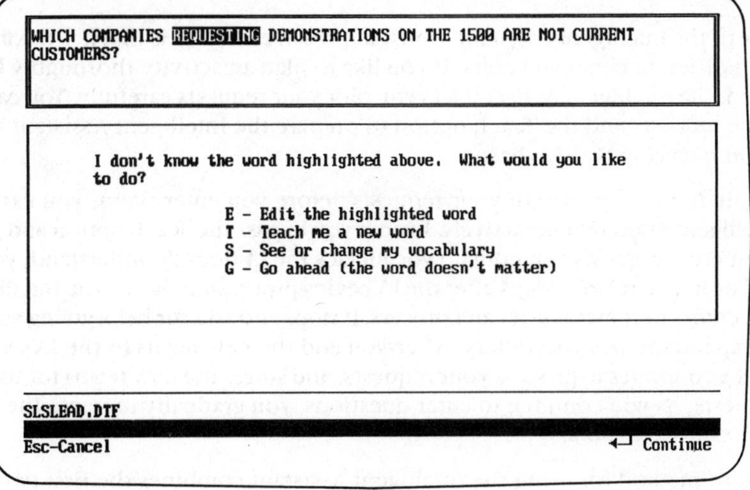


**Fig. 18.3** *The IA asking for clarification of an unknown word.*

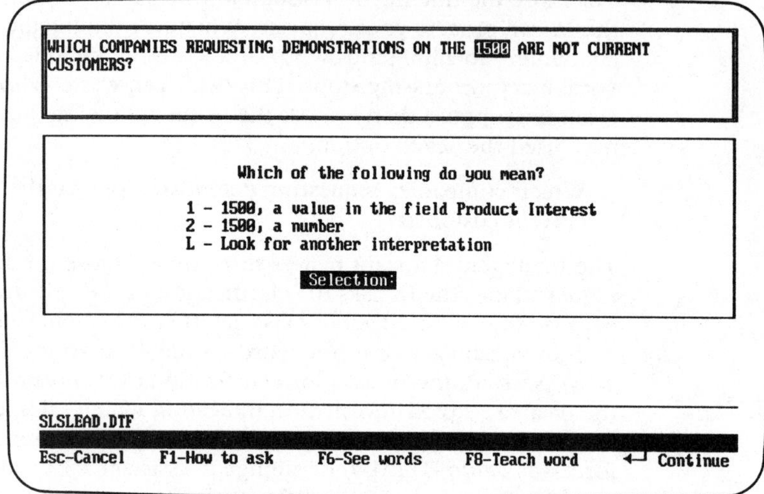
WHICH COMPANIES REQUESTING DEMONSTRATIONS ON THE 1500 ARE NOT CURRENT CUSTOMERS?
Which of the following do you mean?
1 - 1500, a value in the field Product Interest
2 - 1500, a number
L - Look for another interpretation
Selection:
SLSLEAD.DTF
Esc-Cancel
F1-How to ask
F6-See words
F8-Teach word
Continue

**Fig. 18.4** *The IA asking for clarification of an ambiguous term.*

## *Methods for Teaching the IA about Your Database*

One of the Intelligent Assistant's most impressive features is that it is flexible enough to fit different personal habits. If you like to plan an activity thoroughly before you begin, the Intelligent Assistant lets you plot your requests carefully. You can then use these requests and the Teach option to prepare the Intelligent Assistant before you begin querying the database.

If you don't want to plan your requests before you enter them, you can teach the Intelligent Assistant interactively. Even if you bypass the Teach option and go directly to entering requests that contain vocabulary the IA doesn't understand, you can add the terms and relationships after the IA begins processing. When the Intelligent Assistant comes to something it can't process, it stops and asks for help, giving you a chance to expand the IA's vocabulary. After you add the new terms to the IA's vocabulary, the IA continues to process your requests, and stores the new terms for use in future requests. As you continue to enter questions, you gradually increase the Intelligent Assistant's vocabulary.

A third method for using the Intelligent Assistant combines the first two methods. You probably will find this method the most effective. Begin by planning how you want to use the Intelligent Assistant, and then teach it about your database. As you continue to enter questions, add to the information in the Intelligent Assistant's vocabulary by responding to problems that occur when the IA doesn't understand a part of your request.

When you select Teach Me about Your Database from the Assistant menu, the IA responds with a Basic Lessons menu that includes five choices:

- What this database is about
- Which fields identify a form
- Which fields contain locations
- Alternate field names
- Advanced lessons

One of these options is Advanced Lessons; selecting that option displays another five selections:

- What fields contain people's names
- Units of measure
- Advanced vocabulary: adjectives
- Advanced vocabulary: verbs
- Exit lessons

You therefore have a total of nine Teach possibilities. Eight choices are for expanding the IA's information, and a final option is for exiting back to the Main menu. You may not need to use all eight options, but you should select those that best prepare the Intelligent Assistant for your requests. The time you spend working through the lessons on these menus will increase the capability and efficiency of the Intelligent Assistant.

# *Planning Your Requests*

Before you begin the eight lessons, develop a list of as many questions as you can. Think of the questions you will use most often when instructing the Intelligent Assistant to query or sort your database, change or delete information, or provide summary reports.

## *Creating a List of Requests*

The Intelligent Assistant is prepared to respond to simple requests for displaying information in your database. The IA also can perform more complex tasks, such as calculating values, presenting summary reports of information, and changing forms and data in the database.

Begin by determining the types of information your database contains. Next, consider exactly what information you will want to retrieve, how you or others will want information displayed, and what information and forms you will want to change. Think of the kinds of requests you may enter concerning the different types of information. You may want to begin by writing down questions related to each field.

When you write your list of questions, make the list as comprehensive as possible. Consider three elements:

*What task do you want to accomplish?* Do you want to retrieve data or a whole form, create a report, sort forms or data, or change data?

*What type of information do you want?* Do you want information about people or places? Do you want to perform calculations? Do you want answers to yes/no questions?

*How do you want the information displayed?* Do you want one column of information displayed? Do you want a predefined report?

Depending on the complexity of your database, you may want to retrieve many types of information. If you're using the IA with the sales lead database, for example, you may want to enter the following requests about sales leads:

How many sales leads are located in Pennsylvania?

How many sales leads are current customers?

Show all sales leads with annual revenue greater than $1,000,000.

You can enter more specific requests relating to values stored in the fields, such as

Who is the Atlanta sales manager?

What is the address of Hope Laboratories?

How many labs does Hope Laboratories operate?

What is Hope Laboratories' annual revenue?

As you write down possible requests, consider not only the types of information you want, but also the operations you may want the IA to perform with the information in your database. Consider, for example, requests for changing, adding, and sorting information. You may want to make the following requests for changing information in the sales lead database:

Change Hope Laboratories' sales priority to 1.0.

Delete 2600 on the Hope Laboratories form.

Enter 5/3/88 for the Hope Laboratories Demo Date.

Consider requests that ask for types of reports. Notice in the following examples that the first three requests ask for a new report, but the last example asks the IA to display an existing report that was created in the Report module.

Display sales leads where revenue <5,000,000 >1,500,000.

List companies' sales priority = 1.5.

Show sales leads for the Los Angeles district office.

Show the sales priority report.

Decide whether you want the Intelligent Assistant to sum or calculate values in the database, such as

How many sales leads are located in PA?

How many sales leads are current customers?

What is the total annual revenue for all sales leads in the LA sales district?

After you have generated a working set of requests, you need to analyze and revise them so that the Intelligent Assistant can process your requests as quickly as possible.

### Revising Your List of Requests

Although the Intelligent Assistant's flexibility allows for various types of questions, you can save time and avoid problems by putting requests in the simplest form possible. You may want to keep a printed set of your often-used requests for querying, sorting, and changing the form and data in the database. When you design these requests, keep in mind the following guidelines:

- *Use the shortest form possible.* Use direct requests rather than complex questions, and use math symbols to simplify requests. You can replace a question such as "Which sales leads are not current customers?" with "List current customers = N." Notice that the latter request uses a command rather than a question, and math symbols rather than full English syntax. (See Chapter 17 for more information on using math symbols in requests.)
- *Check for any ambiguities and revise to ensure the correct interpretation.* For example, suppose that the sales lead database contains the value *Los Angeles* in both the City and Sales District fields. If you enter a request such as "List all Los Angeles sales leads," the IA cannot process this request without asking you to indicate whether Los Angeles refers to all sales lead companies with Los Angeles addresses or all sales leads that fall under the Los Angeles sales district. To ensure that the Intelligent Assistant interprets this request correctly, you can enter "List sales leads where city = Los Angeles."

## Preparing the IA for Your Requests

Creating a "working set" of requests helps you understand how best to use the Teach option. If you analyze the set of questions you have generated, you can determine what words you need to teach the Intelligent Assistant and how to control report output when you ask the IA to display information in column form. As mentioned previously, the IA Teach option includes two sets of lessons: basic and advanced. The lessons fit in the following categories:

- Providing synonyms for your database and its fields (basic lessons 1 and 4)
- Teaching the IA concepts related to fields (basic lessons 2 and 3; advanced lessons 1 and 2)
- Relating verbs and adjectives to the fields in your database (advanced lessons 3 and 4)
- Telling the IA what to include when you make requests for specific information rather than complete forms (basic lesson 2)

To select an option from the Basic Lessons menu or the Advanced Lessons menu, type the number or move the cursor to the selection and press Enter. Many options display help screens that explain how you can use that particular option. For many selections, the Intelligent Assistant prompts you to enter numbers, words, phrases, and abbreviations that expand the IA's vocabulary and indicate relationships between information and fields in your database.

## *Using Cursor-Movement and Editing Keys in the Lesson Screens*

Whenever you are asked to enter numbers, words, phrases, or abbreviations, use the keys in the following list to move the cursor and edit or delete entries. (Remember, if you are already familiar with WordStar, that the keys you use for editing and moving the cursor in WordStar can also be used in Q&A.)

| *Key* | *Purpose* |
|---|---|
| ↑ | Moves cursor to preceding blank |
| ↓ | Moves cursor to next blank |
| → | Moves cursor to next character |
| ← | Moves cursor to preceding character |
| Ctrl-→ | Moves cursor to next word |
| Ctrl-← | Moves cursor to preceding word |
| Tab | Moves cursor to next blank |
| Shift-Tab | Moves cursor to preceding blank |
| Home | Moves cursor to beginning of text entry |
| End | Moves cursor to end of text entry |
| Del | Deletes character at cursor location |
| Backspace | Deletes preceding character |

## Preparing the IA for Your Vocabulary

Lessons 1 and 4 on the Basic Lessons menu prepare the Intelligent Assistant for the range of requests you will enter about your database. Lesson 1, `What this database is about`, helps the IA process requests that refer to the subject of your database. Lesson 4, `Alternate field names`, prepares the IA for the alternate words and phrases you will use to refer to specific fields. The following sections explain these lessons as they relate to the sample sales lead database.

### Teaching the IA about the Database

When you select the first option on the Basic Lessons menu, the Intelligent Assistant prompts you to list all words, phrases, abbreviations, and acronyms that you may use in your requests. After you have listed all possible words and word combinations, press F10 to save the words (see fig. 18.5).

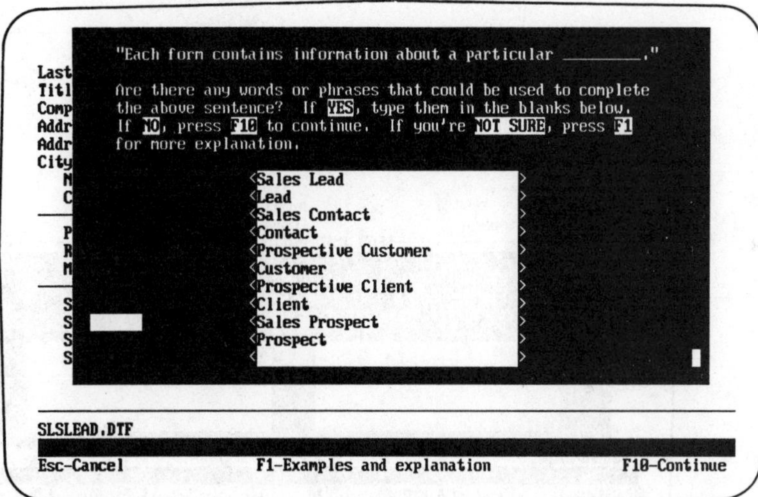


**Fig. 18.5** *Teaching the IA alternative phrases for the database.*

In the sales lead database, you probably will often use the phrase *sales lead*. For example, you may enter questions such as

> Display all sales leads for the New York office.
>
> Which sales leads are current customers?
>
> How many sales leads have annual revenue greater than $2,000,000?

IA requests probably will contain the *sales lead* phrase more often than other phrases, but you will want to use other words and phrases also. Figure 18.5 shows a list of 10 words and phrases that you could enter as alternatives to the primary phrase. For example, the IA can respond to requests such as "Which *leads* are interested in product 1500?" or "Which *sales prospects* would like product demos?" The Intelligent Assistant is able to recognize that *lead* and *sales prospect* are synonymous with *sales lead* and can then respond correctly to your requests.

If you provide many synonyms in the `What this database is about` lesson, the Intelligent Assistant can process your requests more quickly with less action from you. Generating a comprehensive list saves time and effort for you and anyone else who uses your database.

## *Entering Alternative Field Names*

You can use the fourth option in the Basic Lessons menu to teach the IA a wide range of synonyms for field names. When you select the `Alternate field names` lesson, the Intelligent Assistant displays a new screen so that you can enter up to nine alternative field names (see fig. 18.6). The alternative names can be words, phrases, or abbreviations. The original field name is shown as the first entry in the prompt box.

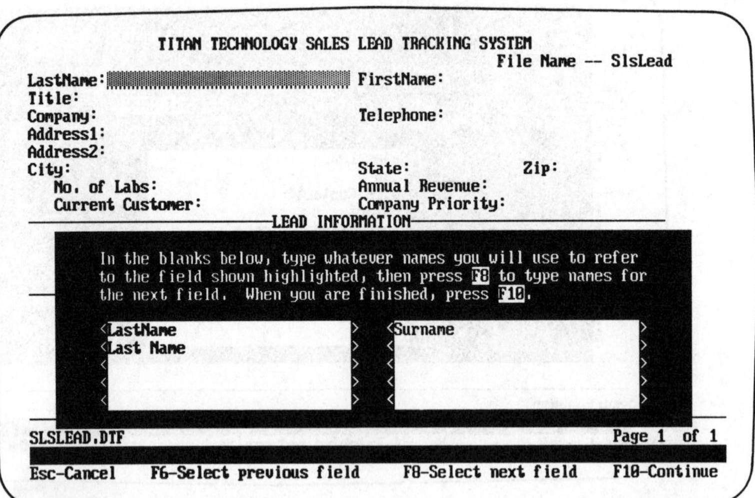


**Fig. 18.6** *Entering synonyms for field names.*

When displaying a columnar report in response to your requests, the IA uses the original field names unless you change the entry by using the `Alternate field names` option (see fig. 18.7). For example, if you want the Company field name to be displayed in capital letters, select Alternate Field names from the Basic Lessons menu, press F8 three times to move the highlight to the company field, move the cursor to the first entry in the Alternate Field names prompt, and change the entry in the prompt box to all capital letters.

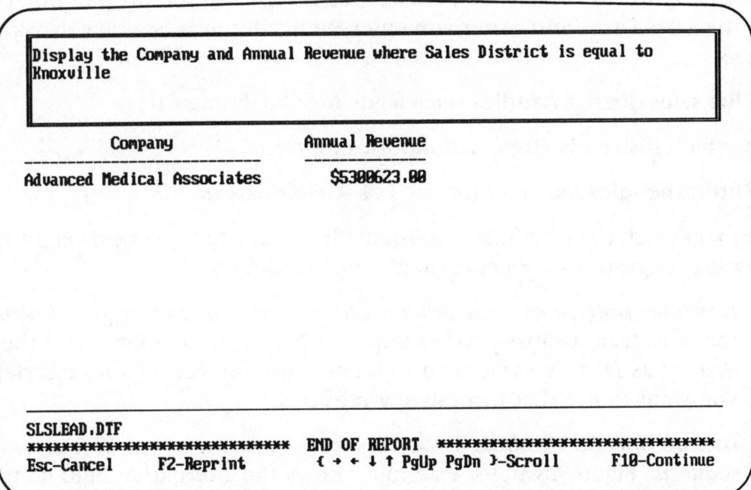


**Fig. 18.7** *The column heads supplied by database field names.*

You can provide synonyms for all fields on your form. If you want to enter synonyms for succeeding fields, press F8; for previous fields, press F6. Keep in mind, however, that Q&A does not accept the same alternative field name in different fields. For example, the sales lead database contains three field names that use the word *priority*: Company Priority, Product Priority, and Sales Priority. If you decide to enter the single word *priority* as an alternative, you can use it with only one field name. If you try to use the same synonym for more than one field, you see the prompt `Sorry. This word/phrase is already used. It must be unique.`

When you enter alternative field names, consider all the possible terms that you may use in requests. Suppose, for example, that you want to enter alternative names for the Sales Dist. field in the sales lead database. Figure 18.8 shows the alternatives entered to cover the range of requests that refer to the Sales Dist. field.

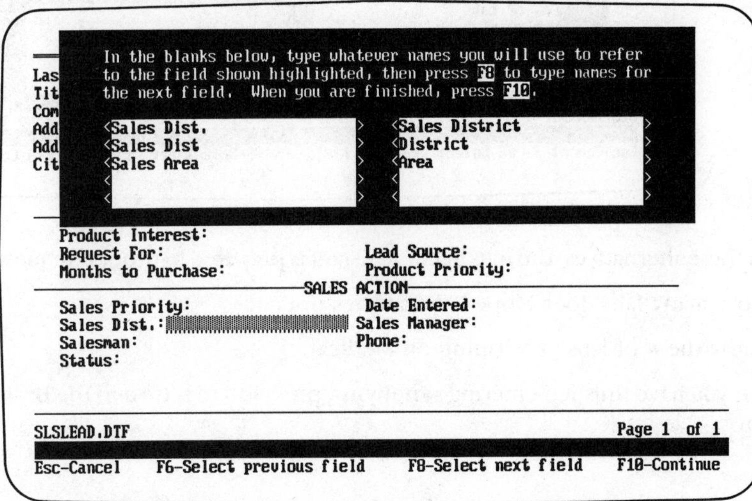


**Fig. 18.8** *Alternative field names for Sales Dist.*

Notice in figure 18.14 that each alternative is typed in the prompt box connected with the Sales Dist. field. After you enter these alternatives, you can ask questions such as

What sales district handles sales leads for Oklahoma City?

In which district is Hope Laboratories located?

Who is the sales manager for the Los Angeles area?

When you teach the Intelligent Assistant alternative field names, keep in mind the following suggestions for generating your list of names:

- *Consider both abbreviations and long forms of existing field names.* In the sales lead database, for example, the field name abbreviates the word *district* as *Dist.*, so you need to include the full form (*sales district*) if you want to use that form in any requests.
- *Include special symbols or acronyms if someone else will use these in requests.* Figure 18.9, for example, shows the alternative field names for the No. of Labs field from the Sales Lead database. Alternative names for this particular field name include the full form, the abbreviated form, and the number symbol (#).

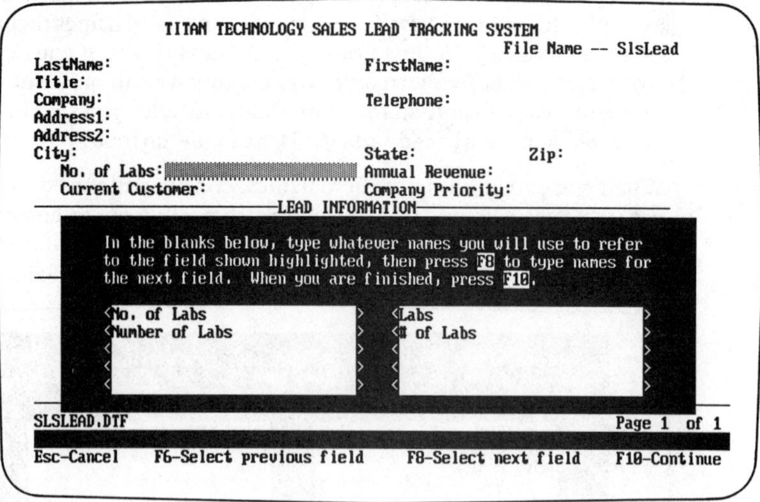


**Fig. 18.9** *Alternative field names for No. of Labs.*

With these alternatives, the Intelligent Assistant is prepared to process requests such as

How many labs does Hope Laboratories operate?

Show the # of labs at Washington Medical.

When you have finished entering synonyms, press F10 to return to the Basic Lessons menu.

## *Teaching the IA To Relate Fields to Names, Locations, and Units of Measure*

Unlike humans, whose language is built on complex relationships between information and concepts, the Intelligent Assistant needs your help to make connections between a few basic concepts and the information in your database. You take for granted the fact that a question such as "Where is Hope Laboratories?" requires an answer specifying a location. You know that "Who sold the model 1500 to Washington Medical Labs?" requires a person's name in response. And "How many months are there before . . . needs delivery on the 2400?" presupposes that you understand months as a unit of time before you can answer. The IA, however, can't process these simple requests without your assistance. Several lessons help you teach the IA about people's names (advanced lesson 1), locations (basic lesson 3), and units of measure (advanced lesson 2).

### *Identifying Name Fields*

If your database includes fields that store the names of individuals—prospective customers, current customers, clients, employees, consultants—you will probably want to make requests for these names. The sales lead database, for example, has five fields that contain either full names or parts of names. The first three fields contain parts of the full name for each sales contact; another field is the name of the district sales manager; and still another field contains the name of the salesperson who followed up on the sales lead. Before the IA can respond to a request like

Who is the lab director at Hope Laboratories?

you must teach the IA to recognize which fields in the sales lead database contain people's names. To do so, choose option 1, `What fields contain people's names`, from the Advanced Lessons menu.

When you select this option, the IA displays a prompt asking you to press F1 if any fields contain a person's name. When you press F1, the Intelligent Assistant directs you to number each field that contains a name (see fig. 18.10).

To tell the Intelligent Assistant which fields are parts of a single name and should be combined into one composite name, enter the same number in each field, followed by a single-letter code to indicate whether the field contains the last name (L), first name (F), middle name (M), or title (T). If a field contains the whole name, use W. Notice in figure 18.10 that 1L, 1F, and 1T are the codes to identify each part of the name for each sales lead. 2W identifies the whole name for the sales manager. You can program the IA to recognize up to nine separate names in each record.

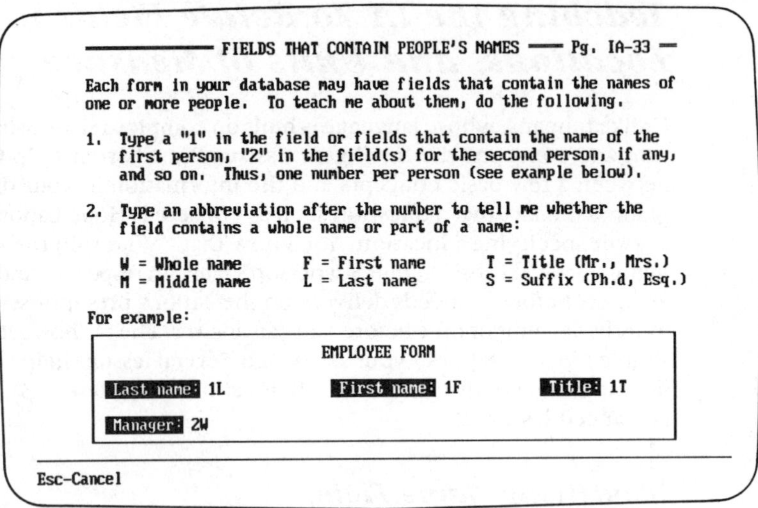
FIELDS THAT CONTAIN PEOPLE'S NAMES — Pg. IA-33 —

Each form in your database may have fields that contain the names of one or more people. To teach me about them, do the following.

1. Type a "1" in the field or fields that contain the name of the first person, "2" in the field(s) for the second person, if any, and so on. Thus, one number per person (see example below).

2. Type an abbreviation after the number to tell me whether the field contains a whole name or part of a name:

W = Whole name F = First name T = Title (Mr., Mrs.)
M = Middle name L = Last name S = Suffix (Ph.d, Esq.)

For example:

EMPLOYEE FORM

Last name: 1L First name: 1F Title: 1T

Manager: 2W

Esc-Cancel

**Fig. 18.10** *Numbering fields that refer to people's names.*

## *Specifying Location Fields*

If you have in your database fields that store address, city, or state information, you need to teach the Intelligent Assistant that these fields refer to locations. For example, to help the Intelligent Assistant process a question such as

> Where is Hope Laboratories?

use the third option from the Basic Lessons menu, `Which fields contain locations`, to identify the Address, City, State, and Zip fields as location fields. Otherwise, the IA may ask a question such as the one shown in figure 18.11. Had you identified Address1, City, State, and Zip as locations, they would appear in the report, even if you had not told the IA these fields help identify a form (see #2 from the Basic Lessons menu).

When you select the third option on the Basic Lessons menu, the Intelligent Assistant prompts you to number each field that refers to a location. You can, for example, identify in the sales lead database seven fields that refer to locations: Address1, Address2, City, State, Zip, and Sales Dist.

To identify fields that refer to locations, select number 3 from the Basic Lessons menu. The Intelligent Assistant then asks you to number each field in the order you want the items to appear in the IA's response. Figure 18.12 illustrates the numbers for each location field in the sales lead database. As you can see, the location fields have been numbered so that they will appear as displayed on the original sales lead form.

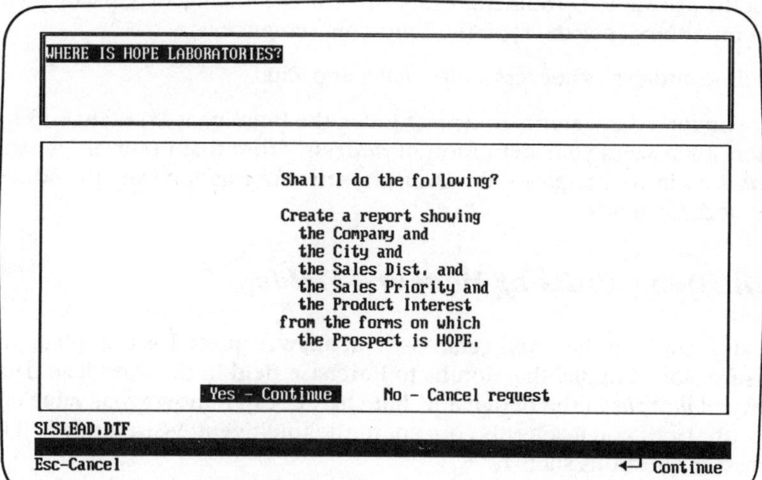

WHERE IS HOPE LABORATORIES?
Shall I do the following?
Create a report showing
the Company and
the City and
the Sales Dist. and
the Sales Priority and
the Product Interest
from the forms on which
the Prospect is HOPE.
Yes - Continue
No - Cancel request
SLSLEAD.DTF
Esc-Cancel
Continue


**Fig. 18.11**
*Before defining location fields.*

```
                 TITAN TECHNOLOGY SALES LEAD TRACKING SYSTEM
                                                   File Name -- SlsLead
LastName:                                FirstName:
Title:
Company:                                 Telephone:
Address1: 1
Address2: 2
City: 3                                  State: 4          Zip: 5
  No. of Labs:                           Annual Revenue:
  Current Customer:                      Company Priority:
                              LEAD INFORMATION
  Pro
  Req    Are there any fields on your form that contain locations,
  Mon    such as addresses, cities, or states?

  Sal    If YES, then number them in the order in which you would
  Sal    like them to appear in reports.  If NO, press F10 to
  Sal    continue.
  Sta
         If you're NOT SURE, press F1 for explanation and examples.

SLSLEAD.DTF                                                  Page 1 of 1
Esc-Cancel              F1-Examples and explanation          F10-Continue
```

**Fig. 18.12**
*Numbering location fields.*

You can limit the IA's response to complex location questions by teaching the Intelligent Assistant to interpret as one address terms or phrases from two or more fields. For example, suppose that you want to ask the question

What is Hope Laboratories' address?

Before the IA can respond correctly by displaying the address, city, state, and ZIP code, you must teach the Intelligent Assistant how to interpret the word *address*.

Select the Ask Me To Do Something option from the Intelligent Assistant menu. When the request box appears, type the following sentence:

Define address as address1, city, state, and Zip.

After you type the sentence and press Enter, the Intelligent Assistant asks for confirmation, then saves your definition of *address*. From that point on, whenever you use *address* in your requests, the IA displays the information from the Address1, City, State, and Zip fields.

### *Identifying Units of Measure Fields*

You also can help the Intelligent Assistant answer questions that relate to units of measure. For example, the Months to Purchase field in the sales lead database has the word *months* in the field name, but Q&A doesn't know what value constitutes a month. Until you teach this concept to the Intelligent Assistant, it will be unable to answer questions such as

How many months are there before Arizona Medical Services needs to purchase the 2400?

How many companies need to purchase the 2400 in 2 months?

Before the Intelligent Assistant can understand that the values entered in the Months to Purchase field are monthly units, you need to use Advanced Lesson 2, `Units of measure`, to identify the units of measure for all numeric fields.

When you select this option, the Intelligent Assistant asks you to indicate the particular unit for the highlighted field. Q&A displays a screen that explains how to specify the units of measure for the field (see fig. 18.13). In the sales lead database, for example, you can enter *months* as the unit of measure in the Months to Purchase field. If you want to change the selected field, press F8 or F6 to move the cursor. After you have identified the measurement types for the fields, press F10 to save the information.

## *Teaching the IA Adjectives and Verbs*

Initially, the Intelligent Assistant's vocabulary is smaller than a young child's. (See fig. 18.28 for a partial list of the built-in vocabulary.) You can scan the IA vocabulary at any time by pressing Shift-F6 when you are in the IA module of Q&A. The more sophisticated your sentence structure and vocabulary, the more difficulty the IA has processing your requests. In Chapter 17, you learned that the IA can process simple requests easily—if they include only words and phrases from your database or from the IA's built-in vocabulary. For example, the IA can respond to the following requests about the sales lead database:

What is Blackson's phone number?

Display forms with demo dates between 7/1/88 and 9/1/88.

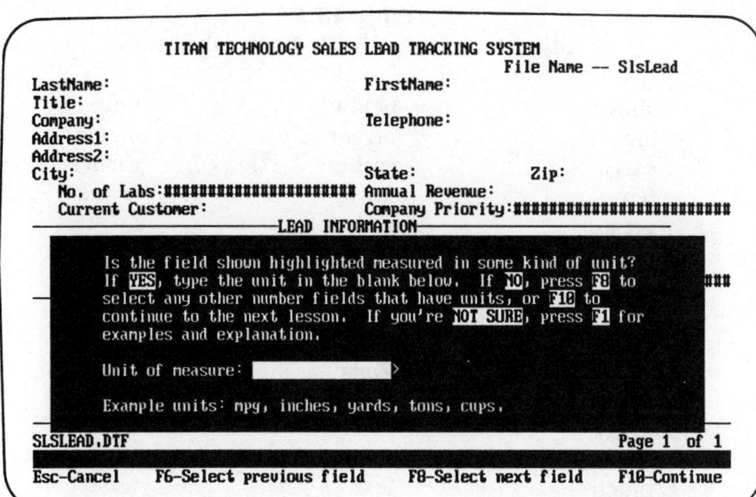


**Fig. 18.13**
*Defining units of measure.*

What company has the greatest annual revenue?

Display the Los Angeles forms.

If you analyze each request, you will find that all words come from either the field names and data in the sales lead database or from words in the IA's vocabulary. In these examples, the words taken from the built-in vocabulary include

| | |
|---|---|
| what | is |
| display | forms |
| with | between |
| and | has |
| the | greatest |

Compared to your vocabulary, the Intelligent Assistant is limited in its range of adjectives and verbs. When you use adjectives and verbs that are new to the IA, it asks for your help in relating the words to the information in your database. Advanced lessons 3 and 4 help you teach the IA how to connect the special adjectives and verbs in your requests with the information in your database.

## *Entering Special Adjectives*

Chapter 17 explains that the IA's built-in vocabulary includes adjectives used in searching and sorting operations. Therefore, the Intelligent Assistant can interpret phrases with words like greatest, highest, least, fewest, and so on (see table 18.1). If you use adjectives that refer to a degree not included in the IA's vocabulary, you need to add these words to the IA's knowledge.

**Table 18.1**
**Adjectives in the Built-In Vocabulary**

| | | |
|---|---|---|
| above | below | under |
| big | bigger | biggest |
| early | earlier | earliest |
| few | fewer | fewest |
| great | greater | greatest |
| high | higher | highest |
| large | larger | largest |
| late | later | latest |
| little | littler | littlest |
| long | longer | longest |
| low | lower | lowest |
| many | more | most |
| maximum | minimum | |
| much | less | least |
| small | smaller | smallest |
| top | bottom | |

For example, if you want to be able to ask the IA a question like "Who is the most successful sales lead?" and receive a report on which sales lead has the highest annual revenue, you must first teach the Intelligent Assistant that *successful* is an adjective referring to the Annual Revenue field. After you establish that relationship, the IA can process your request.

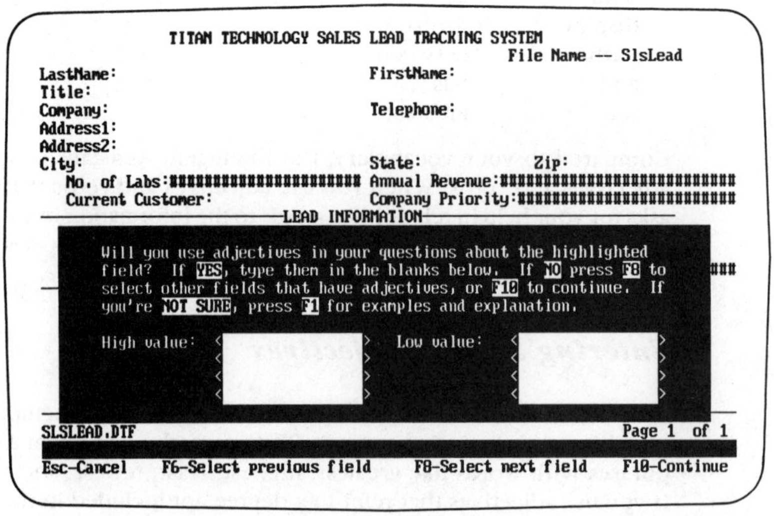

```
                    TITAN TECHNOLOGY SALES LEAD TRACKING SYSTEM
                                                 File Name -- SlsLead
LastName:                              FirstName:
Title:
Company:                               Telephone:
Address1:
Address2:
City:                                  State:          Zip:
  No. of Labs:######################## Annual Revenue:############################
  Current Customer:                    Company Priority:##########################
--------------------------LEAD INFORMATION-----------------------------------------
   Will you use adjectives in your questions about the highlighted
   field?  If YES, type them in the blanks below.  If NO press F8 to
   select other fields that have adjectives, or F10 to continue.  If
   you're NOT SURE, press F1 for examples and explanation.

   High value:  <          >        Low value:  <          >
                <          >                    <          >
                <          >                    <          >
                <          >                    <          >
SLSLEAD.DTF                                                    Page 1  of 1
Esc-Cancel    F6-Select previous field    F8-Select next field    F10-Continue
```

**Fig. 18.14**
*Entering adjectives that relate to your database.*

To teach the IA the special adjectives you plan to use in your requests, select lesson 3, `Advanced vocabulary: adjectives`, from the Advanced Lessons menu. Highlight the field to which the adjectives will relate by pressing F6 for the preceding field and F8 for the next field. When you select this lesson, the Intelligent Assistant displays a screen that explains the purpose and method for using the lesson (see fig. 18.14). Below the explanation are blanks on which you enter pairs or single adjectives to convey high or low values. For the sales lead database, for example, you can enter the following adjectives:

| *High value* | *Low value* |
|---|---|
| rich | poor |
| successful | unsuccessful |
| prosperous | struggling |
| hot | |

You can enter adjectives in one or both columns; you don't need to provide pairs of adjectives in every case. For example, you can enter the adjective *hot* so that you can use the query "Which lead is the hottest?" but you do not have to supply an opposite. You don't need to enter the "est" form of the adjective when you enter the word in the prompt box; Q&A understands that automatically.

You can enter adjectives for every field in your database. If you want to use the same adjective to refer to more than one field, however, you must enter the adjective for each field. When you use the same adjective to refer to more than one field, you have to specify the field in your requests. If you don't make the field reference clear, the IA assumes that you mean the first field that contains the adjective. For example, if you use the adjective *hot* to refer to both the Annual Revenue and Sales Priority fields, you must phrase your questions so that the IA knows to which field *hot* refers. The following queries make the relationship obvious:

Which company has the hottest annual revenue?

Which company is the hottest sales priority?

The Intelligent Assistant can respond easily to a request for the highest or lowest value in a field. If you ask the Intelligent Assistant to determine whether a range of values is high or low, however, the IA can interpret high or low values only as they relate to an average value. For example, if you ask "Which companies are prosperous?" the Intelligent Assistant interprets your request as "Which companies have above the average annual revenue?" Figure 18.15 shows how the IA confirms your request.

## *Entering Special Verbs*

The built-in vocabulary of the Intelligent Assistant contains verbs that you can use to specify operations for displaying, sorting, searching, calculating, or changing data (see table 18.2). In addition, the IA includes a number of other verbs that are used often in requests. When you enter a verb that the Intelligent Assistant does not recognize, however, the IA needs you to define the word and its relationship to the field it references.

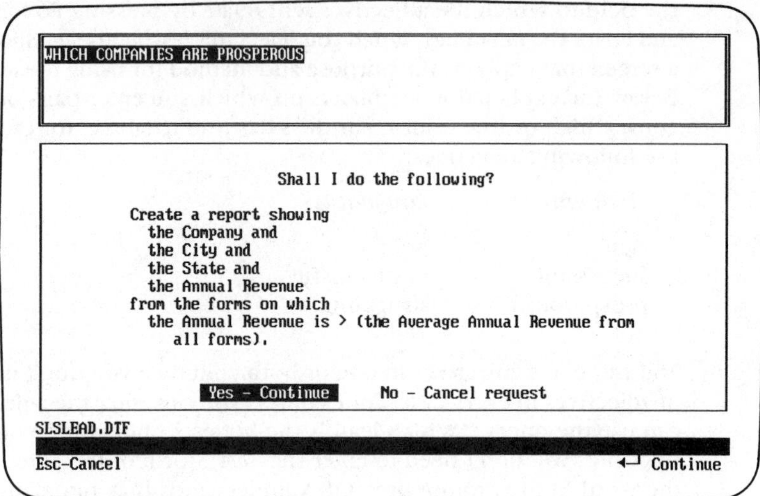

WHICH COMPANIES ARE PROSPEROUS
Shall I do the following?
Create a report showing
the Company and
the City and
the State and
the Annual Revenue
from the forms on which
the Annual Revenue is > (the Average Annual Revenue from
all forms).
Yes - Continue
No - Cancel request
SLSLEAD.DTF
Esc-Cancel
Continue


**Fig. 18.15**
*Interpreting high and low values.*

**Table 18.2**
**Verbs in the IA's Built-in Vocabulary**

| | | | | |
|---|---|---|---|---|
| add | define | find | print | set |
| blank | delete | get | remove | show |
| change | display | increase | replace | sum |
| count | divide | list | report | total |
| create | enter | make | run | |
| decrease | erase | multiply | search | |

For example, the Intelligent Assistant has trouble responding to the following questions:

How many labs does Hope Laboratories administer?

Display all companies that administer 2 or more labs.

Before the IA can process these requests, you need to use the fourth option from the Advanced Lessons menu, `Advanced vocabulary: verbs`, to define the word *administer* and show its relationship to the No. of Labs field.

When you select this lesson, the Intelligent Assistant asks you to enter the verbs you will use to refer to the fields in your database. Figure 18.16 shows that several verbs have been entered for the No. of Labs field. The Intelligent Assistant can then process questions such as

How many labs does Washington Medical Labs direct?

Does Hope Laboratories control 3 labs?

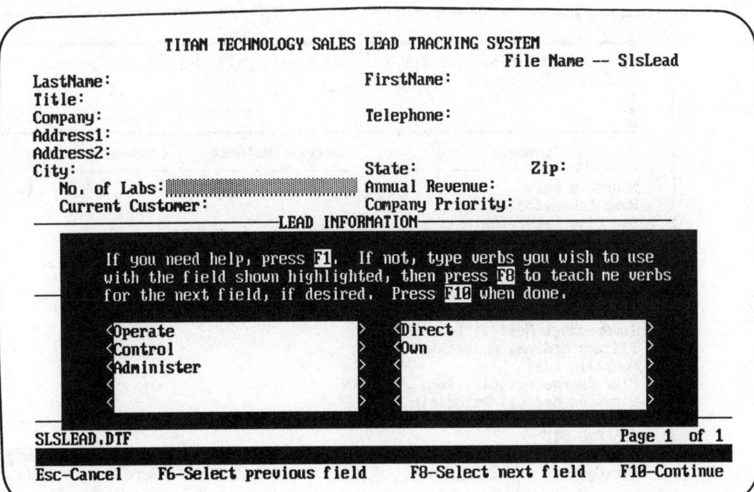
TITAN TECHNOLOGY SALES LEAD TRACKING SYSTEM
File Name -- SlsLead
LastName:
FirstName:
Title:
Company:
Telephone:
Address1:
Address2:
City:
State:
Zip:
No. of Labs:
Annual Revenue:
Current Customer:
Company Priority:
LEAD INFORMATION
If you need help, press F1. If not, type verbs you wish to use with the field shown highlighted, then press F8 to teach me verbs for the next field, if desired. Press F10 when done.
Operate
Control
Administer
Direct
Own
SLSLEAD.DTF
Page 1 of 1
Esc-Cancel
F6-Select previous field
F8-Select next field
F10-Continue

**Fig. 18.16** *Examples of verbs used in the No. of Labs field.*

Although you can enter verbs for any field in your database, you cannot enter the same verb in more than one field. Move to the field you want by pressing F8 for the next field and F6 for the preceding field. When you have finished entering verbs for the fields, press F10 to save the entries.

If you plan to use any irregular verbs (verbs that do not have regular endings such as -s, -es, -en, -ed, or -ing), you must enter all forms of the verb. For example, the verb *sell* plus its irregular past tense form *sold* must be entered in reference to the Salesman field. This entry allows you to ask the IA a question like "Who sold the 2400 to Hope Laboratories?"

## *Controlling the Display of Columnar Reports*

The Intelligent Assistant responds to your requests by displaying complete forms or by listing the results in columnar format (see fig. 18.17). When you ask the IA to "Display all forms for sales leads in the Mobile sales district," however, the IA displays each form (see fig. 18.18). On the other hand, if you ask the IA to answer "Which companies are in PA?" the IA produces a single-column list of those companies (see fig. 18.19). No other information is displayed unless you specify that the IA should include certain fields each time it displays a columnar report.

To specify which fields you want the IA to display in all columnar reports, select the second option, `Which fields identify a form`, from the Basic Lessons menu. On the screen that appears, you can specify the order of the fields in the columnar report. For example, suppose that you want the Intelligent Assistant to display the name and title of the sales lead, the company name, and the telephone number each time a columnar report is produced. To indicate that you want those fields included, number

**Fig. 18.17**
*A columnar report in the Intelligent Assistant.*

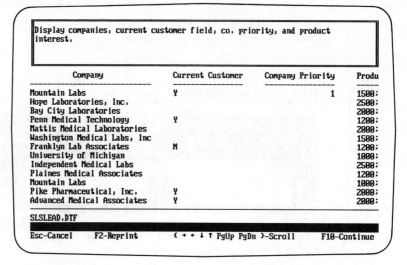

Display companies, current customer field, co. priority, and product interest.

| Company | Current Customer | Company Priority | Produ |
|---|---|---|---|
| Mountain Labs | Y | 1 | 1500; |
| Hope Laboratories, Inc. | | | 2500; |
| Bay City Laboratories | | | 2000; |
| Penn Medical Technology | Y | | 1200; |
| Mattis Medical Laboratories | | | 2000; |
| Washington Medical Labs, Inc | | | 1500; |
| Franklyn Lab Associates | N | | 1200; |
| University of Michigan | | | 1000; |
| Independent Medical Labs | | | 2500; |
| Plaines Medical Associates | | | 1200; |
| Mountain Labs | | | 1000; |
| Pike Pharmaceutical, Inc. | Y | | 2000; |
| Advanced Medical Associates | Y | | 2000; |

SLSLEAD.DTF

Esc-Cancel F2-Reprint {→ ← ↓ ↑ PgUp PgDn }-Scroll F10-Continue

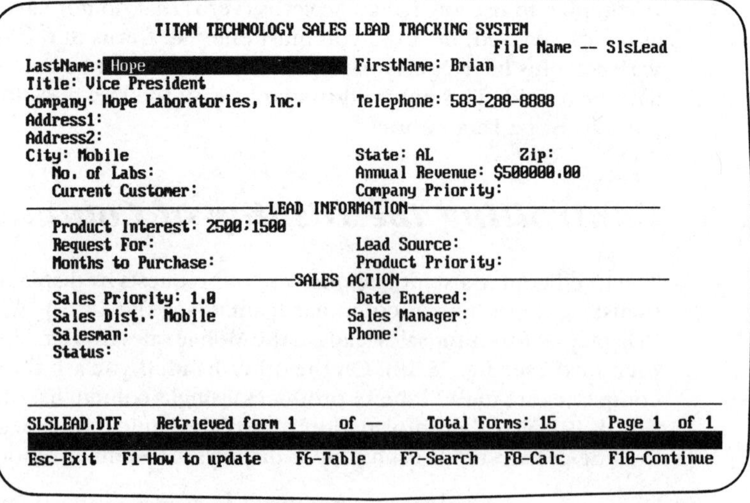
TITAN TECHNOLOGY SALES LEAD TRACKING SYSTEM
File Name -- SlsLead
LastName: Hope FirstName: Brian
Title: Vice President
Company: Hope Laboratories, Inc. Telephone: 503-288-8888
Address1:
Address2:
City: Mobile State: AL Zip:
No. of Labs: Annual Revenue: $500000.00
Current Customer: Company Priority:
LEAD INFORMATION
Product Interest: 2500;1500
Request For: Lead Source:
Months to Purchase: Product Priority:
SALES ACTION
Sales Priority: 1.0 Date Entered:
Sales Dist.: Mobile Sales Manager:
Salesman: Phone:
Status:

SLSLEAD.DTF Retrieved form 1 of — Total Forms: 15 Page 1 of 1
Esc-Exit F1-How to update F6-Table F7-Search F8-Calc F10-Continue

**Fig. 18.18**
*The IA displaying a form as a response.*

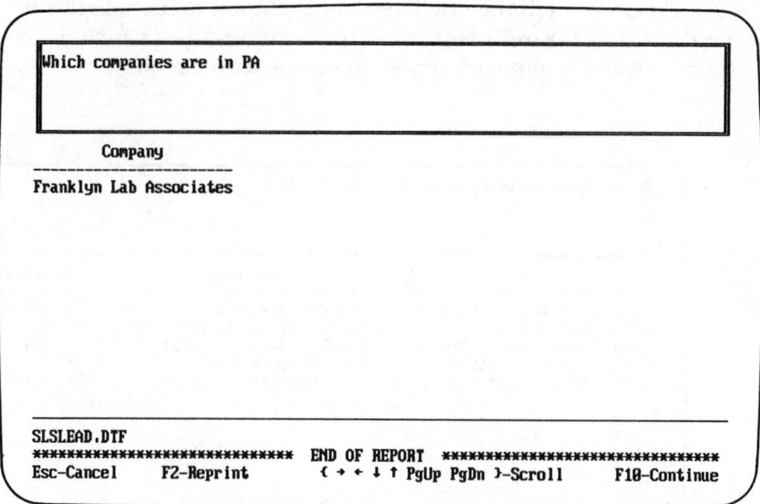


**Fig. 18.19** *The IA displaying a single column.*

the fields in the order you want them to appear. As shown in figure 18.20, for reports generated from the sales lead database, the LastName field has been numbered as 1, FirstName as 2, Title as 3, Company as 4, and Telephone as 5.

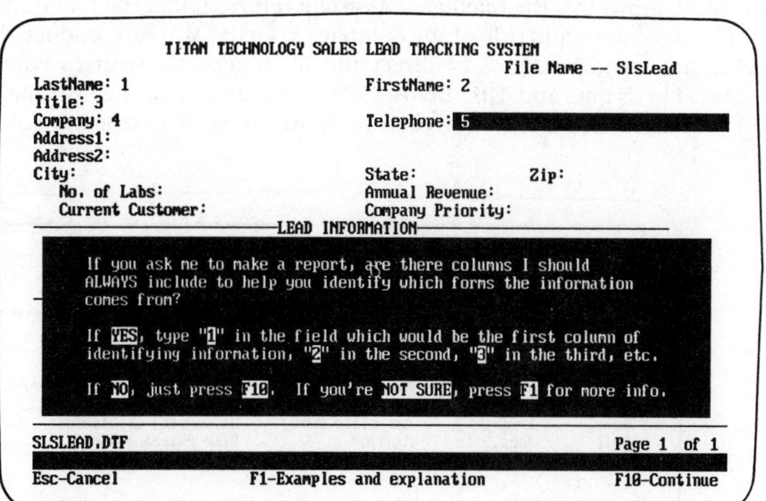


**Fig. 18.20** *Numbering the fields you want included in every report.*

To save your settings, press F10. From that point on, each time you produce a columnar report, the IA includes those fields. For example, if you later ask the IA to list all companies that have a 1.5 sales priority, the IA produces a list of companies, including the name of the contact at the company and the telephone number (see fig. 18.21). Unless you tell the Intelligent Assistant not to include this information (by using the `Which fields identify a form` option), the IA includes these fields every time it creates a summary report in response to a request.

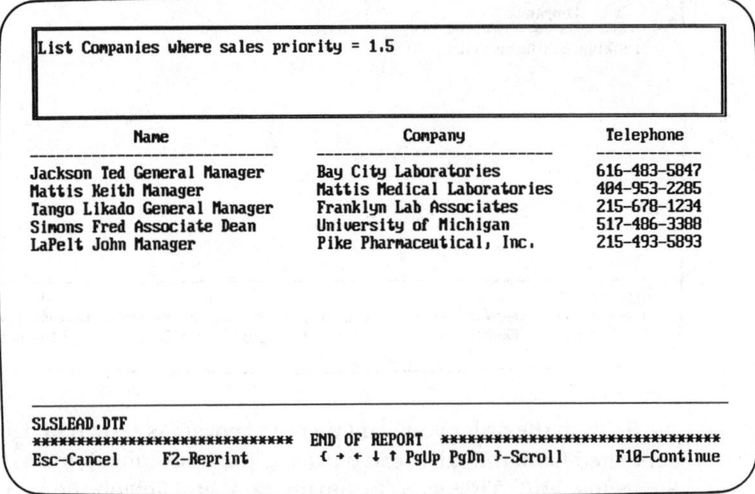

List Companies where sales priority = 1,5

| Name | Company | Telephone |
|---|---|---|
| Jackson Ted General Manager | Bay City Laboratories | 616-483-5847 |
| Mattis Keith Manager | Mattis Medical Laboratories | 404-953-2285 |
| Tango Likado General Manager | Franklyn Lab Associates | 215-678-1234 |
| Simons Fred Associate Dean | University of Michigan | 517-486-3388 |
| LaPelt John Manager | Pike Pharmaceutical, Inc. | 215-493-5893 |

SLSLEAD.DTF
****************************** END OF REPORT ******************************
Esc-Cancel F2-Reprint ← → ← ↓ ↑ PgUp PgDn →-Scroll F10-Continue

**Fig. 18.21** *All columns specified in lesson 1 are displayed in reports.*

Figure 18.21 shows that the Intelligent Assistant returns under the Name column the last name, first name, and title of the company contact. You can produce this result by using Advanced Lesson 1 to direct the Intelligent Assistant to combine the LastName, FirstName, and Title fields. If these fields had not been combined, the report would be displayed with each of those fields as a separate column (see fig. 18.22).

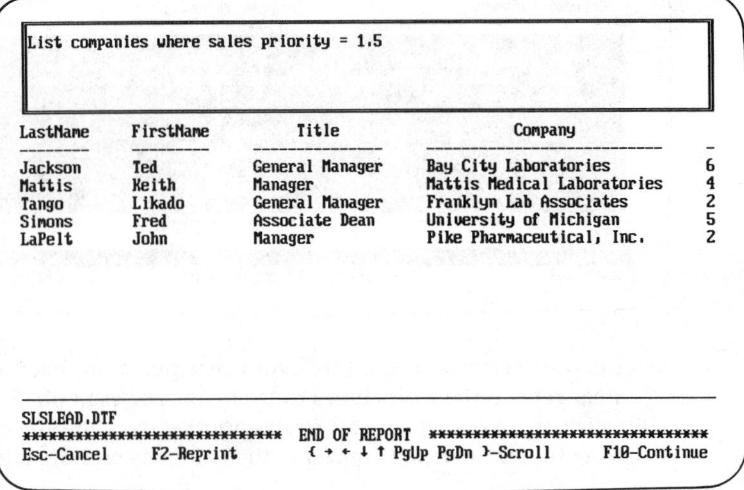

List companies where sales priority = 1.5

| LastName | FirstName | Title | Company | - |
|---|---|---|---|---|
| Jackson | Ted | General Manager | Bay City Laboratories | 6 |
| Mattis | Keith | Manager | Mattis Medical Laboratories | 4 |
| Tango | Likado | General Manager | Franklyn Lab Associates | 2 |
| Simons | Fred | Associate Dean | University of Michigan | 5 |
| LaPelt | John | Manager | Pike Pharmaceutical, Inc. | 2 |

SLSLEAD.DTF
****************************** END OF REPORT ******************************
Esc-Cancel F2-Reprint ← → ← ↓ ↑ PgUp PgDn →-Scroll F10-Continue

**Fig. 18.22** *Each field listed in a column.*

## Displaying Additional Columns

You can add columns to summary reports—without changing the information—through Basic Lesson 2. Suppose, for example, that you decide to display the sales district in addition to the name, company, and telephone number. You can enter the request

List all 1.5 sales priorities and display sales districts.

The Intelligent Assistant understands from this request that you want an additional column displayed in the report. Figure 18.23 shows that the IA asks for confirmation before proceeding with the request.

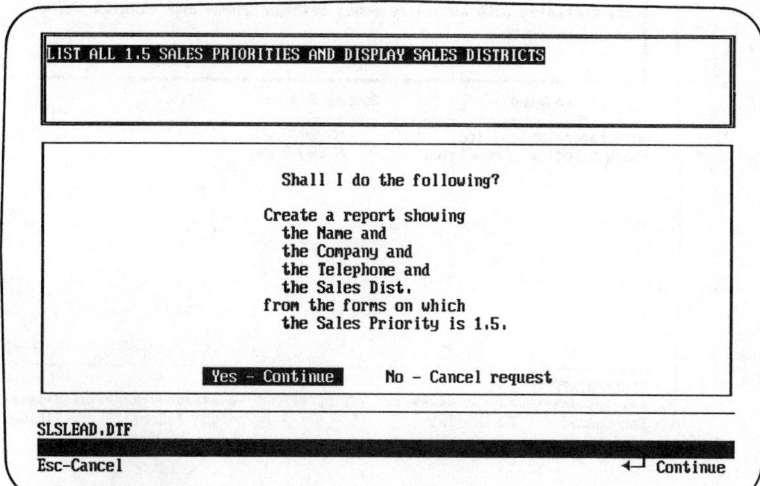
LIST ALL 1.5 SALES PRIORITIES AND DISPLAY SALES DISTRICTS
Shall I do the following?
Create a report showing
the Name and
the Company and
the Telephone and
the Sales Dist.
from the forms on which
the Sales Priority is 1.5.
Yes - Continue
No - Cancel request
SLSLEAD.DTF
Esc-Cancel
Continue

**Fig. 18.23** *The IA asking for confirmation of fields.*

## Restricting Columns

The Intelligent Assistant can "hide" columns of information that you don't want to appear in a summary report. To suppress the column display, you simply add one of three acronyms at the end of your request. The acronyms used to hide columns are listed in table 18.3.

**Table 18.3**
**Suppressing Columns of Information in IA Reports**

| *Acronym* | *Meaning* | *Purpose* |
|---|---|---|
| WNIC | With No Identification Columns | Suppress columns listed in Basic Lesson 2 |
| WNRC | With No Restriction Columns | Suppress restriction columns |
| WNEC | With No Extra Columns | Suppress extra columns |

You can suppress the display of the columns you specified in Basic Lesson 2 (`Which fields identify a form`) so that only the columns affected by your request are displayed. For example, if you want the Intelligent Assistant to display only Company and Annual Revenue columns when you request a report of all companies with annual revenue between $500,000 and $1,000,000, you can enter the following request:

List companies with annual revenues between 500000 and 1000000. WNIC

The IA asks for confirmation that you want only companies and revenues displayed. Figure 18.24 shows the Intelligent Assistant's response to your request.

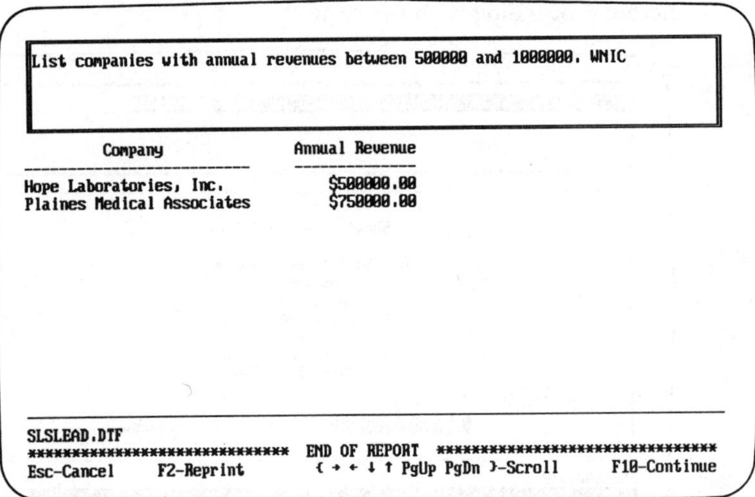


**Fig. 18.24** *Using WNIC in a request.*

The IA has assumed that you want the revenues for each company displayed. The column that shows the revenues, called the restrict column, is the column that defines the limits of your request. If the information in the restrict column is confidential, you can suppress it by entering WNRC (with no restriction columns) at the end of your request. For example,

List companies with annual revenues between 500000 and 1000000. WNRC

The result of this request, shown in figure 18.25, includes all columns of information originally set in lesson 2. The Annual Revenue field, however, is not included.

Using the acronym WNEC (with no extra columns), you can tell the Intelligent Assistant to display only the columns you specify in your request. For example, you can have the IA display only the companies that have an income between $500,000 and $1,000,000 by entering

List companies with annual revenues between 500000 and 1000000. WNEC

The results of this request appear in figure 18.26.

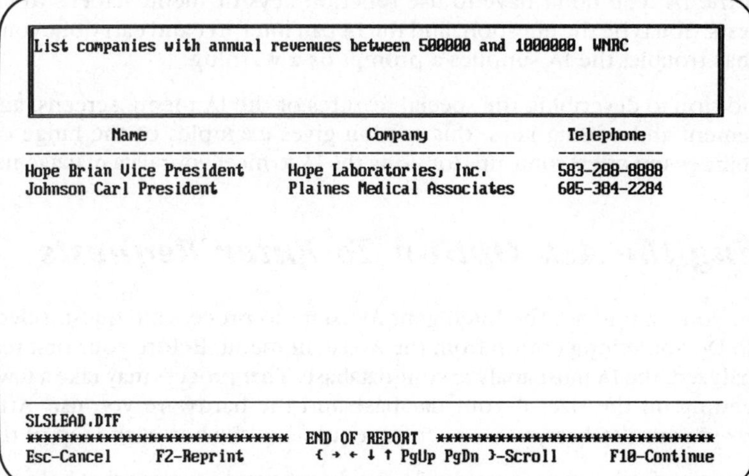

```
List companies with annual revenues between 500000 and 1000000. WNRC

          Name                     Company                    Telephone
--------------------------   ----------------------------   ------------
Hope Brian Vice President    Hope Laboratories, Inc.         503-288-8888
Johnson Carl President       Plaines Medical Associates      605-304-2204

SLSLEAD.DTF
****************************** END OF REPORT ******************************
Esc-Cancel      F2-Reprint      ← → ← ↓ ↑ PgUp PgDn →-Scroll      F10-Continue
```

**Fig. 18.25** *Omitting the restriction column with WNRC.*

```
List companies with annual revenues between 500000 and 1000000. WNEC

          Company
----------------------------
Hope Laboratories, Inc.
Plaines Medical Associates

SLSLEAD.DTF
****************************** END OF REPORT ******************************
Esc-Cancel      F2-Reprint      ← → ← ↓ ↑ PgUp PgDn →-Scroll      F10-Continue
```

**Fig. 18.26** *Using WNEC to display only requested columns.*

# Entering Requests to the Intelligent Assistant

After you enhance the knowledge of the Intelligent Assistant by going through the lessons in the Basic Lessons and Advanced Lessons menus, the IA should be able to respond to most of your requests. And you will find that the IA is much easier to use than File or Report for querying, adding, changing, or reporting information.

With the IA, you don't have to use function keys or menu screens to enter your requests. You type the question, and the IA can interpret and carry out your request. If it has trouble, the IA supplies a prompt or a warning.

In addition to describing the special features of the IA menu, screens, and cursor-movement and editing keys, this section gives examples of the range of the IA's capabilities and offers some tips for using the IA to meet your data management needs.

## *Using the Ask Option To Enter Requests*

When you want to ask the Intelligent Assistant to process a request, select the Ask Me To Do Something option from the Assistant menu. Before your first request can be analyzed, the IA must analyze your database. That process may take a few minutes, depending on the size of your database and the hardware you use. After IA has analyzed your database, you can enter requests in the box at the top of the screen.

The center of the screen is reserved for messages and prompts that help you use the Intelligent Assistant. The bottom of the screen shows the file name of your database and lists explanations of the special keys.

## *Keys Used for Entering Requests*

Many of the editing keys available in Write can be used with the Intelligent Assistant. If you're familiar with the keys used to move the cursor and edit text, you'll find that entering, deleting, and changing information in the request box is easy. (For more information on the keys used in Write, see Chapters 9 and 10.)

Similar to Write, the IA allows you to use Overwrite or Insert mode for entering characters. You also can use the WordStar key combinations for moving the cursor and editing text. You can use the following keys in the IA to move the cursor:

| *Key* | *Moves the cursor* |
|---|---|
| → or Ctrl-D | One character to the right |
| ← or Ctrl-S | One character to the left |
| ↑ or Ctrl-E | Up one line |
| ↓ or Ctrl-X | Down one line |
| Home | To the beginning of the line |
| End | To the end of the line |
| Ctrl-→ or Ctrl-F | One word right |
| Ctrl-← or Ctrl-A | One word left |

Use the following keys to delete characters, words, or lines:

| *Key* | *Deletes* |
|---|---|
| Del | Character at cursor position |
| Backspace | One character to the left |
| Ctrl-G | Character at cursor position |
| F4 | Word to the right |
| Ctrl-Y | Line at cursor position |

The Intelligent Assistant screens display the special uses of keys when you are entering and processing requests. When you are entering requests, for example, the special keys include Esc, F1, F6, F8, and Enter. If you press Esc after entering all or part of a request, you are returned immediately to the Assistant menu. Use F1 when you need to display a help screen about entering a prompt. F6 shows a menu that displays the different portions of the Intelligent Assistant's vocabulary. A menu of options for teaching the IA information about your database is displayed when you press F8. Pressing Enter tells the Intelligent Assistant to begin processing your request.

## Tips for Entering Requests

As you know, you can use the Intelligent Assistant to search, sort, change, add, and calculate data. The IA also can create new forms, produce reports, and delete existing forms. The IA can even respond to requests regarding the date and time and can operate as a calculator for simple equations. This section lists tips for using the Intelligent Assistant to your best advantage.

*When you ask the IA to change information in a text field, enclose the new entry in quotation marks.* Suppose that you want to change the value in the Sales Manager field for all Atlanta sales leads. You enter the request

Change sales manager to "Jim Stevens" in all forms where sales district = Atlanta.

Only text fields require that the new information be enclosed in quotation marks; you can specify number, date, and time fields in the usual way. For example, in the request "Change the sales priority to 1.0 for the University of Michigan," the numeric value needs no quotation marks.

*Save yourself time and keystrokes by using follow-up questions.* Instead of typing a new request every time you query the Intelligent Assistant, you can use phrases that refer to a previous request. If you last requested the IA to list all 1.5 sales priorities, your next request can be "Change these to 2.0 sales priorities."

*Use math symbols to simplify your requests.* Although you probably will want to use English phrases in most of your requests, you can use math symbols to reduce your typing time and help the IA process faster. For example, compare the different versions of these two requests:

> Display annual revenues that are greater than $3,000,000.
> Annual revenue > $3,000,000.

> Display sales leads entered between 4/15/88 and 7/1/88.
> Display leads for date entered >4/15/88 and <7/1/88.

The shorter versions not only include math symbols but also have been written with as few words as possible. The shorter your request, the quicker the IA can respond.

*Use the word "define" in the request box to teach the IA new synonyms.* In addition to teaching the IA new words by using the Teach option, you can enter synonyms with requests such as

> Define address as company, address1, city, state, and Zip.

After you enter this request, the Intelligent Assistant displays the Company, Address1, City, State, and Zip fields whenever you ask for *address*.

*To have the IA display a yes/no field in a columnar report, include the word "field" in your request.* For example, the Current Customer field in the sales lead database is a yes/no field. To ask the IA to display leads from Philadelphia and to indicate whether they are current customers, you type

> Show sales leads from the Philadelphia sales district and the current customers field.

After processing this request, the Intelligent Assistant responds with the report shown in figure 18.27.

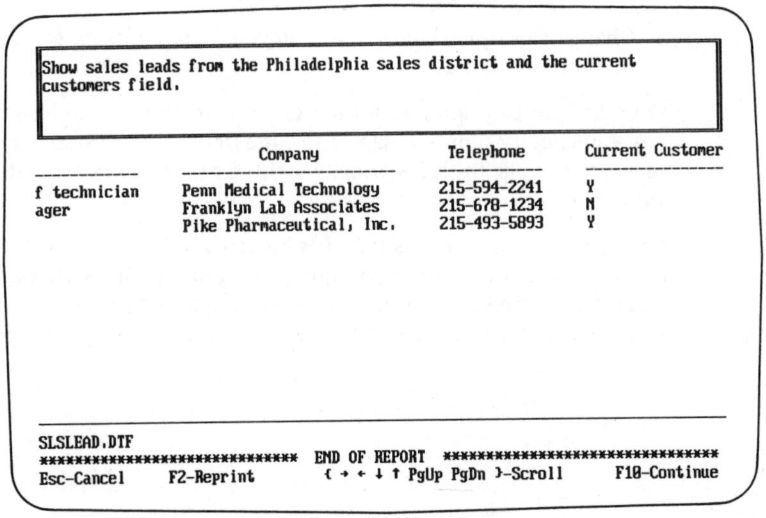

**Fig. 18.27**
*Displaying yes/no fields.*

```
Show sales leads from the Philadelphia sales district and the current
customers field.

                    Company                    Telephone      Current Customer
-------------  ------------------------------  ------------   ----------------
f technician   Penn Medical Technology         215-594-2241   Y
ager           Franklyn Lab Associates         215-678-1234   N
               Pike Pharmaceutical, Inc.       215-493-5893   Y

SLSLEAD.DTF
******************************** END OF REPORT **********************************
Esc-Cancel     F2-Reprint       ← → ← ↓ ↑ PgUp PgDn }-Scroll       F10-Continue
```

# Updating the IA's Knowledge of Your Database

As you enter requests to the IA, you will probably need to add to the information you originally specified with the Teach option. Instead of returning to the Teach option, however, you can add to the IA's vocabulary and help the IA process requests while you're working with the Ask option on the request screen. By pressing F1, you can display a help screen that lists the function keys available for reviewing and adding vocabulary.

The Intelligent Assistant provides two options for updating information. First, you can use the F6 and F8 function keys when entering a request. Second, you can update the IA when it is unable to process a request because of an unknown or ambiguous term.

## Checking and Changing Vocabulary

If you begin to enter a request in the request box and suspect that the IA will have difficulty processing a word or phrase, press the F6 function key. When you press F6, the IA displays a menu of options for checking the built-in vocabulary, adding synonyms to field names, and adding synonyms that you have created by using the word *define.*

Selecting Built-in Words displays a list of the IA's vocabulary. Scroll through the list by pressing PgDn (see fig. 18.28). When you choose Field Names, the IA displays a series of screens in which you can enter the synonyms. For example, if you want to add the synonym ***home office*** to the Sales Dist. field, you can do so at this point. Choosing the third option, Synonyms, displays a list of the synonyms that you have created with the word *define.*

```
                         BUILT-IN VOCABULARY

A             AT         COLUMN      DIVIDE       FEW        HELP         LARGE
ABOUT         AUGUST     COMMENCING  DURING       FIELD      HER          LAST
ABOVE         AVERAGE    CONCERN     EACH         FILE       HIGH         LATE
ACCORDING     AWAY       CONSTRAINT  EARLY        FILL       HIM          LEAST
ADD           BE         CONTAIN     EITHER       FIND       HIS          LESS
AFTER         BEFORE     COUNT       EMPTY        FIRST      HOUR         LET
AGAIN         BEGIN      CREATE      END          FOLLOWING  HOW          LIST
ALL           BELOW      DATE        ENTER        FOR        I            LITTLE
ALONG         BEST       DAY         ENTRY        FORM       IF           LOOK
ALPHA         BETTER     DECEMBER    EQUAL        FOUND      IN           LOW
ALPHABETICAL  BETWEEN    DECREASE    ERASE        FROM       INCLUDE      MAKE
AN            BIG        DEFINE      EVERY        GET        INCLUSIVELY  MANY
AND           BLANK      DEFINITION  EXCEED       GIVE       INCREASE     MARCH
ANY           BOTTOM     DELETE      EXCLUDE      GOOD       IT           MATCH
ANYONE        BUT        DESCENDING  EXCLUSIVELY  GREAT      JANUARY      MAXIMUM
APRIL         BY         DETAIL      F            HALF       JULY         MEAN
AS            CALCULATE  DIFFERENCE  FALSE        HAVE       JUNE         MINIMUM
ASCENDING     CHANGE     DISPLAY     FEBRUARY     HE         KNOW         MINUS

SLSLEAD.DTF

Esc-Cancel                   PgDn-View More Definitions
```

**Fig. 18.28** ***The Intelligent Assistant's built-in vocabulary.***

## Using the F8 Key To Add Information

When you enter a request, press F8 if you want to change or add to information you entered with the Teach option. When you press F8, a menu displays, showing options for changing or adding synonyms or preparing the IA for verbs you are using in your request (see fig. 18.29).

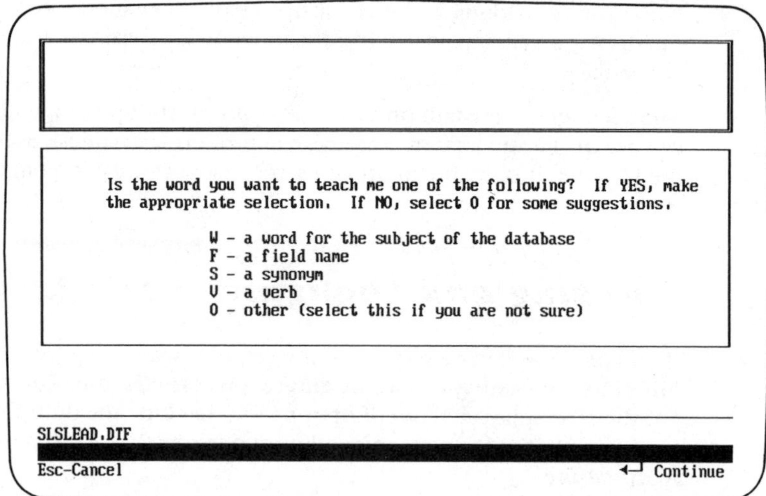

Is the word you want to teach me one of the following? If YES, make the appropriate selection. If NO, select O for some suggestions.
W - a word for the subject of the database
F - a field name
S - a synonym
V - a verb
O - other (select this if you are not sure)
SLSLEAD.DTF
Esc-Cancel
Continue


**Fig. 18.29**
*The menu for changing or adding synonyms or teaching verbs.*

## Helping the IA Interpret a Word

Whenever the Intelligent Assistant has problems with a word in your request, the IA pauses and displays a menu that gives you a chance to add to or change vocabulary. Suppose, for example, that in a request you use the phrase *home office* to refer to the Sales Dist. field in the sales lead database. If you do not prepare the IA for that phrase, the IA indicates that it is having trouble processing one or both of the words (see fig. 18.30).

If you choose the second option on this menu, `Teach me a new word`, the IA displays another menu from which you can add synonyms or verbs.

# Automating the IA with Macros

Similar to the macro capability available in other business applications programs, Q&A's macro capability allows you to automate your frequently used operations. With macros, you can record a sequence of keystrokes required for any program function

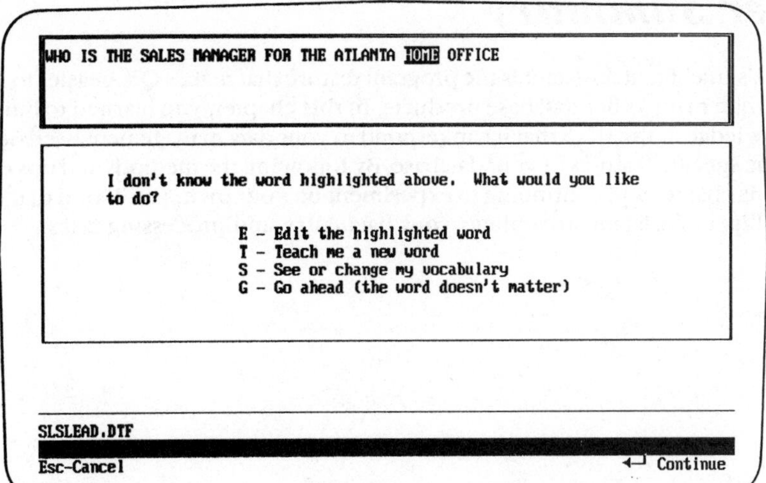


**Fig. 18.30** *The warning displayed when the IA has trouble processing a word.*

and play back those keystrokes by pressing one or two keys. If you often enter the same request when you use the Intelligent Assistant, you can save yourself time and effort by automating the operation with a Q&A macro.

Suppose that you enter the same request every week, asking the Intelligent Assistant to create a report of weekly sales. To automate the process, you can create a macro to make the request for you. Creating a macro for automating requests entered in the Intelligent Assistant involves six steps:

1. Select the screen in which you want the macro to begin. For example, if you want the macro to begin running at the Q&A Main menu, display that screen.

2. Press Shift-F2 to access Q&A's Macro menu.

3. Select the Define Macro option.

4. Press the keys that make up the operation you want to automate.

5. When you are finished entering keystrokes, press Shift-F2 to turn off Macro Record mode.

6. To save the macro for future use, enter a file name, or press Enter to accept the displayed file name.

You can test your macro by moving back to the screen where you defined the macro and pressing the key you supplied as the macro name. For more information on Q&A's macro capability, see Chapter 19, "Creating and Using Macros."

## *Chapter Summary*

Q&A's Intelligent Assistant is the program feature that makes Q&A easier to learn and use than many other database products. In this chapter, you learned to build on the knowledge of the IA so that it can respond to your data management needs according to the specific features of your database. By following the methods and tips explained in this chapter and continuing to experiment on your own, you'll find that using the Intelligent Assistant streamlines your data entry and processing tasks.

## Part VI

# Advanced Q&A Applications

Includes

Creating and Using Q&A Macros

Importing and Exporting Data in Q&A

Networking—Using Q&A in a Multi-User Environment

Chapter 19

# Creating and Using Q&A Macros

Many business applications programs on the market include macro capabilities. When first introduced in early versions of 1-2-3, macro capability was thought to be only for advanced users. Q&A, however, like many recent programs, provides macro capabilities even beginners can use.

This chapter introduces you to Q&A macros and describes how to create and use macros to save time when you use File, Write, Report, and the Intelligent Assistant.

## What Are Macros?

Q&A macros are special programs that store series of commands or text entries that "play back" with one keystroke. You can use macros in any Q&A module—File, Write, Report, and the Intelligent Assistant—to duplicate command sequences and data entry procedures that are repeated frequently. If, for example, you often use the same temporary margin or tab settings while working in Write, you can create a macro to enter these settings automatically.

Once you begin using macros, you will discover how much time they save. Q&A macros can save you from having to look up special printer codes for print enhancements; you can store codes and play the macro any time you need to enter them. You also can create macros to save a text file, enter special print settings, and automatically print the file. Macros are ideal for inserting frequently used paragraphs, sentences, or phrases in your documents. Macros also can reassign the keys on your keyboard.

# *The Basics of Creating Macros*

Two methods are available to create Q&A macros. First, you can have Q&A automatically record a series of keystrokes as you enter them. To use the recording method, direct Q&A to store your keystrokes as a macro program. Q&A does all the work; all you do is tell Q&A when to begin recording keystrokes, when to stop, and what name to assign the recorded keystrokes. Second, you can create macros by typing each one. To use the interactive method, you must open a text file and type the special commands that represent each keystroke and indicate where the macro begins and ends.

You may want to use the interactive method when trying out a new macro because this method allows you to see the definition as you enter the command sequence. You also will use the interactive method when editing a macro created with the recording method (see the ''Editing Macros'' section of this chapter).

In most cases, however, a macro is easier to create with the recording method. When you record a macro, you don't have to leave the current document, and all Q&A's normal keystrokes are available for defining the macro. When you have completed the sequence, turn off the recording feature; no programming is involved.

## *Defining Macros in Record Mode*

Recording macros is easy with Q&A. You press Shift-F2, select Define Macro from the menu, type the key sequence and finish the definition by pressing Shift-F2 again. When you press Shift-F2 initially, a Macro menu appears; and you can choose to define new macros, get existing macros, save macros you created, or clear all macros from memory. If you want to exit the Macro menu without making a selection, press the Esc key.

To define a macro, press D. You are then prompted to type the letter that will become the macro's name. Also called the identifier key, the macro's name can be one key or a combination of keys. Entering the identifier key executes the command sequence you specified.

### *Naming a Macro*

When you name a macro, use Shift, Ctrl, or Alt with the key you assign as the name. For example, suppose that you want to create a macro which moves the cursor from any position on the form to the Company field. If you assign a letter to the macro, the macro will be executed each time you type that letter.

To avoid this problem, use Shift, Ctrl, or Alt with the letter. Then, if you use an Alt-A combination, the macro is executed only when you press both keys. Remember Shift, Ctrl, and Alt cannot be used alone to name a macro.

By combining Ctrl or Alt with a letter, you can choose from more than 80 possible macro names. Table 19.1 lists the keys and combinations already used by Q&A for Write, File, Report, and Intelligent Assistant operations. When you define macros, use names other than those listed in the table unless you want to override Q&A. If, for example, you named a macro Ctrl-F for use within the Write module, you would disable Write's regular use of Ctrl-F for moving the cursor from one word to the next.

**Table 19.1**
**Key Combinations Used by Q&A**
**(Not available for macro names)**

| | | | | |
|---|---|---|---|---|
| Ctrl-A | Ctrl-Bksp | F1 | Shift-F1 | Del |
| Ctrl-C | Ctrl-PrtSc | F2 | Shift-F2 | End |
| Ctrl-D | Ctrl-F2 | F3 | Shift-F3 | Home |
| Ctrl-E | Ctrl-F5 | F4 | Shift-F4 | Ins |
| Ctrl-F | Ctrl-F6 | F5 | Shift-F5 | PgDn |
| Ctrl-G | Ctrl-F7 | F6 | Shift-F6 | PgUp |
| Ctrl-H | Ctrl-F8 | F7 | Shift-F7 | ↓ |
| Ctrl-I | Ctrl-[ | F8 | Shift-F8 | ← |
| Ctrl-M | Ctrl-Home | F9 | Shift-F9 | → |
| Ctrl-R | Ctrl-PgDn | F10 | Shift-F10 | ↑ |
| Ctrl-S | Ctrl-PgUp | | Shift-Bksp | Bksp |
| Ctrl-T | Alt-F2 | | Shift-Esc | Esc |
| Ctrl-V | Alt-F5 | | Shift-Enter | Enter |
| Ctrl-W | Alt-F8 | | Shift-Tab | Tab |
| Ctrl-Y | Alt-F9 | | | |
| Ctrl-Z | | | | |

If you try to define the same key twice or enter a name already used by Q&A, an error message is displayed at the bottom of the Q&A Main menu. Selecting Y in response to the prompt asking whether you want to redefine the key enables you to use that key combination.

## *Using Autostart Macros*

By naming a macro one of the combinations Alt-0 through Alt-9, you make it an autostart macro which executes when Q&A is booted. For example, Q&A executes a macro named Alt-4 when you type (from DOS)

QA-M4

When naming autostart macros, remember 0 through 9 must be typed on the keyboard. The numeric keypad cannot be used to name autostart macros.

### *Recording the Command Sequence*

After you have indicated the key you want to define, a flashing square cursor appears in the lower right corner of the screen. On color monitors, the square flashes alternately red and yellow. This cursor indicates that everything you type is being recorded as part of the new macro.

A macro can contain a pause so that you can enter information. Suppose that you are creating a macro to load a database. You can have the macro make necessary menu selections and then pause so that you can enter the file name. When you press Enter, the macro continues executing.

To insert a pause in the macro, press Alt-F2 and type the keystrokes that will not be included. To resume recording the macro, press Alt-F2 again. When executed, the macro will pause until you press Enter to complete execution.

When you have finished recording the macro, press Shift-F2 again. A message appears, asking whether you want to save your macro now.

### *Playing Back and Changing Recorded Macros*

As soon as you have recorded a macro, you can play it back by pressing the identifier key combination—Alt-A. If the macro doesn't work properly, press Esc to stop execution.

To redefine the macro, press Shift-F2 and select Define Macro from the Macro menu. Press the same identifier keys, and Q&A will tell you the keys are already defined. Choose to redefine the key and attach a revised or new macro to the identifier. Press Shift-F2 again when you have recorded the keystrokes.

### *Saving Recorded Macros*

When you create a recorded macro, you can choose to use the macro only for the current work session or to save the macro for later use. If you use a macro to perform a calculation on a field for a one-time application, you won't need to save it. If you create a macro to perform a recurring function, such as inserting a heading on personal letters, you need to save the macro to disk. Macros created with the recording method are stored in RAM.

To save macros, press Shift-F2 and select S from the Macro menu. Enter a macro file name in answer to the prompt (see fig. 19.1). You can use any name that follows DOS conventions—up to eight characters with an optional three-character extension. The default name, QAMACRO.ASC, is used only if you load QAMACRO.ASC first; otherwise, the new macro will overwrite the old file.

To edit macros later, you can access the macro file from the Write module. Procedures for importing a macro file to Write are included in this chapter under ''Editing Macros.''

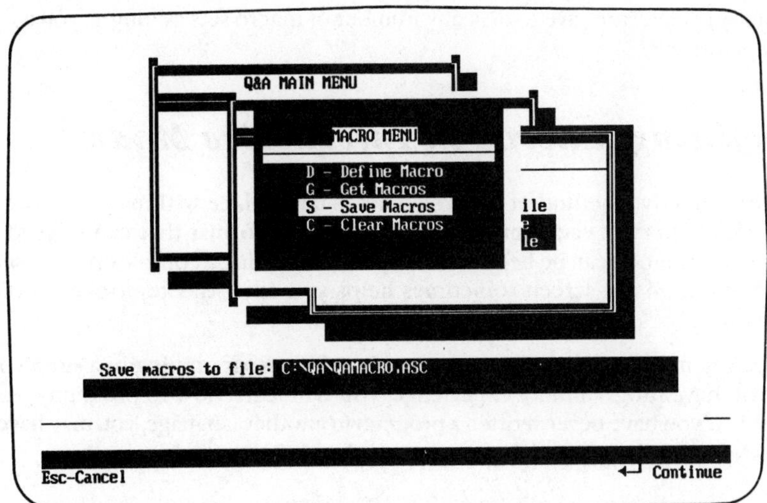


**Fig. 19.1** *Saving the macro file.*

Don't save new macros to a macro file until the file has been loaded in RAM. Suppose that you have already saved several macros in a file and want to save a macro you have just created. If the macro file isn't loaded in RAM and you save the new macro using the same file name, the old file will be replaced by the new file. To save your macros without losing any valuable information,

- Load the file into memory before you record any macros.
- Resave the file after you add new macros.
- Make backups of macro files with different names (Q&A does not make automatic backups).
- Save macro files with names that are easy to identify (with an ASC or MAC extension, for example).

## *Clearing Recorded Macros from Memory*

After you have saved the macros to disk, you can choose Clear from the Macro menu to remove all macros from RAM. This command does not affect macros that have been saved to disk.

The Clear command returns all your macro keys and key combinations to their original functions. Don't press Y until you know which macros will be deleted, because no warning is displayed before macros are erased.

Clearing macros from RAM permits you to work on another set of macros or return the keyboard to its normal state. This capability is useful if you have defined a set of macros for a single application or database and want to use another database or define new macros.

You can create and save to disk any number of macro sets as long as you use different file names.

## *Defining Macros in Interactive Mode*

The interactive method of creating macros takes place within Q&A Write. To write macros, you type each command sequence in a format that can be read by Q&A. Interactive mode can be helpful when you are creating a complex macro; seeing each command on the screen sometimes helps you enter the keystrokes in the correct sequence.

Creating macros in the interactive mode is like programming in a simple language. If you have programming experience, you will learn how to program Q&A macros easily. If you have never written a program in another language, you may have to spend a little extra time grasping the concept, but it is relatively simple.

### *Writing a Macro*

Unlike recorded macros, interactive macros must be entered in a specific format. Q&A creates a command file for you when you record macros, but with the interactive mode, you create the command file. Each macro begins with the code <begdef>, which stands for begin definition. The identifier key is entered next, followed by the keystrokes in the macro. Each keystroke is enclosed within greater-than and less-than signs and typed in lowercase letters. Text that is to appear literally should not be enclosed. The code <enddef> tells Q&A to end the definition.

If you want to create a macro that moves the cursor to the Company field in the sales lead database, you type

<begdef> <alta> <home> <home> <enter> <enter> <enter>
<enddef>
*

The <begdef> code tells Q&A that this is the beginning of the macro; Alt-A is the identifier. The following commands define the actual macro. Q&A now knows that when Alt-A is pressed, the cursor must be moved to the Home position (upper left corner of the screen), and then to the Company field by a series of three Enter keystrokes. The asterisk on the line below the macro is used to separate macros in a file.

When you write and edit interactive macros, the following special keys and key combinations must be entered in a specific format:

| *Key/Combination* | *Written as* |
|---|---|
| Alt-A | <alta> |
| Alt-5 | <alt5> |
| Backspace | <bks> |

| | |
|---|---|
| Ctrl-Home | <ctrlhom> |
| Ctrl-PgUp | <ctrlpgu> |
| Ctrl-Enter | <ctrlent> |
| ↓ | <dn> |
| ↑ | <up> |
| Escape | <esc> |
| Ins | <ins> |
| ← | <lft> |
| → | <rgt> |
| Enter | <enter> |
| Shift-F1 | <capsf1> |
| Shift-Tab | <capstab> |
| Tab | <tab> |
| Alt-F2 | <altf2> |

The Alt-F2 keystroke inserts a pause in a macro definition. When you play back the macro, Q&A waits for you to enter keystrokes at the place where the pause code occurs.

All the keys accessible to you during macro preparation are not shown in this table, but they are entered in the same way. For example, all function keys can be entered as normal, shifted, or with the Alt key by following the F1 and F2 examples given in the table. F10 is entered in a macro as <f10>, for example, and Alt-F10 is <altf10>. When in doubt about how to enter command keystrokes, try what appears logical, and Q&A will tell you if you need to try another combination.

If you can't figure out how to construct a key sequence in the interactive mode, temporarily save the macro and call up the Macro menu with Shift-F2. Select Define Macro and enter the keystrokes you want to add to your interactive macro. Save the RAM-resident macro to a temporary file. Now you can load this file into Write and examine how Q&A constructed the sequence. Either merge this file directly into the interactive macro or type the sequence.

### *Saving Interactive Macros*

Saving macro files you have created with the interactive method takes two steps. First, save the macro as a Q&A Write document. Second, convert this Write text file to an ASCII file. Q&A will read the macro file only in ASCII format.

To save a macro file as a Write text file and convert it to an ASCII file, take the following steps. After you have finished typing all commands for the macro, press Shift-F8 to save the file as a text file. Next, press Esc to return to the Write menu and choose the Utilities option. Finally, as shown in figure 19.2, choose Export To ASCII and assign a new macro file name. Once you have converted the macro file to ASCII format, the file can be used from a Q&A module.

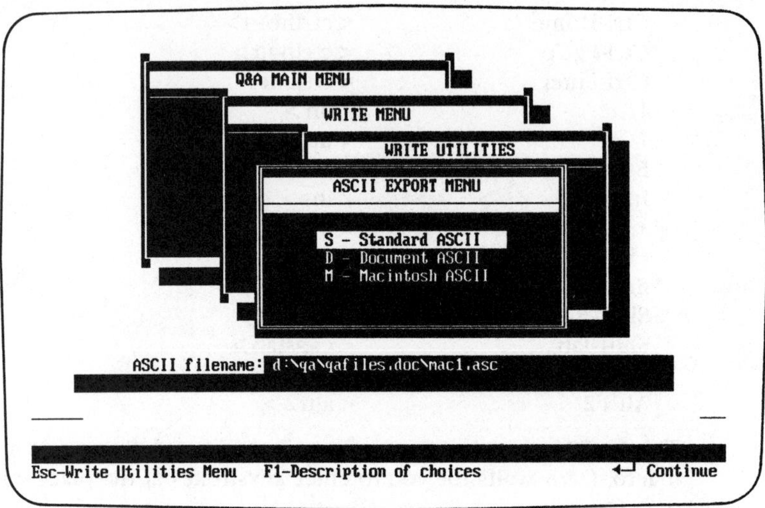


**Fig. 19.2** *Exporting macro files to ASCII.*

When you want to use the macros from within a module, press Shift-F2 to access the Macro menu and select Get Macros. Enter the macro file name at the prompt (be sure to include the path); the macros you created in Write will be loaded.

Remember, you can have as many macro files as you want, but you can use only macros that have been loaded into RAM.

## *Editing Macros*

If you make a spelling error while recording an elaborate sequence of text and commands, you can use the Backspace key to erase the error before the macro is saved. Each time you use the macro, however, it will repeat the same steps, including the error and correction.

You can use the interactive mode to edit the macros you create, but you must save the macro file to disk before editing. If you don't save the current file, any changes you make during your work session will be lost.

In the Write module, use the Get command to load the macro file for editing with standard Write procedures. Q&A will tell you the file is an Unknown Document File Format. As you have read, macro files are written to disk in ASCII format, so you need to select ASCII from the Import Document menu (see fig. 19.3). The file is then converted into Q&A format and can be edited. The Special ASCII option on the Import menu is a document format that strips carriage returns. This selection is not suitable for editing macros.

For example, if you mistakenly type *credentails* in the macro sequence, use the Backspace key to remove characters, and type the correct ending for the word. Q&A records the macro as

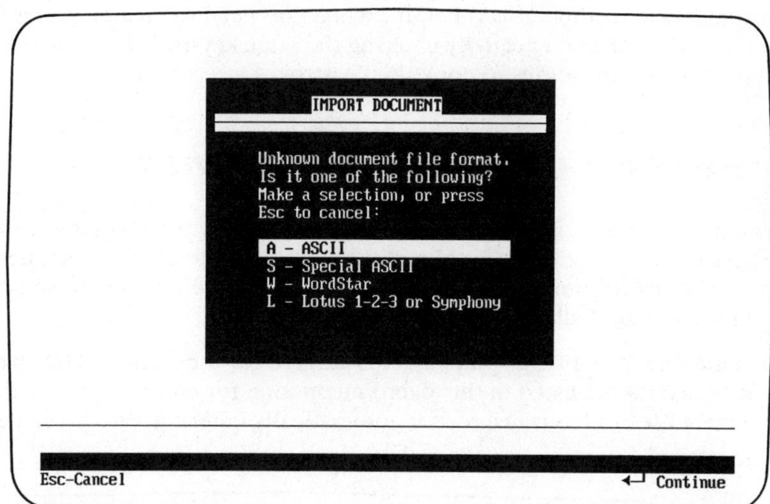


**Fig. 19.3** *Importing a macro file to Write.*

<begdef> <altu>credentails<bks> <bks> <bks> <bks>ials<enddef>

Q&A records the backspace keystroke as <bks> in a macro. The correct ending, *ials*, appears before the ending of the definition.

To remove extra keystrokes in the recorded macro, erase those you don't need. After editing, the correct macro reads

<begdef> <altu>credentials<enddef>

## *Using the Interactive Method To Solve Recorded Macro Problems*

If your recorded macro does not work, you can use the interactive method to fix the problem. Suppose that the final command in a macro instructs Q&A to exit to DOS. You can't save that macro, because the final command deposits you at the DOS prompt before you can select Save a Macro.

Solve the problem by ending the recorded definition before the last command and selecting the Save a Macro option. Then enter the macro file through Q&A Write, find the macro, and add

X<enter>

before the end of the definition (<enddef>). Save the file as explained in the section "Saving Interactive Macros." Now you have in your file a macro that exits Q&A from the Main menu as the final step.

The interactive method also is helpful when you need to create a series of similar macros. To keep from repeatedly entering the same keystrokes, you can use Write's block-copying capabilities to copy the keystrokes to each macro.

## *Remembering Macros You Defined*

If you have defined a large number of macros, you may have trouble remembering the keys used as identifiers. To solve this problem, create a Write document to hold names and descriptions of the macros. Displaying the document on screen will produce a menu of all your macros.

The menu in figure 19.4 displays macros defined for the sales lead database. Three types of macros are listed in the Macro menu: one for entering print settings, one for sorting files and four macros for automatically entering repetitive sales district data.

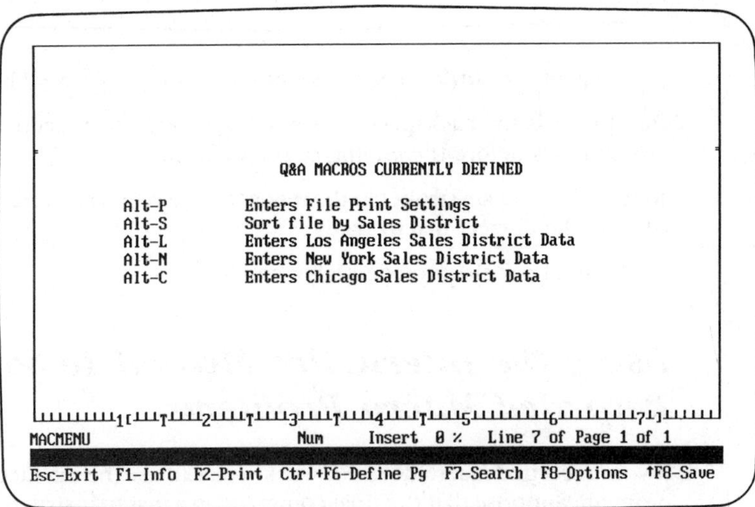


**Fig. 19.4**
*A sample Macro menu.*

Pressing the Enhance key (Shift-F6) will paint the menu with different colors. If you have a monochrome monitor, the Enhance key adds different shades of the displayed color to the text. Ordinarily, this key is used to specify boldface, underline, italic, subscript, or superscript enhancement on a printed document; but the specifications also cause different colors to be displayed on screen. To select an enhancement, choose the option you want and move the cursor to the position where you want the print enhancement to begin. Use the arrow keys to select the text you want enhanced and press F10 to end the feature.

When F10 is pressed, the highlighted area changes. The following list shows colors available for different Q&A text enhancements:

| *Effect* | *Color* |
|---|---|
| Boldface | White |
| Underlining | Green |
| Italic | Red |
| Subscript | Gold |
| Superscript | Cyan |

Don't worry about whether your printer can print these enhancements. This menu screen is used only to remind you of the defined macros. Figure 19.5 shows the file of macros listed in the menu.

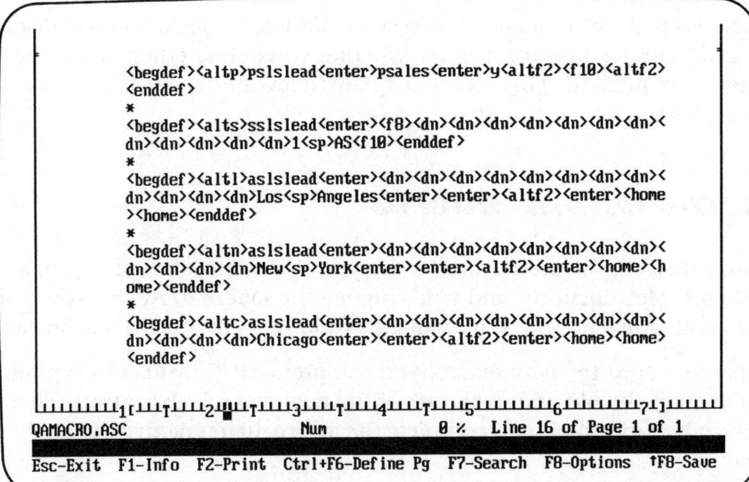


**Fig. 19.5** *Macros from the Macro menu.*

The following macro could be used to call up the new Macro menu:

<begdef><altm><esc><esc><esc><esc><esc><esc>w<enter>
gMACMENU<enter><enddef>

This macro begins with the identifier key (Alt-M) and issues six Esc keystrokes, which return you to the Main menu from any point within Q&A. Six Esc codes are not required from many Q&A positions, but using extra Esc keystrokes will get you to the Main menu from any location. The *w* then selects the Write menu; *g* tells Q&A to Get the file MACMENU, and the Enter keystroke finalizes the selection. By pressing Alt-M, your new Macro menu is displayed.

***Note:*** If you are using Write, save your document before selecting this macro, or unsaved work will be lost. When writing macros in Write, make sure that your commands execute from the proper location and match your Q&A configuration. If you have configured Q&A for single keystroke execution, you don't need <enter> commands after menu selections.

### Reloading Your Macro Files

You can create as many macro files as you have room for on your disk. To retrieve the file you want to use, press Shift-F2 for the Macro menu and G for Get Macros. Enter the macro file name at the prompt; the macro file is then loaded in RAM and ready to use.

## Advanced Macro Techniques

The macros you create can be used in every module of Q&A. You will discover many timesaving applications for macros, whether you defined them using the recording or interactive method. This section explains a few of the advanced techniques that add to Q&A's macro capability.

### Macros within Macros

Suppose that you created a macro to type the name of your regional manager, Jonathan T. McGillicuddy, and you assigned the macro to Alt-N. Now you want to create another macro to type his name and address. This macro will be named Alt-A.

When you record the new macro, you can press Alt-N instead of typing the name again to enter the old macro as part of the new macro's definition. Then, you can add the other information to complete the macro. In interactive mode, these macros appear as

```
<begdef> <altn>Jonathan T. McGillicuddy <enter> <enddef>
*
<begdef> <alta> <altn>, Regional Manager<enter>
Titan Technologies<enter>1234 Main Street<enter>
Lumberyard, PA 12534<enter> <enddef>
*
```

Q&A accepts up to five levels of macros within macros. Only one level is used in the preceding example.

### Autoloading Macros

If you want a macro file to load automatically when you start Q&A, name the file QAMACRO.ASC. When the program is booted, Q&A searches for that macro file. However, only one macro file can be in memory at a time. If you want to use another macro file, choose the Get command from the Macro menu to load the file after the system is booted and the autoloading macros are finished executing.

### *Using Other Word Processors To Create Q&A Macros*

You can create Q&A macro files in any word-processing program that can generate, read, and save files in ASCII. For example, you could use the SideKick editor to create interactive macros from within File or Report modules, without calling up Write. Editors like SideKick and others designed for programmers generate ASCII files directly and do not require the extra step Write needs to save an ASCII file.

## *Sample Macro Applications*

Q&A macros can make your work easier in any of the program's modules. This section offers a few ideas for macro applications and may inspire you to create additional macros.

All macros in this section have been designed to start from the Q&A Main menu, but you can write macros that begin at any point within Q&A. If you record a macro from within a module, however, remember in which module it originates; otherwise, the series of keystrokes and menu selections may be wrong.

### *Querying the Intelligent Assistant*

The following macro accesses the Intelligent Assistant, enters the name of the sales lead database (SLSLEAD.DTF), activates the file, and asks the Intelligent Assistant for a current list of companies in the database:

<begdef> <alts>a<enter>aslslead.dtf<enter> Show me
the companies in the database.<enter>y<enter> <enddef>

The <begdef> code tells Q&A that you are starting a new macro. Alt-S is the identifier key (the one you use to start the macro). The first letter *a* and Enter keystrokes select the Intelligent Assistant from the Main menu. The second letter *a* selects the Ask option from the Intelligent Assistant menu; *SLSLEAD.DTF* tells Q&A the name of the database. The query "Show me the companies in the database" causes Q&A to display a report of the specified data. The remaining entries in the macro are responses to prompts about the query.

If you plan to use a macro repeatedly, type the file name instead of using the arrow keys. The arrow keys work when you define the macro, but if you add a database file, the macro may access the wrong file.

The same macro can be used to ask the Intelligent Assistant questions. Instead of including the name of the database file and query in the macro, you can insert pauses so that the program waits for input. The macro appears as

<begdef> <alts>a<enter>a<altf2> <enter> <altf2> <enter>y
<enter> <enddef>

## *Printing Reports*

Macros, like the following example, can enable you to print a report by pressing only one key:

<begdef> <altr>r<enter>psales.dtf<enter>salesrep<enter>
<enter> <enddef>

After the begin definition code, Alt-R is specified as the identifier key; *r* tells Q&A to select Report from the Main menu, and *p* tells Q&A to print a file; *sales.dtf* is the name of the database. Salesrep is the name of the report, and the remaining Enter keystrokes finish the process.

The following macro uses the Intelligent Assistant to create a report from the sales lead database. The macro tells Q&A to select sales leads from the Indiana district and to print a report of the findings:

<begdef> <altf8>a<enter>aslslead.dtf<enter>List Indiana
companies<enter> <enter> <f2> <lft> <lft> <lft> <lft> <lft> <lft>
<f8> <tab> <tab> <tab> <tab> <tab> <tab> <tab>Sales Leads in the
Indiana District<f10> <esc> <esc> <enddef>

This macro is more complicated than the previous ones. The letter *a* selects the Intelligent Assistant; the database file *slslead.dtf* is specified. The macro then tells the IA to "List Indiana companies" and answers the prompts with Enter keystrokes.

The report is then displayed (see fig. 19.6), and the F2 keystroke in the macro sends results to the printer. The Print Options screen appears before the report is printed, and the destination is changed from SCREEN to LPT1. The macro moves the cursor to a place where a title or header can be entered. In this example "Sales Leads in the Indiana District" was used. The F10 in the macro prints the report (see fig. 19.7).

The concluding Esc keystrokes return you to the Main menu.

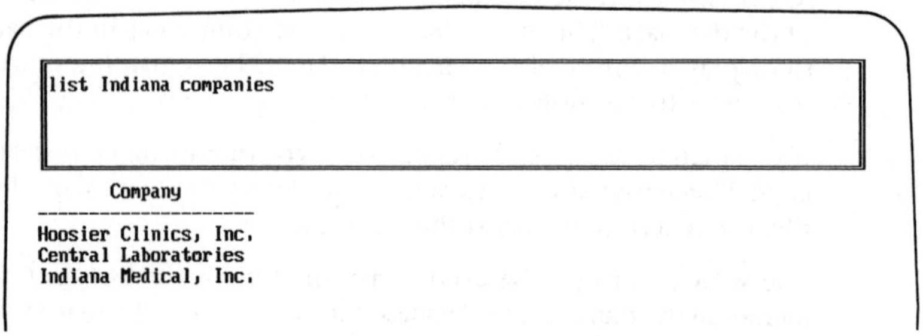

```
list Indiana companies

        Company
--------------------
Hoosier Clinics, Inc.
Central Laboratories
Indiana Medical, Inc.
```

**Fig. 19.6**
*A report generated by a macro.*

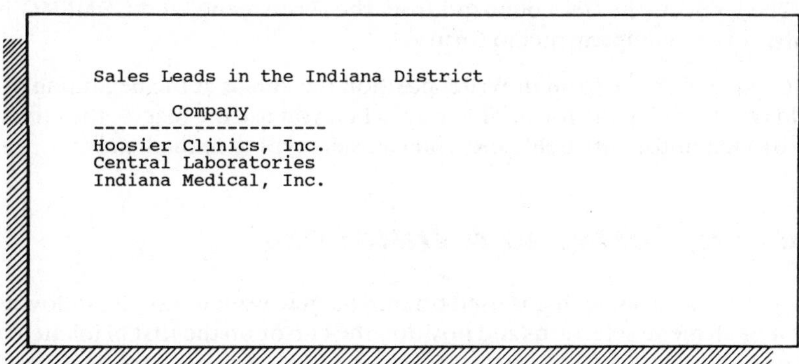
```
Sales Leads in the Indiana District

        Company
---------------------
Hoosier Clinics, Inc.
Central Laboratories
Indiana Medical, Inc.
```

**Fig. 19.7** ***The printed result generated by the macro.***

## *Creating Company Memos*

The process of writing memos can be automated by creating a macro to enter the information that appears on all memos, so you have to enter only the actual text. You can create a blank memo form within Write and call up the form by using the macro. Figure 19.8 shows an example of a blank memo form created in Write. (For more information on creating Write documents, see Chapters 9-13.)

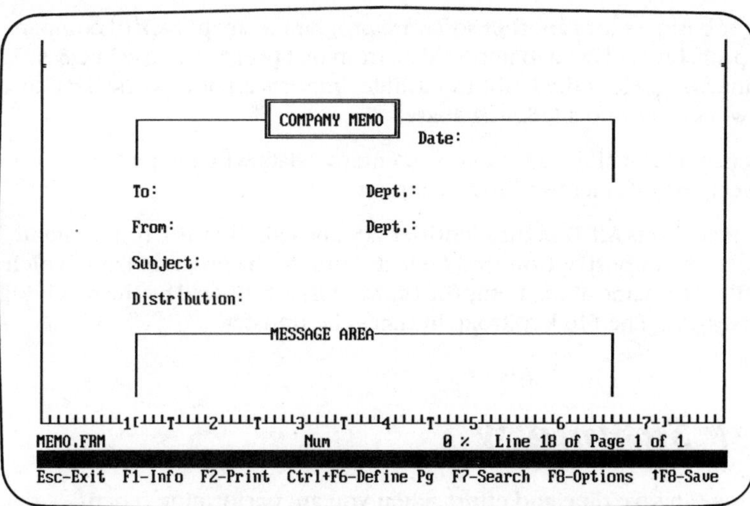


**Fig. 19.8** ***A sample memo form.***

The following macro finds and loads the blank memo file:

<begdef> <altw> w <enter> gcomemo <enter> <enddef>

The macro identifier is Alt-W (for Write), and the letter *w* followed by <enter> selects the Write module from the Main menu. Rememer, if you have configured Q&A for single keystroke operation, you need to remove the <enter> command after the *w*. The *g* selects the Get command from the Write menu, and COMEMO is the file name for the company memo form.

After you create the form in Write, position the cursor at the beginning of the first field before saving the form. This way, when you use the macro, the cursor will be positioned in the first field, and you can start typing immediately.

### *Adding Forms to a Database*

If you have a database that is used often, you may want to use the following macro to enter all menu selections and position the cursor on the first blank field of a new record:

<begdef> <altf>f<enter>aslslead.dtf<enter> <enddef>

This macro can save considerable time by choosing the options from the Q&A menu system for you. Remember, if you have configured Q&A for single keystroke operation, you will need to remove the <enter> command after the *f* that selects the File module.

### *Importing Information*

If your business uses another software program to keep track of company finances, you probably will need to import data from that program to use in Q&A. The following macro accesses the Utilities module, imports a Lotus worksheet, and converts the worksheet into a Q&A database.

<begdef> <altd>u<enter>I<enter>Ldata.wk1<enter>
weekly.dtf<enter> <F10> <enddef>

This macro sets Alt-D as the identifier key and calls up the Utilities menu. The letter *i* selects the Import option, and *l* selects Lotus as the program from which to import the file. The name of the Lotus file (*data.wk1*) is followed by the receiving Q&A file (*weekly.dtf*). The F10 keystroke initiates the transfer.

## *Chapter Summary*

Macros can save time and effort when you are performing repetitive data entry or data management tasks. This chapter explains both the recording method and interactive method of creating macros. The next chapter shows you how to use Q&A's import/export capability to transfer data to and from other popular programs.

Chapter

# 20

# Importing and Exporting Data in Q&A

This chapter deals with a more technical aspect of file operations: importing and exporting data. If you have used other software programs in the past, or if you use additional programs to help you with your record keeping, finances, and word processing, you probably will need to transfer data in and out of Q&A.

## *Importing Data into Q&A*

With the Q&A Utilities module, you can import information from most other software programs. Depending on what other programs you are using, the procedure may be simple or complex.

Before you learn how to import data by using the Utilities module, however, you should know that you can import text files into the Write module without using Utilities at all. A *text file* is a letter, a bulletin, a report—any document that is not a database or spreadsheet file. The next section covers importing text files; then importing databases is covered. The text file shown in figure 20.1 is an excerpt from Titan Technology's annual report.

### *Importing Text Files*

To import a text file into Write, first copy the file to the directory in which you store your Q&A word-processing files. Then use the Get command from the Write menu to select the file.

The program will display the Import Document menu to alert you that the file is not a standard Q&A file. You then indicate whether to import the file as an ASCII file (without wordwrap), a special ASCII file (with wordwrap), a WordStar file, or a 1-2-3 or Symphony file.

**Fig. 20.1**
*A sample text file.*

```
                Titan Technology Report 1988       page 1



                     Titan Technology: A History

        Titan Technology was created in early 1974 to answer a
        fast-growing need in the medical supply business.  Owners
        Bob Lancaster and Dan Evans, working in Bob's unheated
        garage in Chicago, Illinois, packed and shipped their
        first order on February 23, 1974.

        Since that time, Titan Technology has become a leader in
        the medical sales industry.  With over 20,000 customers
        annually, Titan Technology has developed into one of the
        world's most prosperous wholesale medical supply houses.
```

If the document is in WordStar format, the program converts the data to a Q&A file as soon as you press W. You must manually replace the WordStar dot commands and some print-enhancement commands with the corresponding Q&A commands. Print commands for boldface, underline, superscript, and subscript translate into Q&A without adjustment.

Figure 20.2 shows the original WordStar file. Notice the set of dot commands at the top of the page. Two commands set the top and bottom margins, another command specifies the header, and others set the page number and cancel the bottom-of-page page number.

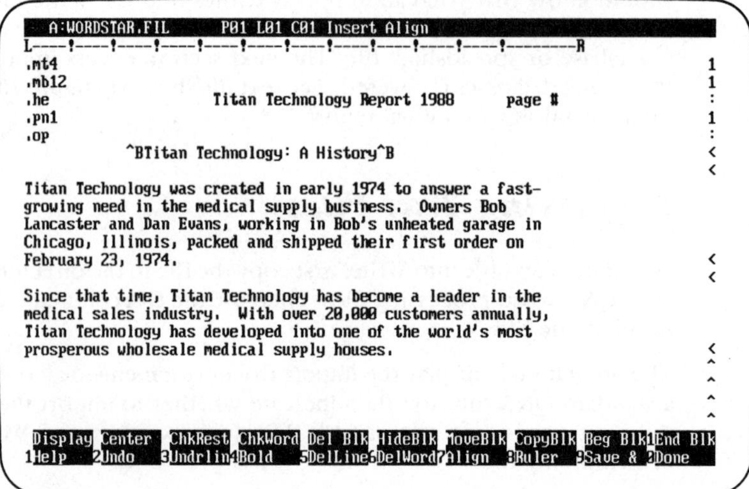

```
   A:WORDSTAR.FIL        P01 L01 C01 Insert Align
L----!----!----!----!----!----!----!----!----!----!---------R
.mt4
.mb12
.he                      Titan Technology Report 1988      page #
.pn1
.op
            ^BTitan Technology: A History^B

Titan Technology was created in early 1974 to answer a fast-
growing need in the medical supply business.  Owners Bob
Lancaster and Dan Evans, working in Bob's unheated garage in
Chicago, Illinois, packed and shipped their first order on
February 23, 1974.

Since that time, Titan Technology has become a leader in the
medical sales industry.  With over 20,000 customers annually,
Titan Technology has developed into one of the world's most
prosperous wholesale medical supply houses.

 Display Center  ChkRest ChkWord Del Blk HideBlk MoveBlk CopyBlk Beg Blk End Blk
1Help   2Undo   3Undrlin4Bold   5DelLine6DelWord7Align  8Ruler  9Save & 0Done
```

**Fig. 20.2**
*The WordStar file.*

Each of these specifications can be duplicated in Q&A, but you must use a different method. First, you must copy the WordStar file into the appropriate Q&A directory. Suppose that the Q&A word-processing files are on the hard disk (drive C) in the QATEXT directory, and the WordStar files are in the WORDSTAR.FIL subdirectory of the WSDIR directory. To copy the files to the appropriate Q&A directory, you would type

copy c:\wsdir\wordstar.fil c:\qatext

When you use the DOS COPY command and you plan to keep the name of the copied file, you don't have to specify the file name in the destination.

When the WordStar file is in the QATEXT directory, you can import the file by selecting the Get command from the Write menu; the Import Document menu appears. Choose WordStar to tell Q&A that the unknown file is a WordStar document.

The file is translated into Q&A format and loaded onto the Type/Edit screen (see fig. 20.3). Notice that the document is slightly different from the original WordStar version. The margins are wider in Q&A, so fewer words appear on each line. The page-number designation has been carried over onto the next line and now appears in the middle of the dot commands.

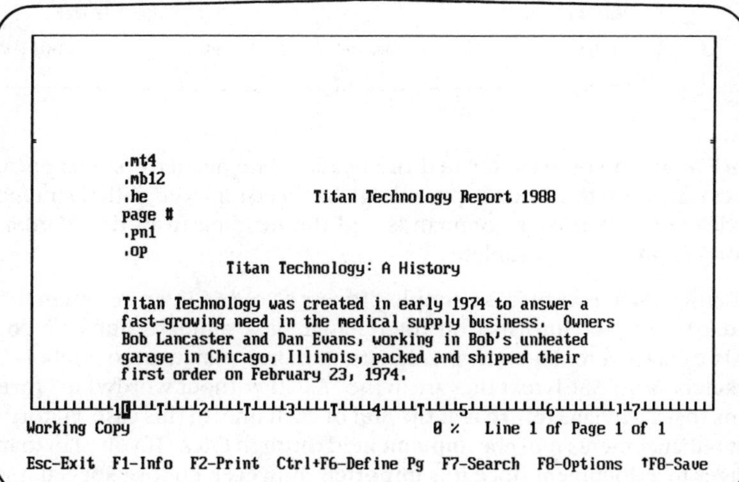

```
.mt4
.mb12
.he                    Titan Technology Report 1988
page #
.pn1
.op
            Titan Technology: A History

Titan Technology was created in early 1974 to answer a
fast-growing need in the medical supply business.  Owners
Bob Lancaster and Dan Evans, working in Bob's unheated
garage in Chicago, Illinois, packed and shipped their
first order on February 23, 1974.

Working Copy                          0 %  Line 1 of Page 1 of 1

Esc-Exit  F1-Info  F2-Print  Ctrl+F6-Define Pg  F7-Search  F8-Options  ↑F8-Save
```

**Fig. 20.3**
*A WordStar file as first imported into Q&A.*

Another difference is that the heading is no longer enclosed in the ^B symbols (WordStar's boldface codes). Q&A recognizes those codes and turns them into the Q&A equivalent for boldface. Although you can't see the result in figure 20.3, Q&A displays the heading in letters that are brighter than the surrounding text, indicating that the heading will appear in boldface on the printout.

You also may notice that the heading is not centered on the screen. WordStar codes cause the heading to be moved to the right, but when the file is printed, the heading appears centered on the page.

To fix this problem, press F8 (Options), and choose the Edit Header command. The cursor moves to the header box, which is displayed at the top of the screen (see fig. 20.4). You then can type the header you want and *Page #*. In WordStar and Q&A, the pound sign specifies automatic page numbering. You also can press F8 and choose the Center Line command to center the header.

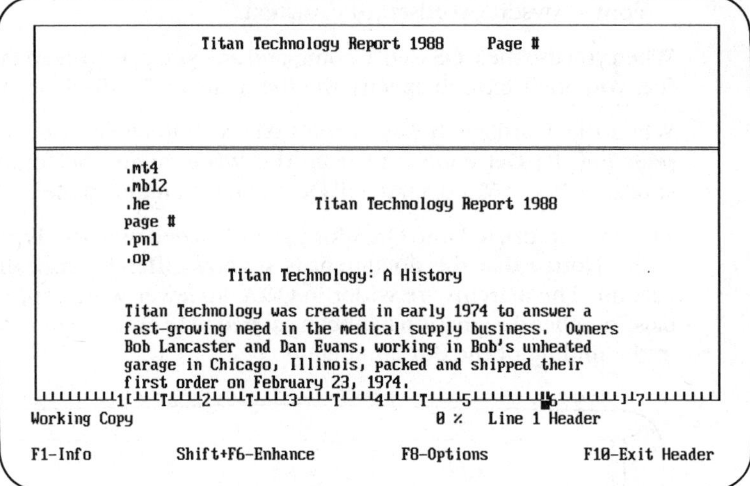


**Fig. 20.4** *Typing the header for the WordStar file.*

Press F10 when you have created the header. The header box disappears, but the header stays on-screen and the pound sign has been replaced with the number *1*. Once you delete the WordStar commands and the heading from the WordStar file, the importing process is complete.

Importing ASCII text files is a simple process also. ASCII, an acronym for American Standard Code for Information Interchange, is a standard numeric code used to translate binary zeros and ones into letters, numbers, punctuation symbols, and special characters. Most ASCII text files are in the "ASCII without wordwrap" format, which means that a carriage return is at the end of each line. In this case, all formatting and print enhancements must be implemented through Q&A. If you plan to make major changes to a document once it is imported, however, choose Special ASCII. In this form, all carriage returns are taken out unless the program encounters two carriage returns in a row, indicating the end of a paragraph.

The last type of file that can be imported to Write is a 1-2-3 or Symphony file. You could use Q&A Write, for example, to import data from 1-2-3 or Symphony for use in a document or mailmerge operation. You import data from these programs by specifying the ranges on the Define Range screen, which is discussed later in this chapter.

## *Importing Files from PFS:FILE and the IBM Filing Assistant*

The Utilities module is used to import database files into Q&A. Q&A supports imported data from a variety of formats:

- PFS:FILE or the IBM Filing Assistant
- dBASE
- 1-2-3 or Symphony
- ASCII or DIF

The general procedure for importing database files into Q&A is similar, whatever the format; however, the specific steps vary according to the kind of file being imported. This discussion begins with a detailed explanation of importing PFS:FILE and the IBM Filing Assistant. Then the other formats are described.

If the file you want to use was created with PFS:FILE or the IBM Filing Assistant, you can import the data and the entire database structure directly. In this chapter, the procedures explained for PFS:FILE apply also to the IBM Filing Assistant. Q&A handles both products the same way.

Before you can import a data file from any of the formats discussed, you must first create a Q&A database to accept the data. The procedures used to import the different programs begin in a similar way.

### *Creating a Q&A Database To Receive Data*

You begin the procedures from the Utilities menu. Select Utilities from the Main menu and call up the Import menu by selecting Import Data. Choose the type of file to import and name the specific file. If you can't remember the name, and the file is located in the default drive and path, press Enter; a list of file names is displayed. Then use the cursor keys to highlight your selection and press Enter. (If the file is in another drive and path, press Ctrl-Y to delete the default drive and path, and enter the correct drive and path.) Then type the name of the Q&A file that will receive the data.

From this point on, the procedure varies according to the kind of file that you're importing. The following sections explain each of the procedures.

When you import data from PFS:FILE into Q&A, you must specify the name of the file that will receive the data. If the Q&A file doesn't exist, it is created with the same structure as the PFS:FILE original. Q&A also will duplicate report and print specifications that have been created for the file.

For example, if you are importing a PFS:FILE database that has eight fields, the same eight fields appear in the Q&A database. The field lengths are the same, although you will have to change the data type to match Q&A specifications (discussed later in this chapter). If the PFS:FILE database has six reports set up to extract and print records for six regional offices, the same six reports are carried into Q&A. If special printer codes are included in the PFS:FILE database, a Print Options screen will be filled in automatically when the file is imported into Q&A.

What happens when you enter the name of a receiving file that is in use? Q&A adds the records from the imported file to the end of the existing records. The restrictions for this procedure are covered later in this chapter.

Remember that in the sections that follow, the procedures for PFS:FILE and the IBM Filing Assistant are identical.

## *Importing the Data*

To import a file from PFS:FILE, first select the program from the Import menu of the Utilities module. Then type the file name or press Enter to display a list of PFS:FILE database files. The list displayed does not contain files exclusively from PFS:FILE; all files in the directory will be listed (see fig. 20.5). Select the file by moving the cursor to the file you want and pressing Enter.

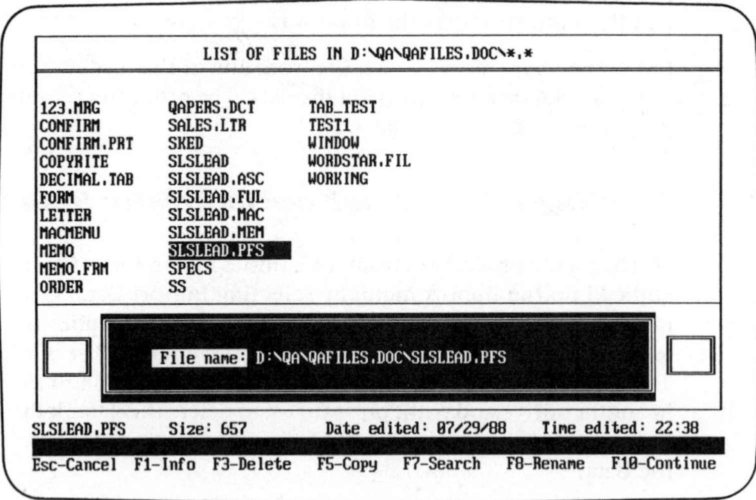


**Fig. 20.5**
*A listing of files in the current directory.*

The Import menu is displayed again. This display doesn't mean that your entry didn't work; you have been returned to the Import menu so that you can enter the name of the new Q&A file to be created. The name of the file to be imported is displayed after the `Import from` prompt, and you will need to answer the prompt **`Q&A file name`**. The drive and directory identification—that is, the path to the file—appears after the prompt. After you type the file name and press Enter, Q&A adds the DTF extension to the name.

## *Specifying Information Types*

Q&A moves from the Import menu to the Format Spec after you enter the file name. Whether the receiving file is new or already existing, you must specify the information type for each field on the Format Spec screen. Each field name is displayed; if you have many fields in the database, you may have more than one screen of information. Press PgDn to display any additional screens.

Each field name is specified initially as a text field (T). This setting is the default, so Q&A assumes that all the fields you are importing are text fields unless you specify otherwise on the Format Spec screen. The field types are

| *Code* | *Field type* |
|---|---|
| T | Text |
| N | Number |
| M | Money |
| D | Date |
| H | Hours (time of day) |
| Y | Logical (requiring a yes/no answer) |
| K | Keywords |

Figure 20.6 shows an example of the Format Spec screen for the SLSLEAD database file. Most of the fields shown on this screen have been specified as text fields. When you specify fields for the imported information, remember that a text field can contain letters, numbers, or both.

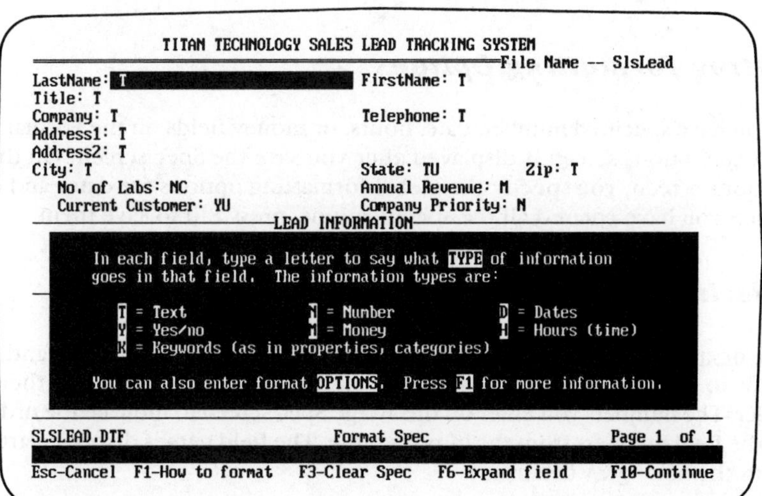


**Fig. 20.6**
*The Format Spec for text fields.*

The fields in the lower part of the Format Spec screen contain several different specifications (see fig. 20.7). The Sales Priority field has been coded to accept numeric values with one decimal place (N1); Sales District is a keyword field (K); and the Date Entered field contains the code for accepting date values (D).

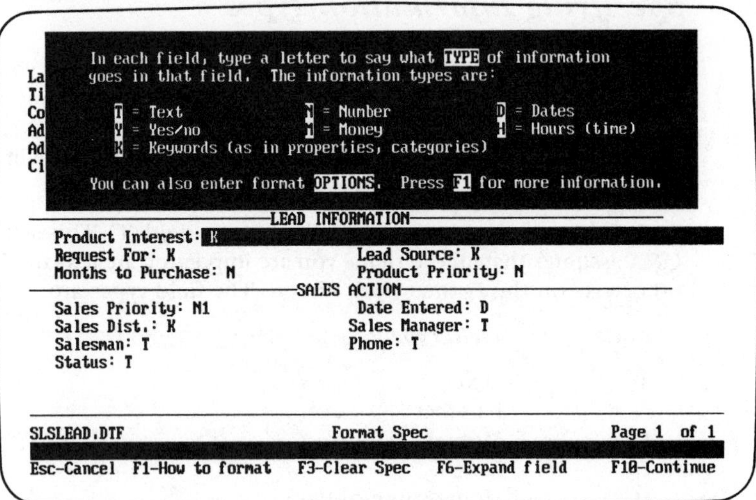


**Fig. 20.7** *The Format Spec with other specifications.*

For more information on entering character types, see Chapter 5, "Setting Up a File." In that chapter you also can review how to specify formatting options, such as justification of text, the use of commas in money fields, and the use of codes to convert text field values to uppercase letters. Remember that you always can display a help screen by pressing F1. When you have specified all information types, press F10 (Continue) to save the Format Spec.

## *Setting Formatting Options*

If you have specified number, date, hours, or money fields on the Format Spec, the Format Options screen is displayed after you save the Spec screen. On the Format Options screen, you specify the global formatting options for dates and currency. When you have entered all the specifications, press F10 to save them.

## *Selecting and Ordering Fields*

The next screen displayed is the Merge Spec. Use this screen to select and order the fields to be imported. If you press F10, all fields will be imported in their original order. The numbers you enter on the Merge Spec screen to indicate the order should be the field numbers from the imported file. The field names displayed are the ones from the new Q&A database.

For example, suppose that when you set up the new database to receive the PFS:FILE information, you want to change the order in which the information is displayed. The Title field may have been field #1 in the PFS:FILE database, but Title is field #3 on the Titan Technology form. To show Q&A where to put the data, you enter a *1* in the Title field on the Merge Spec screen (see fig. 20.8). When you import the data, the contents of field #1 in the PFS:FILE database will be copied to field #3 in the Q&A database.

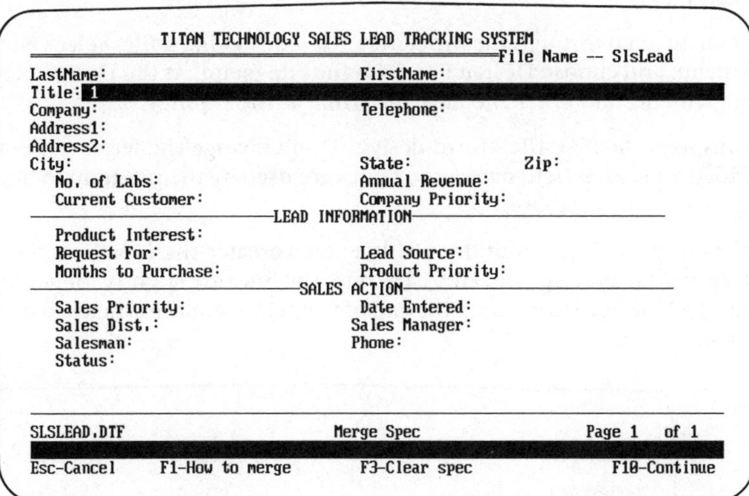


**Fig. 20.8**
*Changing the field order with Merge Spec.*

You also can use the Merge Spec screen to discard fields when you import information. For example, suppose that in the PFS:FILE database you had fields that recorded the name and employee number of the data entry operator, and you don't want those fields to appear on the Titan Technology form. If you don't enter the field numbers of those fields on the Merge Spec screen, the data from the fields will not be imported. Similarly, if the Q&A database has fields that you have not numbered, no data will be transferred to those fields.

When you have filled in the Merge Spec, press F10 to import the data into Q&A.

## *Special Conditions for Importing Data from PFS:FILE*

You should be aware of special conditions as you import files into Q&A from PFS:FILE and the IBM Filing Assistant. If the PFS:FILE database has fields that extend more than one line, you will have to use a different procedure. If you follow the preceding procedure, all data beyond the first line will be lost in the transfer.

You also will have a problem with attachment fields in PFS:FILE and the IBM Filing Assistant. A memo attached to records might be an attachment field, similar to a memo field in dBASE. Q&A cannot transfer attachment fields with the usual importing procedure; but there is a way to solve the problem.

The solution is the same for both programs. First, select the type of file from the Import menu, as you would in a normal import procedure. Then enter the names of the file to be imported and the new Q&A file.

Q&A starts to create the database, and the Format Spec is displayed. In this case, do not change the default settings for the information types (T); press Esc to return to the Main menu.

You then must go through the procedure for redesigning a file. Select File from the Main menu, and choose Design File from the File menu. At the Design menu, select Redesign a File, and enter the new file name at the prompt.

Q&A displays the new file's form design. Don't change the letter codes that Q&A has added after each field name; the codes are used by the program to maintain the structure of your database.

To solve the problem of multiline fields, enter a greater-than symbol (>) where you want the field to end (see fig. 20.9). Because the lines are slightly longer in PFS:FILE than in Q&A, add an extra line at the end of your Q&A multiline fields to guard against data loss.

**Fig. 20.9**
*Specifying a multiline field.*

```
LastName:AA                              FirstName:AB

Address:AC
                                                             >
City:AD                        State:AE         Zip:AF

Telephone:AG                                    Annual Revenue:AH

NEWLEAD                     Num    Insert  0 %   Line 7 of Page 1 of 1

Esc-Cancel          F1-How to design        F8-Options          F10-Continue
```

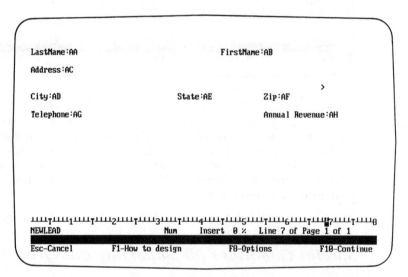

For attachment fields, press PgDn to display a new page in the form design. Type *Attachment:* at the top of the new screen. Move the cursor to the bottom right corner of the screen, and enter a greater-than symbol. When you press F10 (Continue), your modifications are saved, and you have added a full-page attachment field to your form.

After you press F10, the Format Spec is displayed again. Specify the information types for the fields; don't forget the attachment field on the next page. When you are finished, press F10.

Next, select Import Data from the Utilities menu, and enter the name of the file you want to import. After you enter the name of the new Q&A file and press Enter, the Merge Spec is displayed. If you don't need to change the selection or order of the fields, you can skip this step by pressing F10. The file is then imported into Q&A, with multi-line and attachment fields intact.

Importing data can give you some problems if you are using PFS:FILE or the IBM Filing Assistant. For example, you may have trouble importing data into Q&A if you have

- More than 10 pages in the original database
- More than 240 fields on one page
- More than 2,400 fields overall
- A zero-length field
- A page with no fields

You can take two approaches to these problems. You can reduce the number of pages or fields, eliminate or expand the zero-length field, or remove the empty page; or, you can construct a Q&A database that has the same fields and field lengths as the source database. The second method is used later in the chapter to transfer data from other software programs to Q&A.

## *Importing a File from dBASE*

The dBASE programs—dBASE II®, dBASE III®, and dBASE III Plus—are some of the most popular database programs available. Because of the popularity of the programs, Q&A has added an import utility specifically for dBASE files. On the Import menu, only dBASE II and dBASE III are represented, but we have found that dBASE III Plus files also can be imported.

To import a dBASE file, select dBASE II/III from the Import menu and press Enter. Then enter the name of the file you want to import and press Enter. (If you don't remember the file name, you can press Enter again to display a list of files in the current directory.) Then supply the name of the Q&A file. When you import a dBASE file, you don't need to create a database before the import procedure; Q&A creates a database automatically from the dBASE database files.

After the file is created, the same steps apply to dBASE that apply to PFS:FILE or the IBM Filing Assistant. The Format Spec is displayed so that you can identify field types; the default field types should be the same as they appeared in the dBASE database. To accept the default field names, press F10.

The Merge Spec is then displayed, which you use to specify which fields in the source database will be imported. After you make your specifications on the Merge Spec screen, press F10, and the data is imported into the new Q&A database file.

If an existing Q&A database name is used for the new database, only the Merge Spec screen is displayed. After you press F10, the imported data is added to the end of the existing Q&A database.

## *Importing a File from 1-2-3 or Symphony*

If you created a Q&A database to receive the data, Q&A can import a Lotus 1-2-3 or Symphony WKS or WK1 file without first converting it to a PRN file. When you construct the database, remember that each row is a record in a Q&A database. A single column in a 1-2-3 database holds all the field contents for that database. When the data is merged into a Q&A data file, the first column in the 1-2-3 database file or range is transferred to the first Q&A field, the second column goes into the second Q&A field, and so on. Of course, you can use the Merge Spec screen to rearrange the order of these fields. Figure 20.10 shows a Q&A database that has been designed to receive a 1-2-3 file.

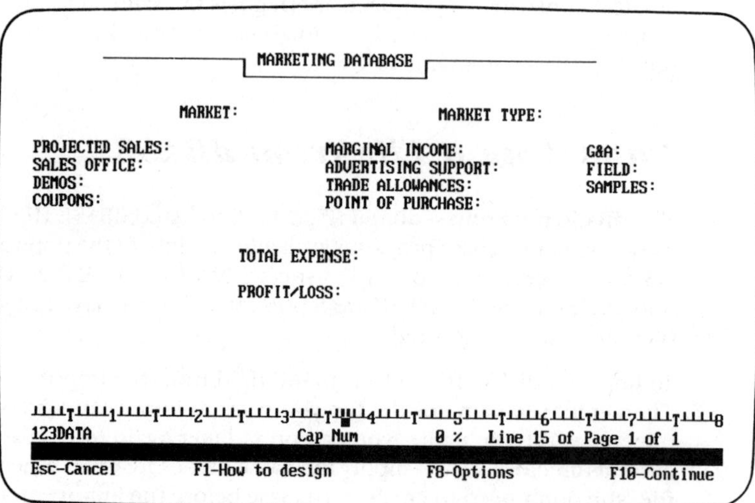


**Fig. 20.10** *Designing a database to receive the 1-2-3 file.*

If you don't provide enough fields in your Q&A database to accommodate the active cells in the worksheet rows, Q&A will discard the rightmost cells for which it has no fields. The other mismatch alternative is less disastrous; if you have more fields in the Q&A database than you have rows in the worksheet, some of the fields in the database will be empty.

Press F10 after you set up your fields; the Format Spec screen is displayed. Be careful when you format the fields for your database. Remember that all Lotus cells are fixed in length. A Q&A field, however, extends to the edge of the screen unless the field length is ended by another field label or by a greater-than symbol (>). Because of this consideration, you won't want to use right-justified fields in the Format Spec. Doing so could cause the value to be separated from the field label by almost the entire screen width.

After you have pressed F10 to complete the Format Spec screen, the Format Options screen is displayed. On this screen, you specify the format options for number, money, date, and hours. When you press F10 again, the new database is ready to use.

Next, select Import Data from the Utilities menu. When the Import menu is displayed, select `LOTUS 123 or Symphony`. You will be asked for the name of the Lotus file you want to import; type your answer (be sure to include the complete path description). If you have copied the worksheet into Q&A, press Enter to display the list of 1-2-3 files in your current directory (see fig. 20.11). Highlight the file you want to use, and press Enter.

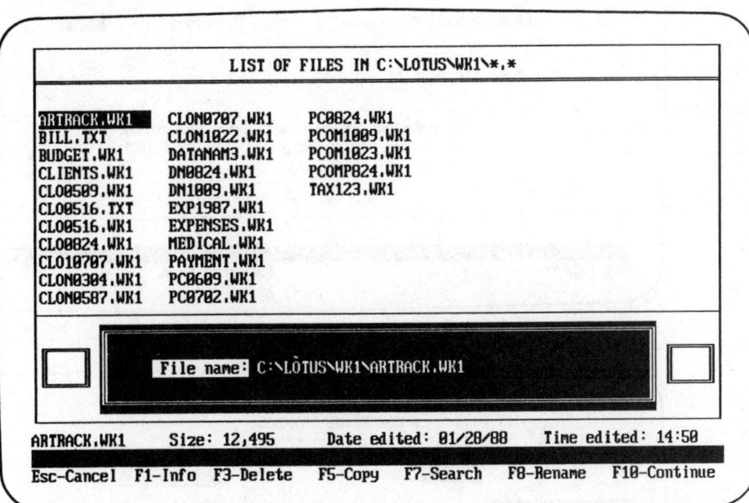


**Fig. 20.11** *Displaying Lotus file names.*

When you are prompted for the name of the Q&A database that will receive the information, type the name and press Enter. (You can redisplay the list of files by pressing Enter. Type the file name and press Enter.)

The Define Range screen is then displayed (see fig. 20.12). On this screen, you can specify a range from the Lotus worksheet to be imported. To do this, you either supply the cell coordinates or type the title of a named range that you created in the 1-2-3 file (see fig. 20.12). If you want to import the entire worksheet, don't specify anything on this screen.

If you want to eliminate cells or alter the order of the cells you are importing, press F8 to display the Merge Spec. The procedure for filling in this screen is the same as the procedure previously explained.

Remember that a field in 1-2-3 is a column in each record, and that columns in Lotus are identified by letters instead of numbers. For example, if the range you're importing begins at the 1-2-3 Home position, column A is the first column to be imported. Refer to column A as field #1 when you fill in the Merge Spec. Similarly, column D will be field #4 on the Merge Spec screen (see fig. 20.13). If the range you want to import begins in column G of the worksheet, start numbering the fields at that point. That makes column G field #1, column H field #2, and so forth.

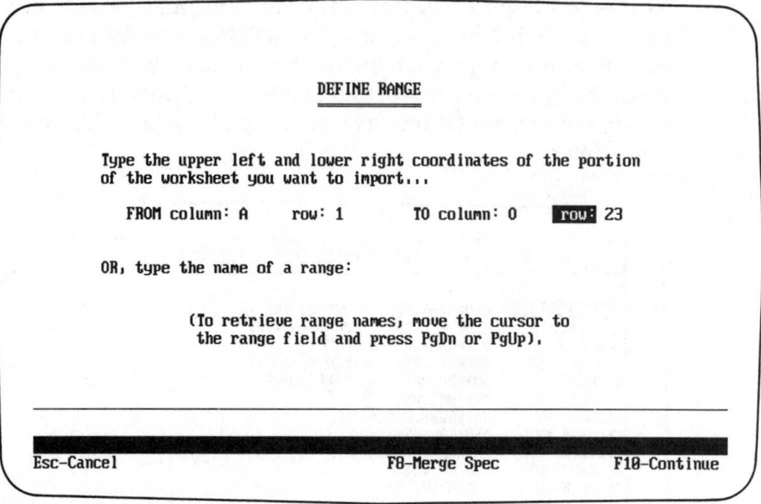

DEFINE RANGE
Type the upper left and lower right coordinates of the portion
of the worksheet you want to import...
FROM column: A row: 1 TO column: O row: 23
OR, type the name of a range:
(To retrieve range names, move the cursor to
the range field and press PgDn or PgUp).
Esc-Cancel
F8-Merge Spec
F10-Continue


**Fig. 20.12**
*Defining a 1-2-3 range to import.*

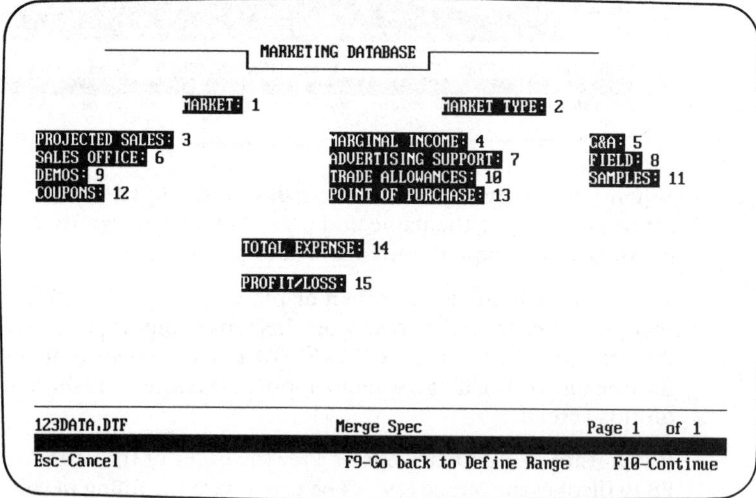


**Fig. 20.13**
*The Merge Spec for importing a 1-2-3 worksheet.*

Whether you use the Define Range and Merge Spec screens or not, press F10 when you are ready to import the worksheet. Each form will be displayed on-screen as the data is imported. When the process is complete, you will have a functioning Q&A database created from your 1-2-3 file.

## Importing an ASCII or DIF File

Database files from other programs can be imported if the programs can export data to a standard ASCII or DIF file. As you know, ASCII is a numeric code used to represent characters. DIF, an acronym for Data Interchange Format, is another type of industry code used for exchanging data. Both types of files can be imported to a Q&A file after the Q&A database has been set up to receive the data.

The import procedure is similar to that described in previous sections of this chapter. To import an ASCII or DIF file, select the file type from the Import menu. Then enter the name of the file to be imported and the Q&A file to receive the data. After you press Enter, the Merge Spec is displayed. You don't need to enter anything on this screen unless you want to change the order or selection of the imported fields. When you press F10, the importing process will begin.

Make sure that the database you create in Q&A has enough fields to accommodate the data you are importing. Remember also that you don't have to create a new database before you import the data; you can add the data as additional records in an existing Q&A database if the field sizes are compatible.

The type of ASCII you choose depends on the way your text file looks. If your text file is similar to the one shown in figure 20.14, choose Fixed ASCII (SDF). If your file appears like the one shown in figure 20.15, select Standard ASCII. When you choose Standard ASCII, an ASCII Options screen appears, giving you the flexibility to decide how the data is saved on disk. In a standard ASCII file the data for each field is enclosed in quotation marks, and fields are separated by commas. However, you can choose whether to use the quotation marks and what symbol to use as the field delimiter.

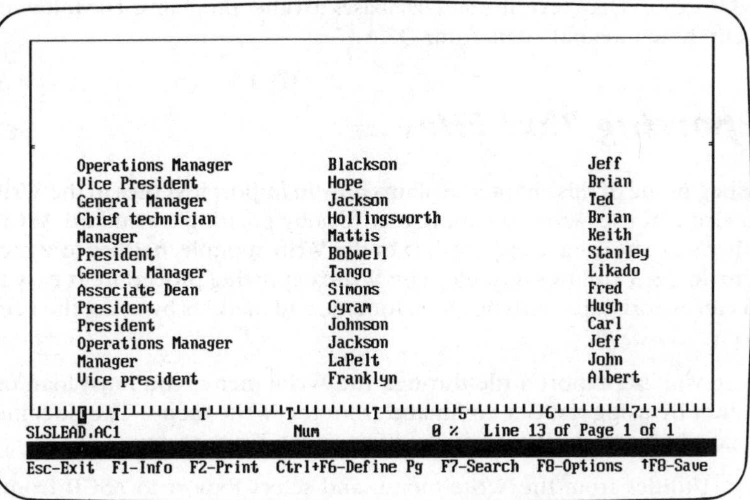


**Fig. 20.14** *A fixed ASCII file.*

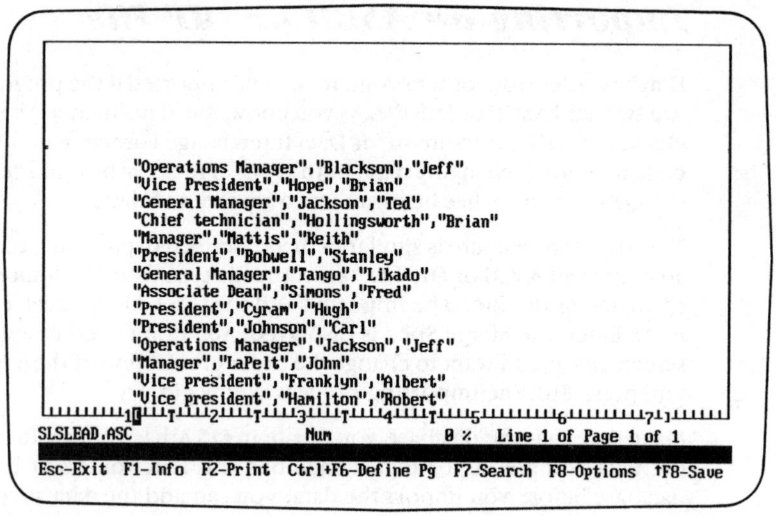

**Fig. 20.15**
*A standard ASCII file.*

```
"Operations Manager","Blackson","Jeff"
"Vice President","Hope","Brian"
"General Manager","Jackson","Ted"
"Chief technician","Hollingsworth","Brian"
"Manager","Mattis","Keith"
"President","Bobwell","Stanley"
"General Manager","Tango","Likado"
"Associate Dean","Simons","Fred"
"President","Cyram","Hugh"
"President","Johnson","Carl"
"Operations Manager","Jackson","Jeff"
"Manager","LaPelt","John"
"Vice president","Franklyn","Albert"
"Vice president","Hamilton","Robert"
SLSLEAD.ASC          Num          0 %   Line 1 of Page 1 of 1
Esc-Exit F1-Info F2-Print Ctrl+F6-Define Pg F7-Search F8-Options ↑F8-Save
```

When a DIF file is generated by another program, the file usually is given a DIF extension. When you import a DIF file, you don't need to specify any special options as you do with Standard ASCII.

# *Exporting Data from Q&A*

Up to this point, the chapter has covered importing data into Q&A. You also may need to export Q&A text files and databases to other programs. The following sections explain how to export data from Q&A.

## *Exporting Text Files*

The beginning of this chapter explains how to import text files in the Write module. You also can use Write to export text files by creating a standard ASCII file. Two methods can be used to export data in the Write module, neither of which involves the main Q&A Utilities module. The Write exporting procedure is easy to use, and you can export a file with headers, footers, and margins by using the Print Options screen.

Before you can export a file through the Write menu, you must load the file into memory by using the Get command from the Write menu. The document is then displayed on-screen. Press Esc to return to the Write menu.

Select Utilities from the Write menu, and select Export to ASCII from the Write Utilities menu. Then choose from a menu of three ASCII formats. When a prompt for the ASCII document appears at the bottom of the screen, enter the name of the

ASCII file that will be created from the Q&A file in memory. *If you are using a version of Q&A prior to Version 3.0, don't press Enter at this time!* If you do, your file will be overwritten immediately by the new ASCII file. At the ASCII file name prompt, type the new name and press Enter.

To export ASCII data from Write, using the Print facility, use the Get command from the Write menu to load the file into memory. Then press F2 to print the document. The Print Options screen is displayed (see fig. 20.16).

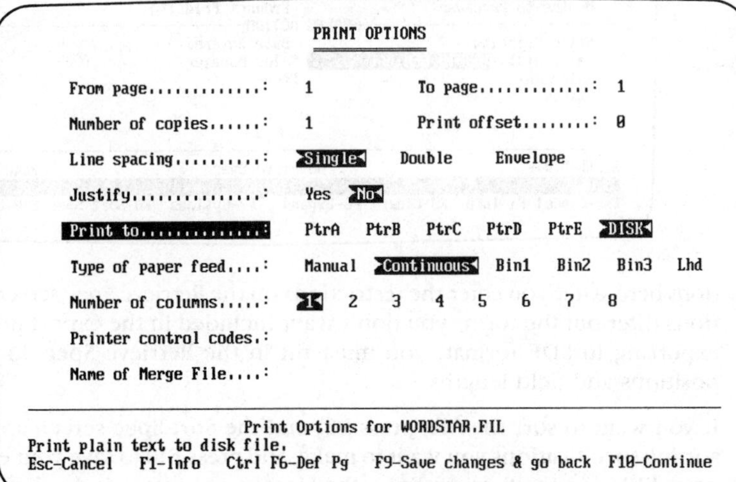


**Fig. 20.16**
*The Print Options screen.*

The Print To option is used to tell Q&A where to send the data. The various Ptr settings assign different printers, but you can use the DISK selection to create an ASCII file. After you choose DISK, press F10 to save the settings. Q&A then displays the Disk Print menu; choose IBM ASCII or Mac ASCII. If the file you are exporting has headers and footers, they are copied to the new file along with the original margin settings.

## Exporting Database Files

Most database programs accept outside files in either ASCII or DIF format. With Q&A you can do more than simply export the data; you can select the forms and fields you want to export, and sort them in a particular order.

For this procedure, select Export Data from the Utilities menu to display the Export menu. This menu has five options, similar to the Import menu. When you select the file type and enter the source and destination file names, the Retrieve Spec is displayed (see fig. 20.17).

You can use the Retrieve Spec screen to restrict the data to be exported. If you want to export the file with no changes, press F10. Otherwise, enter the retrieve specifica-

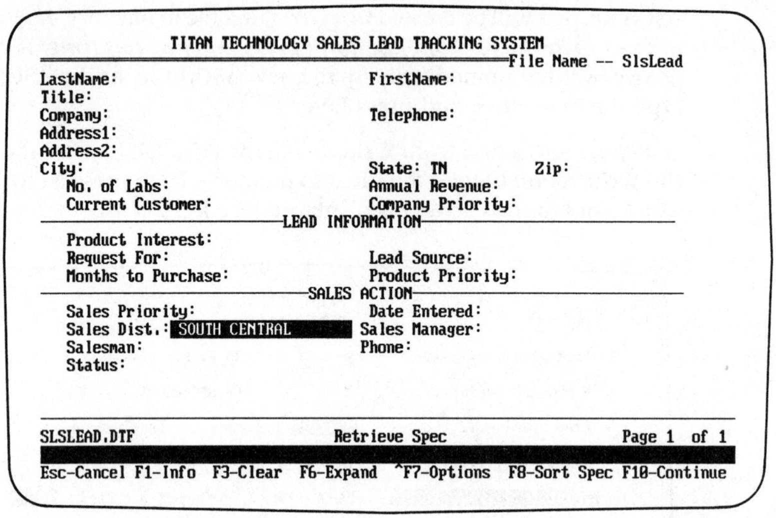

**Fig. 20.17**
*The Retrieve Spec.*

```
                    TITAN TECHNOLOGY SALES LEAD TRACKING SYSTEM
==================================================File Name -- SlsLead
LastName:                              FirstName:
Title:
Company:                               Telephone:
Address1:
Address2:
City:                                  State: TN          Zip:
   No. of Labs:                        Annual Revenue:
   Current Customer:                   Company Priority:
--------------------------LEAD INFORMATION-------------------------------
   Product Interest:
   Request For:                        Lead Source:
   Months to Purchase:                 Product Priority:
-----------------------------SALES ACTION--------------------------------
   Sales Priority:                     Date Entered:
   Sales Dist.: SOUTH CENTRAL          Sales Manager:
   Salesman:                           Phone:
   Status:

SLSLEAD.DTF                    Retrieve Spec                   Page 1 of 1

Esc-Cancel F1-Info  F3-Clear  F6-Expand  ^F7-Options  F8-Sort Spec F10-Continue
```

tions here. After you enter the restrictions on the Retrieve Spec screen, your specifications filter out the forms you don't want included in the export process. If you are exporting to SDF format, you must fill in the Retrieve Spec, to specify column positions and field lengths.

If you want to sort the file, press F8, and the Sort Spec screen appears. Enter any sorting specifications you want to make, and press F10 to save your entries. After you press F10 from the Retrieve Spec, the Merge Spec screen is displayed unless you are exporting to SDF format.

On the Retrieve Spec screen, you specified the forms to be exported; on the Merge Spec screen, you set the field selection and order. (The Merge Spec is discussed in a previous section in this chapter.) After you enter the specifications, press F10.

## *Exporting to ASCII or DIF*

If you are exporting to a DIF file or a standard ASCII file, the export procedure is now finished. If you are creating a standard ASCII file, however, you have one more step. The ASCII Options screen prompts you to specify whether the data in each field will be enclosed in quotation marks and which delimiter will be used to separate fields. You have four choices for the delimiter: carriage return, semicolon, comma, or space. The default delimiter is the comma. The decision you make will depend on the program that is to receive the data. When you press F10, the ASCII file is created.

### *Exporting to dBASE*

The procedures for exporting to dBASE II, dBASE III, and dBASE III Plus are identical, although each program requires a different utility. Simply select one of the utilities, enter the name of the Q&A database, and type the name of the dBASE database. (Be sure not to enter the name of an existing file unless you want it to be overwritten by the exported Q&A file.)

Fill in the Retrieve and Merge Specs, and press F10, creating the database. The database created in dBASE will automatically take on the field type and length characteristics of the Q&A database.

## *Chapter Summary*

Because Q&A's import and export capabilities are so easy to use, Q&A can be used with many of the most popular spreadsheet, database, and word-processing programs. If you have read *Using Q&A*, 2nd Edition, to this point, you are now familiar with all the Q&A operating features; you know how to use Q&A as a self-contained unit and with many other programs. The next chapter explains how to use Q&A in a multi-user environment on a local area network.

### Exporting to dBASE

## Chapter Summary

Chapter 21

# Networking: Using Q&A in a Multi-User Environment

**Microcomputer users increasingly are turning to networking and other methods for multi-user access to programs and data files. With Version 3.0, Q&A addresses this trend by adding multi-user support.**

**This chapter introduces networking and networking concepts, and explains how Q&A fits into that environment. Setting up Q&A on a network is discussed, as well as ideas on configuring Q&A databases for multi-user operation. Differences between using Q&A in a single-user environment and on a network also are covered.**

## Network Concepts

Networks may be an unfamiliar concept to many PC users who are used to single-user systems. The following paragraphs explain computer networks, the benefits of a network, and how Q&A resides on a network.

### What Is a Network?

A *local area network* (LAN) refers to the equipment and software that connects personal computers to each other and usually to a centrally located device called a *server*. The server can be another PC dedicated to server duties, or it can be a minicomputer or mainframe that functions as a server while it conducts other duties.

A LAN uses coaxial cable, telephone wire, or another medium to connect personal computers through a plug-in circuit board. Driver software to support the additional hardware usually must be installed at each PC as well.

Once the physical link is established, PC users can access each other's machine or the server to exchange database information, send and receive electronic mail, and share word-processing files. When a minicomputer or mainframe is part of a network, personal computer users can share the same information and the facilities of the server. Hooking PCs to mainframes or minicomputers also gives users access to any available wide area network. A *wide area network* (WAN) connects computers over a long-distance network using telephone cable, satellite links, or other systems.

## *Why Use a Network?*

One reason for the early popularity of personal computers was because early computer users were linked to large machines controlled by data center personnel. However, installing or changing programs sometimes took weeks or months, if even possible. Also, one user's needs had to coordinate with other users' needs.

Single-user personal computers gave users the freedom to install whatever software they wanted. Within relatively broad budget and procedural limitations, users could do about anything they wanted with their PCs. The refinement of personal computer hardware brought computing power to the people, eliminating what some people have called the "priesthood of computer control."

Within the past few years, however, a growing trend has been to bring PC users back together under some central arrangement that allows them to keep the benefit of personal computer hardware while regaining the strengths of central data and program storage. The local area network has made this change possible.

A LAN offers several advantages over stand-alone PCs. One benefit is that it reduces disk swapping. A LAN also enables many people to work on database maintenance at the same time. Another benefit of a network is that, properly configured, it gives all users simultaneous access to the same versions of database information, word-processing files, electronic mail, and programs. For many users the cost of applications software alone can justify the expense and effort of establishing a network.

Most major software companies offer networked versions of their software so that only one copy of the programs need be installed. The software is stored at the central server, and those who need to use the software access it there rather than from their individual computers. In this way, companies need to purchase only one copy of the software rather than copies for each user. Although multi-user software costs more than single-user software, the total cost of networked software to serve a large number of users frequently is much less than the cost of buying individual copies.

Networked users can share printers as well. Although light-duty printers are available for a few hundred dollars, users increasingly demand high speed, letter quality, graphics, and even color. Printers with these capabilities can be expensive: one popular high-resolution color printer currently sells for nearly $25,000. For most companies, the only way users can access such an expensive device is to share it through a network server, which is much more efficient than carrying floppy disks to a central print station computer.

Disk storage also can be less expensive and more efficient on a network. Moving applications software and data to a central location eliminates most redundant storage requirements. Thus, users can use only floppy disk drives or relatively small hard disks. In fact, some network configurations support disk-free workstations, further reducing the cost of each PC attached to the network.

In addition, central data storage makes maintaining backups easier. Instead of depending on individual users to back up their data regularly, a network management staff backs up the server disk. In this way, everyone's data is backed up at the same time. High-speed, high-capacity tape devices (which frequently provide automatic, timed operations) can be used because only one or two units are required rather than a device for each user.

## *Network Terms*

Networks institute a set of terms that are unfamiliar to many PC users. This section defines a few of the most common network terms.

One definition is especially important for Q&A users. Although network file sharing and multi-user file sharing have some differences, Symantec uses the term *multi-user* to mean networked users. Because Q&A is a microcomputer-based product and multi-user microcomputers are essentially all networked, this is a valid assumption, which this book also adopts.

**Database administrator**. A person charged with maintaining database files and programs. A database administrator's activities generally include backing up files, assigning access rights, installing software upgrades, and designing shared database structures.

**File locking**. A process that denies access to entire database files for more than one user at a time. The first user to access a given file secures all rights to the file. Subsequent users are locked out of the file until the first user releases it.

**Local area network**, or **LAN**. Equipment and software that permits a group of computers to share files and programs. A LAN's operation is usually transparent to the users. The workstations are located relatively close to each other, such as in the same building or on the same campus.

**Multiuser**. Processes and procedures that can be conducted by more than one person simultaneously. Applications software such as Q&A can be established as multiuser programs. Databases and other files, when they can be shared by more than one person at a time, are said to be multiuser files.

**Password**. A group of characters used to uniquely identify a computer user. Passwords typically are entered when a user first accesses a program, such as Q&A.

**Record locking**. A process that denies access to individual database records for more than one user at a time. The first user to access a given record secures modify privileges. Subsequent users are locked out of modify operations until the first user releases the record.

**Security**. A set of processes and procedures to ensure the integrity of computer information. Included are unique user IDs, user-level and group-level passwords, personal paths and directories, and individually assigned access and procedure rights.

**Server**. A central processing unit dedicated to disk, communications, or other shared operations. Disk server functions are the most common server operations of interest to networked Q&A users.

**Wide area network**, or **WAN**. Equipment and software that permits a group of computers to share files and programs. A WAN's operation is usually transparent to the users. A WAN is located over a large distance, such as in different cities or even different countries.

## *The User Versions of Q&A*

The are two ways to use Q&A on a network for simultaneous multi-user access:

- Shared files (single-user Q&A)
- Shared programs and files (multi-user Q&A)

If each user on a network has an individual copy of Q&A, database files still can be stored on the network server and shared among network users. However, these copies are of the single-user version of Q&A. To install a single copy of Q&A on a network server and have multiple users share the program, the single-user version of Q&A must be upgraded to a networked version.

There are no fundamental differences between the single-user version of Q&A and the networked, multi-user version. The single-user software supports shared data access and even record locking to ensure that two or more users don't try to modify the same record at the same time.

The networked version of Q&A operates essentially the same as the single-user version. The multi-user version asks you to provide your identification (usually your name) and a password for some operations, and certain functions cannot be shared. Q&A will display messages to tell you when you are trying to perform an operation that another user already is doing. Also, printing is usually less immediate. See the next section in this chapter for more details on the differences in operation.

# Q&A on a Network

Once any Q&A multi-user software is installed and the data files have been created, little fundamental difference exists between single-user access and multi-user access. However, several aspects of Q&A, such as printing and file access, operate somewhat differently on a network. The following paragraphs describe some differences you should be aware of when you use Q&A under multi-user access.

## Data Access

With most LANs, the network server is accessed as one or more additional disk drives from the users' PCs. DOS sets aside drives A through E as local drives, so the first network drive is drive F.

To access Q&A files or programs from the network, set the appropriate drive default (probably F or above) and run Q&A as if it were on your local drive. Q&A and file access should function virtually the same in the network environment as they do on a single-user PC.

You may occasionally get a message saying that another user is performing the operation you want to perform. You also may notice that some operations are slower than they are in a single-user environment. Otherwise, accessing Q&A data on a network is the same as accessing Q&A on a single-user workstation.

## Record Locking and File Locking Considerations

A law of physics states that no two objects can occupy the same space at the same time. In a sense, multi-user databases follow that law. Although many users can open a file simultaneously, they can modify individual records one at a time only. The first user to display a specific database record locks that record against modification by any other user.

For example, if user A displays a sales lead record on-screen, that user gains modification rights to that record. He can make changes in accordance with his access rights and save the modified record back to disk. While user A is displaying a record, the record is said to be *locked*.

If user B finds the same record while user A is modifying it, Q&A will show user B the following message:

```
Form is being edited by another user. You can't make changes at
this time.
```

User B can only view the information; she cannot change it. This restriction is necessary to ensure data integrity: if both users could modify the record simultaneously, the last user to use the record would overwrite previous changes. By controlling access so that only the first user to access a given record has rights to modify it, user A's changes will be retained. As soon as the first user writes his changes and moves on to another record, subsequent users can then call up that record for editing.

Most Q&A networked operations are open to all users sharing a database at any time. However, some networked operations can be performed by only one user at a time. Table 21.1 shows operations that are *single-user functions on a shared file*. Although multiple users can access the shared file, only one user at a time can perform each operation listed. For example, one user can design a Print Spec and another can assign passwords in the same file simultaneously, but two users cannot design a Print Spec at the same time.

**Table 21.1**
**Single-User Functions on a Shared File**

| *Module* | *Function* |
|---|---|
| File | Design a Print Spec<br>Assign passwords<br>Assign user rights |
| Report | Design a report |

Some operations are critical to database integrity and directly affect the view other users have of the database. These functions are considered *single-user functions on a locked file* and completely lock the file against access by any other user, for any type of operation. The operations that lock the file are listed in table 21.2.

**Table 21.2**
**Single-User Functions on a Locked File**

| *Module* | *Function* |
|---|---|
| File | Redesign a file<br>Customize a file<br>Mass file update<br>Remove file forms |
| IA | Teach<br>Mass file update |
| Utilities | Database recovery<br>DOS commands |

## *Network Messages*

In addition to the normal Q&A messages, other messages and error reports may appear when you operate in a multi-user environment. A summary of networking messages is listed in table 21.3.

**Table 21.3**
**Network Messages**

| *Message* | *Meaning* |
|---|---|
| Form is being edited by another user. You can't make changes at this time. | You attempted to modify a form that already has been accessed by another user. Only one user at a time is given modify rights to individual records. |
| This function is currently in use. Please try again later. Press Esc. | You attempted to perform a single-user operation in a multi-user environment. Two users cannot design a Print Spec at the same time, for example. |
| This function cannot be used while others are using the database. Press Esc. | You attempted to perform a single-user operation while another user is using the file. Some operations, such as file redesign or customize operations, lock the entire file. Only one user at a time can open a file for these operations. |
| File is in use by <Network ID>. | You attempted to access a file that has been locked by another user who is conducting a single-user operation. <Network ID> tells you who is using the file. |
| There are <X> current users out of <Y> permitted under your license. | This message is displayed when Q&A first loads. It shows how many people are using multi-user Q&A and how many users the software is licensed to support. |
| User ID: | Q&A is asking for your name or other code that identifies you. This prompt appears in a password box automatically when required, or when you press F6 at the Main menu. |

**Table 21.3 — *Continued***

| *Message* | *Meaning* |
| --- | --- |
| Password: | Q&A is asking for your unique password to permit you access to shared or protected functions or data. This prompt appears in a password box automatically when required, or when you press F6 at the Main menu. |

## *Q&A Write in a Multi-User Environment*

If you have installed a Network Pack, you can share the Write programs in a network. You can view or modify a Write document and then save it to a network server, where another user can access the document. However, Write documents are essentially single-user files. Two or more users cannot have access to the same Write document simultaneously.

## *The Intelligent Assistant in a Multi-User Environment*

You can use the IA in a shared environment as you normally do—except for Teach. Only one user can access the Teach facilities of the IA at a time.

## *Macros in a Multi-User Environment*

You can use your macros on a network the same as with a single-user environment, with one exception. When the Q&A Main menu is first displayed, press F6 to call up the password box and enter your password. This way, Q&A will remember your password and will not ask for it during other operations. When you enter your password first (before Q&A must ask for it), macros that access password-protected operations won't stop to ask for your password.

## *Printing in a Multi-User Environment*

A shared printer can serve only one user (one print job) at a time. Your network software handles competing requests for the printer by queuing print jobs in a RAM cache or on disk. When you send a job to a networked printer, you should see no difference between printing on a LAN and printing in a single-user environment except that your printout may not be produced immediately. If another user is accessing the printer when you send a report to be printed, your report will move into the queue and print in turn as jobs ahead of yours are finished.

In addition, Q&A handles file contention during report preparation by making a copy of the database at the time you request a report. In this way you can access data for a printout without interfering with other users who may be modifying the data. Of course, your report will not reflect any changes to the database after the report is started.

# Q&A Network Setup

Regardless of which user version of Q&A a network has, one person usually is in charge of setting up Q&A on the LAN. Often, the network administrator will install all applications software, manage the network, and possibly perform other full-time duties.

## Single-User Q&A Vs. Multi-User Q&A

You should consult your dealer and study your network's use of Q&A to determine whether networked software is more economical and efficient than individual copies of the software for each user. Some of the factors to study when you consider a multi-user Q&A upgrade are the size of your user community, the type of hardware each user has, the size and number of databases that will be shared, and the cost of single-user Q&A copies vs. a multi-user license to support all your users.

Remember that sharing multi-user Q&A on a network can slow down access by individual users, because a server has a maximum processing speed. When multiple users share the server and its software, the number of required disks and CPU accesses increases, reducing the performance to any individual user.

Cost is also a major consideration. Check with your dealer and compare the costs of single-user Q&A for each user and the cost of a multi-user license. If the costs are similar, you should consider purchasing single-user software to provide the fastest access time to each user. You still can store Q&A data files on the server for sharing among all your users.

If you decide on single-user copies of Q&A, however, each user should have a hard disk workstation. If most users do not have hard disks on their PCs, you probably should use the multi-user version of Q&A. Q&A can run from floppy disks, but doing so is inconvenient for any but the most simple applications. And adding hard disks to user workstations can be a significant cost.

Remember, too, that with single-user software, when new versions are released you must upgrade each user individually. If you have a large user population, this cost can be significant.

## Networks That Q&A Supports

Q&A probably will work in a multi-user environment on any of the popular networks that run under MS-DOS or PC DOS Version 3.1 or later, as well as the AppleShare network. Symantec specifically mentions support for the 3Plus network, the IBM PC Network and Token-Ring, and networks that use NetWare® software. In fact, any network that adheres to the multi-user procedures of DOS (that is, any network that uses the DOS SHARE program or implements the SHARE protocols) should work with Q&A. Symantec is expanding the list of supported networks regularly. If you have questions about Q&A support for your specific network, contact the network vendor or Symantec.

## Q&A Network Pack

The Q&A Network Pack is additional software that enables simultaneous, multi-user access to Q&A. Without the Network Pack, each Q&A user must have a separate copy of the single-user version of the software. If each user has a single-user copy of Q&A, you don't need the Network Pack. If you want networked users to share Q&A, then you need the Network Pack to enable the multi-user features.

The Network Pack is an enhancement to an existing copy of single-user Q&A. Each Network Pack increases the number of users by three. Thus, the first Pack allows four users to access the Q&A program simultaneously, a second Pack supports up to seven users (the original single user, three users on Network Pack 1, and three users on Network Pack 2), a third Pack supports up to 10 users, and so on.

When you use the Network Pack, you install a single-user copy of Q&A on your network server and then install the network portion. This procedure modifies your installed Q&A so that it runs on a network only. After installing a networked version of the software, you can no longer use the single-user version without violating the terms of your software license.

Included with the Network Pack is the Q&A Network Administrator's Guide, which shows you how to configure Q&A programs for shared access and offers some instruction on network management. The guide is a valuable part of the Network Pack, and you should read it thoroughly before setting up Q&A for network operation.

## Upgrading to Multi-User Q&A

You can easily upgrade single-user copies of Q&A to a networked version by purchasing one or more Network Packs (see the section "Q&A Network Pack" in this chapter). Ask your Q&A dealer or Symantec for information on current costs and procedures for making the upgrade. If you purchase Q&A as a networked package, you will receive one single-user copy and enough Network Packs to support the number of users required for your network.

To set up your system for network access, you may have to alter your system files:

- Determine whether you need to use the DOS SHARE program. This program turns on DOS-level file contention control. Some networks, such as those that use NetWare or 3Plus network, supply these sharing codes for you. Others, such as MS-Net and PC-net, require that you load the SHARE program before using multi-user files. If your network requires you to load SHARE, simply add the SHARE command to your AUTOEXEC.BAT file.
- Make sure that your CONFIG.SYS file contains the statement FILES=20, or a larger number. This limit will ensure that DOS is set up to handle Q&A file access.

For detailed instructions on installing Q&A and configuring the package for your computer environment, see Appendix A. For information on installing a Q&A Network Pack for shared program access, contact Symantec.

# Multi-User Databases

Although there are no fundamental differences between the single-user version of Q&A and the networked version, whoever creates a database—whether the database administrator or someone else—needs to consider some operational factors when setting up a database for multi-user operation. If you are creating a database, you must perform such functions as establish access rights for each database and declare the Sharing mode. You also can assign passwords to each database to restrict user access.

Be aware that true multi-user operation in Q&A is restricted to databases and the support programs for them. A database file can be controlled so that each user can access one record at a time, giving many users simultaneous access to the database file. Networked users also can share word-processing files, but only one person can have access to a given file at a time. The reason is that controlling how more than one person uses and changes a text-based file is difficult or impossible. Therefore, the multi-user instructions in this chapter apply to database access only.

## Designing Multi-User Databases

The basic concepts of designing a database are essentially the same for single-user and multi-user operation. Some additional considerations may apply to some database applications, however.

In a typical Q&A installation, several data files store different kinds of information. You may have an inventory file, a customer file, one or more sales support files, some accounting or bookkeeping files, and personnel files, for example. After you design these files (using some of the techniques described in Chapters 4 through 6), you may want to restrict access to some of these files—for example, to the general payroll files or the inventory information files.

One way to control this level of access easily is to establish user classes or groups. At the simplest level, each member of a group can be assigned a group ID and password. This arrangement reduces the number of different access rights that the database administrator must track. However, this arrangement is less secure than one in which each user is assigned a separate ID and unique password. Such group assignments must be done at the network level.

Q&A supports only user-based access. Several users can share the same ID and password, but the idea of groups, with each user in the group assigned a unique ID and password, is not supported. Some networks (such as NetWare), however, do permit simultaneous group and individual ID and password assignments. You can use the security features of your individual network to enhance Q&A's multi-user access control. Refer to your network configuration manual for more information on this technique.

## *Specifying the Mode*

Before multiple users can share a database file, the file must be configured for sharing. Select Assign Access Rights from the Main/File/Design/Customize menu sequence, calling up the Access menu (see fig. 21.1). Then choose Declare Sharing Mode to call up the screen for setting multi-user access for a file (see fig. 21.2). To turn on Sharing mode, specify Allow from the Declare Sharing Mode screen; to disable Sharing mode, select Disallow from the screen. Because you must declare which file you will customize before the Customize menu is displayed, the operations on the Access menu apply to one file at a time.

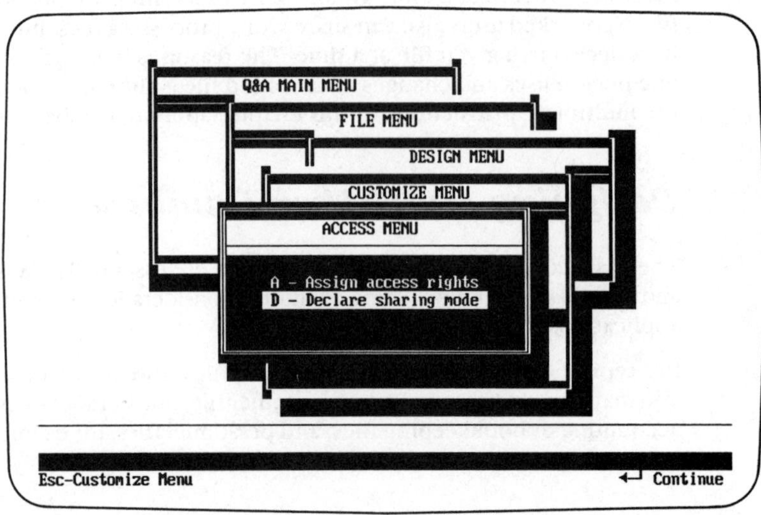


**Fig. 21.1.** *The Access menu.*

```
DECLARE SHARING MODE

On most networks Q&A will automatically allow or disallow
concurrent sharing of a data file depending on whether the
file is on a file server or a local drive. If you want to
make sure that concurrent sharing is either allowed or
disallowed, regardless of the location of the file, make
the appropriate selection below. If the file is to be
used by only one person (or one person at a time), select
"Disallow" to ensure the best performance.

WARNING: Do NOT select "Allow" if this data file is to be
used by only one person or one person at a time.

▸Automatic◂     Disallow     Allow

Esc-Cancel                                      F10-Continue
```

**Fig. 21.2**
*The Declare Sharing Mode screen.*

Q&A can handle file contention automatically by determining whether files are being stored on a server or a local PC. Also, if files are being stored on a network server, Q&A assumes that you want to share them. For some applications, forced Sharing or forced Non-Sharing mode is desirable. If you want to maintain a private, personal database, for example, you can prevent other users from accessing it by disallowing sharing from the Declare Sharing Mode screen. Or you may want to force sharing or non-sharing for some applications software.

## Specifying Access Rights and Passwords

One method of controlling access to network facilities is to assign each user a unique ID and password. Unless the ID and password are entered correctly, a user is denied access to specific network features, programs, or files.

If you want to restrict access to some of the files stored on a network server, choose Assign Access Rights from the Access menu (refer to fig. 21.1). From the Access Control screen you can assign *user rights*: which functions a user will be allowed to perform (see fig. 21.3). From this screen you also can assign user IDs and passwords.

You can use function keys to create and display Access Control screens. See table 21.4 for a list of Access Control screen function keys.

**Fig. 21.3**
*The Access Control screen.*

```
                    ACCESS CONTROL

                   User ID:
          Initial Password: PASSWORD

Make the selections below to indicate what rights this person has:

Administrative rights?...:  Yes  No

Change form design?......:  Yes  No

Change report design?....:  Yes  No

Data access..............:  Read & Write  Read only

SLSLEAD.DTF          Access Control Form 1    of 1

Esc-Cancel  F3-Del  Ctrl F6-Add user  F9-Prev  F10-Next  Shift F10-Continue
```

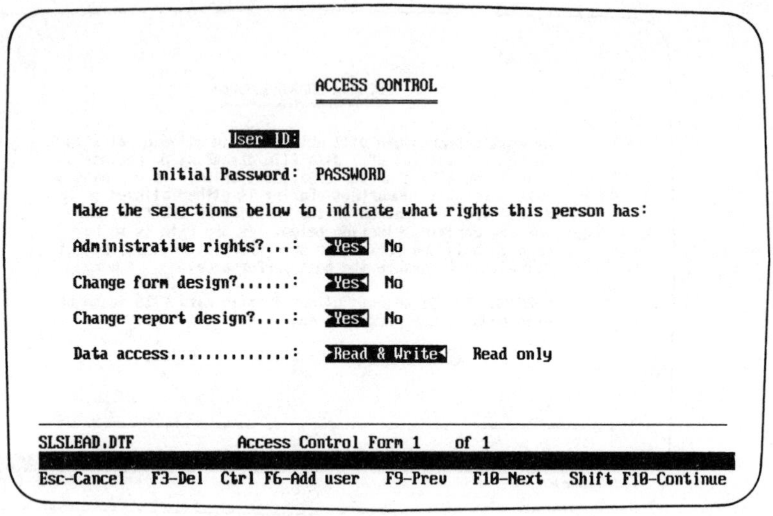

**Table 21.4**
**Access Control Screen Function Keys**

| *Key* | *Function* |
|---|---|
| Ctrl-F6 | Create new Access Control screen |
| F9 | Display preceding Access Control screen |
| F10 | Display next Access Control screen |
| Shift-F10 | Save current Access Control screen and exit |
| Ctrl-Home | Go to first Access Control screen |
| Ctrl-End | Go to last Access Control screen |
| Esc | Cancel changes to current Access Control screen and exit |

The first time you use the Access Control screen, be sure to establish one user as the database administrator. This user should be given all rights to Q&A. Otherwise, you may be locked out of important Q&A functions. The reason is that once any controlled access is established, only those users who have been entered through the Access Control screen can access the database. If you establish a user with less than full rights as the first user, then no one will have access to the full capabilities of the database.

## *Chapter Summary*

This chapter introduces the concept of multi-user access to Q&A programs and data. You learned differences between single-user and multi-user Q&A operation, and how to design and use the networked Q&A.

For detailed instructions on installing Q&A and configuring the package for your computer environment, see Appendix A. For information on installing a Q&A Network Pack for shared program access, contact Symantec.

Appendix

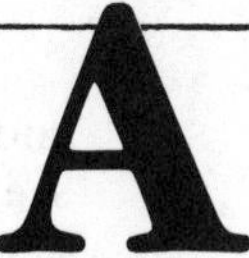

# Installing and Starting Q&A

The Q&A program requires the following hardware:

- IBM PC, IBM PC XT, or IBM Personal Computer AT, or some other compatible computer
- Two floppy disk drives, or one floppy disk drive and one hard disk drive
- Minimum of 512K of RAM (some Q&A operations require as much as 484K; a full 640K of RAM is recommended, especially if you intend to use memory-resident programs with Q&A)
- PC DOS or MS-DOS® operating system, Version 2.0 or higher
- 80-column monochrome or color monitor
- Printer

## *Installing the Q&A Program*

When you have your hardware in place, you can begin the process of installing the Q&A program. The first step is to tailor Q&A to your computer system. This procedure involves specifying the printer to be used, selecting the type of display, and installing the programs on floppies or your hard disk. After also setting the default drive and directory, you must prepare your data disks.

First, check the CONFIG.SYS file in the root directory of your hard disk or boot-up floppy disk. This file should include the following statements, which ensure that Q&A can function properly:

```
FILES = 20
BUFFERS = 10
```

To view an existing CONFIG.SYS file, change to the root directory with the CD\ command. At the DOS prompt, type

```
TYPE CONFIG.SIS
```

and press Enter. If a CONFIG.SYS file exists, text scrolls up the screen. If you do not see FILES and BUFFER statements, use any ASCII text editor to add these statements. Refer to your DOS manual for additional information on preparing CONFIG.SYS files.

If you do not have a CONFIG.SYS file, DOS responds with a `File Not Found` error message.

To create a new CONFIG.SYS file, use an ASCII editor or type the following command at the DOS root directory prompt:

```
COPY CON CONFIG.SYS
```

Then press Enter.

Next, type

```
FILES = 20
BUFFERS = 10
```

(Press Enter at the end of each statement.) Finally, press F6 (or hold down the Ctrl key and press Z), and then press Enter.

***Note:*** If you are short on memory, reduce the number of buffers to 2.

Before you install Q&A, make backup copies of the original disks. The following installation instructions assume that you have made backup copies and that you are using these backup disks for the installation. Your DOS manual can help with the backup procedure.

Installation involves copying the files from the Q&A backup disks to a hard disk or to floppies. Version 3.0 of Q&A includes seven 5 1/4-inch disks or three 3 1/2-inch disks. Symantec will exchange one set of media for another. Refer to your Q&A manual for details on exchanging 5 1/4-inch disks for 3 1/2-inch disks, or vice versa.

## *Installing Q&A on a Hard Disk System*

The following steps enable you to copy the Q&A disks to your hard disk drive so that you can start and use the program without switching the floppy disks in and out of the drives.

1. On each Q&A master disk, cover the write-protect notch with a tab to protect the disk from accidental erasure. If you don't have a disk write-protect notch tab, you can use a one-inch piece of masking or freezer tape.

2. Start your computer. Correct or verify the date and time if necessary. When the prompt (>) appears, make sure that the C drive (or other hard disk prompt) is displayed before the prompt. If not, type *C:* and press Enter.

3. Make a subdirectory to hold the Q&A program and files. To create a subdirectory named QA, type

   MD\QA

   and press Enter. (See the DOS manual for further explanation of subdirectories.)

4. Change to the new directory by typing

   CD\QA

   and pressing Enter.

5. Copy the contents of each Q&A program disk, starting with Disk 1 Start-up Disk, to the hard disk. Place the master Q&A Disk 1 Start-up Disk in drive A. At the C> prompt, type

   COPY A:*.*/V

   and press Enter. (The /V switch verifies the COPY procedure.) When the copying has been completed, remove the master Q&A disk from drive A.

6. Copy the remaining disks, in order, by repeating step 5. To save room on the hard disk, you can elect not to copy disk number 7, but if you want to use the tutorial later you'll have to run it from a floppy drive or copy the programs from the Tutorial Disk to your hard disk.

Q&A now resides on the hard disk, and you may store the Q&A master disks for safekeeping. When installed on your hard disk, Q&A occupies a little more than one megabyte (one million bytes).

## *Installing Q&A on a Floppy Disk System*

The general procedure for preparing the Q&A program disks on a two floppy disk drive system involves two main steps:

1. Format seven 5 1/4-inch or three 3 1/2-inch new disks as backup disks, and copy the operating system onto one disk so that you can start Q&A from this disk. (Refer to your DOS manual for help with formatting disks.)

2. Make backup copies of the four program disks and the Tutorial Disk. Label all the copied disks to match the distribution media, and store the originals in a safe place.

After the disks are formatted, copy all the files from the original (distribution) Q&A media to your newly formatted disks. Make sure that you copy the files from the Q&A System Disk #1 to the formatted disk that also includes the operating system. This disk will become your working start-up disk. You'll also need to format some floppy disks for storing Q&A files.

## *Installing Your Printer*

Q&A operates with many printer brands and models, but the complete range of Q&A print enhancements (condensed print, italic print, and so on) works only with certain printers.

Keep in mind that completing the printer installation process is not essential because of Q&A's "plain vanilla" printer driver, which works with just about anything that connects to a computer and puts ink on paper. Such a printer will reproduce letters, numbers, and symbols but no boldface, underline, or other special text formatting. With a plain vanilla installation, you're wise to avoid any chore that goes beyond printing the basics.

Q&A allows you to assign a printer to each of three parallel ports and two serial ports. Ports are the connectors in the back of the computer that provide access to the printer. Parallel ports are designated LPT; serial ports are designated COM. If the computer has more than one of either type, each port is assigned a number, such as LPT1 and LPT2. If you're not sure what parallel or serial ports you have, check your computer manual or ask your dealer.

If you have a daisy-wheel or a laser printer, it may require a serial port. Most dot-matrix printers are parallel models and are usually connected to the LPT1 port. One or more ports may be used by a modem, mouse, or plotter.

Laser printers come in both parallel and serial configurations. Refer to your laser printer manual to find out which port your printer requires.

To install a printer, you first select the printer port and then attach the printer cable to that port. Follow these steps:

1. Select Install Printer from the Q&A Utilities menu. The Port Selection screen appears, as illustrated in figure A.1.

2. Select the printer port by moving the highlight cursor with the up- and down-arrow keys or the space bar and then pressing Enter. The List of Printers screen displays, as shown in figure A.2.

3. Select the printer by moving the highlight cursor with the arrow keys, the space bar, or the PgDn and PgUp keys and then pressing Enter. If you can't find your printer or a compatible printer on the list, choose Basic (Vanilla) Printer.

   If you select LPT1, LPT2, or LPT3 as the printer port, Q&A continues to the Special Printer Options screen. If you select COM1 or COM2 as the printer port, Q&A first displays the COM (Serial) Port Settings screen, as illustrated in figure A.3.

4. If you are using a serial printer, select the correct COM port settings for your printer according to your serial printer manual. Use the up- and down-arrow keys or the space bar to move the left-column highlight to each of the four communications settings: Baud Rate, Data Bits, Stop

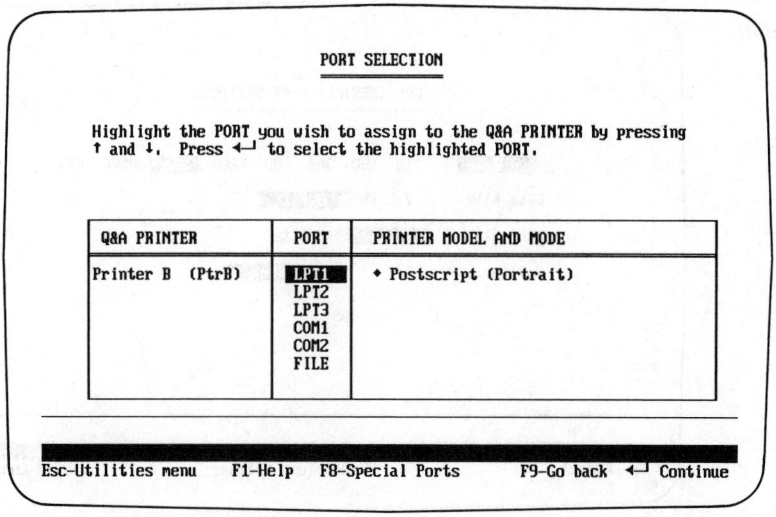

PORT SELECTION

Highlight the PORT you wish to assign to the Q&A PRINTER by pressing ↑ and ↓. Press ←┘ to select the highlighted PORT.

| Q&A PRINTER | PORT | PRINTER MODEL AND MODE |
|---|---|---|
| Printer B (PtrB) | LPT1<br>LPT2<br>LPT3<br>COM1<br>COM2<br>FILE | ◆ Postscript (Portrait) |

Esc-Utilities menu F1-Help F8-Special Ports F9-Go back ←┘ Continue

**Fig. A.1** *The Port Selection screen.*

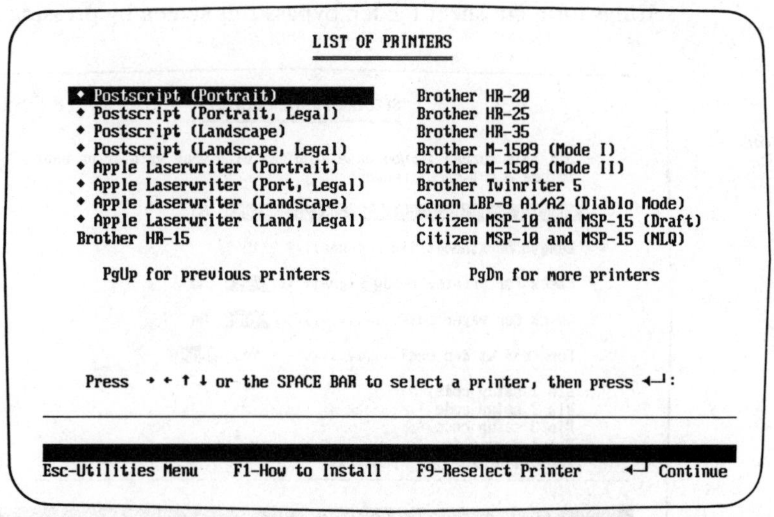

LIST OF PRINTERS

◆ Postscript (Portrait)
◆ Postscript (Portrait, Legal)
◆ Postscript (Landscape)
◆ Postscript (Landscape, Legal)
◆ Apple Laserwriter (Portrait)
◆ Apple Laserwriter (Port, Legal)
◆ Apple Laserwriter (Landscape)
◆ Apple Laserwriter (Land, Legal)
Brother HR-15
Brother HR-20
Brother HR-25
Brother HR-35
Brother M-1509 (Mode I)
Brother M-1509 (Mode II)
Brother Twinriter 5
Canon LBP-8 A1/A2 (Diablo Mode)
Citizen MSP-10 and MSP-15 (Draft)
Citizen MSP-10 and MSP-15 (NLQ)

PgUp for previous printers PgDn for more printers

Press → ← ↑ ↓ or the SPACE BAR to select a printer, then press ←┘:

Esc-Utilities Menu F1-How to Install F9-Reselect Printer ←┘ Continue

**Fig. A.2** *The List of Printers screen.*

Bits, and Parity. At each communications setting, move the highlight, by using the right- and left-arrow keys or the space bar, to the correct setting. Then press Enter. After you have selected all four settings, press F10 to continue to the Special Printer Options screen.

5. At the Special Printer Options screen (see fig. A.4), use the right- and left-arrow keys to highlight your choices for installing a cut sheet feeder or for entering settings for a nonstandard printer. (Check your printer manual for the correct settings.) If you are using one of the

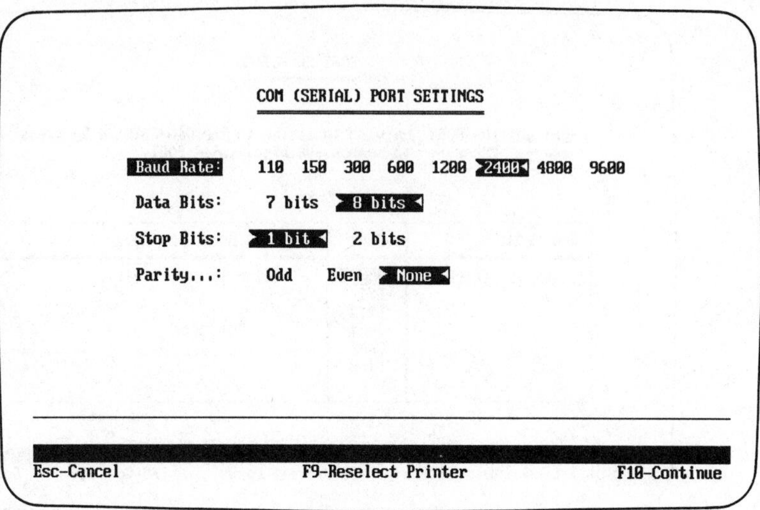
COM (SERIAL) PORT SETTINGS

Baud Rate: 110 150 300 600 1200 2400 4800 9600

Data Bits: 7 bits 8 bits

Stop Bits: 1 bit 2 bits

Parity...: Odd Even None

Esc-Cancel F9-Reselect Printer F10-Continue

**Fig. A.3** *The COM (Serial) Port Settings screen.*

printers from Q&A's List of Printers and do not need to enter special settings for a cut sheet feeder, bypass this screen by pressing F10.

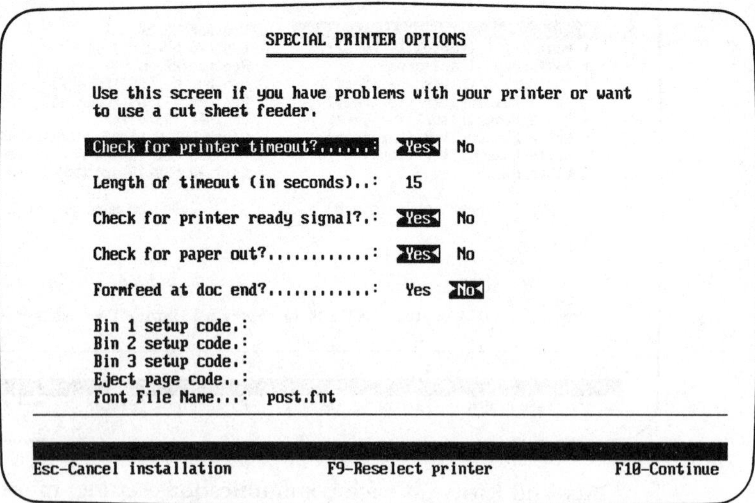
SPECIAL PRINTER OPTIONS

Use this screen if you have problems with your printer or want to use a cut sheet feeder.

Check for printer timeout?......: Yes No

Length of timeout (in seconds)..: 15

Check for printer ready signal?.: Yes No

Check for paper out?...........: Yes No

Formfeed at doc end?...........: Yes No

Bin 1 setup code.:
Bin 2 setup code.:
Bin 3 setup code.:
Eject page code..:
Font File Name...: post.fnt

Esc-Cancel installation F9-Reselect printer F10-Continue

**Fig. A.4** *The Special Printer Options screen.*

After you have made the appropriate selections, Q&A returns you to the Utilities menu.

If you have more than one printer, connect and install each on a different port. Then you can switch printers quickly, just by selecting a different port on the Print Options screen (see fig. A.5).

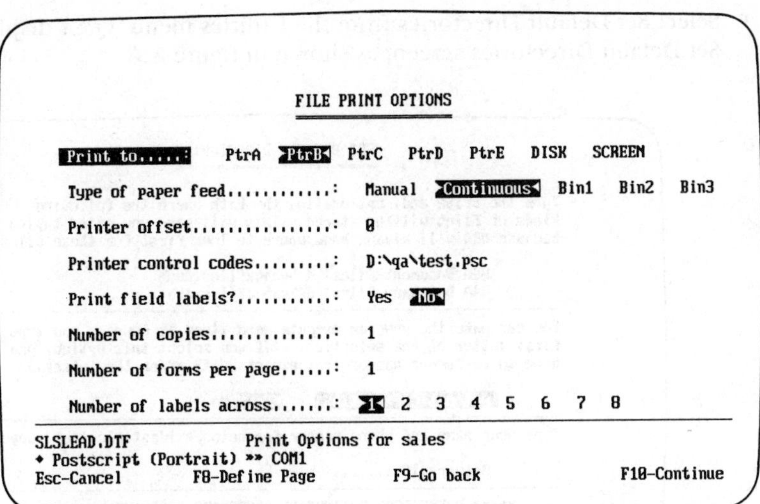
FILE PRINT OPTIONS

Print to.....: PtrA PtrB PtrC PtrD PtrE DISK SCREEN
Type of paper feed...........: Manual Continuous Bin1 Bin2 Bin3
Printer offset...............: 0
Printer control codes........: D:\qa\test.psc
Print field labels?..........: Yes No
Number of copies.............: 1
Number of forms per page.....: 1
Number of labels across......: 1 2 3 4 5 6 7 8

SLSLEAD.DTF Print Options for sales
• Postscript (Portrait) ** COM1
Esc-Cancel F8-Define Page F9-Go back F10-Continue

**Fig. A.5** *Selecting a different printer port.*

## *Setting the Default Drive and Directory*

Default drives and directories are the ones that Q&A automatically selects to save document and database files and drives and directories where the program looks to find and load the files. You can set the drive and the directory in the Set Default Directories option of the Utilities menu. You should set up separate subdirectories for your document and database files.

Why use a document subdirectory? Unless you change the directory, Q&A Write stores documents with the program files and the database files. This method doesn't cause a problem when you have only a few documents. As the number of documents increases, however, the list of files gets longer and longer. The tedious search through that list to find one document is time-consuming and unnecessary. You can avoid this problem by creating a subdirectory—thus creating a separate list of documents.

Why use a database subdirectory? Backing up database files is much easier if they are in a separate subdirectory. You then need only one DOS command to copy everything in your database file directory to your backup disk.

To create subdirectories, use the DOS MD command (see your DOS manual). For example, to create QATEXT and QADATA subdirectories, type the following commands at the `C>` prompt (pressing Enter after each command):

MD\QATEXT
MD\QADATA

To set the default drive and directory within Q&A, follow these steps (using drive C, the QATEXT subdirectory for documents, and the QADATA subdirectory for databases):

1. Select Set Default Directories from the Utilities menu. Q&A displays the Set Default Directories screen, as shown in figure A.6.

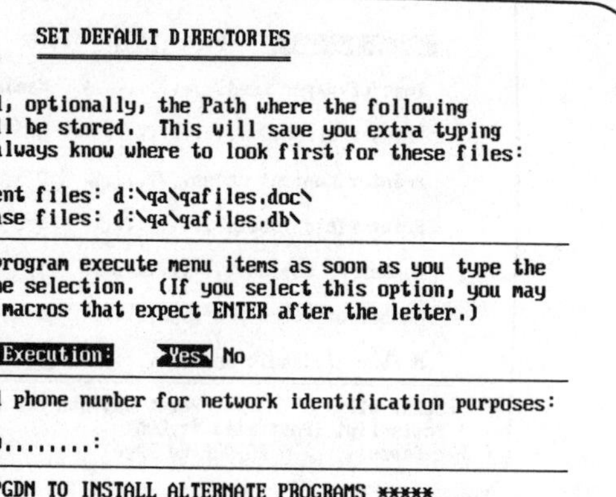

SET DEFAULT DIRECTORIES
Type the Drive and, optionally, the Path where the following kinds of files will be stored. This will save you extra typing because Q&A will always know where to look first for these files:
Q&A Document files: d:\qa\qafiles.doc\
Q&A Database files: d:\qa\qafiles.db\
You can make the program execute menu items as soon as you type the first letter of the selection. (If you select this option, you may have to re-record macros that expect ENTER after the letter.)
Automatic Execution: Yes No
Type your name and phone number for network identification purposes:
Network ID........:
***** PRESS PGDN TO INSTALL ALTERNATE PROGRAMS *****
Esc-Cancel
PgDn-Install alternate programs
F10-Continue


**Fig. A.6.** *The Set Default Directories screen.*

2. To set the default for the Q&A document files, type

   C:\QATEXT

   and press Enter. *C:* sets the default drive to drive C. *\QATEXT* sets the subdirectory. You may select any convenient subdirectory that is compatible with DOS conventions.

3. To set the default for the Q&A database files, type

   C:\QADATA

   and press Enter.

4. Press F10 to return to the Utilities menu, or enter a setting for an alternate program, as explained in the following section.

## *Setting Alternate Programs*

In addition to using the Set Default Directories option from the Utilities menu for selecting the default drive and directory, you can use this option to provide access to other programs from the Q&A Main menu. Use the Alternate Program selection to indicate the subdirectory where the alternate program is stored (see fig. A.7).

If you frequently use another software program (such as Lotus 1-2-3), you can enter it as one of the default alternate programs. If you have installed 1-2-3 in a subdirectory

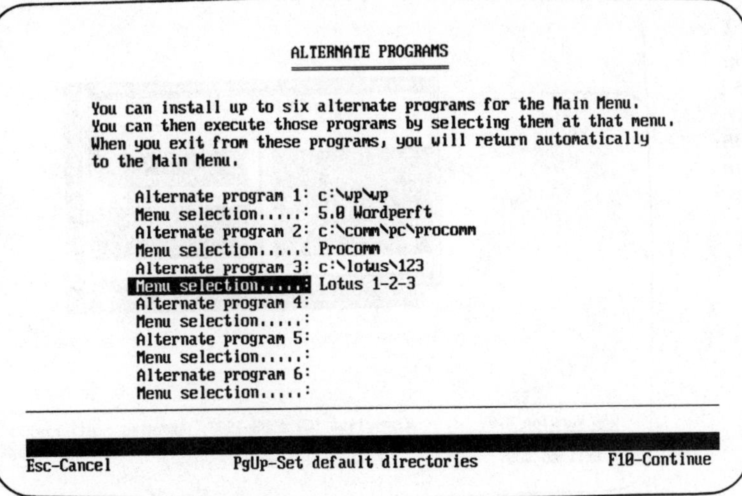
ALTERNATE PROGRAMS

You can install up to six alternate programs for the Main Menu.
You can then execute those programs by selecting them at that menu.
When you exit from these programs, you will return automatically
to the Main Menu.

```
Alternate program 1: c:\wp\wp
Menu selection.....: 5.0 Wordperft
Alternate program 2: c:\comm\pc\procomm
Menu selection.....: Procomm
Alternate program 3: c:\lotus\123
Menu selection.....: Lotus 1-2-3
Alternate program 4:
Menu selection.....:
Alternate program 5:
Menu selection.....:
Alternate program 6:
Menu selection.....:
```

Esc-Cancel PgUp-Set default directories F10-Continue

**Fig. A.7** *The Alternate Program selection from the Set Default Directories screen.*

called \123 on drive C, you can set the default alternate program by using the following procedure:

1. Select Set Default Directories from the Utilities menu.
2. To set Lotus 1-2-3 as a default alternate program, type

   C:\123\LOTUS.COM

   after `Alternate program ...:`.
3. To display `Lotus 1-2-3` as a menu selection on Q&A's Main menu, type

   Lotus 1-2-3

   after `Menu selection ...:`.
4. Repeat these steps for up to five additional alternate programs.

After you have entered settings in the Alternate Program and Menu Selection options and pressed F10, Q&A supplies additional menu items in its Main menu. Figure A.8, for example, shows Lotus 1-2-3, ProComm, and WordPerfect 5.0 as additional menu selections.

Q&A lets you specify nearly any program name as an alternate selection, but if you select a name that begins with the same letter as a standard Q&A selection, your alternate selection replaces the Q&A default. For example, to install WordPerfect as the default word processor, replacing Write, use WordPerfect as the program name. Then when you type *W* at the Main menu, you load WordPerfect rather than the Write module. You can still call up the Write module in this example by typing the number *3* at the Q&A Main menu, or you can specify another name for WordPerfect that does not conflict with Q&A's existing Write program name.

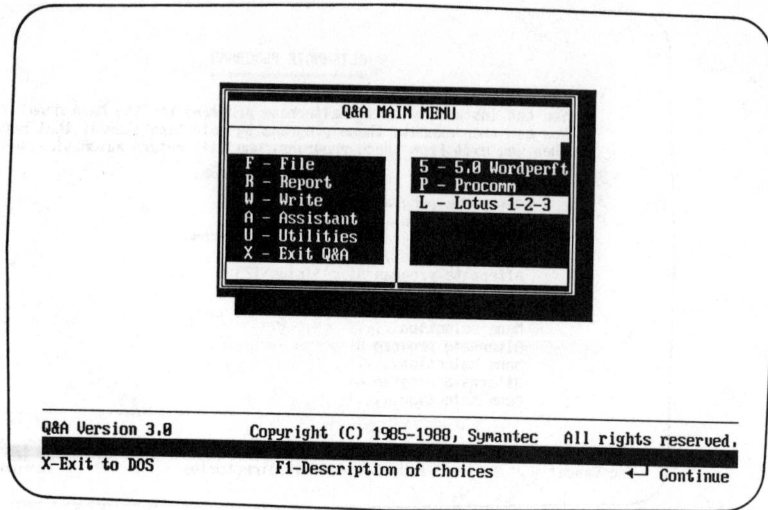


**Fig. A.8.** *Lotus 1-2-3, ProComm, and WordPerfect 5.0 appearing as menu selections on Q&A's Main menu.*

# *Using the Q&A Tutor*

Using the Q&A Tutor is an effective and easy way for you to learn the basics of Q&A. The tutorial program provides a guided tour through Q&A, with instructions and examples that help you begin to master Q&A. The Tutor uses the Q&A program but adds a few menu items, as you can see in figures A.9 and A.10. As an aid to understanding, the Tutor offers on-screen prompts, explanation messages, and working examples.

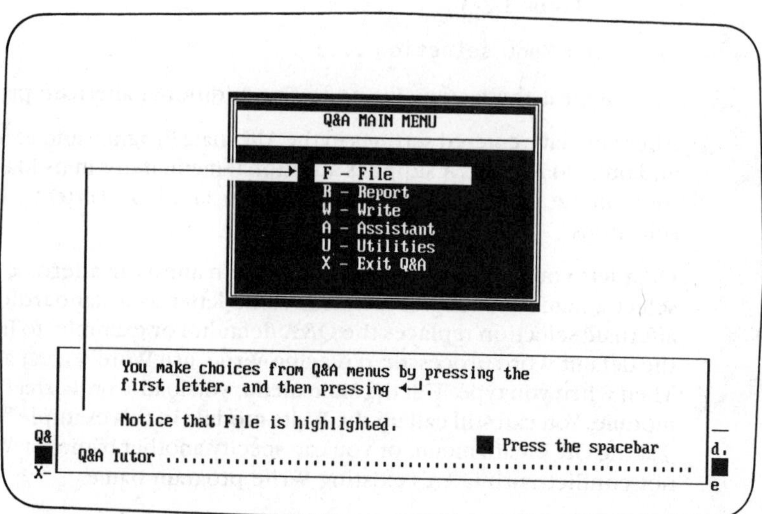


**Fig. A.9** *The Tutor's Main menu.*

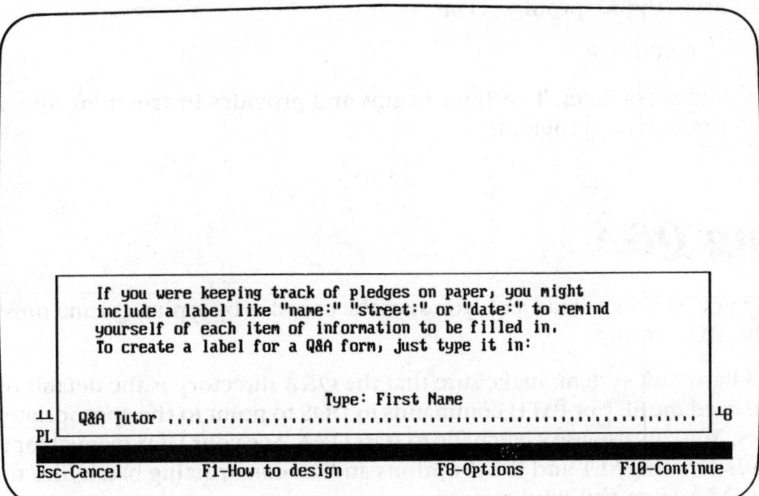


**Fig. A.10** *The Tutor's Design a File screen.*

To use the Tutor on a hard disk system,

1. Start from the DOS `C>` prompt. If you are in Q&A, exit the program and return to DOS.

2. A copy of the Tutor must be located in the same subdirectory in which the Q&A program files are stored. If that subdirectory is not the current subdirectory, change to the Q&A subdirectory. For example, if the Q&A subdirectory is QA, change to that directory by typing

   CD\QA

   and pressing Enter.

3. Copy the contents of the Tutorial Disk to the Q&A subdirectory of the hard disk. (If you completed this process during original installation, you can skip this step.)

4. Start the Tutor from the Q&A subdirectory by typing

   QATUTOR

   and pressing Enter. The Tutor begins.

To use the Tutor on a floppy disk drive system,

1. Start from the DOS `A>` prompt. If you are in Q&A, exit the program and return to DOS.

2. Insert Q&A Disk 1 into drive A.

3. Insert the Tutorial Disk (Disk 5) into drive B.

4. From the A> prompt, type

   QATUTOR

   and press Enter. The Tutor begins and provides instructions to continue through the program.

# Starting Q&A

After you have installed Q&A, you start the program by typing *QA* and pressing Enter at the DOS prompt.

On a hard disk system, make sure that the Q&A directory is the default or that you have used the SET or PATH commands in DOS to point to the appropriate subdirectories. You can also use a batch file to start Q&A. See your DOS manual for additional details on using SET and PATH options and on constructing batch files to help you start Q&A from any subdirectory.

On a floppy-based system, start Q&A with the start-up disk inserted in drive A.

## Customizing Start-up with Q&A Load Switches

Some monitor configurations are incompatible with Q&A's default settings. If you have trouble loading Q&A or if the start-up or menu screens are difficult to read, try using a software switch when you load the program. A software switch is an extra command, appended to the program name, that tells Q&A to reset some internal parameters as the program is started. You turn on a switch by typing *QA*, a space, a hyphen, and a one- to three-letter switch name, as in

QA -SCC

Five software switches are available to correct for differences among display adapters and monitors. One of these should correct your video display problems:

| *Switch* | *Use with* |
|---|---|
| -SCC | Color displays (all) |
| -SMC-A | Monochrome displays |
| -SMM | Monochrome displays |
| -A | Composite displays |
| -ST | Laptops or other LCD displays |

If the first switch that seems appropriate for your system does not work, try another. When you use one of these switches, Q&A remembers that setting and uses it automatically until you change it. Thus, when you have found a switch setting that works, you have to use it only once. After you've turned the switch on once, in subsequent sessions you can load Q&A in the conventional way by typing *QA* and pressing Enter.

Symantec has suggested start-up switches for some systems:

| *System/Display* | *Switch* |
|---|---|
| NEC Multispeed | QA -ST |
| ATT 6300 - Mono Monitor | QA -SMC |
| Any PS/2 with Mono Display | QA -SMC -A |
| Toshiba 1100, 3100 | QA -SMC |
| Zenith laptop | QA -A |
| COMPAQ with color monitor | QA -SCC |
| LCD display computer | QA -A or QA -ST |

## *Configuring for Multi-User Access*

Version 3.0 and later of Q&A supports multi-user operation over local area networks in two ways: data files only, and files and programs. You can share Q&A files over a network with the standard Q&A software as long as each network user has an individual copy of the program. To install a single copy of Q&A program files on a network server and have multiple users share the programs, you must upgrade the single-user version of Q&A to a networked version. Contact Symantec for information on installing a Q&A Network Pack for shared program access.

To set up a database for multi-user access, use the Assign Access Rights option from the Customize menu. This option allows you to turn on or off multi-user mode and assigns individual user rights. For a complete discussion of shared file access, see Chapter 21.

# Index

## A



## B



## C

## D

## G-H



## I

## J-K



## L

## M

## N



## O-P

## Q



## R

## S

## T

## U



## V-W

## X-Z

# SELECT QUE BOOKS TO INCREASE YOUR PERSONAL COMPUTER PRODUCTIVITY

**Upgrading and Repairing PCs**

*by Scott Mueller*

A comprehensive resource to personal computer upgrade, repair, maintenance, and troubleshooting. All types of IBM computers—from the original PC to the new PS/2 models—are covered, as are major IBM compatibles. You will learn about the components inside your computers, as well as how to use this information to troubleshoot problems and make informed decisions about upgrading.

**Using 1-2-3 Release 2.2, Special Edition**

*Developed by Que Corporation*

Learn professional spreadsheet techniques from the world's leading publisher of 1-2-3 books! This comprehensive text leads you step-by-step from worksheet basics to advanced 1-2-3 operations, including Release 2.2's new file linking capabilities, improved graphs, and sophisticated macro commands. Also includes Allways coverage, a Troubleshooting section, a Command Reference, and a tear-out 1-2-3 Menu Map. The most complete resource available for 1-2-3 Release 2.01 and Release 2.2!

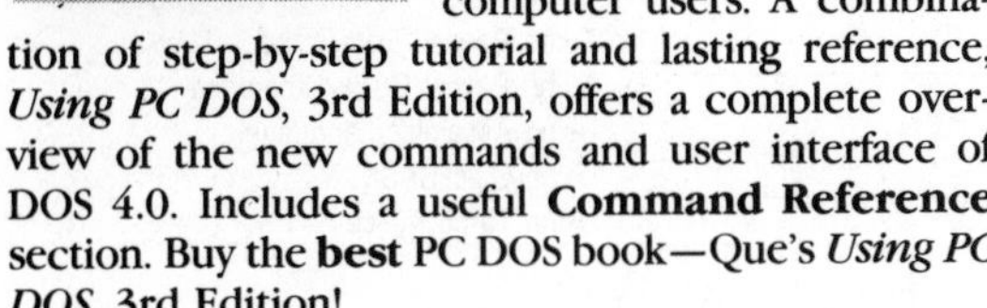


**Using PC DOS, 3rd Edition**

*by Chris DeVoney*

Now covering PC DOS 4.0, this classic text is an essential text for all IBM personal computer users. A combination of step-by-step tutorial and lasting reference, *Using PC DOS*, 3rd Edition, offers a complete overview of the new commands and user interface of DOS 4.0. Includes a useful **Command Reference** section. Buy the **best** PC DOS book—Que's *Using PC DOS*, 3rd Edition!

**Managing Your Hard Disk, 2nd Edition**

*by Don Berliner*

Proper hard disk management is the key to efficient personal computer use, and Que's *Managing Your Hard Disk* provides you with effective methods to best manage your computer's hard disk. This valuable text shows you how to organize programs and data on your hard disk according to their special applications, and helps you extend your understanding of DOS. This new edition features detailed information on DOS 3.3, IBM's PS/2 hardware, and new application and utility software. If you own a personal computer with a hard disk, you need Que's *Managing Your Hard Disk*, 2nd Edition!

FOLD HERE

Place
Stamp
Here

Que Corporation
P.O. Box 90
Carmel, IN 46032

*R856—Using Q&A, 2nd Edition*

# REGISTRATION CARD

Register your copy of *Using Q&A*, 2nd Edition and receive information about Que's newest products. Complete this registration card and return it to Que Corporation, P.O. Box 90, Carmel, IN 46032.

Name ______________ Phone ________

Company ______________ Title ________

Address ______________________

City __________ State ______ ZIP ______

*Please check the appropriate answers:*

Where did you buy *Using Q&A*, 2nd Edition?

- ☐ Bookstore (name: ______________)
- ☐ Computer store (name: ______________)
- ☐ Catalog (name: ______________)
- ☐ Direct from Que ______________
- ☐ Other: ______________

How many computer books do you buy a year?

- ☐ 1 or less ☐ 6-10
- ☐ 2-5 ☐ More than 10

How many Que books do you own?

- ☐ 1 ☐ 6-10
- ☐ 2-5 ☐ More than 10

How long have you been Using Q&A, 2nd Edition ?

- ☐ Less than 6 months
- ☐ 6 months to 1 year
- ☐ 1-3 years
- ☐ More than 3 years

What influenced your purchase of *Using Q&A*, 2nd Edition?

- ☐ Personal recommendation
- ☐ Advertisement ☐ Que catalog
- ☐ In-store display ☐ Que mailing
- ☐ Price ☐ Que reputation
- ☐ Other: ______________

How would you rate the overall content of *Using Q&A*, 2nd Edition?

- ☐ Very good ☐ Satisfactory
- ☐ Good ☐ Poor

How would you rate *Part II—Using Q&A File*?

- ☐ Very good ☐ Satisfactory
- ☐ Good ☐ Poor

How would you rate *Part III—Using Q&A Write*?

- ☐ Very good ☐ Satisfactory
- ☐ Good ☐ Poor

How would you rate *Part V—Using the Intelligent Assistant*?

- ☐ Very good ☐ Satisfactory
- ☐ Good ☐ Poor

What do you like *best* about *Using Q&A*, 2nd Edition?

What do you like *least* about *Using Q&A*, 2nd Edition?

How do you use *Using Q&A*, 2nd Edition?

What other Que products do you own?

For what other programs would a Que book be helpful?

Please feel free to list any other comments you may have about *Using Q&A*, 2nd Edition.

______________________

______________________

______________________

______________________

______________________

______________________

______________________

FOLD HERE

Place
Stamp
Here

Que Corporation
P.O. Box 90
Carmel, IN 46032

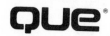

NO POSTAGE
NECESSARY
IF MAILED
IN THE
UNITED STATES

**BUSINESS REPLY MAIL**
First Class Permit No. 9918 Indianapolis, IN

*Postage will be paid by addressee*

**QUE®**

11711 N. College
Carmel, IN 46032


NO POSTAGE
NECESSARY
IF MAILED
IN THE
UNITED STATES

**BUSINESS REPLY MAIL**
First Class Permit No. 9918 Indianapolis, IN

*Postage will be paid by addressee*

**QUE®**

11711 N. College
Carmel, IN 46032